Theories of Human Communication

FOURTH EDITION

Stephen W. Littlejohn   Humboldt State University

Wadsworth Publishing Company

BELMONT, CALIFORNIA

A Division of Wadsworth, Inc.

A study guide has been specially designed to help students master the concepts presented in this textbook. Order from your bookstore.

Communication Editor: Holly Allen
Editorial Assistant: Katherine Hartlove
Production: Ruth Cottrell
Print Buyer: Karen Hunt
Designer: Albert Burkhardt
Cover: Jill Turney
Compositor: Graphic Typesetting Service, Inc.
Printer: Fairfield Graphics

This book is printed on acid-free paper that meets Environmental Protection Agency standards for recycled paper.

3 4 5 6 7 9 10—96 95 94 93

LIBRARY OF CONGRESS CATALOGING-IN-PUBLICATION DATA

Littlejohn, Stephen W.
    Theories of human communication / Stephen W. Littlejohn.—4th ed.
        p.   cm.
    Includes bibliographical references and indexes.
    ISBN 0-534-16134-0
    1. Communication—Philosophy.   I. Title
P80.L48   1991
302.2'01—dc20   91-43561
                CIP

To my daughter

TONYA

Preface

With the publication of the fourth edition, *Theories of Human Communication* is 15 years old. Many changes have occurred in the field during this period, and each revision of the text has attempted to capture the state of communication theory appropriately for its time. No revision of this text has been minor. No revision could have been.

This edition includes many changes and improvements. First and foremost, the book has been lengthened to provide space for more complete coverage of individual theories, more explanation, and better illustration. The text has been updated, with the addition of new material on various theories and the inclusion of some theories that were not mentioned in the previous editions. Sadly, some theories had to be dropped. Numerous brief examples that students can identify from their own experience have been added throughout the text. Students will find this edition more readable than the previous three, and a student workbook is now available to help students with the material.

Another improvement is the addition of research examples for most of the theories. These sections are integrated into the text and range from a paragraph to a page in length. They are not written in a technical style. They serve several functions. First, they give students an idea of how research is done on a particular theory. Second, they illustrate the types of research methods available in the communication field. Third, the research examples help illustrate the ideas of the theory.

Some organizational changes have also taken place. The middle section of the book has been revised to clarify the relationships among theories and to show their historical and conceptual connections. Many of the theories formerly covered in Part III under contexts have been moved to Part II because they help develop concepts introduced there. Part III is now more focused on particular contextual themes—relationships, decision making, networks, and media. These modifications serve to break down artificial divisions that can be misleading in a communication theory course, yet the book still relates to the basic levels of communication on which the field, for better or worse, still depends and which many of our curricula still demand.

New commentary and critique sections have been added to the end of each chapter. These discussions provide perspectives, insights, and criticism of the theories. Many beginning students may wish to skip these sections, but more experienced students will find that they stimulate thought and further investigation.

Professors who have used this book before will need to make some adjustments in their courses, as they have had to do for each subsequent edition. Course changes, however, will not need to be drastic and will hopefully constitute the refinement and improvement that we all seek in our teaching.

These changes have not superseded the essential qualities of this text that reviewers and adopters have requested over the years. The book remains an extensive overview of theories on a wide variety of communication topics. It will continue to inform advanced students and will appeal to less experienced students as well. Although the book continues to include material from a variety of fields, more theories are taken from the communication field, reflecting a natural change in the discipline itself.

I would like to thank the several reviewers whose suggestions made this edition eminently better: David Brenders, Emerson College; Brant Burleson, Purdue University; William Donaghy, University of Wyoming; Valerie Downs, Cal State University, Northridge; William Eadie, Cal State University, Northridge; Mary Anne Fitzpatrick, University of Wisconsin, Madison; Robert Goyer, Arizona State University; Jerold Hale, Miami University; Martha Haun, University of Houston; Edward Hinck, Central Michigan University; Randy Hirokawa, University of Iowa; Devorah Lieberman, Portland State University; Roxanne Parrott, University of Georgia; Susan Shimanoff, San Francisco State University; and Craig Allen Smith, University of North Carolina, Greensboro; the Wadsworth publication team, including Peggy Randall, Holly Allen, Ruth Cottrell, and Betty Duncan; my colleagues at Humbolt State University whose encouragement always keeps the project alive; and my wife, Karen Foss, for her understanding of what it takes to write a book. I would especially like to thank assistant Roberta Gray for her invaluable help throughout the project. I would also like to thank the many students and faculty from around the world who have found this book useful and interesting. One of life's greatest gratifications is to be told that one's work has been beneficial to others.

Brief Contents

Detailed Contents

P A R T I I   Topics in Communication Theory   39

Chapter Three   System Theory   40

Chapter Four   Theories of Signs and Language   63

The Nature of Inquiry and Theory

Communication Theory and Scholarship

As long as people have wondered about the world, they have been intrigued by the mysteries of their own nature. The most commonplace activities of our lives—those realms of human nature we take for granted—become puzzles of the largest magnitude when we try to understand them.

Communication is intertwined with all of human life. Any study of human activity must touch on communication processes in one form or another. Some scholars treat communication as central, whereas others take communication for granted without making it the focus of their study. In this book we are concerned with the idea of communication as central to human life. Our guiding question is how scholars from various traditions have conceptualized, described, and explained human communication.

In a sense this book illustrates a part of our quest to understand ourselves. Specifically, it is a synthesis of many contemporary theories of communication. The book does not provide the answer to questions we ask about communication, but it does present several answers that have been proposed. In other words this book does not complete the puzzle of communication but illustrates how some of the pieces have been shaped and joined.

What Is Communication Theory?

Any attempt to explain or represent something is a theory. As discussed in the next chapter, a theory is someone's conceptualization of an observed set of events. Communication professors often ask their students to devise explanations of certain aspects of communication. This theory-building exercise involves stating clearly what is believed to be happening in communication. Indeed, everybody operates by theory much of the time. Our theories consist of ideas that guide us in making decisions and taking actions. Sometimes our theories are flawed, and we may modify what we think the world is like.

Although the word *theory* can be used to describe the educated guesswork of laypersons, academics use the word somewhat differently. Scholars make it their work to study a particular kind of experience with a keen eye. A theory is the scholar's construction of what an experience is like, based on systematic observation. Thus, theory in this sense is the scholar's best representation of the state of affairs at any given time. As you will see in the next chapter, theory building is not an easy task. A great deal of focused observation, hypothesizing, and revision is required.

The term *communication theory* usually refers to the body of theories for understanding the communication process. Much disagreement exists about what constitutes an adequate theory of communication. This text presents a wide variety of theories, which are discussed in terms of their philosophical assumptions, their claims about what communication involves, and their strengths and weaknesses. You will find a basis for making your own decisions about which theories should and should not be included in our body of knowledge about communication.

Why Study Communication Theory?

Communication is one of our most pervasive, important, and complex clusters of behavior. The ability to communicate on a higher level separates humans from other animals. Our daily lives are strongly affected by our own communication with others as well as by messages from distant and unknown persons. If there is a need to know about our world, that need extends to all aspects of human behavior, especially communication.

Specifically, theories of communication help you become more competent and adaptive. Teachers often provide students with a list of "recipes" when beginning the study of communication, but the communication process is too complex to be approached entirely on the level of simplistic guidelines. Students also need to gain an understanding of what happens during communication and an ability to adapt to circumstances. The study of communication theory is a way to obtain this understanding.

Everybody tries to make sense out of their own experience. We assign meaning to what is going on in and around us. Sometimes the meaning is shared, and sometimes it is not. Sometimes it is clear and other times vague or contradictory. By developing an understanding of the variety of theories to explain communication, students can interpret communication experiences in more flexible, useful, and discriminating ways.

A colleague of mine used to say that the study of communication theory will cause the student to see things he or she never saw before. N. R. Hanson writes, "The paradigm observer is not the man who sees and reports what all normal observers see and report, but the man who sees in familiar objects what no one else has seen before."[1] This widening of perception, the unhitching of blinders, helps one transcend habits and become increasingly adaptable and flexible. To borrow some analogies from Thomas Kuhn, "Looking at a contour map, the student sees lines on paper, the cartographer a picture of a terrain. Looking at a bubble-chamber photograph, the student sees confused and broken lines, the physicist a record of familiar subnuclear events."[2] The basic justification for studying theories of communication is that they provide a set of useful conceptual tools.

The Academic Study of Communication

Although communication has been studied since antiquity,[3] it has become a major topic of concern in the twentieth century. One author has referred to this development as a "revolutionary discovery," largely caused by the rise of communication technologies such as radio, television, telephone, satellites, and computer networking, along with the Industrial Revolution, big business, and

1. N. R. Hanson, *Patterns of Discovery* (Cambridge, Eng.: Cambridge University Press, 1961), p. 30.

2. Thomas S. Kuhn, *The Structure of Scientific Revolutions* (Chicago: University of Chicago Press, 1970), p. 111.

3. See, for example, W. Barnett Pearce and Karen A. Foss, "The Historical Context of Communication as a Science," in *Human Communication: Theory and Research*, eds. G. L. Dahnke and G. W. Clatterbuck (Belmont, Calif.: Wadsworth, 1990), pp. 1–20; Nancy Harper, *Human Communication Theory: The History of a Paradigm* (Rochelle Park, N.J.: Hayden, 1979).

global politics.[4] Clearly, communication has assumed immense importance in our time. It is therefore not surprising that communication should interest teachers, researchers, and theorists.

Intense interest in the academic study of communication began after World War I, as increasing technology and literacy made communication a topic of concern.[5] This concern was stimulated in large measure by the popular ideologies of progressivism and pragmatism, which provoked a desire to advance society and create social change.

A variety of interests supported this early work. One important area of research was the political influence of public messages, which led to considerable research on propaganda and public opinion. This period saw the beginnings of attitude and opinion measurement as researchers attempted to discover the extent to which public opinion was directed by public communication.

At the same time, the social sciences were developing, and both sociology and social psychology emerged. Sociology studied social life, and although their methods differed somewhat, sociology and psychology became preoccupied with research methods. There was considerable experimentation with method, the development of standards for evaluating research, and methodological debates, many of which continue today. Much of the research in sociology in the 1930s investigated the ways in which interaction affects individuals and communities, and popular research topics in social psychology included effects of movies on children, propaganda and persuasion, and group dynamics.

Another research tradition in the early years dealt with communication and education with special attention to the use of new technologies such as radio in education, the teaching of basic communication skills such as public speaking and group discussion, and the effects of various communication practices in the classroom.

The first half of this century was also dominated by commerical interests such as advertising. Much of the early research, even in universities, was driven by the desire of market enterprises to know more about communication.

After World War II, the social sciences became fully recognized as legitimate disciplines, as the interest in psychosocial processes became intense. Persuasion and decisionmaking in groups were central concerns, not only among researchers but also in society at large. After World War II then, the topic of communication was recognized as a legitimate and important study. The approach to communication, however, took rather different turns in Europe and the United States.

In the United States, communication researchers pursued the idea that communication should be studied objectively, primarily with quantitative methods. Although complete consensus was never achieved on this ideal, it was the standard for many years. European investigations, on the other hand, were influenced by historical, cultural, and critical interests and were largely influenced by Marxism. Over the years, tension has been growing between these two traditions, although considerable influence has flowed both ways as scientific work has gotten a toehold in Europe and critical perspectives are taken seriously in North America. Indeed, after about 1960 both the scientific and critical perspectives themselves lost much of their coherence as internal debates and were promulgated within each tradition.

The study of communication as we have understood it in the United States and in Europe is a Western, Eurocentric endeavor. Indeed, virtually all theories discussed in this book are in the Western tradition. This does not mean, however, that thinking common to other parts of the world does not have insights into communication. In a valuable and interesting treatment, Lawrence Kincaid contrasts a variety of Western and Eastern perspectives on communication theory.[6]

Kincaid notes a number of differences between Asian and Western perspectives.[7] For one, Eastern

4, W. Barnett Pearce, *Communication and the Human Condition* (Carbondale: Southern Illinois University Press, 1989).

5. This brief history is based on Jesse G. Delia, "Communication Research: A History," in *Handbook of Communication Science*, eds. C. R. Berger and S. H. Chaffee (Newbury Park, Calif.: Sage, 1987), pp. 20–98.

6. D. Lawrence Kincaid, *Communication Theory: Eastern and Western Perspectives* (San Diego: Academic Press, 1987).

7. Ibid., pp. 331–353.

theories tend to focus on wholeness and unity, whereas Western perspectives are preoccupied with measuring parts and have difficulty relating these pieces to a unified process. Second, much Western theory is dominated by a vision of individual autonomy, action, and purpose. Here, people are considered to be active in achieving personal aims. Most Eastern theories, on the other hand, view communication outcomes as unplanned and natural consequences of events. Even the many Western theories that share the Asian preoccupation with unintended consequences of action tend to be individualistic and highly cognitive, whereas most Eastern traditions stress emotional and spiritual convergence as communication outcomes.

A third difference deals with language and thought. Most Western theories are dominated by language. In the East, verbal symbols, especially speech, are downplayed and viewed with skepticism. Western-style rationality is also mistrusted in the Eastern tradition. What counts in many Asian philosophies is intuitive insights gained from direct experience. Such insight can be gained by nonintervention in natural events, which explains why silence is so important in these traditions.

Finally, relationships are conceptualized rather differently in the two traditions. In Western theories, relationships exist between two or more individuals. In many Eastern traditions, relationships are between social positions, and these differ in terms of role, status, and power.

Today, the study of communication is diverse. Although the academic disciplines most often associated with the study of communication in the United States are journalism and speech communication and many university departments of communication have been formed, communication remains a largely heterogeneous, eclectic, and multidisciplinary endeavor.

The diversity of communication theory reflects the complexity of communication itself. Looking for the best theory of communication is not particularly useful inasmuch as communication is not a single, unified act but a process consisting of numerous clusters of behavior. Each theory looks at the process from a different angle, and each theory provides insights of its own. Of course, all theories are not equally valid or useful, and any particular investigator may find a specific theory or theories more useful for the work to be undertaken. We should welcome rather than avoid a multitheoretical approach to the complex process of communication.[8]

An obstacle to a multitheoretical approach is the tendency to view communication from the narrow confines of specific academic disciplines. Because disciplines are somewhat arbitrary, disciplinary divisions do not necessarily provide the best method of packaging knowledge. Interdisciplinary cooperation is essential for a useful understanding of communication. University courses related to communication are found in many departments, just as the theories described in this book represent a wide array of disciplines. As Dean Barnlund indicates, "While many disciplines have undoubtedly benefited from adopting a communication model, it is equally true that they, in turn, have added greatly to our understanding of human interaction."[9] Remember that when people tell you they are communication experts, they are saying little. Their primary interests may be in the sciences or the arts, mathematics or literature, biology or politics.[10]

Although scholars from a number of disciplines share an interest in communication, the scholar's first loyalty is usually to the general concepts of the discipline itself. Communication is generally considered subordinate. For example, psychologists study individual behavior and view communication as a particular kind of behavior. Sociologists

8. For an excellent case in favor of multiple approaches to communication, see John Waite Bowers and James J. Bradac, "Issues in Communication Theory: A Metatheoretical Analysis," in *Communication Yearbook 5*, ed. M. Burgoon (New Brunswick, N.J.: Transaction, 1982), pp. 1–28.

9. Dean Barnlund, *Interpersonal Communication: Survey and Studies* (New York: Houghton Mifflin, 1968), p. v.

10. The multidisciplinary nature of the study of communication is examined in Stephen W. Littlejohn, "An Overview of the Contributions to Human Communication Theory from Other Disciplines," in *Human Communication Theory: Comparative Essays*, ed. F. E. X. Dance (New York: Harper & Row, 1982), pp. 243–85; and W. Barnett Pearce, "Scientific Research Methods in Communication Studies and Their Implications for Theory and Research," in *Speech Communication in the 20th Century*, ed. T. W. Benson (Carbondale: Southern Illinois University Press, 1985), pp. 255–281.

focus on society and social process, seeing communication as one of several social factors. Anthropologists are interested primarily in culture, and if they investigate communication, they treat it as an aspect of a broader theme. Do we conclude from this that communication is less significant as an academic study than behavior, society, and culture? Of course, we do not.

In recent years scholars have recognized the centrality of communication and have emphasized it in their research and theory. Some of these scholars were trained in traditional disciplines. Others studied in academic departments called communication or speech communication. Regardless of their original academic homes, these scholars have come together in the new field of communication. They have shifted gears to make traditional themes support rather than dominate the study of communication. The field of communication is characterized not only by its focus on communication per se but also by its attention to the entire breadth of communication concerns. The work of such organizations as the International Communication Association and the Speech Communication Association, along with numerous journals devoted to the topic, typify what is happening in the field.

In this book we examine theories that relate directly to communication as a process. The young communication field is now producing fresh theories, many of which are included in this text. As we discuss each theory, we examine the relevance of the theory to the broader study of human communication.

Defining Communication

Because it is complex, communication is difficult to define. The word *communication* is abstract and, like all words, possesses multiple meanings.[11] Scholars have made many attempts to define communication, but seeking a single definition may not be as fruitful as looking at the various concepts behind the term. The term *communication* can be used legitimately in a number of ways. Frank Dance took a major step toward clarifying this muddy concept by outlining fifteen distinct conceptual components in the various definitions.[12] These components are the basic ideas used by an author to distinguish communication from other things. Table 1.1 summarizes the components and provides an example for each. In addition, Dance found three points of "critical conceptual differentiation," which form the basic dimensions along which the various definitions differ. The first is *level of observation*. Definitions vary in level of abstractness. Some definitions are broad and inclusive; others are restrictive. For example, communication as "the means of sending military messages, orders, etc., as by telephone, telegraph, radio, couriers," is a low-level or restricted definition. On the other hand, "communication is the process that links discontinuous parts of the living world to one another," is very general.

The second distinction is *intentionality*. Some definitions include only intentional message sending and receiving; others do not.[13] The following is an example of a definition that includes intentionality: Communication includes "those situations in which a source transmits a message to a receiver with conscious intent to affect the latter's behaviors." A definition that does not require intent is this one: "It is a process that makes common to two or several what was the monopoly of one or some."

The third dimension of definitions is normative *judgment*. Some definitions include a statement of evaluation; other definitions do not contain such implicit judgments of quality. The following definition, for example, presumes that communication is necessarily successful: "Communication is the verbal interchange of a thought or idea." But what if the attempt to exchange a thought fails? The fol-

---

11. There are 126 different definitions of communication listed in Frank E. X. Dance and Carl E. Larson, *The Functions of Human Communication: A Theoretical Approach* (New York: Holt, Rinehart & Winston, 1976), appendix A.

12. Frank E. X. Dance, "The 'Concept' of Communication," *Journal of Communication* 20 (1970): 201–210.

13. Intentionality as a criterion of communication is discussed in detail in Michael Motley, "On Whether One Can(not) Not Communicate: An Examination Via Traditional Communication Postulates," *Western Journal of Speech Communication* 54 (1990): 1–20.

lowing definition does not judge whether the outcome is successful or not: "Communication [is] the transmission of information . . .."

These three dimensions have more than passing significance. Theories of communication contain explicit or implicit definitions of communication, and the definition in large measure sets the boundaries and focus of the theory. For example, a theory

Table 1.1   Conceptual Components in Communication

1. Symbols/verbal/speech	"Communication is the verbal interchange of thought or idea."
2. Understanding	"Communication is the process by which we understand others and in turn endeavor to be understood by them. It is dynamic, constantly changing and shifting in response to the total situation."
3. Interaction/relationship/ social process	"Interaction, even on the biological level, is a kind of communication; otherwise common acts could not occur."
4. Reduction of uncertainty	"Communication arises out of the need to reduce uncertainty, to act effectively, to defend or strengthen the ego."
5. Process	"Communication: the transmission of information, idea, emotion, skills, etc. by the use of symbols—words, pictures, figures, graphs, etc. It is the act or process of transmission that is usually called communication."
6. Transfer/transmission/interchange	"The connecting thread appears to be the idea of something's being transferred from one thing, or person, to another. We use the word 'communication' sometimes to refer to what is so transferred, sometimes to the means by which it is transferred, sometimes to the whole process. In many cases, what is transferred in this way continues to be shared; if I convey information to another person, it does not leave my own possession through coming into his. Accordingly, the word 'communication' acquires also the sense of participation. It is this sense, for example, that religious worshipers are said to communicate."
7. Linking/binding	"Communication is the process that links discontinuous parts of the living world to one another."
8. Commonality	"It (communication) is a process that makes common to two or several what was the monopoly of one or some."
9. Channel/carrier/means/route	"The means of sending military messages, orders, etc., as by telephone, telegraph, radio, couriers."
10. Replicating memories	"Communication is the process of conducting the attention of another person for the purpose of replicating memories."
11. Discriminative response/ behavior modifying response	"Communication is the discriminatory response of an organism to a stimulus."
12. Stimuli	"Every communication act is viewed as a transmission of information, consisting of a discriminative stimuli, from a source to a recipient.
13. Intentional	"In the main, communication has as its central interest those behavioral situations in which a source transmits a message to a receiver (S) *with conscious intent to affect the latter's behaviors*."
14. Time/situation	"The communication process is one of transition from one structural situation-as-a-whole to another, in preferred design."
15. Power	"Communication is the mechanism by which power is exerted."

NOTE: The sources of these definitions are cited in Frank E. X. Dance, "The 'Concept' of Communication," *Journal of Communication* 20 (1970): 204, 208.

adopting a very broad definition of communication—as, say, *linking and binding*—would have to take a sweeping approach and be limited in making substantive distinctions. Such a theory would probably focus on general relationships among elements in a system without identifying very specifically the nature of those relationships. In contrast, a theory using a more restrictive definition of communication—for example, *understanding*—could identify particular kinds of acts without necessarily relating those acts to broader concerns. One of the limitations of any single theory is its definition of communication. Consequently, no single definition of communication can suffice.

Different definitions have different functions; they enable the theorist to do different kinds of things. Always, a definition should be evaluated on the basis of how well it enables a scholar to accomplish the purposes of an investigation. Different sorts of investigations often require different, even contradictory, definitions of communication. Definitions, then, are tools that should be adapted to one's aims.

For example, if you are interested in understanding the ways in which the interaction in a family affects the members' relationship with one another, you would adopt something like the following definition: Communication is the process of defining a relationship. In fact, this definition has been very useful in a whole tradition of research in the field of relational communication (Chapter 12). This definition contains at least two of the key conceptual components outlined by Dance (See Table 1.1)—relationship and process. Researchers in the relational tradition examine the process of interaction, the give and take between people in a small social system, and examine the ways in which that interaction creates certain characteristics of relationships such as dominance, trust, and intimacy.

A rather different research tradition involves the cognitive production of messages (Chapter 6). Here, the central question involves the mental processes employed in creating and sending messages of different sorts. Investigators in this tradition attempt to discover the ways in which people process information about the situation, how they for-

mulate strategies for accomplishing goals, and how they adapt and adjust their actions in various situations. An appropriate definition for this line of work is as follows: Communication is information processing designed to reduce uncertainty. This definition includes several of the conceptual components outlined by Dance, including symbols, reduction of uncertainty, process, transfer/transmission, and replicating memories.

The definitions that guide these two types of research and their corresponding theories are different, but each is essential for the work that needs to be done in communication inquiry. Communication, then, is not just one thing but a number of concepts.

Dance's conclusion is important: "We are trying to make the concept of 'communication' do too much work for us."[14] He calls for a family of concepts. The theories included in the following chapters, seen collectively, represent a step in the direction of specifying the members of this family of concepts.

The Process of Inquiry in Communication

A Basic Model of Inquiry

Inquiry involves systematic, disciplined ordering of experience that leads to the development of understanding and knowledge. Inquiry is what scholars do to "find out." Inquiry is not just one process, of course. Many modes are used, but all are distinguished from mundane or common experience. Inquiry is focused; it involves a planned means or method and has an expected outcome. The investigator is never sure of the exact outcome of inquiry and can anticipate only the general form or nature of the results.

These scholars also share a general approach to inquiry that involves three stages.[15] The first and

14. Dance, "Concept," p. 210.

15. The process of inquiry is described in Gerald E. Miller and Henry Nicholson, *Communication Inquiry* (Reading, Mass.: Addison-Wesley, 1976).

guiding stage of all inquiry is asking questions. Gerald Miller and Henry Nicholson, in fact, believe that inquiry is "nothing more . . . than the process of asking interesting, significant questions . . . and providing disciplined, systematic answers to them."[16] These authors outline common types of questions asked by the scholar. Questions of definition call for concepts as answers, seeking to identify what is observed or inferred (What is it? What will we call it?). Questions of fact ask about properties and relations in what is observed (What does it consist of? How does it relate to other phenomena?). Questions of value probe aesthetic, pragmatic, and ethical qualities of the observed. Such questions result in value judgments about phenomena (Is it beautiful? Is it effective? Is it proper?).

The second stage of inquiry is observation. Here, the scholar looks at the object of inquiry. Methods of observation vary significantly from one tradition to another. Some scholars observe by examining records and artifacts, others by personal involvement, others by using instruments and controlled experiment, others by interviewing people. Whatever form is used, the investigator employs some planned method for answering the questions.

The third stage of inquiry is *constructing answers*. Here, the scholar attempts to define, to describe and explain, to make judgments. This stage, which is the focus of this book, is usually referred to as *theory*.

Students naturally tend to think of the stages of inquiry as linear, occurring one step at a time, but inquiry does not proceed in this fashion. Each stage affects and is affected by the others. Observations often stimulate new questions, and theories are challenged both by observations and questions. Theories lead to new questions, and observations are structured in part by existing theories. Figure 1.1 illustrates the interaction among the stages of inquiry.

Types of Scholarship

The preceding section ignores the important distinctions between the many types of inquiry. These

16. Ibid., p. ix.

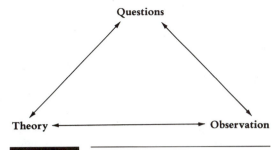

Figure 1.1   The stages of inquiry.

types stem from different methods of observation and lead to different forms of theory. Methods of inquiry often are grouped into three broad forms of scholarship: scientific, humanistic, and social scientific.[17] Although these forms of scholarship share the common elements discussed in the previous section, they also have major differences.[18]

Scientific scholarship. Science often is associated with objectivity. This association is valid or not, depending on how you view objectivity. If by objectivity you mean suspension of values, then science definitely is not objective. However, if by objectivity you mean standardization, then science is indeed objective; or, more accurately, it aims to be objective. The scientist attempts to look at the world in such a way that all other observers, using the same methods, will see the same thing in a given observation. Replications of a study will yield identical results. In addition, science creates generalizations or laws to explain phenomena.

Science typically sees the world as having form and structure apart from differences between indi-

17. An excellent discussion of scholarship can be found in Ernest G. Bormann, *Theory and Research in the Communicative Arts* (New York: Holt, Rinehart & Winston, 1965). See also Nathan Glazer, "The Social Sciences in Liberal Education," in *The Philosophy of the Curriculum*, ed. S. Hook (Buffalo: Prometheus Books, 1975), pp. 145–158; James L. Jarett, *The Humanities and Humanistic Education* (Reading, Mass.: Addison-Wesley, 1973); Gerald Holton, "Science, Science Teaching, and Rationality," in *The Philosophy of the Curriculum*, ed. S. Hook (Buffalo: Prometheus Books, 1975), pp. 101–108.

18. See C. P. Snow, *The Two Cultures and a Second Look* (Cambridge, Eng.: Cambridge University Press, 1964).

vidual observers. The world sits in wait of discovery. Where the scholar has reason to believe that a phenomenon exists in the world, the goal is to observe and explain that phenomenon as accurately as possible. Because no divinely revealed way exists for knowing how accurate one's observations are, the scientist must rely on agreement among observers. This reliance is why objectivity or replicability is so important in science. If all trained observers report the same results, we can be assured that the phenomenon has been accurately observed. If scientists also agree that those accurate observations do not contradict their theory, the explanation is taken as valid. Because of the emphasis on discovering a knowable world, scientific methods are especially well suited to problems of nature.

Humanistic scholarship. Whereas science is associated with objectivity, the humanities are associated with subjectivity. Science aims to standardize observation; the humanities seek creative individuality. If the aim of science is to reduce human differences in what is observed, the aim of the humanities is to understand individual subjective response.[19] Most humanists are more interested in individual cases than generalized theory.

Whereas science is an "out there" activity, humanities stress the "in here." Science focuses on the discovered world; humanities focus on the discovering person. Science seeks consensus; humanities seek alternative interpretations. Humanists often are suspicious of the claim that there is an immutable world to be discovered. The humanities scholar tends not to separate the knower from the known. The classical humanistic position is that who one is determines what one sees. Because of its emphasis on the subjective response, humanistic scholarship is especially well suited to problems of art, personal experience, and values.

This discussion is not intended to lead you to believe that science and humanities are so far apart that they never come together. Almost any program of research and theory building includes some aspects of both scientific and humanistic scholarship. The differences mentioned relate to the primary thrust of the two groups of scholarship; points of crossover also exist between them. At times the scientist is a humanist, using intuition, creativity, interpretation, and insight. Ironically, the scientist must be subjective in creating the mechanisms that will eventually lead to objective observation. Research design is a creative process. At times the humanist, in turn, must be scientific, seeking facts that enable scholars to understand the experiences to which ultimately they will respond subjectively. As we will see in the next section, where science leaves off and humanities begin is not always clear.

The special case of the social sciences. A third form of scholarship is social science. Many social scientists would not separate this type of scholarship from science, seeing it instead as an extension of natural science.[20] In fact, social scientists use numerous methods borrowed from physics. Social science, however, is a world apart. Paradoxically, it includes elements of both science and humanities but is different from both.[21]

Social scholars attempt to understand human beings as objects of study. They seek to observe and interpret patterns of human behavior. In practice, scholars distinguish between behavioral science and social science, the former referring to individual behavior and the latter to human interaction. For our purposes these two branches are combined.

To understand human behavior, the scholar must observe it. If behavioral patterns do in fact exist, then observation must be as objective as possible. In other words the behavioral scientist, like the natural scientist, must establish consensus on

---

19. James A. Diefenbeck, *A Celebration of Subjective Thought* (Carbondale: Southern Illinois University Press, 1984).

20. See, for example, Charles R. Berger and Steven H. Chaffee (eds.), "The Study of Communication as a Science," in *Handbook of Communication Science* (Newbury Park, Calif.: Sage, 1987), pp. 15–19.

21. See, for example, Hubert M. Blalock, *Basic Dilemmas in the Social Sciences* (Beverly Hills, Calif.: Sage, 1984), p. 15; Anthony Giddens, *Profiles and Critiques in Social Theory* (Berkeley: University of California Press, 1983), p. 133; Peter Winch, *The Idea of a Social Science and Its Relation to Philosophy* (London: Routledge & Kegan Paul, 1958).

what is observed. Once the behavioral phenomena are accurately observed, they must be explained or interpreted. Interpreting may be confounded by the fact that the object of observation, the human subject, is itself an active, knowing being. Unlike objects in the natural world, the human subject is capable of having knowledge, of possessing values and making interpretations. Can "scientific" explanation of human behavior take place without consideration of the "humanistic" knowledge of the observed person? This question is the central philosophical issue of social science. It is a question that has provoked considerable concern and debate to the point that some observers believe that the social sciences are in an identity crisis.[22]

Controversy about the nature of inquiry into human life is common in social science. In previous years the majority of social scientists believed that scientific methods alone would suffice to uncover the mysteries of human experience. Today, most social scientists realize that although scientific methods are an important aspect of their scholarship, a strong humanistic element is present as well. Specifically, the individual subjective response must be considered in understanding how people think and evaluate.

The study of communication is a social science. It involves understanding how people behave in creating, exchanging, and interpreting messages. Consequently, communication inquiry combines both scientific and humanistic methods.[23] The theories covered in this book, as examples of social science, vary significantly in their use of science and humanities. Traditionally, in the field of speech communication, humanistic theories of communication have been referred to as *rhetorical theory* and

scientific theories as *communication theory*. This distinction is not particularly useful. All theories we will discuss deal with human communication; both humanistic and scientific theories are worthy of inclusion in our body of knowledge about human communication.

In the field of communication, no universal agreement exists on the limits of science and humanities. We are far from consensus on the questions that can and should be approached scientifically and those that should be the focus of humanistic methods. In the final analysis, scholars defend the traditions in which they are trained and which they enjoy the most. These issues of scholarship are taken up in more detail in Chapter 2 under the heading "Philosophical Issues in the Study of Communication."

The Creation of Knowledge

Inquiry is a process of creating knowledge. On the surface the word *creating* may seem strange in this context. A closer look, however, reveals that knowledge is a product of human activity, a creation. (A more exacting discussion of reality and the ways in which theory approximates it is taken up in Chapter 2.) In this section we begin studying the general ways in which knowledge is created.

Each approach to knowledge makes certain assumptions about what is knowable and how knowledge arises. In brief, each posits a different set of relationships among questions, observations, and theory. Scholars typically make commitments to particular ways of knowing, although a given research project may, at different times, adopt different ways of knowing as appropriate.

In a sense a way of knowing is like a game. It is selected because it is believed to be most appropriate in light of the problem being tackled. It comes with a set of rules that one is obliged to adopt during the course of the game. When playing a knowledge game, the scholar usually does not question the assumptions or rules, though on other occasions these assumptions and rules may be hotly

22. See, for example, Donald W. Fiske and Richard A. Shweder (eds.), "Introduction: Uneasy Social Science," in *Metatheory in Social Science: Pluralisms and Subjectivities* (Chicago: University of Chicago Press, 1986), pp. 1–18; Kenneth J. Gergen, *Toward Transformation in Social Knowledge* (New York: Springer-Verlag, 1982).

23. This position is developed in Thomas B. Farrell, "Beyond Science: Humanities Contributions to Communication Theory," in *Handbook of Communication Science*, eds. C. R. Berger and S. H. Chaffee (Newbury Park, Calif.: Sage, 1987), pp. 123–139.

debated. Although many variants can be found, scholars develop knowledge in three general ways—discovery, interpretation, and criticism.[24]

Knowledge by Discovery

The discovery mode is so prevalent in natural and social sciences that it is often assumed to be the only appropriate route to knowledge, not just one possible avenue. This approach assumes that the world is outside the mind of the observer and lies in wait of discovery. Knowledge, in the discovery game, is something you "get" by "observing." The known is thus revealed to or received by the knower, leading to the label "the received view." The standard of good knowledge in the discovery mode is objective and accurate observation, making validity the goal.

Knowledge by Interpretation

For the interpretive scholar, knowledge cannot be discovered intact because reality is not independent from the human mind. Although a set of knowable events are assumed to exist, those events can be conceptualized in a variety of useful ways and can never be ascertained purely without the imposition of a set of concepts by the knower. Thus, knowledge is a transactional product of the knower and the known. Different observers will see different things in the stream of events because they assign different meanings to those events and conceptualize them in different ways. What mediates between knower and known, then, is a perspective, and knowledge is always colored by that perspective. Objectivity as defined in the classical sciences is therefore not a very useful construct for the interpretivist.

Because "reality" can be conceptualized in a variety of ways, no one way of seeing the world is believed to be best by the interpretive scholar. Although interpretations may be debated and crit-

icized, the underlying assumption is that several theories may be good candidates for expressing what is known. If the discovery mode seeks to eliminate "incorrect" versions of reality, interpretive scholarship seeks to identify the powers and limits of various interpretations. What makes a good interpretation is not a question of validity in the traditional sense but a question of utility. The question for interpretivists is this: Does the interpretation help us talk about, understand, operate on, intervene in, teach, or fulfill some other cognitive or pragmatic goal? The interpretations that "make sense" to a community of scholars will prevail, at least for a time.

Knowledge by Criticism

Many scholars are not satisfied to develop interpretations of events; instead they imagine ways in which change and improvement can be attained. Although there are numerous critical traditions, all share this common goal. Besides a perspective, certain values are brought to bear on the interpretation. The knower's judgment is valued as a tool of knowledge, and the basic criterion of good knowledge in the critical mode is the potential for achieving desired change. Clearly, interpretive and critical approaches to knowledge are commonplace in the humanities and are becoming increasingly popular in the social sciences, including communication.

Two key questions are relevant to these three approaches: (1) What counts as data, and (2) what do data count as?[25] In other words, what do we observe, and what are these observations taken to mean? In the discovery mode, objective observations, often made through instruments, are taken as data, and these observations count as instances of a structural reality in the world. In the interpretive mode, the scholar as a person is often treated as the "instrument," and data are the meanings and

---

24. For a more complete discussion of these three, see Brian Fay, *Social Theory and Political Practice* (London: George Allen & Unwin, 1975). See also Arthur P. Bochner, "Perspectives on Inquiry: Representation, Conversation, and Reflection," in *Handbook of Interpersonal Communication*, eds. M. L. Knapp and G. R. Miller (Beverly Hills, Calif.: Sage, 1985), pp. 27–58.

25. W. Barnett Pearce, Vernon E. Cronen, and Linda M. Harris, "Methodological Considerations in Building Human Communication Theory," in *Human Communication Theory: Comparative Essays*, ed. F. E. X. Dance (New York: Harper & Row, 1982), p. 5.

interpretations of the knowing scholar. Such data count as useful conceptualizations of events. In the critical approach, judgments are taken as data; these data then point to areas for social improvement and change.

Genres of Communication Theory

The many distinguishing issues and dimensions of communication theory defy clear classification. No system of categories is perfectly appropriate for organizing this material, although several schemes could, with qualification, be used.

Five generic labels can be used to classify theories of communication:

- Structural and functional theories
- Cognitive and behavioral theories
- Interactional and conventional theories
- Interpretive theories
- Critical theories

These genres capture some important philosophical similarities and differences among the communication theories now in vogue. These genres also approximate the current divisions in the social sciences and as such constitute angles from which communication has been viewed. Although the theories within each of these genres share some philosophical assumptions, they are not mutually exclusive. Numerous differences exist among the theories in each group, and you will detect similarities and overlaps among groups as well. Some theories cross generic boundaries.[26]

26. This analysis adapts material from Fred R. Dallmayr, *Language and Politics* (Notre Dame, Ind.: University of Notre Dame Press, 1984); Lawrence Grossberg, "Does Communication Theory Need Intersubjectivity? Toward An Immanent Philosophy of Interpersonal Relations," in *Communication Yearbook* 6, ed. M. Burgoon (Beverly Hills, Calif.: Sage, 1984), pp. 171–205; and Jon Stewart, "Speech and Human Being," *Quarterly Journal of Speech* 72 (1986): 55–73. These categories also approximate those of Gibson Winter, *Elements for a Social Ethic: Scientific and Ethical Perspectives on Social Process* (New York: Macmillan, 1966). Winter's scheme was later elaborated by Richard McKeon, "Gibson Winter's Elements for a Social Ethic:

Structural and Functional Theories

This genre includes a broad group of loosely associated approaches to social science. Although the meanings for the terms *structuralism* and *functionalism* are imprecise, these approaches are generally characterized by a belief in real functioning structures outside the observing person.[27]

These approaches probably go back as far as Plato,[28] who believed that truth is ascertained through careful reflective thought, and Aristotle,[29] who believed in knowledge through observation and classification. System theory (Chapter 3), as far back as Georg Hegel's idea of dialectical materialism, is firmly planted in the structural-functional tradition.[30] Modern structuralism generally recognizes Emile Durkheim, who promoted the idea of social structure, and Ferdinand de Saussure, the father of structural linguistics, as important seminal figures.[31]

Although structural and functional approaches are often considered in combination, they differ in emphasis. Structuralism, which is rooted in linguistics, stresses the organization of language and social systems. Functionalism, which is rooted in biology, stresses the ways in which organized systems work to sustain themselves. Systems consist of variables that are causally related to other variables in a net-

A Review," *Journal of Religion* 49 (1969): 77–84; and by Ted J. Smith III, "Diversity and Order in Communication Theory: The Uses of Philosophical Analysis," *Communication Quarterly* 36 (1988): 28–40. The above categories are also similar to the model by G. Burrell and G. Morgan, *Sociological Paradigms and Organizational Analysis* (London: Heinemann, 1979).

27. For an excellent discussion of structuralism and functionalism, see Anthony Giddens, *Central Problems in Social Theory* (Berkeley: University of California Press, 1979). The distinction between structural and functional theory is clearly made by Paul E. Meehl, "What Social Scientists Don't Understand," in *Metatheory in Social Science: Pluralisms and Subjectivities*, eds. D. W. Fiske and R. A. Shweder (Chicago: University of Chicago Press, 1986), pp. 317–319.

28. *Meno.*

29. *Prior Analytics; Posterior Analytics.*

30. G. W. F. Hegel, *Phenomenology of Spirit*, trans. A. V. Miller (Oxford, Eng.: Oxford University Press, 1977).

31. Emile Durkheim, *The Division of Labor in Society* (London: Collier-Macmillan, 1964); Ferdinand de Saussure, *Course in General Linguistics* (London: Peter Owen, 1960).

work of functions. A change in one variable *functions* to create change in others. Putting these two approaches together results in a picture of a system as a structure of elements with functional relations.

Structural and functional theories share certain characteristics. First, they stress synchrony over diachrony. *Synchrony* means stability over time, and *diachrony* means change over time. In other words, these approaches emphasize generalizations about structures believed to be invariant, or nearly so. In contrast, many theories not identified with this genre focus on change and situational contingencies.

Second, these approaches tend to focus on the unintended consequences of action rather than purposeful outcomes. Structuralists mistrust concepts like "subjectivity" and "consciousness" and look for factors that are beyond the control and awareness of human actors. For this reason, such theories are sometimes called antihumanist.

Third, such theorists share a belief in independent reality. They therefore subscribe to the discovery method discussed earlier in the chapter, in which knowledge is discovered through careful observation.

Fourth, the theories tend to be dualist because they separate language and symbols from the thoughts and objects being symbolized in communication. For these scholars, the world exists in and of itself, and language is just a tool for representing what already exists. This belief necessitates the fifth characteristic—the use of the correspondence theory of truth. The *correspondence theory* requires that language must correspond with reality; symbols must accurately represent things.

Structural and functional theories of communication apply these general philosophical commitments.[32] These theorists see communication as a process in which individuals use language to convey meanings to others. The language and symbol systems used in communication have a life of their own apart from the people who employ these tools.

Predictably then, structuralists judge good communication as accurate and clear and view communication competence as the accurate, precise, and skillful use of language and other symbol systems.

Such theories have been extremely influential in the field of communication and have probably determined in large measure how many scholars in the United States view communication today. Several theories in chapters 4 and 5 illustrate the structural approach. In recent years, however, communication theories of this genre have come under scrutiny, and other traditions have assumed equal importance.

Cognitive and Behavioral Theories

Like its structural-functional cousin, this genre is a fusion of two traditions that are not the same but share many characteristics. These theories tend to espouse the same general assumptions about knowledge as do structural-functional theories, and they adopt almost exclusively discovery methods of generating knowledge. The primary difference between the two genres is in their focus and history. Structural and functional theories, which come out of sociology and other social sciences, tend to focus on social and cultural structures, whereas cognitive and behavioral theories, which come out of psychology and other behavioral sciences, tend to focus on the individual.

Psychology is the primary source of the cognitive and behavioral theories of human life. Psychological behaviorism throughout the twentieth century has dealt with the connection between stimuli (S), or inputs, and behavioral responses (R), or outputs. Cognitivism recognizes the S–R link but deals mostly with the information processing that occurs between stimulus and response. Until the mid-1960s or so, *behaviorism* was the favored term. Today, psychologists of this tradition identify themselves as *cognitivists*.[33]

These theorists are "variable-analytic" in that they attempt to catalog important cognitive vari-

32. For a discussion of the effects of this tradition on communication theory, see Lawrence Grossberg, "Communication Theory"; George Lakoff and Mark Johnson, *Metaphors We Live By* (Chicago: University of Chicago Press, 1980).

33. For a good general discussion of cognitivism, see John O. Greene, "Evaluating Cognitive Explanations of Communicative Phenomena," *Quarterly Journal of Speech* 70 (1984): 241–254.

ables and show ways in which these variables are correlated. They are also interested in the ways in which information- and cognitive-processing variables cause certain behavioral outputs. Some of these theories take a systems view, and others do not.

Communication is understood in these theories as a matter of individual behavior, individual thought processes, and bioneural functioning. Consequently, the most important aspects of your cognitive equipment, including language, are usually beyond your awareness and control.

A large and respectable body of literature in communication has emerged in the cognitive tradition. Most of this deals with the ways in which people generate and process messages. These studies tell us how information is organized and used by the individual to produce and evaluate messages and other people. Chapters 6 and 7 cover theories of this type.

Interactional and Conventional Theories

In brief, the theories of this genre view social life as a process of *interaction*, which establishes, maintains, and changes certain *conventions*, including language and symbols. Communication is usually viewed by interactional theorists as the glue of society. This genre is an important part of communication theory because it upholds communication as the preeminent force of social life. Theories in this genre tend to adopt discovery or interpretation modes of knowledge.

These theorists view social structure and function as products, not determinants, of interaction. Whereas structuralism puts structure ahead of interaction, interactionism reverses this order. The focus here is not on structures that permit communication but on how language is used to enact or create social structures and on how language and other symbol systems are reproduced, maintained, and changed through use. Meaning is not something objective to be transferred but emerges from and is created by communication.

Structuralism imagines that organized and objective structures function to accomplish outcomes; interactionism imagines that those structures are

themselves a product of the use of language and symbols in interaction. Interaction therefore leads to or reinforces shared meaning and establishes conventions like rules, roles, and norms that enable further interaction to take place.

Meanings themselves are conventions that are worked out through interaction; therefore, meanings change from time to time, from context to context, and from one group to another. In the final analysis then, interaction within actual groups is both the seat of tradition and the origin of change. Symbolic interactionism (Chapter 8), certain rule-using theories (Chapter 9), and theories of the social construction of reality (Chapter 9) illustrate this genre. These theories have had a major impact on our thinking about communication today.

Interpretive Theories

This genre includes theories that involve the discovery of meaning in action and texts. It includes theories of *phenomenology*, or the experience of the person, and of *hermeneutics*, or the process of interpretation. The theories of this genre describe the process by which understanding occurs, making a distinction between understanding and scientific explanation. The goal of interpretation is not to posit laws that govern events, but to uncover the ways in which people actually understand their own experience or the meanings within texts and objects of interpretation.[34]

Interpretive theories celebrate subjectivism, or the preeminence of individual experience, ascribing great importance to individuals' understandings of their experience. They usually emphasize the importance of language as the center of experience, believing that language creates a world of meaning within which the person lives and through which all experience is interpreted.

Interpretive theories describe the active mind attempting to uncover the meanings of experience in whatever form it may take. Sometimes under-

34. For a general source on interpretive theories, see M. Truzzi, *Verstehen: Subjective Understanding in the Social Sciences* (Reading, Mass: Addison-Wesley, 1974). See also Steward, "Speech and Human Being".

standing involves interpretation of culture, sometimes of texts or artifacts of various kinds. These theories tend to avoid prescriptive judgments about observed phenomena, and interpretations are often cast in tentative and relative terms.

A number of theories of communication are interpretive in nature. These include theories of cultural interpretation, ethnography, organizational culture, and textual interpretation (Chapter 10). Interpretive and interactional theories have a strong kindship based on their mutual concern for language and meaning and their use of interpretive methods.

Critical Theories

Critical theories consist of a loose confederation of ideas held together by their common interest in the quality of communication and human life. Critical theories do not merely observe; they also criticize. Most critical theories are concerned with the conflict of interests in society and the ways in which communication perpetuates domination. Many critical theories are based on Marxism (Chapter 11), although many have extended well beyond original Marxist thought.[35]

An important branch of critical theories is feminist thought (Chapter 11). Feminist scholarship examines and questions the meaning of the division of experience into the categories of masculine and feminine. It too is concerned with oppression and the distribution of power in society.[36]

Critical theories borrow heavily from most of the other genres. Although they reject functionalism and cognitivism, many of these theories are highly structural in orientation because they are looking for the underlying social structures that affect class and gender relations in society. This genre borrows from interactional-conventional theories by

35. For an overview of critical theories, see Thomas B. Farrell and James A. Aune, "Critical Theory and Communication: A Selective Review," *Quarterly Journal of Speech* 65 (1979): 93–120.

36. See, for example, Karen A. Foss and Sonja K. Foss, "Incorporating the Feminist Perspective in Communication Scholarship: A Research Commentary," in *Doing Research on Women's Communication: Alternative Perspectives in Theory and Method,* eds. C. Spitzack and K. Carter (Norwood, N.J.: Ablex, 1989), pp. 65–94.

acknowledging the importance of culture and the ways in which material practices, or praxis, reproduces, and sometimes changes culture. Indeed, one of the important contributions of critical theories is their recognition that communication forms define culture. Critical theories share with interpretive approaches the central concern for language and the ways in which language affects experience. They also make heavy use of interpretive methods.

Important differences exist among these five genres in what is assumed about knowledge, reality, and values. Each genre has its own powers and limits. Each enables theorists to do some things and not others. The various schools of thought within each genre also have their own powers and limits, as do individual theories themselves.

Structural and functional theories specify general categories and relations among variables in systems of all types. Such theories are weak in revealing the tone and color of individual events and particular human experiences. For example, a functional theory of organizations could indicate on a general level the consequences of certain supervisorial styles in terms of productivity, but it would not help you understand the feelings that individual workers might have about their supervisors and the stories they tell to help them cope with the job.

Cognitive theories describe and explain the mechanisms of individual information processing that operate in a variety of situations. Such theories tell us a lot about the psychology of persons, but they say little about the dynamics of social groups. Cognitive theories are designed to show how individuals think, but they are not well suited to explain how action is accomplished conjointly, between people. For example, a cognitive theory of message processing might tell how an individual person weighs information in forming an attitude about a topic, but it cannot reveal the ways in which meanings are created over time by interaction in groups or how attitudes are affected by cultural values.

Interactional and conventional theories are designed to uncover social processes and to show how behavior is affected by group norms and rules. These theories also show how communication can change social conventions. Thus, the power of these theories is to describe and explain interpersonal dynamics and relationships. They are good at expressing the ways in which people and groups change from situation to situation and from moment to moment; but they are weak in uncovering the structures of human life that exist across all situations. For example, an interactional theory might show how your self-concept changes from one occasion to another, depending on the values and rules of the group with which you affiliate. The same theory, however, would not do a very good job of helping you understand your enduring personality.

Interpretive theories are very powerful for revealing the meanings of individual experiences, texts, and social structures. Critical theories stress values or interests for judging events, situations, and institutions. Such theories can be powerful agents for change, which the other genres are not. At the same time, interpretive and critical theories are not suited for making scientific statements about the laws that govern human affairs. Thus, for example, a critical theory might help an observer analyze the speeches of a certain group, show what these speeches mean, and reveal the ways in they reflect the group's oppression in society at large. Such a theory would lead to certain conclusions about institutional changes to reduce or eliminate the oppression in the lives of certain groups of people. On the other hand, these theories would not tell us much about the general process of persuasion and how it operates.

Contexts of Communication

Communication is frequently discussed in terms of the "levels" or "contexts" in which it occurs. In fact, handbooks, textbooks, and college curricula often are divided into sections corresponding to these levels.

Although there is some variation in how contexts are labeled, four levels, which obviously range from narrow to very broad in focus, are commonly encountered in the literature and in college

courses: interpersonal communication, group communication, organizational communication, and mass communication.

• *Interpersonal communication* deals with communication between people, usually in face-to-face, private settings. These chapters include theories relevant to characteristics of communicators, discourse, and relationships.
• *Group communication* relates to the interaction of people in small groups, usually in decision-making settings. Group communication necessarily involves interpersonal interaction, and most of the theories of interpersonal communication apply also in the group context.
• *Organizational communication* occurs in large cooperative networks and includes virtually all aspects of both interpersonal and group communication and includes topics such as the structure and function of organizations, human relations, communication and the process of organizing, and organizational culture.
• *Mass communication* deals with public and mediated communication. Many of the aspects of interpersonal, group, and organizational communication enter into the process of mass communication.

The disadvantage of organizing theories of communication in this way is that it reinforces the already unfortunate tendency to think of these levels of communication as "types" that are different from one another. Although the contexts make a convenient way to organize theories, they should not be considered substantially different. There has been considerable concern of late for the division of the field into these levels, especially the division between mass communication and the others, and some work has been done to bridge these two groups.[37] Figure 1.2 illustrates that each context includes elements of the others as well as adding something of its own.

The chapters in Part III are designed to address a focal theoretical concern relevant to each context.

37. See, for example, Joseph N. Cappella (ed.), "Symposium on Mass and Interpersonal Communication," *Human Communication Research* 15 (1988): 236–318; Robert P. Hawkins, John M. Wiemann, and Suzanne Pingree (eds.), *Advancing Communication Science* (Newbury Park, Calif.: Sage, 1988).

Chapter 12 deals with relationships, which is a central concern of interpersonal communication. Chapter 13 deals with decision making as a key topic in group communication theory. Chapter 14 addresses communication and networks, and the central focal topic of Chapter 15 is media and communication. These chapters are not designed to cover all of the mainstream theories of each context. In fact, you will find theories relevant to these four contexts throughout this book.

Developing Core Communication Theory

Many of the theories you will encounter in this book deal with special aspects of communication. As we saw in the previous section, some theories explain particular contexts of communication, whereas others focus on general concepts and processes common to all communication. We can refer to general treatments as core communication theory.

Core theory is especially significant because it helps us understand communication in general. Core theories provide insight into processes that operate whenever communication takes place in any context. Special theories that deal with particular aspects or contexts of communication may also provide insights into the core process, and, if we want to advance our understanding of communication, looking for such insights in all communication theories is essential. The following list illustrates the types of elements included in core communication theories.

First, core theories can tell us something about the *development of messages*. How do we create what we write, say, and express to others? What mental processes are involved? To what extent and in what ways are messages created in interaction with others? How does the process of message development differ from culture to culture, and what are the cultural mechanisms that enter into the message development process?

Second, core theories often address *interpretation* and the *generation of meaning*. How do humans understand messages, and how does meaning arise in interaction with other people? How does the mind process information and interpret experience? To what extent and in what ways are meaning and understanding a product of culture?

Third, core theories sometimes discuss *message structure*. Message structure consists of the elements of texts in the form of writings, the spoken word, and other nonverbal forms. How are messages put together, and how are they organized? In what ways does the organization of a message possess meaning? How are communicators' messages in a dialogue organized together, and how do the participants in a conversation mesh their talk?

The fourth element often addressed by core theories is *interactional dynamics*. This involves relationships and interdependency among communicators and the joint creation of discourse and meaning. It addresses the give and take, the production and reception, between parties in a communication transaction, whether those parties are individuals or groups.

Finally, core theories may also help us understand *institutional* and *societal dynamics*, or the ways in which power and resources are distributed in society, the ways in which culture is produced, and the interaction among segments of society.

Naturally, no single theory will address all these elements, and when one or more elements are included in a theory, others may be implicated because of the relationship between elements. For example, a theory may focus on interactional dynamics and tell us something indirectly about how messages are organized. This eventuality is made possible because interactional dynamics and message structure are related to one another. Similarly, a theory that discusses message production may also inform us about message reception because the cognitive mechanisms involved in processing information in both production and reception may be similar.

As you study the various theories in this book, always look for the ways in which each might contribute to core theory. You will find that many of

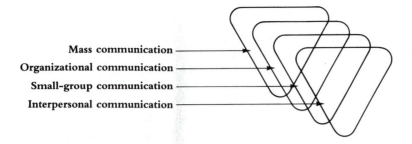

Mass communication
Organizational communication
Small-group communication
Interpersonal communication

Figure 1.2   The hierarchy of communication contexts.

Concepts and Commentary

the theories in Part II address core concepts and processes directly and as a group tell us a great deal about communication. Other theories in Part II and all those in Part III relate more to individual contexts, but they too can provide core insights if you examine them closely. In the final chapter, Chapter 16, we return again to core communication theory to assess its development at this point in the history of the communication field.

Concepts and Commentary

This chapter is important because it sets the stage for the entire book. Here, you learned about the nature of theory and inquiry and how communication has been studied. Remember that communication theory is *not* just a mental exercise. Although working with concepts can be rewarding in and of itself, understanding the process of communication by studying theories also provides insights that can make you a better, more adaptive communicator. Communication has assumed great importance in our times, and this is not going to change. Studying communication theory can make you a more informed member of society and can help you understand some of the problems you will face in many areas of your life. Communication theory is also empowering because it can suggest ideas about how to intervene or institute change.

It is probably not very important for you to memorize a list of definitions of communication; you

can certainly create enough of your own. It is important to remember that definitions are created to focus attention on certain observations and experiences that are important at the moment. In theory building, definitions are skeletal images of the central concerns of the theory builder. Having a single simple definition of communication would be nice; but in our field, this tidy state of affairs is not possible. The study of communication is too diverse, and multiple definitions are unavoidable, as are multiple theories.

In this chapter and the next, you begin to learn how people think as they create knowledge. This may be the most important learning of the entire text. The content of what we know about communication will change, but the basic approaches to knowledge will not. You will be able to use what you learn about communication for a time, but you will be able to use what you learn about inquiry and critical thinking for the rest of your life. If you go on professionally in communication or some other field in the social sciences, this overview of the theory-building process should be especially valuable.

Remember that there are a variety of ways in which to create knowledge, and each has its own powers and limits. You will develop preferences based on your own aptitudes and interests in scientific or humanistic methods, and you may even become proficient in moving from one way of knowing to another. Just keep in mind what these tools can and cannot do for you. Keep in mind also that social processes such as communication can never be completely understood from the vantage point of any single way of knowing, and significant contributions have been made by a variety of discovery, interpretation, and critical methods.

One of the most important points in this chapter is that a theory is not just a simple exposition of fact or reality. Theories are based on certain assumptions about knowledge, values, and things, and theories therefore differ in not only content but also form and philosophical perspective. Theoretical genres are useful for understanding similarities and differences among theories, but they are not pure types. Differences abound within each category, and you will even see that theories placed in one category may have some similarities with those placed in another. Theories can also be organized around contexts, which can be useful, as long as you keep the substantial overlap among contexts in mind.

CHAPTER 2

Theory in the Process of Inquiry

In the study of human communication, as in all branches of knowledge, it is appropriate, even compelling, to ask ourselves, How did we come to profess what we know or think we know? The question of truth, discovery, and inquiry is a particularly important place to begin this book because each chapter presents a kind of truth. Every theorist presented here has taken a stab at truth. This chapter discusses the special role of theory in the process of inquiry.

The Nature of Theory

What is theory? Uses of the term range from farmer Jones's theory about when his pullets will start laying eggs to Einstein's theory of relativity. People sometimes use the term *theory* to mean any unsubstantiated guess about something. Theory often is contrasted with "fact." Even among scientists, writers, and philosophers, the term is used in a variety of ways. The purpose of this book is to represent a wide range of thought about the communication process. Therefore, the term *theory* is used in its broadest sense as any conceptual representation or explanation of a phenomenon.[1] In their most general form, communication theories are attempts of various scholars to represent what is conceived as important in the process of communication. We can make two generalizations about theories.

First, all theories are abstractions. Theories of communication are not themselves the process being conceptualized. As a result, every theory is partial; every theory leaves something out. Theories focus on certain aspects of the process at the expense of other aspects. This truism about theory

1. For definitions of the terms *theory* and *model*, see Karl W. Deutsch, "On Communication Models in the Social Sciences," *Public Opinion Quarterly* 16 (1952): 357; Frank E. X. Dance and Carl E. Larson, *The Functions of Human Communication: A Theoretical Approach* (New York: Holt, Rinehart & Winston, 1976), p. 3; Leonard Hawes, *Pragmatics of Analoguing: Theory and Model Construction in Communication* (Reading, Mass.: Addison-Wesley, 1975), pp. 122–123. See also Steven H. Chaffee and Charles R. Berger, "What Communication Scientists Do," in *Handbook of Communication Science*, eds. C. R. Berger and S. H. Chaffee (Newbury Park, Calif.: Sage, 1987), pp. 91–122. For a discussion of the several senses of the term *theory*, see Ernest G. Bormann, *Communication Theory* (New York: Holt, Rinehart & Winston, 1980), pp. 24–25.

is important because it reveals the basic inadequacy of theory. No single theory will ever reveal Truth.

Second, all theories must be viewed as constructions. Theories are created by people, not ordained by God. Theories represent various ways in which observers see their environments, but theories themselves are not reality.[2] Many readers and theorists forget this principle, and students often are trapped by the conception that reality can be seen in this or that theory. Abraham Kaplan writes, "The formation of a theory is not just the discovery of a hidden fact; the theory is a way of looking at the facts, of organizing and representing them. . . . A theory must somehow fit God's world, but in an important sense it creates a world of its own."[3]

Let us take an analogy from biology. Two observers using microscopes may see different things in an amoeba, depending on their theoretical points of view. One observer sees a one-celled animal; the other sees an organism without cells. The first viewer stresses the properties of an amoeba that resemble all other cells—the wall, the nucleus, the cytoplasm. The second observer concentrates on the analogy between the amoeba and other whole animals. This observer sees ingestion of food, excretion, reproduction, mobility. Neither observer is wrong. Their theoretical frameworks simply stress different aspects of the observed object.[4] We will see this point again and again in the following chapters. Because theories are constructions, questioning a theory's usefulness is wiser than questioning its truthfulness. This statement is not intended to imply that theories do not represent reality but that any given "truth" can be represented in a variety of ways, depending on the theorist's orientation.

In one manner of speaking, this book is like an art gallery. As you stroll through the gallery, you do not question the truthfulness of a painting or sculpture. You think some are more artistic, more appealing, or more useful for providing a particular perspective than others. You may even question the composition or representativeness of a piece of art, but on some level you can enjoy them all as different creations, each with its own values and limits

Basic Elements of Theory

Concepts in Theories

The first and most basic aspect of a theory is concepts. We as persons are by nature concept-processing beings. Our entire symbolic world—everything known—stems from concept formation. Thomas Kuhn writes, "Neither scientists nor laymen learn to see the world piecemeal or item by item; . . . both scientists and laymen sort out whole areas together from the flux of experience."[5] Although the process of conceptualizing is complex, basically it consists of grouping things and events into categories according to observed commonalities. The communication theorist observes many variables in communication and classifies and labels them according to perceived patterns. A goal of theory is to present useful concepts.

An important part of conceptualizing is labeling. We mark our concepts by symbols, usually words. Hence, an integral part of any theory is the set of terms that captures the theory's concepts. Concepts and definitions cannot be separated. Together they tell us what the theorist is looking at and what is considered important.

Some theories stop at the concept level, providing only a list of concepts and definitions without explaining how the concepts interrelate or affect one another. Such theories are known as *taxonomies*. (Note that many scholars believe that taxonomies are *not* theories.) Introductory communication texts often include basic taxonomies that list the "parts" of the communication process, including such concepts as source, message,

2. See Max Black, *Models and Metaphors* (Ithaca, N.Y.: Cornell University Press, 1962).

3. Abraham Kaplan, *The Conduct of Inquiry* (San Francisco: Chandler, 1964), p. 309.

4. Examples from N. R. Hanson, *Patterns of Discovery* (Cambridge, Mass.: Cambridge University Press, 1961), pp. 4–5.

5. Thomas S. Kuhn, *The Structure of Scientific Revolutions* (Chicago: University of Chicago Press, 1970), p. 28.

receiver, feedback, and so forth. The best theories, however, go beyond concepts to provide explanations, statements about how concepts interrelate. These explanations tell us why variables are connected. Theories that stop at the concept level are primitive at best because the goal of theory building is to provide an understanding of how things work.

Explanation in Theories

The second element common to many theories is explanation. Explanation goes beyond naming and defining variables. It identifies regularities in the relationships among those variables. Explanations account for an event by referring to what is going on within that event or between it and some other event. In simplest terms, explanation answers the question, Why? Explanation relies primarily on the principle of necessity.

The principle of necessity. An explanation designates some logical force among variables that makes particular outcomes necessary. If *x* occurs, then *y* is necessary or probable. Necessity is rarely taken as absolute, and a probablistic model is more appropriate. There are a variety of kinds of necessity and therefore a variety of kinds of explanation.[6]

Causal necessity explains events in terms of cause-effect, where behavior is seen as an outcome of causal forces. *Practical necessity* explains events in terms of act-consequence, where behavior is seen as intentional action designed to achieve some goal or future state. Causal necessity explains behavior as response to stimuli, whereas practical necessity attributes volition to the person or object. In causal necessity, the consequent event is a necessary outcome of the antecedent event. In practical necessity, however, behavior is "necessary"

because the actor makes it so. (In fact, in practical explanation, the term *necessity* may be inappropriate.)

To better understand the difference between causal and practical necessity, consider how you might explain to a friend why you failed a test. If you said that you just aren't very good at this subject and had bad teachers in high school, you would be using causal necessity: My bad grade was caused by things I can't control. On the other hand, if you did quite well on the test, you would probably use practical necessity: I studied hard and needed to increase my grade-point average.

A useful model of theoretical explanation is that of Kenneth Gergen and Mary Gergen[7] (Figure 2.1). In this scheme, explanations are *empowered* when they use causal explanation, and explanations are *enabling* when they use practical explanation. Empowered explanations imagine that human behavior is determined or brought about by outside forces, whereas enabling explanations attribute intention and volition to the acts of human beings.

Explanations can also be divided into two further categories. *Person-centered explanations* concentrate on factors inside the acting person, whereas *situation-centered explanations* involve primarily outside factors. Some situation-centered explanations focus on factors occurring before the action being explained, and some focus on those occurring after the action. As Figure 2.1 illustrates, six types of explanation result.

Chaining explanations. Theories often put together an elaborate explanatory framework. In such a framework, statements are linked by logical connection so that by accepting certain statements other statements follow logically. This is logical chaining, which relies on the force of logical consistency. In the overall scheme of a theory, it is the glue that holds together the various theoretical statements. Logical necessity relies on a series of

6. Based on P. Achinstein, *Laws and Explanation* (New York: Oxford University Press, 1971); see also Donald P. Cushman and W. Barnett Pearce, "Generality and Necessity in Three Types of Theory About Human Communication, with Special Attention to Rules Theory," *Human Communication Research* 3 (1977): 344–353. For an excellent discussion of explanation in the social sciences, see Paul F. Secord (ed.), *Explaining Human Behavior: Consciousness, Human Action, and Social Structure* (Beverly Hills, Calif.: Sage, 1982).

7. Kenneth J. Gergen and Mary M. Gergen, "Explaining Human Conduct: Form and Function," in *Explaining Human Behavior: Consciousness, Human Action, and Social Structure*, ed. P. F. Secord (Beverly Hills, Calif.: Sage, 1982), pp. 127–154.

	Empowered explanations (Causal)	Enabling explanations (Practical)
Situation-centered (Prior)	"He was required to . . ." "She was raised to . . ."	"She used certain information." "Someone suggested it."
Person-centered	"It is a habit." "It is a trait."	"He decided." "She felt like it."
Situation-centered (Post)	"He is destined to . . ."	"He did it to reach a goal."

Figure 2.1   Forms of behavioral explanation.

internally consistent definitions and a set of correspondence rules among events. Consider the example of relational communication theory (explained in Chapter 12). The following list is a set of propositions contained in that theory. As you read through these propositions, notice how each presents an explanation of its own, yet the explanatory power of the entire set of propositions is made complete by the logic among them.

1. A complementary relationship exists when the behavior of one person follows naturally from the behavior of another (prior situation-centered/ enabling).

2. One person's behavior will follow naturally from another's when the relational rules are both understood and accepted by the partners (person-centered/enabling).

3. Power is the ability to control relational rules (person-centered/enabling).

4. One-up behavior asserts control over the relational rules (situation-centered/enabling).

5. One-down behavior accepts control by the other in a relationship (situation-centered/ enabling).

6. In a complementary relationship, the person consistently behaving in a one-up fashion has the power (person-centered/enabling).

Laws, rules, and systems. Traditionally, in the field of communication, theories have been separated into three types, depending on their primary method of explanation. *Law theories* are believed to rely primarily on causal necessity, embodying the spirit of science. They make use of covering laws that specify universal causal relations among variables. *Rule theories*, which rely on practical necessity, are believed to be more humanistic, claiming that people choose and change rules. In between lies the *systems approach*, which purportedly relies on logical chaining. This type of theory is believed to center on the logical relations among elements of a system. Such theories stress the intercorrelations among events.

Doubt has been cast on the utility of this laws–rules–systems trichotomy.[8] Differences may not be

8. This controversy is well summarized in Bormann, *Communication Theory*, chap. 7. See also Charles R. Berger, "The Covering Law Perspective as a Theoretical Basis for the Study of Human Communication," *Communication Quarterly* 25 (1977): 7–18; Donald P. Cushman, "The Rules Perspective as a Theoretical Basis for the Study of Human Communication," *Communication Quarterly* 25 (1977): 30–45; Peter R. Monge, "The Systems Perspective as a Theoretical Basis for the Study of Human Communication," *Communication Quarterly* 25 (1977): 19–29. See also Ted Smith III, "Diversity and Order in Communication Theory: The Uses of Philosophical Analysis," *Communication Quarterly* 36 (1988): 28–40.

as clear as suggested by its advocates. Although the covering law approach clearly embodies a scientific epistemology, the difference between systems and rules appears to be more a matter of generality or abstractness than method of explanation. Besides, there are important differences in explanation even among theories that are classed as systems or those classed as rules. For example, rules theorists disagree among themselves as to how much power rules exert over people's actions, and systems theorists equivocate about whether systems relations are causal, correlational, or both. Keep in mind that we are not discarding the terms laws, rules, and systems. In fact, they are a useful way to classify theories. The problem comes when they are used to distinguish forms of explanation.

The Traditional Ideal of Theory

Traditional social science has been dominated by an approach to theory and research modeled on the experimental natural sciences.[9] Traditional social science methods are based on a fourfold approach: (1) developing questions, (2) forming hypotheses, (3) testing the hypotheses, and (4) formulating theory. This approach is known as the *hypothetico-deductive method*. A theory then becomes a codification of hypotheses and/or findings from a series of tests. This approach is based on the assumption that complex phenomena are best understood in terms of fine analysis of parts, giving rise to the alternate label, the *variable-analytic tradition*. It also assumes that social life consists of cause–effect relations.

Hypothesis testing is a painstakingly slow process in which theories are developed and fine-tuned by numerous tests. The fourfold process is

thus repeated to generate new questions and improved hypotheses in an incremental building-block process. Figures 2.2 and 2.3 illustrate the hypothetical deductive method.[10]

The hypothetico-deductive method is based on five major concepts—hypothesis, operationism, control and manipulation, covering laws, and prediction. The first concept is hypothesis. An *hypothesis* is a well-formed guess about a relationship between variables. It is based on intuition, personal experience, or, most desirably, previous research and theory. In fact, hypothesis testing is often preceded by an inductive process of looking for generalizations.

An hypothesis must be testable; in other words, the variables brought together must be carefully defined so that any trained researcher can observe them in precisely the same way. Further, the relationship posited by the hypothesis must be framed so that potential rejection is possible. If it is not, any test will yield either a positive result or an equivocal one, and it is impossible to discover whether the hypothesis is wrong. Hypothesis testing, then, is really a process of looking for exceptions.

Operationism states that all variables in a hypothesis should be stated in ways that provide means of observation. An operational definition answers the question, How do you know when you see what you're seeking? Operational definitions are the most precise possible definitions because they tell you how the concept is to be seen. An operational definition of intelligence, for example, is the Stanford–Binet intelligence test. An operational definition of dominance might be a particular set of observer ratings on dominant versus submissive messages.

Operationism relies on *measurement*, in which precise, usually numerical, indices of observations are made. Measurement enables one to detect differences on an observed variable. Measurement is

9. See, for example, Steven H. Chaffee and Charles R. Berger, "What Communication Scientists Do"; Myron W. Lustig, "Theorizing About Human Communication," *Communication Quarterly* 34 (1986): 451–459; Fred N. Kerlinger, *Foundations of Behavioral Research* (New York: Holt, Rinehart & Winston, 1964), pp. 3–50; Robert J. Kibler, "Basic Communication Research Considerations," in *Methods of Research in Communication*, eds. P. Emmert and W. Brooks (Boston: Houghton Mifflin, 1970), pp. 9–50; Gerald Miller and Henry Nicholson, *Communication Inquiry* (Reading, Mass.: Addison-Wesley, 1976).

10. Figure 2.2 adapted from Walter L. Wallace, *Sociological Theory: An Introduction* (Chicago: Aldine, 1969), p. ix.; Figure 2.3 from Irwin B. J. Bross, *Design for Decision* (New York: Macmillan, 1952), pp. 161–177.

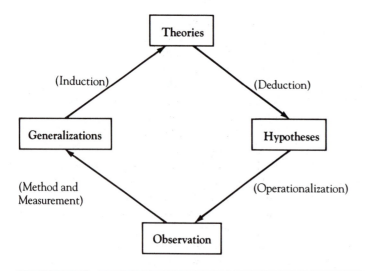

Figure 2.2   The classical ideal of science.

Reprinted with permission: Walter L. Wallace, (ed.) *Sociological Theory, An Introduction* (New York: Aldine de Gruyter). Copyright © 1969 by Walter L. Wallace.

evaluated in terms of two criteria: validity and reliability. *Validity* is the degree to which an observation measures what it is intended to measure. How do we know, for example, that the observer's ratings really measure dominance in communication? Perhaps what is really influencing the ratings is some other hidden factor, or perhaps the ratings reflect nothing in particular. Researchers have methods of estimating whether such measures are valid.

Reliability is the degree to which the construct is measured accurately, and reliability is most often estimated by consistency. If your bathroom scale gives you a different weight each day, even though you have not gained or lost, it is unreliable. And an intelligence test that yields a different result for the same person when administered on separate occasions is also unreliable. If all items on a test are designed to measure the same thing and they prove not to be very consistent with one another, the test is said to be unreliable. Clearly, validity and reliability are related to one another. Reliability is a necessary but not sufficient condition for validity. A measure cannot be valid if it is not first reliable.

The third concept of traditional science is *control* and *manipulation* in observation. These factors are

considered important because they are the only way in which causality can be ascertained. If one set of variables is held constant (control) and another set is systematically varied (manipulation), then the researcher can detect the effect of the manipulated variables without worrying about whether other variables were hidden causes. Control and manipulation can be exercised directly, as in experiments, or can be accomplished through particular kinds of statistical manipulation.

The fourth concept is the *covering law*. The covering law is a theoretical statement of cause and effect relevant to a particular set of variables across situations. In traditional science, the covering law is believed to be very significant because of its power in explaining events. Covering laws also enable the researcher to make predictions about future events. Theories in the classical tradition are statements of related covering laws, or more realistically, hypothesized laws.

Prediction is the final concept of classical social science inquiry. Prediction is an important outcome of inquiry; as an outcome, prediction gives people power over their environment. If, for example, I can predict that certain kinds of communi-

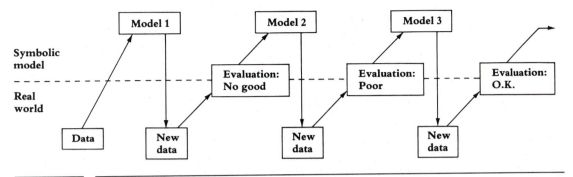

Figure 2.3   The decision-making process.

From *Design for Decision* by Irwin Bross. Copyright © 1953 by Macmillan Publishing Company. Reprinted with permission of the publisher. Copyright renewed 1981 by Irwin D. J. Bross.

cation will lead to particular relationships, I may be able to control relationships by carefully designing communication messages. Prediction is also crucial in the process of inquiry. Hypotheses are often stated in the form of a prediction: If x and y, then z.

This classical approach to research and theory is firmly planted in the tradition of "knowledge as discovery," as explained in Chapter 1. As our previous discussion points out, however, the discovery method is often rejected by scholars in the interpretive and critical traditions. In general terms these critics refer to the classical ideal as "old paradigm" social science and their own work as that of the "new paradigm."[11] A less biased designation is "traditional" and "alternative" paradigms.

Later in this chapter, we will discuss the paradigms and the issues that divide these schools of thought. In brief, alternative-paradigm scholars question two of the assumptions made by the older approach. First, they believe that reality does not have a singular, static structure to be discovered and represented by theory. Rather, reality itself changes and can be represented in a variety of useful ways. This shift questions the whole approach of hypothesis testing and validity in theory. Second, these researchers are suspicious of the view

that human behavior can be broken down into a set of variables that are determined by causal forces. These researchers therefore eschew covering laws and prediction in favor of interpretation.

Theory Development and Change

Although it is important to understand that theory is an abstraction from reality, realizing the relationship between the two is also necessary. Theory is not purely abstract, without grounding in actual experience. Experience affects theory, and theory in turn affects one's conception of experience.

From original experiences (including research), we formulate theory. Good theory development, then, is a constant process of testing and formulating. For the traditionalist, this testing is a process of improving hypotheses about the "real" world. For the alternative-paradigm theorist, it is a process of fine-tuning interpretive frameworks for understanding the flow of events.

The theory development process stresses the need for research, which allows for

1. Specific investigation of facts that are considered significant.

2. Testing the theory's predictive power or interpretive utility.

11. See, for example, R. Harré and P. F. Secord, *The Explanation of Social Behavior* (Totowa, N.J.: Littlefield, Adams, 1979), pp. 19–25.

3. Further developing and articulating the theory.[12]

Theories may change in three ways. The first is *growth by extension*. Here, knowledge is expanded piece-by-piece, moving from an understanding of one bit of reality to an adjoining bit by adding new concepts to the old. The second way, *growth by intension*, is the process of developing an increasingly precise understanding of individual concepts.[13] For example, you might develop a theory of the use of insults in conflict situations. Your theory would change by extension if you added ideas about how compliments and jokes also occur in conflict situations. It would change by intension if you could elaborate more and more on the role of insults. Obviously, a theory could change by extension and intension at the same time.

The third way in which theories change is through *revolution*.[14] In his well-known monograph on scientific revolutions, Thomas Kuhn states that "normal science" is a process of developing theory through extension and intension with relative consensus on the basic nature of the reality being modeled. At some point an extraordinary case is discovered that runs counter to prevailing assumptions of the theories in use. At this point a crisis develops, leading to the development of a new theoretical approach. The new theory (or set of theories) represents a different, competing way of looking at the world. For example, you might discover that conflict has nothing to do with insults at all. Gradually, the revolutionary theory is accepted by more and more members of the field until it becomes the primary theoretical approach in a new normal science.

In a scientific revolution, two paradigms are pitted against one another. The old paradigm represents normal science, and the new represents the revised view. Paradigms are sets of concepts and variables that a group of scholars believe to be important to study, accompanied by a particular opinion of how these things operate. In normal science most scholars agree that a certain set of phenomena, defined by a known set of concepts, are important and should be studied. These scholars also share a notion of how these variables are related.

In a scientific revolution, the concepts and operations come to be conceptualized in a radically different fashion, requiring redefinition of an entire field of knowledge. Previous areas of study may die, others may be born, and new weddings may occur. "What were ducks in the scientist's world before the revolution are rabbits afterwards. The man who saw the exterior of the box from above later sees its interior from below."[15] We can now see why critics of traditional social science are quick to call their approach "new paradigm" and why traditionalists dislike this term.

The Functions of Theory

Nine important and overlapping functions of theory can be identified. The first function of theory is to *organize* and *summarize* knowledge. We do not see the world in bits of data. We need to organize and synthesize the world. Patterns must be sought and connections discovered. Theories and models are one way of accomplishing this organization of knowledge. An added benefit of this function is theory's contribution to accumulated knowledge. The student, practitioner, or scientist does not have to start anew with each investigation. Knowledge is organized into a body of theories, and the investigator begins a study with the organized knowledge of generations of previous scholars.

The second function is that of *focusing*. Theories, besides organizing data, focus attention on important variables and relationships, as a map depicts terrain. From the overall surface, a map points out recreation spots, communities, picnic grounds, and shopping centers. To the persistent

12. Kuhn, *Structure*, pp. 25–27.

13. Kaplan, *Conduct*, p. 305.

14. Kuhn, *Structure*. See also Ellen K. Coughlin, "Thomas Kuhn's Ideas About Science," *Chronicle of Higher Education* 22 September 1982, pp. 21–23.

15. Kuhn, *Structure*, p. 111.

question of "What will I look at?" the theory points out areas for investigation.

Third, theories *clarify* what is observed. The clarification not only helps the observer to understand relationships in communication but also to interpret specific events. Theories provide guideposts for interpreting, explaining, and understanding the complexity of human relations.

Fourth, theories offer an *observational* aid. Closely related to the focus function, the observational function points out not only what to observe but how to observe. Especially for those theories that provide operational definitions, the theorist gives the most precise indication possible about what is meant by a particular concept. Thus, by following directions the reader is led to observe details elaborated by the theory.

The fifth function of theories, to *predict*, is one of the most widely discussed purposes of scientific inquiry. Many theories allow the inquirer to make predictions about outcomes and effects in the data. This ability to predict is important in the applied communication areas such as persuasion and attitude change, psychotherapy, small-group dynamics, organizational communication, advertising, public relations, and mass media. Teachers work toward developing skills and abilities to improve communication competence. Various communication theories aid this process by helping the student substitute well-founded predictions for good guesses.

The sixth theoretical function, the *heuristic function*, is also frequently discussed. A familiar axiom is that a good theory generates research. The speculation forwarded in theories of communication often provides a guide about the direction the research will take and thus aids in furthering the investigation. This heuristic function of aiding discovery is vital to the growth of knowledge and is in a sense an outgrowth of each of the other functions of theory.

Seventh, theories serve an indispensable *communicative function*. Most investigators want and need to publish their observations and speculations for other interested persons. Theory provides a framework for this communication and provides an open forum for discussion, debate, and criticism.

Through the communication of numerous explanations of the phenomena we study, comparison and theory improvement become possible.

The eighth function of theories is *control*. This function grows out of value questions, in which the theorist seeks to judge the effectiveness and propriety of certain behavior. Such theory is often referred to as normative, in that it seeks to establish norms of performance. Much theory, of course, does not seek to fulfill this function at all, remaining on the descriptive level.

The final function of theory is the *generative function*. This is particularly relevant to the interpretive and critical traditions of alternative-paradigm social science. In short, it means using theory to challenge existing cultural life and to generate new ways of living. It is, in other words, the use of theory to achieve change. Kenneth Gergen states the generative function in these terms: "the capacity to challenge the guiding assumptions of the culture, to raise fundamental questions regarding contemporary social life, to foster reconsideration of that which is 'taken for granted,' and thereby to generate fresh alternatives for social action."[16]

Philosophical Issues in the Study of Communication

Communication Metatheory

Metatheory, as the prefix *meta-* suggests, is a body of speculation on the nature of inquiry that goes beyond the specific content of given theories. It addresses such questions as what should be observed, how observation should take place, and what form theory should take. Metatheoretical debates are a natural consequence of uncertainty over the status of knowledge in a field. In the last twenty years, metatheory has dominated the communication field. Communication scholars have come to question the adequacy of their methods,

16. Kenneth J. Gergen, *Toward Transformation in Social Knowledge* (New York: Springer-Verlag, 1982), p. 109.

precisely because of the problems of social science summarized in Chapter 1.[17]

Philosophy as a discipline deals with problems of knowledge and reality. Philosophy questions the basic assumptions and methods of proof used in generating knowledge in all walks of life. Thus, the kind of metatheoretical discussion that has occurred in communication constitutes an important philosophical analysis of communication research and theory. This philosophical examination is complex, yet it can be grouped into three major themes: epistemology (questions of knowledge), ontology (questions of existence), and axiology (questions of value).

Figure 2.4 identifies and briefly outlines the major issue areas of the field.[18] It is divided into three general levels–the metatheoretical, the hypothetical, and the descriptive. The *metatheoretical level* is the most general and includes one's basic assumptions. The *hypothetical level* is the level of theory in which one's picture of reality is painted, and the framework for knowledge is established. The *descriptive level* includes actual statements of operations and findings closest to the thing observed. These three levels cannot be separated as distinct entities. When operating on one level, the scholar always examines the other two at the same time. The three levels within any knowledge tradition reinforce one another. Let us now look more closely at some of the actual issues within each area.

17. For an excellent discussion of metatheoretical issues, see Donald W. Fiske and Richard A Shweder (eds.), *Metatheory in Social Science: Pluralisms and Subjectivities* (Chicago: University of Chicago Press, 1986); W. Barnett Pearce, Vernon E. Cronen, and Linda M. Harris, "Methodological Considerations in Building Human Communication Theory," in *Human Communication Theory: Comparative Approaches*, ed. F. E. X. Dance (New York: Harper & Row, 1982), pp. 1–41. See also John Waite Bowers and James J. Bradac, "Issues in Communication Theory: A Metatheoretical Analysis," in *Communication Yearbook 5*, ed. M. Burgoon (New Brunswick, N.J.: Transaction, 1982), pp. 1–28. For a thorough discussion of many of the issues in communication, see George Gerbner (ed.), *Ferment in the Field*, a special issue of *Journal of Communication* 33 (Summer 1983); and Brenda Dervin, Lawrence Grossberg, Barbara O'Keefe, and Ellen Wartella (eds.), *Rethinking Communication: Paradigm Issues* (Newbury Park, Calif.: Sage, 1989).

18. Adapted from Stanley Deetz, unpublished handout.

Issues of Epistemology

Epistemology is the branch of philosophy that studies knowledge. Epistemologists ask how people know what they claim to know. These scholars question observations and claims as a way of understanding the nature of knowledge and the processes by which it is gained. Any good discussion of inquiry and theory will inevitably come back to epistemological issues.

Because of the diversity of disciplines involved in the study of communication and the resulting divergence of thought about research and theory, epistemological issues are important in this field. Some of the most basic of these issues can be expressed as questions.[19]

To what extent can knowledge exist before experience? Many theorists believe that all knowledge arises from experience. We observe the world and thereby come to know about it. Yet is there something in our basic nature that provides a kind of knowledge even before we experience the world? Many philosophers believe so. This kind of "knowledge" would consist of inherent mechanisms of thinking and perceiving. For example, strong evidence exists that children do not learn language entirely from hearing it spoken. Rather, they may acquire language by using innate models to test what they hear. (We will discuss this idea more in Chapter 5.)

To what extent can knowledge be certain? Is knowledge certain, there for the taking by whoever can ascertain it? Or is knowledge relative and changing? The debate over this issue has persisted for hundreds of years. Communication theorists vary in terms of assumptions about the certainty of truth. Those who take a universal stance will admit

19. This analysis from Stephen W. Littlejohn, "Epistemology and the Study of Human Communication" (Paper delivered at the Speech Communication Association, New York, November 1980). See also Stephen W. Littlejohn, "An Overview of Contributions to Human Communication Theory from Other Disciplines," in *Human Communication Theory: Comparative Essays*, ed. F. E. X. Dance (New York: Harper & Row, 1982), pp. 247–249. For another approach, see W. Barnett Pearce, "Metatheoretical Concerns in Communication," *Communication Quarterly* 25 (1977): 3–6.

	Epistemological	Ontological	Perspectival	Axiological
Metatheory	Methodological questions	Metaphysical questions	Definitional questions	Aesthetic and value questions
Hypothetical	Methods and procedures	Theories, concepts, hypotheses, laws, and interpretive schemas	Definitions and metaphors	Ethical and moral premises and values
Descriptive	Instruments and techniques	Observational statements	Substantive focuses	Judgments
Things-in-Themselves	Flow of events			

Figure 2.4   Philosophical areas affecting theory

to errors in their theories, but they believe that these errors are merely a result of not yet having discovered the complete truth. Relativists would have us believe that knowledge will never be certain because there is no universal reality that can be comprehended.

By *what process does knowledge arise?* This question is extremely complex, and the debate on the issue lies at the heart of epistemology. There are at least four positions on the issue. Mentalism, or *rationalism,* suggests that knowledge arises out of the sheer power of the human mind. This position places ultimate faith in human reasoning. *Empiricism* states that knowledge arises in perception. We experience the world and literally "see" what is going on. *Constructivism* holds that people create knowledge in order to function pragmatically in life. People project themselves into what they experience. Constructivists believe that phenomena in the world can be fruitfully conceptualized many different ways, knowledge being what the person has made of the world. Finally, taking constructivism one step further, *social constructionism* teaches that knowledge is a product of symbolic interaction within social groups. In other words,

reality is socially constructed and a product of group and cultural life.

Is knowledge best conceived in parts or wholes? Gestaltists teach that true knowledge consists of general, indivisible understandings. They believe that phenomena are highly interrelated and operate as a system. Analysts, on the other hand, believe that knowledge consists of understanding how parts operate separately.

To what extent is knowledge explicit? Many philosophers and scholars believe that you cannot know something unless you can state it. Knowledge is thus seen as explicit. Others claim that much of knowledge is hidden, that people operate on the basis of sensibilities that are not conscious and that they may be unable to express. Such knowledge is said to be tacit.[20]

The way in which scholars conduct inquiry and construct theories depends largely on their epistemological assumptions. Many basic positions arise from the issues just described. These positions can be called *worldviews.* Numerous fine distinctions

20. See Michael Polanyi, *Personal Knowledge* (London: Routledge & Kegan Paul, 1958).

can be made among these positions, but our discussion groups them into two broad opposing worldviews that affect thinking about communication.[21]

The *Worldview I* tradition is based on empiricist and rationalist ideas. It treats reality as distinct from the human being, something that people discover outside themselves. It assumes a physical, knowable reality that is self-evident to the trained observer.

Discovery is important in this position; the world is waiting for the scientist to find it. Because knowledge is viewed as something acquired from outside oneself, Worldview I is often called the *received view*. Objectivity is all important, with investigators being required to define the exact operations to be used in observing events. Most mainstream physical science is Worldview I, and much behavioral and social sciences follow suit.

Worldview I aims to make lawful statements about phenomena, developing generalizations that hold true across situations and over time. Scholars in this tradition try to reveal how phenomena appear and how they work. In so doing the scholar is highly analytical, attempting to define each part and subpart of the object of interest.

Worldview II takes a different turn by relying heavily on constructivism, viewing the world in process. In this view people take an active role in creating knowledge. A world of things exists outside the person, but the individual can conceptualize these things in a variety of useful ways. Knowledge therefore arises not out of discovery but from interaction between knower and known. For this reason perceptual and interpretive processes of the individuals are important objects for study.

Worldview II attempts not to uncover universal laws but to describe the rich context in which individuals operate. It is humanistic in that it stresses the individual subjective response. Knowing is interpreting, an activity in which everybody is believed to engage. Many theories of communication take a Worldview II stance, being based on the assumption that communication itself is a vital vehicle in the social construction of reality.[22]

Issues of Ontology

Whereas epistemology is the study of knowledge, *ontology* is the branch of philosophy that deals with the nature of being, or more narrowly, the nature of the phenomena we seek to know.[23] Actually, epistemology and ontology go hand-in-hand because our conception of knowledge depends in part on our notions about the nature of the knowable. In the social sciences, ontology deals largely with the nature of human existence. Thus, ontological issues in the study of communication deal with the nature of human social interaction.

Ontological issues are important because the way a theorist conceptualizes communication depends in large measure on how the communicator is viewed. All communication theories begin with assumptions about being. Issues in this area reflect disagreements about the nature of human experience. Four issues are important.[24]

To what extent do humans make real choices? Although all investigators probably would agree that people perceive choice, there is a long-standing philosophical debate on whether real choice is

21. This particular analysis is supported in part by Georg H. von Wright, *Explanation and Understanding* (Ithaca, N.Y.: Cornell University Press, 1971); and Joseph Hanna, "Two Ideals of Scientific Theorizing," in *Communication Yearbook 5*, ed. M. Burgoon (New Brunswick, N.J.: Transaction, 1982), pp. 29–48. Many other schemes have been devised to classify epistemological approaches. See, for example, Stephen Pepper, *World Hypotheses* (Berkeley: University of California Press, 1942); B. Aubrey Fisher, *Perspectives on Human Communication* (New York: Macmillan, 1978); Kenneth Williams, "Reflections on a Human Science of Communication," *Journal of Communication* 23 (1973): 239–250; Barry Brummett, "Some Implications of 'Process' or 'Intersubjectivity': Postmodern Rhetoric," *Philosophy and Rhetoric* 9 (1976): 21–51; Gerald Miller, "The Current Status of Theory and Research in Interpersonal Communication," *Human Communication Research* 4 (1978): 175.

22. See, for example, Peter Berger and Thomas Luckmann, *The Social Construction of Reality* (Garden City, N.Y.: Doubleday, 1966); Alfred Schutz, *The Phenomenology of the Social World*, trans. George Walsh and Frederick Lehnert (Evanston, Ill.: Northwestern University Press, 1967); Kenneth Gergen, "The Social Constructionist Movement in Modern Psychology," *American Psychologist* 40 (March 1985): 266–275; Harré and Secord, *Explanation*.

23. For a discussion of ontology, see Alasdair MacIntyre, "Ontology," in *The Encyclopedia of Philosophy*, vol. 5, ed. P. Edwards (New York: Macmillan, 1967): 542–543.

24. For an ontological discussion of communication theory, see Bowers and Bradac, "Issues."

possible. On one side of the issue are the determin-
ists, who state that people's behavior is caused by a
multitude of prior conditions and that humans are
basically reactive and passive. On the other side of
the debate are the pragmatists, who claim that people plan their behavior to meet future goals. This
school sees people as decision-making, active
beings who affect their own destinies. Middle positions also exist, suggesting either that people make
choices within a restricted range or that some
behavior is determined while other behavior is a
matter of free will.

*To what extent are humans best understood in terms
of states versus traits?*[25] States are temporary conditions through which people pass. The state view
believes that humans change and go through
numerous states in the course of a day, year, or lifetime. The state view characterizes humans as
dynamic. The trait view believes that people are
mostly predictable because they display more or less
constant characteristics. People may change
because their traits have changed, but traits do not
change easily. For the most part, humans are static.
Many social scientists, of course, believe that both
traits and states characterize human behavior.

*To what extent is human experience basically indi-
vidual versus social?* Many social scientists view
humans as individuals. Although these scholars
understand that people are not in fact isolated from
one another and that interaction is important, they
interpret behavior as if it stems primarily from the
individual. The unit of analysis for such scholars is
the individual human life. Many other social scientists, however, focus on social life as the primary
unit of analysis. These scholars believe that
humans cannot be understood apart from their
relationships with others in groups and cultures.
This issue is especially important to communication scholars because of our focus on interaction.[26]

To what extent is communication contextualized?
The question is whether behavior is governed by
universal principles or whether it depends on situational factors. Some philosophers believe that
human life and action are best understood by looking at universal factors; others believe that behavior is richly contextual and cannot be generalized
beyond the immediate situation. The middle
ground on this issue is that behavior is affected by
both general and situational factors.

Although numerous ontological positions can be
seen in communication theory, this book groups
them into two basic opposing positions: actional
and nonactional. *Actional theory* assumes that individuals create meanings, have intentions, and
make real choices. Theorists of the actional tradition are reluctant to seek covering laws because
they assume that individual behavior is not governed entirely by prior events. Instead, they assume
that people behave differently in different situations because rules change from one situation to
another.

Nonactional theory assumes that behavior basically is determined by and is responsive to biology
and environment. Covering laws are usually
viewed as appropriate in this tradition; active interpretation by the individual is downplayed.

Axiological Issues

Axiology is the branch of philosophy studying
values. For the communication scholar, three axiological issues are especially important.

Can theory be value-free? Classical science claims
that theories and research are value-free; scholarship is neutral, attempting to get the facts as they
are manifest in the real world. When a scientist's
values impinge on his or her work, the result is bad
science.[27] Another position on this issue is that
scholarship is free of substantive values but embodies such metavalues as the pursuit of truth, the
importance of ideas, objectivity, and the value of
science itself. Here, the contention is that science
is not value-free because the researcher's work is

25. This debate is summarized by Peter A. Andersen, "The
Trait Debate: A Critical Examination of the Individual Differences Paradigm in the Communication Sciences," in *Progress in
Communication Sciences*, eds. B. Dervin and M. J. Voigt (Norwood, N.J.: Ablex, 1986).

26. See, for example, Berger and Luckmann, *Social Construction*; Gergen, "Social Constructionist Movement."

27. See, for example, Kaplan, *Conduct*, p. 372.

guided by an interest in certain ways of conducting inquiry.[28]

Finally, some scholars contend that theory can never be value-free, in method or in substance. Scientists choose what to study, and those choices are affected by personal as well as institutional values. Government and private organizational values determine what research is funded; political and economic ideologies both feed and are fed by particular ways of viewing the world embodied by different forms of theory and research.[29]

A substantial political argument on values exists in science. Traditional scientists claim that they are not responsible for the ways scientific knowledge is used, that it can be used for good or ill. Critics object that scientific knowledge by its very nature is instrumentalist and control-oriented and that it necessarily promotes power domination in society. Traditional communication knowledge, especially as derived by media research, is believed by Marxists to be a necessary administrative tool of the power elite. The critics of science do not themselves claim to be above power, but they see themselves as making a choice in favor of a set of values that challenges domination in society rather than perpetuates it. This debate is discussed in more detail in Chapter 11.

To what extent does the practice of inquiry influence that which is studied? This second major value issue centers on the question of whether scholars intrude upon and thereby affect the process being studied. The traditional scientific viewpoint is that scientists observe carefully, but without interference, such that observational fidelity is maintained. Critics doubt this is possible. Observation by its very nature distorts that which is being observed. Sometimes the distortion is great, sometimes small, but it is always there.

On a higher level, some critics maintain that theory and knowledge themselves affect the course

of human life.[30] This presents two potential problems. First, the scholar, by virtue of scholarly work, becomes an agent of change. That role must be actively understood and reckoned with. At the very least, the scholar must consider ethical issues involved. Second, studying human life changes that life, so that what you believe you know at one time may not be true at another time. This second point has particularly profound epistemological implications.[31]

Finally, *to what extent should scholarship attempt to achieve social change?* Should scholars remain objective, or should they make conscious efforts to help society change in positive ways? Many believe that the proper role of the scholar is to produce knowledge: Let the technicians and politicians do what they will with it. Other scholars vociferously disagree: Responsible scholarship involves an obligation to promote positive change. Obviously, this second view is consistent with the critical approach to the development of knowledge.[32]

Overall then, two general positions reside in these axiological issues. First, *value-conscious scholarship* recognizes the importance of values to research and theory and makes a concerted effort to direct those values in positive directions. What those directions should be, of course, is a matter of debate. Second, *value-neutral scholarship* believes that science is aloof from values.

How to Evaluate a Communication Theory

As you encounter theories of communication, you will need a basis for judging one against

28. See, for example, Juergen Habermas, *Knowledge and Human Interests*, trans. J. J. Shapiro (Boston: Beacon Press, 1971), p. 302; Kaplan, *Conduct*, pp. 370–397.

29. See, for example, Brian Fay, *Social Theory and Political Practice* (London: George Allen & Unwin, 1975).

30. See, for example, Fay, *Social Theory*; Gergen, *Transformation*, pp. 21–34.

31. This issue is explored by Sheila McNamee, "Research as Social Intervention: A Research Methodology for the New Epistemology" (Paper presented at the Fifth International Conference on Culture and Communication, Philadelphia, October 1988).

32. See, for example, Cees. J. Hamelink, "Emancipation or Domestication: Toward a Utopian Science of Communication," *Journal of Communication* 33 (1983): 74–79.

another. The following is a list of criteria that can be applied to the evaluation of any theory.[33] Remember that no theory is perfect; all can be faulted. Therefore, the following criteria are goal ideals.

Theoretical Scope

A theory's scope is its comprehensiveness or inclusiveness. Theoretical scope relies on the principle of generality.[34] This principle states that a theory's explanation must be sufficiently general to cover a range of events beyond a single observation. People continually provide explanations for events, but their explanations are not always theoretical. When an explanation is a mere speculation about a single event, it is not a theoretical explanation. However, when an explanation goes beyond a single instance to cover a range of events, it is theoretical.

Two types of generality exist. The first is the coverage of a broad domain. Theories that meet the test of generality in this way deal with many phenomena. A communication theory that meets this test would explain a variety of communication-related behaviors. This has been one of the appeals of system theory, for example. It explains an incredibly wide spectrum of events. A theory need not cover a large number of phenomena to be judged as good, however. Indeed, many fine theories are narrow in coverage. Such theories possess the second type of generality. Although they deal with a narrow range of events, their explanations of these events apply to a large number of situations. Such theories are said to be powerful. Certain theories of relationship breakups illustrate this type of generality.

Appropriateness

Are the theory's epistemological, ontological, and axiological assumptions appropriate for the theoretical questions addressed and the research methods used? In the last chapter, we discussed the fact that different genres of theory allow scholars to do different kinds of things. One criterion by which theories can be evaluated is whether their claims are consistent with their assumptions. If you assume that people make choices and plan actions to accomplish goals, it would be inappropriate to predict behavior on the basis of causal events. If you believe that the real structures affecting behavior are normally out of awareness, it would be inconsistent to report survey data in which subjects were asked why they did certain things. If you believe that theory should be value-free, it would be inconsistent to base your definition of communication on some standard of effectiveness.

In a way then, appropriateness is a kind of logical consistency between theories and presuppositions. For example, many writers from the cognitive tradition state that people actively process information and make plans to accomplish personal goals. Yet theories produced by these researchers often make lawlike statements about universal behaviors, which, if true, would leave little room for purposeful action.

Heuristic Value

Does the theory have potential for generating research and additional theory? One of the primary functions of theory is to help investigators decide what to observe and how to observe it. For example, a major contribution of Bales's interaction process theory (Chapter 13) is that it has spawned much research and further theorizing about group communication. Even Bales's critics find his ideas useful as springboards to develop new concepts.

Validity

Generally speaking, validity is the truth value of a theory. Of course, we must be careful to understand that "truth" is not intended to mean absolute, single-minded fact. Rather, there may be a variety of "truth values" to a theory. Consequently,

33. Evaluation is discussed in greater depth in Bross, *Design*, pp. 161–77; Deutsch, "On Communication Models," pp. 362–363; Calvin S. Hall and Gardner Lindzey, *Theories of Personality* (New York: Wiley, 1970), chap. 1; Kaplan, *Conduct*, pp. 312–322; Kuhn, *Structure*, pp. 100–101, 152–156.

34. Achinstein, *Laws*; Cushman and Pearce, "Generality."

validity as a criterion of theory has at least three meanings.[35]

One kind of validity is that of *value*, or *worth*. This definition of validity concerns the question of importance or utility, whether the theory has conceptual or pragmatic value. This is the primary form of validity in interpretive and critical theories.

The second kind of validity is that of *correspondence*, or *fit*. Here the question is whether the concepts and relations specified by the theory can be seen in observations of ongoing life. Both classical and interpretive-critical theories require fit as a form of validity, and one of the most important functions of research in both traditions is to establish that correspondence. Classical science assumes that one and only one representation will fit, whereas interpretive sciences believe that a number of theories may simultaneously fit. When this is the case, we judge between those theories on the basis of the first kind of validity: value, or worth.

The third kind of validity is *generalizability*, which refers to the extent to which the tenets of the theory apply across situations. This is the classical definition of validity and applies almost exclusively to traditional, discovery-oriented theories with covering laws.

Parsimony

The test of parsimony can be called logical simplicity. If two theories are equally valid, the theory with the simplest logical explanation is said to be the best. For example, although classical information theory can be faulted on other grounds, it is highly parsimonious. A few core assumptions and premises lead logically to a variety of claims about channels, signals, messages, and transmission.

Concepts and Commentary

As mentioned in the previous chapter, the material in Part I may be the most important in the

35. This analysis adapted from David Brinberg and Joseph E. McGrath, *Validity and the Research Process* (Beverly Hills, Calif.: Sage, 1985).

entire book. Here you have learned how communication is studied, the nature of theory, and the various forms that theory building can take. You have also learned what theories can do for us and how to evaluate a communication theory.

Theories are constructions: They are created by human interpreters just as all discourse is created. Theories cannot be taken as truth because they are abstractions, and different scholars will see different things in the same observation. Therefore, the constructions employed to understand communication are extremely diverse. They vary in not only what is covered but also their form and style; and a good deal of disagreement exists about what constitutes a legitimate theory. This state of affairs forces us to take a rather broad view of theory as any conceptual representation of communication. This broad coverage should be seen as an opportunity, rather than an obstacle, because it will help you explore a wide variety of representations and styles. It will let you see examples of a whole range of ways of depicting knowledge. Although a theory course in certain narrow fields is like a tour of a Renaissance portrait gallery, ours is like a tour of the full museum with numerous types and forms of art.

Regardless of their differences, however, all theories are basically composed of concepts, or labeled categories used to classify observations. Many theories also have explanations, which tell us why communication works as it does. Several models of explanation are discussed in this chapter, but what is most important to remember is that all rely on some form of necessity, or logical relations among concepts. The logic employed by the theory creates a kind of "force" that makes one statement follow naturally from another.

Traditionally, you have learned, theory is hypothetical and deductive. In other words, the theory is built on hypotheses and research. One posits a relationship, tests that relationship, and forms revised hypotheses on the basis of the research. Theory building in this traditional view is incremental and grows on the basis of repeated hypothesis testing. Not all theories follow this traditional norm, however, because scholars debate a number of metatheoretical issues affecting the development of communication theory. The assumptions a researcher makes about knowledge, reality, and value determine his or her methods, the form of theoretical statements, and the ways in which norms and values are treated.

Whatever their form, theories constantly change and develop. Often they grow incrementally, as envisioned in traditional science, by extension from one bit of knowledge to the next. Here, the theory becomes more and more extensive as it grows in coverage. Often, however, theories change in another way, by intension, so that they look deeper and deeper into the subject at hand. More and more detail about the subject is revealed within the theory. The third form of change is revolution, in which the old theory is dumped and a brand new conceptualization comes into being.

As you examine the theories in the following pages, consider the ways in which they meet a variety of functions. How do they organize our knowledge about communication? What elements of the communication process do they focus our attention on? What do they clarify? How do they tell us to observe communication events? Do they enable us to make any predictions? What new research questions do they suggest, and what holes do they leave unfilled? How have scholars used these theories to communicate with one another about their ideas? And what ideas are generated by these theories about how to improve social life?

And as you look closely at each theory, you will find some that appeal to you and others that do not. You will find some very helpful in your personal quest for understanding, and you will find others that are less so. As you evaluate these theories, think about their scope: How much do they tell us? Think about the appropriateness of their claims: Are they logically consistent? Think about their heuristic value: Do they suggest ideas for further research? And their parsimony: Are they simple but elegant?

Now take a deep breath and plunge in.

Topics in Communication Theory

CHAPTER 3

System Theory

Perhaps the most general theoretical approach to communication is system theory, the subject of this chapter. We will discuss system theory and two related fields, cybernetics and information theory. These approaches offer broad perspectives on how to look at the world and have been useful in capturing the general nature of the communication process.[1] In general, system theory deals with the interrelatedness of the parts of an organization, cybernetics deals with control and regulation in the system, and information theory focuses on the measurement and transmission of signals.

System theory, cybernetics, and information theory direct us to observe features of a wide variety of physical, biological, social, and behavioral phenomena. As such, they are not communication theories per se but have had important applications in the study of communication and other sociocultural events. Many communication theories and related theories are based on the system concept, and we will address several of them later in the chapter.

The roots of system thinking began at least as far back as the last century with the theory of Georg Hegel. For Hegel, the world is in process, and it is controlled by a dialectical tension between opposites. A state of affairs would be followed historically by an antithesis, and the tension would be resolved through a synthesis of the two poles. The synthesis itself becomes a new balanced position, only to be brought out of balance once again by a new antithesis, beginning the dialectical process again. Hegel explained historical development in terms of this dynamic process.[2] Karl Marx quickly applied Hegel's thinking to the distribution of power in society, using it as the basis for his goal of uniting labor in opposition to the power elite.[3]

1. For excellent discussions of general system theory and other systems approaches, see Peter Monge, "The Systems Perspective as a Theoretical Basis for the Study of Human Communication," *Communication Quarterly* 25 (1977): 19–29; and Brent D. Ruben and John Y. Kim (eds.), *General Systems Theory and Human Communication* (Rochelle Park, N.J.: Hayden, 1975). One of the foremost proponents of system theory in the communication field is B. Aubrey Fisher, *Perspectives on Human Communication* (New York: Macmillan, 1978), especially chap. 7.

2. See, for example, Walter Kaufmann (ed.), *Hegel: Texts and Commentary* (Garden City, N.Y.: Anchor Books, 1966).

3. See, for example, Anthony Giddens, *Profiles and Critiques in Social Theory* (Berkeley: University of California Press, 1982), especially chaps. 8 and 9.

Charles Darwin, too, relied on the idea that organisms evolve and adapt to pressures from outside. However, his explanatory mechanism was different from that of Hegel and Marx. For Darwin, change is brought about by adaptations and accommodations, and history, at least in the biological world, is governed by these processes.[4] Herbert Spencer, in a once popular but now disreputed theory, applied Darwinian thinking to differences in human class and race.[5]

System theory as we know it today was probably best codified by Ludwig von Bertalanffy, whose ideas are summarized in more detail later in the chapter. Before we discuss this recent history, however, let us turn to the basic idea of system.

Fundamental System Concepts

What Is a System?

A *system* is a set of objects or entities that interrelate with one another to form a whole. One of the most common distinctions is between closed and open systems.[6] A *closed system* has no interchange with its environment. It moves toward progressive internal chaos (entropy), disintegration, and death. The closed-system model most often applies to physical systems like stars, which do not have life-sustaining qualities. An *open system* receives matter and energy from its environment and passes matter and energy to its environment.

The open system is oriented toward life and growth. Biological, psychological, and social systems follow an open model. General system theory deals with systems primarily from this open perspective. When we speak of systems in this chapter, we are concerned with only the open model.

From the simplest perspective, a system can be said to consist of four things.[7] The first is *objects*. The objects are the parts, elements, or variables of the system. These objects may be physical or abstract or both, depending on the nature of the system. Second, a system consists of *attributes*, or the qualities or properties of the system and its objects. Third, a system must possess *internal relationships* among its objects. This characteristic is a crucial defining quality of systems and a primary theme in this chapter. A relationship among objects implies a mutual effect (interdependence) and constraint.[8] This idea will be elaborated in the following section. Fourth, systems also possess an *environment*. They do not exist in a vacuum but are affected by their surroundings.

A family is an excellent example of a system.[9] The members of the family are the objects of the system. Their characteristics as individuals are attributes, and their interaction forms relationships among the members. Families also exist in a social and cultural environment, which affects and is affected by them. Family members are not isolated persons, but their relations among one another must be taken into account to fully understand the individuals and the family as a unit.

The advocates of general system theory maintain that biological, psychological, and sociocultural systems possess certain common characteristics. Collectively, these qualities are used to define the system concept; they are not separate, and to a large extent, they define one another.

4. Marjorie Grene, *The Knower and the Known* (Berkeley: University of California Press, 1974), chap. 7.

5. See, for example, Marvin Harris, *The Rise of Anthropological Theory* (New York: Crowell, 1968), chap. 5.

6. A. D. Hall and R. E. Fagen, "Definition of System," in *Modern Systems Research for the Behavioral Scientist*, ed. W. Buckley (Chicago: Aldine, 1968), pp. 81–92; Anatol Rapoport, "Foreword," in *Modern Systems Research for the Behavioral Scientist*, ed. W. Buckley (Chicago: Aldine, 1968), pp. xiii–xxv. For an excellent short description of open versus closed systems, see Ludwig von Bertalanffy, *General Systems Theory: Foundations, Development, Applications* (New York: Braziller, 1968).

7. Hall and Fagen, "Definition."

8. Walter Buckley (ed.), "Society as a Complex Adaptive System," in *Modern Systems Research for the Behavorial Scientist*, (Chicago: Aldine, 1968) pp. 490–513.

9. Considerable research has been done over the years on family communication. See, for example, Arthur P. Bochner and Eric M. Eisenberg, "Family Process: System Perspectives," in *Handbook of Communication Science*, eds. C. R. Berger and S. H. Chaffee (Newbury Park, Calif.: Sage, 1987), pp. 540–563.

Wholeness and interdependence. A system by definition constitutes a unique whole.[10] To understand this idea, examine for a moment the opposite view—physical summativity. In the summative model, a "whole" is merely a collection with no unique qualities apart from its components, like a box of stones. But in a system, the whole is more than the sum of its parts. It is a product of the forces or interactions among the parts.

We view a system as a whole because its parts interrelate and cannot be understood separately. An object, person, concept, or other part of a system is always constrained by its dependence on other parts. This pattern of interdependence is what creates organization in the system.

Interdependence is easily illustrated in families. A family is a system of interacting individuals, and each member is constrained by the actions of the other members. Although each person has some freedom, none has complete freedom because of their bonds with one another. Therefore, the behaviors in a family are not independent, free, or random; instead, they are patterned and structured. What one family member does or says follows from or leads to an action of another.

Because interdependence is the most important defining characteristic of systems and has been such an important influence on communication research, it is worth exploring in some detail here. When a researcher examines a system, several interacting variables must be accounted for. The interdependence among the variables in a system are understood as *correlations*. In a correlation, when one variable changes, so does the other. Correlations are rarely pure or perfect, but they are a matter of degree. Some associations are very strong, others quite weak. In a complex system, many variables interrelate with one another in a web of influences that vary in strength.

Two variables may be directly associated so that one is said to cause the other. For example, use of power by one family member may cause another family member to give in to a demand. Here, power is directly correlated causally with compliance. Tra-

ditionally, causality is considered one-way, whereby variable A affects variable B. In systems, however, causality often runs both ways, such that variable A and variable B influence each other. An example of this would be nagging and withdrawing. As the father nags, the son withdraws; and as the son withdraws, the father nags. Each causes the other to continue in a spiral. Causation in a system is difficult to confirm, and many system researchers believe it is a waste of time to try to do so. These researchers are more interested in discovering associations without attributing cause, although they are often interested in how the participants in a system *perceive* the causes. For example, the father may perceive that the son's withdrawal causes him to nag, while the son perceives that the father's nagging causes him to withdraw.

Besides causal relations, variables also may be associated indirectly. In an indirect relationship, the two variables are correlated but do not cause one another directly. Rather, they share the influence of a third causal variable. For example, performance in school and in doing housework could be correlated: Children who get their jobs done at home also seem to do well in school, and children who do not do very well at school are also remiss in getting house chores done. If this correlation were discovered, the researcher might try to find out why and uncover a third variable, perhaps the amount of time parents spend with the child. Here, the hypothesized relationship might be that spending more time with a child brings about greater cooperation at home and school.

A more complex form of indirect relationship occurs in a chain of influence. Variable A causes B, which causes C, which causes D, which causes E, which causes A. Because of the causal ring, these five variables would be correlated, but they are not causally related directly to one another.

Complex systems consist of a network of relationships. In other words, a variable is related not just to one other variable but to a potentially large number of other variables. You can see that interdependence can get complicated and difficult to study. Researchers deal with this problem by taking the system apart and examining the relationship of

10. Rapoport, "Foreword"; Hall and Fagen, "Definition."

one or two variables with a manageable set of other variables. There are several ways of doing this, which as a group are known as *multivariate analysis*.[11] An example is multiple regression analysis. Here, one variable, which is called the *independent variable*, is correlated with several other *dependent variables*. An equation is used to reveal the stength of the correlation between the independent variable and the group of dependent variables.

Hierarchy. Systems tend to be embedded within one another. In other words, one system is a part of a higher system.[12] Arthur Koestler expresses this idea in the following tale:

> There were once two Swiss watchmakers named Bios and Mekhos, who made very fine and expensive watches. Their names may sound a little strange, but their fathers had a smattering of Greek and were fond of riddles. Although their watches were in equal demand, Bios prospered, while Mekhos just struggled along; in the end he had to close his shop and take a job as a mechanic with Bios. The people in the town argued for a long time over the reasons for this development and each had a different theory to offer, until the true explanation leaked out and proved to be both simple and surprising.
>
> The watches they made consisted of about one thousand parts each, but the two rivals had used different methods to put them together. Mekhos had assembled his watches bit by bit—rather like making a mosaic floor out of small coloured stones. Thus each time when he was disturbed in his work and had to put down a partly assembled watch, it fell to pieces and he had to start again from scratch.
>
> Bios, on the other hand, had designed a method of making watches by constructing, for a start, subassemblies of about ten components, each of which held together as an independent unit. Ten of these sub-assemblies could then be fitted together into a

sub-system of a higher order; and ten of these subsystems constituted the whole watch. . . .

> Now it is easy to show mathematically that if a watch consists of a thousand bits, and if some disturbance occurs at an average of once in every hundred assembling operations—then Mekhos will take four thousand times longer to assemble a watch than Bios. Instead of a single day, it will take him eleven years. And if for mechanical bits, we substitute amino acids, protein molecules, organelles, and so on, the ratio between time-scales becomes astronomical; some calculations indicate that the whole life-time of the earth would be insufficient for producing even an amoeba—unless he [Mekhos] becomes converted to Bios' method and proceeds hierarchically, from simple subassemblies to more complex ones.[13]

Every complex system consists of a number of subsystems. The system is therefore a series of levels of increasing complexity. Figure 3.1 illustrates the idea of system hierarchy with a "tree" model. Families illustrate hierarchy very well. The suprasystem is the extended family, which itself is part of the larger system of society. Several small family units are part of the extended family, and each family unit may have subsystems such as parents, children, and parent–child units.

Koestler calls system hierarchy the Janus effect:

> The members of a hierarchy, like the Roman god Janus, all have two faces looking in opposite directions: the face turned toward the subordinate levels is that of a self-contained whole; the face turned upward toward the apex, that of a dependent part. One is the face of the master, the other the face of the servant.[14]

The natural question at this point is, Where does a system end and its environment begin? Because systems are part of other systems, the system's boundary may be arbitrary and can only be established by the observer. One can take a very broad view—observing a number of interacting systems in a large *suprasystem*—or a narrower view—observing one or two smaller *subsystems* interacting with the larger system as environment—as Figure 3.1 outlines.

11. See, for example, Peter R. Monge and Joseph N. Cappella, *Multivariate Techniques in Human Communication Research* (New York: Academic Press, 1980).

12. For excellent discussions of hierarchy, see Donna Wilson, "Forms of Hierarchy: A Selected Bibliography," *General Systems* 14 (1969): 3–15; Arthur Koestler, *The Ghost in the Machine* (New York: Macmillan, 1967); W. Ross Ashby, "Principles of the Self-Organizing System," in *Principles of Self-Organization*, eds. H. von Foerster and G. Zopf (New York: Pergamon Press, 1962), pp. 255–278.

13. Koestler, *Ghost*, pp. 45–47.

14. Ibid., p. 48.

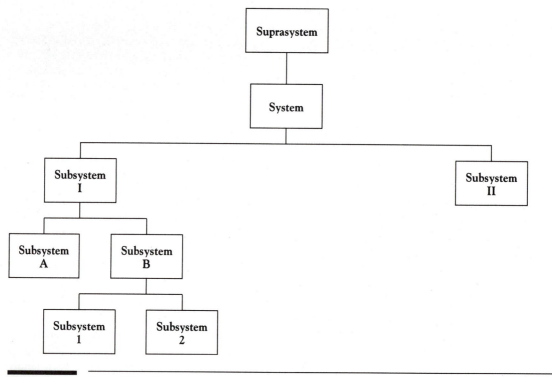

Figure 3.1   System hierarchy.

Self-regulation and control. Systems are most often viewed as goal-oriented organisms. They are governed by their purposes. A system's activities are controlled by its aims, and the system regulates its behavior to achieve those aims. The parts of a system must behave according to guidelines and must adapt to the environment on the basis of feedback. This aspect of system functioning, known as cybernetics, is examined in detail in the next section.

Again, families illustrate this quality of systems. A family may have a variety of control mechanisms. For example, the family may rely on one dominant member for making decisions and providing guidance. This person monitors the family and asserts control as necessary whenever signs of deviation from family standards (feedback) are detected. Other families may handle control very differently, as in the case of families that have strict role divisions that permit each member to exert control over certain kinds of decisions and not others.

Interchange with the environment. Remember that open systems interchange with their environment. They take in and let out matter and energy. Thus, systems are said to have *inputs* and *outputs*. This concept follows logically from the ideas of hierarchy and cybernetics. Therefore, the system both affects and is affected by the environment.[15] For example, parents must adjust constantly to their children's relationships outside the family and deal with influences from friends, teachers, and television.

15. Gordon Allport, "The Open System in Personality Theory," in *Modern Systems Research for the Behavioral Scientist,* ed. W. Buckley (Chicago: Aldine, 1968), pp. 343–350; Hall and Fagen, "Definition."

Balance. Balance, sometimes referred to as *homeostasis*, is self-maintenance.[16] One task of a system, if it is to remain alive, is to maintain some level of balance. The system must somehow detect when it is off kilter and make adjustments to get back on track. Deviation and change does occur and can be tolerated by a system, but only so long. Eventually, the system will fall apart if it does not work to maintain itself.

This necessity explains why families seem to struggle so hard to keep things on an even keel. For example, why do parents keep nagging children to behave? Why do couples who are having serious relational problems frequently keep trying to get back together? From a system perspective, these kinds of efforts are a natural attempt to maintain homeostasis. Indeed, it seems as though families have trouble maintaining balance in a complex social environment, and many do not survive.

Change and adaptability. Because it exists in a dynamic environment, the system must be adaptable.[17] Paradoxically, adaptation often means homeostasis or counteracting outside forces. More than that, however, complex systems sometimes have to change structurally to adapt to the environment, and that kind of change means getting out of balance for a time. Advanced systems must be able to reorder themselves on the basis of environmental pressures. The technical term for system change is *morphogenesis*. To continue our example, families change. As its members age and develop, as new members come and old members leave, and as the family faces new challenges from the environment, it adapts and changes.

Equifinality. Finality is the goal achievement or task accomplishment of a system. *Equifinality* means that a particular final state may be accomplished in different ways and from different starting points. The adaptable system, which has a final state as a goal, can achieve that goal in a variety of

environmental conditions. The system is capable of processing inputs in different ways to produce its output.[18] Families can accomplish their goals in a variety of ways. Smart parents know that their children's behavior can be affected by a variety of techniques. Family decision making can occur in more than one way. And children learn a variety of methods for securing the compliance of the adults in their world.

Cybernetics

Cybernetics is the study of regulation and control in systems, with emphasis on *feedback*.[19] An important feature of open systems, as we have just seen, is that they are regulated, seek goals, and therefore are purposeful.

Cybernetics deals with the ways systems gauge their effect and make necessary adjustments. The simplest cybernetic device consists of a sensor, a comparator, and an activator. The sensor provides feedback to the comparator, which determines whether the machine is deviating from its established norm. The comparator then provides guidance to the activator, which produces an output that affects the environment in some way. This fundamental process of output-feedback-adjustment is the basis of cybernetics.

Obviously, feedback mechanisms vary in complexity. Figure 3.2 illustrates different levels of complexity in feedback and control.[20] The model demonstrates that the most basic distinction is

16. Ashby, "Principles."

17. Hall and Fagen, "Definition"; Buckley, "Adaptive System"; Koestler, *Ghost*.

18. Bertalanffy, *General System Theory*, chap. 3.

19. Rollo Handy and Paul Kurtz, "A Current Appraisal of the Behavioral Sciences: Communication Theory," *American Behavioral Scientist* 7, no. 6 (1964): 99–104. Supplementary information is found in Gordon Pask, *An Approach to Cybernetics* (New York: Harper & Row, 1961); G. T. Guilbaud, *What Is Cybernetics?* (New York: Grove Press, 1959). For a historical review, see Norbert Wiener, *Cybernetics or Control and Communication in the Animal and the Machine* (Cambridge, Mass.: MIT Press, 1961), pp. 1–29. For a cybernetic approach to communication, see D. J. Crowley, *Understanding Communication: The Signifying Web* (New York: Gordon and Breach, 1982), especially chap. 1.

20. Arturo Rosenblueth, Norbert Wiener, and Julian Bigelow, "Behavior, Purpose, and Teleology," *Philosophy of Science* 10 (1943): 18–24 [reprinted in *Modern Systems Research for the Behavioral Scientist*, ed. W. Buckley (Chicago: Aldine, 1968), pp. 221–225].

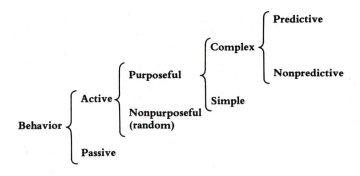

between active and passive behavior. An organism displaying *active behavior* is the primary source of energy initiating that behavior. *Passive behavior* is any response to outside stimulation. People have all kinds of bodily motions that are merely responses to stimulation, such as scratching an itch, although much bodily activity is active nervous energy. Within the category of active behavior, a further division can be made between purposeless, or random, and purposeful behavior. *Purposeful behavior* is directed toward an objective or aim, whereas *random behavior* is not. Rubbing one's face or moving a hand may be just a random action, but when done to express an idea or emphasize a point, the action is clearly achieving a purpose. All purposeful behavior requires feedback; the nature of that feedback may be more or less complex, as indicated in the model.

Purposeful behavior may be further subdivided into complex and simple feedback mechanisms.[21] In *simple systems* the organism responds to feedback only by turning on or off. A thermostat is a perfect example of a simple feedback mechanism. *Complex systems*, however, use positive and negative feedback to adjust and adapt during the action itself. Further, complex systems may be predictive or nonpredictive. *Predictive behavior* is based on antic-

ipated position or response rather than actual position or response. A good quarterback passes the football to the spot where his receiver will be, not directly to the receiver. Usually, the quarterback releases the ball before the receiver turns to look for it.

A simple feedback model is represented in Figure 3.3. In the figure, B is an energy source directing outputs to C. A is the control mechanism responding to feedback from C. Depending on the complexity of the system and the nature of the output, the control mechanism itself is restricted in the kind of control it can exert. Figure 3.4 illustrates some possible situations.[22]

The first model in Figure 3.4 demonstrates a situation where the signal itself is modified (e.g., amplified) by A. The high-pitched squeal in a loudspeaker system is an example. The next model illustrates a simple switch such as a thermostat or circuit breaker. The third model illustrates selection control in which A chooses a channel or position on the basis of criteria. In a guided missile, for example, the guidance system may specify turning in one direction or another, based on feedback from the target.

The process of system regulation through feedback involves several facets. The regulated system must possess certain control guidelines. The con-

21. I have changed the original nomenclature here to avoid confusion and inconsistency with previous word usage in this chapter. The authors' intent is unchanged.

22. Adapted from Guilbaud, *Cybernetics.*

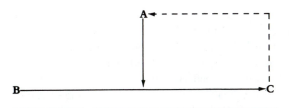

Figure 3.3   A simple feedback model.

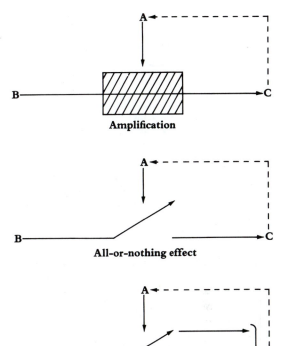

Amplification

All-or-nothing effect

Selector

Figure 3.4   Illustrative control models.

trol center must "know" what environmental conditions to respond to and how. It must possess a sensitivity to aspects of the environment that are critical to its goal seeking.[23]

Feedback can be classified as positive or negative, depending on the way the system responds to it. *Negative feedback* is an error message indicating deviation; the system adjusts by reducing or counteracting the deviation. Negative feedback is the most important type of feedback in homeostasis because negative feedback maintains a steady state.

A system can also respond by amplifying or maintaining deviation. When this happens, the feedback is said to be *positive*. This kind of interaction is important in morphogenesis, or system growth (e.g., learning). The inflationary cycle in economics is an example of positive-feedback effects. The growth of a city is another. In communication when a speaker receives negative feedback from a listener, the speaker knows he or she is missing the aim. Negative feedback from a fellow communicator usually calls for a shift in strategy to close the gap between how the speaker wants the listener to respond and the actual response. Whether in mechanical or human systems, the response to negative feedback is "cut back, slow down, discontinue." Response to positive feedback is "increase, maintain, keep going."

Figure 3.5 illustrates three feedback states. The first is a steady state, the second a growth state, and the third a change state. A *steady state* involves the use of negative feedback to keep the system on track. Negative feedback signals deviation from the

standard, and the system adjusts in order to return to the line. Notice that the system is always moving; it is constantly changing, but it never gets too far from the desired state because of negative feedback. For example, a manager may want to maintain a supportive relationship with all her subordinates. She continually tries to be supportive, and when employees are feeling unsupported, she detects the dissatisfaction and tries harder to make them feel included. This manager may waver from time to time but, because of negative feedback, can maintain supportiveness most of the time.

The second state is *growth*. Here as the system deviates, positive feedback maintains the deviation, and the result is further and further movement from the original state. The system acceler-

23. Walter Buckley, *Sociology and Modern Systems Theory* (Englewood Cliffs, N.J.: Prentice-Hall, 1967), pp. 52–53.

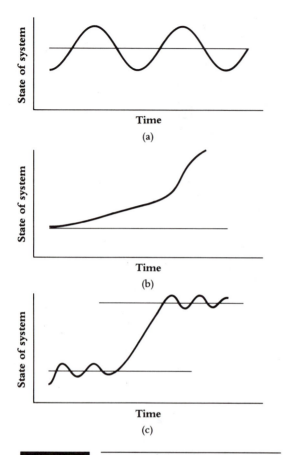

Figure 3.5   Three feedback states: (a) steady state, (b) growth state, and (c) change state.

ates some behavior, and if this continues indefinitely, the system will disintegrate. Relational spirals are an example. A relational spiral occurs when partners increase the intensity of their responses to one another. Imagine, for example, that a woman goes out with friends without telling her boyfriend, and when he discovers this, he gets irritated. She thinks that his irritation is unjustified and decides to go out with her friends again. Now he gets even more upset, and she goes out again just to make the point that she has the right to do so. In time, she is going out very frequently with her friends, and he is exploding in anger and jealousy. Here, each partner's actions are taken as positive feedback, creating even more deviation from the original state. If the spiral does not stop, the relationship will not survive. Notice that positive feedback does not mean "good" feedback; indeed, it may be very bad. And negative feedback is not necessarily "bad" because it is needed by the system to maintain balance.

The third state is *change*. Here, the system moves from one state to another state. It requires both negative and positive feedback. Positive feedback gets the system moving in a new direction, but negative feedback comes into play at some level to return the system to balance. Let us return to our original example of the supportive manager. As sometimes happens too much support causes the suppression of productive conflict and the stifling of needed change. Assume that our manager begins to get feedback saying that her department is not productive enough. She responds by criticizing her employee's work habits and in the process becomes less supportive. At some point the workers' productivity increases, and she reduces her criticism. At this point the system has moved to a new state of somewhat less supportiveness and a bit more scrutiny.

Our discussion of feedback thus far has given the impression that a system responds as a unit to feedback from the outside. This impression is realistic only for the simplest systems such as a heater-thermostat arrangement. As a series of hierarchically ordered subsystems, advanced systems are more complex. A subsystem at any moment may be part of the larger system or part of the environment.[24] Further, we know that subsystems respond to one another in mutual interdependence. As a result the concept of feedback is expanded for complex systems. In a complex system, a series of feedback loops exist within and among subsystems, forming *networks*. At some points the feedback loops are positive, at other points negative. But always, consistent with the basic feedback principle, system

24. Magoroh Maruyama, "The Second Cybernetics: Deviation-Amplifying Mutual Causal Processes," *American Scientist* 51 (1963): 164–179 [reprinted in *Modern Systems Research for the Behavioral Scientist*, ed. W. Buckley (Chicago: Aldine, 1968), pp. 304–316].

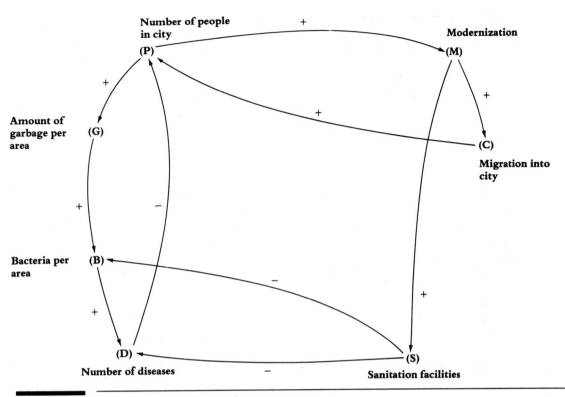

Figure 3.6   A simplified feedback network.

From *American Scientist*, "The Second Cybernetics," by Magoroh Maruyama. Copyright © 1963. Reprinted by permission of the publisher.

output returns as feedback input. No matter how complicated the network, one always comes back to the beginning.

A simple illustration of a system network is the example of urbanization in Figure 3.6.[25] In this figure the pluses (+) represent positive relationships, the minuses (−) negative relationships. In a positive relationship, variables increase or decrease together. In a negative relationship, as one increases, the other decreases. For example, as the number of people in the city (P) increases, modernization also increases. With increased modernization comes increased migration, which in turn further increases the population. This relationship is an example of a positive-feedback loop. A negative

relationship is illustrated by the effect of the number of diseases (D) on population (P).

Earlier we mentioned multivariate analysis as a way of assessing the interdependency among variables in a system. One multivariate technique that is especially useful for describing complex feedback networks is *causal modeling*.[26] The researcher creates a network of probable correlations among several variables, each with a corresponding equation, and the overall model is then tested with actual data.

As our discussion up to this point indicates, cybernetics is a central concept in system theory. The cybernetic elements of control, regulation,

26. Causal modeling actually consists of several methods. For an introduction see Herbert B. Asher, *Causal Modeling* (Beverly Hills, Calif.: Sage, 1976).

25. Ibid.

and feedback provide a concrete explanation of such system qualities as wholeness (a portion of the system cannot be understood apart from its loops among subsystems); interdependence (subsystems are constrained by mutual feedbacks); self-regulation (a system maintains balance and changes by responding appropriately to positive and negative feedbacks); and interchange with the environment (inputs and outputs can be largely explained in terms of feedback loops).

Although these cybernetic concepts originated in the fields of physiology, engineering, and mathematics, they have tremendous implications in the behavioral and social sciences as well.[27] As Norbert Wiener, the founder of cybernetics, states, "This principle [feedback] in control applies not merely to the Panama locks, but to states, armies, and individual human beings. . . . This matter of social feedback is of very great sociological and anthropological interest."[28]

Information Theory

The area of study most concerned with communication in systems is information theory. Information theory grew out of the boom in the telecommunications industry after World War II. A perspective that focuses on the measurement of information, *information theory* deals with the quantitative study of information in messages and the flow of information between senders and receivers. It has practical applications in the electronic sciences of communication that need to compute information quantities and design channels, transmitters, receivers, and codes that facilitate efficient handling of information. It has also been used widely in the behavioral and social sciences.[29]

Information theory developed out of investigations in physics, engineering, and mathematics, which were concerned with the organization among events. The primary work that drew all this work together into a single theoretical approach was that of Claude Shannon, a telecommunications engineer at the Bell Telephone Laboratories. His classic book with Warren Weaver, *The Mathematical Theory of Communication*, is the basic source on information theory.[30]

Basic Concepts

Information theory provides a precise definition of *information*. Perhaps it is easier to understand information by starting with a related concept, entropy, borrowed from thermodynamics. *Entropy is randomness, or lack of organization in a situation.* A totally entropic situation is unpredictable. Entropy is best thought of as variable. Most of the situations you are confronted with are partially predictable. If dark clouds come over the sky, you might predict rain, and you would probably be right. Because weather is an organized system, certain probable relationships (e.g., clouds and rain) exist. On the other hand, you cannot predict rain conclusively. The entropy existing in the situation causes some uncertainty. In short, the more entropy, the less organization and predictability.

What does this have to do with information? *Information is a measure of uncertainty, or entropy, in a situation.* The greater the uncertainty, the more the information. When a situation is completely predictable, no information is present. This is a condition known as negentropy. Most people associate information with certainty or knowledge; consequently, this definition from information theory can be confusing. As used by the information theorist, the concept does not refer to a message,

27. See Karl Deutsch, "Toward a Cybernetic Model of Man and Society," in *Modern Systems Research for the Behavioral Scientist*, ed. W. Buckley (Chicago: Aldine, 1968), pp. 387–400.

28. Norbert Wiener, *The Human Use of Human Beings: Cybernetics in Society* (Boston: Houghton Mifflin, 1954), pp. 49–50.

29. Several brief histories of the movement are available. See, for example, Wendell R. Garner, *Uncertainty and Structure as Psychological Concepts* (New York: Wiley, 1962), p. 8.

30. Claude Shannon and Warren Weaver, *The Mathematical Theory of Communication* (Urbana: University of Illinois Press, 1949). For a number of excellent brief secondary sources, see the Bibliography. Two sources were particularly helpful in the preparation of this section: Allan R. Broadhurst and Donald K. Darnell, "An Introduction to Cybernetics and Information Theory," *Quarterly Journal of Speech* 51 (1965): 442–453; Klaus Krippendorf, "Information Theory," in *Communication and Behavior*, eds. G. Hanneman and W. McEwen (Reading, Mass.: Addison-Wesley, 1975), pp. 351–389.

facts, or meaning. It is a concept bound only to the quantification of stimuli or signals in a situation.

On closer examination, this idea of information is not as distant from common sense as it first appears. We have said that information is the amount of uncertainty in the situation. Another way of thinking of it is to consider information as the number of messages required to completely reduce the uncertainty in the situation. For example, your friend is about to flip a coin. Will it land heads up or tails up? You are uncertain; you cannot predict. This uncertainty, which results from the entropy in the situation, will be eliminated by seeing the result of the flip. Now suppose that you have received a tip that your friend's coin is two-headed. The flip is "fixed." There is no uncertainty and therefore no information. In other words, you could not receive any message that would make you predict any better than you already can. In short, a situation with which you are completely familiar has no new information for you.

We have now related information to uncertainty and to the number of messages necessary to reduce uncertainty. There is yet a third way to view information. Information can be thought of as the number of *choices*, or *alternatives*, available to a person in predicting the outcome of a situation. In a complex situation of many possible outcomes, more information is available than in a simple situation with few outcomes. In other words, a person would need more messages to predict the outcome of a complex situation than to predict the outcome of a simple one. For example, there is more information in a two-dice toss than in the toss of a single die and more information in a single-die toss than in a coin flip. Because information is a function of the number of alternatives, it reflects the degree of freedom in making choices within a situation. The more information in a situation, the freer you are to choose alternatives within that situation.

Another important concept is *redundancy*. Redundancy is a function of its sister concept, relative entropy. *Relative entropy* is the proportion of entropy present compared with the maximum amount possible. Entropy is maximum when all alternatives are equally probable. In qualitative terms redundancy is the proportion of a situation

that is predictable; it is a measure of certainty. If one alternative follows from another, it is predictable and therefore redundant. It should be apparent from this discussion that information theory is basically a tool for measuring and describing the pattern and structure of a system.

Language and Information

Most messages consist of a sequence of stimuli received serially, and information theory can be applied to the predictability of the sequential arrangement of a message. If the letters in a sentence were arranged randomly, there would be 100 percent entropy. Decoding would be difficult because of the great amount of information in the message. But letters (or sounds in speech) are not organized randomly. Various predictable patterns are found. These patterns make decoding easier because there is less information, lower relative entropy, and high redundancy. For example, an adjective has a high probability of being followed by a noun. A *q* is always followed by a *u* in English. Thus, the overall arrangement of a sentence is patterned and partially predictable. On the other hand, a sentence does contain some information because redundancy or predictability is never 100 percent. If it were, there would be no freedom of choice. Once the first letter was written, all other letters would follow automatically. Actually, language is blessed with moderate redundancy, allowing ease in decoding, with freedom of encoding.

Language information is an example of a *Markov process*, in which things that come earlier in a chain create a probability that other things will come later. A Markov chain is a series of events, one happening after another in time, such that the occurrence of one element in the chain establishes a probability that another particular element will come next. In English, for example, there is a 100 percent probability that *u* will follow *q* in a string of letters. There is a much lower probability that *i* will follow *t*. Although language is an example of a Markov chain, many other phenomena follow the same pattern.

Markov chains like language must be discussed in terms of average relative entropy and average redundancy because the actual amounts vary from point to point in the chain. For example, the average relative entropy-redundancy in English is about 50 percent.

One interesting application of Markov chains in communication research is in the study of communication control. Markov models have been used to study the likelihood that dominance will be followed by submission in a series of interactions between two people. We discuss this application in more detail later in this chapter.

Information Transmission

Technical information theory is not concerned with the meaning of messages, only with their transmission and reception. This application is particularly important in electronic communication. The basic model of communication developed by Shannon and Weaver is shown in Figure 3.7.[31] In this model communication begins at the source. The *source* formulates or selects a *message*, consisting of signs to be transmitted. The *transmitter* converts the message into a set of *signals* that are sent over a *channel* to a *receiver*. The receiver converts the signals into a message. This model can be applied to a variety of situations. In the electronic arena, a television message is a good example. The producers, directors, and announcers constitute the source. The message is transmitted by airwaves (channel) to the home receiver, which converts electromagnetic waves back into a visual impression for the viewer. In the interpersonal arena the speaker's brain is the source, the vocal system the transmitter, and the air medium the channel. The listener's ear is the receiver, and the listener's brain the destination.

The final element in Shannon and Weaver's model is noise. *Noise* is any disturbance in the channel that distorts or otherwise masks the signal. The disturbance may be, literally, noise in auditory communication, but any kind of interference is included.

Whether the message is coded into regular language, electronic signals, or some other verbal or nonverbal code, the problem of transmission is the same—to reconstruct the message accurately at the destination. Any television viewer with poor

31. Shannon and Weaver, *Mathematical Theory*, p. 5.

reception is painfully aware of the problem. Accurate transmission would be no problem were it not for certain factors such as noise.

Now you can begin to see the role of redundancy in a message. Redundancy compensates noise. As noise distorts, masks, or replaces signals, redundancy allows the receiver to correct or fill in missing or distorted stimuli. For example, suppose you receive from a friend a letter that has been smeared by rain. The first sentences might look like this: "How --- yo-? I a- fine." Or perhaps because of static, a sentence of radio news comes across as, "The Pres-- --ed States has -clared. . . ." You can make some sense out of these distorted sentences because of the predictability or redundancy in the language.

Another factor limiting accurate transmission is channel capacity. *Channel capacity* is usually defined in terms of the maximum amount of information that can be transmitted over a channel per second. The actual amount of information in the channel is *throughput*. If throughput exceeds channel capacity, distortion will occur.

What, then, is necessary for efficient transmission? Efficient transmission involves coding at a maximum rate that will not exceed channel capacity. It also means using a code with sufficient redundancy to compensate the amount of noise present in the channel. If there is too much redundancy, transmission will be inefficient; if too little, it will be inaccurate.

The major contribution of classical information theory to human sciences is that it has used the technical model as an analogy for interpersonal communication. Witness the fact that Shannon and Weaver's model (Figure 3.7) is one of the most frequently reproduced depictions of communication in textbooks.

General System Theory as an Approach to Knowledge

General system theory (GST) is a broad, multi-disciplinary approach to knowledge based on the system concept. GST was developed primarily by

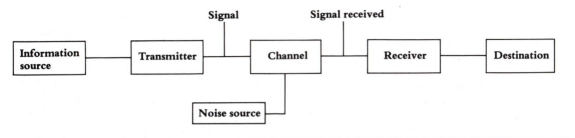

Ludwig von Bertalanffy, a well-known biologist.[32] Basically, GST postulates concepts governing systems in general and applies these generalizations to numerous phenomena.[33] Here is how Bertalanffy describes GST:

> It seems legitimate to ask for a theory, not of systems of a more or less special kind, but of universal principles applying to systems in general.
>
> In this way we postulate a new discipline called General System Theory. . . .
>
> General System Theory, therefore, is a general science of "wholeness" which up till now was considered a vague, hazy, and semi-metaphysical concept. In elaborate form it would be a logico-mathematical discipline, in itself purely formal but applicable to the various empirical sciences.[34]

GST is not a singular theory developed by one person. Although GST itself was promoted by Bertalanffy, others were doing similar work in other fields. The two most important cognate areas, which were developed almost simultaneously with Bertalanffy's work, were Wiener's cybernetics and Shannon and Weaver's information theory. In fact, these three approaches so completely support one another that they are like tributaries of the same river.

A primary aim of GST is to integrate accumulated knowledge into a clear and universal framework. General system theorists attempt to do this through the principle of isomorphism. An *isomorphism* is a structural similarity between two models or between an abstract model and an observed phenomenon. Two systems that are widely different are said to be isomorphic if their behaviors are governed by the same principles. A generalized model such as GST attempts to clarify these principles. The following is an example:

> An exponential law of growth applies to certain cells, to populations of bacteria, of animals or humans, and to progress of scientific research measured by the number of publications in genetics or science in general. The entities in question . . . are completely different. . . . Nevertheless, the mathematical law is the same.[35]

Many believe that there is a need to better integrate knowledge from various disciplines like communication. Kenneth Boulding provides a compelling argument for the use of GST as an integrator of knowledge:

> The need for general systems theory is accentuated by the present sociological situation in science. . . . The crisis of science today arises because of the increasing difficulty of such profitable talk among scientists as a whole. Specialization has outrun Trade. Communication between the disciplines becomes increasingly difficult, and the Republic of Learning is breaking up into isolated subcultures with only tenuous lines of communication between them. . . . One wonders sometimes if science will grind to a stop in an assemblage of walled-in hermits, each mumbling to

32. For a biographical sketch of Bertalanffy, see "Ludwig von Bertalanffy," *General Systems* 17 (1972): 219–228.

33. For an example of formalized GST, see Masanao Toda and Emir H. Shuford, "Logic of Systems: Introduction to a Formal Theory of Structure," *General Systems* 10 (1965): 3–27.

34. Bertalanffy, *General System Theory*, pp. 32–37.

35. Ibid., p. 33.

s p.

---

himself words in a private language that only he can understand. . . . The spread of specialized deafness means that someone who ought to know something that someone else knows isn't able to find it out for lack of generalized ears.

It is one of the main objectives of General System Theory to develop these generalized ears.[36]

System Theory and the Study of Communication

System theory has had a major influence on the study of human communication and can be seen in many corners of the field in one form or another. It would be impossible to mention all lines of work that show system influences, but several important projects warrant discussion at this point. Not only do these theories illustrate the ways in which system theory can be applied, but they have also been important research–theory programs in their own right.

System Theory and Communication in Relationships

That aspect of the communication field now known as *relational communication* is discussed in detail in Chapter 12. There, you will see a diverse set of theories dealing with communication in relationships, and much of this work has been influenced by system theory. At the core of relational communication is the assumption that interpersonal communication functions to establish, maintain, and change relationships, whereas the relationship in turn cybernetically determines the nature of the interpersonal communication.

This idea is deeply rooted in system thinking, in which the processes by which a system works creates its structure. Communication consists of interaction, and interaction patterns constitute the structure of the system. In a family, for instance, the

individual members by themselves do not make a system, but when they interact with one another, the resulting pattern of relationships among the members gives the family its form, texture, and structure. This is a very important system idea largely adopted in the communication field: Process and form are two sides of a coin; they are interdependent and cannot be separated.

Anthropologist Gregory Bateson is founder of the line of theory that has come to be known as relational communication.[37] His work led to the development of two foundational propositions on which most relational theories still rest. The first is the proposition of the dual nature of messages. Every interpersonal exchange bears two messages, a "report" message and a "command" message. The *report message* contains the substance or content of the communication, whereas the *command message* makes a statement about the relationship.[38] These two elements have come to be known as the content message and the relationship message, or *communication* and *metacommunication*, respectively. The report message addresses what is being talked about, and the command message addresses the relationship between the communicators. A simple content message like "I love you" can be delivered in a variety of ways, each of which says something different about the relationship. This phrase could be said in a domineering, submissive, pleading, doubtful, or trustful way. The content message is the same, but the relationship message would be different in each case.

Bateson's second proposition is that relationships can be characterized by complementarity or symmetry. In *complementary* relationships the dominant behavior of one participant elicits submissive behavior from the other. In *symmetry*,

---

36. Kenneth Boulding, "General Systems Theory—The Skeleton of Science," in *Modern Systems Research*, ed. W. Buckley (Chicago: Aldine, 1968), p. 4.

37. Bateson began to formulate his ideas on relationships from his field observations of the Iatmul tribe of New Guinea in the 1930s. See *Naven* (Stanford, Calif.: Stanford University Press, 1958).

38. This proposition was first presented in the theory of communication by Juergen Ruesch and Gregory Bateson, *Communication and the Social Matrix of Society* (New York: Norton, 1951). For a summary of this theory, see the first edition of this book: Stephen W. Littlejohn, *Theories of Human Communication* (Columbus, Ohio: Merrill, 1978), pp. 43–47.

dominance is met by dominance, or submissiveness by submissiveness. Here, we begin to see how the process of interaction creates the structure of the system. How we respond to one another determines the kind of relationship we have. A system structure of a series of submissive messages is very different from the structure of a series of domineering ones. And a structure of mixed domineering and submissive messages is different yet.

Although Bateson's ideas originated in anthropological research, they were quickly picked up in psychiatry and applied to pathological relationships. In the 1950s and 1960s, Bateson led an active group of researchers and clinicians in a program to further develop and apply ideas on relational communication. These scholars became known as the Palo Alto Group. Although their interests were primarily clinical, their work had enormous impact on the study of interpersonal communication in general. About 1960 psychiatrist Paul Watzlawick joined the group and quickly became one of its leaders. This group received wide publicity and popularity through the publication of *Pragmatics of Human Communication*.[39]

Several communication researchers have made use of the work of Bateson and the Palo Alto Group. Aubrey Fisher, one of the most well known of these, is a leading system theorist. In *Perspectives on Human Communication*, he applies system concepts to communication in what he calls the *pragmatic perspective*.[40]

Fisher's analysis begins with behavior as the smallest unit of analysis in the communication system. Individuals communicate by behaving in ways that have potential for eliciting meanings in others, and these observable behaviors are the sole vehicles for linking individuals in the communication system. From a system point of view, the behavior itself is what counts because behavioral patterns are organized to form the system's structure.

A communication pattern is a sequence of interaction. In other words, when we communicate we take turns acting and reacting in sequence, making an interaction between people a flow of messages. Fisher believes that this flow of talk by itself says little about the communication system; rather, it must be broken up into units consisting of acts and responses. Fisher developed a coding method to uncover the overall pattern of a conversation, which consists of coding messages, so that the pattern of responses can be ascertained.

The most basic unit of analysis used by Fisher is the *interact*, or a set of two contiguous messages between two people. An example is a question by one person followed by an answer from the second person. Another example is an assertion by one speaker followed by an opposing one by another speaker. The interact is coded on the basis of the pattern established by the two acts together. For example, a question followed by an answer is different from a demand followed by compliance. A request followed by an offer is different from a suggestion followed by an objection. In hierarchical fashion, interacts are combined into larger units called double interacts (three acts), and the latter are combined yet again into triple interacts (four acts). The structure of the entire interaction system is composed of larger and larger sets of interactions.

Most of Fisher's work involves decision making in small groups.[41] In his research he codes what people say in group discussions and analyzes this interaction in such a fashion that the overall pattern, or structure, of the discussion can be described. Fisher shows how interactions combine to form group decision-making phases. His theory of small-group decision making is covered in more detail in Chapter 13.

Among the most well-known researchers in the communication field to develop relational system theory are Edna Rogers and Frank Millar. Millar and Rogers's landmark work in relational communication is a direct application of Bateson's ideas

39. Paul Watzlawick, Janet Beavin, and Don Jackson, *Pragmatics of Human Communication: A Study in Interactional Patterns, Pathologies, and Paradoxes* (New York: Norton, 1967).

40. Fisher, *Perspectives*.

41. B. Aubrey Fisher, *Small Group Decision Making: Communication and the Group Process* (New York: McGraw-Hill, 1980).

and is consistent with that of Fisher.[42] Specifically, they are responsible for developing a research method for codifying and classifying relational patterns. Like Fisher, Millar and Rogers observe conversations and code the actions of the communicators in such a way as to discover the pattern that is created by the interaction. From their research they have developed a theory of relational patterns that shows how a relationship consists of structures of control, trust, and intimacy. These ideas are discussed in greater detail in Chapter 12.

System Theory and Large Networks

In the previous section, we looked at the ways in which interaction can be understood as a building block of systems. Relationships and groups are easily understood in system terms when interaction is made central. The significance of interaction patterns can also be seen in even larger systems such as organizations and society at large, and a number of theorists have explored communication in large networks.

Carl Weick has shown why interaction is so important in the process of organizing.[43] Weick sees organizations not as structures or entities but as activities. It is more proper to speak of *organizing* than of *organizations* because organizations are always something that people accomplish through interaction. In the same tradition as Millar and Rogers and Fisher, Weick believes that people's behaviors are interlocked so that one person's behavior is contingent on another's. Whereas Millar and Rogers and Fisher have been most concerned about interacts, Weick thinks that organizing occurs at the level of the double interact: an act followed by a response followed by an adjustment. The executive asks the secretary to type a letter, the secretary asks for clarification, and the executive explains. One worker asks another for a tool, the other hands it to the first worker, and the the first worker says, "Thanks."

These types of interaction lead to complex links within the organization that create large interaction structures often referred to as networks. A network is a large system of interaction patterns, and organizations are nothing more nor less than a series of networks. Again, we see a case of how structure and process go hand-in-hand. The communication process, actual interaction among individuals, creates a structure known as the system.

Although many writers have discussed networks, perhaps the most well-known network researchers in organizational communication are Peter Monge and his colleagues.[44] These researchers have shown that networks consist of groups connected to one another by communication ties. Just as relationships and groups are structured through interaction, groups themselves are connected in the same way. A network is established by individuals' passing information from one group to another. Organizations can be characterized by a number of structures, each depending on some pattern of communication within the organization. These networks can be described by using computers to analyze who talks to whom within the organization.

42. This work is explained in several sources. See, for example, Frank E. Millar and L. Edna Rogers, "A Relational Approach to Interpersonal Communication," in *Explorations in Interpersonal Communication*, ed. G. Miller (Beverly Hills, Calif.: Sage, 1976), pp. 87–203; Frank E. Millar and L. Edna Rogers, "Relational Dimensions of Interpersonal Dynamics," in *Interpersonal Processes: New Directions in Communication Research*, eds. M. Roloff and G. Miller (Newbury Park, Calif.: Sage, 1987); L. Edna Rogers, "Relational Communication Processes and Patterns," in *Rethinking Communication: Paradigm Exemplars*, eds. B. Dervin et al. (Newbury Park, Calif.: Sage, 1989), pp. 280–290.

43. Carl Weick, *The Social Psychology of Organizing* (Reading, Mass: Addison-Wesley, 1969).

44. Peter R. Monge, "The Network Level of Analysis," in *Handbook of Communication Science*, eds. C. R. Berger and S. H. Chaffee (Newbury Park, Calif.: Sage, 1987), pp. 239–270; Peter R. Monge and E. M. Eisenberg, "Emergent Networks," in *Handbook of Organizational Communication*, eds. F. Jablin, L. Putnam, K. Roberts, and L. Porter (Newbury Park, Calif.: Sage, 1987); Peter R. Monge and Gerald R. Miller, "Communication Networks," in *The Social Science Encyclopedia*, eds. A. Kuper and J. Kuper (London: Routledge & Kegan Paul, 1985); Richard V. Farace, Peter R. Monge, and Hamish Russell, *Communicating and Organizing* (Reading, Mass: Addison-Wesley, 1977).

Even society at large can be understood in terms of communication networks. Mass-communication researchers have shown that innovations and information are disseminated in society through interpersonal networks.[45] Although mass media are instrumental, ideas and information are actually spread by word of mouth through interpersonal networks. In this dissemination process within a culture, people often come together in establishing common ground and similar ways of thinking. This process of coming together, which has been called convergence, is explored in the following section.

Networks and Convergence Theory

A natural extension of network theory is the work on convergence, which is attributable to Lawrence Kincaid and his colleagues.[46] Kincaid sees groups and cultures as open systems that sustain themselves by expending effort. The work required to sustain a human group is communication, or the transfer of information, among individuals, groups, and cultures. With this premise, convergence theory is consistent with network theory and has been closely associated with it. Communication creates a network of relations among people that comprises the structure of society. Networks connect groups with one another and enable them to exchange information.

Society consists of connected groups that cluster together according to common beliefs, values, and behavior. Convergence theory explains why there is similarity within groups and differences between them. You can imagine two extreme types of groups, those in which everybody has exactly the same beliefs, values, and behavior and those in which nothing is shared. Although no group matches these extremes, all groups lie somewhere in between. In other words, groups vary in the extent to which they share common ideas. Groups that come to share more and more are said to have *convergence*, and groups that share less and less are said to have *divergence*.

Convergence and divergence can be explained in terms of information theory. Where there is little work in the form of communication, the amount of variation increases, the structure of the system comes apart, and entropy prevails. This would be the fate of a hypothetical group with no communication. As communication increases within a group, more and more is shared, structure develops, and convergence results. Generally speaking then, the more the communication, the greater the convergence; and the less the communication, the greater the divergence. People within a group come to share common ideas as they communicate with greater frequency, and people within a group come to lose common ground when they communicate less frequently. The same principle holds between groups: As two groups increase their contact, they become more similar, and as they lose contact, they become less similar. Perhaps you have experienced this yourself when you lost touch with old friends and made new ones.

Kincaid believes that this process is the basis for cultural differences. Cultures are nothing more than common ways of thinking and doing, and they develop because of relatively isolated in-group communication. Cultures differ from one another because there is less contact between cultures than within a culture. If everybody communicated with others outside their culture as much as they do with others in the group, cultures would soon disappear.

Kincaid and his colleagues have done some interesting research in Hawaii on acculturation

45. See, for example, Everett M. Rogers, *Diffusion of Innovations* (New York: Free Press, 1962); Everett M. Rogers and Ronny Adhikarya," Diffusion of Innovations: An Up-to-Date Review and Commentary," in *Communication Yearbook 3*, ed. D. Nimmo (New Brunswick, N.J.: Transaction Books, 1979), pp. 67–82; Everett M. Rogers and D. Lawrence Kincaid, *Communication Networks: Toward a New Paradigm for Research* (New York: Free Press, 1981).

46. D. Lawrence Kincaid, "The Convergence Theory of Communication, Self-Organization, and Cultural Evolution," in *Communication Theory: Eastern and Western Perspectives*, ed. D. L. Kincaid (San Diego: Academic Press, 1987), p. 15; June O. Yum, "The Communication Network Paradigm and Intercultural Communication," in *Rethinking Communication: Paradigm Exemplars*, eds. B. Dervin et al. (Newbury Park, Calif.: Sage, 1989), pp. 486–496; Rogers and Kincaid, *Communication Networks*, pp. 31–78.

that seems to support convergence theory.[47] They have found that the more contacts members of an ethnic group have outside the group, the more information they can get and the more they share certain attitudes.

Commentary and Critique

System theory has been a popular and influential tradition in communication. You can easily see why this has been the case. Communication is a complex of variables that interrelate with one another. As such, it seems to be a natural topic for the application of system principles. System theory can be useful for understanding communication in general as well as instances of communication as they occur in such settings as families and organizations.

System theory also shows us concretely how functionalism works. Functional approaches to theory examine the links, influences, and associations among concrete parts of a system; and many of the ideas presented in this chapter demonstrate how this is done.

Fundamental system concepts are common to all systems and form the basis of system principles used in one way or another in every system application. In the abstract these concepts may not make a lot of sense, but when you see them in actual operation in communication theories, they take on new meaning. The most important system principle is probably wholeness and interdependence. What really makes a system is the interaction among its parts. Even other system qualities such as self-regulation and interchange with environment are

basically extensions of the interdependence principle.

One of the most important aspects of interdependence is cybernetics, which is the study of how system parts influence one another for purposes of control. Although the simple feedback loop is basic to cybernetics, most complex systems—certainly all human systems—make use of networks of influence.

System ideas have been criticized on several fronts, although its supporters remain undaunted.[48] Six major issues have emerged:

1. Does the breadth and generality of system theory provide the advantage of integration or the disadvantage of ambiguity?

2. Does the theory's openness provide flexibility in application or confusing equivocality?

3. Is system theory merely a philosophical perspective, or does it provide useful explanation?

4. Has system theory generated useful research?

5. Is the system paradigm an arbitrary convention, or does it reflect reality in nature?

6. Does system theory help to simplify, or does it make things more complicated than they really are?

The first issue clearly relates to theoretical scope. From the beginning supporters have claimed that system theory provides a common vocabulary to integrate the sciences, that establishes useful logics that can be fruitfully applied to a broad range of phenomena. Others, however, claim that system theory merely confuses. If it is everything, it is really nothing. If all phenomena follow the same system principles, we have no basis for understanding anything apart from anything else.

Along the same line, some critics point out that system theory cannot have its cake and eat it too. Either it must remain a general framework without explaining real-world events, or it must abandon general integration in favor of making substantive claims. Jesse Delia expresses this concern: "General

47. See, for example, D. Lawrence Kincaid, June Ock Yum, and Joseph Woelfel, "The Cultural Convergence of Korean Immigrants in Hawaii: An Empirical Test of a Mathematical Theory," *Quality and Quantity* 18 (1983): 59–78; June Ock Yum, "Communication Diversity and Information Acquisition Among Korean Immigrants in Hawaii," *Human Communication Research* 8 (1982): 154-169; June Ock Yum, "Social Network Patterns of Five Ethnic Groups in Hawaii," in *Communication Yearbook 7*, ed. R. Bostrom (New Brunswick, N.J.: Transaction Books, 1983), pp. 574–591.

48. For arguments supporting system theory, see especially Ludwig von Bertalanffy, "General System Theory: A Critical Review," *General Systems* 7 (1962): 1–20; Buckley, *Sociology*; Monge, "Systems Perspective"; Fisher, *Perspectives*.

System Theory manifests a fundamental ambiguity in that at points it seems to present a substantive perspective making specific theoretical claims and at other points to present a general abstract language devoid of specific theoretical substance for the unification of alternative theoretical views."[49]

The second issue relates to the first. Does the theory's openness provide flexibility of thought or confusing equivocality? Detractors claim that the theory embodies what Delia calls "a fancy form of the fallacy of equivocation." In other words, by permitting a variety of applications in different theoretical domains, it cannot prevent inconsistencies among these applications. Two theories using a system framework may even contradict each other. Where, then, Delia asks, is the supposed unity brought about by system theory? This problem is exacerbated by the fact that system theories can employ various logics, which are not necessarily consistent with one another.[50] Supporters answer that this openness is one of the main advantages of system theory: It does not bias the researcher with an a priori notion of what to expect. Consequently, it promotes research that sees things as they are without imposing arbitrary theoretical categories.[51]

The third issue is also a matter of appropriateness. Some critics question whether the systems approach is a theory at all, claiming that it has no explanatory power. Although it gives us a perspective or way of conceptualizing, it provides little basis for understanding why things occur as they do. Fisher agrees:

> These principles are quite abstract (that is to say, general). Consequently, they can be applied in numerous ways by differing theorists with equally different results. In fact, system "theory" is probably a misno-

mer. . . . In short, system theory is a loosely organized and highly abstract set of principles, which serve to direct our thinking but which are subject to numerous interpretations.[52]

System advocates probably would agree with this assessment of general system theory but point out that any given system theory of communication could be highly explanatory.

The fourth issue relates to system theory's heuristic value, questioning its ability to generate research. According to Donald Cushman, "Systems is a perspective which has produced more staunch advocates than theoretical empirical research."[53] Again, critics return to the extreme generality of the approach as the basis of their criticism. They claim that the theory simply does not suggest substantive questions for investigation.

In contrast, advocates claim that the fresh perspective provided by system theory suggests new ways of looking at old problems and thus is highly heuristic. Wayne Beach points out, for example, that a great deal of fruitful research followed Aubrey Fisher and Leonard Hawes's 1971 article on small-group systems.[54] Fisher himself has done research on small-group interaction, and, as we have seen, Millar and Rogers, Monge, Kincaid, and their associates have also produced a respectable quantity of research.

The fifth issue relates to the validity of system theory. Critics question whether system theory was developed to reflect what really happens in nature or to represent a useful convention for conceptualizing complex processes. In fact, system advocates themselves differ in their views of the function of the approach in this regard. Critics place system theory in a dilemma. If the theory attempts to describe phenomena as they really are, it is invalid.

49. Jesse Delia, "Alternative Perspectives for the Study of Human Communication: Critique and Response," *Communication Quarterly* 25 (1977): 51. See also Edgan Taschjan, "The Entropy of Complex Dynamic Systems," *Behavioral Science* 19 (1975): 3.

50. Delia, "Alternative Perspectives," 51–52.

51. Wayne Beach, "Stocktaking Open-Systems Research and Theory: A Critique and Proposals for Action" (Paper delivered at the meeting of the Western Speech Communication Association, Phoenix, November 1977).

52. Fisher, *Perspectives*, p. 196. See also Bertalanffy, "Critical Review."

53. Donald Cushman, "The Rules Perspective as a Theoretical Basis for the Study of Human Communication," *Communication Quarterly* 25 (1977): 30–45.

54. B. Aubrey Fisher and Leonard C. Hawes, "An Interact System Model: Generating a Grounded Theory of Small Groups," *Quarterly Journal of Speech* 57 (1971): 444–453. See also Beach, "Stocktaking."

It posits similarities among events that are not really there. If, on the other hand, the theory provides merely a useful vocabulary, attributed similarities among events are only semantic and are therefore useless for providing understanding of those events. As Delia points out: "[Events] have different referents; they require different explanations; calling them the same thing ... does not make them the same."[55] Bertalanffy calls this objection the "so what?" argument: If we find an analogy between two events, it is meaningless.[56]

The final issue of system theory is parsimony. Adherents claim that the world is so complex that a sensible framework such as system theory is necessary to sort out the elements of world processes. Critics generally doubt that events are that complex. They claim that system theory overcomplicates events that are essentially simple. Charles Berger states the case against overcomplication:

> In the behavioral sciences ... we may be the victims of what I call irrelevant variety. Irrelevant variety is generated by the presence of attributes in a situation which have little to do with the phenomenon we are studying but which give the impression that what we are studying is very complex.... Merely because persons differ along a larger number of physical, psychological, and social dimensions, does not mean that all of these differences will make a difference in terms of the phenomena we are studying.... It is probably the case that relatively few variables ultimately can account for most of the action.[57]

These six criticisms of general system theory are probably fair. However, actual system theories of communication must be evaluated on their own merit. The many theories of communication that make use of system principles are specific and help us understand concrete experiences, as we can see

from the examples earlier in this chapter. You will also notice that these theories tend to be consistent and mutually supportive. Because of system influences, a common vocabulary make these theories coherent and useful as a group.

For example, the relationship theories of Fisher and of Millar and Rogers are based on the idea that individual acts or behaviors have no meaning apart from their relations with other acts. By interacting in certain ways, the structure of a relationship is created, and in a cybernetic fashion, that relationship form in turn influences the nature of the interaction. This is why relationship theorists say that communication defines and maintains the relationship. Weick shows how the same thing happens in organizations.

The coherence among system theories of communication does not invalidate the criticism that general system theory can be applied in inconsistent ways, but at least in the study of communication we find instances of consistent application in which the use of system principles clarifies rather than obscures. Further, although general system theory is not very explanatory, various applications of system theory can be quite explanatory. For example, the character of a particular relationship can be explained by the interaction pattern within the relationship, and Fisher and Millar and Rogers do a fine job of demonstrating how interaction patterns define relationships. Similarly, organizational differences may reflect different patterns of enactment, and Weick's interaction theory explains how enactment occurs.

As for heuristic value, each theory described in the previous section has generated much research and suggests ideas for more. And on the final point of parsimony, these theories are among the most parsimonious in the field. Within their domains each theory previewed here explains a great deal with just a few explanatory concepts.

Network–convergence theory is an excellent example of parsimony. This is really a very simple theory, yet it explains a great deal in communication, culture, and society. The point to be made by this discussion is that although general system theory does have a number of problems, system prin-

55. Delia, "Alternative Perspectives," p. 51.

56. Bertalanffy, "Critical Review."

57. Charles Berger, "The Covering Law Perspective as a Theoretical Basis for the Study of Human Communication," *Communication Quarterly* 75 (1977): 7–18. See also Gerald R. Miller, "The Pervasiveness and Marvelous Complexity of Human Communication: A Note of Skepticism" (Keynote address delivered at the Fourth Annual Conference in Communication, California State University, Fresno, May 1977). See also Beach, "Stocktaking."

ciples can be applied on a lower level in very useful and productive ways. Further, much of the commentary about system theory relates to system principles as a general explanatory approach and not with specific uses of that approach to explain particular events.

Information theory is a topic your instructor may or may not emphasize. No study of communication is complete without touching on this subject because it has been influential in a variety of ways. Convergence theory, which is contemporary, makes heavy use of it. However, the concepts of information theory are often considered somewhat arcane these days. If you are technical-minded, enjoy mathematics, and tinker with electronics or broadcasting equipment, you will probably enjoy information theory and see its relevance. If you like analogies and enjoy looking at human experience by applying physical concepts, you will see the relevance of information theory. It is not surprising, however, that most students of human communication today find information theory difficult to apply and less relevant than many of the other theories you will encounter in this book. The most directly applicable topic from information theory as presented in this chapter is Shannon and Weaver's model of transmission, which has been immensely useful, though somewhat oversimple, in teaching the basic elements of communication for the past forty years.

Although it is indispensable for developing advanced electronic communication devices, some of the original information theorists, system theorists, and other scholars looked to information theory for answers it could not provide. Shannon and Weaver hoped to use the theory as a covering model for all human and machine communication. However, even Colin Cherry, whose famous 1957 treatise on communication was based largely on information theory, now argues in his 1978 third edition that "the language of physical science is inadequate for discussion of what is essentially human about human communication."[58]

Most criticism of information theory relates to the standard of appropriateness.[59] The philosophical assumptions of the theory are not considered appropriate for understanding many aspects of human communication. Roger Conant captures the essence of the argument:

> When Shannon's theory first appeared it provoked a lot of optimism, not only in the telephone company for which it had clear technical applications, but also among biologists, psychologists, and the like who hoped it would illuminate the ways in which cells, animals, people, and perhaps even societies use information. Although the theory has been put to use in these ways, the results have not been spectacular at all. . . . Shannon's theory provides practically no help in understanding everyday communication.[60]

Many critics have centered on the ill-advised use of the term *information* as a symptom of this problem. Because the usage of the term is at such odds with popular meanings for information, much confusion has resulted. Ironically, information theory is not at all about information as we commonly understand it. One critic has suggested that the approach be retitled the "theory of signal transmission."[61] Because the term *information* as used by these theorists is so difficult to apply to human communication, other scholars have developed new definitions of the term under the old rubric of information theory, which have caused even more befuddlement.[62] Of course, terminological confusion is only a symptom of the problems involved in stretching the concept to fit alien domains. Three

58. Colin Cherry, *On Human Communication*, 3rd. ed. (Cambridge: MIT Press, 1978), p. ix.

59. Criticism of information theory can be found in many sources, including the following, on which my summary relies: Anatol Rapoport, "The Promise and Pitfalls of Information Theory," *Behavioral Science* 1 (1956): 303–309 [reprinted in *Modern Systems Research for the Behavioral Scientist*, ed. W. Buckley (Chicago: Aldine, 1968), pp. 137–142]. See also Handy and Kurtz, " Current Appraisal"; Roger C. Conant, "A Vector Theory of Information," in *Communication Yearbook 3*, ed. D. Nimmo (New Brunswick, N.J.: Transaction Books, 1979), pp. 177–196.

60. Conant, "Vector Theory," p. 178.

61. Yehoshua Bar-Hillel, "Concluding Review," in *Information Theory in Psychology*, ed. H. Quastler (Glencoe, Ill.: Free Press, 1955), p. 3.

62. See, for example, Krippendorf, "Information Theory."

such problems have been cited frequently in the literature.

The first is that information theory is designed as a measurement tool based on statistical procedures. Human messages in their full complexity are not easily broken down into observable, measurable signals. Although the phonetic structure of language is amenable to analysis, when you add vocal cues, not to mention body language, information theory becomes virtually useless. Also, many of the codes used in human communication are continuous, not discrete; that is, they do not consist of off-on signals. Such codes are difficult to fit into the mathematical paradigm.

A second problem of applying information theory to human communication is that the theory downplays meaning. Even if we could predict the amount of information received by a listener, we would know nothing of the degree of shared understanding among the communicators or the impact of the message on them. Convergence theory shows that within limits shared understanding can be included as an outcome of information processes.

Finally, information theory does not deal with the contextual or personal factors affecting an individual's channel capacity. For example, individual learning, which changes one's ability to comprehend certain types of messages and ultimately one's capacity to receive signals, is left untouched in classical theory. Indeed, a shortcoming of convergence theory is that it ignores situational factors. It relies on a single explanatory variable: the amount of communication in the network. Much research shows that many other contextual factors affect convergence.[63]

63. See, for example, Arthur P. Bochner, "The Functions of Human Communication in Interpersonal Bonding," in *Handbook of Rhetorical and Communication Theory*, eds. C. C. Arnold and J. W. Bowers (Boston: Allyn and Bacon, 1984), pp. 544–621.

CHAPTER 4

Theories of Signs and Language

In this chapter and the next, we discuss one of the most important applications of the structural tradition in communication—theories of signs and meaning. Theories of language and other symbolic forms have been a mainstay in the communication literature. Here, we examine theories of signs, language, and nonverbal communication. In the following chapter, we discuss theories of discourse. These chapters go hand-in-hand because the study of discourse is a natural extension of the study of language and other symbolic forms.

A *sign*, whether linguistic or nonlinguistic, designates something other than itself. Meaning is the interpretation that arises from the use of signs. This basic idea ties together an amazingly broad array of theories related to signs, language, discourse, and nonverbal forms. These theories explain systems of representation, including the signs themselves, their relations to objects, and their syntax or organization. The study of organizational relations and patterns within sign systems has been particularly important in this tradition. For example, structural linguistics investigates the organization of sounds within sentences. Similarly, the study of discourse deals with the organization of speech and conversation. A large body of literature in this tradition examines the nature and organization of nonverbal sign systems as well.

Semiotics

The first modern theory of signs was developed by the great nineteenth-century philosopher and logician Charles Saunders Peirce.[1] Over his lifetime, Peirce developed a comprehensive and wide-ranging theory of signs. Peirce is known as the father of modern *semiotics*, or the study of signs, which is very much alive and well even now, and it

1. Charles Saunders Peirce, *Charles S. Peirce: Selected Writings*, ed. P. O. Wiener (New York: Dover, 1958). See also, for example, Christopher Hookway, *Peirce* (London: Routledge & Kegan Paul, 1985); Max H. Fisch, *Peirce, Semiotic, and Pragmatism* (Bloomington: Indiana University Press, 1986); Thomas A. Goudge, *The Thought of Peirce* (Toronto: University of Toronto Press, 1950); John R. Lyne, "Rhetoric and Semiotic in C. S. Peirce," Quarterly Journal of Speech 66 (1980): 155–168. For an overview of semiotics, see Kaja Silverman, *The Subject of Semiotics* (New York: Oxford University Press, 1983). See also Arthur Asa Berger, *Signs in Contemporary Culture: An Introduction to Semiotics* (Salem, Wis.: Sheffield, 1989).

has had a major influence on the study of communication.

Peirce defined *semiosis* as a triadic relationship among three elements—a sign, an object, and a meaning. The sign represents the object, or referent, in the mind of an interpreter. Peirce referred to the representation of an object by a sign as the *interpretant*. For example, the word *dog* is associated, in your mind, with a certain animal. The word is not the animal, and the association you make (the interpretant) between the word and the animal is yet a third element in the system. All three elements are required together in an irreducible triad in order for meaning to arise.

This three-part relationship is clearly depicted in a well-known model created by C. K. Ogden and I.A. Richards.[2] The triangle of meaning (Figure 4.1) shows that the symbol is related to the object by a thought or reference, the interpretant.

An interesting and significant illustration of semiosis as a triad of meaning is the study of generic pronouns by Wendy Martyna.[3] Traditionally, the pronoun *he* is used to designate both males and females when a singular pronoun is required, as in the sentence, "When a teacher returns tests, he usually discusses them with the class." Martyna was interested in finding out what generic pronouns people would actually use and their meanings for these. Forty students at Stanford completed a series of sentences requiring the use of a generic pronoun. Some of the sentences referred to people normally thought of as male ("Before a judge can give a final ruling, he must weigh the evidence"). Some referred to people normally considered female ("After a nurse has completed training, she goes to work"). And some were neutral ("When a person loses money, he is apt to feel bad").

The researcher found that the participants usually used a pronoun that was consistent with sex stereotypes such as using *he* for judge and *she* for nurse. In the neutral sentences, *he* was most often used. Some participants deliberately suggested role

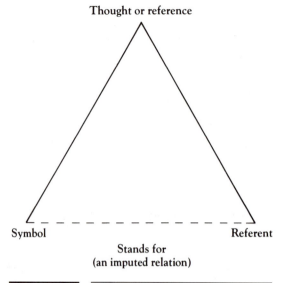

2. C. K. Ogden and I. A. Richards, *The Meaning of Meaning* (London: Kegan, Paul, Trench, Trubner, 1923)

3. Wendy Martyna, "What Does 'He' Mean?" *Journal of Communication* 28 (1978): 131–138.

Figure 4.1   Ogden and Richards's meaning triangle.

From *The Meaning of Meaning*, by C. K. Ogden and I. A. Richards. Copyright © 1923. Reprinted by permission of Harcourt Brace Jovanovich and Routledge & Kegan Paul.

reversals by switching the pronouns, and others tried to avoid sexism by using a combination as in *he or she*. In general, women were less likely to use the masculine generic form than men.

After the participants completed the sentences, the researcher asked them what image they had when they completed the sentence. Most often, they imagined a man in male-stereotyped sentences and a woman in female-stereotyped ones. In neutral sentences, the image was almost exclusively male. Martyna concludes that the prescribed use of the generic *he* is ambiguous and inequitable.

This study clearly illustrates that the sign, in this case a prounoun, is connected to its referent through the mind of the user. Meaning thus depends on the image or thought of the person in relation to the sign and the object being signified. Many semiotic thinkers have elaborated and expanded this basic idea. Here, we will discuss three of the most well known—Charles Morris, Susanne Langer, and Umberto Eco.

Morris on Signs, Behavior, and Interaction

Charles Morris is a well-known philosopher who wrote for many years about signs and values. His theory has undergone an interesting evolution. Over the years he broadened his rather narrow initial approach to integrate notions of signs, behavior, values, and interaction.[4]

We have already defined a sign generally as something taken to represent something other than itself. A sign operates by eliciting a readiness to respond in the organism. Morris has created labels for various aspects of this process: The *interpreter* is the organism that takes a stimulus as a sign; the *interpretant* is a disposition to respond in a certain way because of the sign; the *denotatum* is anything designated by the sign that enables the organism to respond apppropriately; and the *significatum* is the conditions making the response possible.

Let's take a look at some simple examples. In classical conditioning a dog is taught to respond to a buzzer as a sign of food. When the conditioned buzzer is sounded, the dog readies itself for food. Here, the buzzer is a sign, and the dog is the interpreter. The dog's readiness for food is the interpretant; and because the food itself will enable the dog to eat, the food is the denotatum. The edible quality of the food is the significatum, which is signified by the buzzer.

Suppose, in a second example, that a mother says to her toddler, "Let's go get some toys." The word *toys* is the sign, the child is the interpreter, her disposition to go to the toy box is the interpretant, the presence of the toys in the box is the denotatum, and the fact that they can be played with is the significatum.

All sign behavior involves three major factors—the designative, the appraisive, and the prescriptive.[5] The *designative factor* of signs directs the interpreter to specific objects or particular types of denotata. The *appraisive factor* orients the interpreter to particular qualities of relevance of the denoted objects, and the *prescriptive factor* restricts the responses available to the interpreter. In the dog–food example above, the designative factor directs the dog to food specifically located at a particular place and time. The dog may even come to expect a certain kind of food. The appraisive factor in this situation is seen in the dog's positive orientation to the food; the dog values the food as relevant to internal needs. The prescriptive factor compels the dog to eat the food.

The use of generic pronouns is another example. Generic pronouns designate an unknown person. Contrary to popular belief, they are not neutral but include an appraisive dimension, normally involving a male image; and they may also be prescriptive in affecting one's response to actual and imagined persons.

In language, signs are combined into phrases, clauses, and sentences called *ascriptors*, which designate an object and signify something else about that object. The sentence *The boy is happy* is an ascriptor designating boy and signifying happiness. Like signs, ascriptors can be designative, appraisive, or prescriptive. For example, a physician might say, "Here is an ointment that will stop your itching. Rub it in three times a day." *Here is an ointment* designates the object; *that will stop your itching* is an appraisal of the value of the object; and *Rub it in three times a day* is an obvious prescription.

Like all theorists, Morris was a product of his day. His theory was very much influenced by the thinking that predominated at the time he wrote and was influenced by the prominence of behavioral psychology during the middle part of this century. This explains why his early semiotic theory was so behavioristic and why it seems so simplistic. Later, as you will see, his theory broadened quite a bit because of other intellectual influences between 1930 and 1960.

4. Morris's classic work on signs is *Signs, Language, and Behavior* (New York: Braziller, 1946). A shorter version can be found in "Foundations of the Theory of Signs," in *International Encyclopedia of Unified Science*, vol. I, part 1 (Chicago: University of Chicago Press, 1955), p. 84. A unified theory of signs and values is developed in *Signification and Significance* (Cambridge, Mass.: MIT Press, 1964).

5. A fourth factor, the formative, is vaguely defined, and Morris himself later equivocated on it (See *Signification*, chap. 1).

Although these basic ideas about signs are very limited, they do help us understand the nature of signs. Morris's later expanded theory is a much fuller, more human conception.

The expanded theory is influenced by system theory and symbolic interactionism among others. Specifically, Morris makes use of George Herbert Mead's concept of the act (see Chapter 8), which consists of the three stages of perception, manipulation, and consummation.[6] In *perception* the person becomes aware of some impulse that is a sign. In the *manipulation* stage, the person interprets the sign and decides how to respond to it. Then the act is *consummated* by actual behavior. The three modes of signification correspond to these three stages. Designative signs predominate in the perceptual stage, prescriptive signs predominate in manipulation, and appraisive signs mark consummation. So our itchy patient becomes aware of the medication because of the doctor's mentioning it in a perceptual stage, decides to try it in the manipulation stage because of the physician's prescription, and actually applies the ointment in the consummation stage because of the doctor's appraisal of the effectiveness of the medicine.

Morris's most important innovation is his application of values to the signification process. Morris outlines three dimensions of values—dependence, detachment, and dominance. Certain values stress dependence, others emphasize detachment, and still others relate to dominance. As we recall from system theory, a system influences and is influenced

by other systems. When one system is being affected by another, it is said to be *dependent* on the other system. When it is affecting another system, it is *dominant* over that other system. A state of *detachment* exists when a system is more or less autonomous. Detachment corresponds to perception and the designative mode of signification. Dominance corresponds to manipulation and prescriptive signs, and dependence corresponds to consummation and appraisive signs. Table 4.1 summarizes these relationships.[7]

Now let's consider an example of this model. Suppose you are watching television one evening, and you see a new commercial for some product you do not currently use. Viewing the commercial represents the perceptual stage of the act. After seeing the commercial, you may spend some time thinking about it. You might think about what was meant by some of the statements in the advertisement. Perhaps you will determine the relevance of the product for yourself. This stage is manipulation. The third stage would occur in actually purchasing the new product (consummation). In the first stage, you are detached—you are simply maintaining your present system. In the second stage of manipulation, you are dominating by processing the information you have received. At this point you are making your decision to buy or not to buy. If you decide to buy, the final consummation stage will occur: You will receive the product (dependence). At each point in this process, signs are used. In the first stage, the product is identified, and various aspects are designated. In the manipulation

6. George Herbert Mead, *Mind, Self, and Society* (Chicago: University of Chicago Press, 1934). See also Chapter 8.

7. Morris, *Signification*, p. 22.

Table 4.1   Stages of Action in Relation to Dimensions of Signifying and Value

Stages of action	Dimensions of signifying	Dimensions of value
Perceptual	Designative	Detachment
Manipulatory	Prescriptive	Dominance
Consummatory	Appraisive	Dependence

SOURCE: From *Signification and Significance* by Charles Morris (Cambridge, Mass.: MIT Press, 1964).

stage, you are deciding how to act toward the product (whether or not to buy), thus using primarily prescriptive signs. Finally, in consummation you discover and signify to yourself your like or dislike for the product.

Acts may be individual (accomplished by a single person) or social (accomplished by a group). In the case of social acts, the group will go through the same stages outlined above. With role specialization some people may be primarily responsible for perceptual aspects of the social act, others for manipulation, and still others for consummation. In addition, a given individual may show a preference for certain aspects of individual and social acts. This preference, expressed in terms of detachment, dominance, or dependence, represents the person's values.

In studies on human values, Morris found five basic value factors, which correspond to the three-point model developed in Table 4.1:

- Factor A: Social restraint and self-control (social detachment)
- Factor B: Enjoyment and practice in action (social and individual dominance)
- Factor C: Withdrawal and self-sufficiency (individual detachment)
- Factor D: Deceptivity and sympathetic concern (social dependence)
- Factor E: Self-indulgence (individual dependence)

Social value factors deal with the individual's relationship to social acts, and individual value factors deal with individual acts. Figure 4.2 shows the relationship of these five factors to the three-point model of the act developed earlier.[8]

One of Morris's most enduring contributions, and one that has significance for communication, is his three fields of sign theory. The first is *semantics*, or the study of how signs relate to things. Here we are interested in what a sign is taken to designate, the relationship between the world of signs and the world of things. The second is *syntactics*, or the study of how signs relate to other signs. This field examines grammar and system structure and

points to the ways in which signs are organized into larger sign systems. Finally, the field of *pragmatics* is interested in the effects of signs on human behavior. Pragmatic scholars look at communication effects and outcomes.

In Morris's work we see an interesting evolution of theory. Combining behavioral psychology, symbolic interactionism, value theory, and system theory, he developed a taxonomy of signs, a theory of values, and a joint theory of signs and value. Although Morris's theory provides a good backdrop on the general nature of signs, it is limited. The richness of coding will be revealed as we work through the theories of signs, language, discourse, and nonverbal communication in the following pages.

Langer's Theory of Symbols

One of the most important topics of philosophy in the past century has been the relationship between language and meaning. Any investigation of knowledge, or epistemology, must include a view of these central issues. A most useful concept of language is that of Susanne Langer, whose *Philosophy in a New Key* has received considerable attention by students of symbolism.[9]

Langer considers symbolism to be the key issue of philosophy, an issue that underlies all human knowing and understanding. According to Langer, all animal life is dominated by feeling, but human feeling includes the additional ability to conceive of objects in their absence via symbols and language.

Langer distinguishes between signs and symbols. Langer uses the term *sign* in a more restricted sense than Morris as a stimulus that signals the presence of something else. It corresponds closely with the actual signified object. In this sense clouds may be a sign of rain, laughter is often associated with happiness, and a red light means cross traffic. A *symbol* is more complex: "Symbols are not proxy of their

---

8. Ibid., p. 26.

9. Susanne Langer, *Philosophy in a New Key* (Cambridge, Mass.: Harvard University Press, 1942). See also *Mind: An Essay on Human Feeling,* 3 volumes (Baltimore: Johns Hopkins University Press, 1967, 1972, 1982).

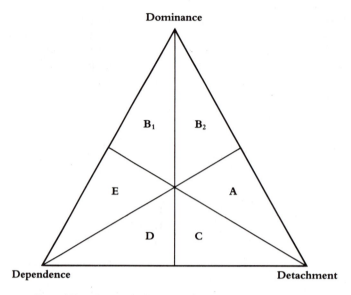

Figure 4.2   Model of the relation of values, signs, and the act.

From *Signification and Significance* by Charles Morris. (Cambridge, Mass.: MIT Press, 1964).

objects, but are *vehicles for the conception of objects.*[10] Symbols allow a person to think about something apart from its immediate presence. Langer calls the symbol "an instrument of thought."[11]

Not only do people have an increased capacity to use symbols, but the human also has a basic need to symbolize apart from the practical necessities of living. Further, the symbol-making process is a continuous function in humans tantamount to eating and sleeping. A good deal of human behavior is to be explained, then, in terms of meeting the symbolic need.

Like Peirce and Morris, Langer sees meaning as the complex relation among the symbol, the object, and the person. As she puts it, "If there is

not at least one thing meant and one mind for which it is meant, then there is not a complete meaning."[12] Thus, we have both a logical and psychological sense of symbol meaning, the logical being the relation between the symbol and referent and the psychological the relation between the symbol and the person.

The real significance of language, however, is not in words, but in *discourse.* Words name things, but "before terms are built into propositions, they assert nothing, preclude nothing . . . say nothing."[13] By tying words together, grammatical structure plays an important symbolic role. A *proposition* is a complex symbol that presents a picture of something. The word *dog* brings up a conception, but its combination with other words in a proposi-

10. Langer, *Philosophy in a New Key*, p. 61.

11. Ibid., p. 63.

12. Ibid., p. 56.

13. Ibid., p. 67.

tion provides a unified picture: The little brown dog is nestled against my foot. In this sense language truly makes us human. Through language we communicate, we think, and we feel.

How, then, do symbols work? Any symbol, including a proposition expressed in language, communicates a common *concept.* The concept is the general idea, pattern, or form embodied by the symbol. It is, in short, common meaning among communicators. But each communicator also will have a private image or meaning, which fills in the details of the common picture. This private image is the person's *conception.* Meaning therefore consists of the individual's conception and the common concept. For example, van Gogh's paintings are filled with symbols, both common and private. The common symbols in these paintings are accessible to anybody who views them; they are the commonly recognized images in the scene. The private meanings are those of van Gogh himself and those who are told or read about these conceptions.[14]

For example, his painting *Open Bible* is a view of a large open Bible sitting next to a candle. Next to the Bible is a small copy of a novel, Zola's *The Joy of Living.* For the common viewer, these images denote the objects depicted, and various private meanings might be assigned to them. For the artist, these images have very particular private meanings. As a whole the painting symbolizes the life and death of the artist's father. Van Gogh's father was a minister, symbolized by the open Bible. His death is symbolized by the candle, which casts a light on a passage from Isaiah about the suffering servant. The title of the smaller book symbolizes the elder van Gogh's life.

Van Gogh discussed the symbolism of his work in a letter to his brother:

> I want to paint men and women with that something of the eternal which the halo used to symbolize, and which we seek to convey by the actual radiance and vibration of our coloring. . . . I am always in the hope of being able to express the love of two lovers by

a wedding of two complementary colors, their mingling and their opposition, the mysterious vibration of kindred tones. To express the thought of a brow by the radiance of a light tone against a somber background. To express hope by some star, the eagerness of a soul by a sunset radiance.[15]

Three terms help explain Langer's ideas: signification, denotation, connotation. *Signification* is the meaning of a sign. A sign, as defined earlier, is a simple stimulus announcing the presence of some object. Signification therefore is a one-to-one relationship between sign and object, as between a stop sign and cross traffic. *Denotation* is the relation of the symbol to its object via the conception of the person. The *connotation* of a symbol is the direct relationship between the symbol and the conception itself. For example, the denotation of the symbol *dog* is its relation to the little brown puppy at your feet. This relationship occurs only in your mind through your idea of the animal. Even when the puppy is not present, you can think of it because of the relationship between the symbol and conception—the connotation of the word. Connotation includes all of one's personal feelings and associations attached to a symbol.

Langer notes that humans possess a built-in tendency to *abstract.* Abstraction, which leads to the ability to deal with concepts, is a crucial human function. It is the essence of rationality. Consistent with her notion of meaning, Langer defines abstraction as a process of forming a general conception from a variety of concrete experiences. Abstraction is a process of leaving out details in conceiving of an object, event, or situation in ever more general terms. For example, the word *dog* brings to mind a conception, a connotation, but this conception is incomplete; it always leaves something out. The more abstract the symbol, the more sketchy the conception: A *dog* is a *mammal,* which is an *animal;* an animal is a *living thing,* which is an *object.* All these terms can be used to symbolize the little brown puppy, but they constitute a hierarchy of abstraction, each successive term leaving out more details in the conception.

14. A semiotic analysis of van Gogh's work was done by Mark Roskill, " 'Public' and 'Private' Meanings: The Paintings of Van Gogh," *Journal of Communication* 29 (1979): 157–169.

15. Quoted in Roskill, " 'Public' and 'Private' Meanings," p. 157.

Two important types of symbols are language and ritual. Language symbols are discursive, and ritual symbols are presentational. *Discursive symbols* involve the combination of smaller language units into larger ones. Individual word meanings are combined into larger concepts. Words are combined into sentences, and sentences are combined into larger blocks of discourse. In *presentational symbolism* individual units may not have distinct meaning. Such forms may not be translatable or definable in other terms. The meanings of presentational forms are understood only through the whole. A Catholic mass or commencement ceremony illustrates this idea.

Other philosophers have excluded presentational forms from rationality, but Langer believes that all experience, including thought (discursive symbolism) and feeling (presentational symbolism), is rational. Some of the most important human experiences are emotional and are best communicated through presentational forms such as art and music. Langer summarizes her quest in the following passage:

> The continual pursuit of meanings—wider, clearer, more negotiable, more articulate meanings—is philosophy. It permeates all mental life; sometimes in conscious form of metaphysical thought, sometimes in the free confident manipulation of established ideas to derive their more precise, detailed implications, and sometimes—in the greatest creative periods—in the form of passionate mythical, ritual, and devotional expression.[16]

Eco's Semiotics

In this section we describe the work of Italian semiotician Umberto Eco, who has produced perhaps the most comprehensive and contemporary theory of signs.[17] Eco's theory is important because it is highly developed and integrates so much earlier semiotic thinking. Because the theory refuses to separate code structure from cultural practice, it overlaps somewhat with interactional-conven-

tional theories, which are summarized in Chapters 8 and 9.

Eco believes that semiotics should include both a "theory of codes" and a "theory of sign production." The theory of codes must come to grips with structural and functional features of language and other coding systems; the complementary theory of sign production must explain the ways in which coding systems are both used and changed through communication in actual sociocultural contexts. Thus, Eco tacks back-and-forth between assumptions of stability in coding structure and rich variation in cultural practice. In so doing he hopes to create a general theory that encompasses a number of symbolic and communicative concerns.

Eco's system of semiotics begins with the concept of a sign. A sign is anything taken by social convention to represent something else. The process of representing things by signs is signification or semiosis. Signification is best viewed as a four-part system:

1. Conditions or objects in the world
2. Signs
3. A repertoire of responses
4. A set of correspondence rules

The correspondence rules pair the signs with objects, defining what represents what, or they link signals with responses, thereby regulating a person's actions.

Eco uses the example of a dam in which a set of sensors activates a series of lights to tell an operator how high the water level is. The water levels are the worldly conditions, the lights are the signs, and the actions that an operator can take are the responses. Notice how these elements cannot function as a signification system without a set of correspondence rules. The rules tell the operator what water level each light represents and what should be done.

The system of objects, signs, and response possibilities constitutes an s-code or code system. The *s-code* is a structure in and of itself apart from its actual use and can be studied as such. A *code*, however, is a particular set of correspondence rules and cannot be studied apart from the person or group

---

16. Langer, *Philosophy in a New Key*, pp. 293–294.

17. Eco's primary semiotic works include *A Theory of Semiotics* (Bloomington: Indiana University Press, 1976); and *Semiotics and the Philosophy of Language* (Bloomington: Indiana University Press, 1984).

using it. Any s-code can be restructured time-and-time again because people can use and create a variety of codes or sets of rules for different purposes. For example, the formal grammar of a language is an s-code; the way people adapt and use the grammar in everyday life is a code. We can better understand the difference between a code and an s-code by examining signs in more detail.

Eco discusses four modes of sign production, or ways in which people use signs. First, there is *recognition*, in which a person identifies or views an object or event as an expression of some content. Recognizing symptoms and clues is an example. Second, there is *ostension*, the most elementary form of active signification. Here the person uses the object itself to signify a content. You might, for example, hold up an empty soda can to signal someone to buy you a soda at the store. Third, *replica* is the use of arbitrary signs in combination with other signs to signify. The use of language, certain gestures, emblems, musical notes, and so forth are examples of replica. Finally, there is *invention*, or proposing a new way to organize a field of stimuli to create a code. This involves suggesting new ways in which signs might be used. Art is a good example of invention.

When a rule associates a sign with something else, a *sign-function* is said to exist. The sign-function is the relationship between the sign and the signified, between an expression and a content. It is tempting to think of the content as an existing thing or a referent; however, Eco is careful to point out that the content is never the thing itself but a cultural conception of the thing. He designates a sign with slashes, as in /dog/, and the actual object with double slashes, as in //dog//. The content of the sign function, however, is designated <<dog>>, which is a concept of "dogness." Sometimes the referent simply does not exist, as in the case of fantasies like mermaids, lies, and jokes. In the example of the dam, the real content of the sign-function is not the water level per se but one's meanings for the water level, for example, <<safe>>, <<danger>>, and <<flood>>.

Codes are organized sets of rules that relate to and define one another. Signs as expressions can be broken down into further expressions and con-

tents, and contents, too, can be subdivided in this way. So the expression /red light/ has the subcode of /flood/, which means <<danger>>. The content <<high water>> can also be broken down into a subcode of /open valve/ with a meaning of <<let water out>>. In fact, code systems are completely defined in terms of their internal relations. All sign-functions are defined ultimately in terms of other sign-functions.

Eco defines *denotations* as a simple sign-content relation. *Connotation* is a sign that is related to a content via one or more other sign-functions. For example, the sign-function /dog/ — <<dog>> is a denotation; a connotation would be /dog/ — <<stinky>>, which is derived from a more complicated link: <<dog>> — /hairy/ — /smells/ — <<stinky>>.

Now we can see more clearly the difference between an s-code and a code. Any system of contents, signs, and responses can be related to one another in innumerable ways. Any sign can have many possible contents or sign-functions. Complex combinations of sign-functions are often used to elaborate an idea or feeling, which Eco calls text, message, or discourse. Because of the possibility of multiple meanings then, communication always involves interpretation, which is the use of sign-functions to translate and explain other sign-functions.

An *interpretant* is the relationship between one sign-function and another; it is the means by which people understand and interpret texts. For example, I might ask you, "What is a /fire/?" You would then answer, "/Fire/ is <<burning>>." "What," I then ask, "is /burning/?" "/Burning/ is <<hot>>." Children in the process of learning codes drive parents crazy by their interminable quest for interpretants. Eco shows how dictionaries are simple catalogs of interpretants, one sign being related to another. Human interpretation, however, is more similar to the working of an encyclopedia because of the nearly infinite number of possible sign-functions that are related to one another in a complex web of actual and possible relations. Remember, interpretants are not facts or truths but cultural conceptions that establish the representational meaning of signs.

Codes establish what correspondence rules are in force in a particular context. These codes are established by convention within cultural groups. Meanings are therefore cultural units. Not only is meaning cultural, but cultures are semiotic; as Eco describes,

> Perhaps we are, somewhere, the deep impulse which generates semiosis. And yet we recognize ourselves only as semiosis in process, signifying systems and communicational processes. The map of semiosis, as defined at a given stage of historical development (with the debris carried over from previous semiosis), tells us who we are and what (or how) we think.[18]

The Structure of Language

The study of language and linguistics has been heavily influenced by semiotics and the structural tradition. The modern founder of structural linguistics was Ferdinand de Saussure, who along with figures such as Peirce, Ogden, Morris, Langer, and Eco made substantial contributions to the structural tradition in communication early in this century. Later, significant questions arose concerning the ways in which language is actually produced, understood, and acquired, leading to contemporary cognitive approaches. We will review each of these briefly in the following pages.

Classical Foundations

Saussure taught that signs, including language, are arbitrary.[19] He noted that different languages use different words for the same thing and that there is no physical connection between a word and its referent. Therefore, signs are conventions governed by rules. Not only does this axiom support the idea that language is a structure, but it also reinforces the general assumption that language

18. Eco, *Semiotics and Philosophy*, p. 45.

19. Ferdinand de Saussure's primary work on this subject is *Course in General Linguistics* (London: Peter Owen, 1960). Excellent secondary sources include Anthony Giddens, *Central Problems in Social Theory: Action, Structure, and Contradiction in Social Analysis* (Berkeley: University of California Press, 1979); and Fred Dallmayr, *Language and Politics* (Notre Dame, Ind.: University of Notre Dame Press, 1984).

and reality are separate. Saussure himself referred to language as both a system and as a structure. As such, he believed that linguistic researchers must pay attention to language forms, such as sounds, word parts, and grammar.

The arbitrariness of language, however, is not absolute. Although language conventions are arbitrary, individual speakers are required to follow the conventions that are established, making language use not at all arbitrary. Further, because some words are based on other words, arbitrariness is a matter of degree. Basic words like *his* and *story* are "radically arbitrary," whereas a derived word like *history* is "relatively arbitrary."

Language described in these terms is strictly a system of formal relations without substance. The key to understanding the structure of the system is difference: The elements and relations embedded in language are distinguished by their differences. One sound differs from another (as *p* and *b*); one word differs from another (as *pat* and *bat*); one grammatical form differs from another (as *has run* and *will run*). This system of differences constitutes the structure of the language. Both in spoken and written language, distinctions among signified objects in the world are identified by corresponding distinctions among linguistic signs. No linguistic unit has significance in and of itself; only in conjunction with other linguistic units does a particular unit acquire meaning.

Saussure believed that language and meaning are inseparable and that all a person knows of the world is determined by language. Unlike other semioticians, then Saussure does not see signs as referential. Signs do not designate objects but constitute them. In this regard, Saussure's work set the stage for much twentieth-century thought not only in structural linguistics but also interactionist theory (Chapters 8 and 9) and interpretive and critical theories (Chapters 10 and 11).[20]

Saussure made an important distinction between formal language, which he called *langue*, and the actual use of language in communication, which he referred to as *parole*. These two terms correspond to language and speech. Language (langue) is a formal

20. See Art Berman, *From the New Criticism to Deconstruction* (Urbana: University of Illinois Press, 1988), pp. 114–143.

system with a life of its own apart from the people who use it. Speech (parole) is the use of language to accomplish purposes. Language is not created by users, but speech is. Indeed, speech makes use of language, but it is less regular and more variable than the formal system of language from which it derives. Linguistics, to Saussure, is the study of langue, not parole: "Taken as a whole, speech is many-sided and heterogeneous; straddling several areas simultaneously . . . we cannot put it into any category of human facts, for we cannot discover its unity. Language, on the contrary, is a self-contained whole and a principle of classification."[21] This distinction has had a significant impact on the study of language and communication to the present day.

One difference between langue and parole, according to Saussure, is stability. Language is characterized by *synchrony*, meaning that it changes very little over time. Speech, on the other hand, is characterized by *diachrony*, meaning that it changes constantly from situation to situation. Because of its constant flux, speech is not particularly suitable for scientific study, which is why linguistics must take a language-oriented, synchronic focus. The point here is not that language does not change, only that language form cannot be understood unless a synchronic perspective is adopted. As we will see in Chapters 8 and 9, however, the distinction between language and speech, and that between synchrony and diachrony, is sharply criticized by theorists from other traditions. We return to the topic of language in Chapter 5 where we explore in more detail theories of how language functions in discourse.

Let us turn now to a more detailed discussion of language structure itself. Influenced by the work of Saussure, the standard model of sentence structure was developed between about 1930 and 1950 in the classical structural period.[22] Numerous linguists contributed to this model, but the most important include Leonard Bloomfield, Charles Fries, and Zellig Harris.[23] Basically, this model breaks down a sentence into component parts in hierarchical fashion. Sounds and sound groups combine to form word roots and word parts, which in turn combine to form words and phrases. Phrases are put together to make clauses or sentences. Thus, language can be analyzed on various levels, roughly corresponding to sounds, words, and phrases.

The first level of sounds involves the study of *phonetics*. An isolatable speech sound is a *phone*. Phones of a particular type are grouped into a sound family called *phoneme*, which is the basic building block of any language. Any dialect of a language contains a number of phonemes. These phonemes are combined according to rules to produce *morphemes*, the smallest meaningful linguistic unit. On the syntax level, words are combined according to rules to form grammatical *phrases*, which are linked together into clauses and sentences. This structural approach provides an orderly classification of language parts. Actual observed segments are put into classes of a given type (phoneme, morpheme, etc.), and these segments are sequenced in a sentence-building process. At each level of analysis is a finite set of classes (e.g., phonemes or morphemes) that can be observed in the native language. Sentences are always built up from the bottom of the hierarchy, so that succeeding levels depend on the formation of lower levels. This scheme is known as phrase-structure grammar.

For example, a sentence can be broken down according to the following rewrite rule:

$$\text{sentence} = \text{noun phrase (NP)} + \text{verb phrase (VP)}$$

The verb phrase can be broken down further according to the following rewrite rule:

$$VP = V + NP$$

This process continues until all units of the sentence are accounted for, including small parts such as the articles (A) *the* or *an*. Phrase structures are

21. Saussure, *Course*, p. 9.

22. An excellent summary and critique of this period can be found in J. A. Fodor, T. G. Bever, and M. F. Garrett, *The Psychology of Language: An Introduction to Psycholinguistics and Generative Grammar* (New York: McGraw-Hill, 1974).

23. Leonard Bloomfield, *Language* (New York: Holt, Rinehart & Winston, 1933); Charles Fries, *The Structure of English* (New York: Harcourt, Brace & World, 1952); Zellig Harris, *Structural Lingusitics* (Chicago: University of Chicago Press, 1951).

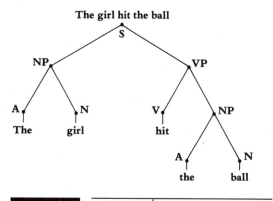

The girl hit the ball

Figure 4.3   A simple tree diagram.

often illustrated by a tree diagram, as shown in Figure 4.3.

Although this approach provides a useful description of the structure of language, it fails to explain how people use language. This latter question, far more central to communication than language structure, has demanded the attention of psycholinguists since about 1950. We know that people must possess an intuitive knowledge of their language in order to produce meaningful, grammatical speech. What is the nature of this knowledge? How is it acquired? How is it used? The literature that has emerged from this work is extensive, controversial, and somewhat technical.

Old-fashioned phrase-structure grammar is no longer believed to be adequate by itself to explain the generation of sentences.[24] The primary objection to classical linguistics is that although it is useful as a taxonomic, or descriptive, approach, it is powerless to explain how language is generated. A simple example will suffice to illustrate this weakness. Phrase-structure grammar would analyze the following two sentences exactly the same way, even though their syntactical origins are different.[25]

John is easy to please.
John is eager to please.

These sentences have entirely different syntactical meanings. In the first sentence, John is the object of the infinitive *to please*. In the second John is the noun phrase of the sentence. Regular phrase structure provides no easy way by examining the actual sentence itself to explain these different grammatical meanings.

Problems such as this lead to a series of questions that traditional phrase-structure grammar cannot answer:

• How can a speaker produce an infinite number of novel sentences from just a few rules?
• By what cognitive process are sentences generated and understood?
• How is syntactical ambiguity to be accounted for?
• How is language acquired?

To answer questions such as these, generative grammar has been developed.

Noam Chomsky is the primary force behind generative grammar. As a young linguist in the 1950s, Chomsky parted company with the classical theorists to develop an approach that since has become the foundation of contemporary linguistics.[26] Like any theoretical tradition, generative grammar now has several positions within it, although the tradition as a whole is built on a cluster of essential ideas.

First, generative grammar rests on the believed centrality of sentence generation, which is seen as far more important than sentence description. Old-style linguistics was powerful in describing the structure of a sentence, but it did not explain how sentences are actually produced by the individual. Further, there is the suspicion that the surface structure of a sentence may actually mislead us about how sentences are really structured within the mind.

Second, the objective of generative grammar is to isolate a set of rules that will parsimoniously explain how any sentence could be generated. Parsimony is the key. Inventing a new rule for each

24. For an explanation and critique of finite-state and phrase-structure grammar, see Noam Chomsky, "Three Models for the Description of Language," *Transactions on Information Theory* 1T-2 (1956): 113–124; and Jerry Fodor, James Jenkins, and Sol Saporta, "Psycholinguistics and Communication Theory," in *Human Communication Theory*, ed. F. E. X. Dance (New York: Holt, Rinehart & Winston, 1967), pp. 160–201.

25. Examples from Gilbert Harmon, *On Noam Chomsky: Critical Essays* (Garden City, N.Y.: Anchor Books, 1974), p. 5.

26. For a list of Chomsky's works, see the Bibliography.

construction is not workable. Indeed, the brain is finite and cannot operate on an infinitely expanding set of linguistic rules. Yet people can produce and understand an infinite number of sentences. An adequate grammar must explain this paradox. The answer lies in a relatively small number of rules that can be used over and over again to produce novel sentences.

The third essential feature of generative grammar is the transformation. (In fact, generative grammar is alternatively named transformational grammar.) At some point the surface structure of a sentence must have been transformed from some other, deeper structure; and generative grammar seeks to explain this transformation process.

In treating the study of mind as a natural science, Chomsky believes that elements of language and mind are universal and available for discovery. He is analytical in approach, seeking inherent mechanisms of mind. However, he also sees the individual as distinctly human and creative. He believes also in the a priori nature of knowledge and that much knowledge is tacit or implicit. He follows the notion that knowledge arises from an application of innate categories onto the world of experience.[27] In short, Chomsky is a champion of a point of view that has not been popular in this century—rationalism. He has revived the basic idea of René Descartes of the seventeenth century, that the mind is given its power by a priori qualities and that knowledge arises from the use of this power in understanding experience.[28]

Let us now look more specifically at the ideas in Chomsky's theory. Original generative theory posits four basic components of grammar. Deep structures are believed to be underlying sentence models constructed by the use of base phrase-structure rules. The deep structure of any sentence is modified by transformation rules, resulting in an uttered (or utterable) surface structure. Sentence generation proceeds along the following lines.

Deep structure is created with base rules. The deep structure is a sentence model, a mental structure, not utterable as speech. It is a model of sentence parts resembling a simple declarative form. The rules used to generate the deep structure are rewrite rules that follow lines originally developed in phrase-structure grammar.

Next, a surface structure is generated by transformation rules, which are instructions of movement: Move component x to location y. For example, the active transformation moves components so that they appear in the order NP + VP (Sally hit the ball). The passive transformation prescribes NP + auxiliary + VP + NP (The ball is hit by Sally). A sufficient but parsimoniously small number of phrase-structure and transformation rules will permit the generation of any proper sentence.

Because this book is not a linguistics text, we will not cover the range of possible transformation rules of English. To understand the basics of the theory, however, we will look at an example. Our example uses two transformation rules: the passive transformation and the adjective transformation.[29] The passive transformation inverts the noun phrase and verb phrase, puts the verb in the passive form, and adds the preposition *by*:

> John loves Mary.
> Mary is loved by John. (passive)

The adjective transformation occurs by deleting the verb form *be* and placing the adjective in front of the noun:

> John loves Mary.
> Mary is pretty.
> John loves pretty Mary. (adjective)

Suppose you wish to generate the sentence, *Ripe mushrooms are loved by hobbits.*[30] You would do this in two stages. First, with the phrase-structure rules, you would generate a deep tree, as shown in Figure 4.4. This deep tree provides the basic semantic interpretation of the sentence. All basic logical grammatical relations are present, and the meaning of the sentence is set. Don't worry that this deep

27. Chomsky discusses features of his epistemology in *Rules and Representations* (New York: Columbia University Press, 1980).

28. René Descartes, *Meditations on First Philosophy*, trans. Laurence J. LaFleur (Indianapolis: Bobbs-Merrill, 1960).

29. Several English transformations are explained in brief form by Peter Salus, *Linguistics* (Indianapolis: Bobbs-Merrill, 1969).

30. Example from Salus, *Linguistics*.

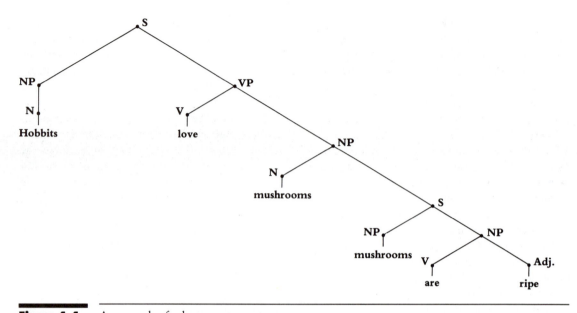

Figure 4.4   An example of a deep tree structure.

From *Linguistics* by Peter H. Salus. Copyright © 1969 by Macmillan Publishing Company. Reprinted by permission of the publisher.

structure does not resemble the intended surface structure. The deep structure is an abstract model from which the actual sentence will be generated in the next stage.

The surface tree—the actual sentence—is generated by applying the two transformations described above, passive and adjective. Figure 4.5 illustrates the surface tree.

With a relatively small number of phrase-structure rules and transformation rules, a speaker can generate any novel grammatical sentence. The basic semantic structure is generated on the deep or abstract level with phrase structure, and sentences are generated by subjecting the underlying structure to transformations. In essence, this process is what a speaker intuitively "knows" about the language. The two-stage sentence-generation model is a parsimonious and descriptively adequate explanation of how the speaker uses this knowledge.

An essential feature of generative theory is that a singular correspondence exists between a surface structure and its deep structure. Any meaningful sentence structure has one, and only one, deep

structure. If an uttered sentence has more than one syntactical meaning, each meaning is derivable from a separate deep structure. For example, the sentence *She is a dancing teacher* has two possible meanings. No analysis of surface structure alone can explain this inconsistency. The two interpretations stem from separate deep structures with dif-

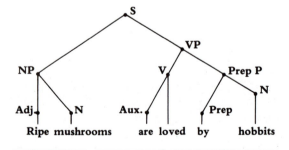

Figure 4.5   An example of a surface structure.

From *Linguistics* by Peter H. Salus. Copyright © 1969 by Macmillan Publishing Company. Reprinted by permission of the publisher.

ferent configurations. One stems from a structure with the following components: NP (She) + VP (teaches dancing). The other is transformed from a deep structure of two clauses—(1) NP (She) + VP (dances), and (2) NP (She) + VP (teaches)—that have been combined into a single deep structure of the following form: NP (She) + S (who dances) + VP (teaches).

Obviously, this theory explains surface ambiguities, whereas the classical structure cannot. It also illustrates that in standard theory meaning must always be located at the deep level.

Theories of Nonverbal Communication

Nonverbal communication is difficult to conceptualize. Scholars disagree about what nonverbal communication is, as Randall Harrison points out:

> The term "nonverbal communication" has been applied to a broad range of phenomena: everything from facial expression and gesture to fashion and status symbol, from dance and drama to music and mime, from the flow of affect to the flow of traffic, from the territoriality of animals to the protocol of diplomats, from extrasensory perception to analog computers, and from the rhetoric of violence to the rhetoric of topless dancers.[31]

Because of the uncertainties about what counts as nonverbal communication, classifying and organizing this material is difficult. Judee Burgoon suggests a threefold scheme:

1. The structure of nonverbal code systems
2. Cultural variation and patterns
3. Social functions of nonverbal codes[32]

Many of the topics relevant to the second and third categories are covered later in the book; for now, we concentrate on structural approaches to nonverbal coding.

Burgoon characterizes nonverbal code systems as possessing several structural properties. First, nonverbal codes tend to be *analogic* rather than digital. Whereas digital signals are discrete, like numbers and letters, analogic signals are continuous, forming a spectrum or range, like sound volume and the brightness of light. Therefore, nonverbal signals like facial expression and vocal intonation cannot simply be classed into one category or another.

A second feature found in some, but not all, nonverbal codes is *iconicity*, or resemblance. Iconic codes resemble the thing being symbolized (like depicting the shape of something with your hands.) Third, certain nonverbal codes seem to elicit *universal meaning*. This is especially the case with such signals as threats and emotional displays, which may be biologically determined. Fourth, nonverbal codes enable the *simultaneous transmission* of several messages. With the face, body, voice, and other signals, several different messages can be sent at once. Fifth, nonverbal signals often evoke an *automatic response* without thinking. An example would be stepping on the brake at a red light. Sixth, nonverbal signals are often emitted quite *spontaneously*, as when you let off nervous energy.

Finally, nonverbal code systems have several things in common with language, though Burgoon is careful to point out that there are also many differences. Both language and nonverbal code systems can be broken down into particular units, as we will see in the next section.

We can use Morris's three dimensions of semantics, syntactics, and pragmatics to characterize both language and nonverbal forms. *Semantics* refers to

31. Randall Harrison, "Nonverbal Communcation," in *Handbook of Communcation*, eds. I. de sola Pool et al. (Chicago: Rand McNally, 1973). Conceptual issues are discussed in Judee K. Burgoon, "Nonverbal Communication Research in the 1970s: An Overview," in *Communication Yearbook 4*, ed. D. Nimmo (New Brunswick, N.J.: Transaction Books, 1980), p. 179; see also Mark Knapp, *Nonverbal Communciation in Human Interaction* (New York: Holt, Rinehart & Winston, 1978); Mark Knapp, John Wiemann, and Johy Daly, "Nonverbal Communication: Issues and Appraisal," *Human Communication Research 4* (1978): 271–280; Robert G. Harper, Arthur Weiss, and Joseph Motarozzo, *Nonverbal Communcation: The State of the Art* (New York: Wiley, 1978).

32. This analysis from Judee K. Burgoon, "Nonverbal Signals," in *Handbook of Interpersonal Communication*, eds. M. L. Knapp and G. L. Miller (Beverly Hills, Calif.: Sage, 1985), pp. 350–353.

the meanings of a sign. For example, two fingers held up behind someone's head is a way of calling him a "devil." *Syntactics* refers to the ways in which signs are organized into systems with other signs. One might, for example, hold up two fingers behind someone's head, laugh, and say "Joke's on you!" Here a gesture, a vocal sign (laughing), facial expressions, and language combine to create an overall effect. *Pragmatics* refers to the effects or behaviors elicited by a sign or group of signs, as when the "devil" sign is taken as a joke and brings about a lighthearted feeling in the group.

The meanings attached to both verbal and non-verbal forms are context-bound, or determined in part by the context in which they are produced and read. Further, both language and nonverbal forms allow communicators to combine relatively few signs into an almost limitless variety of complex expressions of meaning.

Nonverbal code systems are often classed according to the type of activity used in the code. Burgoon suggests seven types:

- Kinesics, or bodily activity
- Proxemics, or use of space
- Physical appearance
- Haptics, or use of touch
- Vocalics, or use of voice
- Chronemics, or use of time
- Artifacts, or use of objects[33]

In this chapter we will look at three prominent theories of the first two types of nonverbal coding—kinesics and proxemics.

Kinesics

Ray Birdwhistell is considered the originator of kinesics.[34] An anthropologist interested in language, Birdwhistell uses linguistics as a model for his kinesic work. In fact, kinesics is popularly referred to as body language, although critics doubt

the validity of the language analogy. Let us look at the foundation ideas of Birdwhistell's theory.

In *Kinesics and Context* Birdwhistell lists seven assumptions on which he bases his theory:[35]

1. All body movements have potential meaning in communicative contexts. Somebody can always assign meaning to any bodily activity.

2. Behavior can be analyzed because it is patterned. The organization of bodily activity can be subjected to systematic analysis.

3. Although bodily activity has biological limitations, the use of body motion in interaction is considered to be a part of the social system. Different groups will therefore use gestures differently.

4. People are influenced by the visible bodily activity of others.

5. The ways in which body activity functions in communication can be investigated.

6. The meanings discovered in research on kinesics result from the behavior being studied as well as the methods used for research.

7. A person's use of bodily activity will have idiosyncratic features but will also be part of a larger social system shared with others.

Birdwhistell's work is based largely on the perceived similarities between bodily activity and language, which has been called the *linguistic-kinesic analogy*. This analogy extends classical linguistics into the realm of kinesics:

> This original study of gestures gave the first indication that kinesic structure is parallel to language structure. By the study of gestures in context, it became clear that the kinesic system has forms which are astonishingly like words in language. The discovery in turn led to the investigation of the components of these forms and to the discovery of the larger complexes of which they were components. . . . It has become clear that there are body behaviors which function like significant sounds, that combine into simple or relatively complex units like words, which are combined into much longer stretches of structured behavior like sentences or even paragraphs.[36]

33. Burgoon, "Nonverbal Signals," pp. 349–350.

34. Birdwhistell's major works include *Introduction to Kinesics* (Louisville: University of Louisville Press, 1952); *Kinesics and Context* (Philadelphia: University of Pennsylvania Press, 1970).

35. Birdwhistell, *Kinesics and Context*, pp. 183–184.

36. Ibid., p. 80.

The similarity of hierarchical structure in kinesics to that of linguistics is striking. The problem of the kinesicist is similar to that of the linguist: "Kinesics is concerned with abstracting from the continuous muscular shifts which are characteristics of living physiological systems those groupings of movement which are of significance to the communicational process and thus to the interactional systems of particular social groups."[37]

Out of the thousands of perceptible bodily motions produced in a short period of time, certain of these emerge as functional in communication. Such movements are called kines. A *kine* is a range of motions or positions seen as a single motion or position. A perceptible movement of the eyelid or a turn of the hand are examples of kines. What is defined as a kine in one cultural group may not be in another. Kines are further grouped into *kinemes*, elements that have distinct meanings. Like the phoneme in linguistics, the kineme is a group of relatively interchangeable kines. For example, up to twenty-three different positions (kines) of the eyelids can be discerned, but they can be grouped into about four kinemes. Kinemes, like phonemes, occur in context. A complex combination of kinemes throughout the body such as a wink, a smile, and a wave of the hand are called a *kinemorphs*.

Proxemics

Edward Hall shares the view of his fellow anthropologist Birdwhistell that communication is a multichannel affair.[38] Hall believes that just as language varies from culture to culture, so do the other media. Specifically, *proxemics* refers to the use of space in communication: "the study of how man unconsciously structures microspace—the distance between men in conduct of daily transactions, the organization of space in his houses and buildings,

and ultimately the layout of his towns."[39] Although this definition of proxemics is broad, most work in the area has been limited to the use of interpersonal space.

According to Hall, the way space is used in interaction is very much a cultural matter. In different cultures various sensory modalities assume importance. In some cultures, such as the American, sight and hearing predominate; in other cultures, such as the Arabian, smell is also important. Some cultures rely on touching more than others. In any case, a necessary relation is present between the use of senses in interaction and interpersonal distances. Another reason that proxemic relations vary among cultures involves the definition of the self. People in most Western cultures learn to identify the self through the skin and clothes. Arabs, however, place the self deeper in the middle of the body.

For these reasons then, the people of a particular culture structure their space in particular ways. Hall defines three basic types of space. *Fixed-feature space* consists of the unmovable structural arrangements around us. Walls and rooms are examples. *Semifixed-feature space* is the way that movable obstacles, such as furniture, are arranged. *Informal space* is the personal territory around the body that travels with a person. Informal space determines the interpersonal distance among individuals. American culture uses four discernible distances: intimate (0 to 18 inches), personal (1½ to 4 feet), social (4 to 12 feet), and public (over 12 feet).

When people are engaged in conversation, eight possible factors are involved in the distance between them. Hall lists these factors as primary categories:

1. Posture–sex factors: These include the sex of the participant and the basic position (standing, sitting, lying).

2. Sociofugal-sociopetal axis: The word *sociofugal* implies discouragement of interaction; *sociopetal* implies the opposite. This dimension refers to the angle of the shoulders relative to the other person.

---

37. Ibid., p. 192.

38. Edward Hall's major works include *The Silent Language* (Greenwich, Conn.: Fawcett Books, 1959); "A System for the Notation of Proxemic Behavior," *American Anthropologist* 65 (1963): 1003–1026: and *The Hidden Dimension* (New York: Random House, 1966).

39. Hall, "A System for Notation," p. 1003.

The speakers may be facing each other, may be back-to-back, or may be positioned toward any other angle in the radius.

3. Kinesthetic factors: This is the closeness of the individuals in terms of touchability. Individuals may be in physical contact or within close distance, they may be outside body contact distance, or they may be positioned anywhere in between these extremes. This factor also includes the positioning of body parts as well as which parts are touching.

4. Touching behavior: People may be involved in any of the following tactile relations: caressing and holding, feeling, prolonged holding, pressing against, spot touching, accidental brushing, or no contact.

5. Visual code: This category includes the manner of eye contact ranging from direct (eye-to-eye) to no contact.

6. Thermal code: This element involves the perceived heat from the other communicator.

7. Olfactory code: This factor includes the kind and degree of odor perceived in the conversation.

8. Voice loudness: The loudness of speech relates directly to interpersonal space.

Ekman and Friesen

For many years Paul Ekman and Wallace Friesen have collaborated on nonverbal research that has led to an excellent general model of nonverbal signs.[40] They have concentrated their work on kinesic behavior (e.g., face and hands). Their goal has been ambitious: "Our aim has been to increase understanding of the individual, his feelings, mood, personality, and attitudes, and to increase understanding of any given interpersonal interaction, the nature of the relationship, the status or quality of communication, what impressions are formed, and

40. Ekman and Friesen's major works include "Nonverbal Behavior in Psychotherapy Research," in *Research in Psychotherapy*, vol. III, ed. J. Shlien, (Washington, D.C.: American Psychological Association, 1968), pp. 179–216; "The Repertoire of Nonverbal Behavior: Categories, Origins, Usage, and Coding," *Semiotica* 1 (1969): 49–98; *Emotion in the Human Face: Guidelines for Research and an Integration of Findings* (New York: Pergamon Press, 1972); *Unmasking the Face* (Englewood Cliffs, N.J.: Prentice-Hall, 1975).

what is revealed about interpersonal style or skill."[41]

These authors have approached nonverbal activity from three perspectives: origin, coding, and usage. *Origin* is the source of an act. A nonverbal behavior may be *innate* (built into the nervous system), *species-constant* (universal behavior required for survival), or *variant* across cultures, groups, and individuals. As examples, one could speculate that eyebrow raising as a response to surprise is innate, that territoriality is species-constant, and that shaking the head back-and-forth to indicate "no" is culture specific.

Coding is the relationship of the act to its meaning. An act may be arbitrary; that is, no indication of meaning is inherent in the sign itself. Head nodding is a good example. By convention, in our culture we agree that nodding is an indication of "yes", but this coding is purely arbitrary. Other nonverbal signs are *iconic*. Iconic signs resemble what is being signified. For instance, we often draw pictures in the air or position our hands to illustrate what we are talking about. The third category of coding is *intrinsic*. Intrinsically coded cues contain their meaning within them; such cues are themselves part of what is being signified. Crying is an example of intrinsic coding. Crying is a sign of emotion, but it is also part of the emotion itself.

The third way to analyze a behavior is by *usage*, which is affected by such factors as external conditions around the behavior, awareness or nonawareness of the act, reactions from others, and the type of information conveyed. Usage also includes the degree to which a nonverbal behavior is intended to convey information. A *communicative act* is one used deliberately to convey meaning. *Interactive acts* are those that influence the behavior of the other participants. An act is both communicative and interactive if it is intentional and influential. For example, if you deliberately wave to a friend as a sign of greeting and the friend waves back, your cue is communicative and interactive. A third category of behaviors are those not intended to be communicative but that nevertheless provide

41. Paul Ekman and Wallace Friesen, "Hand Movements," *Journal of Communication* 22 (1972): 353.

information for the perceiver. Such acts are said to be *informative*. On a day when you are feeling less than friendly, you may duck into a hallway to avoid meeting an acquaintance coming your way. If the other person sees the avoidance, your behavior has been informative even though you did not intend to communicate.

All nonverbal behavior is one of five types, depending on origin, coding, and usage. The first type is the *emblem*. Emblems have a verbal translation of a rather precise meaning for a social group. They are normally used in a deliberate fashion to communicate a particular message. The victory "V" and the black power fist are examples. The origin of emblems is cultural learning; emblems may be either arbitrary or iconic in coding.

Illustrators are the second kind of nonverbal cues. Illustrators have a high relation to speech because they are used to illustrate what is being said verbally. They are intentional, though we may not always be directly aware of them. They include eight types:

• *Batons* Movements that accent or emphasize
• *Ideographs* "Sketching" the direction of a thought
• *Deictic movements* Pointing
• *Spatial movements* Depicting or outlining space
• *Rhythmic movements* Pacing motions
• *Kinetographs* Depicting physical actions
• *Pictographs* Drawing a picture in the air
• *Emblematic movements* Illustrating a verbal statement

These types are not mutually exclusive; some motions are combinations of types. Illustrators are informative or communicative in use and occasionally may be interactive. They are also learned.

The third type of nonverbal behavior is the *adaptor*, which serves to facilitate release of bodily tension. Examples are hand wringing, head scratching, or foot jiggling. *Self-adaptors*, which usually occur in private, are directed to one's own body. They include scratching, stroking, grooming, squeezing. *Alter-adaptors* are directed to another's body. *Object-adaptors* are directed at things. In any case, adaptors can be iconic or intrinsic. Rarely are they

intentional, and one is usually not aware of one's own adaptive behaviors. They may occur when the individual is communicating with another, but they usually occur with greater frequency when the person is alone. Although they are rarely communicative, they are sometimes interactive and often informative.

Regulators, the fourth type of behavior, are used directly to regulate, control, or coordinate interaction. For example, we use eye contact to signal speaking and listening roles in a conversation. Regulators are primarily interactive. They are coded intrinsically or iconically, and their origin is cultural learning.

The final category of behavior is the *affect display*. These behaviors, which may be in part innate, involve the display of feelings and emotions. The face is a particularly rich source for affect display, although other parts of the body also may be involved. Affect displays are intrinsically coded. They are rarely communicative, often interactive, and always informative.

Research on Nonverbal Communication

Nonverbal communication theories have been used in a variety of research applications.[42] For example, the development of nonverbal codes has been investigated, and individual, cultural, and universal nonverbal signs have been discovered. In addition, research has dealt with nonverbal skills in sending information to others and interpreting the behavior of other people. Cultural norms, gender differences, and other nonverbal differences between age groups, races, and socioeconomic status have also been explored.

Various functions of nonverbal communication such as information processing, learning, expression of emotion, and impression formation have received considerable attention by researchers. Investigators have also looked at the role of nonverbal communication in relationships, including attraction, emotion, dominance, and other factors. One of the most popular topics related to nonver-

42. Many of these are discussed in Burgoon, "Nonverbal Signals."

bal communication has been deception, including its use and detection.

One of the most important subjects in communication theory is social influence and persuasion. Nonverbal communication has been examined in this context as well. An example of nonverbal persuasion research is that of Judee Burgoon, Thomas Birk, and Michael Pfau, who studied the relationship of a public speaker's nonverbal cues to audience perception of credibility and persuasiveness.[43] In this study, students in a basic speech class rated one another's speeches in terms of credibility and persuasiveness. At the same time, expert raters also judged each speaker's use of sixteen different nonverbal behaviors, including certain kinesic behaviors such as smiling, facial expressiveness, and gestures; proxemic behaviors such as eye contact, distance, and body lean; and a variety of voice qualities such as pitch and tempo.

These researchers found that many of these behaviors were indeed correlated with perceived persuasiveness and credibility. For example, a speaker's perceived character is related in part to vocal pitch, eye contact, and even facial expression. Perceived competence is related to such behaviors as fluency, pitch, smiling, and facial expression.

This study is a good example because it not only illustrates the utility of nonverbal communication research and the kinds of things done in this area but also shows the assumptions of semiotics at work. A sign is taken by a person to represent a referent. In this case the nonverbal sign is a referent for some quality in the speaker. Attributions about the speaker are made on the basis of these signified traits.

Commentary and Critique

Theories of signs and language form an important core in the study of communication. They not only provide a way of looking at communication

43. Judee K. Burgoon, Thomas Birk, and Michael Pfau, "Nonverbal Behaviors, Persuasion, and Credibility," *Human Communication Research* 17 (Fall 1990): 140-169.

but also have had a powerful impact on almost all perspectives now employed in communication theory. At the heart of semiosis is the basic notion of the triad of meaning. Although various theorists have defined the elements of the triad somewhat differently or have stressed different aspects of it, it constitutes the heart of semiotic thinking. Whatever disagreements they may have, structuralists almost always agree that the triad is an inseparable unit that lies at the base of signification in its various forms.

Semiotic thinking has gone through a variety of versions. Peirce was primarily responsible for developing the idea of the sign–referent–interpretation unit, and others have built on this basic notion. Saussure made use of the basic semiotic idea with an exclusive interest in language, whereas others like Birdwhistell and Hall emphasize nonlanguage forms.

Saussure's idea of *difference* has been a key concept in our understanding of language, but it applies equally well to any sign system. Signs do not have a life of their own as independent markers. They assume significance only in relation to other signs by virtue of the difference among signs. Thus, semiotics can never be applied to a single sign-meaning relation but is always useful only when viewing a system of signs together. Semiotics, then, always makes distinctions.

For Morris, signification is a behavioral phenomenon, and a sign is understood in terms of how it predisposes people and animals to respond in certain ways that other signs do not. Much of human life, including meaning, action, interaction, and values are behavioral and semiotic processes for Morris. If Morris's semiotic is behavioristic, Langer's is cognitive-emotive. For Langer, meaning consists of feeling and conception. This is why symbols are so important for Langer: They are the tools of thought. Langer, unlike so many other semiotic theorists, tries to convey the complexity and holistic nature of meaning and communication. She is less analytic than most theorists in this tradition because she recognizes the complex nature of expression.

Morris's three-fold division of semiotics into semantics, syntactics, and pragmatics has been especially useful in understanding the structural tradition. Many semioticians, including Morris, Langer, and Eco, have been preoccupied with the semantic dimension, in which the sign brings an idea, feeling, or conception into the mind of the person.

Syntactics, or the relationship among signs, has dominated the study of language and nonverbal communication. Saussure's idea of difference is especially important because it captures that character of signs making organization possible. Individual signs differ, making it possible to distinguish one from another; and organizational patterns differ as well, causing any grammatical structure to imply a meaning different from that implied by other structures.

Pragmatics is the study of how signs make a difference in people's lives. It is the study of the practical effects of signs, both linguistic and nonlinguistic. In a general sense, many communication theories are pragmatic because they deal with the outcomes or effects of communication. We begin looking at some pragmatic elements in the next chapter, and we will encounter them again at various points in this book.

Classical semiotics, which today may seem self-evident and simplistic, laid the foundation for much linguistic and communication theory in the twentieth century. Although these ideas have a certain intuitive appeal, they have been criticized.[44] Most critics agree that language is certainly conventional, but its arbitrariness is more in question. Arbitrariness makes sense only if one accepts the tenets that language and speech are separate and that signs are separate from their referents. Indeed, we know that some signs are intrinsic and part of the very thing they represent. Even Saussure acknowledged that for all practical purposes our knowledge of the world is completely determined by language. Further, critics of the structuralist tradition believe that language and communication cannot be separated in the way that Saussure does with his *langue–parole* distinction or Chomsky with his notion of *competence* and *performance* because

speech and other communicative forms are the mechanisms by which language and signs are created, maintained, and changed. Later semioticians like Eco acknowledge this difficulty and attempt to deal with it. At the same time, interactionists and certain interpretive scholars attack the problem head-on by focusing on the uses of language and nonverbal forms in actual interaction rather than on the structure of the sign system itself.

Chomskian linguistics has been described as a true Kuhnian revolution (see Chapter 2). It is generally praised as providing answers to questions that classical and behavioristic linguistics could not handle. Its major strengths are usually seen as its parsimony and explanatory power. However, language is one of our most difficult intellectual puzzles, and even generative grammar has its weaknesses. Basically, generative grammar has been criticized on two fronts, its scope and its validity.

Two problems of scope warrant discussion here. First, generative grammar generally ignores or downplays semantics. Primarily, it is a theory of grammar, of syntax; problems of individual lexical units and their meanings are ignored as unimportant. Second, critics are bothered by the failure of generative grammarians to consider problems of language as used in everyday life. Generative grammar treats language as an abstraction, claiming that an understanding of the anomalies of language use is unimportant to an understanding of language itself. This approach makes a sharp distinction between language *competence* and language *performance*. The former is knowledge of grammar; the latter is language use. Staying within the tradition of structural linguistics, generative grammarians steadfastly have maintained that performance is not a linguistic concern. Consequently, they are not interested in how language is used in social interaction. The theory therefore does not account for local and cultural variations of language, nor does it account for the commonly observed phenomenon of ungrammatical speech.

Much of the criticism of generative grammar questions its validity. A good deal of disagreement exists within the generative movement itself about the locus of meaning. Where in the process of sentence generation is meaning established? Chomsky

44. For a critique of structuralism, see Giddens, *Central Problems.*

has shown that meaningfulness cannot reside strictly at the surface level, yet deep analysis by itself may not be adequate for the establishment of meaning.

Transformational theory's key problems result from the difficulty of observing generative processes. Linguists must rely on inferences made from observing spoken sentences. Classical linguistics failed to make this inferential leap from observed behavior to hidden processes, and thus it fell short. As a result of its strong reliance on inference, generative theory operates primarily from logical force (see Chapter 2). Its explanations rest on the strength of the logical connections among inferences. It also relies heavily on reasoning from "residues." In other words, alternative explanations are attacked and shown to be inadequate. What cannot be disproved, the residue, is taken as the best explanation. Linguistic writings are filled with demonstrations of how this or that explanation will not work in explaining a particular construction. The use of inference, logical necessity, and residues in the development of generative theory is not inherently weak, and it is the only available method for developing theory in the absence of direct observation.

The work on nonverbal communication has been important because it shows us that communication consists of many types of signs, both language and otherwise. At the same time, by emphasizing the nonverbal, most of these theories distract us from the holistic nature of the communication code. Indeed, the analytical nature of both linguistics and nonverbal research belies the complexity of the communication process.[45] This problem is the *fallacy of analysis.*

Ironically, as nonverbal communication research separates language behavior from other behavior, much of it has relied heavily on a linguistic analogy. In other words, nonverbal codes are believed by some to be organized essentially the same way as language. This belief is not surprising because of the common semiotic heritage of the two lines of research. As the early semioticians so clearly spelled out, the syntax or organization among signs is the most important constituent of meaning. Saussure applied this idea to language, and theorists like Birdwhistell adopted lingustic ideas about syntax to nonlinguistic signs.

This problem is the *fallacy of the linguistic analogy.* Although some superficial similarities may be observed between language and bodily behavior, more differences than similarities exist. Language is presented sequentially and involves discrete signs; nonverbal codes are not presented in a sequential manner and usually do not consist of discrete behaviors. Although language is organized hierarchically, no good evidence shows that nonverbal acts are organized in this way. Language tends to be used consciously, and nonverbal signs are often displayed unconsciously.

One of the limits of most of the theories in this chapter is that they focus on the smallest units of meaning—signs and low-level organizations of signs. The true richness of communication occurs at a higher level, when signs are combined into complex messages. We turn to this concern Chapter 5 in our discussion of discourse.

45. For a discussion of the limitations of nonverbal communication theories, see Judee Burgoon and Thomas Saine, *The Unspoken Dialogue: An Introduction to Nonverbal Communication* (Boston: Houghton Mifflin, 1978), chap. 2; and Knapp, Wiemann, and Daly, "Nonverbal Communication."

CHAPTER 5

Theories of Discourse

In the previous chapter, we discussed the structure of language and other code systems. We saw that communication involves single signs and combinations of signs, including sentences and sentence parts. It is clear, however, that communication usually involves much more than simple utterances and actions. Even the most mundane communication in everyday life consists of messages and complex acts embedded in ongoing talk. These larger units are referred to as *discourse*.

The study of message structure in communication goes by the general label *discourse analysis*.[1] Although writing is sometimes considered discourse, most work in this area concentrates on naturally occurring talk. Most of this chapter deals with discourse analysis in one form or another, but at the end of the chapter, we will look at a critical alternative to this tradition.

Although there are several strands of discourse

analysis, many share a common set of concerns.[2] First, all are concerned with the ways in which discourse is organized. This means discovering the principles used by communicators to generate and understand talk. Second, discourse is viewed as action; it is a way of doing things, a means of communication. Discourse analysts assume that language users know not only the rules of sentence grammar but also the rules for using larger segments of talk to accomplish pragmatic goals in social situations. This means that language is used strategically to achieve desired ends. Third, discourse analysis is a search for principles used by actual communicators *from their perspective*.

Just as linguistics is concerned with rules of language, so too is discourse analysis interested in rules. We will therefore begin this chapter by addressing the rules tradition as it affects discourse analysis. Beyond that, three other major discourse traditions will be covered. The first is speech act theory, which has not only affected other

---

1. For a brief summary of the field, see Scott Jacobs, "Recent Advances in Discourse Analysis," *Quarterly Journal of Speech* 66 (1980): 450–472. For a more recent and detailed treatment, see Donald G. Ellis and William A. Donohue (eds.), *Contemporary Issues in Language and Discourse Processes* (Hillsdale, N.J.:Erlbaum, 1986).

2. For a brief discussion of the various uses of the term *discourse analysis*, see Jonathan Potter and Margaret Wetherall, *Discourse and Social Psychology: Beyond Attitudes and Behavior* (London: Sage, 1987), pp. 6–7.

approaches to discourse and communication but has become an important tradition in its own right. The second is conversation analysis, which is perhaps the most well-developed and prominent application of discourse analysis in the communication field. The third is the poststructuralist movement with special attention to the work of Michel Foucault. Poststructuralism presents an entirely different and alternative view of discourse.

The Rules Approach to Communication

The rules tradition has had a major impact on the field of communication. The idea that people operate by rules in the use of language, discourse, and social action has become a mainstay in the literature.[3] Susan Shimanoff discusses the importance of rules in social life:

> In order for communication to exist, or continue, two or more interacting individuals must share rules for using symbols. Not only must they have rules for individual symbols, but they must also agree on such matters as how to take turns at speaking, how to be polite or how to insult, to greet, and so forth. If every symbol user manipulated symbols at random, the result would be chaos rather than communication.[4]

Despite its diversity the rules approach is held together by certain common assumptions.[5] The

3. Susan B. Shimanoff, *Communication Rules: Theory and Research* (Beverly Hills, Calif.: Sage, 1980), pp. 31–88, lists some of the major scholars who have studied rules as well as a variety of definitions and explanations of rules.

4. Ibid., pp. 31–32.

5. The similarities and differences among rules theories are discussed in such sources as Donald P. Cushman, "The Rules Perspective as a Theoretical Basis for the Study of Human Communication," *Communication Quarterly* 25 (1977): 30–45; W. Barnett Pearce, "Rules Theories of Communication: Varieties, Limitations, and Potentials" (Paper presented at the meeting of the Speech Communication Association, New York, 1980); Stuart J. Sigman, "On Communication Rules from a Social Perspective," *Human Communication Research* 7 (1980): 37–51; Shimanoff, *Communication Rules;* and Donald Cushman, "The Rules Approach to Communication Theory: A Philosophical and Operational Perspective," in *Communication Theory: Eastern and Western Perpsectives*, ed. D. L. Kincaid (San Diego: Academic Press, 1987), pp. 223–234.

action principle generally is considered to be a primary assumption of the rules approach. Although some human activity is mechanical and determined by uncontrollable factors, the most important behaviors are considered to be actively initiated by the individual. People are thought to choose courses of action within situations to accomplish their intentions. Rules theorists generally agree that the most significant human behavior is not governed by laws. For this reason the rule-governed approach to communication theory often is set in opposition to the law-governed approach.

Although a rule is normally viewed as something a person can choose not to follow, much linguistic analysis assumes that certain rules deeply embedded in language do in fact bring about actions in an almost causal way. For example, you cannot really choose to violate semantic and syntactic rules of language because by definition to speak the language is to follow its rules. Some discourse analysis also uses rules in this highly programmed way, and when this is the case, the distinction between rules and laws becomes very fuzzy, indeed.

Another basic assumption of most rules theories is that social behavior is structured and organized. Certain behaviors recur in similar situations. Social interaction patterns, however, vary in different settings. Although these patterns are organized, they are not universal but highly situational. Thus, most rules theories emphasize the relationship between the way people act and the culture and situation wherein the action occurs. In fact, rules scholars criticize law-governed theories precisely because of their failure to reflect such variation.

Rules are considered to be the mechanism through which social action is organized. The structure of interaction can be understood in terms of the rules governing it. Rules affect the options available in a given situation. Because rules are thought to be contextual, they explain why people behave similarly in similar situations and differently in different situations.

We encounter rules at various points in this book. Here, we examine some of the ways in which rules affect our use of discourse. Later, we will look at rules in social action and in personal relationships.

Approaches to Rules

The rules perspective can be divided into three main groups of rule conceptions.[6] These are the rule-following approach, the rule-governed approach, and the rule-using approach.

Rule-following approach. In this view rules are seen simply as observed behavioral regularities. A recurring pattern is said to happen "as a rule." Barnett Pearce calls such rules weak laws because they are cast in the form of a statement of what is expected to happen under certain circumstances. This approach is highly descriptive but does not explain why particular patterns recur; it aims only to catalog predictable behaviors. Linguistic and discourse theories typically are of this type, suggesting that speakers follow rules of grammar and discourse with a high degree of regularity.

Rule-governed approach. Here, rules are beliefs about what should or should not be done to achieve an objective in a given situation. The rule-governed approach attempts to uncover people's intentions and to define the socially acceptable ways in which people accomplish their intentions. For example, if a person wishes to engage another person in conversation at a party and the other person is talking with someone else, one would approach the two individuals and not speak until recognized nonverbally. To interrupt or to break in too quickly would be a rules violation that could prevent the desired conversation from occurring. This approach presumes that people know the rules and have the power to follow or to violate them. It also assumes that people usually act consciously, intentionally, and rationally.

The use of discourse is governed by rules in this sense. Because people use speech in a variety of ways to achieve their goals, they must know how to use talk effectively and appropriately. When you want to accomplish a goal such as greeting, requesting, objecting, or bonding, you employ the rules necessary to achieve it within whatever situation you find yourself. You are free to choose your goals,

but once having done so, you must employ certain rules to achieve them.

Rule-using approach. This view is consistent with the rule-governed approach except that it posits a more complex social situation. The actor potentially is confronted with a variety of rules for accomplishing various intentions. The actor chooses which rules to follow (or, more properly, to use) in carrying out an intention. People are rule critics and choose to follow some rules and discard others. This approach thereby provides a basis for evaluating what choices a person makes in a social situation and even allows for people to create new options.

Rule using also helps the theorist discuss communication competence by observing how well a person sorts through the matrix of objectives and rules to plan a strategy. In a highly homogeneous situation, such as breaking into a cocktail party conversation, the rules are few and simple. Here, the rule-governed approach suffices to explain what occurs. The broader rule-using approach is better suited for understanding the preparation of a speech, the organization of a meeting, the writing of a letter, and other heterogeneous rule situations. We return to rule-governed and rule-using approaches later in Chapter 9.

We turn now to two traditions that have incorporated the concept of rules.

Speech Act Theory

Ludwig Wittgenstein, a German philosopher, was the originator of *ordinary language philosophy*. His early works were based strongly in the formal structural tradition, but he repudiated this approach in one of the most dramatic turnarounds in modern philosophy.[7] He later taught that the

---

6. Pearce, "Rules Theories." See also Joan Ganz, *Rules: A Systematic Study* (Paris: Mouton, 1971).

7. Wittgenstein's best-known early work was *Tractatus Logico-Philosophicus* (London: Routledge & Kegan Paul, 1922); his later work, which forms the foundation for ordinary language philosophy, is *Philosophical Investigations* (Oxford, Eng.: Basil Blackwell, 1953). See also the excellent summary by David Silverman and Brian Torode, *The Material Word: Some Theories of*

meaning of language depends on the context of use. Language, as used in ordinary life, constitutes a *language game*. In other words, people follow rules for accomplishing verbal acts. Giving and obeying orders, asking and answering questions, and describing events are examples of ordinary uses of language that follow rules and hence constitute language games.

Whereas the philosophical groundwork of ordinary language philosophy was laid by Wittgenstein, J. L. Austin developed the basic concepts of what his protégé, John Searle, later called speech acts.[8]

Building on the foundation laid by Wittgenstein and Austin, Searle developed the well-known theory of speech acts.[9] Although Searle is not solely responsible for speech act theory, he is clearly the leader of the movement, and his name is most often associated with the theory.

The *speech act* is the basic unit of language for expressing meaning. It is an utterance that expresses an intention. Normally, the speech act is a sentence, but it can be a word or phrase as long as it follows the rules necessary to accomplish the intention (or, in Wittgenstein's terms, to play the language game). When one speaks, one performs an act. The act may involve stating, questioning, commanding, promising, or any of a number of other acts. Speech therefore is conceived of as a form of action or intentional behavior.

An important characteristic of a speech act is that the recipient understand the speaker's intention. Unlike the representational view of meaning, speech act theory does not stress the individual referents of symbols but the intent of the act as a whole. If you make a promise, you are communicating an intention about something you will do in the future; but more importantly, you are expecting the other communicator to realize from what you have said what your intention is.

Searle's classification divides speech acts into four types. The first is an *utterance act*. Such acts are the simple pronunciation, an utterance and nothing more. An example is an actor doing voice exercises. The *propositional act* is what Austin refers to as a *locution*. It is the utterance of a sentence that expresses a reference. In other words, the individual wishes to make an association between a subject and verb or to designate an object and refer this object to something else. An *illocutionary act* is designed to fulfill an intention vis-à-vis another person. Here one uses the speech act to elicit response in another. Finally, the *perlocutionary act* is designed to have effects or consequences on other peoples' behavior. Because the difference between illocution and perlocution is sometimes hard to grasp, let's pursue it a little further.

An illocution is an act in which the speaker's primary concern is that the listener understand the speaker's intention. A perlocution is an act in which the speaker expects the listener not only to understand but to act in a particular way because of that understanding. If I say, "I am thirsty," with the intention of having you understand that I need something to drink, I am performing an illocutionary act. If I make the same statement expecting you to bring me a glass of water, my act is perlocutionary.

Now let us pursue propositional acts and illocutionary acts in more detail. The proposition can be understood as one aspect of the content of a statement. It designates some quality or association of an object, situation, or event. "The cake is good," "Salt is harmful to the body," "Her name is Karen"

Language and Its Limits (London: Routledge and Kegan Paul, 1980); Richard Buttney, "The Ascription of Meaning: A Wittgensteinian Perspective," *Quarterly Journal of Speech* 72 (1986): 261–273; and Allan Janik and Stephen Toulmin, *Wittgenstein's Vienna* (New York: Simon & Schuster, 1973).

8. J. L. Austin, *How to Do Things with Words* (Cambridge, Mass.: Harvard University Press, 1962); *Philosophy of Language* (Englewood Cliffs, N.J.: Prentice-Hall, 1964). For a general summary of Austin's ideas, see also Potter and Wetherall, *Discourse and Social Psychology*, pp. 14–18.

9. John Searle, *Speech Acts: An Essay in the Philosophy of Language* (Cambridge, Eng.: Cambridge University Press, 1969); "Human Communication Theory and the Philosophy of Language: Some Remarks," in *Human Communcation Theory*, ed. F. E. X. Dance (New York: Holt, Rinehart & Winston, 1967), pp. 116–129. Good secondary sources include John Stewart, "Concepts of Language and Meaning: A Comparative Study," *Quarterly Journal of Speech* 58 (1972): 123–133; Paul N. Campbell, "A Rhetorical View of Locutionary, Illocutionary, and Perlocutionary Acts," *Quarterly Journal of Speech* 59 (1973): 284–296; Robert Gaines, "Doing by Saying: Toward a Theory of Perlocution," *Quarterly Journal of Speech* 65 (1979): 207–217.

are all examples of propositions. Propositions can be evaluated in terms of their truth value. In speech act theory, however, truth and logic are not considered central. Rather, the question is what a speaker intends to do by uttering a proposition. The meaning of an illocutionary act is determined in part by establishing how the speaker wishes others to take the stated proposition. Hence, for Searle, propositions must always be viewed as part of a larger context, the illocution. Searle would be interested in acts such as the following: I *ask* whether the cake is good; I *warn* you that salt is harmful to the body; I *state* that her name is Karen. What the speaker is doing with the proposition is the speech act, and how the proposition is to be taken by the audience is the *illocutionary force* of the statement. You could, for example, state the proposition "The cake is good" in such a way to convey to the listener that you were speaking ironically, meaning to imply just the opposite: This cake is the worst I ever ate.

Searle states fundamentally that "speaking a language is engaging in a rule-governed form of behavior."[10] Two types of rules are important—constitutive and regulative. *Constitutive rules* create new forms of behavior; that is, acts are created by the establishment of rules. For example, football as a game exists only by virtue of its rules. The rules constitute the game. When you observe people following a certain set of rules, you know the game of football is being played. These rules therefore tell you what to interpret as football. In speech acts one's intention is largely understood by another person by virtue of constitutive rules because these rules tell others what to count as a particular kind of act.

As an example of the use of constitutive rules, let us look at one of Searle's extended analyses of a speech act, the act of making a promise. Promising involves five basic rules. First, promising involves uttering a sentence that indicates the speaker will do some future act (propositional content rule). Second, the sentence is uttered only if the listener would rather that the speaker do the act than not do it (preparatory rule). Third, a statement is a

10. Searle, *Speech Acts*, p. 22.

promise only when it would not otherwise be obvious to the speaker and hearer that the act would be done in the normal course of events (preparatory rule). Fourth, the speaker must intend to do the act (sincerity rule). Finally, a promise involves the establishment of an obligation for the speaker to do the act (essential rule). These five rules "constitute" a sufficient set of conditions for an act to count as a promise.

The second kind of rule is regulative. *Regulative rules* provide guidelines for acting out already-established behavior. The behaviors are known and available before being used in the act, and the regulative rules tell one how to use speech to accomplish a particular intention. For example, if I want something, I make a request. When I request something of you, you are obligated either to grant the request or to turn it down.

Any illocutionary act must have the basic kinds of constitutive rules discussed above. The *propositional content rule* specifies some condition of the referenced object. *Preparatory rules* involve the presumed preconditions in the speaker and hearer necessary for the act to take place. The *sincerity rule* requires the speaker to mean what is said. The *essential rule* states that the act is indeed taken by the hearer and speaker to represent what it appears to be on the face. Of course, many acts are not successful in these ways, and speech acts can be evaluated in terms of the degree to which they meet these criteria. Whereas propositions are evaluated in terms of truth or validity, speech acts are evaluated in terms of *felicity*, or the degree to which the conditions of the act are met. These constitutive rules are believed to apply to a wide variety of illocutionary acts, including at least requesting, asserting, questioning, thanking, advising, warning, greeting, and congratulating.

Although many speech acts are direct, involving the use of an explicit statement of intention, other speech acts are indirect. For example, in requesting that his family come to the table, a father might say, "Is anybody hungry?" On the face this appears to be a question, but in actuality it is a request.

Searle outlines five types of illocutionary acts. The first is called *assertives*. An assertive is a statement that commits the speaker to advocate the truth of a proposition. In direct form such acts might contain such performative verbs as *state*, *affirm*, *conclude*, and *believe*. The second are *directives*, illocutions that attempt to get the listener to do something. They are commands, requests, pleadings, prayers, entreaties, invitations, and so forth. *Commissives*, the third, commit the speaker to a future act. They consist of such things as promising, vowing, pledging, contracting, and guaranteeing. The fourth, *expressives*, are acts that communicate some aspect of the speaker's psychological state, such as thanking, congratulating, apologizing, condoling, and welcoming. Finally, a *declaration* is designed to create a proposition that, by its very assertion, makes it so. Examples include appointing, marrying, firing, and resigning.

Speech-act theory has been adopted by a variety of other traditions in the field, as we will see in the following section.

Conversation Analysis

One of the most interesting and popular lines of work in communication is conversation analysis.[11] Most conversation analysis is in the tradition of *ethnomethodology*, which is the careful and detailed study of how people organize their everyday lives.[12] From an ethnomethodological standpoint, social life is a joint achievement of communicators. How people use language is an important part of this process of organizing interaction.

Conversations, like any aspect of social life, are viewed as the achievements of actors within social situations as they attempt to accomplish tasks cooperatively through talk.[13] Conversation analysis attempts to discover by careful examination exactly what those achievements are. The primary concern of conversation analysis is *sequential organization*, or the ways in which speakers organize their talk turn-by-turn.

Of utmost importance in conversation analysis is the assumption that conversations are stable and orderly. Even when they appear sloppy on the surface, there is an underlying organization to all talk, and the participants themselves create, recognize, and appreciate this organization as an accomplishment.

The conversation analyst does not hypothesize possible organizational patterns and then look for their presence in actual conversations. Rather, the analyst works inductively by first examining the details of actual conversations—many conversations—and then positing possible principles by which the participants themselves are organizing their own talk.

As an example, consider the simple task of telling a story. On the surface it may appear that a story is just "told" by someone in a conversation while others just listen. In fact, a story is a joint achievement by both "tellers" and "listeners." Although the teller usually takes an extended turn, the story is made possible by the cooperation of others in carefully organized turns. First, the teller has to get the floor by offering to tell a story, and the other members acknowledge and permit the extended turn to be taken. During the story itself, listeners

11. This section deals with conversation in the discourse analysis tradition, emphasizing the verbal structure of conversational texts. There is also a tradition that studies the management of conversations in a broader sense, including the nonverbal elements. See Joseph N. Cappella, "The Management of Conversations," in *Handbook of Interpersonal Communication*, eds. M. L. Knapp and G. R. Miller, (Beverly Hills, Calif.: Sage, 1985), pp. 393–439.

12. Ethnomethodology is most often associated with its originator, sociologist Harold Garfinkel, *Studies in Ethnomethodology* (Englewood Cliffs, N.J.: Prentice-Hall, 1967). For a brief description of this tradition, see Potter and Wetherall, *Discourse and Social Psychology*, pp. 18–23.

13. For an excellent detailed discussion of conversation analysis, see Robert Nofsinger, *Everyday Conversation* (Newbury Park, Calif.: Sage, 1991). For a briefer account, see Don H. Zimmerman, "On Conversation: The Conversation Analytic Perspective," in *Communication Yearbook 11*, ed. J. Anderson (Newbury Park, Calif.: Sage, 1988), pp. 406–432. See also Wayne Beach, "Orienting to the Phenomenon," in *Communication Yearbook 13*, ed. J. Anderson (Newbury Park, Calif.: Sage, 1990), pp. 216–244; Robert Hopper, Susan Koch, and Jennifer Mandelbaum, "Conversation Analysis Methods," in *Contemporary Issues in Language and Discourse Processes*, eds. D. G. Ellis and W. A. Donohue (Hillsdale, N.J.: Erlbaum, 1986), pp. 169–186; and Charles Goodwin, "Turn Construction and Conversational Organization," in *Rethinking Communication: Paradigm Exemplars*, vol. 2, eds. B. Dervin, et al. (Newbury Park, Calif.: Sage, 1989), pp. 88–102.

may take various types of turns to recognize and reinforce the teller's story, to indicate understanding, to give further permission to continue the extended turn, to direct or affect the story in some way, or to correct or repair something the teller said. All of this requires work and organization on the part of the participants.[14]

Conversation analysis has been concerned with a variety of issues.[15] First, it deals with what speakers need to know to have a conversation. This means, for the most part, knowledge of the rules of conversation. Interactional features of conversation such as turn taking, silences and gaps, and overlaps have been of special interest. Conversation analysis has also been concerned with rule violation and the ways in which people prevent and repair errors in talk.

Certainly the most popular, and perhaps the most significant, aspect of conversation analysis is *conversational coherence*.[16] Simply defined, coherence is connectedness and meaningfulness in conversation. Coherent conversation seems well structured and sensible to the participants. It is a quality we normally take for granted; yet the production of coherence is highly complex and not altogether understood.

We cannot summarize here the large and growing literature in conversation analysis. This section therefore concentrates on three areas: foundational work on conversational maxims, the problem of conversational coherence, and conversational argument.

Conversational Maxims

Perhaps the most important foundational theory of conversation is that of H. Paul Grice.[17] Grice proposed a set of very general assumptions to which all conversationalists must subscribe in order to be perceived as competent. The first is the most general principle of all conversation, the *cooperative principle*: One's contribution must be appropriate. Cooperation here does not necessarily mean expression of agreement, but it does mean that one is willing to contribute in a way that is in line with the purpose of the conversation. More specifically, cooperation is achieved by following four maxims. The first is the *quantity maxim*: One's contribution should provide sufficient, but not too much, information. The quantity maxim is violated when one's comments are too brief or too verbose. The second is the *quality maxim*: One's contribution should be truthful. The quality maxim is violated when one deliberately lies or communicates in a way that does not reflect one's honest intention. The third is the *relevancy maxim*: One's comment must be pertinent to the context of the conversation at the moment. It is violated when one makes an "off the wall" or irrelevant comment in a conversation. The fourth maxim is the *manner maxim*: One should not be obscure, ambiguous, or disorganized.

On the surface, these maxims may seem absurdly simple and obvious, but the associated question of how speakers actually use these maxims and how they handle apparent violations is far more complicated. Grice's maxims constitute basic ideas that have provided structure for much research on these questions. Of course, the cooperative principle and attendant maxims are often violated, sometimes for strategic purposes; but what makes the maxims so important is that they are never violated without disrupting the flow of conversation or affecting the perceptions of others in the conversation. In other words, violations are a problem communicators must deal with cooperatively.

When a maxim appears to be violated, communicators wonder about what is going on and make attributions that accommodate the apparent violation. These interpretations are called *conversational implicatures*. The question being considered through implicature is this: What is being implied or implicated by this apparent violation? To assume that the violator is living up to the cooperative principle, the listener must attribute some addi-

14. Jenny Mandelbaum, "Interpersonal Activities in Conversational Storytelling," *Western Journal of Speech Communication* 53 (1989): 114–126.

15. These issues are outlined in Margaret L. McLaughlin, *Conversation: How Talk Is Organized* (Beverly Hills, Calif.: Sage, 1984).

16. See Robert T. Craig and Karen Tracy (eds.), *Conversational Coherence: Form, Structure, and Strategy* (Beverly Hills, Calif.: Sage, 1983).

17. H. Paul Grice, "Logic and Conversation," in *Syntax and Semantics*, vol. 3, eds. P. Cole and J. Morgan (New York: Academic Press, 1975), pp. 41–58.

tional meaning that will make the speaker's contribution seem to conform to the principle. In fact, many deliberate violations are predicated on the assumpion that the hearer will, through conversational implicature, understand that one indeed intends to be cooperative. If, for example, I say, "It is raining cats and dogs," I am literally violating the quality maxim; but I know that you will realize that I am speaking metaphorically.

Conversational implicature allows communicators to use all kinds of strategically interesting, indirect statements to achieve their purposes, without risking the judgment of incompetence; in fact, competence itself requires the effective use of implicature.

One of the most common types of violation is to say something indirectly. Indirect communication is important for a variety of social and personal reasons such as politeness. If, for example, someone asks me how much my house cost, I might say, "Oh, quite a bit." Now, on the surface, that violates the maxim of quantity and appears uncooperative, but most competent conversationalists will realize that it is really an indirect statement: "It's none of your business." Here, one concludes that I am indeed not being cooperative but that there is sufficient reason for me not to be. In fact, one of the important functions of talk is to justify rule violations. The study of conversational implicature is really the study of the rules people use to understand or justify violations of other rules; and these implicatures are very important for the overall management of conversations.

As an example of how people manage the cooperative principle, consider the ways in which they use qualifications as a cue that they are violating a maxim but do not intend to be uncooperative. These qualifications are *licenses for violations* because they enable one to violate a maxim without objection. For example, after being asked where she came from, one student indicated Philadelphia. The other student said, "Did you grow up in Philadelphia?" and the first one replied, "In the Philadelphia area. Not really *in* Philadelphia. Uhm, this is embarrassing to admit, I was a Main Line kid. In the uh, there's a stream of cities or towns that go

around Philadelphia . . . that are called the Main Line and they range from suburban to rural." This qualification essentially says, I am not being absolutely honest, but I don't mean to deceive.

Another licensing move occurs in the following example in which one person shifts the responsibility of the violation of the quantity maxim onto the other person:

PERSON ONE: How did you and your husband meet?
PERSON TWO: Well, that's a long story.
PERSON ONE: Okay, I'm not going anywhere, let's hear it.

Here Person Two essentially gets the other's permission to talk longer than might otherwise be permitted.[18]

Conversational Coherence

Coherence involves the question of how communicators tell whether statements are meaningfully structured. How do communicators know what is appropriate and what is inappropriate for keeping a conversation well organized? A variety of theories have been proposed.[19] Some of these use *local principles*: They explain coherence in terms of the connection between adjacent statements. Local coherence assumes that communicators follow rules for what constitutes a permissible response to a statement. If I say, "Hi, how are you?" you are obligated to respond, "Fine." Other theories use *global principles* or rules that relate a given statement to the broad meaning of a larger segment of conversation. Communication scholars generally agree that coherence cannot be explained with strictly local rules; it is easy to identify sequences that are obviously coherent to the communicators but have contiguous statements that by themselves do not appear consistent. We return to the local-global issue later.

18. Examples of violations are from Susan Swan Mura, "Licensing Violations: Legitimate Violations of Grice's Conversational Principle," in *Conversational Coherence: Form, Structure, and Strategy*, eds. R. T. Craig and K. Tracy (Beverly Hills, Calif.: Sage, 1983), pp. 101–115.

19. For a summary of some of the approaches, see Craig and Tracy, *Conversational Coherence*.

Theories of coherence also differ in terms of the explanatory mechanism used. Three such approaches are common: the propositional, the sequential, and the pragmatic.[20] *Propositional theories* explain coherence by referring to the meaning of statements. Here, the rules state that the meaning of one's sentences must somehow relate to or be consistent with the meaning of other sentences or the meaning of the whole segment of conversation. The *sequence approach* looks for the rules governing the kinds of acts that are permissible after another act. The *pragmatic approach* relies on rules for accomplishing actual intentions. Thus, in propositional theories, coherence is a matter of the consistency of meaning; in sequencing theories, coherence is a matter of syntactical organization; and in pragmatic theories, coherence is a matter of appropriate practical action. Three representative theories are discussed next.

A propositional approach. An example of a propositional approach is the theory of Teun van Dijk.[21] Although this theory concentrates on single utterances and written documents rather than conversation, van Dijk believes the principles governing these utterances are also important for the overall coherence of a conversation. Van Dijk uses a global approach, relating each proposition to a larger proposition through the use of rules. In simplified form a message is considered to be an assertion of a thesis that is supported by subpoints in a coherent fashion.

A whole text has at least one thesis or general proposition, which is supported or elaborated by the various other statements. This overall proposition is called the *macrostructure* of the discourse. The organization of the text is built up by a hierarchy of propositions, such that each lower-level statement enters into a higher one until the general proposition of the text is reached. For example, "I can go outside now" is supported by the proposition "I am dressed," which is further supported by the proposition "I have on pants, shirt, shoes, and socks."

Macrorules are used to build this structure of propositions within the discourse. For example, the *deletion–insertion rule* states that propositions unnecessary for understanding other propositions should be deleted, and those necessary as building blocks for a higher-order proposition should be included. There may be, for example, descriptions of an event that are not relevant to the overall point being made, and these should be deleted when developing the general sense of the utterance.

The *generalization rule* requires that propositions be grouped into more general ones according to their common topic. This rule helps communicators find the general concept that holds individual propositions together. In describing one's garden, for example, there may be several descriptions of flowers and other descriptions of vegetables. The flower statements might consist of propositions about color and shape, whereas the vegetable statements are dominated by descriptions of taste and food. In this example, the higher-order propositions would be that flowers are judged by aesthetic qualities, whereas vegetables are judged by culinary ones.

Another macrorule is *construction*, or the principle that general propositions should combine the elements of lower-level ones. In other words, the "facts" proposed in the lower propositions are integrated or combined in some way in the higher propositions. For example, if I say that (a) my gladiolus are colorful and make a good arrangement, (b) the sweet peas are abundant and stay fresh long after being picked, and (c) the carnations look especially pretty when mixed together in a vase, then a permissible higher-order proposition would be that flowers are valued as decoration.

Thus, with knowledge of macrorules, individuals can construct coherent discourse; the sentences in a lengthy utterance are ordered and make sense on

20. These are summarized in McLaughlin, *Conversation*, pp. 35–90. The local-global issue is also discussed by Stuart J. Sigman, *A Perspective on Social Communication* (Lexington, Mass.: Lexington Books, 1987), pp. 17–26.

21. Teun A. van Dijk, *Macrostructures: An Interdisciplinary Study of Global Structures in Discourse, Interaction, and Cognition* (Hillsdale, N.J.: Erlbaum, 1980); *Studies in the Pragmatics of Discourse* (The Hague: Mouton, 1981).

a larger level by virtue of the organization of the propositions contained in the discourse. If an utterance seems incoherent to a listener, either the speaker did not make proper use of macrorules, or the listener cannot find the necessary rules to make sense of it. If such rules are not yet learned by a speaker, as in the case of child, or not retained, as in the case of a brain-damaged person, then the discourse will seem incoherent in this propositional sense.

Van Dijk has applied this theory to the study of news reports.[22] In his analyses, he breaks down a news report into its propositional structures and shows how the overall coherence of the article is achieved by following the macrorules. For instance, one article in 1984 had the headline "East Timor's Plight: Schultz Joins Critics of Indonesian Rule." This article is about the Secretary of State's visit to a region of Indonesia known as East Timor in which he protested the actions of the Indonesian military in the region. The headline of this article—as is often the case—states the most general proposition of the article. The article itself contains several propositions that support the overall thesis, and these are organized into a hierarchy. Figure 5.1 illustrates the structure of this discourse.[23] For simplicity, Figure 5.1 is expressed as themes, but you can easily see how each theme would consist of statements. Although this example is not conversation, the coherence of statements made in a conversation can be evaluated in the same way.

The propositional approach is useful when explaining the semantic sense of an utterance or document—what it means or refers to. The weakness of this approach, however, is that most utterances are part of a conversation and fulfill functions other than mere reference. Utterances are acts that are used to accomplish intentions, and the coherence of a conversation depends on an organization of speech acts apart from logical propositional organization. Most theories of coherence therefore make use of speech act theory. These theories understand coherence as the organization of

intentions and the rules by which those intentions are translated into actual conversational utterances. Both of the following theories are speech act approaches to conversational coherence.

A sequencing approach. The idea behind sequence-structure approaches to coherence is that a conversation consists of a series of speech acts, the order of which is governed by rules. As such, these approaches are strictly local theories of coherence. For example, the greeting "How are you?" is a question and demands an answer. Therefore, "How are you?" would not normally be answered by "See you later." More typically, the sequence would go like this: "How are you?" "Fine. How are you?"

Sequencing approaches center on the *adjacency pair*, which are two speech act utterances in a row. The *first-pair part* (FPP) is the first utterance, and the *second-pair part* (SPP) is the following utterance. By this approach, a conversation is coherent if proper rules of sequencing are consistently used between the FPP and the SPP.

Perhaps the most influential sequencing model is that of Harvey Sacks, Emanuel Schegloff, and Gail Jefferson.[24] This is basically a turn-taking theory, which stipulates that the next turn in a conversation must be a proper response to complete a particular adjacency-pair type. For instance, a question is to be followed by an answer, a greeting by another greeting, an offer by an acceptance, a request by an acceptance or a rejection. A number of adjacency-pair types have been discussed in the literature: assertion-assent/dissent, question-answer, summons-answer, greeting-greeting, closing-closing, request-grant/denial, insult-response, apology-acceptance/refusal, compliment-acceptance/rejection, threat-response, challenge-response, accusation-denial/confession, and boast-appreciation/derision.

When one speech act is completed, that signals a next turn for another speaker, who is obligated to respond according to appropriate rules. The

22. Teun van Dijk, *News as Discourse* (Hillsdale, N.J.: Erlbaum, 1988).

23. Ibid., p. 42.

24. Harvey Sacks, Emanuel Schegloff, and Gail Jefferson, "A Simplest Systematics for the Organization of Turn Taking for Conversation," *Language* 50 (1974): 696–735.

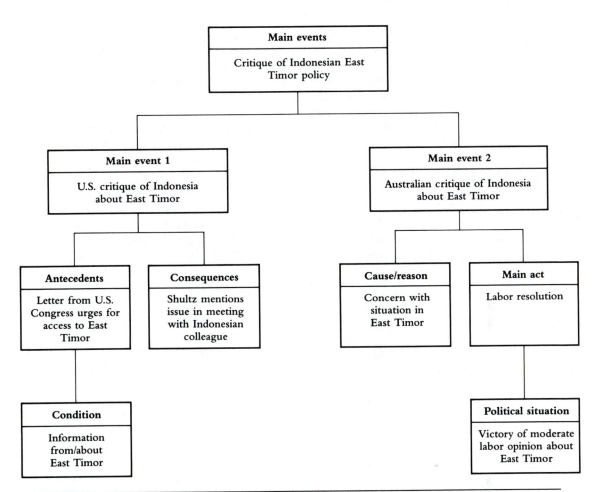

Figure 5.1   Representation of the simplified thematic structure of the news report about Shultz/East Timor. From *News as Discourse*, by Teun van Dijk. © 1988 Laurence Earlbaum Associates. Reprinted by permission of the publishers.

speaker may designate who the next speaker is to be, or another speaker can appropriately take a turn, as long as a proper response is given. Failing a response, the speaker may continue talking.

Further, adjacency pairs include a *preference for agreement*. In other words, the SPP is normally expected to agree with the FPP. For example, a statement is normally followed by an agreement ("Don't you just love the sun?" "Sure do.") and a request is followed by an acceptance ("Can I borrow your pen?" "Sure."). This does not mean that people always agree, but disagreement calls for special action in the form of an account, excuse, or argument.

Of course, conversations are usually more complex than the simple adjacency-pair concept implies. This theory is adapted to more complex situations by recognizing presequences and insertions. A *presequence* is an adjacency pair whose meaning depends on another series of acts that has not yet been uttered. They are prefatory to another set of acts. The initial FPP is an invitation for a subsequent one. Here is an example:

FPP: Have you washed your hands? ⌐   (presequence)
SPP: No, why? ⌐
FPP: 'Cause dinner's ready.
SPP: Okay, I'll do it.

The second sequence of acts is really a request, but it cannot be understood as such without the first set.

An *insertion* is an adjacency pair that is between the two parts of another pair and is subordinate to the main pair. Such insertions are necessary to clarify the intention of the initial FPP. Here is an example:

FPP$_1$: Would you like to go out sometime?
FPP$_2$: With you? ⌐ (insertion)
SPP$_2$: Yeah, me. ⌐
SPP$_1$: Oh, okay.

Such a move is an example of an *expansion*, which means that a subsequent speaker expands the sequence to include additional or subsidiary intentions. An expansion is involved whenever a directed segment of talk like a greeting, compliment, or request is played out turn-after-turn. Sequences of utterances can, by this system, be parsed, as one would diagram a sentence with rules of grammar. The conversation would therefore be analyzed into adjacency pairs, pair parts, and expansions. (Table 5.1).

A pragmatic approach. Pragmatic, or rational, approaches assume practical action in conversation and predicate coherence on the reasoning process of the communicators. In other words, communicators make decisions about what to say and how

Table 5-1   A Conversational Sequence

Greeting-greeting		FPP	Hi.
	FPP	SPP	Hi. Great dress.
Compliment-acceptance			
	SPP	FPP	Thanks. My mom bought it for me this weekend.
Assertion-assent			
	FPP	SPP	Yeah, it looks great on you.
Compliment-rejection			
	SPP		Well, not that great really.
		FPP	How's Terry?
Question-answer			
		SPP	He's okay, getting better and better.
		FPP	Will he be out of the hospital soon?
Question-answer			
	FPP	SPP	In about three days, I think.
Assertion-assent			
	SPP		Great.
		FPP	Well, I gotta go.
Closing-closing			
		SPP	Yeah, me too. See ya.

to achieve their intentions, and coherence is really judged in accordance with this act–consequent link. If the sequence of acts appears rational vis-à-vis a set of goals, it is judged coherent regardless of whether an act is consistent with other adjacent acts. This theory is definitely a global approach. The rational approach is primarily the product of Sally Jackson and Scott Jacobs.[25]

Jackson and Jacobs use the game analogy to explain how conversation works. The game itself is controlled by a set of rules, which players must know. The players have objectives in the game, and they use the rules of the game to achieve those objectives. The game is coherent because the appropriate use of rules accomplishes rational objectives. So players must have two kinds of knowledge: They must know the rules of the game and what constitutes rational play within the parameters of the rules. For example, in playing Monopoly you are expected to collect properties and cash by purchasing property when you land on it and building houses and hotels, and you must do this according to rules. In Monopoly your moves are not judged rational or coherent based on whether they are consistent with the moves that came before or after but whether they are consistent with the overall objectives of the game.

Communication is complicated because conversation, like a game, is played in interaction with another, so that the moves of one person must mesh with those of the other, and this requires agreement on purpose and some reciprocity of perspective.

The rational model is also based on speech act theory. Utterances have a force that obliges a hearer to understand the speaker's intent, and the speaker must meet certain felicity conditions in order for understanding to occur. Communicators respond not to each individual speech act but to the intentions of others as expressed by those acts. The coherence of a conversation is judged, then,

not by whether a particular type of act is followed by some other permissible act but by whether the unfolding sequence of acts is consistent with the perceived plan of goals.

Jackson and Jacobs stipulate two kinds of rules necessary for coherence. *Validity rules* establish the conditions necessary for an act to be judged as a sincere move in a plan of goals. For example, a promise must meet a variety of conditions: It must state that the speaker will do some future act; the future act must be something the hearer wants; the hearer has reason to believe that the future act would not otherwise be done in the normal course of events; and the speaker sincerely intends and feels obligated to do the act.

Reason rules require the speaker to adjust statements to the beliefs and perspectives of the other conversationalists. This does not mean that speakers say only what listeners want to hear but that they frame their statements in a way that makes logical sense within the perspective of the other person. Reason rules do not prescribe agreement, but they set up a situation in which communicators are invited and somewhat pressured to agree. These rules require the use of a common set of concepts in which disagreement can be expressed, justified, and understood. For example, a statement of preference on the part of a speaker must be relevant to some perspective of the listener, such that if the listener does not have a preference, he or she will come to agree with the speaker, or, if the listener already disagrees, he or she will consider agreeing or be able to express and justify the disagreement. The reason rule is an application of Grice's cooperative principle.

Basically, these rules help communicators set up a logical system within which utterances and utterance sequences can be judged as coherent or not. Remember that these rules may be violated, and coherence is not always achieved. Communicators may also disagree about whether a sequence meets the required conditions of validity and reason; such disagreement is often the basis for conflict in communication. Ultimately, because conversations are practical, goal-oriented acts, communicators must constantly judge whether the interaction is leading toward the desired goal and, if not, whether and

25. Scott Jacobs, "Language," in *Handbook of Interpersonal Communication*, eds. M. L. Knapp and G. R. Miller (Beverly Hills, Calif.: Sage, 1985), pp. 330–335, also see Scott Jacobs and Sally Jackson, "Speech Act Structure in Conversation: Rational Aspects of Pragmatic Coherence," in *Conversational Coherence: Form, Structure, and Strategy*, eds. R. T. Craig and K. Tracy (Beverly Hills, Calif.: Sage, 1983), pp. 47–66.

what kinds of adjustments must be made in the conversational moves. This fact makes conversation a dynamic process of practical reasoning.

This theory views adjacency pairs as a special case of a logical context for action. The FPP invites the listener to join into a kind of microplan for achieving a goal. The SPP is coherent with the first if it joins into that plan. For example, a statement of greeting invites the listener to make contact, and a returned greeting fulfills a kind of greeting contract. Responses to an FPP may simply and directly cooperate, may indirectly cooperate, may approximate agreement, or may attempt to extend, change, or refuse the goal set up by the first utterance. Over a sequence of utterances, communicators may actually negotiate a goal-achievement plan. Jackson and Jacobs call this "the transformation of belief/want contexts." Communicators ask themselves mentally, What do we want to accomplish here and what logical moves are required by each of us to accomplish this? If agreement is achieved on the goals and the actions of the conversationalists seem appropriate for achieving these goals, then the conversation is coherent.

To see more concretely how these ideas can be applied, let us look at Jackson and Jacobs's applications of their theory to requests.[26] Actually, requests are among the most studied of all speech acts, and this theory provides an excellent extension and modification of a whole line of such research.

Recall that coherent conversation consists of moves within a common goal-oriented frame negotiated by the communicators. A variety of request-and-response moves are possible. Such moves range on a continuum from very direct through indirect to irrelevant. The clearer and more direct a request and the clearer and more direct a response, the more coherent the request sequence. This is because directness supports clarity of goals

26. Scott Jacobs and Sally Jackson, "Strategy and Structure in Conversational Influence Attempts," *Communication Monographs* 50 (1983): 285–304; Sally Jackson and Scott Jacobs, "Conversational Relevance: Three Experiments on Pragmatic Connectedness in Conversation," in *Communication Yearbook 10*, ed. M. McLaughlin (Newbury Park, Calif.: Sage, 1987), pp. 323–347.

and relevance of moves toward meeting those goals. Therefore, if I say, "Please pass the butter," my goal is clear and your response, "Sure," is obviously relevant. On the other hand, if I say, "My toast is dry," my goal of getting you to pass the butter is less clear; and your response, "You should turn the toaster down a little," is not at all coherent with my desire to get butter.

Jackson and Jacobs provide a list of utterance types that may be taken as a request. These range from very direct to irrelevant. "Please pass the butter" is an absolutely direct request. An indirect request would be less clear: "My toast is dry." A hint is even less direct: "Some people at this table have something I sure would like." There is also an entire group of utterances commonly found in conversations that function as a prerequest. These set up the listener for a request in the future. An example is, "Could I interrupt to ask for something?"

Once a request or prerequest is made, a listener can respond in a variety of direct or indirect ways. If the communicator recognizes the intent of a request, he or she can make the conversation coherent by responding directly. An example would be an anticipatory move, in which the listener recognizes the hidden or indirect request and grants it immediately ("My toast is sure dry." "Here, have some butter."). Such moves provide coherence because they are oriented to the apparent goals of the other communicator. Less coherent would be responses that misinterpret the speaker's statement, as in the case of someone who takes an innocent statement to be a request that was never intended as such. A communicator may also make a move to avoid being influenced by a request, indirect request, or prerequest. Such responses create a problem in the conversation that results in frustration, avoidance, or readjustment of interactional goals. Such responses often lead to conversational argument.

Conversational Argument

The study of conversational argument is an interesting extension of discourse analysis. As proposed by Jackson and Jacobs, this theory is built on rule theory, speech act theory, and principles of conversation analysis.[27] It began as an application of the sequencing approach but has become the major application of the rational model explained in the previous section. As such it illustrates the rational model very well.

Earlier we saw that there is a preference for agreement in conversations. This does not mean that people always agree, however, and the theory of conversational argument deals with how people manage disagreement. Managing disagreement, like any of the structural features of talk, is a rule-governed, cooperative achievement.

There can be a number of levels of disagreement in conversation. In the prototypical case, both parties openly disagree and state reasons for their positions. More typically, however, the level of disagreement may be less open. In its most primitive forms, conversational disagreement may be nothing more than an exchange of "tis-taint" objections ("My daddy makes better cookies than your daddy." "No he doesn't." "Yes, he does." "No he doesn't."").

Because of the preference for agreement, the goal of conversational argument is to achieve agreement. Each turn must be rational in trying to bring agreement about, and the coherence of an argument is largely judged in terms of the rationality of moves toward this end. Thus, conversational argument is a method of managing disagreement so that it is minimized and so that agreement is achieved as quickly as possible.

Disagreement may be over the truthfulness of statements that people make (their propositional value) or over the felicity of their speech acts. When one's "performance" is questioned, the

truthfulness of what one is saying is not a central concern. Rather, the argument occurs because one person does not confirm or accept a speech act of the first. For example, George may tell Harry that he wants to mow his lawn and asks Harry if he can borrow his mower. If Harry is worried that the mower will not be returned as promised, he may argue with George about whether the felicity conditions of George's promise are properly met.

There are basically two kinds of arguments. Argument$_1$ involves *making* an argument, which involves stating your case by giving reasons. Argument$_2$ is *having* an argument, or exchanging objections in some form or another. People can make an argument without having one, and they can have an argument without making one.[28] Conversational argument involves argument$_2$, although argument$_1$ may be employed in the process. One makes an argument by presenting a case or supporting one's position with reasons. Making an argument involves supporting the felicity conditions of the speech acts being questioned. In other words, one uses a turn at talk to support or deny one's position. Let's take a closer look at the argument between George and Harry:

GEORGE: Well, I better get this grass cut.
HARRY: Yeah, me too.
GEORGE: Can I borrow your mower?
HARRY: Well, I really need it myself.
GEORGE: I'll return it right away.
HARRY: Last time you kept it two weeks.
GEORGE: No, I'll return it.
HARRY: Last spring you kept it a month.
GEORGE: Gosh, Harry, I really will get it back to you today.

Here, George makes a request and a promise. The argument ensues because Harry does not grant the request as would normally be expected and he challenges George's promise. In objecting, Harry makes an argument (argument$_1$) by saying that George has not been reliable in the past, and George comes back by supporting his intent to return the item. For purposes of illustration, this

27. The clearest statement of this theory is Scott Jacobs and Sally Jackson, "Argument as a Natural Category: The Routine Grounds for Arguing in Conversation," *Western Journal of Speech Communication* 45 (1981): 118–132. See also Sally Jackson and Scott Jacobs, "Structure of Conversational Argument: Pragmatic Bases for the Enthymeme," *Quarterly Journal of Speech* 66 (1980): 251–265; Sally Jackson and Scott Jacobs, "The Collaborative Production of Proposals in Conversational Argument and Persuasion: A Study of Disagreement Regulation," *Journal of the American Forensic Association* 18 (1981): 77–90; Scott Jacobs and Sally Jackson, "Building a Model of Conversational Argument," in *Rethinking Communication: Paradigm Exemplars*, vol. 2, eds. B. Dervin et al. (Newbury Park, Calif.: Sage, 1989), pp. 153–171.

28. This distinction was originally made by Daniel J. O'Keefe, "Two Concepts of Argument," *Journal of the American Forensic Association* 13 (1977): 121–128.

argument is direct and clear. Real conversational arguments are often indirect, and the participants are left to infer the reasons for objection. Here is another example:

SUSIE: Time to get up!
TIM: Uhhhhhhhhhh.
SUSIE: Gotta get up.
TIM: Uhhhhhhhhhhhhhhh.
SUSIE: We'll be late for work.
TIM: Just a few minutes.
SUSIE: You'll miss breakfast.
TIM: Uhhhhhhhhhhhhhhhhhh.
SUSIE: (Goes into the bathroom)

This may not seem like an argument, but technically it is because the comments of each person are not in agreement or consistent with what would normally be expected under the preference for agreement.

Although the theory of conversational argument originally subscribed to sequencing rules of coherence, Jackson and Jacobs have developed a more global approach in recent years, and now the theory is clearly in the rational tradition. In other words, one does not judge the coherence of conversational arguments by whether individual speech acts cohere with one another on a local level but whether the overall sequence is consistent with the goals negotiated by the communicators themselves. As described in the previous section, this is a process of coordination of plans designed to solve a problem, in this case to manage disagreement. In the following modified version of Susie and Tim's conversation, notice that the individual speech acts are not organized into proper adjacency pairs, but they still make sense within a broader frame:

SUSIE: Time to get up.
TIM: I have a headache.
SUSIE: We'll be late for work.
TIM: It's cold.
SUSIE: You'll miss breakfast.
TIM: I have a headache.
SUSIE: (Goes into the bathroom)

In this segment Susie and Tim are negotiating the organization of their getting-out-of-bed routine, and they disagree about it. Susie wants to get up, and Tim wants to stay in bed. Their respective turns violate the relevancy maxim if viewed as adjacency pairs because they do not seem related to one another; but from a global perspective, within the overall context of managing their disagreement, the conversation does make sense.

A Poststructural View of Discourse

Poststructuralism is a movement that began in the 1960s and continues today. It is most generally understood as a reaction against structural theories of language and discourse, including most of the theories discussed in this chapter and the previous one.

Most of the theories discussed so far have treated language and discourse as a product and instrument of human communicators. By analyzing the structure of discourse, one can understand the meanings conveyed and the functions fulfilled for human beings by speech. Poststructuralists have a somewhat different view of discourse. For one, discourse is not limited to speech. In fact, for some, everyday speech is considered unimportant and attention is given to written texts as the central object of study.

Most poststructuralists reject the idea that discourse is primarily a tool of communication. It may be considered that by communicators, but in fact it functions in far more profound ways that defy the traditional methods of discourse analysis discussed in this chapter. The three most well known poststructuralists are Jacques Derrida, Jacques Lacan, and Michel Foucault. Little theoretical coherence exists among these theorists. In fact, calling poststructuralism theoretical at all is stretching the truth. If anything, it is probably antitheoretical because of its rejection of the truth claims of discourse, including theoretical discourse.[29]

29. For an excellent discussion of poststructuralism, see Art Berman, *From the New Criticism to Deconstruction: The Reception of Structuralism and Post-structuralism* (Urbana: University of Illinois Press, 1988). A briefer treatment is Robert Young (ed.), "Post-structuralism: An Introduction," in *Untying the Text: A Post-structuralist Reader* (Boston: Routledge & Kegan Paul, 1981), pp. 1–28.

Jacques Derrida rejects absolutely the idea that language means anything of certainty.[30] He believes that there are always alternative meanings in a text and that any proposed meaning for a text is only one alternative to that which it is not. Derrida's method of *deconstruction* is designed to take meaning apart and show that texts cannot be understood as expressions of particular meanings or truths.

Jacques Lacan, a student of Freud, deals with the effects of discourse on the idea of self.[31] He shows how, at an early age when the child is beginning to see the self as a unified being, language shapes and represses the developing ideas of the self. At that time both conscious and unconscious images of self emerge. The self is thus nothing in and of itself but is a product of discourse.

Because his work is most closely related to the topic of this chapter, we will concentrate here on the theory of Michel Foucault.[32] Foucault is not a traditional structuralist and is, in fact, impossible to classify neatly. Although he denies a structuralist bias in his work, his work does show some similarity to the other theories in this chapter because of his concern for the structure and function of discourse.

Foucault says that each period has a distinct worldview, or conceptual structure, that determines the nature of knowledge in that period. The character of knowledge in a given epoch Foucault calls the *episteme* or *discursive formation*. The vision of each age is exclusive and incompatible with those of other ages, making it impossible for people in one period to think like those of another. The episteme, or way of thinking, is determined not by people but by the predominant discursive structures of the day. These discursive structures are deeply embedded ways of practicing or expressing ideas. Consequently, you cannot separate what people know and the structure of discourse used to express that knowledge. For Foucault, discourse includes written texts, but it also includes spoken language and nonverbal forms such as architecture, institutional practices, even charts and graphs.

An intriguing analysis of nonverbal forms as discourse is Sonja Foss and Ann Gill's application of Foucault to Disneyland.[33] In this study they look at the architectural layout of Disneyland, the creation of artificial reality, and the appearance of employees in the park as elements that express dimensions of knowledge in our own time.

Another example of how discourse shapes knowledge is Nixon's famous "Checkers" speech. Martha Cooper applied Foucault's ideas to this speech to show how the discourse as an event made use of, indeed created, standards for responding to an accusation.[34] In the presidential campaign of 1952, vice presidential candidate Richard Nixon was accused of harboring a secret campaign fund. He responded to this accusation by denying the charge, opening his private finances to public scrutiny, and claiming that the only possible illegitimate contribution he had received was a little dog named "Checkers."

This speech has been analyzed by several scholars in the rhetorical tradition, each looking at the

30. Derrida's chief work is *Of Grammatology*, trans. G. Spivak (Baltimore: Johns Hopkins University Press, 1974, 1976). For a brief overview, see the third edition of this book, *Theories of Human Communication* (Belmont, Calif.: Wadsworth, 1989), pp. 58–60. A more thorough treatment is that of Berman, *From the New Criticism*, pp. 199–222. See also Anthony Giddens, *Central Problems in Social Theory: Action, Structure and Contradiction in Social Analysis* (Berkeley: University of California Press, 1979), pp. 28–48.

31. See Jacques Lacan, *The Four Fundamental Concepts of Psycho-Analysis*, trans. A. Sheridan (New York: Norton, 1981). See also, Berman, *From the New Criticism*, pp. 185–194.

32. Foucault's primary works on this subject include *The Archaeology of Knowledge*, trans. A. M. Sheridan Smith (New York: Pantheon, 1972); *The Order of Things: An Archaeology of the Human Sciences* (New York: Pantheon, 1970); and *Power/Knowledge: Selected Interviews and Other Writings 1927–1977*, trans. Colin Gordon et. al., ed. Colin Gordon (New York: Pantheon, 1980). For an excellent short summary, see Sonja K. Foss, Karen A. Foss, and Robert Trapp, *Contemporary Perpsectives on Rhetoric* (Prospect Heights, Il.: Waveland Press, 1991). See also, Carole Blair, "The Statement: Foundation of Foucault's Historical Criticism," *Western Journal of Speech Communication* 51 (1987): 364–383; Sonja K. Foss and Ann Gill, "Michel Foucault's Theory of Rhetoric as Epistemic," *Western Journal of Speech Communication* 51 (1987): 384–402; Nancy Fraser, *Unruly Practices: Power, Discourse, and Gender in Contemporary Social Theory* (Minneapolis: University of Minnesota Press, 1989), pp. 17–68.

33. Foss and Gill, "Michel Foucault's Theory."

34. Martha Cooper, "Rhetorical Criticism and Foucault's Philosophy of Discursive Events," *Central States Speech Journal* 39 (1988): 1–17.

ways in which this particular speaker used strategies to appeal to the national audience at that time. For Foucault, this kind of analysis is irrelevant. Cooper shows how this speech is a discursive event that serves to create and reinforce knowledge structures in our culture. In particular, this speech defines what it means to respond to an accusation, reinforcing the rule that when accused, people should respond.

The structure of discourse is a set of inherent rules that determines the form and substance of discursive practice. Foucault's use of rules is not entirely like that of the other theories in this chapter because for him rules apply across the culture in a variety of types of discourse and function on a deep and powerful level. These are not merely rules for how to talk but rules that determine the very nature of our knowledge, power, and ethics as expressed in discourse. These rules control what can be talked or written about and who may talk or write (or whose talk is to be taken seriously). Such rules also prescribe the conceptual form that discourse must take. In our own day, for example, "scientific authorities" are given great credibility, and the form of "objective studies" is preferred in matters of "fact" over the form of conjecture or myth.

So in the "Checkers" speech, for example, we see what counts as good evidence for a claim that a politician is corrupt (or not corrupt as the case may be). We learn from this discourse that politicians must speak out when accused of wrongdoing, and the persona of the honest, average American is created here as a model.

Contrary to popular belief, according to Foucault, people are not responsible for establishing the conditions of discourse. Rather, discursive formation itself determines the definition and place of the person in the scheme of the world. Our present discursive structure makes humans the foundation and origin of knowledge, but people have never before achieved this status in any other period and will soon lose it. Foucault believes that the episteme will again shift, and humans will once again disappear from their central place in the world: "It is comforting . . . and a source of profound relief to think that man is only a recent invention, a figure

not yet two centuries old, a new wrinkle in our knowledge, and that he will disappear again as soon as that knowledge has discovered a new form."[35]

This radical idea does not mean that humans do not produce discourse. Indeed, they do; but any number of individuals could have produced a statement, and any given speaker or writer is merely fulfilling a role in making a statement. That Nixon was the speaker of the "Checkers" speech is unimportant. Nixon took the role of agent in this case, and since then any number of other politicians have done essentially the same thing. Discourse, then, does not require a knowing subject, a person who creates it, consumes it, understands it, and uses it. Rather, language itself prefigures personhood: Language creates the person. A Nixon-type was created by the language in the "Checkers" speech.

In our own era, persons are believed to obtain and have knowledge and power, but this idea is a creation of the predominant discursive formation of our day, and the rules of expression with which we communicate establish this notion. In other times, entirely different ideas about knowledge and power emerged from the discourse in use.

Foucault's research on the penal system is a good example of this.[36] He found a dramatic shift in the eighteenth and nineteenth centuries away from torture and public punishment to incarceration and protection of the criminal from bodily harm. Prior to this period, convicts were publicly tortured or executed in a kind of spectacle. In the discursive formation of the day, the body was seen as the central object of political relations. It was very natural that power should be exerted against the body and that punishment should involve bodily pain. In the latter discursive formation, the body lost this status, as power became more a matter of individual human psyche or soul.

Foucault's work centers on analyzing discourse in a way that reveals its rules and structure. This he calls *archaeology*. Archaeology seeks to uncover,

35. Foucault, *The Order of Things*, p. xxii.

36. Michel Foucault, *Discipline and Punish: The Birth of the Prison*, trans. A. Sheridan (New York: Vintage Books, 1979).

through careful description, the regularities of discourse. It displays disparities or contradictions, rather than coherence, and reveals a succession of one form of discourse to another. For this reason, Foucault places emphasis on comparative descriptions of more than one piece of discourse.

Interpretation, or establishing the meaning of a text, cannot be avoided in text analysis, but it should be minimized because interpretation does not reveal discursive structure and, in fact, may obscure it. Foucault thinks that analysts should avoid associating discourse with authors because authors are merely fulfilling the discourse's function and are not instrumental in any fundamental way in establishing the structure of the texts they produce. This is why Nixon as the speaker in the "Checkers" event is unimportant. We look to what the discourse says about knowledge, power, and ethics rather than viewing it as an instrument of one particular author.

Foucault's writings are preoccupied with the subject of power. He believes that power is an inherent part of all discursive formation. As such, power is a function of discourse or knowledge and not a human or institutional property. The episteme, as expressed in language, grants power. Thus, power and knowledge cannot be divided. Power, however, is a good, creative force that finds its zenith in "disciplinary power" or the prescription of standards of correct behavior.

Commentary and Critique

No discussion of language or communication is complete without addressing discourse. Discourse is message units larger than sentences that are part of ongoing talk. For some scholars, it is even written texts and nonverbal forms. Although language and other symbol systems are the building blocks of communication, discourse is the product of communication itself.

Discourse as a part of everyday life is governed by rules, and much has been written about this topic. Rules are guidelines for action, and they govern how language is used at every level, semantic, syntactic, and pragmatic. In other words, communicators use rules to determine how a sentence should be uttered, what words mean, and how to use language in ongoing communication. In this chapter we have seen how rules are used in the production of speech acts and in conversations.

The rule concept has been popular in communication studies because it acknowledges that people can make choices but provides a way of studying regularity and pattern at the same time. Rules are even an important part of Foucault's theory, although he uses the concept in a strictly rule-following way and, in fact, grants great power to rules to shape the very nature of knowledge and personhood in a particular discursive formation. Foucault would be the last to say that people choose rules.

Rule theory has had its share of critics. Criticism of rules theory has centered around two issues: conceptual coherence and explanatory power. Even its adherents admit that the rules tradition lacks unity and coherence. Jesse Delia verbalizes this objection in strong terms:

> The terrain covered by notions of "rules," then, is broad, grossly diffuse, and imprecisely articulated. And the real problem for any position purporting to be a general rules perspective is that the meaning of "rule" does not remain constant either within or across these domains. The "rules" territory taken as a whole is, in fact, little short of chaotic. At the least, it is clear that there is no unifying conception of the rule construct, of the domain of phenomena to which the construct has reference, of whether rules have generative power in producing and directing behavior . . . or of the proper way to give an account of some domain of phenomena utilizing the construct. The idea of "rules" as a general construct represents only a diffuse notion devoid of specific theoretical substance.[37]

The theories we have covered illustrate this lack of coherence. Linguistic rules are bound to an inherent structure of language and as such pretty much determine how sentences are generated and understood. As described by Searle, speech acts too

37. Jesse Delia, "Alternative Perspectives for the Study of Human Communication: Critique and Response," *Communication Quarterly* 25 (1977): 54.

are regulated by strict rules that are violated by default rather than by design. Wittgenstein on the other hand, considers the rules of language games to be malleable and changeable, much as in the rule-using tradition. The original conversation-analysis work, especially that governed by adjacency sequencing used rules in the narrower, more restrictive sense; but Jackson and Jacobs in their global, rational approach see rules as something that communicators negotiate in the conversation itself.

The second issue related to rules theory involves its explanatory power. Critics generally believe that rules approaches cannot be explanatory as long as they fail to develop general principles that cut across contexts. To identify the rules in operation within a particular context is not sufficient to explain communication processes. Charles Berger believes that "at some point one must go beyond the description of 'what the rules are' and ask why some rules are selected over others . . . [and] what social forces produced the kinds of conventions and appropriate modes of behavior we now observe."[38] Berger's view is that a covering law approach is ultimately necessary to provide explanation; attempts of rules theorists to provide generic principles are nothing more than covering laws in disguise.

Most rules advocates do not go along with this argument. Shimanoff points out that most rules explanations, in contrast to laws explanations, are practical, or reason-giving. Behaviors are explained in terms of their practical impact on creating desired outcomes. Such explanations can be generalized. Although developing universal explanations would not be desirable, and perhaps not possible, rules theories should seek reason-giving explanations that cover relatively broad classes of situations, even to the point of allowing for prediction.[39]

The appropriate question here is not whether rules theories are explanatory but what kind of explanation the critic believes is necessary. Clearly, Berger and Shimanoff disagree on the level of generality necessary for adequate explanation. We must also keep in mind that different rules theories possess different levels of explanatory power.

Recall from Chapter 2 that explanation is made possible by principles of necessity and generality. Pearce discusses rules approaches in terms of these criteria.[40] Rule-following approaches tend not to be explanatory because they merely describe recurring behavior without indicating any form of necessity. Rule-governed approaches explain in terms of practical necessity, although their generality is somewhat limited. Pearce believes that the rule-using approach has the highest potential for explanatory power in terms of both practical and logical necessity and generality.

An important application of rule theory has been ordinary language philosophy and the work on speech acts, one of the most productive and useful creations of contemporary philosophy and social science. It has had a major impact on the communication field. The power of speech act theory is in its explanation of intent as a kind of meaning. When we communicate we not only convey content, referential meaning, or our own version of truth but also an intent to do something with the words we use. This idea expresses so clearly how people use language to act or to accomplish objectives. Poststructuralism takes an entirely different tack. Here, discourse is not seen primarily as a strategic method of accomplishing individual objectives. In Foucault's theory, discourse forms the very structure of knowledge in an era. The rules embedded in discourse dictate how we do what we do, and speakers are merely taking roles established in the discursive formation.

Still, speech act theory has influenced a number of other theoretical lines of work, including conversation analysis. As researchers have worked with the concept of speech acts and applied it to various contexts, a number of weaknesses have been brought to light.

Critics generally agree that intentions are an

---

38. Charles R. Berger, "The Covering Law Perspective as a Theoretical Basis for the Study of Human Communication," *Communication Quarterly* 25 (1977): 12.

39. Shimanoff, *Communication Rules*, pp. 217–234.

40. Pearce, "Rules Theories."

important aspect of meaning, that speech constitutes a form of action, and that speech acts are governed by rules; but they argue that the conceptual categories of speech act theory are vague or meaningless. Austin's threefold distinction among locutionary, illocutionary, and perlocutionary acts has been severely criticized from this standpoint, prompting one critic to state: "And now Austin has, in my judgment, erected a structure that is in imminent danger of collapse."[41]

Critics question the utility of locution as a concept, if the utterance of a locution automatically constitutes an illocution, as Austin claims it does. The distinction between illocutionary and perlocutionary acts is equally unclear to many readers, who point out that even if one could observe the difference between these concepts, it is doubtful that they constitute a useful conceptual framework for guiding our understanding of speech acts. It would perhaps be more fruitful to recognize that any given speech act may be fulfilling a variety of intents and may be taken in a variety of different ways by different listeners.[42] Conceptually, the terms *illocution* and *perlocution* may apply more directly to types of force and effects than to types of acts per se.

The distinction between regulative and constitutive rules is equally fuzzy.[43] The problem here is that once any act becomes standardized, as in the case of almost all illocutionary acts, rules no longer are constitutive in the sense of creating new acts. Hence, rules that regulate can be taken as constitutive, and rules that constitute an act also regulate.

Another application of rules theory, and one heavily influenced also by speech acts, is conversation analysis. This is the ethnomethodological study of the ways in which actors cooperate in organizing interaction. It involves the careful examination of the details of actual conversations in an attempt to discover what people do to accomplish tasks and solve problems together.

Basically, conversation is a cooperative endeavor. People must play the game by the same rules or they would never know what was going on in a conversation. For cooperation to occur, participants make certain assumptions about the other person, that he or she is conversing in good faith with the intent to speak in accordance with the rules. Even blatant violations of conversational rules are interpreted through implicature as being cooperative. Indeed, the combination of basic rules of cooperation such as appropriate quantity of talk, truthfulness, relevance, and organization with the flexibility permitted by conversational implicature makes it possible for humans to enact an infinite number of often creative expansions of talk to meet a whole array of intentions.

Perhaps the most important aspect of conversation analysis is the discovery of ways in which conversations are made coherent. This is also one of the most problematic aspects of this field. Originally, conversation analysts explained coherence strictly in terms of local rules, or the ways in which adjacent pairs of turns were consistent with one another. Most analysts now agree, however, that strictly local, adjacency explanations are inadequate.[44]

The problem with the theory is that it cannot explain certain conversational sequences. For example, some coherent sequences do not follow the sequencing rules stipulated by the theory. Also, some speech acts that could be a first-pair part have no apparent structural preference for any particular other kind of act as a second-pair part. What, for example, would be the preferred response to a promise or an accusation? This problem seems to result from the rather arbitrary system by which speech acts are classified: The system labels acts according to type without much sensitivity to their actual function in the conversation.

41. Campbell, "A Rhetorical View," p. 287.

42. This point is made by John Lyne, "Speech Acts in a Semiotic Frame, *Communication Quarterly* 29 (1981): 202–208; and by Robert Trapp, "The Role of Disagreement in Interactional Argument," *Journal of the American Forensic Association* 23 (1986): 23–41.

43. Shimanoff, *Communication Rules*, pp. 84–85. For additional critique, see McLaughlin, *Conversation*, pp. 63–68.

44. Jacobs, "Language."

These weaknesses have given rise to more global explanations of coherence. Perhaps the most interesting of these is the rational model of Jackson and Jacobs. In this more humanistic explanation, communicators understand what is going on within a broader context than the simple sequence of acts at a given moment. They use conversation to negotiate plans, and the overall conversation itself is rational within this negotiation context. Acts that appear unrelated to one another if examined locally become consistent when you understand the broader context in which they appear.

A significant application of the rational approach is Jackson and Jacobs's work on conversational argument, which looks at the ways in which communicators manage disagreements in conversations. It examines the ways in which speakers and listeners have an argument and the ways in which they make arguments in conversations. The distinction between *making* an argument and *having* an argument is important and captures two dimensions of conversations, the individual speech act and the organization of interactions.

One major objection to conversation analysis is that it works entirely within the confines of the discourse itself. The researcher makes observations and inferences entirely on the basis of the text, without reference to outside factors or even the opinions of the participants themselves. The researcher relies solely on his or her own intuitions as a member of the culture in analyzing the discourse.[45] Although this procedure has merits, it is insensitive to the problem of possible multiple interpretations of speech acts. The participants in a conversation may not understand what is going on in the same way as the researcher thinks they do. Kathy Kellermann and Carra Sleight have written that coherence is not in the text but is in the cognitive system of the perceiver.[46] Although cues

may be presented in the discourse, the actual coherence itself results from the application of a knowledge structure in the mind of the communicator to the discourse.

Considerable disagreement exists about whether conversation analysts do accurately intuit what is going on in a conversation. Robert Trapp claims, for example, that the subjects in a study did not identify sequences as arguments that Jacobs and Jackson had identified as such.[47] Jacobs and Jackson, on the other hand, have presented data that subjects can and do operate by the same intuitions as do conversational analysis.[48]

A related issue is whether conversational organization is correlated without other outside factors such as characteristics of the communicators or social situation. Without going outside the discourse itself, the researcher cannot know whether such associations exist. Most conversational analysts agree that they are not concerned with these kinds of issues and leave such questions to others who use non–conversational analysis methods.[49]

A natural tension exists between discourse analysis and poststructural approaches to text. Discourse analysts of every variety assume that the meaning and function of talk can be uncovered by careful examination of the structure of the text. Poststructuralists deny this assumption out of hand. For Foucault, as one poststructuralist, the text precedes the talk in the sense that language has both knowledge and action embedded in it and predetermines how actors will respond in their use of speech. Here, we see two drastically different approaches to texts.

In the next two chapters, we move to a set of theories that deal with communicators apart from discourse. We will examine the cognitive structures and processes that affect discourse production and processing.

---

45. This process is discussed in some depth by Wayne Beach, "Orienting to the Phenomenon."

46. Kathy Kellermann and Carra Sleight, "Coherence: A Meaningful Adhesive for Discourse," in *Communication Yearbook 12*, ed. J. Anderson (Newbury Park, Calif.: Sage, 1989), pp. 95–129.

47. Trapp, "The Role of Disagreement."

48. Sally Jackson and Scott Jacobs, "Characterizing Ordinary Argument: Substantive and Methodological Issues," *Journal of the American Forensic Association* 22 (1986): 42–57.

49. This issue is discussed at some length by Don Zimmerman, "On Conversation."

CHAPTER 6

Theories of Message Production

Communication is a process that relies on messages and information, and much communication theory has been developed to explain how the production and reception of messages and the management of information occur. Although we separate theories of message production from those of reception in this book for purposes of organization, the processes cannot themselves be divided. Because of the systemic nature of communication and the give and take between communicators, the processes of message production and reception are closely intertwined.

The theories discussed in this chapter and the next center on the role of the individual in the communication process. Most of these theories acknowledge the social nature of communication, but they do not use social explanations. Rather, these theories see message production and reception as psychological processes. In Chapters 8 and 9, we look at another set of theories that do not view communication primarily as a psychological process but as a social one.

Traits, States, and Processes

The theories of message production, reception, and processing use three types of psychological explanations—trait explanations, state explanations, and process explanations. *Trait explanations* focus on relatively static characteristics of individuals and the ways in which they correlate with other traits and variables. This type of theory associates particular personality types with certain sorts of messages. In essence, they teach that when you have a certain personality trait, you will tend to communicate in certain ways. For example, one of the traits we discuss later is argumentativeness. Highly argumentative people tend to defend their beliefs and refute opposing ones.

State explanations focus on states of mind that persons experience for a period of time. Unlike traits, states are relatively unstable and transitory. These theories are interested in how certain states affect the sorts of messages sent and how messages are understood. For example, a popular theory discussed in the Chapter 7 associates ego involvement with the perception of messages. This theory shows that when you are highly involved in a topic because it is important to your life, you tend to misperceive certain messages about that topic.

Trait and state explanations can be used in concert with one another. They recognize that many of our characteristics are relatively stable. At the same time, they realize that our behavior is not entirely determined by traits. Therefore, an observer might attempt to determine which behaviors are traitlike and which are statelike. Further, both trait and state theories rely on the measurement of dispositions. In the case of traits, we try to measure a person's predispositions that seem to be operating most of the time, and in the case of state research, we are measuring a person's dispositions of the moment. In addition, certain states are the outcome of an interaction between traits and situation. In other words, the way you communicate may result from some combination of who you are and the situation in which you find yourself. Situations are important in the production of messages, and we devote considerable space to this subject later in this chapter.

The third type of explanation often found in theories of message production and reception is *process explanation*. Here, the interest is in the ways in which communication actually occurs rather than the traits or states of the communicators themselves. Process explanations attempt to capture the mechanisms of the human mind. They focus on the ways in which information is acquired and organized; how memory is used in communication, both in the production and reception of messages; how people decide how to act; and a host of other similar concerns.

Trait and state approaches are not incompatible with process explanations. In fact, you can find many examples of combinations of these in communication research. For example, one theory covered later in this chapter shows how a trait called cognitive complexity is related to message production. According to this theory, cognitively complex individuals adapt messages to others more effec-

tively than do cognitively simple individuals. This theory combines a communication trait (cognitive complexity) with a process (adapting messages to persons).

Behavioral and Cognitive Explanations

The theories in this and the next chapters come out of the tradition of behaviorism and cognitive psychology. Cognitive and behavioral approaches to the study of communication share an interest in the ways in which stimuli lead to responses. Behaviorism has a long history in modern psychology, going back at least to the work of J. B. Watson and C. L. Hull early in this century.[1] Strict behaviorists wanted to account for stimulus and response variables in a way that would make overt behavior predictable. These early behaviorists considered internal "thought" processes inaccessible and uninteresting. Thinking and feeling were considered to be hidden in a "black box," and "mentalism" was discredited. Early behaviorism was therefore known as S–R (stimulus–response) psychology.

Today, strict behaviorism is out of favor among most behavioral and social scientists. In its place is "cognitivism," which attempts to crack the black box between stimulus and response. Old-style behaviorism is now believed to be too narrow to capture the truly essential variables of human action. Cognitive sciences arose, too, from the popularity of information theory (Chapter 3) in the behavioral sciences, so that cognitivism focuses on the ways in which people process information about their environment. Cognitivism, like behaviorism, remains interested in what is now termed

---

1. J. B. Watson, *Psychology from the Standpoint of the Behaviorist* (Philadelphia: Lippincott, 1919); C. L. Hull, *Principles of Behavior: An Introduction to Behavior Theory* (New York: Appleton, 1943).

inputs and *outputs*, but only in the context of the thought processes that bridge the two.

The Behavioral Tradition

Behaviorism is a perspective that focuses on responses to external and internal stimuli. As such, it looks for predictable patterns between stimulus and response. There have been numerous ways of looking at the S–R relationship, but overall, two major traditions have emerged.[2] The first of these, classical conditioning, examines the way in which stimuli in the environment produce new responses in the organism. The common example of classical conditioning is Pavlov's early experiment, in which a bell was paired with a dog's food so that the dog came to salivate to the sound of the bell.

Instrumental, or operant, theory concentrates not on the paired association of prior stimuli in the environment but on reinforcement elicited by behavior. Whereas classical conditioning views behavior as dependent on prior stimulation, the operant school holds that the actual behavior of the organism is instrumental in causing consequences in the environment and is reinforced by those consequences. Animal training, in which behavior is shaped by administering rewards and punishments, is a good example of operant conditioning.

The behaviorist tradition has influenced three areas of communication theory—language, persuasion, and meaning. Early theories that attempted to explain how language is acquired were behavioristic in orientation. These theories tended to treat language as any learned behavior that is acquired through reinforcement.[3] Such explanations are not now generally considered to be sufficient.

The second area of communication in which behaviorism has been influential is persuasion. Up

through the 1960s, almost all persuasion research had a strong behaviorist bias. The most significant persuasion research program during this time was the Yale project.[4] This decade-long research program in the psychology department at Yale University, which is still influential today, was heavily behaviorist in orientation. It was devoted primarily to analyzing the complex interaction among variables in the communication situation, the predispositions of the communicators, and the observable effects. Although the Yale researchers certainly acknowledged the importance of "internal mediating processes," these were never very well defined or examined, and persuasion was viewed primarily as an S–R operation.

The third area in which behaviorism has had an impact is in the theory of meaning. This influence is most evident in the work of Charles Osgood. As a behaviorist, Osgood is especially interested in how meanings are learned and how they relate to internal and external behavior. His theory is one of the most elaborate of the behavioral theories of language and meaning, and because of its concern for internal processes, it has a foot in both the behavioral and cognitive traditions. Osgood's theory is covered in some detail in Chapter 7.

The Cognitive Tradition

Like behaviorists, latter-day cognitivists are variable-analytic; in other words, they tend to see behavior as a complex of variables that can be directly or indirectly observed, measured, and analyzed. Cognitivists believe in the fruitfulness of examining S–R patterns, but unlike strict behaviorists, they concentrate on the mental processes that mediate between the two.[5]

2. J. W. Kling, "Learning: Introductory Survey," in *Woodward and Schlosberg's Experimental Psychology*, eds. J. W. Kling and L. Riggs (New York: Holt, Rinehart & Winston, 1971), pp. 551–613.

3. See, for example, B. F. Skinner, *Verbal Behavior* (New York: Appleton-Century-Crofts, 1957).

4. For a brief summary of the findings of the Yale research, see Mary John Smith, *Persuasion and Human Action* (Belmont, Calif: Wadsworth, 1982), pp. 213–240.

5. Sally Planalp and Dean E. Hewes, "A Cognitive Approach to Communication Theory: *Cogito Ergo Dico?*" *Communication Yearbook 5*, ed. M. Burgoon (New Brunswick, N.J.: Transaction Books, 1982), pp. 49–78; John O. Greene, "Evaluating Cognitive Explanations of Communicative Phenomena," *Quarterly Journal of Speech* 70 (1984): 241–254.

Behaviorism was almost completely deterministic in that it aimed to predict behavior on the basis of antecedent conditions and afforded little power to the individual as a creative agent. One of its chief adherents, B. F. Skinner, stated this deterministic assumption in definite terms: "Science insists that action is initiated by forces impinging upon the individual, and that caprice is only another name for behavior for which we have not yet found a cause."[6] Most cognitive theorists disagree with this assumption. Cognitive theories assume that individuals are purposeful and capable of creating action alternatives and choosing options.

Given their emphasis on human powers, cognitive theories deal with mental processes that make action possible. These theories deal with the cognitive system that helps individuals organize and understand information, act, and choose among behavioral options. Cognitive theories deal with

1. The structure of the cognitive system, or the manner in which information is organized in the system.

2. The processes by which that organization is achieved.

3. The content of the cognitive system.

The content is what is contained in the cognitive system—the information, thoughts, feelings, attitudes, and so forth. The structure is the pattern in which the content is organized in one's memory, and the process is the operations by which content is handled and transformed, including a variety of information-processing mechanisms. Typical topics of cognitive theories are meaning, memory, selection, plans of action, and inference making.

The cognitive approach is one of the most prominent perspectives in contemporary communication theory. Because information is the basic commodity of communication, the study of information processing becomes very important. Many of the theories not only in this chapter and the next, but in other chapters as well, are cognitive in orientation.

Communication States: Traits and Situations

Perhaps the most commonly held belief among researchers today is that communication states are determined by a combination of traits and situational factors. How you communicate at any given moment depends on certain traits you may have and your understanding of the situation in which you find yourself. Numerous traits have been studied in communication research, and we cannot begin to cover them all here. In this section we concentrate on several prominent communication traits. We later discuss the role of the situation in determining behavior.

Some Communication Traits

Communication apprehension. Many people are afraid of communication. Since about 1970 there has been much research on the problem of *communication apprehension* and related concepts. Perhaps the most well developed of these programs is that of James McCroskey and his colleagues, who have discovered that fear of communicating is a serious practical problem for many people.[7]

Communication apprehension (CA) can be a trait or a state. Traitlike CA is an enduring tendency to be apprehensive about communication in a variety of contexts. Individuals who suffer from this kind of fear may avoid all sorts of oral communication. Some people are afraid of a certain kind of communication—like public speaking—but may exhibit very little fear of other types of communication. Such fear is called generalized-context CA. Still others are afraid of communicating with certain specific people or groups. This form of CA, person–group CA, is not a personality trait but is more situational. Almost everybody suf-

6. B. F. Skinner, *Cumulative Record: A Selection of Papers*, 3rd ed. (New York: Appleton-Century-Crofts, 1972), p. 8.

7. This work is summarized in James C. McCroskey, "The Communication Apprehension Perspective," in *Avoiding Communication: Shyness, Reticence, and Communication Apprehension*, eds. J. A. Daly and J. C. McCroskey (Beverly Hills, Calif.: Sage, 1984), pp. 13–38.

fers from time to time from the state of CA. There are times when the threat is high or the situation is nerve-wracking, and you will feel afraid, but normal anxiety does not mean that you have the trait of high CA. Normal stage fright is a good example of normal anxiety.

These forms of CA are variables. In other words, every person has some degree of apprehension ranging from low to high. Normal apprehension is not especially problematic. Of special concern, however, is pathological CA, in which an individual suffers high traitlike fear of communication. Abnormally high CA creates serious personal problems, including most notably extreme discomfort and avoidance of communication, to the point of preventing productive and happy participation in society.

For example, McCroskey and others have found that CA has a serious effect on students at school.[8] Students high in CA score lower on the ACT aptitude test, and they tend to have lower grade-point averages than do less apprehensive students. Highly apprehensive students have special difficulty in small classes because of the expectations for students in small classes. These students also have difficulty with individualized instruction because they have to interact one-on-one with the instructor, which frightens them. Highly apprehensive students tend to do best in large lecture classes, where they can hide in the crowd.

Communication apprehension, though it may have an hereditary base, is probably primarily a learned response. Although behavioristic learning theory and modeling may explain some CA, McCroskey believes that the best explanations of CA are cognitive. He suggests that people create expectations about how encounters with others will turn out. When one's expectations are accurate, the resulting confidence reduces apprehension because the individual experiences less uncertainty about future encounters; but when expectations turn out to be wrong, the individual

loses confidence. Communication apprehension may be the result of repeated inaccurate expectations about communication situations, which is essentially a pattern of learned helplessness.

One of the bright spots in the research on CA is the discovery that the problem is treatable. Consequently, the practical application of this line of research has had a significant effect. One of the most successful interventions for CA is *systematic desensitization*.[9] In this treatment, subjects are first taught techniques that they can use to put themselves into a state of deep relaxation. With the help of a counselor or teacher, they construct a list of communication situations that frighten them. This list is put in order from the least frightening to the most frightening. For example, at the bottom of the list might be the mere thought of having to give a speech, which is only mildly irritating; at the top of the list might be actually standing up and walking to a lectern to give a talk, which is extremely frightening. Very gradually, through several sessions, the therapist or teacher helps the client pair the images on the list in order from the lowest to highest with deep relaxation, and the fear is slowly and effectively eradicated.

Rhetorical sensitivity. Rhetorical sensitivity is the ability and willingness to adapt messages to audiences. This construct is attributable to Roderick Hart and his colleagues.[10] For these theorists,

8. James C. McCroskey, "Classroom Consequences of Communication Apprehension," *Communication Education* 26 (1977): 27–33.

9. James C. McCroskey, David C. Ralph, and James E. Barrick, "The Effect of Systematic Desensitization on Speech Anxiety," *Speech Teacher* 19 (1970): 32–36; James C. McCroskey, "The Implementation of a Large-Scale Program of Systematic Desensitization for Communication Apprehension," *Speech Teacher* 21 (1971): 255–264; Gustav Friedrich and Blaine Goss, "Systematic Desensitization," in *Avoiding Communication: Shyness, Reticence, and Communication Apprehension*, eds. J. A. Daly and J. C. McCroskey (Beverly Hills, Calif.: Sage, 1984), pp. 173–188.

10. Roderick P. Hart and Don M. Burks, "Rhetorical Sensitivity and Social Interaction," *Speech Monographs* 39 (1972): 75–91; Roderick P. Hart, Robert E. Carlson, and William F. Eadie, "Attitudes Toward Communication and the Assessment of Rhetorical Sensitivity," *Communication Monographs* 47 (1980): 1–22. See also Steven A. Ward, Dale L. Bluman, and Arthur Dauria, "Rhetorical Sensitivity Recast: Theoretical Assumptions of an Informal Interpersonal Rhetoric," *Communication Quarterly* 30 (1982): 189–195.

effective communication does not arise from blatant openness and disclosure but from sensitivity and care in adjusting what you say to the listener. Relying on the categories of Donald Darnell and Wayne Brockriede, Hart contrasts three general types of communicators.[11] *Noble selves* stick to their personal ideals without variation and without adapting or adjusting to others. *Rhetorical reflectors* are individuals who, at the opposite extreme, mold themselves to others' wishes, with no personal scruples to follow.

Rhetorically sensitive individuals, as a third type, moderate these extremes. Rhetorical sensitivity embodies concern for self, concern for others, and a situational attitude. For Hart, this type is clearly superior to the other two. It leads to more effective understanding and acceptance of one's ideas.

Rhetorically sensitive people accept personal complexity; they understand that each individual is a composite of many selves. There is no real self to communicate to others. Instead, one must be in touch with the "self" that is operating in the situation. You are not the same person in a professor's office as you are at a party with your friends, and you are not going to communicate the same way in these two situations.

Rhetorically adaptive individuals avoid rigidity in communicating with others, and they attempt to balance self-interests with the interests of others. These people try to adjust what they say to the level, mood, and beliefs of the other person. They do not forsake their own values, but they realize that they can communicate those values in a variety of ways. Rhetorically sensitive people are aware of the appropriateness of communicating or not communicating particular ideas in different situations. An idea can be expressed in many ways and can be adapted to the audience in the particular situation.

To better understand the rhetorically sensitive person in contrast with the noble self and rhetorical reflector, Hart and his colleagues created a questionnaire called RHETSEN and administered it to over 3000 students at forty-nine universities.[12] In this study the researchers found substantial variation among people in their tendencies to possess the different types. Most people have varying degrees of all three types with one predominate type.

The variation between persons seems to be associated with a variety of factors, including philosophical, economic, geographic, and cultural differences. Certain groups such as families and ethnic groups may teach and reinforce the values of particular types. For example, noble selves tend to be politically liberal, young, Jewish, and competitive. Rhetorical reflectors tend to be conservative, midwestern churchgoers, and they are older than the average noble self. Rhetorical sensitivity seems to be a white middle-class trait found especially among groups that are politically independent, do not attend church, and have few ethnic ties.

Hart also administered RHETSEN to a group of about 500 nurses and found very similar patterns.[13] For example, nurses under the age of 35 were more rhetorically sensitive than the average, and those over 55 were more rhetorically reflective. The nurses with more education were more rhetorically sensitive than those with less education. Registered nurses tended to have more of the noble self than other types of nurses, and aides and LPNs tended to exhibit rhetorical reflector behaviors.

Communicator style. The idea of rhetorical sensitivity suggests that individuals have a predominant manner or style in which they communicate. *Communicator style* has been investigated by Robert Norton and his colleagues.[14] The style construct is predicated on the idea that we communicate on two levels. Not only do we give others informational content, but we also use words and actions to give form to the content of the primary message.

11. Donald Darnell and Wayne Brockriede, *Persons Communicating* (Englewood Cliffs, N.J.: Prentice-Hall, 1976).

12. Hart, Carlson, and Eadie, "Attitudes," p. 19.

13. Ibid.

14. Robert Norton, *Communicator Style: Theory, Applications, and Measures* (Beverly Hills, Calif.: Sage, 1983).

This higher-order communication tells others how to understand and how to respond to a message. For example, on the content level, you might tell a friend about an experience; on a higher level, you might signal that your message is to be taken with authority, with levity, with disinterest, with humor, or with any number of different attitudes. Norton believes that a speaker's higher-order communication functions as a "style message" by "signaling how a literal (primary) message should be taken, filtered, interpreted, or understood."[15] Style messages accompany content messages, but they may be delivered before, during, or after the primary message. Norton further believes that the tendency to expect style messages is so strong that if faced with ambiguous or contradictory messages, people look for style-level cues that will inform them of how the message is to be taken. For example, a comment that could be taken either seriously or jokingly will be interpreted in accordance with what the receiver believes to be the style of the speaker.

Over time, as an individual gains experience interacting with another person, various types of style messages will recur. For example, one might be viewed repeatedly as being gruff, laid-back, whimsical, serious, and so on. Norton's thesis is that characteristics repeatedly associated with a person constitute that individual's dominant style. Styles, of course, are not totally individual. Cultures, for example, affect how people behave and how they perceive others, as in the case of Hispanic machismo.

Although a person's style constitutes the individual's predominant way of communicating, it is not the only way in which the person communicates, and in fact a person's style can be multifaceted and include several different aspects.

There are numerous possible styles. Each style is a combination of certain traits or variables. Norton has found nine variables that can enter into an individual's overall style. These variables are not independent from one another, and considerable

overlap exists among them. They include dominance, dramatic behavior, contentiousness, animation, impression leaving, relaxation, attentiveness, openness, and friendliness. Of these, dramatic behavior and animation seem to go together, as do attentiveness and friendliness. Dominance and contentiousness also go together.

Aggression. Aggression, or the application of pressure on another person, is commonly observed in communication. Dominick Infante and his colleagues have been responsible for developing this concept in the communication literature.[16] These authors note that aggression can be constructive when it aims to improve communication or enhance a relationship, or it can be destructive when it causes dissatisfaction or harms the relationship in some way.

Aggression, as conceptualized by Infante, consists of four traits—assertiveness, argumentativeness, hostility, and verbal aggressiveness. The first two are positive traits, and the second two are negative. *Assertiveness* involves putting one's own rights forward without hampering other individuals' rights. As a trait, it is the tendency to act forthrightly in your own best interest. It may involve such practices as asserting leadership, initiating conversations, defending one's rights in social situations, and resisting pressure from others to conform.

Argumentativeness is the tendency to engage in conversations about controversial topics, to sup-

15. Ibid., p. 31.

16. For a summary of this work, see Dominic A. Infante, Andrew S. Rancer, and Deanna F. Womack, *Building Communication Theory* (Prospect Heights, Ill.: Waveland Press, 1990), pp. 155–161. See also Dominick A. Infante, *Arguing Constructively* (Prospect Heights, Ill.: Waveland Press, 1988); "Aggressiveness," in *Personality and Interpersonal Communication*, eds. J. C. McCroskey and J. A. Daly (Newbury Park, Calif.: Sage, 1987), pp. 305–316; Dominick A. Infante and Charles J. Wigley, "Verbal Aggressiveness: An Interpersonal Model and Measure," *Communication Monographs* 53 (1986): 61–69; Dominick A. Infante, J. David Trebing, Patricia E. Shepherd, and Dale E. Seeds, "The Relationship of Argumentativeness to Verbal Aggression," *Southern Speech Communication Journal* 50 (1984): 67–77; Dominick A. Infante and Andrew S. Rancer, "A Conceptualization and Measure of Argumentativeness," *Journal of Personality Assessment* 46 (1982): 72–80.

port one's own point of view, and to refute opposing beliefs. Infante is positive toward argumentativeness because he believes that it can improve learning, help people see others' points of view, enhance credibility, and build communication skill. Argumentative individuals are by definition assertive, although not all assertive people are argumentative.

Hostility is the tendency to feel and display anger. It is important to note that one can be assertive, even argumentative, without anger. Unlike assertiveness and argumentativeness then, hostility involves irritability, negativism, resentment, and suspicion. It is clearly a negative trait.

Verbal aggressiveness is often, though not always, associated with hostility. It is the attempt to hurt someone, not physically, but emotionally. Whereas arguments attack ideas and beliefs, verbal aggression attacks the ego or self-concept. Whereas arguments are reasoned, verbal aggressiveness includes such tactics as insults, profanity, threats, and emotional outbursts. It results in anger, embarrassment, hurt feelings, and other negative reactions.

It is important to understand that verbal aggressiveness and hostility are not the same thing as argumentativeness. In fact, Infante believes that when people are unable to argue constructively, they may lash out with verbal aggressiveness, especially if they are hostile. Knowing how to argue properly may be a solution to otherwise hurtful aggressive tendencies. As a case in point, Dominick Infante, Teresa Chandler, and Jill Rudd studied husbands and wives in violent relationships and discovered that violent marriages are characterized by higher verbal aggressiveness and lower argumentativeness than are nonviolent ones.[17] It seems that many nonviolent spouses deal with their problems by arguing constructively, whereas violent spouses may be unable to solve their differences in this way.

Keep in mind that these four traits are variables. In other words, people differ in their predispositions to be assertive, argumentative, hostile, or ver-

bally aggressive. Some people often behave in one or more of these ways, and others seldom do. However, Infante is quick to point out that these traits do not always determine one's behavior. Highly aggressive people do not always aggress, and individuals who have little aggressiveness sometimes do act assertively, argumentatively, or even hostilely. Thus, these traits can also be states that are affected by the situation. For example, highly argumentative people will often refrain from arguing if they perceive that they cannot win or that winning may not be important, and highly hostile people will sometimes refrain from being hostile toward authority figures.

The Role of the Situation

The manner in which one communicates is only partially determined by traits. Indeed, your state of mind and communication behavior are very much affected by external factors, especially your perception of the situation. Perhaps the most well-developed program on the role of the situation is that of Michael Cody, Margaret McLaughlin, and their colleagues.[18] Their ideas are based on their own research and a copious review of other studies on this subject.

A communication situation is the entire communication event, including the participants (who), the setting (where), and the activities being done (what). Obviously, when you communicate in a situation, you take much of this overall situation into account, and your behavior is affected by it. This truism makes trait explanations inadequate by themselves to explain behavior. So, for example, someone who is typed as an aggressive individual would not always behave aggressively because of the constraints of various situations.

Individuals use their knowledge about the situation in a number of ways. They use it to evaluate other people in the situation. For example, in the classroom you will probably give a professor a cer-

17. Dominick A. Infante, Teresa A. Chandler, and Jill E. Rudd, "Test of an Argumentative Skill Deficiency Model of Interspousal Violence," *Communication Monographs* 56 (1989): 163–177.

18. Michael J. Cody and Margaret L. McLaughlin, "The Situation as a Construct in Interpersonal Communication Research," in *Handbook of Interpersonal Communication*, eds. M. L. Knapp and G. R. Miller (Beverly Hills, Calif.: Sage, 1985), pp. 263–312.

tain amount of deference just because of his or her role. In another situation such as church or a sporting event, you might perceive the same individual very differently. People also use situational knowledge to establish their communication goals. Why are they there, and what do they want to accomplish? Situational knowledge helps us answer such questions. Obviously, the way people communicate depends at least partially on their goals as defined in the situation.

One's manner and behavior are often affected by situational knowledge. How you see yourself within the situation, including what you believe your skills and abilities to be, affect how you define the situation, whether you choose to be part of it, and what kind of changes you might want to try to achieve within the situation. You may eagerly seek out certain situations such as leading a youth group or writing articles for the college magazine, and you might steer clear of other situations such as intercollegiate athletics or community activism.

Finally, and perhaps most importantly, people use their knowledge of the situation to guide their behavior. Will I try to persuade other people to change? How will I do so? Will I speak up? Will I remain quiet? Will I be witty and charming or strict and formal? You answer questions like these on the basis of your definition of the situation.

Of course, answers to questions such as these will vary from person to person, largely because of different traits. Here, we see most vividly the interaction between traits and situational factors. A person will not behave the same way at all times because of situational constraints, but on the other hand, different people will define those situational constraints somewhat differently because of their own individual differences.

Two general principles seem to govern communication behavior. First, how one chooses to communicate depends on how effective various strategies are believed to be within a particular situation. The same strategy, making an excuse perhaps, might work very well in one situation such as communicating with someone who is not very familiar with you, but not at all well in another such as communicating with a someone who knows you

well. Second, strategies are also chosen in terms of their cost. Within any situation one will choose those messages that are believed to maximize gains and minimize costs. In any given situation, you will adopt those communication strategies that you think will lead to the most beneficial outcomes with the least cost. So, for example, you will make an excuse because it is easy if you think it will be effective in helping you to save face, but you will probably not do so if you think it won't work. Or perhaps an excuse might be effective, but explaining it to the other person might require more effort than you are willing to put forth.

From their own and others' studies, Cody, McLaughlin, and their colleagues have identified six factors that probably enter into most perceptions of situations. These are intimacy, friendliness, pleasantness, apprehension, involvement, and dominance. Specific types of situations such as persuasive ones may have additional factors as well.

A more difficult question appears to be the relationship between such factors of situational perception and actual communication behavior. These researchers point out that we really do not know very well how to predict a person's behavior on the basis of his or her definition of the situation. Cody and several colleagues explored this issue in a study of over 1000 students in three states.[19] The researchers developed forty-two illustrative communication situations in which participants were trying to influence someone else, such as trying to talk their apartment owner into fixing the plumbing. Specifically, students were asked to think of a situation similar to one of these examples in which they had been personally involved. They were asked several questions about their perception of the situation and how they actually tried to persuade the other person. The researchers then examined the compliance-gaining messages used and categorized them into several types, such as giving evidence, indicating how the other person would benefit, or promising to do something in return.

19. Michael J. Cody et al., "Situation Perception and Message Strategy Selection," in *Communication Yearbook 9*, ed. M. L. McLaughlin (Beverly Hills, Calif.: Sage, 1986), pp. 390–422.

The researchers found that perceptions of the situation did make a difference in the kind of strategy used to gain compliance. For example, one is more apt to give evidence when one perceives that there will be resistance, when the intimacy level between the two communicators is low, and when people believe they have a right to ask for compliance. On the other hand, one is more apt to tell the other persons how they will benefit when the following conditions apply: (1) One's own benefits are small, (2) apprehension is low, (3) long-term relational consequences are expected, (4) resistance to persuasion is high, (5) one thinks he or she may not have the right to persuade, and (6) the other person is not dominant. Several other similar findings resulted from this study.

The work of Cody and his associates has advanced our understanding of these situational complexities, but even they admit that many questions remain unanswered. Not only do we need to know about how people interact behaviorally with their environments, but we also do not yet fully understand the processes that operate in communication message selection. Let us turn to this subject now.

Process Theories

Unlike trait and state theories, *process theories* attempt to explain the mechanism by which communicators produce messages, or as we will see in the following chapter, how they process information in the reception of messages. Here we will look at theories related to several processes—accommodating, assembling, constructing, and gaining compliance.

Accommodation

Howard Giles and his colleagues have developed speech accommodation theory to explain the ways in which communicators adjust their speech and other communicative behaviors in interaction with others.[20] Numerous researchers have observed that communicators often seem to copy one another's speech. For example, two speakers may adjust their accents to sound more alike, they may begin to speak at the same speed, or to use mirrorlike gestures. Sometimes speakers do just the opposite and actually exaggerate their differences. The process of *convergence*, or coming together, and *divergence*, or moving apart, is the subject of speech accommodation theory. Accommodation has been seen in almost all imaginable communication behaviors, including accent, rate, loudness, vocabulary, grammar, voice, gestures, and other features.

Convergence or divergence can be *mutual*, in which case both communicators come together or go apart, or it can be *nonmutual*, in which one person accommodates to or diverges from the other. Convergence can also be *partial* or *complete*. For example, one might speak somewhat faster to come closer to another person's speech rate or go all the way and speak just as fast as the other person.

Although accommodation may be done consciously, it is usually out of awareness. The use of accommodation is similar to any number of other highly functional but subconscious processes that are scripted. Scripts are sets of behavior that are enacted as a whole without having to attend to all the details of each behavior. People are probably more aware of their divergence than of their convergence.

Accommodation researchers have found that accommodation can be very important in communication. It can lead to social identity and bonding or disapproval and distance. For example, convergence often happens in situations in which individuals seek the approval of others. This can occur in groups that are already alike in certain ways because such groups consist of similar individuals who already can coordinate their actions. The

20. Giles and others have written extensively about speech accommodation theory. One of the most recent and complete expositions is Howard Giles, Anthony Mulac, James J. Bradac, and Patricia Johnson, "Speech Accommodation Theory: The First Decade and Beyond," in *Communication Yearbook 10*, ed. M. L. McLaughlin (Newbury Park, Calif.: Sage, 1987), pp. 13–48.

result of convergence can be increased attractiveness, predictability, intelligibility, and mutual involvement.

When persons converge, they rely on their perception of the other person's speech qualities. Often they are correct in their perception, but sometimes they are wrong, which can lead to negative results. For example, an individual sometimes converges not with the other person's actual speech but to a stereotype. This kind of accommodation can result from discrimination, as, for example, when a nurse speaks to an elderly patient using "baby talk" or when someone speaks loudly and slowly to a blind person.

Observing how people evaluate the convergence of others is interesting. Typically, some convergence is appreciated. You tend to respond favorably to someone who makes an attempt to speak in your style. But too much convergence can be evaluated negatively if it is viewed as inappropriate. People tend to appreciate convergence from others that is accurate, well intended, and appropriate in the situation.

Whether converging is evaluated positively or negatively depends in part on the attributed motive for doing so. Studies have shown that when listeners perceive that the speaker is intentionally speaking in a style close to their own, they will tend to evaluate the behavior positively, but when convergence is seen as out of the speaker's control, the convergence may criticized. Almost certainly, any convergence move that is seen as inappropriate in the situation or done out of ill will would be evaluated negatively. This would include, for example, mocking, teasing, insensitivity to social norms, or inflexibility.

Convergence is not always done to seek approval. Often higher-status speakers will slow their speech or use simpler vocabulary when talking with a lower-status individual in an attempt to increase understanding, whereas lower-status communicators will upgrade their speech to match the higher-status person, not to increase understanding, but to seek the approval of the high-status speaker.

Accommodation often seems to be associated with power. For example, in New York City where blacks are viewed as having more power than Puerto Ricans, the latter converge more to the accent of the former. In organizations, subordinates have been observed to converge with superiors more often than the opposite.

Convergence is far from an automatic strategy for identifying with other people. Although the rewards of speech convergence can be substantial, so are the costs. Accommodations require effort, even though they are often unconscious, and they may mean the loss of personal identity. Sometimes they are even viewed as abnormal and may be frowned on.

Instead of converging, people sometimes maintain their own style or actually change in the opposite direction. People will work to maintain their style when they want to symbolize their identity. This would be the case, for example, among members of an ethnic group with a strong accent, who work to perpetuate the accent in the face of threats from homogenizing influences outside. Divergence often functions to accentuate in-group identity vis-à-vis members of an out-group.

Sometimes members of a group will even accentuate their speech characteristics in a strange community to elicit sympathy from the host group. This is a kind of "self-handicapping" method that frees the speaker from responsibility for violation of certain social norms with which they may not be familiar. Sometimes, too, speakers will diverge from the style of other speakers in order to affect the others' behavior in some way. Teachers may deliberately talk above the heads of students in order to "challenge" the students to learn. You might speak extra slowly when talking with a very fast speaker in order to get him or her to slow down.

Action Assembly

One of the problems of cognition is to organize knowledge in order to act appropriately in given situations. *Action-assembly theory* has been developed by John Greene as a first step toward explaining possible structures and processes involved in the production of communicative behavior.[21] Action-assembly theory closely examines the ways in which knowledge is ordered and used.

The theory begins with the claim that individuals have *content knowledge* and *procedural knowledge*: They know *about* things and they know *how to do* things. Procedural knowledge consists of an awareness of the consequences of various actions in different situations. Our overall procedural knowledge consists of a large number of "procedural records," each of which is composed of knowledge about an action, its outcomes, and the situations in which it is appropriate. Because people remember the results of actions, they can behave effectively on future occasions.

For example, how do you know how to introduce yourself to another person at a party? From experience and watching others do it, you have knowledge of various procedures that could be used to do this. These memories tell you not only how to introduce yourself but also the possible outcomes of various methods and the situations in which they would be used. You would probably introduce yourself differently to a person you had never met than to someone you have met before. You have formal and informal methods of introducing yourself. You have methods you use when you really want to get to know someone, and other methods when you are merely fulfilling an obligation.

Thus, acting involves "assembling" appropriate possible actions. Out of all the actions in your procedural memory, you must select the most appropriate procedures in any situation. How do you do this? An action sequence is selected or triggered when the conditions and desired outcome are similar to those encountered by the individual on a prior occasion. In communication a number of outcomes may be desired, including the achievement of a particular objective with another person,

expressing information, managing conversation, producing intelligible speech, and other results. So when introducing yourself to another person, you may want to meet the other person, make yourself look good, and have a good time, all in one set of actions. You essentially assemble the procedures necessary to accomplish these objectives. This organized "plan" is called the *output representation.*

No single action can stand by itself. Every action implicates other actions in one way or another. To introduce yourself, you have to use a variety of actions from moving your vocal chords to using certain words and gestures. Actions, then, are integrated into a hierarchy of knowledge. Each piece of knowledge in the organization is a representation of something that needs to be done.

The most abstract level in the hierarchy is the *interactional representation*, or a sense of the overall objective to be achieved by the action within the communication itself, such as making an introduction. Next is *ideational representation*, or the ideas to be expressed in the course of achieving the interactional objectives. To continue our example, introducing yourself requires that you know your name and information about yourself. The third level is the *utterance representation*, which includes the linguistic requirements necessary to express the idea or content of the message. In other words, one must know how to use language appropriately in a given situation. Finally, the *sensorimotor representation* helps one activate the proper neural commands to produce the message, which may include use of the speech mechanism. The example of making an introduction is very simple, but the same general process is used in all communication actions, even the most complex ones such as giving a speech, managing a conflict, or writing a book.

Thus, the cognitive system must coordinate very different levels of behavior in a single action sequence, requiring knowledge of how to speak (sensorimotor), language structures (utterances), appropriate content (knowledge), and the larger goal-oriented interactional behavior. In the process of composing this paragraph, for example, my cognitive system had to integrate into a coherent action at least four levels of representation: typing

21. John O. Greene, "Action-Assembly Theory: Metatheoretical Commitments, Theoretical Propositions, and Empirical Applications," in *Rethinking Communication: Paradigm Exemplars*, eds. B. Dervin et al. (Newbury Park, Calif.: Sage, 1989), pp. 117–128; "A Cognitive Approach to Human Communication: An Action Assembly Theory," *Communication Monographs* 51 (1984): 289–306.

(sensorimotor), sentence structure (language), knowledge of action-assembly theory, and general strategy for communicating the theory clearly. All were stored in my procedural memory and were selected from a variety of possible representations.

Action assembly takes time and effort. Thinking is work. The more complex the assembly task, the more time and effort it takes. Introducing yourself is probably not as difficult as giving a speech. Even though communicators seem to respond to a situation immediately without effort, research shows that every response does take time, if only a fraction of a second, and that more complex tasks take more time than simple ones. You know from your own experience that you think through and struggle with communicating in situations with which you are unfamiliar. The difficulty in processing information in communication can be seen in the pausing and disfluency patterns of a person's speech. When people take a long time to say something, pause or stutter a lot, or generally seem confused, they are displaying some difficulty in integrating procedural knowledge and formulating an action. When people respond very quickly and fluently, they are demonstrating that the task is relatively easy for them in this situation.

Constructivism

This section deals with a theory that shows how understanding is constructed and how the structure of cognition affects message production. *Constructivism* is the label most commonly associated with this theory, which was developed by Jesse Delia and his colleagues.[22] This project has had immense impact on the field of communication. The theory suggests that individuals interpret and act according to conceptual categories in the cognitive system. This theory is like many other cognitive approaches in explaining that an event does not just present itself to the individual in raw form; rather, the person constructs experience according to the organization of the cognitive system.

Constructivism is based partially on George Kelly's theory of personal constructs.[23] Kelly proposes that persons understand experience by grouping events according to similarities. A construct is a distinction between opposites, such as tall-short, hot-cold, black-white, that is used to understand events and things. An individual's cognitive system consists of numerous such distinctions. By classifying an experience into categories, the individual gives meaning to the experience. So, for example, one may see mother as tall and father as short, coffee as hot and milk as cold, a favorite jacket as black and a favorite hat as white.

Constructs are organized into interpretive schemes, which identify what something is and place the object in a category. With interpretive schemes, we make sense out of an event by placing it in a larger context of meanings. Interpretive schemes are developed during the maturation of the individual according to the *orthogenetic principle*, by moving from relative simplicity and generality to relative complexity and specificity.[24] Thus, very young children have quite simple construct systems, and adults have much more sophisticated ones.

Constructivism has been included in this chapter because it is clearly a cognitive approach, but it recognizes at base that constructs have social origins; they are learned through interaction with other people. One's construct system is a direct result of a history of interaction in social groups

22. For a summary of the theory and its various tributaries and applications, see Brant R. Burleson, "The Constructivist Approach to Person-Centered Communication: Analysis of a Research Exemplar," in *Rethinking Communication: Paradigm Exemplars*, eds. B. Dervin et al. (Newbury Park, Calif.: Sage, 1989), pp. 29–46; Jesse G. Delia, "Interpersonal Cognition, Message Goals, and Organization of Communication: Recent Constructivist Research," in *Communication Theory: Eastern and Western Perspectives*, ed. D. L. Kincaid (San Diego: Academic Press, 1987), pp. 255–274; Jesse G. Delia, Barbara J. O'Keefe, and Daniel J. O'Keefe, "The Constructivist Approach to Communication," in *Human Communication Theory: Comparative Essays*, ed. F. E. X. Dance (New York: Harper & Row, 1982), pp. 147–191.

23. George Kelly, *The Psychology of Personal Constructs* (New York: North, 1955).

24. H. Werner, "The Concept of Development from a Comparative and Organismic Point of View," in *The Concept of Development*, ed. D. B. Harris (Minneapolis: University of Minnesota Press, 1957).

and cannot be divorced from social life. Consequently, culture seems especially significant in determining the meanings of events. Culture can influence the way in which communication goals are defined, how goals should be achieved, as well as the types of constructs employed in the cognitive schema.[25]

Although it acknowledges the impact of social interaction and culture on the cognitive system, constructivism has been a primarily psychological and cognitive endeavor. This theory deals primarily with individual differences in construct complexity and strategies used in communication.

Individuals with highly developed interpretive schemes make more discriminations than those who see the world simplistically. Although the construct system develops throughout childhood and adolescence as the person matures, even adults differ widely in their cognitive complexity. Also, different parts of the construct system of a single individual can also differ in complexity, so that you might have elaborate thoughts about music but simple ideas about international relations.

Because cognitive complexity plays an important role in communication, this concept is a mainstay of constructivism.[26] Complexity or simplicity in the system is a function of the relative number of constructs and the degree of differentiation one can make between the elements of experience. Individuals vary in their own cognitive complexity across topics and over time. The number of constructs used by an individual to organize a perceptual field is called *cognitive differentiation*. Cognitively sophisticated individuals can make more distinctions in a situation than can cognitively uncomplicated people.

Cognitive differentiation also affects the number of goals one can achieve through action. Often an action involves multiple intentions and may embody several strategies simultaneously. Messages vary in the extent to which they can achieve multiple, sometimes conflicting, objectives. Delia and his colleagues have shown that messages can be classified according to a hierarchy of complexity. Simple messages attack only one goal, more complex messages separate goals and deal with each in turn, and the most sophisticated messages actually integrate several goals in one message.[27] Goal achievement is often attached to one's own desires in a transaction. Simpleminded persuasive messages attempt only to achieve one's own desires without consideration of the other person's needs, whereas more adaptive, complex persuasive messages are designed to meet one's own needs and the needs of the other person or to transcend both by creating a new context.

For example, if you want to get a person to change his or her behavior, to stop smoking perhaps, you want to do this in a way that would help the other person protect his or her ego or save face. This would require you to achieve at least two objectives in the same message. Simple messages cannot do this, but more complex messages can be employed precisely for this purpose. Constructivists have found that one's tendency to help the other person save face is directly related to his or her construct differentiation.

Interpersonal constructs are especially important because they guide how we understand other people. Individuals differ in the complexity with which they view others. Cognitive simplicity leads to stereotyping other people, whereas differentiation allows more subtle and sensitive distinctions to be made.

The research of the constructivism team has shown that cognitive complexity in the interpersonal construct system generally leads to greater understanding of others' perspectives and better

25. For a discussion of the effects of culture on the cognitive system, see James L. Applegate and Howard E. Sypher, "A Constructivist Theory of Communication and Culture," in *Theories in Intercultural Communication*, eds. Y. Y. Kim and W. B. Gudykunst (Newbury Park, Calif.: Sage, 1988), pp. 41–65.

26. The idea of cognitive complexity was originally developed by Walter H. Crockett, "Cognitive Complexity and Impression Formation," in *Progress in Experimental Personality Research*, vol. 2, ed. B. A. Maher (New York: Academic Press, 1965), pp. 47–90. See also Harold M. Schroder, Michael S. Driver, and Siegfried Streufert, *Human Information Processing: Individuals and Groups Functioning in Complex Social Situations* (New York: Holt, Rinehart & Winston, 1967).

27. Multiple goal achievement is developed in detail by Barbara J. O'Keefe and Gregory J. Shepherd, "The Pursuit of Multiple Objectives in Face-to-Face Persuasive Interactions: Effects of Construct Differentiation on Message Organization," *Communication Monographs* 54 (1987): 396–419.

ability to frame messages in terms understandable to others, an ability called *perspective taking*. Perspective taking seems to lead to more sophisticated arguments and appeals.[28] Adjusting one's communication to others is referred to as *person-centered communication*. People vary in the extent to which they use person-centered messages, and higher-level cognitive differentiation leads to greater use of such messages.

Compliance gaining is one of the several types of communication that has been studied from a person-centered perspective.[29] Persuasive messages range from those that do not take the needs of other people into account to those that adapt in rather elaborate ways. On the simplest level, for example, one could attempt to achieve the single objective of compliance by commanding or threatening. On a more complex level, one might also try to help this person understand why compliance is necessary by offering reasons for complying. On an even higher level of complexity, a communicator could even try to elicit sympathy by building empathy or insight into the situation. As one's messages become more complex, they necessarily involve more goals.

As an example of how person-centered communication works, consider the study of Susan Kline and Janet Ceropski on doctor–patient communication.[30] This study involved forty-six medical students, who completed a variety of tests, participated in videotaped interviews with patients, and wrote statements on what they thought the purpose of medical interviews to be. The interviews were carefully examined by the researchers in terms of three types of communication—persuading patients to do something, handling patients' distress, and gathering information. Messages in each category were classified according to person centeredness. The person-centered messages used by the medical students were found to be more complex than messages that were not person-centered.

The researchers found that about 40 percent of the medical students were person-centered in persuading patients. These individuals explained why compliance was necessary and took patients' feelings into consideration. About 50 percent of the subjects used person-centered communication in dealing with distress by acknowledging rather than denying patients' feelings, helping patients to understand their discomfort, and giving advice for how to relieve the distress. Finally, about 70 percent of those studied used person-centered communication in gathering information. Their questions were more detailed, and they gave patients more leeway in telling their story.

This research confirmed that those who used person-centered strategies had more complex cognitive schema for understanding other people, and they were better able to take the perspective of others and to have empathy for others.

Recently, Barbara O'Keefe has suggested that different message strategies may embody more than mere differences in construct differentiation.[31] People may actually employ different message logics, which reflect varying conceptions of what communication itself is. O'Keefe outlines three possible message design logics. The *expressive logic* sees communication as a mode of self-expression for communicating feelings and thoughts. It results in messages that are open and reactive in nature, with little attention to the needs or desires of others. An example of a message resulting from this logic would be an angry response to a friend who forgot to get tickets to a concert:

> Now we are not going to get our tickets. I was counting on getting to go to this concert. This is my favorite group and I really really wanted to hear them.

28. This literature is reviewed by Claudia Hale, "Cognitive Complexity-Simplicity as a Determinant of Communication Effectiveness," *Communication Monographs* 47 (1980): 304–311.

29. See, for example, Jesse G. Delia, Susan L. Kline, and Brant R. Burleson, "The Development of Persuasive Communication Strategies in Kindergarteners Through Twelfth-Graders," *Communication Monographs* 46 (1979): 241–256; James L. Applegate, "The Impact of Construct System Development on Communication and Impression Formation in Persuasive Messages," *Communication Monographs* 49 (1982): 277–289.

30. Susan L. Kline and Janet M. Ceropski, "Person-Centered Communication in Medical Practice," in *Emergent Issues in Human Decision Making*, eds. G. M. Phillips and J. T. Wood (Carbondale: Southern Illinois University Press, 1984), pp. 120–141.

31. Barbara J. O'Keefe, "The Logic of Message Design: Individual Differences in Reasoning About Communication," *Communication Monographs* 55 (1988): 80–103.

I have been thinking about this for weeks. Nothing I really want to do ever works out. I am going to be mad at you for a long time about this.[32]

The *conventional logic* sees communication as a game to be played by rules. It also views communication as a means of self-expression, but it acknowledges the importance of communicating according to accepted rules and norms. It tends to be polite and appropriate. A response to the ticket situation from a conventional logic might go like this:

> It was your responsibility to pick up the tickets. Everyone decided what job they would do in organizing this evening, and that was the job you picked. So you will just have to figure out some way to get them yourself, even if you have to pay a taxi to deliver them.[33]

The *rhetorical logic* views communication as a way of changing the rules through negotiation. Messages designed with this logic tend to be flexible and insightful into the perspectives of other people. These three logics differ roughly from least person-centered to most person-centered as the following example of a rhetorical message illustrates:

> Gee, I'm sorry you have been so pressed. This really has put us in a pickle. I know what you can do. Bob has to go right by the ticket office on his way home from work. Call the ticket office and charge the tickets on your Master Card. Then call Bob and see if he can stop and pick up the tickets. Or maybe he could just pick you up and run you by the ticket office.[34]

Compliance Gaining

One of the most common communication situations is *compliance gaining*, or trying to get other people to do what you want them to do. This type of situation is one of the most researched areas in the field and as such requires special treatment here. A number of approaches have been taken to this topic, far too many to cover in this brief treat-

ment.[35] Here, we will look at three of the most influential.

Marwell and Schmitt. The prolific research program on compliance-gaining strategies in the communication field received its impetus from the groundbreaking studies of Gerald Marwell and David Schmitt.[36] These researchers isolated sixteen strategies they believed to be commonly used in gaining the compliance of other people. These include the following list:

- *Promising*   Promising a reward for compliance
- *Threatening*   Indicating that punishment will be applied for noncompliance
- *Showing expertise about positive outcomes*   Showing how good things will happen to those who comply
- *Showing expertise about negative outcomes*   Showing how bad things will happen to those who do not comply
- *Liking*   Displaying friendliness
- *Pregiving*   Giving a reward before asking for compliance
- *Applying aversive stimulation*   Applying punishment until compliance is received
- *Calling in a debt*   Saying the person owes something for past favors
- *Making moral appeals*   Describing compliance as the morally right thing to do
- *Attributing positive feelings*   Telling the other person how good he or she will feel if there is compliance
- *Attributing negative feelings*   Telling the other

32. Ibid., p. 100.

33. Ibid., p. 102.

34. Ibid., p. 103.

35. For some recent reviews of this work, see Daniel J. O'Keefe, *Persuasion: Theory and Research* (Newbury Park, Calif.: Sage, 1990), pp. 201–223; Michael G. Garko, "Perspectives on and Conceptualizations of Compliance and Compliance-Gaining," *Communication Quarterly* 38 (1990): 138–157; Gerald R. Miller, "Persuasion," in *Handbook of Communication Science*, eds. C. R. Berger and S. H. Chaffee (Newbury Park, Calif.: Sage, 1987), pp. 446–483; David R. Siebold, James G. Cantrill, and Renee A. Meyers, "Communication and Interpersonal Influence," in *Handbook of Interpersonal Communication*, eds. M. L. Knapp and G. R. Miller (Beverly Hills, Calif.: Sage, 1985), pp. 551–614.

36. Gerald Marwell and David R. Schmitt, "Dimensions of Compliance-Gaining Strategies: A Dimensional Analysis," *Sociometry* 30 (1967): 350–364.

person how bad he or she will feel if there is noncompliance
• *Positive altercasting* Associating compliance with people with good qualities
• *Negative altercasting* Associating noncompliance with people with bad qualities
• *Seeking altruistic compliance* Seeking compliance simply as a favor
• *Showing positive esteem* Saying that the person will be liked by others more if he or she complies
• *Showing negative esteem* Saying that the person will be liked less by others if he or she does not comply

Marwell and Schmitt use an exchange-theory approach: Compliance is an exchange for some other resources supplied by the compliance seeker. This is a common approach to a variety of social issues, and it rests on the assumption that people basically act to gain something from others in exchange for something else. Why might one comply with the requests of others? To gain esteem, approval, rewards, relief from obligations, positive identification, good feelings, and many other things. Such a model is inherently power-oriented. In other words, you can gain the compliance of others if you have sufficient resources to give them what they want. The power dimension of compliance gaining is discussed in more detail later in this section.

One of the most important theoretical questions about compliance-gaining tactics has been how to reduce the list of all possible tactics to a manageable set of general strategies or dimensions. A long list of how people persuade others does not tell you much more than you already know. A shorter list would crystallize the tactics into essential qualities, functions, goals, or some other set of dimensions that would help explain what people are actually accomplishing when they try to persuade other people. In an attempt to answer this question, Marwell and Schmitt asked subjects to apply the sixteen items to various compliance-gaining situations, and from these data the items were analyzed. Five general strategies (or clusters of tactics) emerged. These included *rewarding* (e.g., promis-

ing), *punishing* (e.g., threatening), *expertise* (e.g., showing expertise about positive outcomes), *impersonal commitments* (e.g., moral appeals), and *personal commitments* (e.g., debts).

These items and others like them have been analyzed by other researchers in a number of ways. It seems that the dimensions of compliance-gaining strategies change with every study that has been done, and we do not have sufficient space to describe all of these. We turn now to one of the most prominent challenges to the Marwell and Schmitt typology.

Schenck-Hamlin, Wiseman, and Georgacarakos. Concerned about the lack of a theoretical basis for taxonomies such as Marwell and Schmitt's, William Schenck-Hamlin, Richard Wiseman, and G. N. Georgecarakos developed a scheme based on strategies that subjects indicated that they actually used.[37] Specifically, four elements are isolated in this model. The first is the degree to which the persuader reveals the compliance-gaining goals. In other words, does the communicator make his or her objective known? Some strategies are straightforward and *direct*, others are *indirect*, and still others are *misleading*. You might, for example, ask your roommate directly to turn off the stereo because you have to study. Or you might go about it indirectly by hinting that you need some peace and quiet. Or your might be downright deceptive and tell your roommate that the neighbors had complained about the noise.

The second element of compliance gaining is whether the strategy is based on *sanctions* such as rewards and punishments or on *reasons* and *explanations*. For example, you might tell your roommate that if she does not turn off the stereo, you will be noisy when she wants to study. This threat is a kind of sanction. Other strategies are based on explana-

37. William J. Schenck-Hamlin, Richard L. Wiseman, and G. N. Georgacarakos, "A Model of Properties of Compliance-Gaining Strategies," *Communication Quarterly* 30 (1982): 92–100; Richard L. Wiseman and William Schenck-Hamlin, "A Multidimensional Scaling Validation of an Inductively-Derived Set of Compliance-Gaining Strategies," *Communication Monographs* 48 (1981): 251–270.

tion and reasons. For example, you might tell your roommate how hard it is for you to study when there is a lot of noise.

The third element of compliance gaining is whether the rationale for the required action is stated or implied. A simple request implies a reason but does not state it, whereas an explanation actually provides the rationale. This is the difference between simply saying, "Please turn off the stereo," versus, "Could you turn off the stereo 'cause I have a hard time studying around noise."

The fourth element of compliance gaining has to do with who, if anyone, controls the situation. In the case of a threat or promise, for example, the persuader controls the outcome. In the case of a guilt appeal, the control is in the hands of the other person. When you suggest that your roommate will feel guilty if she does not turn off the stereo, you are relying on a state of affairs that she herself controls. Table 6.1 summarizes these elements and the fourteen associated compliance-gaining tactics. Table 6.2 gives some examples of each tactic in the stereo case.

Wheeless, Barraclough, and Stewart. One of the most comprehensive analyses of the compliance-gaining literature is that of Lawrence Wheeless, Robert Barraclough, and Robert Stewart, who review and integrate the variety of compliance-gaining schemes.[38] These researchers believe that compliance-gaining messages are best classified according to the kinds of power employed by communicators when attempting to gain the compliance of another individual. Power is access to influential resources, and it is a result of interpersonal perception: People have as much power as others perceive that they have.

Wheeless and his colleagues isolate three general types of power. The first is the perception that someone can *manipulate behavior consequences* or a person's expectation about the outcome of a certain course of action. Parents often use this kind of

38. Lawrence R. Wheeless, Robert Barraclough, and Robert Stewart, "Compliance-Gaining and Power in Persuasion," in *Communication Yearbook 7*, ed. R. N. Bostrom (Beverly Hills, Calif.: Sage, 1983), pp. 105–145.

power in administering punishments and rewards. The second kind of power is the perception that a person is in an important *relational position* or is a source of identification with another individual. Here, the powerful person can identify certain elements of the relationship to bring about compliance or can act as a model or example to others. For example, people in romantic relationships often attribute a great deal of power to their partners because they fear that if things don't go exactly right, the partner will leave them.

The third type of power involves the perceived ability to *define values* and/or obligations. For example, one might be able to relate another person's behavior to something that should be done because of shared values.

In a compliance gaining situation then, one assesses his or her power and chooses tactics that invoke that power. Wheeless lists a number of tactics that are associated with the three classes of power. For example, the ability to affect another person's expectations and consequences will lead to such tactics as promises, threats, and warnings. The ability to affect the relationship with the other person may lead one to choose such tactics as expressing liking for the other person, attributing positive or negative esteem, making emotional appeals, flattering, and so on. The third category of power—defining values and obligations—will give rise to the use of moral appeals, debt, guilt, and other similar techniques.

Commentary and Critique

Communication is a process involving the exchange of messages, and it is not surprising that this topic has received so much attention by communication scholars. Although message production can be understood from a variety of perspectives—including social, interpretive, and critical, all of which will be discussed in some detail later in this book—the predominant approach has been individual and cognitive.

Table 6.1   Definitions of the Strategies

I. Sanction Strategies
A. Reward Appeals
  1. Rewards are controlled by the actor.
     a. *Ingratiation:* Actor's profferred [sic] goods, sentiments, or services precede the request for compliance. They range from subtle verbal or nonverbal positive reinforcement to more blatant formulas of "apple polishing" or "brown-nosing." Manipulations in behavior include gift giving, supportive listening, love and affection, or favor-doing. Form: Present reward from actor implies compliance.
     b. *Promise:* Actor's profferred [sic] goods, sentiments, or services are promised the target in exchange for compliance. This may include a bribe or trade. A variant is compromise, in which gains and losses are perceived in relative terms, so that both actor and target give in order to receive. Sometimes compromise is called trading-off, log-rolling, or finding a "middle-of-the-road" solution. Form: Compliance implies future reward from actor.
     c. *Debt:* Actor recall obligations owed him or her as a way of inducing the target to comply. Past debts may be as tangible as favors or loans, or as general as the catch-all "After all I've done for you . . ." Form: Past reward from actor implies compliance
  2. Rewards are controlled by the target.
     Esteem: Target's compliance will result in automatic increase of self-worth. Actor's appeal promises this increase in areas of target's power, success, status, moral/ethical standing, attention and affection of others, competence, ability to handle failure and uncertainty well, and/or attempts to aspire. "Everyone loves a winner" is the fundamental basis for appeal. "Just think how good you will feel if you would do this." Form: Compliance implies future reward because of target's action.
  3. Rewards are controlled by circumstance.
     Allurement: Target's reward arises from persons or conditions other than the actor. The target's compliance could result in a *circumstance* in which other people become satisfied, pleased, or happy. These positive attitudes will be beneficial to the target. "You'll always have their respect" is an example. Form: Compliance implies future reward because of the action of forces other than the actor or target.
B. Punishment Appeals
  1. Punishments are controlled by the actor.
     a. *Aversive stimulation:* Actor continuously punishes target, making cessation contingent on compliance. Pouting, sulking, crying, acting angry, whining, "the silent treatment," and ridicule would all be examples of aversive stimulation. Form: Non-compliance implies present punishment.
     b. *Threat:* Actor's proposed actions will have negative consequences for the target if he or she does not comply. Black-mailing or the suggestion of firing, violence, or breaking off a friendship would all be examples of threats. Form: Non-compliance implies future punishment.
  2. Punishments are controlled by the target.
     Guilt: Target's failure to comply will result in automatic decrease of self-worth. Areas of inadequacy might include professional ineptness, social irresponsibility, or ethical/moral transgressions. Form: Non-compliance implies future punishment because of target's actions.
  3. Punishments are controlled by circumstance.
     Warning: Target's punishment arises from persons or conditions other than the actor. The target's non-compliance could lead to a *circumstance* in which other people become embarrassed, offended, or hurt. Resulting negative attitudes from those people will have harmful consequences for the target. "You'll make the boss unhappy" and "What will the neighbors say" are examples. Form: Non-compliance implies future punishment because of the action of forces other than the actor or target.

II. Altruism Strategies
  Altruism: Actor requests the target to engage in behavior designed to benefit the actor rather than the target. Asking the target for help is typical. Intensity of the appeal may be manipulated by making the target feel unselfish, generous, self-sacrificing, heroic or helpful. "It would help me if you would do this," and "Do a favor for me" exemplify the direct approach of the altruistic strategy. Two variants are sympathy ("I am in big trouble, so help me.") and empathy ("You would ask for help if you were me.") Form: Comply for my sake.

(Continues)

Table 6.1   Definitions of the Strategies (continued)

III. Argument Strategies
   A. Response controlled by the Rationale, and Rationale *not* revealed by the actor.
      Direct request: The actor simply asks the target to comply. The motivation or inducement for complying is not provided by the actor, but must be inferred by the target. In some cases the actor's message appears to offer as little influence as possible, so that the target is given the maximum latitude of choice. "If I were you, I would . . ." and "Why don't you think about . . ." are instances of direct request. In other cases the strategy takes on a form where the actor demands the target's compliance. Examples would be "I want you to do this" and "Do this." Form: You (might) comply.
   B. Response controlled by the Rationale, and Rationale revealed by the actor.
      Explanation: One of several reasons are advanced for believing or doing something. A reason may include the following: (1) credibility, "I know from experience." Form: The reason for complying is my trustworthiness, integrity, exemplary action or expertise; (2) reference to a value system, "It's in the best interests to . . ." Form: Since we value this, you should comply; (3) inference from empirical evidence, "Everything points to the logic of this step." Form: The reason for complying is based on the following evidence.
   C. Response controlled by Rationale; situational context revealed by actor.
      Hinting: Actor represents the situational context in such a way that the target is lead [sic] to conclude the desired action or response. Rather than directly requesting the desired response, the actor might say, "It sure is hot in here," rather than directly asking the target to turn down the heat. Form: Given this context, target should infer desired response.

IV. Circumvention Strategies
   Deceit: Actor gains target's compliance by intentionally *misrepresenting* the characteristics or consequences of the desired response. "It's easy," when in fact it is neither simple nor easy. "By doing this, you'll be handsomely rewarded," but the actor does not have the ability to give that reward. Form: Given false rationale or reward, compliance is requested.

The theories summarized in this chapter see message generation as an individual process leading to observable behaviors in the form of messages. Some of these theories focus on the traits of individuals and how they are correlated with various message behaviors, others deal with the effects of the situation on message behavior, and still others concentrate on the actual cognitive processes that operate in the production of messages.

Although these theories have many differences, they share a common concern for behavior and the generative mechanisms that produce it. These concerns are not new. Indeed, the behavioral and cognitive traditions have dominated the human sciences throughout the twentieth century. For the first half of the century, theorists were preoccupied with behavioristic explanations and with cognitive ones in the second half. Cognitive explanations do not abandon concern for behavior but attempt to explain it on a deeper, more complex level than was possible during earlier times.

The individualistic approach common in the study of communication, indeed in the behavioral and social sciences at large, is understandable in our cultural milieu. Western thought since the enlightenment (eighteenth century) has been dominated by the individual. The autonomous person is the primary unit of analysis in much Western, especially American, thinking.[39] We naturally

39. See, for example, Robert N. Bellah et al. *Habits of the Heart* (Berkeley: University of California Press, 1985); Alistair MacIntyre, *After Virtue* (Notre Dame, Ind.: University of Notre Dame Press, 1984); Floyd W. Matson, *The Idea of Man* (New York: Delacorte Press, 1976). A critique of the assumptions of the individual mind is presented in Rom Harré, "Language Games and Texts of Identity," in *Texts of Identity*, eds. J. Shotter and K. Gergen (London: Sage, 1989), pp. 20–35.

tend to see persons as entities with characteristics that lead them to behave in independent ways. We view the single human mind as the locus for processing and understanding information and generating messages. It is hardly surprising, then, that psychological explanations have been so appealing to many communication scholars.

Yet the individualistic approach by no means exhausts the ways in which communication and other social processes can be understood. Ironically, what distinguishes communication is something that happens between people, and communication cannot be explained solely from the perspective of the individual mind. Indeed, many believe that strictly psychological explanations miss the target completely. This point of view is explored in greater detail in Chapters 8 and 9.

Psychological theories of communication respond to this criticism in two ways. One is to acknowledge the social nature of communication but to argue that social explanations by themselves are also inadequate. Communication in this view is both social and individual. The individual is involved in the process and must be studied. Focusing on the individual does not negate the value of social theories, but it does provide a vital link in our overall understanding of communication.[40]

The second answer to the criticism is to refute it straightforwardly. Although communication involves people acting together in some fashion, everything that happens in this process is filtered through and generated by the separate minds of the individuals involved. Although the outcome of communication may be social in nature, its ulti-

40. For an example of this response, see Dean E. Hewes and Sally Planalp, "The Individual's Place in Communication Science," in *Handbook of Communication Science*, eds. C. R. Berger and S. H. Chaffee (Newbury Park, Calif.: Sage, 1987), pp. 146–183.

Table 6.2   Persuasive Messages for the Stereo Situation

---

1. *Ingratiation:* I would be nice and polite to my roommate, then ask her to turn off the stereo.

2. *Promise:* I would promise to do a favor for my roommate if she will turn off the stereo now.

3. *Debt:* I would recall past favors I've done and say my roommate owes me a few hours of quiet.

4. *Esteem:* I would tell my roommate that it would be very thoughtful of her to turn off the stereo.

5. *Allurement:* I would tell my roommate that our apartment will be a more comfortable place for us to study if the stereo is turned off.

6. *Aversive Stimulation:* I would act irritated toward my roommate until she turns off the stereo.

7. *Threat:* I would tell my roommate to turn off the stereo now or I will not cooperate when she wants to study.

8. *Guilt:* I would tell my roommate that it was inconsiderate of her to play the stereo while I'm trying to study.

9. *Warning:* I would tell my roommate that our neighbors will complain if she does not turn off the stereo.

10. *Altruism:* I would ask my roommate to turn off the stereo for my sake.

11. *Direct Request:* I would simply ask my roommate to turn off the stereo.

12. *Explanation:* I would explain to my roommate that the stereo's volume is too loud to study by.

13. *Hinting:* I would drop subtle hints about how hard it is to study.

14. *Deceit:* I would lie, implying that our neighbors had complained about the loud stereo.

From *Communication Monographs*, "A Multidimensional Scaling Validation of an Inductively-Derived Set of Compliance-Gaining Strategies," by Richard L. Wiseman and William Schenck-Hamlin. Copyright © 1981. Used by permission of the publisher.

mate genesis is individual, making psychological explanation crucial.[41]

Psychological theories of communication are of three types—traits, states, and processes. Trait and state theories deal with dispositions of individuals and the correlates of these dispositions. Process theories attempt to explain the mechanisms that are employed in processing information and in acting on the basis of that information. Although most theories of message production and processing focus on one or more of these types of explanation, few deal strictly with only one. For example, the theory of communication apprehension deals with the state of apprehension in its various forms, only one of which is traitlike.

Trait theories of communication abound. Not only have "communication traits" been developed, but much research has made use of other related traits such as self-monitoring, self-esteem, and dogmatism. Here, we can only present a few of the more prominent trait theories, and these include strictly communication traits. In this chapter, communication apprehension is treated as a trait theory because most of the work in this area has concentrated on traitlike communication apprehension. We also discuss communicator style, aggressiveness, and rhetorical sensitivity. In this chapter constructivism is treated as a process theory, although it is heavily involved with the trait of cognitive complexity.

Most of these theories have proved interesting and useful; but like most theories that concentrate mostly on traits, they do not go far enough in explaining the cognitive processes involved in the linkage between traits and actions. Dean Hewes and Sally Planalp make this point in rather strong terms:

> Predispositions do not explain much. Whenever trait theorists have been pressed to explain why a trait works, they have been forced to look for the mechanisms *behind* that trait, mechanisms outside the realm of predispositions that almost always involve processes

of interpretation and production of behavior or adaptation. Trait approaches, when successful, *do* warn us that something about individuals is the locus of causality for social action, but by oversimplifying explanations of individuals' capabilities they do not take us far enough. They tell us *that* individuals are important in the study of human communication but not *how* or *why*.[42]

Communication apprehension illustrates this weakness. Although McCroskey has offered an explanation of how apprehension is learned, there has been little explication of the cognitive processes involved in communication avoidance. In fact, the project has taken a rather behavioral tack in defining, measuring, and treating communication apprehension, without a great deal of conceptual explanation of the phenomenon.

To address the issue more fully, these researchers could relate communication apprehension to a variety of general cognitive theories. For example, how does communication apprehension affect one's constructs of the communication situation? Or, inversely, how does an apprehensive individual conceptualize communication? How are communication action plans and their assembly affected by apprehension, or, conversely, how is apprehension itself a cognitive definition within some larger action-assembly set?[43]

Trait theories, although they do not ignore the situation, certainly downplay it. If a trait is stable across contexts, then by definition it will usually override situational factors. The entire idea of testing for a trait is predicated on this assumption. And yet much research such as that of Cody and McLaughlin shows that people do behave differently in different situations. A natural theoretical tension exists between trait explanations and situational ones. A challenge for both trait and situa-

---

41. For an example of this point of view, see Greene, "Action-Assembly Theory."

42. Hewes and Planalp, "Individual's Place."

43. Actually, this problem has been studied briefly by action-assembly researchers, not CA researchers. See John O. Greene and Glenn G. Sparks, "Explication and Test of a Cognitive Model of Communication Apprehension: A New Look at an Old Construct," *Human Communication Research* 9 (1983): 349–366.

tional theories is to deal with this tension in some way.[44]

One answer to this dilemma is to combine trait and situational explanations, suggesting that a certain amount of variation is caused by situational factors and another portion of variation by traits. This solution is inherently problematic because of the assumption in trait measurement of stability. Trait instruments are designed and tested to capture stability, and correlating such a measure with other measures of situational difference is methodologically and conceptually inconsistent.

Trait theories are designed to identify qualities in persons. This is a semantic process. In other words, the theorist must label the qualities believed to exist. Thus, like all theoretical concepts, traits are constructed by the theorist. Indeed, some sophisticated data analysis will be required to verify the fit of the hypothesized trait to research subjects' actual behaviors and perceptions, but ultimately a name is attached and an abstraction is reified.

This process of construction can lead to problems. One is clarity and distinctiveness of traits. For example, what is the difference between communication apprehension, shyness, reticence, and avoidance? Are these the same trait, similar ones, or are they conceptually different? Among communication apprehension researchers, little agreement exists on the overall dimensions that bind this cluster of variables.[45]

Confusion can easily result from labeling. For example, Infante divides aggression into four categories of traits—assertiveness, argumentativeness, hostility, and verbal aggressiveness. Here, the term *aggression* is used to label both positive and negative traits, but *verbal aggressiveness* labels only a negative trait. How, then, can assertive and argumentative behaviors, which are largely verbal, be positive? This may sound like a word game, but it illustrates the kinds of semantic difficulties that trait labeling can involve.

A second problem created by trait construction is the endless number of traits that can and are "discovered." Virtually any tendency can be defined as a trait. According to trait theory, a person is not only a bundle of traits but a very large bundle at that. How can we say in any given situation which traits predominate over others, and, indeed, how can any trait predominate over another if traits are stable across contexts?

The key question for evaluating trait theories, then, is not whether the traits actually exist but how useful they are in communication scholarship, teaching, and intervention. What are the limits of the utility of trait definition? We know, for example, that communication apprehension has been very useful for communication teachers who must deal with a practical difficulty that many students face in communication situations.

The third problem resulting from the constructed nature of traits is their value orientation. Trait theories often originate in an attempt to identify individuals who have particular positive or negative communication qualities. This is certainly the case with at least three of the theories discussed in this chapter—communication apprehension, rhetorical sensitivity, and aggressiveness. Other trait theories end up making value judgments by virtue of the correlations discovered in research. The results of research on communicator style and cognitive complexity have been applied, at least implicitly, in this way.

Consequently, trait definitions are often value-laden. This feature makes such theories normative, or prescriptive, in orientation. For example, we learn from the theories in this chapter that it is better to be low in communication apprehension than to be high; it is better to be rhetorically adaptive than to be a noble self; it is better to be argumentative and assertive than to be hostile and verbally aggressive; it is better to have more construct dif-

44. These issues are explored by Peter A. Anderson, "The Trait Debate: A Critical Examination of the Individual Differences Paradigm in the Communication Sciences," in *Progress in Communication Sciences*, eds. B. Dervin and M. J. Voigt (Norwood, N.J.: Ablex, 1986).

45. A critique of this line of work can be found in Gerald R. Miller, "Some (Moderately) Apprehensive Thoughts on Avoiding Communication," in *Avoiding Communication: Shyness, Reticence, and Communication Apprehension*, eds. J. A. Daly and J. C. McCroskey (Beverly Hills, Calif.: Sage, 1984), pp. 237–246.

ferentiation than less; and it is probably better to have a dramatic style than a nondramatic one (at least if you are a teacher).

Normative theories have a place and can serve very positive functions in the study of communication. Indeed, some argue that all theories are at least implicitly value-laden and ideological, as we will see in Chapter 11. A potential problem occurs when one confuses the researcher's value concept with an objective trait. The way in which traits are described and measured will often lead the reader to believe that something in the person is being discovered objectively, when in fact the researcher has carefully designed a test to find instances of thoughts, behaviors, and feelings that exemplify the theorist's own positive and negative values.

This state of affairs can create theoretical difficulties. What, for example, do we do with people who display a negative trait? Because traits are defined as stable predispositions, do we merely condemn and avoid these individuals, or do we reform them? If people can change their traits—and most trait theorists would at least entertain the possibility—then perhaps the trait is merely a state. Then the important theoretical questions deal with how, when, and under what conditions people behave one way as opposed to another.

The theory of rhetorical sensitivity makes an excellent case in point. This theory arose as a reaction to the humanistic movement of the 1960s and 1970s, which was dominated by what Hart and his colleagues came to call the noble self. Hart and Burks clearly advocate rhetorical sensitivity over other possible responses.

The theory treats rhetorical sensitivity as a trait, implying that individuals may exercise little choice over whether they are noble selves, rhetorical reflectors, or rhetorically sensitive individuals, yet the very idea of rhetorical sensitivity implies change and choice. Indeed, the original formulation arose from a desire to help people become more effective communicators. There is a definite change in the tone of reporting used by Hart and his associates in the early articles and the later ones. The original response to humanistic psychology was quite pejorative in tone, whereas the later

research report on the RHETSEN scale was stated in the vocabulary of objective realism.

Is rhetorical sensitivity a trait or is it a desired state? The theory is unclear on this question. If rhetorical sensitivity is a trait, then RHETSEN tells us who is good and who is bad at communication according to the authors' ideology of effectiveness. A particular danger of this theory is that it identifies rhetorical sensitivity (a valued trait) and its foils (disvalued traits) with certain groups of people of particular religions, geographic locations, cultural identities, and occupational affiliations. Does this mean that certain classes and groups of people are better communicators than others?

These difficulties raise the point that "traits" such as rhetorical sensitivity might be better conceptualized as transitory states. This shift opens a variety of research possibilities designed to discover whether, or under what conditions, an individual may act as noble self, rhetorical reflector, or rhetorically sensitive person. Such an approach would lead us to ask under what conditions people are assertive, argumentative, hostile, or verbally aggressive. We would want to know what leads people to be dramatic, attentive, or open.

Process theories are designed in part to overcome many of the problems encountered by trait theories. Three kinds of process theories are encountered in this chapter. The first, represented by compliance-gaining research, consists of observing behavioral regularities. These theories describe what people do, in this case, what messages they use to gain compliance. Often such theories deduce the implicit strategic choices people are making on the basis of an analysis of message types. The work of Schenck-Hamlin and his colleagues illustrates this move well. This theory shows that people choose between direct, indirect, and deceptive options; that they choose between sanctions and arguments; and that they decide whether to use messages that maintain or abdicate control in some way. The Wheeless group makes the same kind of move with power, indicating what power choices people have available to them.

By inferring strategic choice from behavior, both theories are "cognitive" in a weak sense. The problem here is that you can never be sure, based on an external analysis of behavior, what actual cognitive mechanisms are in operation. Just because one makes a promise, for example, does not mean that the individual has strategically chosen to be direct, to use sanctions, and to maintain control over the consequences of interaction. In fact, some entirely different set of dimensions may have been operating.

The second type of process theory goes one step further to correlate message choices with other behaviors and traits. Speech accommodation theory and constructivism are examples. The former looks at the relationship between accommodation and a variety of social functions, and the latter associates cognitive complexity with message production. Unlike theories of the first type, these actually measure some states of mind or perceptions in some way and correlate those with observed messages or communication behaviors. In fact, the associations observed between message choices and other variables can be taken as evidence that the proposed cognitive mechanism is valid. Indeed, constructivism has done this again and again by correlating perspective taking with cognitive complexity.

The third kind of process theory represented here attempts to explain the cognitive mechanism that generates actions. Action-assembly theory is an example. This kind of problem is very difficult to study. The behaviorists were correct in asserting that cognitive processes cannot be observed directly. Indeed, one reason why so much trait research has been done is that it is relatively easy in comparison to cognitive process research.

All cognitive research involves indirect observation and a great deal of inference. The theorist posits certain cognitive mechanisms and looks for evidence of them in behavior. Action-assembly research, for example, looks for differences in the amount of time it takes to process information in difficult versus simple tasks. Because the action-assembly process takes time, these differences are taken as evidence for the existence of the proposed mechanism. The problem is that such evidence indicates only that the proposed model could be operating, not that it is operating. Many other cognitive models might lead to the same behavioral differences.

The coverage of this chapter is admittedly limited. This chapter is the first in a two-chapter set on theories of message production, reception, and processing. As such, it tells only part of the story of how people process information to generate and understand messages. Although it is necessary to divide this material in some way in order to study it, these chapters should be read in concert with each other. Together, they present a variety of interrelated theories on the role of the individual in communication. To complete the picture, we turn now to theories of message processing and communication outcomes.

CHAPTER 7

Theories of Message Reception and Processing

This is the second chapter in a two-part series on behavioral and cognitive theories of message production and processing. In Chapter 6 we dealt with theories explaining how messages are produced. Here we concentrate on how they are received and processed. The central question of the theories in this chapter is how human beings come to understand, organize, and use the information contained in messages.

These theories emerge from the same behavioral and cognitive traditions discussed previously. They are interested, in one way or another, in the relationship between information inputs, processing, and outputs. The amount of theorizing on this topic is vast, and we can only touch on it here. This chapter includes some classic treatments of the subject of message processing as well as some recent extensions.

Most of the theories in this chapter are firmly in the cognitive tradition, which has been described in Chapters 1 and 6. Briefly, cognition is the study of thinking, or information processing. Dean

Hewes and Sally Planalp have provided a useful summary of some cognitive research as it relates to communication.[1] According to these authors, cognition requires two central elements—knowledge structures and cognitive processes.

Knowledge structures are the organization of information in the person's cognitive system, the body of knowledge that a person has accrued. Even the simplest messages require much information to understand, and that is provided in the individual's knowledge structure. As important as the content of one's knowledge is its organization. Pieces of information are connected to one another in particular ways, and one person's organization may be different from another's. These organizational patterns, which have been called such names as *scripts*

---

1. Dean E. Hewes and Sally Planalp, "The Individual's Place in Communication Science," in *Handbook of Communication Science*, eds. C. R. Berger and S. H. Chaffee (Newbury Park, Calif.: Sage, 1987), pp. 146–183; Sally Planalp and Dean E. Hewes, "A Cognitive Approach to Communication Theory: Cogito Ergo Dico?," in *Communication Yearbook 5*, ed. M. Burgoon (New Brunswick, N.J.: Transaction, 1982), pp. 49–78.

and *schemas*, determine in large measure how one sees the world and how messages will be perceived.

Cognitive processes are the mechanisms by which information is handled in the mind. Hewes and Planalp outline seven major interrelated processes, the first of which is focusing. *Focusing* is a process of attending to certain details of information. How and what is processed depends on what one pays attention to, and the overall impact of a message depends ultimately on this element.

The second process is *integration*, or making connections between pieces of information, and is the process of incorporating what is seen and heard into the overall organization of knowledge. The third is *inference*, a "filling in" process, in which a person makes assumptions about unobserved things on the basis of things that are observed.

The fourth and fifth processes involve memory—*storage* and *retrieval*. The knowledge structure must be stored for future use, and it must be remembered appropriately. Storage and retrieval, or memory, are essential for all other cognitive processes.

The sixth and seventh processes, *selection* and *implementation*, also go together. Selection is choosing behavior from one's repertoire, and implementation is acting in accord with the chosen behavior, doing it. In actual practice these elements of knowledge structures and cognitive processing cannot be separated: Each influences the other. All theories in this chapter address one or more of these elements, although their views differ substantially.

The chapter is divided into three segments. The first deals with processes of *interpretation*, which involves understanding and meaning. The theories summarized here show how meaning develops and the dimensions of meaning, how the content of messages and intentions of communicators are understood, how the causes of behavior are assessed, and how and why people reinterpret messages.

The second section deals with *information organization*. These theories tell us how information is integrated into the cognitive system and how it affects attitudes, how we think about information

that relates to our attitudes, and how consistency is used as an organizing principle.

The third section of the chapter relates to the process of making *judgments*. These theories deal with how information is compared to what we already know and expect, the role of deviations from expectations, and how the value of information is assessed.

Message Interpretation

Interpretation is a process of assigning meaning and of understanding experience. Chapter 10 presents a number of theories of interpretation from a textual and philosophical perspective, but in this chapter we approach the subject psychologically.

The theories in this section touch on four aspects of interpretation central to communication. The first is the meanings assigned to concepts. The second deals with understanding communicators' intentions. The third has to do with understanding the causes of behavior, and the fourth relates to the recognition of bias and inaccuracy in messages.

Interpreting Concepts: Osgood on Meaning

As a behaviorist, Charles Osgood is especially interested in how meanings are learned and how they relate to internal and external behavior. His theory is one of the most elaborate of the behavioral theories of language and meaning and has its basis in both the behavioral and cognitive traditions.[2] Osgood follows the classical learning tradition, which teaches that learning is a process of developing new internal and external behavioral associations. In this tradition learning theory begins with the assumption that individuals respond to stimuli in the environment. Osgood believes that the basic S–R association is responsible for the establishment of meaning. Although

2. Charles Osgood, "On Understanding and Creating Sentences," *American Psychologist* 18 (1963): 735–751.

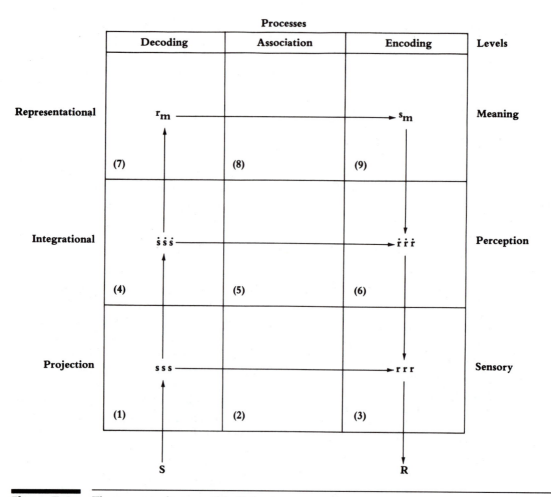

Figure 7.1   Three-stage mediation model of behavior.

The letter s refers to internal stimuli, the letter r to internal responses, both differentiated by level. The letters S and R refer to external stimulus and response.

individuals can respond overtly to actual environmental stimuli, they also have an internal representation of the stimulus and response. The uppercase letters S and R represent the overt stimulus and response, and the lowercase letters s and r designate the internal representation. Meaning occurs on this internal (s–r) level.

Osgood proposes a three-stage behavioral model, illustrated in Figure 7.1.[3] This model can be used to analyze any behavior, but he applies it to language

3. Ibid., p. 740.

and meaning in particular. Three basic processes are involved: encoding (receiving stimuli), association (pairing stimuli and responses), and decoding (responding). These processes occur on one of three levels, depending on the complexity of the behavior involved. The *projection level* is the simple neural pathway system between sensor and effector organs such as eye and hand. Behavior on this level is reflexive, such as knee jerks and eye blinks. Here the stimulus and response are linked automatically and directly. On the *integration level*, the s–r link is not automatic. Stimulus and response must be integrated by the brain through perceived association. An example is the routine greeting ritual: "How are you?" "I am fine."

The *representational level* is the level on which meaning occurs. The stimulus from the environment is projected onto the brain, where an internal response leads to an internal stimulus (meaning), which in turn leads to the individual's overt response. Osgood sees the first level as sensory, the second as perceptual, and the third as meaningful.

The internal response or meaning, then, is a learned association between certain actual responses to the object and a sign of the object on the representational level. Thus, the sign such as a word will elicit a particular meaning or set of meanings, which stem from the association of the sign and the object.

To use a rather dramatic example, suppose that a dog bit you recently. In the immediate future, a picture of the dog, the sight of another dog, or even the word *dog* will elicit an image (r_m) in your head that influences how you will respond. This internal response (fear or pain) is part of your meaning for the sign. In real life, meanings are more complex than in this example, but they are formed, Osgood believes, through the same basic associational process.

Figure 7.2 illustrates the development of meaning by associating a sign with an environmental stimulus. This figure shows the development of a sign $\boxed{S}$ as the result of its association with a natural stimulus S. A portion of one's complex response to the natural stimulus R_T becomes represented in the form of an internal response r_m, which in turn becomes an internal stimulus to a new but related overt response R_x. Meaning is the internal mediating process represented in Figure 7.2 as $r_m \dashrightarrow s_m$. Such meaning, because it is internal and unique to the person's own experience with the natural stimulus, is said to be *connotative*.

Osgood presents a good example of this process. For a particular person, a spider (S) elicits a complex response R_T. When the word *spider* is associated with the object as it might be by a small child, a portion of the response r_m (fear) becomes associated with the label. This internal meaning medi-

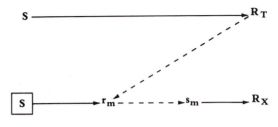

Figure 7.2   Development of a sign.

From *The Measurement of Meaning* by Charles Osgood, George Suci, and Percy Tannenbaum. Copyright © 1957 by the Board of Trustees of the University of Illinois. Reprinted by permission of the University of Illinois Press.

ates the person's response to the word, even when the actual object is not present.[4]

Most meanings are not learned as a result of direct experience with the natural stimulus. In other words, they are learned by associations between one sign and another, a process that may occur in the abstract out of physical contact with the original stimulus. Figure 7.3 is Osgood's illustration of this more complex process.[5] This figure depicts a series of signs, $\boxed{S}$, each of which elicits meanings in the individual because of previous associations (r_m). These signs are associated with another new sign /S/, and their internal responses (meanings) "rub off" on the new sign (r_{ma}). To continue our example, imagine that the child who had already established internal responses to the words *spider*, *big*, and *hairy* listens to a story about a tarantula. In the story the *tarantula* was characterized as a "big, hairy spider." Through association the child will now have a meaning for the new word *tarantula*. This word may also carry some mixture of the connotations earlier attached to the other words because of its association with these words. If the child associated *spider* with fear, *big* with dangerous, and *hairy* with feeling creepy, then the child might well react to a real or imagined tarantula by run-

4. Charles Osgood, "The Nature of Measurement of Meaning," in *The Semantic Differential Technique*, eds. J. Snider and C. Osgood (Chicago: Aldine, 1969), pp. 9–10.

5. Ibid., p. 11.

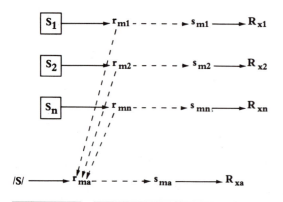

Figure 7.3   Development of an assign

From *The Measurement of Meaning* by Charles Osgood, George Suci, and Percy Tannenbaum. Copyright © 1957 by the Board of Trustees of the University of Illinois. Reprinted by permission of the University of Illinois Press.

ning away. In this example the words *spider*, *big*, and *hairy* are $\boxed{S_1}$, $\boxed{S_2}$, and $\boxed{S_3}$; r_{m1} is fear, r_{m2} is dangerous, and r_{m3} is creepy. The new word /S/ (tarantula), when associated with the other words, comes to elicit the internal response of avoidance (r_{ma}), which itself becomes a stimulus (s_{ma}) to cause the child to run away (R_{xa}) when threatened by a real or imagined tarantula.

Osgood is perhaps best known for the semantic differential technique, a method for measuring meaning.[6] This measurement technique assumes that one's meanings can be expressed by the use of words. The method begins by finding a set of adjectives that could be used to express individuals' connotations for some stimulus or sign. These adjectives are set against one another as opposites, such as good-bad, high-low, slow-fast. Individuals are given a topic, word, or other stimulus and are asked to indicate on a seven-point scale how they associate the stimulus with the adjective pairs. A scale looks like this:

good __:__:__:__:__:__:__ bad

The subject places a check mark on any space between these adjectives to indicate the degree of good or bad associated with the stimulus. The sub-

6. Osgood, "Nature."

ject may fill out as many as fifty such scales for each stimulus, each with a different set of bipolar adjectives. Osgood then uses a statistical technique called factor analysis to find the basic dimensions of meaning that are operating in a person's connotations of the stimulus. His findings in this research have led to the theory of semantic space.[7]

One's meaning for any sign is said to be located in a metaphorical space of three major dimensions: evaluation, activity, and potency. A given sign, perhaps a word or concept, elicits a reaction in the person, consisting of a sense of evaluation (good or bad), activity (active or inactive), and potency (strong or weak). The person's connotative meaning will lie somewhere in this hypothetical space, depending on the responses of the person on the three factors. Figure 7.4 illustrates semantic space.

Take the concept of *mother*, for example. For any given person, this sign will elicit an internal response embodying some combination of the three factors. One person might judge *mother* as good, passive, weak; another as good, active, strong. In any case one's connotative meaning for *mother* will depend on learned associations in the individual's own life.

Osgood and others have done semantic differential research on a variety of types of concepts, including words, music, art, and even sonar sounds.[8] In addition, they have done research among a number of groups of people representing a wide range of cultures. Osgood believes that the three factors of meaning—evaluation, potency, and activity—apply across all people and all concepts.[9] If these dimensions are universal as Osgood

7. More recently Osgood has hypothesized that bipolarity is the basic factor in all language and human thought. See Charles Osgood and Meredith Richards, "From Yang and Yin to *and* or *but*," *Language* 49 (1973): 380–412.

8. A sampling of studies illustrating the applications can be found in James Snider and Charles Osgood (eds.), *The Semantic Differential Technique* (Chacago: Aldine, 1969). This work also includes an atlas of approximately 550 concepts and their semantic profiles.

9. This point of view is expressed in Charles Osgood, "Semantic Differential Technique in the Comparative Study of Cultures," in *The Semantic Differential Technique*, eds. J. Snider and C. Osgood (Chicago: Aldine, 1969), pp. 303–323; and *Cross Cultural Universals of Affective Meaning* (Urbana: University of Illinois Press, 1975).

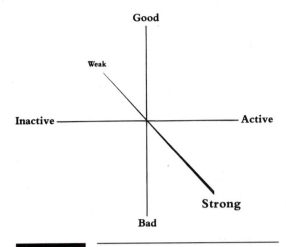

Figure 7.4   Three-dimensional semantic space.

believes they are, then he has significantly advanced our understanding of meaning. We examine this claim more carefully in the concluding section of this chapter.

Osgood's theory has been useful to describe and explain the meaning of individual concepts. Concepts, however, are only part of communication. In the next theory, we look at a more complex level of meaning—the communicator's intention.

Interpreting Intentions: Relevance Theory

Relevance theory by Dan Sperber and Deirdre Wilson attempts to explain how listeners come to understand the intentions of speakers in communication.[10] Two approaches have been used to tackle this problem, the coding model and the inferential model. The *coding model,* as explained in Chapter 4, is most often associated with semiotics. It suggests that words and other symbols convey meaning. The *inference model* suggests that meaning is not simply transferred but must be inferred by communicators from evidence in the message. Sperber and Wilson believe both models are useful because communication occurs in both ways; however, sophisticated human communication cannot

be explained entirely from a coding perspective, requiring an elaboration of the inferential approach.

In the coding model, meaning is a simple association between a symbol or stimulus and a referent, but in human communication meaning is more complex, for it involves the intentions of the communicators. People produce messages not merely to represent referents but to communicate intentions. We have already explored this idea in the context of speech acts in more detail in Chapter 5. The chief problem for the sender is to get the intention across accurately, and the chief problem for the receiver is to understand the other person's intention. The receiver can only do this inferentially. Even when much knowledge is already shared between the communicators, they can only understand each other from the perspective of their own knowledge because one can never be sure what the other person knows.

A simple example illustrates the role of inference in understanding messages. Suppose that a friend tells you that the weather is nice today. With coding you can easily understand the literal meaning of the sentence, but what is the intention of the speaker in telling you this? Unless she is explicit about the intention, you will have to make an inference. It may be nothing more than a simple piece of information that will brighten your day, but it may involve more.

A communicator will always have two levels of intent. The *informative intention* is the desire to have the listener become aware of something, and the *communicative intention* is to have that person realize one's informative intent. In the example above, your friend obviously wants you to become aware of the good weather; but she also wants you to know that she intends to inform you of this; or perhaps she even wants you to be aware of another less obvious intent. Whenever you say anything to another person with the intention to communicate, you want that person to realize your intention. How, then, is the informative intention understood?

Context is the key for inferring an intention. The *context* is the set of assumptions one uses to understand a message. The chief problem here is

10. Dan Sperber and Deirdre Wilson, *Relevance: Communication and Cognition* (Cambridge, Mass.: Harvard University Press, 1986).

that different people have different assumptions and thereby operate with different contexts. These differences result because people live in different cognitive environments. Your *cognitive environment* is all facts (or believed facts) that are apparent to you through observation and inference. It is the set of assumptions you use to understand your experience. Here Sperber and Wilson use *assumption* to be anything you take to be true.

Human cognition is designed to be efficient. In other words, it is designed to reach certain goals with the least possible effort. New information is considered *relevant* when it can be combined with what one already knows to make inferences. When you combine new information with old information in this way, the new information is said to have a *contextual effect*. In other words, it affects the context by strengthening existing assumptions, leading to the abandonment of former assumptions or adding new ones. By definition then, relevant information has greater impact on the cognitive environment than does irrelevant information.

Suppose your friend told you recently that she would like to go on a picnic. That has become a new assumption in your immediate context; so when she later tells you that the weather is good, you can put these two assumptions together and infer that today is the appropriate time for the picnic. The new information about the weather has had a contextual effect and is therefore relevant.

Relevance is obviously a matter of degree, depending on the magnitude of contextual effect and the cognitive effort required to process the information. To be efficient, people try to maximize the effect of the information and minimize the effort involved in processing it; and when this is successfully done, we can say that they have maximized the relevance of the information.

Now let's look more closely at communication itself. Inferential communication always involves *ostension*, which is the process of making information known to someone, pointing something out, or drawing someone's attention to something believed to be relevant to them. It always involves intending to make information known and having the intention itself known by the audience. Thus,

communication is an attempt to modify in some way the cognitive environment of the other person by affecting his or her assumptions, what he or she takes to be true. The change in the cognitive environment may be concrete, as in a factual claim, or vague, as in a feeling or impression.

Communication will be successful to the extent that the listener accurately interprets the intentions of the speaker. Because of the need for efficiency, the listener cannot use the entire cognitive environment as the context for understanding the message because of the demands it would put on memory. Even if you could remember all of your cognitive environment at once, the effort required would be tremendous and very inefficient. Imagine how hard it would be to interpret a message if you had to use everything you knew to understand its relevance.

Therefore, the listener must select a smaller context in which to understand the intentions of the other communicator. According to this theory, contexts are first narrowed down on the basis of what is available in the immediate memory in the particular time and place (the physical environment) of the communication. Then a context is chosen on the basis of maximizing the relevance of the information in the message. In other words, you ask yourself, From what is available to me right now, what do I need to assume to make sense of this message with the least amount of effort? The speaker will help you with this. Here is how.

Speakers know that they have two primary tasks—to get your attention and to present a message that is potentially relevant to you. (It makes no sense to send a message that is not relevant to the other person.) Thus, relevance itself is always a major goal of the communicator. The speaker always presents you with a *guarantee of relevance*. You can assume when anybody communicates with you that they think what they have to say is relevant. This is the *presumption of relevance* on your part. The speaker then gives you evidence or signs of the relevance of the message, and you look for those signs.

Now, as a listener you have only to hypothesize various intentions by testing any possible intention that occurs to you with the relevancy principle. So you ask, Can this possible intention be relevant to me based on the chosen context? If not, it probably is not the intention of the speaker. The first hypothesized intention that works will be assumed to be the correct one. In some cases, you may immediately see that more than one intention could work, which will result in ambiguity.

For example, if in addition to saying that she wanted to go on a picnic, your friend also mentioned that she would like your help with the yard work, you would have two assumptions as part of the context for interpreting her subsequent weather report. You hypothesize almost simultaneously that you could go on a picnic or stay home and work in the yard. Suddenly, your friend's intention is ambiguous. In this case, you would probably resolve the ambiguity by expanding your assumptions by asking her what she wants to do.

Language is especially useful in communicating intent. Because it is so much more explicit than nonverbal signs and because it contains its own rules for what words mean and how to put words together into expressions of intent, language provides direct evidence of what the communicator is trying to do. The problem with language is that it is often used indirectly, so that what is said is not what is meant. Here the listener must infer an appropriate *implicature,* or implied intent. Recall from Chapter 5 that conversations are peppered with such implied intent and that, to be competent in conversations, you must have the ability to infer intentions from implicatures.

Again, the principle of relevance is used here to determine the actual intent of the speaker. If the direct statement does not seem relevant, you will naturally explore implied intentions that will turn out to be relevant. Actually, unless she just wants you to know that it is a nice day, your friend's statement about the weather involves an implicature. Surely, you think, she is not just commenting on the weather. What is her real intent? You determine that by figuring out how the weather comment is relevant to you at that moment.

In this section we have dealt with inferences about communicative intentions. As we see in the following section, inferring intent is a common yet difficult task.

Interpreting Causes: Attribution Theory

Attribution theory, also known as "naive psychology," deals with the ways people infer the causes of behavior. It explains the processes by which people come to understand their own behavior and that of others. Unlike scientific psychology, which attempts to ascertain the actual causes of behavior, naive psychology centers on the perceived causes of behavior by ordinary people in ongoing interaction.

Attribution theory has three basic assumptions.[11] First, people attempt to determine the causes of behavior. When in doubt, they look for information that will help them answer the question, Why is she doing that? Harold Kelley puts it this way:

> In the course of my interaction with other people, I often wonder why they act as they do. I may wonder how to interpret a compliment a student makes of a lecture I recently gave, why my friend is so critical of a certain common acquaintance, or why my colleague has not done his share of work on our joint project. These are questions about the attribution of the other people's behavior—what causes it, what is responsible for it, to what is it to be attributed?[12]

The second assumption of attribution theory is that people assign causes systematically. Kelley likens this occurrence to the scientific method: "The lay attributor . . . generally acts like a good scientist, examining the covariation between a given effect and various possible causes."[13] As we will see later in this section, some research evidence challenges this assumption. The third assumption is that the attributed cause has impact on the perceiver's own feelings and behavior. The communicator's attri-

11. The basic assumptions in attribution theory are outlined in Edward E. Jones et al. (eds.), *Attribution: Perceiving the Causes of Behavior* (Morristown, N.J.: General Learning Press, 1972), p. xi.

12. Harold H. Kelley, "Attribution in Social Interaction," in *Attribution: Perceiving the Causes of Behavior,* (eds. E. E. Jones et al. (Morristown, N.J.: General Learning Press, 1972), p. 1.

13. Ibid., p. 2.

butions determine in large part the meaning for the situation. In this section we look first at some early foundations of attribution theory and some more recent extensions.

The foundations of attribution theory are to be found in social psychology. Here we examine two leaders in this field. The first is Fritz Heider, who can easily be called the father of attribution theory.[14] It was he who coined the term *naive psychology*. His early work has been extended by a number of later theorists.

Heider presents the basic idea that people try to figure out whether an observed behavior has been caused by situational or personal attributes. Some commonly perceived attributes that can combine to cause behavior include situational causes (being affected by the environment), personal effects (influencing things personally), ability (being able to do something), effort (trying to do something), desire (wanting to do it), sentiment (feeling like it), belonging (going along with something), obligation (feeling you ought to), and permission (being permitted to).

Attribution is largely a process of indirect perception, in which one infers causes from observations of overt behavior. There is not a one-to-one relationship between the observed behavior and the cause. A variety of behaviors may be perceived as stemming from a single cause, or, conversely, one behavior may be thought to arise from multiple possible causes. One task of the perceiver is to resolve such ambiguities. For example, a supervisor in a company may notice that an employee is particularly industrious. The supervisor must infer the cause of the employee's hard work. Virtually any of the causes listed would fit. For example, the employee may be working hard because he is being forced to, he wants to, he is able to, he feels he should, or any of a number of other causes. Of course, every behavior occurs in a situation, and you make use of this context to help you resolve ambiguities. You may also have the benefit of getting additional information by observing a situation repeatedly over time.

14. Fritz Heider, *The Psychology of Interpersonal Relations* (New York: Wiley, 1958).

Causal perception is mediated by psychological variables in the perceiver. One of these variables is meaning. You always assign meaning to what you observe, and your meanings are crucial in interpersonal perception. Meanings serve as integrators in perception, organizing observations into patterns that help you make sense of the world. Because of a need for consistency, you define things in such a way that causal attribution makes logical sense, which makes the overall attribution process integrated and consistent. The way in which you resolve ambiguities and establish a consistent pattern of perception may be different from the way in which other people do so.

The lack of one-to-one correspondence between behavior and motive makes multiple interpretations of a given event possible. Heider calls individual patterns of perception *perceptual styles*. He recognizes that any state of affairs may give rise to a number of interpretations, each of which seems true to the person involved.

One of the most common attributions is purposeful action. If you think that someone did something on purpose, you are recognizing two underlying attributes, ability and motivation. Suppose, for example, that your friend fails to show up for a meeting. You will wonder why. Here are the possibilities: Either your friend could not make it, or she didn't try. If she wasn't able, something might have been wrong with her (e.g., illness), or some situational cause (e.g., snowstorm) prevented her appearance. If she did not try, she either didn't want to (an attribution of intent) or was too lazy (an attribution of exertion). Now you can see what happens in interpersonal perception. In this instance you will infer the causes of your friend's behavior according to your overall experience, your meanings, the situational factors, and your own perceptual style.

The attribution of obligation, as when a person thinks he "ought" to do something, is particularly interesting. An obligation is seen as an impersonal, objective demand embedded in a situation. It has interpersonal validity in that most people would agree that the demand is present. Thus, a person says, "You ought to go to the dentist," or "I ought to report the theft." But "oughts" do not necessarily correspond with values. I may dread going to the dentist even though I think I ought to. Because people seek congruity among attributions, they will balance their obligations and values:

> There exists a tendency to be in harmony with the requirements of the objective order. Thus the situation is balanced if one likes to do what one ought to do, if one likes and enjoys the entities one believes are valuable, if happiness and goodness go together, if p [perceiver] admires the person he likes and likes the person with whom he shares values, if what ought to be conforms with what really is, etc.[15]

Heider's theory has influenced virtually every other attribution theory. One important early theorist influenced by Heider's thinking is Harold Kelley, who created a theory of how people think when making attributions.[16] Kelley developed two postulates about causal attribution, which apply to both self-perception and perception of others.

The first postulate is the *covariation principle:* "An effect is attributed to the one of its possible causes with which, over time, it covaries."[17] This principle applies to situations in which the perceiver has information from more than one observation. The person sees which effects are associated (covary) with which causes. For example, if you observe that every time you stay up late to study, your roommate goes out, you might conclude that he does not want to be in the room late in the evening when you are there.

The second principle is the *discounting effect:* "The role of a given cause in producing a given effect is discounted if other plausible causes are also present."[18] In other words, the perceiver tends to weigh possible causes in relation to one another to determine which is the most plausible. So, for example, if your roommate's girlfriend calls him just before he leaves in the evening, you have two possible causes—your presence in the room and his

desire to see his girlfriend. The second cause makes the first seem less plausible.

These two postulates describe attribution as a rational process in which the individual carefully examines the various causal possibilities and generalizes on the basis of the best available data.

The covariation principle applies when the person has multiple observations from which to generalize. The perceiver goes through a process of "analysis of variance," which is similar to a statistical procedure often used in experimental research. It allows the researcher to weigh the various sources of variation in such a way as to determine the causes in operation. By analogy, people use the same basic pattern in making attributions: They treat possible causes as independent variables and effects as dependent variables. Figure 7.5 illustrates a three-way contingency model used in causal inference.[19] The three dimensions in this model include the several persons observed, the various times in which observation took place, and the objects of the behavior (entities). You can attribute the cause of a behavior to the person, to time, or to entity. So, for example, you might conclude that your roommate leaves the room in the evening because he does not like you (person), because of the time of day (evening), or because of his girlfriend (entity). You can also make more complicated attributions that combine causes, which Kelley calls an *interaction effect.* You might, for example, conclude that your roommate is leaving for all three reasons.

You can easily fit this example into Figure 7.5:

1. Attribution to person *(He doesn't want to be around when I am studying.)*

2. Attribution to entity *(He leaves to be with his girlfriend.)*

3. Attribution to time *(He likes to take off in the evening.)*

4. Attribution to person and entity *(My studying gives him an opportunity to meet his girlfriend.)*

5. Attribution to circumstances *(He likes to go out in the evening, and my studying gives him an opportunity to meet his girlfriend at that time.)*

---

15. Ibid., p. 233.

16. See the Bibliography for a list of Kelley's works.

17. Harold Kelley, "The Process of Causal Attribution," *American Psychologist* 28 (1973): 108.

18. Ibid., p. 113.

19. Ibid., p. 110.

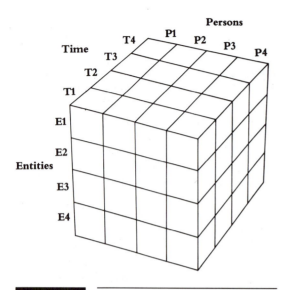

Persons

Time

T4 P1 P2 P3 P4
T3
T2
T1

E1

E2

Entities

E3

E4

Figure 7.5   Analysis of variance model of attribution.

From *American Psychologist*, "The Process of Causal Attribution," by Harold Kelley. Copyright © 1973 by the American Psychological Association. Reprinted by permission of the publisher and the author.

With the covariation principle, the perceiver observes the covariation (association) of particular causes and effects in different situations over time. By putting these various observations together, the observer sees patterns emerge, and the causal inferences outlined above occur. Much of the time, however, we do not have the advantage of a complete data block such as that shown in Figure 7.5 because we do not have the opportunity to make many observations over time. At these times we use the discounting principle.

The *discounting effect* applies when the perceiver must rely on a single observation. The various possible causes of an observed effect are weighed against one another. The process itself is no different from the analysis of variance as explained above. What is different is the way the data block is filled in. In the discounting model, most of the data (causal patterns) are assumed, not observed. One makes assumptions about cause–effect rela-

tionships on the basis of past experience and learning. As Kelley puts it,

> The mature individual ... has a repertoire of abstract ideas about the operation and interaction of causal factors. These conceptions [enable one to make an] economical and fast attributional analysis, by providing a framework within which bits and pieces of relevant information can be fitted in order to draw reasonably good causal inferences.[20]

By using experience and learning, the attributor brings various causal assumptions into play. A particularly good example of this occurs when you have both an assumed internal cause (in the person) and a competing external cause (in the situation). For example, your friend has just received an A on a term paper. You assume that this outcome occurred because of your friend's ability or because the assignment was easy. A couple of causal schemata are possible here. If you follow the schema of *multiple necessary causes*, you will reason that your friend got the A because she is able and the task was easy. This schema is illustrated in Figure 7.6(a). Or perhaps you will use the schema of *multiple sufficient causes*, in which you reason that either your friend is able or the task was easy or both. Figure 7.6(b) illustrates this possibility.

Kelley summarizes the importance of the attribution process:

> There is much evidence ... that attributions do matter. Man's concern with the reasons for events does not leave him "lost in thought" about those reasons. Rather, his causal explanations play an important role in providing his impetus to action and in his decisions among alternative courses of action. When the attributions are appropriate, the person undoubtedly fares better in his decisions and actions than he would in the absence of the causal analysis.[21]

Brant Burleson has shown how attribution works in ordinary communication.[22] He tape-recorded a

20. Harold Kelley, *Causal Schemata and the Attribution Process* (Morristown, N.J.: General Learning Press, 1972), p. 2.

21. Kelley, "Process," p. 127.

22. Brant R. Burleson, "Attribution Schemes and Causal Inference in Natural Conversations," in *Contemporary Issues in Language and Discourse Processes*, eds. D. G. Ellis and W. A. Donohue (Hillsdale, N.J.: Erlbaum, 1986), pp. 63–86.

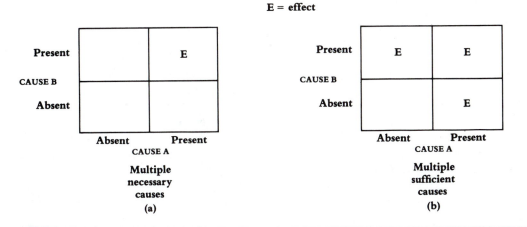

Figure 7.6   Causal schemata.

From *American Psychologist*, "The Process of Causal Attribution," by Harold Kelley. Copyright © 1973 by the American Psychological Association. Reprinted by permission of the publisher and the author.

conversation between two teaching assistants about a student. In this conversation Don complains to Bob that one of his students, who had the opportunity to retake the midterm examination, failed it three times. Don is very concerned and explores with Bob what the reasons might be. This is a classic case of attribution, and it shows how it is often done jointly with other people in a conversation. In this conversation these teachers use primarily the covariation principle to establish what they consider the cause to be.

They first explore the possibility that the test was too hard, but Don says that the test was not changed and that no one else failed it. They also establish that the student's behavior is consistent over time. Thus, they are able to rule out test difficulty as a cause. They then conclude that it must be something about the student herself that led to the failures. Either she did not have the ability or she was not trying. Because of the fact that she completed all assignments and took the test three times, she appeared to be trying. By deduction then, they conclude that she just does not have the ability to pass the test. In the end Don says that he will ask her to drop the class because he doesn't think she can pass the course.

The literature on attribution theory is vast.[23] We do not have the space here to summarize all findings, but one of the most common findings is that attribution is often biased. In other words, people are not very objective when making causal inferences about themselves and other people. Rather than weighing all factors, as Kelley's theory suggests, people seem to make quick judgments based on salient cues and emotional factors. Research also shows that people's prior judgments are hard to dislodge, no matter how compelling the evidence. Thus, once you make an attribution, you are apt to stick with it.

How, then, do we reconcile these research findings with the idea found in attribution theory that human beings are logical and systematic? Several researchers have adopted the position that people can process information in both logical and nonlogical ways, depending on the circumstances. One

23. For summaries, see David R. Seibold and Brian H. Spitzberg, "Attribution Theory and Research: Formalization, Review, and Implications for Communication," in *Progress in Communication Sciences*, vol. 3, eds. B. Dervin and M. J. Voigt (Norwood, N.J.: Ablex, 1981), pp. 85–125; Alan L. Sillars, "Attribution and Communication," in *Social Cognition and Communication*, eds. M. E. Roloff and C. R. Berger (Beverly Hills, Calif.: Sage, 1982), pp. 73–106.

factor that may operate here is motivation. For example, where motivation to promote the self is high, as when we need to save face, there is probably a tendency to be biased in favor of self-serving, situational attributions. Where motivation is high to control the situation, there will probably be a bias toward attributions of personal responsibility (as opposed to situational causes).

One of the most persistent findings in attribution research is the so-called *fundamental attribution error*. This is the tendency to attribute the cause of events to personal action, the feeling that people are personally to blame for what happens to them. An insensitivity to many circumstantial factors causing events seems to exist. This tendency, however, is mitigated in the case of one's own responsibility. You tend to blame other people for what happens to them, but you blame the situation for what happens to you. If your roommate fails a test, you are apt to claim that she did not study hard enough; but if you fail the test, you will probably say that the test was too hard.

Alan Sillars conducted a landmark study on the effects of attribution in conflict resolution among college roommates, which shows how attribution can affect communication in everyday life.[24] Sillars conducted both a questionnaire and a live study of roommates. In the first study, he asked them to write about a conflict they had had with their roommates, and in the second study, he actually videotaped roommates discussing problems such as irritability, boyfriend or girlfriend problems, and disagreements about music. He then looked for three types of conflict strategies that have been discussed in the literature, including passive methods such as avoidance or submission; competitive strategies such as requests, demands, and threats; and integrative strategies such as problem solving. He found that the roommates' attributions very much

affected the kinds of strategies they employed in managing their conflicts.

If, for example, the students saw their roommates as cooperative, they were more likely to use an integrative strategy. Attributing self-blame led to the use of integrative strategies, whereas attributing blame to the other person led to competitive ones. The attribution of certain negative personality traits to the other person also seemed to prevent the use of integrative solutions. Sillars also found that, because of the fundamental attribution error, both partners tended to blame the other for the conflict and saw themselves as merely responding.

Reinterpreting Messages: Second-Guessing Theory

We often encounter messages that we believe are not accurate. This happens when communicators are lying or merely mistaken. It happens, too, when communicators are biased. Or perhaps the speaker is perfectly honest, but the listener has reason to doubt the accuracy of the message for some reason. Second-guessing theory was developed by Dean Hewes and his colleagues to explain how communicators respond to this situation.[25]

Second guessing is a process we go through whenever we believe a message is biased and we have a need for accurate information. When the motivation for accurate information is high, second guessing can be accurate in assessing the truth of a situation. Second guessing occurs when there is something "fishy" about a message that is personally relevant or is interesting or important for some reason. It involves the use of prior knowledge to question what is being said. In some cases, of course, second guessing is not possible because the claims made by the speaker are strictly subjective and not verifiable.

Second guessing consists of four phases—vigilance, reinterpretation, reinterpretation assessment, and social tactic choice. In the *vigilance*

24. Alan L. Sillars, "Attributions and Communication in Roommate Conflicts," *Communication Monographs* 47 (1980): 180–200; "The Sequential and Distributional Structure of Conflict Interaction as a Function of Attributions Concerning the Locus of Responsibility and Stability of Conflict," in *Communication Yearbook 4*, ed. D. Nimmo (New Brunswick, N.J.: Transaction Books, 1980), pp. 217–236.

25. For a summary of the growing literature related to this theory, see Dean E. Hewes and Maudie L. Graham, "Second-Guessing Theory: Review and Extension," in *Communication Yearbook 12*, ed. J. A. Anderson (Newbury Park, Calif.: Sage, 1989), pp. 213–248.

phase, the listener becomes aware of a problem in the message. One's need for certainty in the situation will be a primary motivation for detecting inaccuracies and biases. Some people are probably more likely to detect biases than others. For example, people who have a high need to understand and control a situation will probably be more aware of problems than will individuals who do not have such a need.

Vigilance, then, involves the detection of a problem. This is called *cue extraction*. Cues in the message content, message form, or context can signal inaccuracy or bias. When survey respondents were asked to recall three cases of second guessing in which they had participated, they could do so with ease.[26] These subjects also could recall what cues had led them to undertake second guessing and to suggest other cues that are used in these kinds of situations. Table 7.1 lists the cues found in this survey.

In another study, these researchers found that when presented with potentially deceptive messages about such subjects as how well a friend had done on a test, they could use cues planted into these messages to determine whether they were biased and to correctly identify those cues.[27]

Imagine that a neighbor in your apartment building tells you that the rent was going to increase. Would you have reason to doubt this statement? You might. For example, if another neighbor had recently told you that he had talked to the owner, who said that no rent increases were planned, you would probably begin second-guessing these messages.

How are bias cues used? Two methods could be employed. The first is to become more sensitive to cues that would reveal the need for second guessing, and the second is to attempt to eliminate ambiguous cues and concentrate on just a few clear ones. Research evidence suggests that most people may favor the second method. This preference

makes sense because there are a number of potential cues for inaccuracy in any message. We would drive ourselves crazy questioning everything if all cues were taken into account; but when one or two major indicators are present, then doubt is more apt to arise. Your neighbors' inconsistent reports are a good example of the use of a single, clear cue that something is wrong.

The second phase of second guessing is *reinterpretation*. Here the listener becomes reflective and examines the message critically, attempting to determine the real state of affairs. At this point the listener decides whether it is worth the effort to reinterpret the message to get a more accurate picture of what is actually going on. Even in a doubtful situation, you will accept a message at face value if there is no particular reason to get at the truth. But if you have a need for accurate information and you doubt the message, you will engage in some form of second guessing.

In the case of a rent increase, the message is highly relevant, so you would undoubtedly reinterpret the messages. You would probably think about what you know about these two neighbors and what they have told you in the past. You might consider their relationship with the owner and which one is most apt to have the accurate information.

The third phase is *reinterpretation assessment*, or judging the adequacy of your reinterpretation. Whether you will assess your interpretation depends on how important accuracy is and how much effort reinterpretation will require. At this point you can either stop interpreting and settle for what you know, reinterpret based on the available evidence, or seek new information from other people. If the need for accuracy is acute, you will probably seek additional information. Another factor, however, is social constraints. Sometimes it is not appropriate to seek additional information from other people, and you may stop second-guessing because you are unwilling to ask for more information. This would be the case, for example, when inquiries might offend other people.

If you received contradictory information about the rent, you might discount the message that the

26. Joel A. Doelger, Dean E. Hewes, and Maudie L. Graham, "Knowing When to 'Second Guess': The Mindful Analysis of Messages," *Human Communication Research* 12 (1986): 301–338.

27. Ibid.

Table 7.1   Second-Guessing Cues

1. Target

1.1a   Inconsistency: Message from the source is inconsistent with prior knowledge of the target. (This includes baseline probabilities on events—norms, regularities, etc.—as related to the target.)

2. Source Cues

2.1   Motivational (self-interest) Cues

2.1a   Source distorts for his or her benefit.

2.1b   Source distorts for altruistic reasons; for example, to avoid embarrassing me or another person.

2.1c   Consistency bias: Distortion resorts from source's attempt to keep his or her attitudes or beliefs consistent.

2.2   Dispositional Cues

2.2a   Rigid use of knowledge structures: Source always sees things in a particular way (e.g., from a Marxist perspective) even when such a perspective is inappropriate. Could be the implied result of the source's group membership.

2.2b   Dispositional distortions: Source is a habitual liar, exaggerator, distorter, and so on. [Or, source has distorted information in similar context previously.]

2.2c   Personal preference differences: Not necessarily implying bias or distortion, but acknowledging the role of personal tastes. Source holds different judgmental criteria when evaluating the target. Therefore, he or she cannot provide accurate information for me.

2.2d   Diagnosticity: Source is not skilled in picking discriminant clues.

2.3   Consistency Cues

2.3a   Behavioral consistency: Source's typical behavior patterns are deviated from (would not be a cue for anyone though: these are deviations particular to this source's typical behavior) [Uses *this* source's typical behavior as a baseline, not a baseline of all human behavior (for the latter see 4.1b).]

2.4   Informational Cues

2.4a   Availability heuristic: Source's account of the target was influenced by the availability of objects or events, that is, their accessibility in the processes of perception, memory, or recall; not their actual occurrence. Specific type: Egocentric bias—One's own efforts and actions may be disproportionately available and their frequency compared to others' may be overestimated ("I helped the group more than they did").

2.4b   Representativeness heuristic: Application of simple resemblance or goodness-of-fit criteria to problems of categorization. Deals with the degree to which salient features of the object are representative of, or similar to, features presumed to be characteristic of the category. Source has not considered the relevant base-rate information in drawing conclusions about the target.

2.4c   Fundamental attribution error: Source's comment on the target reflects his or her view that behavior is caused by enduring dispositions of the actor rather than characteristics of the situation.

2.4d   Data sufficiency: Source does not have sufficient data to reach the stated conclusion about the target. [This includes the area of expertise normally associated with source credibility.]

3. Receiver Cues

3.1a   Dispositional traits: Receiver makes a global self-attribution, "I just distrust people."

4. Message Cues

4.1a   Message is internally inconsistent: Components of the message are contradictory. Anyone could hear the inconsistency; not based on prior knowledge of the source or target. [May also include violations of expected content for this type of message or implausibility of explanation generally, *not* implausibility for a specific target.]

4.1b   Message deviates from expected form: Represents clues that would be evident if provided by any source, for example, too smooth, cocky, nervous.

Source: From Joel A. Doelger, Dean E. Hewes, Maudie L. Graham, "Knowing When to 'Second Guess': The Mindful Analysis of Messages," *Human Communication Research* 12 (1986): 333–335.

rent is going to increase, but you would probably would not leave it at that. You would undoubtedly ask other neighbors what they have heard, and you might even ask the manager.

If you decide to seek additional information from other people, you have to decide how to go about it, which occurs in the final stage, *social tactic choice*. Little research has been done on this aspect of second guessing, although we know that it is fairly common. In one survey, researchers asked a group of college students to recall an incident of second guessing that they had done, to describe it, and to answer several questions about it. They found that only 9 percent of the students were satisfied with their first reinterpretation of the message, 21 percent continued second-guessing, and 70 percent actually sought additional information to test their reassessments.[28]

In this section we have dealt with a variety of levels of interpretation. All interpretation is made possible by information processing, which is discussed in greater detail in the following section.

Information Organization

The theories outlined in this section deal with the ways in which people integrate and operate on information that is received in messages. The central question of each of these theories is how information is organized and managed and how it affects the cognitive system. The first theory deals with the ways in which information is combined with what is already believed and how this organization comes to affect attitude change, and the second theory addresses consistency as an organizing principle.

Organizing Beliefs: Information-Integration Theory

The information-integration approach centers on the ways people accumulate and organize infor-

mation about some person, object, situation, or idea to form attitudes toward a concept. The construct *attitude* has been an important one in research on persuasion because much persuasion is aimed at changing attitudes. An attitude usually is defined as a predisposition to act in a positive or negative way toward an object. The information-integration approach is one of the most credible models of the nature of attitudes and attitude change.[29]

According to this theory, an individual's attitude system can be affected by information that is received and integrated into the attitude-information system. All information has the potential of affecting one's attitudes, but the degree to which it affects attitudes depends on two variables. The first is valence. *Valence* is the degree to which the information is good news or bad news. A piece of information will be evaluated in terms of a scale from highly positive to highly negative. If it supports one's beliefs and attitudes, it generally will be viewed as positive; if not, it probably will be seen as negative.

The second variable that affects the importance of information to a person is the weight assigned to the information. *Weight* is a function of credibility. If the person thinks the information is probably true, a higher weight will be assigned to the information; if not, a lower weight will be given. Valence affects how information influences attitudes; weight affects the degree to which it does so. When the assigned weight is low, the information will have little effect, no matter what its valence.

For example, suppose that you have two friends, one who is strongly in favor of legalizing marijuana and the other strongly opposed to legalization. Suppose further that your friends read that three states have recently increased penalties for possession. How will this information affect your friends' attitudes toward the issue? If your two friends accept this information as true, they will assign a high

---

28. Dean E. Hewes, Maudie L. Graham, Michael Monsour, and Joel A. Doelger, "Cognition and Social Information-Gathering Strategies: Reinterpretation Assessment in Second-Guessing," *Human Communication Research* 16 (1989): 297–321.

29. Contributors include Norman H. Anderson, "Integration Theory and Attitude Change," *Psychological Review* 78 (1971): 171–206; Martin Fishbein and Icek Ajzen, *Belief, Attitude, Intention, and Behavior* (Reading, Mass.: Addison-Wesley, 1975); Robert S. Wyer, *Cognitive Organization and Change* (Hillsdale, N.J.: Erlbaum, 1974).

weight to it, and it will affect their attitudes one way or the other. One of your friends definitely will define the information as bad news, and his attitude toward legalization will likely become more positive. The other will define it as positive information, causing a more negative attitude.

An attitude is considered to be an accumulation of information about an object, person, situation, or experience, each piece of information having been evaluated as indicated. Thus, attitude change occurs because of new information or changing judgments of truthfulness or value.

One of the best-known and respected information integration theorists is Martin Fishbein.[30] Fishbein highlights the complex and interactive nature of attitudes in what is known as *expectancy-value theory*. According to Fishbein, there are two kinds of belief. The first is what he terms *belief in* a thing. When one believes in something, he or she predicts a high probability of the thing existing. The second kind of belief, *belief about*, is the predicted probability that a particular relationship exists between the belief object and some other quality or thing. For example, one may believe in God, that God exists. One may also believe that God is loving—a statement of a relationship between God and love.

Attitudes differ from beliefs in that they are evaluative. Attitudes are correlated with beliefs and predispose a person to behave a certain way toward the attitude object. Attitudes are learned as part of one's concept formation. They may change as new learnings occur throughout life. Furthermore, Fishbein sees attitudes as hierarchically organized. In other words, general attitudes are predicted from specific ones in a summative fashion. An attitude toward an object is the sum of the specific factors, including beliefs and evaluations, in the hierarchy.

This formula is represented algebraically as follows:[31]

$$A_o = \sum_1^N B_i a_i$$

where

A_o = attitude toward object o

B_i = strength of belief i about o; that is, the probability or improbability that o is associated with some other concept x

a_i = evaluative aspect of B; that is, the evaluation of x

N = number of beliefs about o

The distinctive feature of Fishbein's formula is that it stresses the interactive nature of attitudes. Attitudes are a function of a complex factor that involves both beliefs (probability predictions) and evaluations. The example in Table 7.2 helps clarify this model. According to this conceptualization, attitude change can occur from any of three sources. First, information can alter the believability (weight) of particular beliefs. Second, information can change the value of a belief. Finally, information can add new beliefs to the attitude structure.

This theory suggests some of the ways in which information affects the cognitive system, but how, then, do the resultant attitudes affect behavior? This is a more complicated issue. In the *theory of reasoned action*, Icek Ajzen and Martin Fishbein argue that behavior results in part from intentions and that intentions are a complex outcome of attitudes.[32]

Specifically, one's intention to behave in a certain way is determined by that individual's attitude toward the behavior and a set of beliefs about how other people would like one to behave. Consider

---

30. Fishbein has published several articles on this topic. See the Bibliography. For an excellent secondary source, see David T. Burhans, "The Attitude-Behavior Discrepancy Problem: Revisited," *Quarterly Journal of Speech* 57 (1971): 418–428. For a more recent treatments, see Fishbein and Ajzen, *Belief*; Daniel J. O'Keefe, *Persuasion: Theory and Research* (Newbury Park, Calif.: Sage, 1990), pp. 45–60.

31. Martin Fishbein (ed.), "A Behavior Theory Approach to the Relations Between Beliefs About an Object and the Attitude Toward the Object," in *Readings in Attitude Theory and Measurement* (New York: Wiley, 1967), P. 394.

32. Fishbein and Ajzen, *Belief*; Icek Ajzen and Martin Fishbein, *Understanding Attitudes and Predicting Social Behavior* (Englewood Cliffs, N.J.: Prentice-Hall, 1980).

your progress in college as an example. Do you plan to continue until you get your degree or drop out for a while? The answer to this question depends on your attitude toward school and what you think other people want you to do. Each factor—your attitude and others' opinions—is weighted according to its importance. Sometimes your attitude is most important, sometimes others' opinions are most important, and sometimes they are more or less equal in weight. The formula is as follows:

$$BI = A_B w_1 + (SN)w_2$$

where

BI = behavioral intention
A_B = attitude toward behavior
SN = subjective norm (what others think)
w_1 = weight of attitude
w_2 = weight of subjective norm

The attitude toward the behavior itself is formed in the same way that any attitude is formed, by a combination of beliefs and evaluations. One's estimate of what others want them to do, the so-called *subjective norm*, is a sum of a person's estimate of what each of several other people think times his or her motivation to comply with these people:

$$SN = \sum NB_i MC_i$$

where

SN = subjective norm
NB_i = beliefs attributed to others
MC_i = motivation to conform to others beliefs

Now let us return again to the example of your intention regarding school. If you have developed a poor attitude toward school and your friends are encouraging you to drop out for a semester to work, that is probably what you will intend to do. On the other hand, if your friends are encouraging you to stick it out and their opinions are very important to you, you will probably stay despite your negative attitude. If your friends' opinions don't matter that much, your attitude will win out, and your intention will be to get a job.

Of course, one's intention may not always lead to the desired behavior. The preceding formulas predict one's behavioral intention, but they do not necessarily predict the actual behavior. We know that people are notorious for going against their own best intentions. Sometimes, for example, people cannot fulfill their intentions because they cannot. Smokers may intend to stop smoking but do not because of the addiction. You might well intend to drop out of school, but your parents' threat to cut off your support might keep you from doing so.

Table 7.2   A Simplified Example of an Attitude Hierarchy According to Fishbein Model

Attitude object (o) → jogging $N = 6$ (number of beliefs in system)

Associated concepts (x_i)	Probability of association (B_i)	Evaluation (a_i)
x_1 Cardiovascular health	B_1 Jogging promotes cardiovascular vigor.	a_1 Cardiovascular vigor is good.
x_2 Disease	B_2 Jogging reduces the chance of disease.	a_2 Disease is bad.
x_3 Obesity	B_3 Jogging reduces weight.	a_3 Being overweight is bad.
x_4 Mental health	B_4 Jogging promotes peace of mind.	a_4 Letting off mental tensions is good.
x_5 Friendship	B_5 Jogging introduces a person to new friends.	a_5 Friendship is important.
x_6 Physique	B_6 Jogging builds better bodies.	a_6 A beautiful body is appealing.

Information-integration theory shows some factors that contribute to one's organization of information. Let us turn now to one of the most commonly advocated principles of cognitive organization.

Maintaining Balance: Consistency Theories

Undoubtedly, one of the largest bodies of research related to attitude, attitude change, and persuasion is consistency theory. All consistency theories begin with the same premise: People are more comfortable with consistency than inconsistency. Consistency, then, is a primary organizing principle in cognitive processing, and attitude change can result from information that disrupts this balance.

Although the vocabulary and concepts of these theories differ, the basic assumption of consistency is present in all of them. In system language (Chapter 3), people seek homeostasis; persons are open systems that aim to achieve self-maintenance and balance.

In the remainder of this section, two theories of cognitive consistency are summarized. These were chosen because of their prominence in the field and their relative completeness of explanation. The first is Leon Festinger's theory of cognitive dissonance, and the second is Milton Rokeach's theory of attitudes, beliefs, and values.

The theory of cognitive dissonance. Leon Festinger's theory of cognitive dissonance is the most significant and influential consistency theory. In fact, it is one of the most important theories in the history of social psychology. Over the years it has produced a prodigious quantity of research and volumes of criticism, interpretation, and extrapolation.[33]

Festinger teaches that any two cognitive elements, including attitudes, perceptions, knowledge, and behaviors, will have one of three kinds of relationships. The first of these is null, or *irrelevant;* the second is consistent, or *consonant;* and the third is inconsistent, or *dissonant.* Dissonance occurs when one element would not be expected to follow from the other. What is consonant or dissonant for one person may not be so for another, so we must always ask what is consistent or inconsistent within a person's own psychological system.

Two overriding premises govern dissonance theory. The first is that dissonance produces tension or stress that pressures the individual to change so that the dissonance is thereby reduced. Second, when dissonance is present, the individual will not only attempt to reduce it but will also avoid situations in which additional dissonance might be produced.

These tendencies to reduce dissonance and to avoid dissonance-producing information are a direct function of the amount of dissonance: the greater the dissonance, the greater the need for change. For example, the more a person's smoking is inconsistent with his or her knowledge of the negative effects of smoking, the greater the pressure to stop smoking. Dissonance itself is a result of two other variables, the importance of the cognitive elements and the number of elements involved in the dissonant relation. In other words, if you have several things that are inconsistent and if they are important to you, you will experience greater dissonance.

How, then, do you deal with cognitive dissonance? Understanding that dissonance produces a tension for reduction, we can imagine a number of "methods" for reducing the dissonance. First, you might change one or more of the cognitive elements. For example, as a smoker, you might stop smoking. Second, new elements might be added to one side of the tension or the other. For example, you might switch to a pipe. Third, you might come

33. Leon Festinger, A *Theory of Cognitive Dissonance* (Stanford, Calif.: Stanford University Press, 1957). Many short reviews of dissonance theory are available, including Charles A. Kiesler, Barry E. Collins, and Norman Miller, *Attitude Change: A Critical Analysis of Theoretical Approaches* (New York: Wiley, 1969); Robert Zajonc, "The Concepts of Balance, Congruity, and Dissonance," *Public Opinion Quarterly* 24 (1960): 280–296; Roger Brown, *Social Psychology* (New York: Free Press, 1965), chap. 11. For a readable exposition showing the practical applications of cognitive dissonance theory, see Elliot Aronson, The *Social Animal* (New York: Viking Press, 1972), chap. 4. For a detailed examination of the theory and related research, see J. W. Brehm and A. R. Cohen, *Explorations in Cognitive Dissonance* (New York: Wiley, 1962). A recent brief summary can also be found in O'Keefe, *Persuasion.*

to see the elements as less important than they used to be. Fourth, you might seek consonant information such as evidence for the benefits of smoking. Fifth, you might reduce dissonance by distorting or misinterpreting the information involved. For example, you might say that the evidence for the ill effects of smoking is not really very strong.

Much of the theory and research on cognitive dissonance has centered around the various situations in which dissonance is likely to result. These include such situations as decision making, forced compliance, initiation, social support, and effort. Decision making has received a great deal of research attention. Salespeople call dissonance that occurs after buying something "buyer's remorse." The popular saying goes, "The grass is always greener on the other side." The amount of dissonance one experiences as a result of a decision depends on four variables, the first of which is the *importance of the decision*. Certain decisions, such as that to skip breakfast, may be unimportant and produce little dissonance. Buying a house, seeking a new job, or moving to a new community, however, might involve a great deal of dissonance. The second variable is the *attractiveness of the chosen alternative*. Other things being equal, the less attractive the chosen alternative, the greater the dissonance. Third, the greater the *perceived attractiveness of the unchosen alternative*, the more the felt dissonance. Fourth, the greater the degree of *similarity or overlap between the alternatives*, the less the dissonance.

In 1970 an interesting study was published about automobile buying.[34] Often, while waiting for delivery of a car, a customer will cancel the purchase because of postdecisional dissonance. In this study, a group of automobile customers were called twice during the period of time between signing the contract and actual delivery to reassure them about their purchase. Members of a control group were not called. As expected, significantly more of those who were not called canceled the order (about twice as many).

Another situation in which dissonance is apt to result is forced compliance or being induced to do or say something contrary to one's beliefs or values. This situation usually occurs when a reward is involved for complying or a punishment for not complying. Dissonance theory predicts that the less the pressure to conform, the greater the dissonance. If you were asked to do something you didn't like doing but you were paid quite a bit for doing it, you would not feel as much dissonance as if you were paid very little. The less external justification (such as reward or punishment), the more one must focus on the internal inconsistency within the self. This is why, according to the dissonance theorist, "soft" social pressures can be so powerful: They can cause a great deal of dissonance.

After completing a very boring task, subjects in a well-known experiment were "bribed" to tell other subjects that the task would be fun.[35] Some of these participants were paid $1 to lie, and the others were paid $20. As expected, because they experienced more dissonance, the $1 liars tended to change their opinion of the task to actually believe it was fun, whereas the $20 liars tended to maintain their belief that the task was dull.

Dissonance theory also makes several other situational predictions. The theory predicts, for example, that the more difficult one's initiation to a group, the greater commitment one will have to that group. The more social support one receives from friends on an idea or action, the greater the pressure to believe in that idea or action. The greater the amount of effort one puts into a task, the more one will rationalize the value of that task.

The theory of cognitive dissonance sets the stage for a more detailed look at the cognitive system and consistency as an organizing principle.

Rokeach: Attitudes, beliefs, and values. One of the finest theories on attitude and change is that of Milton Rokeach. He has developed an extensive explanation of human behavior based on beliefs, attitudes, and values.[36] His theory builds on the

34. J. H. Donnelly and J. M. Ivancevich, "Post-purchase Reinforcement and Back-Out Behavior," *Journal of Marketing Research* 7 (1970): 399–400.

35. Leon Festinger and James M. Carlsmith, "Cognitive Consequences of Forced Compliance," *Journal of Abnormal and Social Psychology* 58 (1959): 203–210.

36. Milton Rokeach, *Beliefs, Attitudes, and Values: A Theory of Organization and Change* (San Francisco: Jossey-Bass, 1969); *The Nature of Human Values* (New York: Free Press, 1973).

theories of the past and provides some interesting and valuable extensions.

Rokeach believes that each person has a highly organized belief–attitude–value system, which guides the behavior. The system consists of "countless beliefs, their organizations into thousands of attitudes, the several dozen of hierarchically arranged terminal values . . . organized to form a single, functionally interconnected belief system."[37]

Beliefs are the hundreds of thousands of statements (usually inferences) that we make about self and the world. Beliefs are general or specific, and they are arranged within the system in terms of their centrality or importance to the ego. At the center of the belief system are those well-established, relatively unchangeable beliefs that literally form the core view of self and world. At the periphery of the system lie numerous insignificant beliefs.

The more central a belief, the more resistant it is to change and the more impact such change will have on the overall system. In other words, if one of your central beliefs changes, expect rather profound changes in how you think about many things. This is why religious conversion has such a great impact on one's life.

Groups of beliefs that are organized around a focal object and predispose a person to behave in a particular way toward that object are *attitudes*. If a

37. Rokeach, *Human Values*, p. 215.

belief system has hundreds of thousands of beliefs, it similarly will have perhaps thousands of attitudes, each consisting of a number of beliefs about the attitude object. Figure 7.7 illustrates, in overly simple form, the organization of an attitude.

Rokeach believes attitudes are of two important kinds that must always be viewed together. These are *attitude toward object* and *attitude toward situation*. One's behavior in a particular situation is a function of these two in combination. If you do not behave in a given situation consistently with your attitudes toward certain things, it is probably because your attitude toward the situation prevents it. An example of this kind of inconsistency is eating foods you do not like when they are served to you as a guest. For example, you might dislike cabbage, brussels sprouts, and broccoli, but because of your attitude toward being a guest, if they were served, you would not complain. The point here is that behavior is a complex function of a variety of sets of attitudes, and the system consists of many beliefs ranging in their centrality.

Rokeach believes that of the three concepts in explaining human behavior, value is the most important. *Values* are specific types of beliefs that are central in the system and act as life guides. Values are of two kinds. *Instrumental values* are guidelines for living on which we base our daily behavior, such as hard work and loyalty. *Terminal values* are the ultimate aims of life toward which we work, such as wealth and happiness.

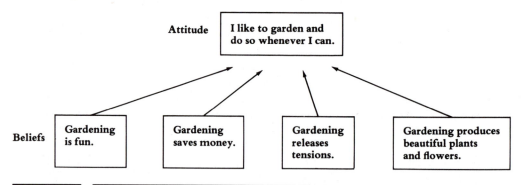

Figure 7.7 A simple example of the belief structure of an attitude.

In his research on values, Rokeach isolated what he considers the most common values in our society and has developed a ranking scale to assess individuals' value systems. Assuming that values vary in terms of centrality, people were asked to rank order these values from the most important to the least important. Table 7.3 lists the eighteen terminal and instrumental values isolated in the theory.[38] The numbers in the columns indicate the composite rankings for American men and women discovered in a massive survey. A world at peace is the most important terminal value for men and women, and honesty is the most important instrumental value. Rokeach has conducted several studies with his scale and provides a breakdown of attitude rankings into various categories of age, race, and education.[39]

Another component in the belief–attitude–value system that assumes great overall importance is *self-concept*. Self-concept consists of one's beliefs about the self. It is the individual's answer to the question, Who am I? Self-concept is particularly important to the system because "the ultimate purpose of one's total belief system, which includes one's values, is to maintain and enhance . . . the sentiment of self-regard."[40] Thus, whereas beliefs, attitudes, and values constitute the components of the system, self-concept is its guiding goal or purpose. With these four concepts, Rokeach has tied the theory into a cohesive package.

Rokeach is basically a consistency theorist. He includes a number of significant hypotheses about attitudes, beliefs, and values, but he concludes that people are guided by a need for consistency and that inconsistency creates a pressure to change

Rokeach has broadened his explanation of consistency far beyond the other theories of this tradition. Taking the total system into consideration, he sees consistency as extremely complex. An individual may be inconsistent on several different levels.

38. Ibid., pp. 57–58.
39. Ibid., chap. 3.
40. Ibid., p. 216.

In all, ten areas in the psychological system interrelate and bear the potential for inconsistency. Table 7.4, adapted from Rokeach's book, is a matrix of all the possible relations among elements

Table 7.3 Value Rankings (Composite) for American Men and Women

Values	Men	Women
Terminal Values		
A comfortable life	4	13
An exciting life	18	18
A sense of accomplishment	7	10
A world at peace	1	1
A world of beauty	15	15
Equality	9	8
Family security	2	2
Freedom	3	3
Happiness	5	5
Inner harmony	13	12
Mature love	14	14
National security	10	11
Pleasure	17	16
Salvation	12	4
Self-respect	6	6
Social recognition	16	17
True friendship	11	9
Wisdom	8	7
Instrumental Values		
Ambitious	2	4
Broadminded	4	5
Capable	8	12
Cheerful	12	10
Clean	9	8
Courageous	5	6
Forgiving	6	2
Helpful	7	7
Honest	1	1
Imaginative	18	18
Independent	11	14
Intellectual	15	16
Logical	16	17
Loving	14	9
Obedient	17	15
Polite	13	13
Responsible	3	3
Self-controlled	10	11

in the belief–attitude–value system.[41] Rokeach calls his own theory a comprehensive theory of change:

> A comprehensive theory should ideally be able to address itself to the conditions that will lead to long-range as well as short-range change, behavioral change as well as cognitive change, personality change as well as cognitive and behavioral change, and a rising or lowering of self-conceptions as well as their maintenance. A major objective of this book is to build a theoretical framework that will, it is hoped,

address itself to such issues, one that at least attempts to bridge the current gap between various personality, social-psychological, and behavior theories that for the most part do not speak to each other.[42]

Rokeach believes that the most important inconsistencies in a person's psychological system are those in row A (Table 7.4), involving cognitions about the self. Only when inconsistencies involve the self-conception will there be significant, lasting change. The reason for this is that such contradictions increase self-dissatisfaction.

41. Ibid., pp. 220–221.

42. Ibid., p. 224.

Table 7.4 Matrix of Contradictory Relations Possible Within the Total Belief System

	A	B	C	D	E	F	G	H	I	J	
A Cognitions about self											
B Terminal value system											
C Instrumental-value system											
D Attitude system											
E Attitude											
F Cognitions about own behavior											
G Cognitions about significant others' attitudes											
H Cognitions about significant others' values											
I Cognitions about significant others' behavior											
J Cognitions about behavior nonsocial objects											

Because maintenance of self-regard is the overall aim of the psychological system, it is natural that this should be so.

Judgment Processes

The theories in this section deal with the ways in which individuals make judgments about messages. A theory of the general process of message evaluation is presented first, followed by theories related to three general types of judgments—judgments of nonverbal behavior, judgments of belief claims, and judgments of attitudes.

Evaluation: Elaboration Likelihood Theory

Social psychologists Richard Petty and John Cacioppo developed elaboration likelihood theory as a general summation of insights from many other attitude-change theories.[43] It has received a good deal of research in its own right and has thereby become one of the most popular persuasion theories today.

The basic thesis of this theory is that people process information from persuasive messages with varying degrees of *elaboration,* which involves active, critical thinking about arguments and issues. Sometimes you are thoughtful about arguments, and other times you are not. Elaboration likelihood, the probability of critical evaluation of arguments, is a continuum from very little to a great deal.

People process information in one of two ways: through a *central route* or a *peripheral route.* Elaboration occurs in the central route and nonelaboration in the peripheral one. Thus, processing information through the central route means that you actively think about the information and weigh it against what you already know. When you process through the peripheral route, you tend to be influenced by factors other than the argument itself.

43. Richard E. Petty and John T. Cacioppo, *Communication and Persuasion: Central and Peripheral Routes to Attitude Change* (New York: Springer-Verlag, 1986). For an excellent brief summary, see O'Keefe, *Persuasion,* pp. 95–116.

When you use the central route, arguments are carefully considered; and if attitude change results, it is apt to be relatively enduring and will probably affect your behavior. On the other hand, if you use the peripheral route, any resulting change is probably temporary and may have less effect on how you actually act. Keep in mind, however, that because elaboration likelihood is a variable, you will probably use both routes somewhat, depending on the degree of elaboration expected.

The likelihood of elaboration depends upon two general factors—motivation and ability. When you are highly *motivated,* you are likely to use central processing, and when motivation is low, peripheral processing is more likely. You cannot use central processing unless you have the *ability* to do so. Consequently, low ability leads to more peripheral processing, whereas higher ability at least makes central processing possible.

Motivation consists of at least three things. The first is *involvement,* or the personal relevance of the topic to the person. The more important the topic, the more likely that the individual will think critically about the issues involved. The second factor of motivation is *diversity of argument.* People tend to think more about multiple arguments that come from several sources. The reason for this is that when several people are addressing an issue in a variety of ways, making snap judgments is not as easy. Other things being equal then, where multiple sources and multiple arguments are involved, receivers tend to process the information centrally. The third factor of motivation is the *need for cognition,* or the enjoyment of thinking. People who enjoy mulling over arguments will probably use more central processing that those who do not.

Motivation is obviously important in determining elaboration likelihood, but motivation by itself is not sufficient. One must also be able to give a message the kind of attention required of central processing. There are a variety of reasons why one may not have this ability. For example, you might be distracted by other things, or you may have insufficient knowledge about the topic to think carefully about the arguments and issues. In these cases you will have to rely on less complicated decision-making rules in deciding whether to believe what you hear.

Let us turn now to the differences between central and peripheral processing and their potential outcomes. Figure 7.8 illustrates the two processing routes.[44] According to this figure, if one is neither motivated nor has the ability to process the message, peripheral cues will be monitored with the possibility of peripheral influence. If the receiver is motivated and can process the message, the information in the message will be compared with what he or she already knows. If knowledge is insufficient to make these kinds of judgments, peripheral processing will occur. Otherwise, arguments will be weighed and judgments made about their adequacy, and change may occur in the individual's attitudes and behavior.

When processing information in the central route, you will carefully consider the arguments. What might persuade you under these conditions? Certainly the degree to which the message matches your previous attitude would have an effect here. Messages that are more favorable to your view would probably be evaluated more positively than those that are not. On the other hand, the strength of the argument will certainly play a role because in central processing you are thinking critically. You will identify good and bad arguments, and you will tend to be influenced more by good ones.

In peripheral processing, you do not look closely at the strength of the argument. Indeed, you make judgments quickly about whether to believe what you hear or read on the basis of certain simple cues. For example, the *credibility* of the source can be used as a cue. When source credibility is high, the message may be believed. *Liking* is another cue: You tend to believe people you like. The *number of arguments* can also be a cue in that you may rely on the sheer number of arguments to determine whether to accept a message. Probably, many types of cues are used in the peripheral route.

As an example of how central and peripheral processing work, consider the following experiment. Petty and his colleagues asked 145 students to evaluate audiotapes of arguments in favor of instituting comprehensive examinations for seniors at their college.[45] Two versions were used, one with strong arguments and the other with weak ones. Half of the students were told that the examination could go into effect the following year, but the other half were led to believe that the change would not occur for 10 years. Obviously, the first group would find the message more personally relevant than the second group and would therefore be more motivated to scrutinize the arguments carefully. It was expected that these students would be less susceptible to peripheral cues.

To test this hypothesis, the researchers told half of the high-relevance group and half of the low-relevance group that the tape was based on a report from a high school class, and the other half of these groups was told that it was based on a report of the Carnegie Commission. Thus, the first group was presented with a low-source credibility cue, whereas the other group was presented with a high-credibility cue. In a typical experimental design then, the subjects were divided so that an eighth of them heard each variation of the tape: (1) a highly relevant message with strong arguments by a highly credible source, (2) a highly relevant message with strong arguments by a less credible source, (3) a highly relevant message with weak arguments by a highly credible source, (4) a highly relevant message with weak arguments by a less credible source, (5) a nonrelevant message with strong arguments by a highly credible source, (6) a nonrelevant message with strong arguments by a less credible source, (7) a nonrelevant message with weak arguments by a highly credible source, and (8) a nonrelevant message with weak arguments by a less credible source.

As expected, the students who heard the highly relevant message were motivated to pay careful attention to the quality of the arguments and were more influenced by the arguments than were the students who heard the less relevant message. Those students who heard the less relevant message

44. Petty and Cacioppo, *Communication*, p. 4.

45. Richard E. Petty, John T. Cacioppo, and R. Goldman, "Personal Involvement as a Determinant of Argument-Based Persuasion," *Journal of Personality and Social Psychology* 41 (1981): 847–855.

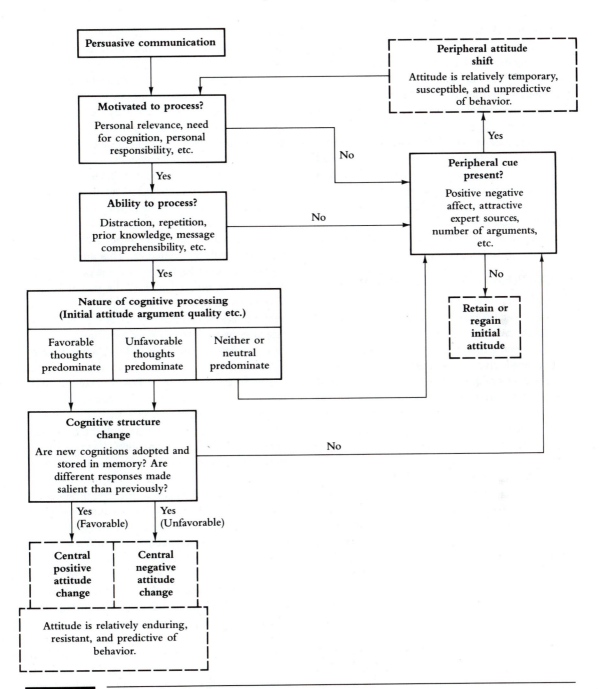

Figure 7.8   Schematic depiction of the two routes to persuasion.

From *Communication and Persuasion: Central and Peripheral Routes to Attitude Change* by Richard E. Petty and John T. Cacioppo. © 1986 by Springer-Uerlag. Reprinted by permission of the publisher.

were more influenced by credibility as a peripheral cue than were the other students. Petty, Cacioppo, and their colleagues have done a number of similar studies with the same results.

It might seem that the lesson from this theory is always to be critical in evaluating messages, but, practically, people cannot always attend carefully to every message. Some combination of central and peripheral processing is always to be expected. Most of the time, you are probably influenced by both. Even when motivation and ability are low, you might still be influenced somewhat by strong arguments; and even when you are processing in the central route, other less critical factors can also affect your attitudes.

Judging Behavior: Expectancy-Violation Theory

People usually behave according to accepted norms, but this is not always the case. How do we respond when other communicators violate our expectations? This interesting question has been the subject of a number of theories.[46] Here, we look at one particularly promising approach developed on the basis of a number of research studies by communication researcher Judee Burgoon and her colleagues. It is called the *nonverbal expectancy-violation model.*[47]

According to this theory, we have expectations about the behavior of another person based on social norms as well as our previous experience with the other person and the situation in which the behavior occurs. These expectations can involve virtually any nonverbal behavior, including, for example, eye contact, distance, and body angle. (Actually, we probably have expectations for verbal behavior as well, but this theory does not address this subject.)

The common assumption is that when expectancies are met, the other person's behaviors are judged as positive, and when they are violated, the behaviors are judged as negative; however, Burgoon has found that this is not always the case. Violations are often judged favorably.

Whether judged as good or bad, violations cause arousal on the part of the perceiver. In other words, if someone stands too close to you or too far away, if a another person's eye contact is abnormal, or if an individual violates some other set of expectations, you will feel different. This arousal is not necessarily negative. In fact, in some cases it might feel pleasant, especially when the violation communicates affiliation or liking. Sometimes, however, violations can make you feel uncomfortable. Apparently, we learn to have expectations and to detect violations very early in life, even in infancy.

Researchers in this area have also found that people are quick to make judgments about the nonverbal behavior of other people. Sometimes these judgments are positive and sometimes negative. This theory deals in large part with the conditions under which violations are appreciated and when they are disliked and the consequences of these judgments.

What seems to happen in the case of violations is that the perceiver's attention is drawn to behavior that would otherwise go unnoticed. When expectations are met, behavior is out of awareness; when they are violated, we become distracted by the behavior. This distraction may be what causes the arousal. When we notice behaviors that are normally out of awareness, we tend to pay more attention to interpreting those behaviors, which in turn leads to the evaluation process.

Imagine, for example, that you have just been introduced to an attractive person. In getting to know each other, you talk about everything from the weather to family. Suddenly you become aware that this person is standing unusually close to you. You try to back off, but your new acquaintance continues to move in. Your first tendency will be to

46. See, for example, P. A. Andersen, "Nonverbal Immediacy in Interpersonal Communication," in *Multichannel Integrations of Nonverbal Behavior,* eds. A. W. Siegman and S. Feldstein (Hillsdale, N.J.: Erlbaum, 1985), pp. 1–36; Joseph N. Cappella and John O. Greene, "A Discrepancy-Arousal Explanation of Mutual Influence in Expressive Behavior for Adult-Adult and Infant-Adult Interaction," *Communication Monographs* 49 (1982): 89–114; M. L. Patterson, *Nonverbal Behavior: A Functional Perspective* (New York: Springer-Verlag, 1983).

47. Judee K. Burgoon and Jerold L. Hale, "Nonverbal Expectancy Violations: Model Elaboration and Application," *Communication Monographs* 55 (1988): 58-79.

interpret this behavior: What does it mean? Then you will make a judgment about it: Is it good or bad? You might, for example, interpret the behavior as a "come on" and evaluate it positively.

An important variable in the evaluation process is the *communicator reward valence*, or the degree to which you find the interaction rewarding. You might be rewarded because you like the person, because the interaction will lead to positive outcomes, or because of a variety of situations in which the benefits for interaction outweigh the costs. On the other hand, the communicator valence could be negative because it entails more costs than benefits.

Your evaluation of the communicator affects your subsequent evaluation of the violation by influencing your interpretation of the behavior and thereby your judgment. In the example above, if you like the other person and are attracted to this individual, you will probably see the violation of interpersonal space as a sign that this person is also attracted to you and evaluate it positively.

Figure 7.9 illustrates the violation-evaluation process. The figure shows that expectancies arise from one's perception of the communicator's characteristics, the state of the relationship, and the context in which the behavior occurs. If the behavior is expected, arousal is not heightened, and the evaluation of the behavior will be pretty much in line with the perceiver's view of the communicator and the interpretation of the behavior. If you find communication with this person rewarding and the behavior has a positive connotation, you will probably evaluate the behavior positively; if these conditions do not exist, you will probably evaluate it negatively.

Violations of expectancies accentuate the judgments you make in this process. Here the reward valence of the other communicator is especially strong: Violations cause arousal, which in turn accentuate evaluation of communication with the other person and the meaning of the message. If the exchange is valued and the behavior has a positive meaning, then a positive outcome will result.

Figure 7.9 includes two other possibilities that can be important. The first is that the message can

be disregarded (discounted) as unimportant and ignored. Another possibility is that the meaning of the behavior may be ambiguous, and one is not sure what to make of it. This theory predicts that ambiguous behavior by a valued communicator will be taken as positive, but such behavior by an unrewarding communicator will be taken as negative. Again, this effect will be accentuated in cases of a violation.

An interesting study of eye gaze shows how violations can affect judgments of behavior and communication outcomes.[48] The researchers trained four confederates to manipulate their eye behavior to effect seemingly natural violations in an interview. About 150 students in an organizational communication course volunteered to participate in the study as part of an interviewing assignment. They took the role of an employment interviewer, and each interviewed one of the confederates. In preparation for half of the interviews, the subjects were given a high-status résumé, and the other half were given a low-status one. The first group was set up to find interview rewarding, whereas the other would obviously find it less so. Some interviewers got a confederate who gave them normal eye contact, some got a person who gave them no eye contact, and some got a confederate who gave above-normal eye gaze.

The experiment aimed to test the effects of eye-gaze violations in high- and low-reward interactions. After the interview, each subject completed a set of scales related to the credibility of the applicant, how likely they would be to hire this individual, how attracted they were to this person, and other aspects of the relationship that developed between them in the interview.

The results of this experiment showed that the failure to have eye contact with the interviewer definitely hurt the applicants' images whether they were high or low status. A higher-than-normal level of eye gaze was also found to be a violation, but it was interpreted somewhat differently

48. Judee K. Burgoon, "Communicative Effects of Gaze Behavior: A Test of Two Contrasting Explanations," *Human Communication Research* 12 (1986): 495–524.

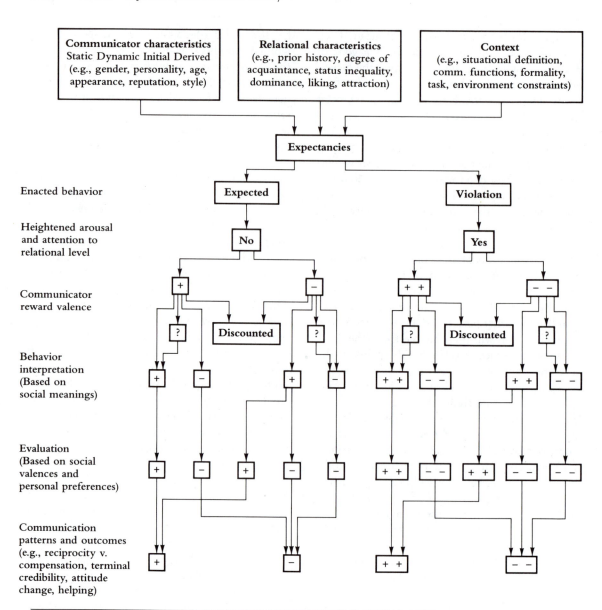

Enacted behavior

Heightened arousal
and attention to
relational level

Communicator
reward valence

Behavior
interpretation
(Based on
social meanings)

Evaluation
(Based on social
valences and
personal preferences)

Communication
patterns and outcomes
(e.g., reciprocity v.
compensation, terminal
credibility, attitude
change, helping)

NOTE: For simplicity, communicator reward valence, behavior interpretation, and behavior evaluation valence have been dichotomized into positive and negative but should be understood to represent continua. Double pluses and minuses denote greater magnitude of effect.

Figure 7.9   Nonverbal Expectancy Violations Model.

From Judee K. Burgoon and Jerold L. Hale, "Nonverbal Expectancy Violations: Model Elaboration and Applica-tion," *Communication Monographs* 55 (1988): 64. Reprinted by permission of Speech Communication Association and the authors.

between the two conditions. High-status applicants with nearly constant eye contact were judged more favorably than were low-status applicants with constant eye contact.

Judging Claims: Cognitive Argument

Argument is a commonly studied topic in the field of communication. Typically, arguments have been viewed in two ways, which have been designated argument$_1$ and argument$_2$. *Argument$_1$* is *making* an argument, and *argument$_2$* is *having* one.[49] The first form is the structure of an argument within a message, and the second is the interaction between people embroiled in a dispute.

Dale Hample has suggested that there is a third form called *cognitive argument*.[50] He labels this form *argument$_0$* because he believes it to be fundamental to the other two.[51] Cognitive argument is the mental process involved in evaluating beliefs, which lies at the heart of both message reception and production. It entails all basic cognitive processes outlined at the beginning of this chapter. As such cognitive argument is internal, private, and prior to any public manifestations of argumentation. Hample believes that all public forms of argument require cognitive argument as a foundation.

In addition, cognitive argument is a natural part of all message reception because the information processing that receivers go through involves weighing, integrating, and evaluating claims. From this perspective then, receivers actively make arguments out of the material provided by message senders. Public arguments are stimuli, but the real work occurs mentally in the mind of the receiver. This kind of internal argument can create new beliefs, reinforce old ones, change beliefs, alter the salience of certain beliefs within the system, or cause beliefs to be related to one another in new ways.

Cognition is designed to produce order, and argument is a central process in this organizational function. Hample relates argument to three types of organizational patterns—evaluation, probability, and semantics. *Evaluation* is a process in which values and judgments are organized into a consistent pattern. This type of evaluation is determined by argument—weighing information and comparing it with what is already felt or valued in some way. For example, when you get your grades at the end of the semester, you test your feelings about them with how you already feel about grades in general and the value you assign to them. You then make some sort of judgment about your grades for that term.

Probability is the organization of information into a consistent belief pattern. This pattern is used to answer questions about the probability of truth. Again, probabilistic consistency is achieved by internal argument. For example, you may use your grades as evidence for certain beliefs about your abilities, perhaps a confirmation that you are smart.

Finally, *semantics* involves meaning, and cognition via argument operates to maintain consistency of meanings. So, for example, your meanings for the grades of A, B, and C are constantly reinforced by your performance each semester.

Cognitive argument is basically a process of evaluating claims. Each new claim is evaluated in terms of the context of existing beliefs within the mind of the communicator. A message presents new claims, and you evaluate these in terms of your overall *cognitive context*. Whether you accept the claim depends on the weight you give to the new information versus that assigned to the overall context of relevant beliefs.[52] If, for example, you assign

49. Daniel J. O'Keefe, "Two Concepts of Argument," *Journal of the American Forensic Association* 13 (1977): 121–128.

50. Dale Hample, "A Cognitive View of Argument," *Journal of the American Forensic Association* 16 (1980): 151–158; "The Cognitive Context of Argument" *Western Journal of Speech Communication* 45 (1981): 148–158; "A Third Perspective on Argument," *Philosophy and Rhetoric* 18 (1985): 1–22; "Argument: Public, Private, Social and Cognitive," *Argumentation and Advocacy* 25 (1988): 13–19.

51. Actually, Hample now seems to see cognitive argument as one of several dimensions of a singular process rather than a separate type that is fundamental to the others. See Hample, "Argument: Public, Private."

52. This idea is based in part on a theory of belief evaluation by William J. McGuire, "A Syllogistic Analysis of Cognitive Relationships," in *Attitude Organization and Change*, eds. M. J. Rosenberg et al. (New Haven, Conn.: Yale University Press, 1960), pp. 65–111; and Robert S. Wyer and Lee Goldberg, "A Probabilistic Analysis of the Relationship Between Beliefs and Attitudes," *Psychological Review* 77 (1970): 100–120.

very heavy weight to a set of beliefs about the importance of grades, an instructor's comments that grades don't matter will probably be rejected. On the other hand, if you are not very confident in what you already believe about, say, the depletion of the ozone layer, you might evaluate a professor's claims on this subject quite positively.

Hample summarizes the importance of cognitive argument in this way: "Argument is a way—perhaps our only way—of ordering the world. By processing 'evidence' into 'conclusions,' we make inferences and build up associations among cognitive items which hopefully have analogues in objective reality."[53]

Judging Attitudes: Social Judgment Theory

Social judgment theory is associated primarily with the work of the social psychologist Muzafer Sherif and his associates.[54] This theory finds its roots in the early psychophysical research in which persons were tested in their ability to judge physical stimuli. Using this work as an analogy, Sherif investigated the ways individuals judge social stimuli such as attitudes. He learned that many principles of psychophysics hold for social judgment as well.

Sherif and his colleagues found that individual judgments of things and people are highly situational and depend on one's initial orientation toward the world. The psychological literature shows that people make judgments about things based on anchors, or reference points. Suppose that you are involved in an experimental situation in which you are asked to judge the relative weight of five objects. On what would you base your judgment? If the experimenter handed you a weight and

told you it was 10 pounds, you would first feel the reference weight and then make judgments about the other objects based on the feeling of the known weight. The known weight would act as an anchor, influencing your perception of the others. In fact, with a different initial weight, you would judge the same objects differently.

To demonstrate this idea of anchors, try a simple experiment. Take three bowls. Fill the first with hot water, the second with cold water, the third with tepid water. Put one hand in the hot water, the other in the cold water; and after a few moments, place both hands in the third bowl. Your perceptions of the warm water will be different for each hand because each hand had a different anchor, or reference.

Sherif reasons that similar processes operate in judging communication messages. In social perception anchors are internal; they are based on past experience. The internal anchor, or reference point, is always present and influences the way a person responds in communication with others. The more important the issue is to one's ego, the stronger the anchor will influence what is understood.

In a social judgment experiment, you would be given a large number of statements about some issue. You then would be asked to sort these messages into groups according to similarity of position. You could use as many groups as you wished. Then you would order these groups in terms of position on a negative-positive scale and indicate which groups are acceptable to you personally, which are not acceptable, and which are neutral. The first measures your *latitude of acceptance*, the second your *latitude of rejection*, and the third your *latitude of noncommitment*. On any issue, there will usually be a range of statements, pro or con, that the person can tolerate; there will also be a range that one cannot accept.

Another important concept from social judgment is *ego-involvement*. Previously, an attitude was thought to be measured primarily in terms of valence (direction, pro or con) and the degree of agreement or disagreement. But Sherif demonstrates that ego-involvement is significant apart

53. Hample, "Cognitive View," p. 157.

54. The first major work in this area was Muzafer Sherif and Carl I. Hovland, *Social Judgment* (New Haven, Conn.: Yale University Press, 1961). See also Muzafer Sherif, Carolyn Sherif, and Roger Nebergall, *Attitude and Attitude Change: The Social Judgment-Involvement Approach* (Philadelphia: Saunders, 1965). For a brief overview of the theory, see Muzafer Sherif, *Social Interaction—Process and Products* (Chicago: Aldine, 1967), chaps. 16–18. Several secondary sources are also available; see, for example, Mary John Smith, *Persuasion and Human Action: A Review and Critique of Social Influence Theories* (Belmont, Calif.: Wadsworth, 1982), pp. 264–283; O'Keefe, *Persuasion*, pp. 29–44.

from either of these other two dimensions of attitude. Ego-involvement is the degree to which one's attitude toward something affects the self-concept. It is the importance of the issue to the individual.

For example, you may have read much about the depletion of the ozone layer and have come to believe that this is a serious problem. If you have not yet experienced any personal difficulties because of this problem, it may be academic to you, and your ego-involvement is low. On the other hand, if you have already been treated for skin cancer, the issue might be considerably more ego-involving.

Ego-involvement makes a great deal of difference in how you respond to messages related to the issue. A relatively high correlation exists between involvement and extremity, but it is not a perfect correlation. In fact, it is possible for a person to have a moderate position yet be highly ego-involved.

Now let us consider what social judgment theory says about the communication process. The social judgment theory is a fine contribution to our understanding of communication because it explains two important behaviors of audiences in receiving messages. First, we know from Sherif's work that individuals judge the favorability of a message based on their own internal anchors and ego-involvement. On a given issue, such as legalization of marijuana, a person may distort the message by contrast or assimilation. The *contrast effect* occurs when individuals judge a message to be farther from their point of view than it actually is. The *assimilation effect* occurs when persons judge the message to be closer to their point of view than it is.

Basically, when a message is relatively close to one's own position, that message will be assimilated, and more distant messages are apt to be contrasted. These assimilation and contrast effects are heightened by ego-involvement. So, for example, if you believe strongly that industry should be regulated to stop ozone depletion, a moderately favorable statement to that effect might seem like a strong positive statement because of your assimilation, whereas a slightly unfavorable statement

might be perceived to be strongly opposed to regulation because of contrast. If you were highly ego-involved in the issue, this effect would be even greater.

The second area in which social judgment theory aids our understanding of communication is attitude change. The predictions made by social judgment theory are the following:

1. Messages falling within the latitude of acceptance facilitate attitude change.

2. If a message is judged by the person to lie within the latitude of rejection, attitude change will be reduced or nonexistent. In fact, a boomerang effect may occur in which the discrepant message actually reinforces one's own position on the issue.

3. Within the latitude of acceptance and noncommitment, the more discrepant the message from the person's own stand, the greater the expected attitude change. However, once the message hits the latitude of rejection, change will not be expected.

4. The greater one's ego-involvement in the issue, the larger the latitude of rejection, the smaller the latitude of noncommitment, and thus the less the expected attitude change.

In summary, social judgment theory predicts a curvilinear relationship between discrepancy and attitude change, as Figure 7.10 illustrates.

To illustrate how social judgment works, consider an interesting experiment done by a group of researchers shortly after Oklahoma passed a prohibition law in the 1950s.[55] The researchers recruited a number of people who were deeply involved in the issue on one side or the other and several who were moderate and not very involved in the issue. They found that those who were highly ego-involved and extreme in their opinions had much wider latitudes of rejection than did moderates, and the moderate subjects had much wider latitudes of noncommitment than did those who held extreme

55. Carl I. Hovland, O. J. Harvey, and Muzafer Sherif, "Assimilation and Contrast Effects in Reactions to Communication and Attitude Change," *Journal of Abnormal and Social Psychology* 55 (1957): 244–252.

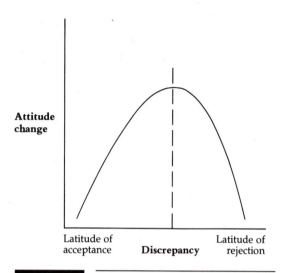

Attitude
change

Latitude of
acceptance   **Discrepancy**   Latitude of
rejection

Figure 7.10   Theoretical relationship between
discrepancy and change.

opinions. Interestingly, when presented with the same moderate message, the extreme "drys" judged it to be much more toward the nonprohibition side than did other subjects, and the "wets" judged it to be much more toward the prohibition side than the other subjects. In other words, both extreme groups had a contrast effect. Generally, the attitude change experienced by the moderates after hearing a message on the issue was about twice as much as the attitude change experienced by those who were highly involved in the issue.

Commentary and Critique

The theories discussed in this chapter explain how people process information in messages. For the most part, these are receiver-oriented theories, which is not to suggest that they are divorced from message production. Indeed, message production and reception are two sides of the same coin and cannot be separated in actual practice.

Still, these theories show us that communication depends on how messages are understood and judged. All these theories tell us in one form or another what message receivers do and how they

do it. As a group these theories address three major accomplishments—interpreting, organizing, and judging.

The first of these accomplishments is interpretation. We assign meaning to concepts, we try to figure out intentions, and we attribute causes. Interpretation is continuous so that we often reinterpret messages as well. The second accomplishment is organization, in which new information is integrated into a system of existing beliefs and attitudes. One of the central principles for organizing information seems to be consistency. Finally, people constantly make judgments on the basis of information. We sometimes evaluate arguments carefully, and sometimes we attend to less central aspects of the message or source. As part of the judgment process, we evaluate nonverbal behaviors, argument claims, and attitude statements.

The theories in this chapter are organized around these three elements of information processing, and each theory is discussed within the context that seems most applicable to it; however, each theory in this chapter tells us something about all three accomplishments outlined above. Indeed, interpretation, organization, and judgment are basically different aspects of the same process.

The theories in this chapter share a number of ideas about how people process information. Four general processes are suggested by the theories in this chapter. The first is *assigning meaning*. Although meaning is central to interpretation, it also relates to organization and judgment. Obviously, one's meaning for a piece of information will govern how that information is organized and evaluated. Osgood's theory of meaning shows us how individual concepts are interpreted on the basis of evaluation, potency, and activity. Relevance theory states that relevance is the key to interpreting intentions, and attribution theory addresses the causal nature of meaning. Even the nonverbal expectancy-violation model shows that interpretation is a vital part of how nonverbal behaviors are judged.

Another mechanism that permits information processing is *reasoning*, or inference making. Reasoning enters into interpretation, organization, and judgment in a variety of ways. Several theories in this chapter address this concern. For example, cognitive argument theory shows how virtually every aspect of cognition is involved in argument formation. It explains the ways in which contextual information is combined with new information to evaluate the probability of a claim. Relevance theory uses this same idea to show how communicators use messages to infer intentions. Attribution theory also reveals the reasoning process that people use to assess causes.

Several of the theories in this chapter also address the process of *comparing ideas*. This is the central idea of social judgment theory, and a number of other theories also provide insights into this process. Consistency theory and information-integration theory are examples. Consistency theories show us how new information is compared with the other elements of cognition and how inconsistency is handled. Information-integration theory shows us that various pieces of information are weighted in terms of their overall effects within the cognitive system.

Finally, several of these theories deal with processes of attitude, belief, and value *change*. Information-integration theory shows how change occurs as a result of newly integrated information. Consistency theory shows how imbalance leads to change. Social judgment theory shows how change results from the perception of attitude statements. Elaboration likelihood theory shows the relative effects of central and peripheral processing on attitude change. The theory of cognitive argument addresses the ways in which one's internally formed arguments are crucial to persuasion.

Virtually all theories in the chapter follow the rational-person model. As a group these theories share the idea that people think through problems and situations rationally and objectively. There are exceptions, of course. For example, some adherents to attribution theory have made the point that people are often inaccurate and irrational in their judgments. Social judgment theory indicates that people often distort information, and elaboration likelihood theory says that people weigh evidence and evaluate arguments only part of the time. Vir-

tually all theorists in this chapter, however, admit to the possibility of rational decision making, and few of them would deny that people can be rational and objective.

The rational-person model makes a clear assumption about the nature of human thought. Humans are conceived as independent, rational, choice-making beings. This view is deeply embedded in Western philosophy and is part of many Western cultural views. Many other cultures, however, would find this description of people very strange. Like all theory then, these approaches are definitely products of a particular worldview.

This is a worldview that explains human experience in terms of individual cognition. It is a view that assumes a universal cognitive mechanism behind all action. The point of the experiments, measurements, hypotheses, and theories of message processing is to discover these underlying mechanisms. Many theories in this chapter exemplify this type of thinking directly; others are more specific in explaining certain types of behaviors.

Examples of general theories of cognition are Osgood's theory of meaning and semantic space, information integration, consistency, elaboration likelihood, and cognitive argument. Each theory posits certain principles, operations, or mechanisms that drive human thought and action. Other theories such as expectancy violation, second guessing, and attribution address particular types of thought and action. By extrapolation, all the latter theories also tell us indirectly something about general mechanisms as well.

Given their overall aim then, the chief strengths of all these theories are their parsimony and intuitive appeal. Most explain a great deal with only a few key variables. Osgood narrows all of connotative meaning down to three dimensions. Sperber and Wilson show how relevance lies at the heart of interpretation. Fishbein and Ajzen show how a vast array of thought and behavior can be explained by a simple integrative mechanism. Festinger and even Rokeach reduce cognitive organization to a single principle of consistency. And so it goes. These theories are appealing because they truly help us understand rather esoteric processes normally baffling to the average person. One of the reasons cognitive explanations are so popular is the common "aha" response they produce.

Cognitive consistency theories are a good example of this strength. These theories have had a major impact on our thinking about attitude and attitude change. A mainstay of social psychology for many years, cognitive consistency is appealing because of its parsimony and heuristic value. For a 20-year period, it stimulated a great deal of research. The popularity of consistency theory is understandable, given the goal of this field to discover a few important variables that would predict social behavior. Consistency theories do just that. They isolate certain elements of cognition and show how manipulations among these variables can predict a person's feelings, thoughts, or actions. They also appeal to the scientist's sense of logic, providing an explanation for behavior that makes intuitive sense. At one time consistency theories were so well accepted that debates centered not on whether people respond to dissonance but on ways to improve the precision of predictions based on these theories.

At the same time, however, there are serious hazards in this kind of theorizing. The nagging question remains: Are cognitive processes really universal, and if not, how wide a scope do these theories cover? Osgood's three "universal" dimensions of meaning offer a good example of the problem.

Although most behavioral researchers admit the usefulness of semantic differential technique for measuring a certain aspect of connotative meaning, they question the view that the factors of meaning—evaluation, potency, and activity—are invariant and universal across situations, concepts, and cultures. Although these factors have shown up in an amazingly diverse set of studies, they do not always appear; to suggest that they are universal is a gross overgeneralization. What appears as universal may in fact not be so.

For example, similar responses may result from the use of the highly structured semantic differential test. The semantic differential always involves adjective scales, and subjects are often presented with many of the same scales in study after study.

Subjects may respond more to the form of the instrument than to the real meanings of the concepts. Also, the semantic differential relies heavily on a statistical procedure called factor analysis. This technique shows how the several scales intercorrelate to form factors, but the researcher must subjectively interpret and name the factors. If a theorist such as Osgood believes that three factors are universal, a strong tendency may develop to interpret the factor structure in just that way. In short, the claim that factors of meaning are universal may be the result of a self-fulfilling prophecy.

Another problem in trying to discover cognitive universals is the mistaken idea that if one's hypothesized mechanism fits the data, it alone can explain the data, when any number of hypothesized mechanisms may explain what is going on. How, then, do we choose from among competing explanations? This is a difficult problem. The theory of cognitive dissonance, as an example, has been criticized for precisely this problem.[56]

The basic standard for any predictive theory—and the theory of cognitive dissonance is precisely that—is to be stated in such a way that contradictory evidence could prove the theory wrong in its predictions. In other words, the theory must be falsifiable. The problem with dissonance theory is that it can be used to explain various, contradictory results and cannot be proved wrong, which creates a situation wherein the dissonance theorist wins no matter how an experiment comes out. If attitude change results from the manipulations, one can argue that the change was caused by dissonance; if attitude change does not occur, one can say that dissonance did not exist.

Furthermore, dissonance is such a general concept that it can take any number of forms. Thus, the experimenter can claim that a particular result was caused by one kind of dissonance but that an entirely different result was produced by another kind of dissonance. This circular reasoning results because dissonance researchers do not measure dis-

56. Natalia P. Chapanis and Alphonse Chapanis, "Cognitive Dissonance: Five Years Later," *Psychological Bulletin* 61 (1964): 21.

sonance per se but infer dissonance from behavior. Indeed, there is some question about whether dissonance is directly observable at all. This is the case of virtually all cognitive processes.

Cognitive processes do not present themselves in self-defined form. Despite the scientific leanings of many researchers, cognitive processes do not lie in wait of discovery. They must be defined by the theorist. Inquiry into information processing involves inferring underlying processes from observed behavior and naming the variables believed to be operating. As we have seen in the history of the social sciences, there is no end to the number of constructs that can be created and named. Theoretical definitions are abstract and partial, which always leaves room for additional constructing, naming, and defining.

In this chapter we have encountered a wide variety of constructs, which have been given a host of interesting names: dissonance, elaboration, attitude, argument, expectancy, relevance, attribution, ego-involvement, and more. The mere fact that these concepts vie for our attention as competing explanations of thought and action demonstrates the challenge of explaining cognition and action.

There are a variety of responses to this state of affairs. One is competition: Which theory will win? This response is problematic because of the impossibility of falsifying all but one explanation. Another response is integration: How can the theories be combined? This response is appealing because it recognizes the utility of all theories, but it is a pretext, resulting in a loss of parsimony and failure to discover cognitive universals. A third response is flexibility: How can each theory be used appropriately for certain purposes without denying the utility of the others? This approach has the benefit of enabling us to see more than could be viewed from the confines of a single theory, but it can only be done after abandoning the attempt to find a parsimonious, central mechanism of thought and action.

The creation and definition of constructs can lead to a self-fulfilling prophecy on the part of the theorist. In other words, once a set of constructs is found to fit, even if only partially, there is a strong

tendency to see the same things no matter where you look. Osgood always "saw" evaluation, potency, and activity in his factor-analysis results. No matter what a person processes in a message, one could call it "central" or "peripheral." No matter what one says about another person, you could identify it as "attribution."

Social judgment theory is a good example of how researcher biases affect the interpretation of results. In many of their experiments, researchers compared individuals who were highly ego-involved with people less involved and concluded that the differences were due to their level of involvement. Actually, these groups of people could have been different for other reasons as well, which would invalidate the interpretation offered by social judgment theory.[57]

Like the interpretation of any research results, social judgment theorists had to make certain assumptions in their interpretations. The theory assumes, for example, that there is a sequential, causal mechanism whereby judgment as a cognitive activity precedes attitude change, and social judgment research was unable to prove this assumption.

Looked at objectively, the results of many experiments on cognitive processes are less clear than the author believes them to be. For example, most of the negative criticism of information-integration theory relates to the validity of measurement. Although the idea that attitudes consist of accumulated and weighted beliefs is generally accepted, much doubt exists that one can measure the overall accumulated weight and value of a belief system with any degree of reliability. In the natural setting, a researcher would first have to isolate beliefs contributing to an attitude, measure them accurately, and factor out the influence of other elements of the system. Because this process is difficult or impossible to do, most research in this tradition is artificial, hypothetical, and controlled. This problem thus casts doubt on the external validity of the claims. A related problem is that disagreement exists about the way one accumulates information to form an attitude. The research evidence is

57. This point is made by O'Keefe, *Persuasion*.

equivocal on this point and casts doubt on the validity of the approach.[58]

All these objections to theories of message processing are "easy punches." They belie the intelligence and hard work that has gone into the devel-

opment of these theories. In Chapter 2, we noted that no theory has a direct line to truth. Theories are based on guess, inference, and creativity, and that is the best we can do. Whether or not you believe in universal processes of mind, the theories presented in this chapter and others like them provide insights that are intriguing and useful in our attempt to understand communication.

58. For a review of the issues in this dispute, see Mary John Smith, *Persuasion and Human Action*, pp. 245–248; and O'Keefe, *Persuasion*, pp. 55–59.

CHAPTER 8

Theories of Symbolic Interaction, Dramatism, and Narrative

The theories discussed in this chapter take quite a turn from the cognitive theories discussed in the previous two chapters. For the scholars in the interactional tradition, communication and meaning are unabashedly social. Unlike the theories discussed previously, these approaches do not seek meaning in intrinsic properties of the mind. Rather, meaning is created through and sustained by interaction in the social group. Interaction establishes, maintains, and changes certain conventions—roles, norms, rules, and meanings—within a social group or culture. Those conventions literally define the reality of the culture.

We discuss this group of theories in two chapters. This chapter covers the foundational literature in symbolic interactionism and closely related ideas on dramatism and narrative. Chapter 9 examines theories of the social construction of reality, rules, and culture. An affinity also exists between this genre and some of the interpretive theories that are addressed in Chapter 10.

Symbolic Interactionism

Symbolic interactionism contains a core of common premises about communication and society. Jerome Manis and Bernard Meltzer isolate seven basic theoretical and methodological propositions from symbolic interactionism, each identifying a central concept of the tradition:[1]

1. "The meaning component in human conduct: Distinctly human behavior and interaction are carried on through the medium of symbols and their meanings." All human understanding occurs by assigning meaning to experience. Human perception is always mediated by a filter of symbols.

2. "The social sources of humanness: The individual becomes humanized through interaction

---

1. Jerome G. Manis and Bernard N. Meltzer (eds.), *Symbolic Interaction* (Boston: Allyn and Bacon, 1978), p. 437.

with other persons." Meanings are learned in interaction. Meanings arise from the exchange of symbols in social groups.

3. "Society as process: Human society is most usefully conceived as consisting of people in interaction." All social structures and institutions are created by actual individuals in interaction with one another.

4. "The voluntaristic component in human conduct: Human beings are active in shaping their own behavior." Individual behavior is not strictly determined by prior events. Rather, through interaction, individuals re-create social realities.

5. "A dialectical conception of mind: Consciousness, or thinking, involves interaction within oneself." Mind is nothing more than an internal conversation, which mirrors interactions one has had with others.

6. "The constructive, emergent nature of human conduct: Human beings construct their behavior in the course of its execution." Behavior is enacted. It is created in the social group in the course of interaction.

7. "The necessity of sympathetic introspection: An understanding of human conduct requires study of the actors' covert behavior." One cannot understand human experience by observing overt behavior. People's understandings, their meanings, for events must be ascertained.

The picture painted by symbolic interactionism, then, is one of individuals who attempt to achieve goals through interaction with other people. Their experience is always shaped by the meanings that arise from the use of symbols within the social group. Meaning, which is the heart of experience, is a product of interaction, making communication the core of human experience.

Manford Kuhn divides the time line of symbolic interactionism into two major portions. The first, which he calls the *oral tradition*, was the early period when the primary foundations of symbolic interaction developed. Following the posthumous publication of George Herbert Mead's *Mind, Self, and Society*, the second period, which can be

termed the *age of inquiry*, came to flower.[2] Of course, the ideas of symbolic interaction did not emerge overnight from the mind of a lone thinker. They can be traced to the early psychology of William James. The primary interactionists in the early tradition were Charles Cooley, John Dewey, I. A. Thomas, and George Herbert Mead. Before Mead's ideas on communication were published, the interactionist perspective found life and sustenance primarily through oral transmission, especially in Mead's classroom. Although Mead did not publish his ideas during his lifetime, he is considered the prime mover of symbolic interactionism.

During this early Meadian period, the important ideas of the theory were developed. Mead and other interactionists departed from earlier sociological perspectives that had distinguished between the person and the society. Mead viewed individuals and society as inseparable and interdependent. Early interactionism stressed both the importance of social development and innate biological factors. Further, the early symbolic interactionists were not as concerned with how people communicated as they were with the impact of this communication on society and individuals. Above all, the early interactionists stressed the role of the shared meaning of symbols as the binding factor in society. The early theorists were strongly concerned with studying people in relation to their social situation. They maintained that a person's behavior could not be studied apart from the setting in which the behavior occurred or apart from the individual's perception of the environment. A result of this concern was that these early interactionists favored case histories as a research method.[3]

During the age of inquiry—the years that followed the publication of *Mind, Self, and Society*—two divergent schools began to develop within the arena of symbolic interactionism. The original for-

2. Manford H. Kuhn, "Major Trends in Symbolic Interaction Theory in the Past Twenty-Five Years," *Sociological Quarterly* 5 (1964): 61–84.

3. Bernard N. Meltzer and John W. Petras, "The Chicago and Iowa Schools of Symbolic Interactionism," in *Human Nature and Collective Behavior*, ed. T. Shibutani (Englewood Cliffs, N.J.: Prentice-Hall, 1970).

mulations of Mead were not altogether consistent, leaving room for divergent interpretation and extension. As a result the Chicago and Iowa schools developed. The Chicago School, led primarily by Herbert Blumer, continued the humanistic tradition begun by Mead. Blumer above all believes that the study of humans cannot be conducted in the same manner as the study of things. The goals of the researcher must be to empathize with the subject, to enter the subject's realm of experience, and to attempt to understand the value of the person as an individual. Blumer and his followers avoid quantitative and scientific approaches to studying human behavior. They stress life histories, autobiographies, case studies, diaries, letters, and nondirective interviews. Blumer particularly stresses the importance of participant observation in the study of communication. Further, the Chicago tradition sees people as creative, innovative, and free to define each situation in individual and unpredictable ways. Self and society are viewed as process, not structure; to freeze the process would be to lose the essence of person–society relationships.

The Iowa School takes a more scientific approach to studying interaction. Manford Kuhn, its leader, believes that interactionist concepts can be operationalized. Although Kuhn admits the process nature of behavior, he advocates that the objective structural approach is more fruitful than the "soft" methods employed by Blumer. As we will see later in the chapter, Kuhn is responsible for a well-known measurement technique used in symbolic interaction research.[4]

The Chicago School

George Herbert Mead is usually viewed as the major source of the interactionist movement, and his work certainly forms the core of the Chicago School.[5] Herbert Blumer, Mead's foremost apostle,

invented the term *symbolic interactionism*, an expression Mead himself never used. Blumer refers to this label as "a somewhat barbaric neologism that I coined in an offhand way. . . . The term somehow caught on."[6]

The three cardinal concepts in Mead's theory, captured in the title of his best-known work, are society, self, and mind. These categories are different aspects of the same general process, the *social act*. Basic to Mead's thought is the notion that people are actors, not reactors. The social act is an umbrella concept under which nearly all other psychological and social processes fall. The act is a complete unit of conduct, a gestalt, that cannot be analyzed into specific subparts. An act may be short, such as tying a shoe, or it may be the fulfillment of a life plan. Acts interrelate and are built on one another in hierarchical form throughout a lifetime. Acts begin with an impulse; they involve perception and assignment of meaning, covert rehearsal, weighing of alternatives in one's head, and consummation.

In its most basic form, a social act involves a three-part relationship: an initial gesture from one individual, a response to that gesture by another (covertly or overtly), and a result of the act, its meaning, which is perceived or imagined by both parties. In a holdup, for example, the robber indicates to the victim what is intended. The victim responds by giving money or belongings, and in the initial gesture and response, the defined result (a holdup) has occurred. Even individual acts, such as

4. Ibid.

5. Mead's primary work in symbolic interactionism is *Mind, Self, and Society* (Chicago: University of Chicago Press, 1934). For a general discussion of the history, influence, and methods of the Chicago School, see Jesse G. Delia, "Communication Research: A History," in *Handbook of Communication Science*, eds. C. R. Berger and S. H. Chaffee (Newbury Park, Calif.: Sage, 1987), pp. 30–37. For outstanding secondary sources on Mead, see Bernard N. Meltzer, "Mead's Social Psychology," in *Symbolic Interaction*, eds. J. G. Manis and B. N. Meltzer (Boston: Allyn and Bacon, 1972), pp. 4–22; and Charles Morris, "George H. Mead as Social Psychologist and Social Philosopher" (Introduction), in *Mind, Self, and Society*; and C. David Johnson and J. Stephen Picou, "The Foundations of Symbolic Interactionism Reconsidered," in *Micro-Sociological Theory: Perspectives on Sociological Theory*, vol. 2, eds. H. J. Helle and S. N. Eisenstadt (Beverly Hills, Calif.: Sage, 1985), pp. 54–70.

6. Herbert Blumer, *Symbolic Interactionism: Perspective and Method* (Englewood Cliffs: N.J.: Prentice-Hall, 1969), p. 1.

taking a solitary walk, are interactional in that they are based on gestures and responses that occurred many times in the past and continue in the mind of the individual. One never takes a walk by oneself without relying on meanings and actions learned in social interaction in the past. This capacity to act implies that the individual can deal with problem situations: "Instead of being merely an organism that responds to the play of factors on or through it, the human being is seen as an organism that has to deal with what it notes."[7]

Societal or group action is merely the extended process of many individuals accommodating their actions to one another. A *joint action* of a group of people consists of an *interlinkage* of their separate actions. Such institutions as marriage, trade, war, and church worship are joint actions. Group action is based in individual acts. Hence, we must consider group conduct as the combined independent actions of the individual participants; Blumer states, "The participants still have to guide their respective acts by forming and using meanings."[8]

Blumer notes that in an advanced society the largest portion of group action consists of highly recurrent and stable patterns. These group actions possess common and established meanings in their social context. Because of the high frequency of such patterns and the stability of their meanings, scholars have tended to treat the actions as structures, or entities. Blumer warns us not to forget that new situations present problems requiring adjustment and redefinition. Even in highly repetitious group patterns, nothing is permanent. Each case must begin anew with individual action. No matter how solid a group action appears to be, it is still rooted in individual human choices: "It is the social process in group life that creates and upholds the rules, not the rules that create and uphold group life."[9]

Interlinkages may be pervasive and extended. Individual actions may be connected through complicated networks. Distant actors may be inter-

linked ultimately in diverse ways, but contrary to popular sociological thinking, "a network or an institution does not function automatically because of some inner dynamics or system requirements: it functions because people at different points do something, and what they do is a result of how they define the situation in which they are called on to act."[10]

With this outline in mind then, let us look more closely at the first facet of Meadian analysis—society. *Society*, or group life, is a cluster of cooperative behaviors on the part of society's members. Lower animals have societies, too, but they are based on biological necessity and are physiologically determined. As a result an animal society behaves in predictable, stable, and unchanging ways. What, then, distinguishes human cooperative behavior?

Human cooperation requires understanding the intentions of the other communicator. Because "minding" or thinking is a process of figuring out what actions one will undertake in the future, part of "feeling out" the other person is assessing what that person will do next. Thus, cooperation consists of "reading" the other person's actions and intentions and responding in an appropriate way. Such cooperation is the heart of interpersonal communication. The notion of mutual response with the use of language makes symbolic interactionism a vital approach to communication theory.

Human beings use symbols in their communication. People consciously conduct a process of mental manipulation, delaying of response, and assigning meaning to the gestures of others. The symbol is interpreted by the receiver, which makes meaning central to social life. Blumer develops three points about the centrality of meaning:

> Human beings act toward things on the basis of the meanings that the things have for them.
> The meaning of such things is derived from, or arises out of, the social interaction that one has with one's fellows.
> These meanings are handled in, and modified through, an interpretive process used by the person in dealing with the things he encounters.[11]

7. Ibid., p. 14.
8. Ibid., p. 17.
9. Ibid., p. 19.

10. Ibid., p. 19.
11. Ibid., p. 2.

Meaning is a product of social life. Whatever meaning a person possesses for a thing is the result of interaction with others about the object being defined. An object has no meaning for a person apart from the interaction with other humans. So, for example, although you may never have heard of a "toilet telephone," inmates know it well because they have learned that they can communicate by listening to voices that travel through the sewer pipes in the prison.

What is distinctive about the interactionist view of meaning is its stress on conscious interpretation. An object has meaning for the person at the point when the individual thinks about or interprets the object. This process of handling meanings is basically an internal conversation: "The actor selects, checks, suspends, regroups, and transforms the meanings in light of the situation in which he is placed and the direction of his actions."[12]

Clearly, symbols must possess shared meaning for society to exist. Mead called a gesture with shared meaning a *significant symbol.* Society arises in the significant symbols of the group. Because of the ability to vocalize symbols, we literally can hear ourselves and thus can respond to the self as others respond to us. We can imagine what it is like to receive our own messages, and we can empathize with the listener and take the listener's role, mentally completing the other's response.

Society, then, consists of a network of social interactions in which participants assign meaning to their own and other's actions by the use of symbols. Even the various institutions of society are just built up by the interactions of people involved in those institutions. Consider the court system in the United States as an example. The courts are nothing more than the actions and interactions among judges, juries, attorneys, witnesses, clerks, reporters, and others who use language to interact with one another. *Court* has no meaning apart from the interpretations of the actions that occur in and around court by those involved. The same can be said for school, church, government, industry, and any other segment of society.

12. Ibid., p. 5.

This interplay between responding to others and responding to self is an important concept in Mead's theory, and it provides an excellent transition to the second member of the troika—*the self.* To state that a person has a self implies that the individual can act toward the self as toward others. A person may react favorably to the self and feel pride, happiness, encouragement; or one may become angry or disgusted with the self. The primary way that a person comes to see the self as others see it (possess a self-concept) is through *role taking* or behaving as others behave. Of course, this act would not be possible without language (significant symbols), for through language the child learns the responses, intentions, and definitions of others.

The idea of the *generalized other* is central to Mead's notion of self. The generalized other is the unified role from which the individual sees the self. It is our individual perception of the overall way that others see us. The self-concept is unified and organized through internalization of this generalized other. Your generalized other is your concept of how others in general perceive you. You have learned this self-picture from years of symbolic interaction with other people in your life.

Consider, for example, the self-image of an adolescent. As a result of their interactions with significant others such as parents, siblings, and peers, teenagers come to view themselves as they perceive others have viewed them. They come to take on the persona that has been reflected to them in their many interactions with other people. As they behave in ways that affirm this image, it is strengthened as others respond accordingly in a cyclical fashion. So, for example, if a young person feels socially inept, he or she may withdraw, further reinforcing the image of being "dorky."

The self has two facets, each serving an essential function in the person's life. The *I* is the impulsive, unorganized, undirected, unpredictable part of the person. The *me* is the generalized other, made up of the organized and consistent patterns shared with others. Every act begins with an impulse from the I and quickly becomes controlled by the me. The I is the driving force in action, whereas the me provides direction and guidance. Mead used the concept of me to explain socially acceptable and adaptive behavior and the I to explain creative, unpredictable impulses within the person.

For example, many people will deliberately change their life's situation in order to alter their own self-concept. Here, the I moves the person to change in ways that the me would not permit. An example might.be a high school student's going on to college. Many "dorky" high school students decide that they will use college to establish a new me by associating with a new group of significant others and by establishing a new generalized other. This is what people mean when they say that they got a new start.

The ability to use significant symbols to respond to oneself leads to the possibility of inner experience and thought that may or may not be consummated in overt conduct. This latter idea constitutes the third part of Mead's theory—the *mind*. The mind can be defined as the process of interacting with oneself. This ability, which develops along with the self, is crucial to human life, for it is part of every act. "Minding" involves hesitating (postponing overt action) while one consciously assigns meaning to the stimuli. Mind often arises around problem situations in which the individual must think through future actions. The person imagines various outcomes, selecting and testing possible alternative actions.

Because people possess significant symbols that allow them to name their concepts, the person can transform mere stimuli into real objects. Objects do not exist apart from people. The object is always defined by the individual in terms of the kinds of acts that a person might make toward the object. A seascape is a seascape when I value looking at it. A glass of lemonade is a drink when I conceive of drinking it or not drinking it. Objects become the objects they are through the individual's symbolic minding process; when the individual envisions new or different actions toward an object, the object is changed.

For Blumer, objects are of three types: physical (things), social (people), and abstract (ideas). Objects acquire meaning through symbolic interaction. Objects can hold different meanings for dif-

ferent people, depending on the nature of others' actions toward the person regarding the defined object. A police officer may mean one thing to the residents of an inner-city ghetto and something else to the inhabitants of a posh residential area; the different interactions among the residents of these two vastly different communities may determine different meanings.

A fascinating study of marijuana using by Howard Becker illustrates the ideas of the Chicago School very well.[13] Becker found that users learn at least three sets of meanings and actions through interaction with other users. The first is to smoke the drug properly. Virtually everyone Becker talked to said that they had trouble getting high at first until others showed them how to do it. Second, smokers must learn to define the sensation produced by the drug as a "high." In other words, the individual learns to discriminate the effects of marijuana and to associate these with smoking. Becker claims that this association does not happen automatically and must be learned through social interaction with other users. In fact, some experienced users reported that novices were absolutely stoned and didn't know it until they were taught to identify the feeling. Finally, users must learn to define the effects as pleasant and desirable. Again, this is not automatic; many beginners do not find the effects pleasant at all until they are told that they should consider them so.

Here, we see that marijuana is a social object. Its meanings are created in the process of interaction. How people think about the drug (mind) is determined by those meanings, and the assumptions of the group (society) is also a product of interaction. Although Becker does not report information about self-concept specifically, it is easy to see that a part of the self may also be defined in terms of interactions in the marijuana-smoking community.

The Iowa School

Manford Kuhn and his students, although maintaining basic interactionist principles, take two

13. Howard Becker, "Becoming a Marihuana User," *American Journal of Sociology* 59 (1953): 235–242.

new steps not previously seen in the old-line inter-actionist theory. The first is to make the interac-tionist concept of self more concrete; the second, which makes the first possible, is the use of quanti-tative research. In this latter area, the Iowa and Chicago schools part company. Blumer strongly criticizes the trend in the behavioral sciences to operationalize; Kuhn makes a point to do just that! As a result Kuhn's work moves more toward micro-scopic analysis than does the traditional Chicago approach.

Like many of the interactionists, Kuhn never published a truly unified work. The closest may be C. A. Hickman and Manford Kuhn's *Individuals, Groups, and Economic Behavior*, published in 1956.[14] (For an excellent short synthesis see Charles Tucker's critique.[15])

Kuhn's theoretical premises are consistent with Mead's thought. Kuhn conceives of the basis of all action as symbolic interaction. The child is social-ized through interaction with others in the society into which he or she is born. The person has mean-ing for and thereby deals with objects in the envi-ronment through social interaction. To Kuhn, the naming of an object is important, for naming is a way of conveying the object's meaning in commu-nicable terms. Kuhn agrees with his colleagues that the individual is not a passive reactor but an active planner. He reinforces the view that individuals undertake self-conversations as part of the process of acting. Kuhn also stresses the importance of lan-guage in thinking and communicating.

Like Mead and Blumer, Kuhn discusses the importance of objects in the actor's world. The *object* can be any aspect of the person's reality: a thing, a quality, an event, or a state of affairs. The only requirement for something to become an object for a person is that the person name it, rep-resent it symbolically. Reality for persons is the totality of their social objects. Kuhn agrees with other interactionists that meaning is socially

derived. Meaning is assigned to an object from group norms regulating how people deal with the object in question.

A second concept important to Kuhn is the plan of action. A *plan of action* is a person's total behav-ior pattern toward a given object, including whether to seek or avoid it, how the object is thought to behave (because this determines how the person will behave toward the object), and feelings about the object as it is defined. *Attitudes* constitute a subset of the plan of action. Attitudes are verbal statements that act as blueprints for one's behavior. The attitude indicates the end toward which action will be directed as well as the evalu-ation of the object. Because attitudes are verbal statements, they can be observed and measured.

Consider, for example, the variety of plans of action that people hold in regard to marijuana and other drugs. For some, drugs are a central part of life and daily activity; for others, drugs are to be avoided at all costs. Many people in our society have a disdain for illegal drugs but use legal ones such as alcohol and tobacco with gusto. For the most part, these plans of action are determined by a person's attitudes toward drugs, which are learned in social interaction with other people.

A third concept important to Kuhn is the orien-tational other. *Orientational others* are those who have been particularly influential in a person's life. They possess four qualities. First, they are people to whom the individual is emotionally and psycholog-ically committed. Second, they are the ones who provide the person with general vocabulary, central concepts, and categories. Third, they provide the individual with the basic distinction between self and others, including one's perceived role differ-entiation. Fourth, the orientational others' com-munications continually sustain the individual's self-concept. Orientational others may be in the present or past; they may be present or absent. The important idea behind the concept is that the individual comes to see the world through interac-tion with particular other persons who have touched one's life in important ways.

Finally, we come to Kuhn's most important con-cept—*the self*. Kuhn's theory and method revolve

14. C. A. Hickman and Manford Kuhn, *Individuals, Groups, and Economic Behavior* (New York: Holt, Rinehart & Winston, 1956).

15. Charles Tucker, "Some Methodological Problems of Kuhn's Self Theory," *Sociological Quarterly* 7 (1966): 345–358.

around self, and it is in this area that Kuhn most dramatically extends symbolic interactionist thinking. Kuhn is primarily responsible for a technique known as the twenty-statements self-attitudes test. His rationale for developing this procedure is stated succinctly: "If as we suppose, human behavior is organized and directed, and if, as we further suppose, the organization and direction are supplied by the individual's attitudes toward himself, it ought to be of crucial significance to social psychology to be able to identify and measure self-attitudes."[16]

A subject taking the twenty-statements test would be confronted with twenty blank spaces preceded by the following simple instructions:

> There are twenty numbered blanks on the page below. Please write twenty answers to the simple question, "Who am I?" in the blanks. Just give twenty different answers to this question. Answer as if you were giving the answers to yourself, not to somebody else. Write the answers in the order that they occur to you. Don't worry about logic or "importance." Go along fairly fast, for time is limited.[17]

There are a number of ways to analyze the responses from this test, with each method tapping a different aspect of self. The self-conception is seen as the individual's plans of action toward the self as an object. This self-concept consists of the individual's identities (roles and statuses), interests and aversions, goals, ideologies, and self-evaluations. Such self-conceptions are anchoring attitudes, for they act as one's most common frame of reference for judging other objects. All subsequent plans of action stem primarily from the self-concept.

Two major aspects of the self may be termed the ordering variable and the locus variable. The *ordering variable* is the relative salience of identifications the individual possesses. It is observable in the order of statements listed by the subject in the twenty-statements task. For example, if the person lists "Baptist" a great deal higher than "father," the

researcher may conclude that the person identifies more readily with religious affiliation than with family affiliation. The *locus variable* is the extent to which the subject in a general way tends to identify with consensual groupings rather than idiosyncratic, subjective qualities.

In scoring the self-attitude test, the analyst may place statements in one of two categories. A statement can be said to be *consensual* if it consists of a discrete group or class identification, such as student, girl, husband, Baptist, from Chicago, premedical student, daughter, oldest child, engineering student. Other statements are not descriptions of commonly agreed-on categories. Examples of *subconsensual* responses are happy, bored, pretty, good student, too heavy, good wife, interesting. The number of statements in the consensual group is the individual's locus score.

The idea of locus is important to Kuhn: "Persons vary over a rather wide range in the relative volume of consensual and subconsensual components in their self-conceptions. It is in this finding that our empirical investigation has given the greatest advance over the purely deductive and more or less literary formulations of George Herbert Mead."[18]

The conflict between the Chicago and Iowa schools is apparent. In fact, the work of Kuhn and his associates has become so estranged from mainstream symbolic interactionism that it has lost its support among those who espouse the basic tenets of the movement. Kuhn's methods simply are not adequate for investigating processal behavior, an essential element of interaction. As a result a group of followers, who believe in both the central ideas of symbolic interactionism and the expressed need to examine social life in concrete ways, has emerged as the "new" Iowa School. One of its leaders, Carl Couch, describes the situation:

> By the mid-1960s most of us affiliated with Kuhn had become disenchanted with the use of the TST [twenty-statements test] and allied instruments. There was an increasing awareness that this set of procedures was not generating the data required for serious testing, revision, and elaboration of the theory. Some

---

16. Manford H. Kuhn and Thomas S. McPartland, "An Empirical Investigation of Self-Attitudes," *American Sociological Review* 19 (1954): 68.

17. Ibid., p. 69.

18. Ibid., p. 76.

turned to naturalistic observation. . . . Some gave up the search; others foundered.[19]

Couch and his associates began studying the structure of coordinated behavior by using videotaped sequences. They have produced research on how interaction begins (openings) and ends (closings), how disagreements are negotiated, and how unanticipated consequences that block achievement of interaction objectives are explained. By studying these areas, they attempt to isolate general principles of symbolic interaction. Such principles may form the basis for a grounded theory of symbolic interaction in the future.[20]

Dramatism and Narrative

Dramatism and narrative are two closely associated movements that fit well under the interactionist umbrella. Theories of dramatism and narrative deal with one of the most important ways in which people use symbols and create meaning, the story. *Dramatism* is distinguished by its heavy reliance on a theatrical metaphor, and *narrative* is characterized by its use of story sequence.

The dramaturgical movement is closely aligned with symbolic interactionism and has been heavily influenced by it. The dramaturgists see people as actors on a metaphorical stage playing out roles in interaction with others. Bruce Gronbeck sketches the basic idea of dramatism, as shown in Figure 8.1.[21] Here action is seen as performance, or the use of symbols to present a story or script to interpret-

ers. In the process of performance, meanings and actions are produced within a scene or sociocultural context.

In this sense, several theorists might be termed *dramaturgical*, but dramaturgical theory lacks the unity required to be called a school. This section reviews the work of two very different dramaturgical theories. The first is the landmark theory of symbols by Kenneth Burke, and the second is the influential role theory of Erving Goffman.

An increasingly popular approach to communication is the narrative paradigm, which is akin to dramatism and consistent with the tenets of symbolic interactionism. Narrative theories focus on the ways in which people structure reality by telling stories. The story is not only a way of organizing a message but is also a common, some say universal, format for structuring interaction itself.[22] Howard Kamler expresses the importance of stories in this passage:

> Any communication is a sharing of stories. Most stories seem to cry out to be shared. And getting shared is perhaps the most profound function of stories. Stories are the stuff of communication. And the sharing of them is what transforms persons into communal beings. In trading our stories back and forth for inspection, agreement, disagreement, we are involved in the activity of making ourselves members of a community. Public story trade is at the heart of the social miracle about persons.[23]

In this chapter we look at two theories of narrative. The first, Ernest Bormann's convergence theory, originated in small-group communication theory and has been expanded to cover a great deal more. The second, Walter Fisher's narrative theory, points to the function of stories in all communication.

Dramatistic and narrative theories are difficult to separate. They both deal with the meanings

19.   Carl J. Couch, "Symbolic Interaction and Generic Sociological Principles" (Paper presented at the Symposium on Symbolic Interaction, Boston, 1979), p. 9.

20.   This work is summarized in Carl J. Couch and Robert Hintz (eds.), *Constructing Social Life* (Champaign, Ill.: Stipes, 1975); and Clark McPhail, "Toward a Theory of Collective Behavior" (Paper presented at the Symposium on Symbolic Interaction, Columbia, South Carolina, 1978). See also Carl Couch, "Studying Social Processes" (Videotape presentation, University of Iowa Media Center, Iowa City, 1984).

21.   Adapted from Bruce E. Gronbeck, "Dramaturgical Theory and Criticism: The State of the Art (or Science?)," *Western Journal of Speech Communication* 44 (1980): 317.

22.   Narrative is a popular topic in literature and in communication. See, for example, W. J. T. Mitchell (ed.), *On Narrative* (Chicago: University of Chicago Press, 1980); Howard Kamler, *Communication: Sharing Our Stories of Experience* (Seattle: Psychological Press, 1983); Didier Coste, *Narrative as Communication* (Minneapolis: University of Minnesota Press, 1989).

23.   Kamler, *Communication*, p. 49.

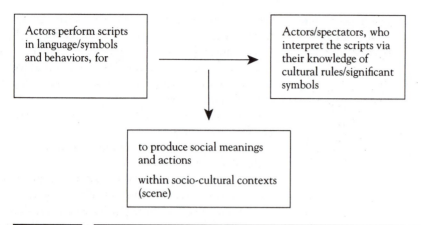

Figure 8.1   Dramaturgical model of society.

assigned to characters playing roles in a sequence of events. For this reason, the dramatistic and narrative theories are grouped together in this book.

The Dramatism of Burke

Kenneth Burke has written widely in many areas: from creative writing, to literary and rhetorical criticism, to social psychology, to linguistic analysis. Burke's concepts are not derived from the work of Mead and the other early sociologists. Some of his most important works, in fact, appeared concurrently with the publication of Mead's ideas. On the other hand, it would be incorrect to exclude Burke from the mainstream of symbolic interactionist thought, for although he has maintained his independence, his theory is highly consistent with the others presented in this chapter.

Burke is no doubt a giant among symbol theorists.[24] He has written over a period of 50 years, and his theory is the most comprehensive of all the interactionists. Hugh Duncan wrote, "It may be said without exaggeration that anyone writing today on communication, however 'original' he may be, is echoing something said by Burke."[25]

Burke has published eight major books, spanning from 1931 to the present.[26] A number of scholars have provided written interpretations of Burke's ideas.[27] In surveying Burke's communication theory, we will begin with a summary of his concept of action; then we will turn to his central concepts of symbols, language, and communication; and finally we will sketch Burke's method.

Burke sees the act as the basic concept in dramatism. His view of human action is consistent with that of Mead, Blumer, and Kuhn. Specifically, Burke distinguishes between action and motion. All objects and animals in the universe can be said to possess motion, but only human beings have action. *Action* consists of purposeful, voluntary behaviors of individuals. Dramatism is the study of action in this sense; the study of motion is mechanism. Burke believes that a dramatistic view of people is needed in all "human" disciplines, for human behavior cannot be properly understood without it.

Burke views the individual as a biological and neurological being, who possesses all the animalistic characteristics of lower species. Consistent with

24. See, for example, Herbert W. Simons and Trevor Melia (eds.), *The Legacy of Kenneth Burke* (Madison: University of Wisconsin Press, 1989).

25. Hugh Duncan, "Communication in Society," *Arts in Society* 3 (1964): 105.

26. See the Bibliography for a listing of Burke's main works.

27. For a comprehensive overview on Kenneth Burke, see William Rueckert (ed.), *Critical Responses to Kenneth Burke* (Minneapolis: University of Minnesota Press, 1969). For a brief and very clear summary, see Sonja K. Foss, Karen A. Foss, and Robert Trapp, *Contemporary Perspectives on Rhetoric* (Prospect Heights, Ill.: Waveland Press, 1991), pp. 169–208.

Mead, Burke distinguishes humans by their symbol-using behavior, the ability to act. People are symbol-creating, symbol-using, and symbol-misusing animals. They create symbols to name things and situations; they use symbols for communication; and they often abuse symbols by misusing them to their disadvantage. Burke's view of symbols is broad, including an array of linguistic and nonverbal elements as well. Especially intriguing for Burke is the notion that a person can symbolize symbols. One can talk about speech and can write about words. This second-level activity is a distinguishing characteristic of symbol use.

People filter reality through the symbolic screen. For an animal reality just is, but for humans reality is mediated through symbols. Burke agrees with Mead that language functions as the vehicle for action. Because of the social need for people to cooperate in their actions, language arises and shapes behavior. Language, as seen by Burke, is always emotionally loaded. No word can be affectively neutral. As a result a person's attitudes, judgments, and feelings invariably are in that person's language. Language is by nature selective and abstract, focusing attention on particular aspects of reality at the expense of others. Language is economical, but it is also ambiguous. Further, language is formal in that it tends to follow certain patterns or forms.

An overriding consideration for all of Burke's work is his concept of guilt. The term *guilt* is Burke's all-purpose word for any feeling of tension within a person: anxiety, embarrassment, self-hatred, disgust, and so forth. For Burke, guilt is a condition caused only in humans by their symbol-using nature. He identifies three interrelated sources of guilt arising out of language. The first is *the negative*. Through language people moralize (animals do not). They construct myriad rules and proscriptions. These rules are never entirely consistent, and in following one rule, you necessarily are breaking another, creating guilt.

Opinions about the conflict in the Persian Gulf are a perfect example. Many people have an opinion about U.S. involvement one way or another but feel uneasy about their opinion. If you supported the administration's offensive action there, you may have felt what Burke would call "guilt" about the lives lost and the tremendous costs of the war. If on the other hand, you had opposed the president's action, you may have felt a certain amount of "guilt" about letting a tyrant destroy a peaceful neighbor, and you quietly worried about what would have happened if Saddam Hussein prevailed.

The second reason for guilt is the *principle of perfection*. People are sensitive to their failings. Humans can imagine (through language) a state of perfection. Then, by their very nature, they spend their lives striving for whatever degree of this perfection they set for themselves. Guilt arises as a result of the discrepancy between the real and the ideal. Many peace activists are motivated by this kind of guilt. For example, a speaker at a rally may say that war is barbaric and inappropriate method of resolving conflict in the twentieth century. This speaker can imagine a world without war and is motivated to speak out because of the principle of perfection.

A third reason for guilt is the *principle of hierarchy*. In seeking order, people structure society in social pyramids or hierarchies (social ratings, social orderings). This ranking is a symbolic phenomenon. Competitions and divisions result among classes and groups in the hierarchy, and guilt results. The Persian Gulf crisis was precipitated by a struggle over dominance in that part of the world. Many who supported the U.S. involvement there worried that without intervention, Saddam would have gotten the upper hand. Others who had opposed the war felt a certain amount of guilt about U.S. supremacy in regions such as the Middle East.

For Burke, guilt is the primary motive behind all action and communication: We communicate to purge our guilt. In discussing communciation Burke uses several inseparable terms: persuasion, identification, consubstantiality, communication, and rhetoric. Let us see how these concepts are integrated in his theory. The underlying concept behind Burke's ideas on communication is that of *substance*. Substance is the general nature, fundamentals, or essence of a thing. Substance must be viewed in holistic terms; it is not a mere summation of the parts or aspects of the thing in consideration. Each person is distinct, possessing separate substance. Crucial to Burke's theory is the understanding that the substances of any two persons always overlap to some extent. The overlap is not perfect, though, and thus prevents ideal communication. Whatever communication occurs between individuals is a direct function of their consubstantiality (sharing of common substance). *Consubstantiality*, or commonality, allows for communication because of the shared meaning it creates for the symbols used. When Barney and Joe are relaxing next to the swimming pool on a warm summer morning, they communicate with each another in a free and understanding manner because they share meanings for the language in use. They are, so to speak, consubstantial. On the other hand, when Mary and Bob ask a question of a harried busboy in a Swiss restaurant, they may feel frustration because of their lack of shared meaning with this individual. To combine Mead and Burke, a significant symbol is one that allows for shared meaning through consubstantiality.

Another important concept of Burke is identification. As generally conceived, *identification* is the same as consubstantiality, or the sharing of substance. The opposite of identification is *division*. Division and the guilt it produces are the primary motives for communication. Through communication, identification is increased. In a spiraling fashion as identification increases, shared meaning increases, thereby improving understanding. Identification thus can be a means to persuasion or improved communication, or it can be an end in itself. Identification can be conscious or unconscious, planned or accidental. Three overlapping sources of identification exist among people. *Material identification* results from goods, possessions, and things. *Idealistic identification* results from ideas, attitudes, feelings, and values. *Formal identification* results from the form or arrangement of the act. If two people who are introduced shake hands, the conventional form of handshaking causes some identification to take place. Speakers can identify better with their audiences if they provide a form that is meaningful to the particular audience.

Before we proceed, let us be cautious. First, identification is not an either-or occurrence but a matter of degree. Some consubstantiality will always be present merely by virtue of the shared humanness of any two persons. Identification can be great or small, and it can be increased or decreased by the actions of the communicators. Second, although identification and division exist side-by-side between any two persons, communication is more successful when identification is greater than division.

An interesting phenomenon that might seem to contradict Burke's view of identification is that people of lower strata in a hierarchy often identify with persons at the top of the hierarchy, despite tremendous apparent division. This kind of identification can be seen, for example, in the mass following of a charismatic leader. Two overlapping factors explain its occurrence. First, individuals perceive in others an embodiment of the perfection for which they themselves strive. Second, the mystery surrounding the charismatic person simultaneously tends to hide the division that exists. This phenomenon can be called identification through *mystification*.

In striving for happiness, each person adopts certain strategies of identification. *Strategies* are analogous to Kuhn's concept of plans of action. They are the tactics for living, the plans for communicating with another. Burke does not attempt to outline all available strategies for relating to others because the list would be indefinitely long. One suggestion he makes for analyzing a rhetorical (communicative) act is to assess the strategies the communicators use to increase their identification. Burke provides a full-blown methodology for studying rhetorical acts. His method, in fact, has proved useful in areas such as rhetorical and literary criticism—the analysis of speeches, poems, books, and other rhetorical devices.

Burke's most basic methodological model is the dramatistic pentad. Pentad, meaning a group of five, is an analytical framework for the most efficient study of any act. The first part is the *act*, what is done by the actor. It is a view of what the actor played, what was accomplished. The second part is the *scene*, the situation or setting in which the act was accomplished. It includes a view of the physical setting and the cultural and social milieu in which the act was carried out. The third component is the *agent*, the actor, including all that is known about the individual. The agent's substance reaches all aspects of his or her being, history, personality, demeanor, and any other contributing factors. The *agency*, the fourth component, is the means, or vehicle, the agent uses in carrying out the act. Agency may include channels of communication, devices, institutions, strategies, or messages. Fifth, the *purpose* is the reason for the act—the rhetorical goal, the hoped-for effect or result of the act.

For example, in writing a paper for your communication theory course, you, the agent, gather information and present it to the instructor (the act). Your course, your university, your library, your desk and room, the social atmosphere of your school, and more constitute the scene; the format of the paper itself is the agency. You have a variety of purposes, including, in all likelihood, getting a good grade.

David Ling shows how Burke's pentad can be used to understand a communication event.[28] In 1969 Edward Kennedy, a senator from Massachusetts, was involved in an automobile accident with an aide, Mary Jo Kopechne, when he accidentally drove a car off of a bridge into a pond. Kennedy escaped, but Kopechne drowned. In a remarkable address to the people of Massachusetts about a week later, he explained what happened and attempted to regain the support of the people. Ling writes that Kennedy wanted to achieve two things—to minimize his own responsibility for the accident and to make the people responsible for whether or not he would continue in office.

Kennedy's appeal on the first point describes himself (agent) as a helpless victim of the events leading to the death of the young woman (scene). He explains his own failure to report the accident (act) as a consequence of his confusion and injuries. Kennedy's depiction makes him out to be a victim of a tragic situation. Later in his speech,

Kennedy essentially offered to resign if the citizens wanted him to. Here, the scene shifted to the public reaction to the accident, the agent became the people of Massachusetts, the act was their decision as to whether he should resign, the agency would be a statement of resignation, and the purpose would be to remove him from office. Ling believes this was a very effective speech. The reaction was overwhelmingly positive, and Kennedy continued in office.

Goffman's Social Approach

One of the most prolific sociologists of our day is Erving Goffman.[29] As a symbolic interactionist of the dramaturgical tradition, Goffman analyzes human behavior with a theatrical metaphor. The ordinary interaction setting is a stage. People are actors, structuring their performances to make impressions on audiences. According to Goffman, interpersonal communication is a presentation through which various aspects of the self are projected.

Goffman's observations of nearly 20 years are spread throughout his books, making synthesis difficult. Fortunately, Goffman provides a theoretical framework that outlines his general approach to human behavior.[30] He begins with the assumption that the person faced with a situation must somehow make sense of or organize the events perceived. What emerges as an organized happening for the individual becomes that person's reality of the moment. This premise states that what is real for a person emerges in that person's *definition of the situation*.

A typical response of a person to a new situation is the question, What is going on here? The person's definition of the situation provides an answer. Often the first definition is not adequate and a rereading may be necessary, as in the case of a prac-

28. David A. Ling, "A Pentadic Analysis of Senator Edward Kennedy's Address to the People of Massachusetts July 25, 1969," *Central States Speech Journal* 21 (1970): 81–86.

29. See Bibliography for a listing of Goffman's works.

30. Erving Goffman, *Frame Analysis: An Essay on the Organization of Experience* (Cambridge, Mass.: Harvard University Press, 1974). See also Jef Verhoeven, "Goffman's Frame Analysis and Modern Micro-Sociological Paradigms," in *Micro-Sociological Theory: Perspectives on Sociological Theory*, vol. 2, eds. H. J. Helle and S. N. Eisenstadt (Beverly Hills, Calif.: Sage, 1985), pp. 71–100; Stuart J. Sigman, *A Perspective on Social Communication* (Lexington, Mass.: Lexington Books, 1987), pp. 41–56.

tical joke, a mistake, or a misunderstanding. Rereading is important because we are often deceptive with one another.

One's definition of a situation can be divided into strips and frames. A *strip* is any arbitrary sequence of activity. It is any sequence of events, such as opening the refrigerator door, removing the milk, pooring it into a glass, drinking it, and putting the glass into the dishwasher. A *frame* is a basic organizational pattern used to define the situation. The strip of activities listed above might be defined as a "snack."

Frame analysis thus consists of examining the ways experience is organized for the individual. What the frame (or framework) does is allow the person to identify and understand otherwise meaningless events; it gives meaning to the ongoing activities of life. A natural framework is an unguided event of nature with which the individual must cope. A social framework, on the other hand, is seen as controllable, guided by some intelligence. Thus, humans have a sense of control when they enter the social frame. These two types of frameworks interrelate because social beings act on and are in turn influenced by the natural order. Goffman demonstrates the importance of frameworks for culture:

> Taken all together, the primary frameworks of a particular social group constitute a central element of its culture, especially insofar as understandings emerge concerning principal classes of schemata, the relations of these classes to one another, and the sum total of forces and agents that these interpretive designs acknowledge to be loose in the world.[31]

Frameworks, then, are the models we use to understand our experience, the ways in which we see things as fitting together into some coherent whole. Many traditional societies, for example, define persons in terms of roles. Women, men, and children have definite roles to be fulfilled, such as authority, food provider, homemaker, child nurturer, and learner, and each person knows his or her place in the world by virtue of this framework. Morality, whether one is good or bad, is judged in

terms of the framework of roles, and a sense of self-fulfillment or failure is also established within this frame. Modern societies, on the other hand, may have very different frameworks with which to understand social relations.

A *primary framework* is a basic organizational unit. Goffman points out in detail various ways that primary frames can be transformed or altered so that similar organizational principles are used to meet different ends. A game, for example, is a secondary framework that is modeled after the primary framework of a fight or competition. A large portion of our frameworks are not primary at all, though they are modeled after primary events. Examples include games, drama, deceptions (both good and bad), experiments, and other fabrications. Indeed, what happens in ordinary communication often involves this kind of secondary activity.

With this general theoretical approach as a base, we come to Goffman's central ideas on communication. Communication activities, like all activities, are viewed in the context of frame analysis. We will begin with the concept of face engagement.[32] A *face engagement* or *encounter* occurs when people engage in focused interaction. Persons in a face engagement have a single focus of attention and a perceived mutual activity. In unfocused interaction people in public places acknowledge the presence of one another without paying attention to one another. In such an unfocused situation, the individual is normally accessible for encounter with others. Once an engagement begins, a mutual contract exists to continue the engagement to some kind of termination. During this time a relationship develops and is mutually sustained. Face engagements are both verbal and nonverbal, and the cues exhibited are important in signifying the nature of the relationship as well as a mutual definition of the situation.

31. Goffman, *Frame*, p. 27.

32. On the nature of face-to-face interaction, see Erving Goffman, *Encounters: Two Studies in the Sociology of Interaction* (Indianapolis: Bobbs-Merrill, 1961); *Behavior in Public Places* (New York: Free Press, 1963); *Interaction Ritual: Essays on Face-to-Face Behavior* (Garden City, N.Y.: Doubleday, 1967); and *Relations in Public* (New York: Basic Books, 1971).

People in face engagements take turns presenting dramas to one another. Story telling—recounting past events—is a matter of impressing the listener by dramatic portrayal. This idea of presenting dramas is central to Goffman's overall theory:

I am suggesting that often what talkers undertake to do is not to provide information to a recipient but to present dramas to an audience. Indeed, it seems that we spend most of our time not engaged in giving information but in giving shows. And observe, this theatricality is not based on mere displays of feelings or faked exhibitions of spontaneity or anything else by way of the huffing and puffing we might derogate by calling theatrical. The parallel between stage and conversation is much, much deeper than that. The point is that ordinarily when an individual says something, he is not saying it as a bold statement of fact on his own behalf. He is recounting. He is running through a strip of already determined events for the engagement of his listeners.[33]

In engaging others, the speaker presents a particular character to the audience. The person divides the self into a number of parts and like the stage actor presents this or that character in a particular engagement role. Thus, in ordinary conversation we have the actor and the character or the animator and the animation; the listener willingly is involved in the characterization being presented.

Of course, the individual has opportunities to present the *self* in situations other than conversation. Even in unfocused interactions, scenes are presented to others.[34] Goffman believes that the self is literally determined by these dramatizations. Here is how he explains the self:

A correctly staged and performed scene leads the audience to impute a self to a performed character, but this imputation—this self—is a product of a scene that comes off, and is not a cause of it. The self, then, as a performed character, is not an organic thing that has a specific location, whose fundamental fate is to be born, to mature, and to die; it is a dramatic effect arising diffusely from a scene that is presented, and the

characteristic issue, the crucial concern, is whether it will be credited or discredited.[35]

To realize the validity of Goffman's ideas about self-presentation as dramatization, you have only to think about the many situations in which you project a certain image of yourself. It is doubtful that you behave the same way with your best friend as you do with your parents; and it is unlikely that the image you project to a professor is the same one you present at a party. In most of the situations in which you participate, you decide on a role and enact it.

In attempting to define a situation, the person goes through a two-part process. First, the person needs information about the other people in the situation. Second, one needs to give information about oneself. This process of exchanging information enables people to know what is expected of them. Usually, this exchange occurs indirectly through observing the behavior of others and structuring one's own behavior to elicit impressions in others. *Self-presentation* is very much a matter of *impression management*. The person influences the definition of a situation by projecting a particular impression:

He may wish them to think highly of him, or to think that he thinks highly of them, or to perceive how in fact he feels toward them or to obtain no clearcut impression; he may wish to insure sufficient harmony so that the interaction can be sustained, or to defraud, get rid of, confuse, mislead, antagonize, or insult them.[36]

An interesting situation that requires special self-presentation is the predicament in which you are likely to get blamed for something. You can respond in a number of ways, including excuses, justifications, apologies, and more. For example, in making an excuse, you might say that you didn't mean to do it, that you did not realize what would happen, or that you couldn't help it. Justifications

33. Goffman, *Frame*, p. 508.

34. The best sources on self-presentation are Erving Goffman, *The Presentation of Self in Everyday Life* (Garden City, N.Y.: Doubleday, 1959); and *Relations in Public*.

35. Goffman, *Presentation*, pp. 252–253.

36. Ibid., p. 3.

include appeals to a higher authority, self-defense, loyalty, or some other set of values.[37]

Because all participants in a situation project images, an overall definition of the situation emerges. This general definition is normally rather unified. Once the definition is set, moral pressure is created to maintain it by suppressing contradictions and doubts. A person may add to the projections but never contradict the image initially set. The very organization of society is based on this principle.

Bormann's Convergence Theory

Convergence theory, often known as *fantasy-theme analysis,* is based on Robert Bales's research on small-group communication. (Chapter 13)[38] Bales found that at moments of tension, groups will often become very dramatic and share stories or *fantasy themes.* Ernest Bormann applied this idea to rhetorical action in society at large.[39] Much of individuals' images of reality consists of narratives of how things are believed to be. These stories are created in symbolic interaction within small groups, and they are chained out from person to person and group to group.

Fantasy themes are part of larger dramas that are longer, more complicated stories called rhetorical visions. A *rhetorical vision* is essentially a view of how things have been, are, or will be. Rhetorical visions structure our sense of reality in areas that we cannot experience directly but can only know by symbolic reproduction. Consequently, such visions give us an image of things in the past, in the future, or in faraway places; in large measure these visions form a set of assumptions on which our knowledge is based.

Fantasy themes, and even the larger rhetorical visions, consist of dramatis personae (characters), a plot line, a scene, and sanctioning agents. The characters can be heroes, villains, and other supporting players. The plot line is the action or development of the story. The scene is the setting, including location, properties, and sociocultural milieu. Finally, the sanctioning agent is a source that legitimizes the story. This source may be an authority who lends credibility to the story or authorizes its telling, a common belief in God or another sanctioning ideal like justice or democracy, or a situation or event that makes telling the story seem appropriate.

Rhetorical visions are never told in their entirety but are built up by sharing associated fantasy themes. To grasp the entire vision, one must attend to the fantasy themes because these comprise the content of conversation in groups of people when the vision is being created and chained out. Fantasy themes are recognizable by their quality of being repeated again and again. In fact, some themes are so frequently discussed and so well known within a particular group or community that the members no longer tell the whole episode. Instead, they abbreviate the telling of the fantasy theme by presenting just a "trigger" or *in-cue.* This is precisely what happens with an inside joke. Fantasy themes that develop to this point of familiarity are known as *fantasy types*—stock situations told over and over within a group.

As people come to share fantasy themes, the resulting rhetorical vision pulls them together and gives them a sense of identification with a shared reality. From the perspective of this theory, people converge or come to hold a common image as they share fantasy themes. In fact, shared rhetorical visions—and especially the use of fantasy types— can be taken as evidence that convergence has occurred.

Fantasy themes therefore constitute an important ingredient in persuasion. Public communica-

37. For a well-developed discussion of impression management in predicaments, see J. T. Tedeschi and M. Reiss, "Verbal Strategies in Impression Management," in *The Psychology of Ordinary Explanations of Social Behavior,* ed. C. Antaki (New York: Academic Press, 1981), pp. 271–309.

38. Robert F. Bales, *Personality and Interpersonal Behavior* (New York: Holt, Rinehart & Winston, 1970).

39. Bormann's major works on fantasy-theme analysis are *Communication Theory* (New York: Holt, Rinehart & Winston, 1980), pp. 184–190; *The Force of Fantasy: Restoring the American Dream* (Carbondale: Southern Illinois University Press, 1985); "Fantasy and Rhetorical Vision: The Rhetorical Criticism of Social Reality," *Quarterly Journal of Speech* 58 (1972): 396–407; and "Fantasy and Rhetorical Vision: Ten Years Later," *Quarterly Journal of Speech* 68 (1982): 288–305. See also John F. Cragan and Donald C. Shields, *Applied Communication Research: A Dramatistic Approach* (Prospect Heights, Ill.: Waveland Press, 1981).

tors—in speeches, articles, books, films, and other media—often tap into or make use of the audience's predominant fantasy themes. Public communication can also add to or modify the rhetorical vision by amplifying, changing, or adding fantasy themes.

An interesting application of fantasy-theme analysis is Karen Foss and Stephen Littlejohn's critique of the television film *The Day After*.[40] These researchers asked about eighty people to write descriptions of what they thought a nuclear war would be like. They then compared these personal statements with the fantasy themes in the film itself and discovered a close association between the two. Actor, setting, and plot themes were found. Actor themes included physical effects, death, confusion, separation, fear, and others. Setting themes included such items as radiation, limited services, and congestion. Examples of the plot themes discovered are destruction, survival, and military action.

The film was watched by a huge television audience, and it appears that it was effective in using a rhetorical vision shared with that audience. Foss and Littlejohn believe that the deep structure of the vision is irony, which consists primarily of the inconsistency of being both a detached observer and an involved participant in the nuclear-attack drama. This kind of irony is typical of the visions presented by films because films draw you in as a participant, but they also rely on you to be an observing and detached audience.

Fisher's Theory of Narrative

Perhaps the most comprehensive narrative theory in the communication field is that of Walter Fisher.[41] Fisher believes that human rationality in all of its forms is based essentially on narrative. Consequently, communication in all its forms can be understood in narrative terms.

Traditionally, narration or story telling has been viewed as a different genre from argumentation. Arguments were viewed as rational, whereas stories were viewed as nonrational. Traditional arguments can be formal, as is the case of technical logic, or informal, as in the case of rhetorical discourse; but in either case, argument has always been viewed traditionally as a set of premises and conclusions based on specialized rules of argument.

In disagreement with this traditional view, Fisher believes that narrative also involves rationality. Narrative can incorporate traditional rationality, but it goes beyond this to include other forms of rationality not often recognized. In other words, reasoning is more diverse than either technical or rhetorical argument realize, and the narrative paradigm encompasses a broader variety of types of rationality. Fisher summarizes:

> [In narrative] no form of discourse is privileged over others because its form is predominantly argumentative. No matter how strictly a case is argued—scientifically, philosophically, or legally—it will always be a story, an interpretation of some aspect of the world that is historically and culturally grounded and shaped by human personality.[42]

Persuasion occurs when people see good reasons for adopting the advocated point of view. Good reasons can be presented in the form of traditional reasoning, or they can be presented in other ways. In the narrative paradigm, positive values constitute good reasons to accept a claim. For example, if you want to persuade a friend to attend an animal rights rally with you, you might outline a number of reasons why animals need to be protected, or you might tell the story of the abuse of beagles in a research lab. If your friend accepts the values in the story, he will probably decide to go along. In fact, for many people the story would be more powerful than a list of reasons presented in traditional style. Of course, the list of reasons in a more customary message is also a kind of narrative and could also be judged in terms of the values it projects.

What is a narration? For Fisher, narration is not merely fictional stories but any verbal or nonverbal

40. Karen A. Foss and Stephen W. Littlejohn, "*The Day After*: Rhetorical Vision in an Ironic Frame," *Critical Studies in Mass Communication* 3 (1986): 317–336.

41. Walter R. Fisher, *Human Communication as Narration: Toward a Philosophy of Reason, Value, and Action* (Columbia: University of South Carolina Press, 1987).

42. Ibid., p. 49.

account that has a sequence of events and to which listeners assign meaning. The narrative paradigm *describes* what people do when they communicate; it does not dictate what they should do, as does traditional argument learned in debate courses.

This does not mean all stories are equally effective. Some stories are better than others, and people do not need special knowledge or skill to tell the difference. Two criteria are used to establish the quality of a narrative—coherence and fidelity. *Coherence* is the degree to which a story makes sense, the extent to which it has meaning. Coherence is measured by the organization and structure of the story: A coherent story is well told. Coherence involves three kinds of consistency. The first is internal consistency, which Fisher calls *argumentative* or *structural coherence.* This is the degree to which the parts of the story "hang together." The second is external consistency, which Fisher calls *material coherence.* This is the congruence between this story and other stories, the degree to which the story seems complete in terms of the events previously learned from other sources. Finally, *characterological coherence* has to do with the believability of the characters in the story, both the narrators and the actors. What kind of choices do these characters make, and what kind of values do they espouse?

You know the difference between a well-told story and one that is confusing. You can tell when a story makes sense, when it is organized in a way that makes you pay attention and appreciate the art in the telling. But coherence is not everything. Indeed, a well-told story may still fail to persuade. It must also have fidelity.

Fidelity is the truthfulness or reliability of the story. A story has fidelity if it seems to ring true to the listener. A story with fidelity presents a "logic of good reasons," or a set of elements such as values that are taken as good reasons by the listener. Here, one judges five aspects of the narrative. First, the story is a tale of values. Second, these values are appropriate for the moral of the story, the decisions being made by characters, or the thesis communicated by the discourse. Third, the values are perceived to have positive consequences in the lives of people. Fourth, the values in the story are consistent with people's own experience. Fifth, the values are part of an ideal vision for human conduct.

Because it is universal, narrative is liberating and empowering. It does not limit argumentation to those who have special skill or knowledge because everyone intuitively knows how to use and to evaluate narrative. Unlike traditional argument then, narrative is an egalitarian form. The lawyer arguing in court with traditional logic uses one kind of narrative, just as does the grandmother telling her grandchild about life during the Great Depression.

The general public will tend to evaluate arguments of all types in terms of narrative forms, making the narrative criteria of coherence and fidelity more effective in winning adherents than traditional logical criteria. This is the case because in its appeal to all the faculties, including reason, emotion, sensation, imagination, and values, narration more nearly captures the experience of the average person than does formal discourse, which is designed to appeal to a rather narrow range of specialized rationality. In addition, narrative ability is cultural knowledge and does not have to be learned in logic classes and law school. Finally, narration creates an identification among people and appeals to the public on an indirect, subconcious level.

For these reasons, narrative is especially powerful in public moral argument. A public moral argument deals with basic questions of good and bad, life and death, ideas about personhood, and how to live a life. It is aimed at all of society, not to small groups or individual communities. Some of the chief public moral arguments of our own time relate to abortion, the right to life, and reproductive choice; war and peace; women's rights; public education; church and state; and many others. Fisher believes that in public moral arguments, the rules of good narrative will win out over the rules of traditional argument. When expert argument is pitted against common narrative, the rhetoric of the experts will fail because it will not stand up to the coherence and fidelity expected by the public.

Fisher uses Jonathan Shell's book *The Fate of the Earth* as an example. This book about the nuclear-weapons buildup was widely read in the early 1980s. It argued that the weapons race must stop and be reversed. Fisher states that the book was highly respected because it met the standards of coherence and fidelity. In other words, it was a well-told story that rang true to many people. It included a set of values that seemed especially relevant at that point in the history of the world. Experts refuted the book on technical grounds, but these technical arguments did not have the fidelity necessary to win public sentiment.

Commentary and Critique

The theories in this chapter see communication as the thread with which the fabric of society is held together. A culture's reality is defined in terms of its meanings, which arise from interaction within social groups. Individual's meanings for words and symbols, objects, stories, and roles are determined by the ways in which symbols are used to define objects and people in actual communication situations. Social institutions are nothing more than grand networks of interaction in which common meanings are generated. The self as an object is especially important; the self, too, is defined in terms of symbols and meanings derived from one's interaction with other people.

As people interact in society, they perform in ways that make social life very much like a drama. They act within scenes, make presentations, represent characters, and tell stories. These communication activities create, sustain, and change the very nature of reality in a group or culture.

Although many specific objections have been raised against symbolic interactionism, for the most part they can be combined into three major criticisms.[43] First, symbolic interactionism is said to be nonempirical. That is, one cannot readily translate

its concepts into observable, researchable units. Second, it is said to be overly restrictive in the variables it takes into account. Critics have charged that it ignores crucial psychological variables on one end and societal variables on the other. Third, it uses concepts in an inexact, inconsistent way. Let us look at each of these objections more closely.

The first major criticism of symbolic interactionism has broad implications. Despite Blumer's protests to the contrary, critics maintain that in actual practice the researcher does not know what to look for in observing interactionist concepts in real life. This problem seems to stem from the vague, intuitive claims of early interactionists. What is mind, for example? How can this concept be observed? We already have noted Kuhn's failure to operationalize interactionist concepts without giving up its assumptions about the process nature of behavior. Most basically, this criticism questions the appropriateness of symbolic interactionism to lead to a more complete understanding of everyday behavior. As such, critics believe it to be more appropriately social philosophy, which may guide our thinking about events but which provides little concrete conceptualization for explaining the events. John Lofland's criticism is especially biting. He claims that interactionists participate in three main activities: "doctrinaire reiteration of the master's teachings, . . . [making] slightly more specific the general imagery, . . . [and connecting] descriptive case studies and interactionism."[44]

As a result of this alleged failure, symbolic interactionism is not thought to be adequately heuristic. It has generated few testable hypotheses, and little research has been produced. Interactionist scholars thus have been unable to elaborate and expand their thinking. Couch, a leading proponent (and house critic) of the movement, points out that interactionists do engage in research but that their observations do not cast light on the theory's key concepts, making revision and elaboration difficult. Couch believes this circumstance need not be

43. For reviews of specific objections to symbolic interactionism, see Jerome G. Manis and Bernard M. Meltzer (eds.), "Appraisals of Symbolic Interactionism," *Symbolic Interaction* (Boston: Allyn and Bacon, 1978), pp. 393–440; Bernard N. Meltzer, John Petras, and Larry Reynolds, *Symbolic Interactionism: Genesis, Varieties, and Criticism* (London: Routledge & Kegan Paul, 1975).

44. John Lofland, "Interactionist Imagery and Analytic Interruptus," in *Human Nature and Collective Behavior*, ed. T. Shibutani (Englewood Cliffs, N.J.: Prentice-Hall, 1970), p. 37.

so, and the "new" Iowa tradition has emerged out of a need for interactionists to do "serious sociological work."[45] The problem associated with this criticism may be that the critics conceive of the movement too narrowly. Indeed, if you include many of the tributaries of the interactionist movement, many of which are outlined in this and the following chapter, this critique crumbles.

The second major criticism is that interactionism has either ignored or downplayed important explanatory variables. Critics say it leaves out the emotions of the individual on one end and societal organization on the other. These arguments as a whole make clear that interactionism is overly restrictive in scope. To cover as much of social life as it pretends to do, interactionism must take into account social structures as well as individual feelings. The problem is not one merely of scope; it casts doubt on the validity of the tradition as well. Again, however, if we turn to the many theories associated with social interactionist thinking, whether they go by the name symbolic interactionism or not, we find that a much wider range of concepts is included. In Chapter 9, for example, we will encounter the work of theorists who deal with such concerns as the social contruction of emotions, values, and morality. We will look at the process of making accounts and enacting social life. All these topics have been well researched and are included in the interactionist tradition broadly conceived.

The alleged failure of symbolic interactionism to deal with social organization is a major concern for interactionists. Social organization or structure removes individual prerogative, a highly valued idea in old-style interactionism. Social structure is normally a matter of power, and interactionists have been loath to admit to power inequality. However, the concept of power can be investigated from an interactionist perspective, and since about 1965 several research programs have begun to look at power.[46]

The third general criticism of symbolic interactionism is that its concepts are not used consistently. As a result such concepts as *I, me, self, role,* and others are vague. However, we must keep in mind that symbolic interactionism is not a unified theory. Rather, it is a general framework, and as we have seen, it has different versions. Therefore, although this is a valid criticism of early interactionism, it is not a fair picture of the movement today.

One inconsistency that persists in most versions of symbolic interactionism involves the problem of determinism. Most mainstream interactionists clearly teach that individuals and groups have the capacity to seek goals, to define situations in new ways, and to change. Yet the idea of the social genesis of meaning creates a kind of determinism. In other words, if the group creates meaning through interaction, the individual has little choice but to see the world in predetermined ways. Mead tried to handle this difficulty with the concept of the *I,* but this is a vague, mystical, and ill-defined concept.

The question that plagues interactionism to today is how people can act in accord with personal goals yet be affected by meanings that have been established through a history of interaction. Perhaps the most serious and credible answer to this problem has been forwarded by Anthony Giddens, who shows how action results in unintended consequences that return to constrain future action. Many believe that Giddens has successfully reconciled structural, deterministic approaches with interactional ones in a unified theory of social life. Gidden's theory is covered in more detail in Chapter 13.

The critical response to dramatism and narrative has been copious and spirited, and it is not possible to review all of these viewpoints.[47] Gronbeck sum-

---

45. Couch, "Symbolic Interaction."

46. This line of work is discussed in Peter M. Hall, "Structuring Symbolic Interaction: Communcation and Power," in *Communciation Yearbook 4,* ed. D. Nimmo (New Brunswick, N.J.: Transaction Books, 1980), pp. 49–60.

47. For a summary of criticisms of Burke, see Foss, Foss, and Trapp, *Contemporary Perspectives,* pp. 199-203. For criticism of Goffman, see Stephen W. Littlejohn, *Theories of Human Communication,* 2nd ed. (Belmont, Calif.: Wadsworth, 1983), pp. 180–181; and Randall Collins, "Erving Goffman and the Development of Modern Social Theory," in *The View from Goffman,* ed. J. Ditton (New York: St. Martin's Press, 1980), pp. 170–209. For criticism of Bormann, see Bormann, "Ten Years Later," and G. P. Mohrmann, "An Essay on Fantasy Theme Criticism," *Quarterly Journal of Speech* 68 (1982): 109–132. A critique and response to Fisher's work are Robert C. Rowland,

marizes the critique against dramaturgy.[48] Dramatism is not a unified theory. It still remains basically an "interest group" or coalition of theories that share a metaphor rather than any particular set of theoretical terms or principles. The theories chosen for this chapter illustrate this lack of coherence in the movement.

Burke's is the grandest and perhaps the most elaborate of the four theories covered here. This breadth and complexity has elicited both praise and blame. Some believe that it has opened vistas of great import; others believe that Burke's lack of focus has led to interminable confusion, if not exhaustion.

Goffman's ideas are perhaps least theoretical in that they are scattered and hard to assemble into a single rubric. His numerous writings are insightful and interesting but hard to integrate. He rarely uses the same vocabulary twice and, until the end of his career, seemed more interested in pointing out idiosynchratic observations than in making a general statement. Fortunately, his final work *Frame Analysis* provides an overall scheme that can be used to integrate a lifetime of work.

Bormann's theory is perhaps the most clearly focused of the dramaturgical and narrative theories presented in this chapter. It, too, has received both praise and blame. Bormann and his associates also put a good deal of work into clarifying and elaborating the vocabulary of fantasy-theme analysis. Bormann's work—and that of his critics and adherents—fulfills one of Gronbeck's suggestions: that the field of communication work to elaborate, clar-

ify, and develop the concepts and terms of narrative.

The narrative paradigm has been very useful. Indeed, telling stories and sharing rhetorical visions is a common, perhaps universal, human activity. The function of stories in communication and persuasion is therefore a significant area of study. Both Bormann and Fisher advance our knowledge of narrative by suggesting some of the elements of this dimension of communication. Both have proved useful in the actual examination of discourse.

Considerable controversy still exists about the place of narrative in communication. In a critique of fantasy-theme analysis, G. P. Mohrmann acknowledges the validity of fantasy themes in groups, but he doubts that they function in public discourse in the ways imagined by Bormann. Narrative has its place, but it does not function outside the group in the manner described in Bormann's theory.[49] Bormann answers by simply pointing to the copious quantity of research that demonstrates the utility of the theory.[50]

Fisher's narrative paradigm has been criticized in similar ways. Robert Rowland, for example, has suggested that although narrative is a powerful dimension of much communication, it cannot be said to characterize all communication.[51] Fisher answers that his brand of narrative indeed underlies all communication and is especially important in persuasion.[52] For Fisher, narrative is more a dimension than a type of communication.

"On Limiting the Narrative Paradigm: Three Case Studies," *Communication Monographs* 56 (1989): 39–54; and Walter R. Fisher, "Clarifying the Narrative Paradigm," *Communication Monographs* 56 (1989): 55–58.

48. Gronbeck, "Dramaturgical Theory."

49. Mohrmann, "Fantasy Theme Criticism."
50. Bormann, "Fantasy and Rhetorical Vision."
51. Rowland, "On Limiting the Narrative Paradigm."
52. Fisher, "Clarifying the Narrative Paradigm."

CHAPTER 9

Theories of Social and Cultural Reality

Because the theories discussed in this chapter are tightly intertwined with those of Chapter 8, these two chapters should be read as a unit. Interactional approaches, represented most generally by symbolic interactionism, deal with the ways in which our understandings, meanings, norms, roles, and rules are worked out interactively in communication. Chapter 8 explored some of the general concepts relevant to that process; here, we take a look at theories that describe more exactly some of the conventions that emerge from interaction and the nature of the process in which those understandings are developed. As a group these conventions constitute the social reality of a group or culture.

People communicate to interpret events and to share those interpretations with others. For this reason it is believed that reality is constructed socially as a product of communication.[1] The idea of the social construction of reality comes from an important intellectual tradition of our century, a tradition that provides a conceptual backdrop for most of the theories to be covered in this chapter.

The Social Construction of Reality

The idea of the social construction of reality was expressed by philosopher Alfred Schutz in these words:

> The world of my daily life is by no means my private world but is from the outset an intersubjective one, shared with my fellow men, experienced and interpreted by others: in brief, it is a world common to all of us. The unique biographical situation in which I find myself within the world at any moment of my existence is only to a very small extent of my own making.[2]

Our meanings and understandings, in short, arise from our communication with others. This notion of reality is deeply embedded in sociological thought; its most well-known proponents are Peter Berger and Thomas Luckmann in their treatise *The Social Construction of Reality*.[3] With the impetus

1. For a good general discussion of this school of thought, see Stuart J. Sigman, *A Perspective on Social Communication* (Lexington, Mass.: Lexington Books, 1987).

2. Alfred Schutz, *On Phenomenology and Social Relations* (Chicago: University of Chicago Press, 1970), p. 163.

3. Peter L. Berger and Thomas Luckmann, *The Social Construction of Reality: A Treatise in the Sociology of Knowledge* (New York: Doubleday, 1966).

from symbolic interactionism and the foundations of the work of Schutz and Berger and Luckmann, the social construction of reality has become a respectable and popular idea in the social sciences. Kenneth Gergen has labeled it "the social constructionist movement."[4] According to Gergen the movement is concerned with the processes by which individuals account for the world and their experience. It is based on four assumptions:

1. The world does not present itself objectively to the observer, but is known through human experience, which is largely influenced by language.
2. The categories in language used to classify things emerge from the social interaction within a group of people at a particular time and in a particular place. Categories of understanding, then, are situational.
3. How reality is understood at a given moment is determined by the conventions of communication in force at that time. The stability of social life therefore determines how concrete our knowledge seems to be.
4. Reality is socially constructed by interconnected patterns of communication behavior. Within a social group or culture, reality is defined not so much by individual acts, but by complex and organized patterns of ongoing actions.[5]

An interesting classroom exercise to illustrate the social construction of reality is to have each class member produce an object. The objects are put on a table in front of the class, and someone is then asked to sort the objects. This is easy to do. One might, for example, put wooden articles in one group, metal ones in another, cloth in another, and plastic in a fourth pile. Another student is then asked to sort the objects again. Someone else is asked to do it a third time. The objects are sorted again and again, each time in a different way. They might be sorted by size, by use, by color, by number of parts, by things you would or would not give a child, by things that could be used as a weapon and things that could not. There is a seemingly endless number of ways to understand each object. You can

see that our language gives us labels that we use to distinguish objects in our world. How things get grouped together depend on the invocation of a particular social reality. How we understand objects and how we behave toward them depend in large measure on the social reality in force.

In this section we look at theories related to three aspects of social construction—the self, emotions, and accounts.

The Social Construction of Self

Among contemporary social scientists who have made constructionist assumptions central to their work is Rom Harré. Recognizing that self is both individual and social, Harré places emphasis on the ways in which individuals account for and explain their own behavior in particular episodes.

Harré and his colleague Paul Secord are responsible for *ethogeny*, which is the study of how people understand their actions within specific episodes.[6] An *episode* is a predictable sequence of acts that all parties define as an event with a beginning and an end. Having dinner, making a speech, holding a commencement ceremony, having an argument, driving to work, making love, and negotiating an agreement are episodes. Ethogeny involves the meaning of the episode and how participants understand the various acts in it. Further, the ordinary language that people use to describe and explain an episode reflects their meaning for it.

The social group or community, through interaction, creates "theories" to explain the experience of reality.[7] A group's theory conceptualizes the experience and includes a scenario of what the logical outcome of a particular action within an episode should be. These "theories" are *structured templates* of the course of action anticipated in the episode. For example, two people who say they are "in love" have a theory of what love is and how it should be acted out, which becomes evident when the lovers are required to describe, explain, or account for their actions.

4. Kenneth J. Gergen, "The Social Constructionist Movement in Modern Psychology," *American Psychologist* 40 (1985): 266–275; see also *Toward Transformation in Social Knowledge* (New York: Springer-Verlag, 1982).

5. Gergen, "Social Constructionist," pp. 266–269.

6. Rom Harré and Paul Secord, *The Explanation of Social Behavior* (Totowa, N.J.: Littlefield, Adams, 1972).

7. Rom Harré, *Social Being: A Theory for Social Psychology* (Totowa, N.J.: Rowman and Littlefield, 1979).

The meanings attached to the events of an episode give rise to rules that guide the participants' actions within the episode. Participants know how to act because of the rules in force at a particular moment. For example, our hypothetical couple may engage in the episode of "making love," which consists of a series of acts with a beginning and an end, which have meaning and an anticipated course. The episode of making love will be different for other couples, who have their own definitions of what it means to make love and the action sequence required. The concept of rules is especially important in constructionist thought and is explained in detail later in the chapter.

The concept of *self*, which is so important in symbolic interactionism (Chapter 8), has been the chief concern of Harré in most of his theoretical work.[8] Harré says that like any other experience, the self is structured by a personal theory. That is, the individual learns to understand the self by employing a theory that defines it.

One's notion of self as a person, then, is a theoretical concept, derived from the ideas of personhood embodied in the culture and expressed through communication. Harré distinguishes between person and self. The *person* is the publicly visible being and carries all attributes and characteristics of persons in general within the culture or social group. The *self* is one's private notion of his or her own unity as a person. Concepts of personhood are *public*, whereas concepts of selfhood, though they may be expressed to others, are ultimately *private*. The character of persons is governed by the group's theory of personhood; the self is governed by the individual's theory of his or her own being as one member of the culture. Personal being is thus two-sided, consisting of a social being (person) and a personal being (self). For example, many traditional cultures conceptualize the person as the embodiment of a role (e.g., mother, father, priest, worker). People in general are seen as manifestations of these roles. An individual within the culture, on the other hand, will assign a particular nature, feeling, and character to the self, as an individual within a role.

One's self theory, like a personhood theory, is learned through a history of interaction with other people. Throughout life people learn that individuals have different perspectives on the world, and the self is an autonomous actor with the power to do things. All our thoughts, intentions, and emotions are cast in terms that are learned through social interaction. The notions of selfhood on which these perceptions are based are highly variable from one culture to another. An individual's personal perspectives and the degree and character of one's personal powers depend on this personal self theory.

For example, most Western industrialized cultures stress theories of self that perceive individuals as whole, undivided, and independent entities. The Javanese, in contrast, see themselves as being two independent parts—an inside of feelings and an outside of observed behaviors. Moroccans have yet another theory of self, as they see persons as embodiments of places and situations, and their identities are always tied to these situations.[9]

The self consists of a set of elements that can be viewed spatially along three dimensions (Figure 9.1). The placement of an aspect of the self in this grid depends on one's theory of self. The first dimension is *display*, whether an aspect of the self is displayed publicly or remains private. For example, with one theory of self, emotions may be kept relatively private, whereas personality is seen as public. The second dimension is *realization*, or source. This dimension involves the degree to which some feature of the self is believed to come from within the individual, as opposed to evolving from a group. Elements of a self that are believed to come from the person are individually realized, whereas those elements believed to derive from the person's relationship to the group are collectively realized. For example, a self theory might treat "purpose" as individually realized because it seems to be something that individuals have on their

8. Ibid; see also *Personal Being: A Theory for Individual Psychology* (Cambridge, Mass.: Harvard University Press, 1984).

9. Clifford Geertz, *Local Knowledge: Further Essays in Interpretive Anthropology* (New York: Basic Books, 1983), p. 60.

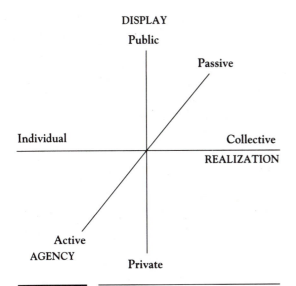

Figure 9.1 Dimensions of personhood.

Adapted from *Personal Being: A Theory for Individual Psychology* by Rom Harré. Copyright © 1984 by Harvard University Press. Reprinted by permission of the publisher.

own. On the other hand, "cooperation" may be collectively realized because it seems to be something that one can only do as a member of a group.

Agency is the degree of active power attributed to the self. Active elements (like "speaking" or "driving") are contrasted with passive elements (like "listening" or "riding"). Individual selves can be drastically different from one another—not only in the concepts used to define self but also in the placement of these concepts in the three-dimensional scheme. For example, people of Anglo-Saxon descent tend to treat emotions as privately displayed, individually realized, and passive. In other words, they feel that emotions just happen to them and are within them. Many southern Europeans on the other hand see emotions as public, collective, and active. In other words, they believe that emotions are something they create as a group and display together.

All self theories have three elements in common. First, they all contain a sense of *self-consciousness*. This means that one thinks of oneself as an object. When I think about myself or talk about myself, I am displaying consciousness of myself as a person. There are, then, two senses of the word *I*—the self that knows and the self that is known about. Consider the following statement: "I_1 know that I_2 am afraid." I_1 reflects one's sense of being aware, and I_2 reflects one's sense of being the object of fear. The second element of all self theories is *agency*. The self is always seen has having certain powers to do things. People see themselves as agents, capable of having intentions and actions. The third element of the self is *autobiography*, or identity as a person with a history and a future. My agency is evident whenever I plan something, and my autobiography is apparent whenever I tell someone about myself.

Harré uses the Eskimo as an example of personal identity.[10] The Eskimo self is viewed in a network of relations with others. An Eskimo may have private feelings, but these are generally considered unimportant. Important matters related to self are generally defined in terms of qualities of relationship with others. In English we would say, "I hear him." The Eskimo equivalent would be something like, "he is making a sound with reference to me." Both positive and negative emotions are considered public displays rather than private feelings. Many visitors have made the interesting observation that Eskimos tend to display emotions as a group. For example, they all laugh together, or they all cry to together. Most Eskimo virtures are all social ones in that they are necessary for the preservation of the community as a whole. Eskimo art illustrates this quality as well. Eskimos do not have a concept for individual creativity. Artists believe they are merely releasing that which is already present in the material. When they carve a log, for example, the figure that results is seen as being revealed from the log and not something created by the carver.

The Social Construction of Emotion

We usually do not think of emotions as "constructed"; yet they are an important outcome of communication. Harré suggests that emotions are

10. Harré, *Personal Being*, p. 87.

constructed concepts, just as any aspect of human experience, because they are determined by the local language and moral orders of the culture or social group.[11] One of the leading scholars in the social construction of emotions is James Averill.[12]

According to Averill, emotions are belief systems that guide one's definition of the situation. As such, emotions consist of internalized social norms and rules, including how to define emotions and how to respond to them. Emotions do have a physiological component, but combining and labeling bodily feelings are learned socially within a culture. In other words, our ability to make sense of emotions is socially constructed.

Averill calls emotions syndromes. A *syndrome* is a cluster or set of responses that go together. No single response is sufficient by itself to define an emotion, but all must be viewed together. Emotional syndromes are socially constructed because people learn through interaction with other people what particular clusters of behavior should be taken to mean and how to perform a particular emotion. Emotions are acted out in specific ways, and we learn these "roles" from communication. What does grief look like? It is different in different societies. People must learn how to take the role of the grieving person, or the angry person, or the jealous person.

Each experience of an emotion has an *object*, which is where the emotion is directed, and each emotion has a limited range of possible objects. When you are angry, you are angry at someone. When you are envious, you have envy about some achievement or possession. When you grieve, you grieve the loss of someone or something. As Averill

points out, you cannot be proud of the stars because pride is something reserved for accomplishment. You may say that you "love" your new car, but you cannot really be "in love" with it. Nor can you say that a friend's angry attack on you makes you feel jealous.

How an emotion is labeled, what it is called, is instrumental in how the emotion is experienced. You may have very different meanings for the same physiological response depending on whether you call it "anger" or "fear." You experience an emotion one way when you call it "jealousy" and quite another when you call it "loneliness." We have rules for what anger, fear, jealousy, and loneliness are, and we have rules for how to respond in these feelings. Such rules are constructed in social interaction throughout a person's lifetime.

Four kinds of learned rules govern emotions. *Rules of appraisal* tell a person what an emotion is, where it is directed, and whether it is positive or negative. *Rules of behavior* tell one how to respond to the feeling. *Rules of prognosis* define the progression and course of the emotion. *Rules of attribution* dictate how an emotion should be explained or justified. Not all these types of rules apply to every emotion, of course.

If you were angry at another person, your rules of appraisal would tell you what you were feeling and who the target of the feeling is. These rules would also define whether that anger is positive (like righteous indignation) or negative (like rage). Behavior rules would guide your behavior, including how to express the anger, whether to lash out or remain quiet, whether to aggress or retreat. Prognosis rules would guide how long the anger episode should last and the different phases through which it might pass. Finally, the rules of attribution would help you explain the anger ("she was acting like a jerk and made me mad").

Thus, emotions are not just things in themselves. They are defined and handled according to rules that are learned in social interaction with other people. We learn emotional rules in childhood and throughout life. Averill is clear that people can and do change emotionally. When you enter a new life situation, you are exposed to new

11. Rom Harré (ed.),"An Outline of the Social Constructionist Viewpoint," in *The Social Construction of Emotions* (New York: Basil Blackwell, 1986), pp. 2–14.

12. Among Averill's most pertinent writings in this line of work are "A Constructivist View of Emotion," in *Theories of Emotion*, eds. K. Plutchik and H. Kellerman (New York: Academic Press, 1980), pp. 305–339; "On the Paucity of Positive Emotions," in *Assessment and Modification of Emotional Behavior*, eds. K. R. Blankstein et al. (New York: Plenum, 1980), pp. 7–45; *Anger and Aggression: An Essay on Emotion* (New York: Springer-Verlag, 1982); "The Acquisition of Emotions During Adulthood," in *The Social Construction of Emotions*, ed. R. Harré (New York: Basil Blackwell, 1986), pp. 98–119.

ways of understanding emotion, and your feelings, their expression, and the ways in which you manage those emotions change.

Averill conducted an interesting study in which he isolated over 500 terms for emotions.[13] This was done systematically to the point that he was confident that he had a truly representative list of emotional terms in the English language. Research subjects rated these terms on a number of dimensions, including evaluation (e.g., pleasant-unpleasant). He found that far more emotional terms were evaluated as negative (e.g., anger, jealousy) than positive (e.g., joy, happiness). This is an interesting puzzle: Why do negative emotions outweigh positive ones by about two to one?

The answer is that emotions do not come prepackaged as positive or negative but that we define them that way based on our social constructions. In our culture positive outcomes tend to be considered as something individuals accomplish through action, whereas negative results tend to be seen as beyond control. So, for example, courage is the result of one's brave actions, whereas jealousy is the consequence of an unfortunate situation. Further, emotions in general tend to be viewed in our society as beyond control, something that just happens to us. So it is logical that postive outcomes are defined less as emotions and more as actions, whereas negative outcomes are more often seen as emotions, which leads to the idea that emotional terms are more often negative than positive.

Accounts in Social Construction

One of the ways in which people construct social realities is by making accounts, or explaining and justifying their behavior. For example, if you forgot your mother's birthday, you would have some explaining to do. You might say that you were busy at school and forgot, which reinforces the idea that being productive is good; or that you lost your calendar, which suggests that record keeping is important; or that you have no excuse and are sorry, which says that family relationships should not be ignored. No matter what you say, you are recon-

structing some aspect of the social reality in force within your family and culture.

Types and functions of accounts. Much has been written about accounts. Margaret McLaughlin, Michael Cody, and their colleagues have codified account types and have done research to show when different types of accounts are used.[14] They see accounting as a method of managing so-called *failure events.* When you have done something that could be criticized by others, you will act in some way to save face. McLaughlin and Cody have shown that in conversations the sequence of talk most frequently associated with accounts is a reproach (criticism), an account (explanation), and an evaluation (acceptance or rejection of the account).

For example, if you were distracted and failed to return the greeting of a friend on the street, your friend might say, "Hey, what's the matter?" You might respond to this reproach by an account such as, "Oh, sorry, I didn't see you," whereupon your friend might evaluate your account by saying, "Oh, okay." Certainly, not all accounting occurs in precisely this way. In fact, you will often anticipate potential criticism and offer an account without an initial reproach.

What kind of events provoke accounts in our society? Cody and McLaughlin suggest at least four. The first is *offenses of taste, attitude, or belief.* These are simple disagreements with other people: "What! You drink black coffee? Yuk." The second involves *personal identity,* when someone says or does something that attacks someone's identity: "John, you're behaving just like a man. Cut it out." The third involves *work* or *school offenses:* "Uh, oh, I'm late again." And the fourth are *interaction offenses:* "That's a dumb question."

Cody and McLaughlin list three types of accounts—concessions, excuses, and justifications.

13. Averill, "On the Paucity of Positive Emotions."

14. Margaret L. McLaughlin, Michael J. Cody, and Nancy E. Rosenstein, "Account Sequences in Conversations Between Strangers," *Communication Monographs* 50 (1983): 102–125; Margaret L. McLaughlin, Michael J. Cody, and H. Dan O'Hair, "The Management of Failure Events: Some Contextual Determinants of Accounting Behavior," *Human Communication Research* 9 (1983): 208–224.

Concessions are admissions of guilt: "I blew it. Sorry." *Excuses* offer reasons why the offender could not help doing what they did: "My car broke down." And *justifications* admit responsibility but deny that the act was without merit: "Okay, I should have come up with something for dinner, but now we can both decide what we want." Of course, we do not always make accounts, and McLaughlin and Cody maintain that the refusal to make an account is itself a management strategy for managing failure events.[15]

A reproach can also assume a number of forms. The first is a *projection*, which is commonly used with intimates and other people with whom we have an ongoing relationship. Projections express an assumption that the other person will have an adequate account for their behavior, and it seems to be designed to protect the relationship itself. For example, a *projected concession* assumes that the other person will just admit guilt: "Cut the crap, John; just say your sorry, okay?" A *projected excuse* communicates an expectation that a partner has some good reason for what was done: "Did your car have problems again this morning, Sue?" A *projected justification* assumes that the offender will explain why it was okay to do what he or she did: "I went ahead and ordered dinner 'cause I thought you would be late, with your work schedule and all this week."

The strategies used with strangers, however, may be more direct. McLaughlin and Cody suggest that we might express simple *surprise* or *disgust*: "Get your hands off, you creep!" We might express *moral* or *intellectual superiority*: "You're old enough to know better, Joey." We also sometimes just issue a *direct request for an account*: "Why did you do that?" Or we might issue a *direct rebuke*: "I told you in class several times that the paper was due March 1!"

Accounts seem to vary in how confrontative they are. For example, if you admit guilt (concession), you present little threat to the other person. On the other hand, if someone criticizes you and you refuse to make an account, you are essentially challenging the other person at that moment. The four strategies can therefore be placed along a spectrum of mitigation-aggravation. Concessions are highly mitigating, excuses are slightly mitigating, justifications are potentially aggravating, and refusals are very aggravating. For this reason people tend to concede more in intimate relationships than they do with strangers. These researchers have also found that an aggravating reproach will probably elicit an aggravating response, and vice versa.

Accounts and moral responsibility. Another important account theorist is John Shotter, whose work provides a useful extension of constructionist thinking into the subjects of responsibility and morality.[16] Shotter believes that human experience cannot be separated from communication. Our speech both reflects and creates our experience of reality. Central to this link between communication and experience is the process of making accounts.

In everyday conversation the "I" cannot be separated from the "you," because the speaker (I) and the listener (you) go back-and-forth. So in a conversation, people are making demands on one another; they are telling others how to behave and what to think. The morality of everyday life is constructed in this process.[17]

Communicators believe they have the power to act, yet they may feel somewhat constrained by rules of action. Rules may be followed or broken, but people are at least expected to explain their actions on the basis of rules or exceptions to those rules. Because of the presence of rules and our personal powers to follow them or to break them, we must think through and plan our actions, and these plans are largely framed in light of what we would have to say to explain what we did. Think about it: When you undertake an action, you often consider ahead of what you would say if you had to explain

15. These categories are adapted from P. A. Schonbach, "A Category System for Account Phases," *European Journal of Social Psychology* 10 (1980): 195–200.

16. John Shotter, *Social Accountability and Selfhood* (Oxford, Eng.: Basil Blackwell, 1984).

17. This argument is developed in John Shotter, "Social Accountability and the Social Construction of 'You,'" in *Texts of Identity*, eds. J. Shotter and K. J. Gergen (London: Sage, 1989), pp. 133–151.

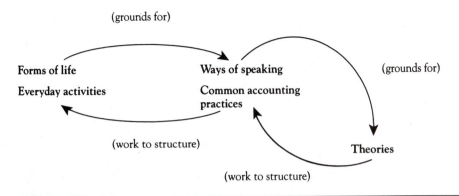

Figure 9.2   Communication–experience loop.

Adapted from *Social Accountability and Selfhood.* by John Shotter. Copyright © 1984 by Basil Blackwell Publishers. Reprinted by permission of the publisher.

that action to others. In other words, potential accounts actually help shape your actions before their occur.

Like other constructionists Shotter believes that people are constantly assigning meaning to and making sense of their experiences. The meanings assigned to an event are closely tied to the language used to account for the event in communication among participants. This idea is further developed by Richard Buttny, who suggests that in any kind of failure event the participants have an interest in controlling the meaning for that event.[18] Accounts serve precisely this function. They are a way of accomplishing goals, such as saving face and preserving relationships. Buttny says that accounts essentially reframe events by creating a context in which to interpret those events.

Buttny presents the example of a student-teacher conference about a speech assignment.[19] The teacher confronts the student on a poor performance, and the student offers an excuse: "It was a bad day, I just, ah, blew a math test before it, so I didn't really feel like speaking." Here, the student is trying to create the context of a bad day, in which

it is okay to do poorly. By giving an account, the student controls the meaning of the situation.

Shotter shows that the relationship between communication (talking and making accounts) and the experience of reality constitutes a loop: Communication determines how reality is experienced, and the experience of reality affects communication. Figure 9.2 illustrates this relationship.[20] To illustrate this diagram, let's return to the birthday example.

Birthdays are an ordinary activity in our culture. Birthday activities are grounds for a variety of forms of talk, including certain kinds of accounts. The standard birthday card that apologizes in an amusing way for forgetting a birthday or being late is a good example of institutionalized accounting. These forms of talk in turn contribute to certain ideas we have about the importance of individuals and their lives. They also address our cultural theories of personal responsibility and interpersonal relations. (You better remember Mom's birthday, or she will think you don't care about her.) When you acknowledge a person's birthday, you are reinforcing the idea that individuals are important in our sociey, which is certainly an important part of our culture's theory of personhood. Those theories in

18. Richard Buttny, "Accounts as a Reconstruction of an Event's Context," *Communication Monographs* 52 (1985): 57–77. See also "Sequence and Structure in Accounts Episodes," *Communication Quarterly* 35 (1987): 67–83.

19. Buttny, "Accounts."

20. Shotter, *Social Accountability*, p. 140.

turn affect how we talk, including the forms of speech used in birthday celebrations.

Shotter takes what he calls an ecological approach. Much like Harré, Shotter believes that the individual and the society are inseparable. Persons are not independent: "Attention is not concentrated upon the supposed relation between people's 'outer' behavior and their 'inner' workings, for it is not focused upon individuals at all, but upon the relations between people."[21] The overall milieu is an *Umwelt*, which is essentially a moral world of rights, duties, privileges, and obligations. The moral framework of human experience is expressed in and through communication: "To preserve their autonomy, people must be able to account, not only for their actions, but also for themselves, i.e. who and what they are."[22]

Rules and Social Action

Rules are an important part of social and cultural reality. Not only are they formed in the process of interaction, but they also govern interaction itself. We discussed rules at some length in Chapter 5. There, rules are defined as guidelines for action and meaning, and three approaches are outlined. The first, *rule following*, treats rules as structurally embedded in language and social life. In the rule-following tradition, rules almost have the force of laws in that people have very little choice about whether to follow them. Rules of grammar are an example.

The other two traditions, the *rule-governed* and the *rule-using approaches*, give individuals much more latitude to create, use, and even reject rules. Here, rules are viewed as conventions that are established as part of the social construction of reality. Rule-governed approaches see rules as guides that can be and are violated. Rule-using approaches suggest that actors have a variety of rules available in a situation and choose those they

believe most appropriate to accomplish their goals. In this section we examine a number of rules theories of social and cultural reality. The first is that of Susan Shimanoff.

Shimanoff's Rule-Governing Approach

Shimanoff surveyed the literature on rules and formulated an overview that incorporates what she judges to be the best thinking in the field.[23] She adds to rules theory in such a way as to make it particularly applicable to communication. Her work is integrative in that it critically considers and analyzes the divergent literature. Shimanoff defines a rule as "a followable prescription that indicates what behavior is obligated, preferred, or prohibited in certain contexts."[24] This definition incorporates the following four elements.

1. *Rules must be followable.* This criterion implies that actors can choose whether to follow or to violate a rule. If a person has no choice in a course of action, then a "rule" is not being followed. The laws of nature are not "followed" because there is no choice; they are fulfilled. Similarly, you are not following a rule by running out of a burning building. On the other hand, rules must deal with the possible. One cannot follow an impossible rule such as visiting your parents every weekend when they live 500 miles away.

2. *Rules are prescriptive.* By this Shimanoff means that a course of action is called for and that the failure to abide by the rule can be criticized. Prescriptions may state what is obligated, preferred, or prohibited, but in any case negative evaluation may ensue if the rule is not followed. If a behavior is permitted, but not preferred or required, it is not governed by a rule because no criticism would follow if the behavior were not chosen. For example, telling a joke may be permissible in certain situations, but it is not a rule if it is not required or preferred.

3. *Rules are contextual.* A rule must do more than govern a single event. At the same time, a rule

---

21. Ibid., p. 94.
22. Ibid., p. 152.

23. Susan B. Shimanoff, *Communication Rules: Theory and Research* (Beverly Hills, Calif.: Sage, 1980).
24. Ibid., p. 57.

cannot be so broad that it governs everything. For example, if you decide on a whim to pick up a hitchhiker, you would not be following a rule because this is an isolated act that you have never done before. On other other hand, if you frequently pick up hitchhikers and you are expected to, you probably are following a rule. If you try to be kind to people in all your dealings, kindness would not be considered rule-governed because it always applies. On the other hand, if you are kind to people in need, you are following a rule: When someone is in need, be kind.

4. *Rules specify appropriate behavior.* They tell us what to do or not do. They do not specify how we must think, feel, or interpret. For example, a rule may require an apology, but it cannot require the apologizer to feel sorry.

To identify a rule properly, an observer must be able to specify its context and its obligated, preferred, or prohibited behavior. The rule also must be stated in a form that demonstrates that it is followable. Shimanoff believes that the "if-then" format allows the observer to do this: "If . . ., then one (must, must not, should). . . ." The "if" clause specifies the nature of the prescription, and the "then" clause specifies the behavior. Consider the following examples:

> If one is not the owner or guest of the owner, *then* one is prohibited from being in the land marked off by this sign.
>
> If one is playing bridge and is the dealer, *then* one must bid first.
>
> If one is wearing a hat and is entering a church, *then* one must remove his/her hat.
>
> If one is playing chess and one's chess pieces are white, *then* one must move his/her piece first.[25]

To verify a rules theory, a researcher must be able to observe rules in operation in everyday interaction. If Shimanoff's rule model is accurate, one will be able to apply her rule criteria to any episode and thereby identify the rules in force. Sometimes this is easy because the rules are explicit. In these situations rules are announced on a sign or in a game-

rules book. Most often, identifying rules is more difficulty because they are implicit. Here, they must be inferred from the behavior of the participants. Shimanoff shows how to do this.

Rules can be found by examining behavior in terms of three criteria:

1. Is the behavior controllable (to assess the degree to which the underlying rule is followable)?

2. Is the behavior criticizable (to assess whether the underlying rule is prescriptive)?

3. Is the behavior contextual (to assess whether people behave differently in various situations)?

If all three are answered by yes, a rule has been found.

Applying these criteria is not necessarily easy. Consider how difficult it would be to determine whether an action is criticized. We know that rule behavior is open to evaluation and that compliance may be praised while violation may be punished. Overt *sanctions* are easiest to identify in observing interactions because they involve verbal or nonverbal rewards and punishments. Sanctions may range from simple frowns or smiles to a stern lecture about rule violation. Besides noting sanctions observers can also look for *repairs*. Here, a rule violator will behave in a way that reveals that a rule was violated. Apologizing is an example. In the absence of overt sanctions or repairs, the observer can simply ask participants whether a given behavior was appropriate or not.

One of Shimanoff's most useful contributions is her model of rule behavior, which indicates the ways people relate to rules in actual interaction (Figure 9.3).[26] This model identifies eight types of rule-related behavior. Four of these are rule conforming, and four are rule deviating. Let us go through these in pairs, beginning at the center of the figure.

Rule-fulfilling and *rule-ignorant behaviors* involve acting without knowing the rule. For example, there is a traditional rule for men to open doors for women. Imagine a little boy who naively opens a door for a woman. He is unaware that he has fol-

25. Ibid., p. 79.

26. Ibid., p. 127.

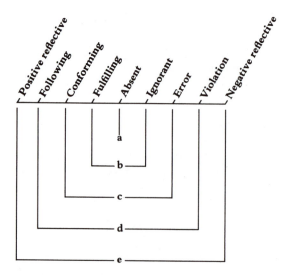

Key: a = noncontrollable, noncriti-
cizable, or noncontextual
b = rule-governed, but no
knowledge of the rule
c = tacit knowledge of a rule
d = conscious knowledge of a rule
e = conscious knowledge, plus
evaluation of a rule

Figure 9.3   Rule-related behavior.

From *Communication Rules: Theory and
Research* by Susan B. Shimanoff. Copyright
© 1980 by Sage Publications. Reprinted by
permission of the publisher.

lowed a rule, but the woman might respond by saying, "What a gentleman you are." This behavior is
rule-fulfilling because the boy didn't know he was
following a prescription. On the other hand, had
the boy failed to open the door in ignorance of the
rule (rule-ignorant behavior), the woman might
whisper to the boy's parents, "You need to teach
your child good manners."

Conforming and *error behaviors* definitely are governed by rules, although the rule is not noted consciously by the individual at the time it is followed
or not followed. Men often unconsciously open
doors for women, and frequently they fail to do so,
not out of ignorance but because they are not
thinking about it at the moment. The first instance

is an example of conforming behavior, the second
of error behavior.

Rule-following behavior is conscious compliance
with the rule. To pursue our example, rule following would apply when a man intentionally steps
ahead of a woman and opens a door. *Rule violation*,
on the other hand, is intentional violation of the
rule. For instance, a man may be tired and simply
may not feel like opening the door for his
companion.

Reflective behavior involves *positive reflection* or
negative reflection (following or violating) of a rule
after evaluating it. The women's movement has
brought many social rules into question. A man
may consciously choose not to open the door for a
woman, precisely because of his evaluation of what
the gesture implies about sex roles. Or a woman
may take the initiative to open a door first. A man
who does not espouse feminist values may make a
point to open the door because, on reflection, he
believes that the rule is a good one.

As an example of how rules operate, consider
Shimanoff's study of marital communication.[27] To
explore communication rules between husbands
and wives, Shimanoff asked twenty couples to tape-
record all their conversations for a day or longer if
necessary to get an hour's worth of talk. She interviewed the couples and analyzed their conversations to determine how husbands and wives express
emotions to each other. Several types of emotional
expressions were explored in this study. *Face-honoring expressions* tell the other person how good you
feel about them. *Face-compensating expressions* tell
another person that you are sorry for an earlier
transgression. *Face-neutral expressions* deal with
emotions about other people, and *face-threatening
expressions* are hostile toward the other person.

Shimanoff found a strong tendency to express
feelings in ways that help the spouse save face and
feel good about himself or herself or at least not
hurt his or her feelings. She therefore posited the
following rules: (1) "When speaking with one's

27. Susan B. Shimanoff, "Rules Governing the Verbal
Expression of Emotions Between Married Couples," *Western
Journal of Speech Communication* 49 (1985): 147–165.

spouse, one should disclose face-honoring, face-compensating, and pleasant face-neutral emotions more frequently than face-threatening emotions"; (2) "When speaking with one's spouse, one should disclose unpleasant face-neutral emotions more often than hostile emotions towards one's spouse or regrets for transgressions against absent others."[28] Now, these are not laws because they are sometimes violated. As we all know, husbands and wives do sometimes express their feelings in face-threatening ways, but as rules these guidelines help couples know how to express emotions in certain ways.

Contingency Rules Theory

Contingency rules theory, originated by Mary John Smith, applies the rule-using approach to compliance-gaining situations.[29] There are three assumptions to the theory:

1. People act with purpose and are influenced in their actions by what they believe the outcome will be.

2. Persuasion is controlled more by people's personal choices than by the influence of others.

3. External threats and rewards are meaningful only if they apply to one's personal goals and standards.

In persuasion people select compliance-gaining message strategies and decide how to respond to the messages of others. They make these choices under the influence of rules that they believe apply in the situation. The individual will normally perceive several choices. Given a goal, a context, and a set of possible actions designed to achieve the goal, the individual will perceive that certain acts are more acceptable and more effective in the context than are others.

Imagine, for example, that a friend asks you to help her move. Would you do it? This depends on what you think the outcome of your agreement or rejection would be, and you will choose rules for

acting on the basis of these judgments. So, for example, if you value the friendship and want to maintain it, you will probably help her move to build the relationship. On the other hand, if you value personal success and have a big test the next day, you might decline. Here, you would have to weigh two rules, one dealing with the maintenance of the relationship and the other dealing with your own sense of personal success.

The rules guiding a person's actions are of two types—self-evaluative and adaptive. *Self-evaluative rules* are tied to one's personal standards and are closely associated with the self-concept. Some self-evaluative rules involve *self-identity* in that they are guided by what an individual believes to be his or her personal characteristics; others involve *image maintenance* because they affect how one wants others view him or her. Actions guided by self-identity rules serve to maintain a self-concept, whereas actions guided by image-maintenance rules serve to maintain a public image. For example, if you are guided more by the self-identity rule of being a good student, you will probably study for the exam rather than help your friend move; but if you are more interested in perpetuating your image as a nice person, you may well decide to postpone studying for the exam and help.

The second class of contingency rules are adaptive rules. These rules tell one what actions will be effective or advantageous within a given situation. *Environmental contingency rules* help a person select behavior that will lead to positive outcomes. For example, you might decide to help your friend move because you see this as a way to win a favor. *Interpersonal relationships rules* are created to help people behave in ways that maintain satisfying relationships with others. You might decide to help your friend move because you value the friendship and want to build it. Finally, *social-normative rules* tell a communicator what is appropriate by standard social norms such as reciprocity. If your friend had helped you move, you would probably follow the social-normative rule of reciprocation and help her move, too.

Rules are contingent, or context-specific, depending on the situation in which the compli-

---

28. Ibid., pp. 159–160.

29. Mary John Smith, "Cognitive Schemata and Persuasive Communication: Toward a Contingency Rules Theory," in *Communication Yearbook* 6, ed. M. Burgoon (Beverly Hills, Calif.: Sage, 1982), pp. 330–363.

ance gaining will take place. Many aspects of context are beyond the communicators' control; others, however, are created by the actions of the communicators themselves. These contextual factors include the nature of the relationship among the communciators, their intentions, and the degree to which they agree or disagree about the subject being discussed. Different rules will come into play in different relationships. When the communicators' intentions change, the rules also change, and rules that apply to situations in which communicators agree do not apply to situations in which they disagree.

For example, you would use various rules to decide whether to help a friend move, depending on the situation. If your relationship is particularly close or intimate, it will be hard to say no. If, on the other hand, she is a mere acquaintance, you might well decline. If you already owe her a favor, you will probably decide to help her move, but if she owes you one, you may decide to study for the test instead.

Contingency rules theory seems to be well supported by research. In one study, Smith asked about 500 students to consider what they would do in a persuasive situation.[30] Specifically, she gave each of them a version of one of two scenarios. One is a situation in which the subject is planning to chop down a tree in the yard, and a neighbor asks him not to. Another is a case in which a co-worker asks the subject not to smoke so much at work. The first scenario is a situation in which people probably feel a strong right to resist, whereas in the second people do not feel they have this right.

Various versions of these situations were created to test a number of contextual factors, including the intimacy of the relationship between the other person and the subject, the extent to which the request is seen as self-serving, and the amount of power the other person has in the situation. For example, in one version of the tree-cutting scenario, the neighbor is a good friend, and in another he is not. In one version of the episode, the reason for the request is to enhance the value of the neigh-

bor's property (self-serving), whereas in another it is to enhance both properties (mutual benefits). In one version the neighbor is the subject's supervisor at work (high power), and in another he is just a neighbor (low power).

Theoretically, a different set of rules should be used to decide how to respond to each of these versions, and Smith found that this was exactly the case. For example, when a self-serving request is made by a good friend and you feel you have the right to reject the request, it will probably be rejected, first, because of rules for relationship maintenance and, second, rules of image. On the other hand, if a mere acquaintance makes the same kind of request, you are more apt to reject it, first, on the grounds of image maintenance and, second, self-identity. Notice that the main issue here is not whether one accepts or rejects a persuasive attempt, but why one does so. As a rules theory, this approach helps us understand the basis on which individuals make their choices.

The contingency rules theory provides an excellent idea of what the rule-using approach is like, and it accents the ways in which rules theory departs from more traditional linear models of communication. With this introduction, we turn to the most comprehensive rule-using theory, the coordinated management of meaning.

Coordinated Management of Meaning

The theory of the coordinated management of meaning (CMM) was developed by Barnett Pearce, Vernon Cronen, and their colleagues as a comprehensive theory of communication.[31] The theory

---

30. Mary John Smith, "Contingency Rules Theory, Context, and Compliance-Behaviors," *Human Communication Research* 10 (1984): 489–512.

31. W. Barnett Pearce and Vernon Cronen, *Communication, Action, and Meaning* (New York: Praeger, 1980); Vernon Cronen, Victoria Chen, and W. Barnett Pearce, "Coordinated Management of Meaning: A Critical Theory," in *Theories in Intercultural Communication*, eds. Y. Y. Kim and W. B. Gudykunst (Newbury Park, Calif.: Sage, 1988), pp. 66–98; Vernon Cronen, W. Barnett Pearce, and Linda Harris, "The Coordinated Management of Meaning," in *Comparative Human Communication Theory*, ed. F. E. X. Dance (New York: Harper & Row, 1982); W. Barnett Pearce, "The Coordinated Management of Meaning: A Rules Based Theory of Interpersonal Communication," in *Explorations in Interpersonal Communication*, ed. G. R. Miller (Beverly Hills, Calif.: Sage, 1976), pp. 17–36; Vernon Cronen, W. Barnett Pearce, and Linda Harris, "The Logic of the Coordinated Management of Meaning," *Communication Education* 28 (1979): 22–38.

integrates work from symbolic interactionism (Chapter 8), ethogeny (Chapter 9), system theory (Chapter 3), speech acts (Chapter 5), and relational communication (Chapter 12). CMM is interesting because not only does it integrate and build on a great deal of previous theoretical work but it also is broadly applicable to a variety of communication situations.

In CMM theory, people are seen as interpreting and acting on the basis of rules. Individuals within any social situation first want to understand what is going on and apply rules to interpret the events they experience. Persons then act on the basis of their understandings, employing rules to decide what kind of action is appropriate. These rules are available to communicators as part of their social realities. In other words, our understandings and actions are determined by interaction in social groups.

Pearce and Cronen make use of the concept of constitutive and regulative rules from speech act theory and make them a central part of their treatment (see Chapter 5). In CMM, *constitutive rules* are essentially *rules of meaning,* used by communicators to interpret or understand an event. *Regulative rules* are essentially *rules of action,* used to determine how to respond or behave.

For example, if a friend says something to you, you decipher the meaning of the message. You interpret it; you figure out what it means. Usually this is a simple and almost unconscious experience because your interpretation rules are immediately available and simply applied. Sometimes interpretation is more difficult, and you may have to dig for appropriate rules of understanding. The point here is not whether you come to understand your friend's statement in the way it was intended but that you develop your own understanding of it, which may or may not correspond with the intended meaning. Once you feel you know what was said, you then respond in some way, and your action rules help you decide what to say.

Rules of meaning and action are always chosen within a context. The *context* is the frame of reference for interpreting an action. Your meanings and actions are always chosen within some context,

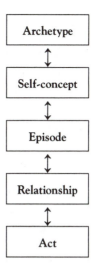

Figure 9.4   Hierarchy of contexts.

Adapted from *Communication, Action, and Meaning* by W. Barnett Pearce and Vernon Cronen. Copyright © 1980 by Praeger Publishers. Reprinted by permission of the author.

and your responses will differ from one context to another.

Pearce and Cronen see contexts as a nested *hierarchy:* One context is embedded within another. In other words, each context is itself part of a bigger context. Figure 9.4 illustrates this idea. Here, four typical contexts are depicted in a hierarchy. The *relationship context* includes mutual expectations among members of a group. The *episode context* is an event. The *self-concept context* is one's sense of personal definition. Finally, the *archetype context* is an image of general truth.

Each context is part of a higher-level context, so that, for instance, one's relationship expectations might be framed within an episode, which in turn would be framed by self-concept. Further, the order of contexts shown in Figure 9.4 is not universal; in fact, it probably shifts constantly. Sometimes, for example, self is understood within the context of the relationship, whereas on other occasions relationships are understood in reference to self. Also, although the contexts listed in Figure 9.4 are representative and common, they by no means exhaust the possible contexts within which interpretations and actions are made. Humans have the ability to create a number of contexts for interpretation and action.

Pearce and Cronen tell of a couple named Jan and Dave who have problems with their relationship. The relationship pattern that troubles the couple is like this: Jan fails to do something important, and Dave nags her to do it. Jan then follows through and does what Dave asks. Neither of them likes this pattern, but they seem unable to change it. Jan and Dave use different contexts to understand their actions. Jan understands her own actions within the context of her self-concept as a lazy person, believing that she requires others to motivate her to do necessary things. Dave understands his actions within his self-concept as a "laid-back" guy, not a domineering person. Within the context of the relationship, Jan defines Dave's actions as being dominant, but within the context of his self-concept, Dave sees his actions as submissive because he is complying with Jan's manipulative desire to be pushed.

Any event or action being interpreted is known as a *text*. Often text and context form a loop (Figure 9.5), such that each is used from time to time to interpret the other.[32] This situation is called *reflexivity* because each context reflects the other. Jan, for example, uses the relationship as a context for interpreting herself as lazy, but she also uses her self-concept as a lazy person to understand her relationship with Dave as one of dominance and submission. Reflexivity enters every context heirarchy at some point because the hierarchy cannot keep going up forever. At some point the ladder of contexts must come to an end and start coming down again.

Where the interpretation rules are consistent throughout the loop, the loop is said to be *charmed*, or self-confirmatory. Jan's charmed loop, for exam-

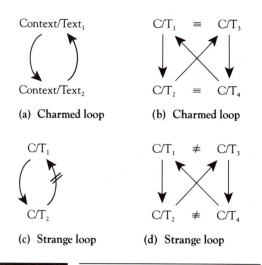

(a) **Charmed loop**   (b) **Charmed loop**

(c) **Strange loop**   (d) **Strange loop**

Figure 9.5   Text-context loop patterns.

Adapted from "Between Text and Context: Toward a Rhetoric of Contextual Reconstruction" by Robert J. Branham and W. Barnett Pearce, in *Quarterly Journal of Speech* 71 (1985): 23, 25. Reprinted by permission of the author and publisher.

ple, is like this: I am lazy and therefore Dave needs to push me; Dave pushes me so that I will do what needs to be done. Often, however, the rules of interpretation change from one point in the loop to another, causing a paradox. Pearce and Cronen refer to a paradoxical loop as a *strange loop*. The strange loop of the alcoholic is illustrated in Figure 9.6.

Here the alcoholic is confused about control. Within the context of the self as a controlled drinker, drinking is accepted as okay; but within the context of the episode of drinking, the self is defined as out of control, making drinking not okay. If you follow the loop in Figure 9.6, you see what many alcoholics go through. First, they drink and come to see themselves as out of control. Then they stop drinking, now believing they are in control, so that they can begin drinking again.

To demonstrate the operation of rules, Pearce and Cronen use a set of symbols denoting rule structures. Three are important here:

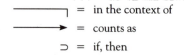

32. Loops are discussed in Vernon E. Cronen, Kenneth M. Johnson, and John W. Lannamann, "Paradoxes, Double Binds, and Reflexive Loops: An Alternative Theoretical Perspective," *Family Process* 20 (1982): 91–112; and Robert J. Branham and W. Barnett Pearce, "Between Text and Context: Toward a Rhetoric of Contextual Reconstruction," *Quarterly Journal of Speech* 71 (1985): 19–36.

The first symbol denotes the context of an act, the second applies to a constitutive rule, and the third is used to stipulate a regulative rule. Consider the following examples:

1.
$$\overline{\text{insult} \longrightarrow \text{joke}}^{\text{play}}$$

In the context of play, an insult is to be taken as a joke. *Constitutive rule*: An insult counts as a joke.

2.
$$\overline{\text{insult} \longrightarrow \text{put down}}^{\text{conflict}}$$

In the context of conflict, an insult is to be taken as a put-down. *Constitutive rule*: An insult counts as a put-down.

3.
$$\overline{\text{husband insults wife's family} \supset \text{wife cries}}^{\text{argument}}$$

When arguing, the wife typically cries after the husband insults her family. *Regulative rule*: When the husband insults, wife cries.

4.
$$\overline{[\text{husband insults wife's family} \supset \text{wife playfully hits husband}] \longrightarrow \text{fun}}^{\text{playful banter}}$$

In play it is considered fun for the wife to "hit" the husband after he insults her family. *Regulative rule*: Wife should respond to husband's insult by "hitting" him. *Constitutive rule*: This sequence of events is to be taken as fun.

These examples are simple, but complex acts can be diagrammed in the same fashion. Whereas simple examples are used here for clarity, most significant interactions are far more complex.

Rules give us a sense of what interpretations and actions appear to be logical or appropriate in a given situation. This sense is called *logical force*. Because people behave in a manner consistent with their rules, rules provide a logical force for acting in certain ways. Four types of logical force operate in communication. The first is *prefigurative* or *causal force*, an antecedent-to-act linkage in which the individual perceives that he or she is being "pressured" to behave in certain ways because of prior conditions. If you think that you are being caused to do something, prefigurative force is at play. For example, you might tell someone that you are in school because your parents made you go.

Practical force is an act-to-consequent linkage in which one behaves in a certain way to achieve a future condition. In any communication encounter, an individual's rules present a series of "oughts" that guide interpretations, responses, and actions. These oughts are perceived logical forces in the interactional system. So, for example, you might believe you are in college because you want to get a better job than you could get with only a high school education.

The third type of logical force is contextual. *Contextual force* is a pressure from the context to the act. Here, you believe that the action or interpretation is a natural part of the context. Within the context of your self-concept, for example, you might feel that going to college is just necessary, just part of who you are.

Finally, *implicative force* is a pressure to transform or change the context in some way. Here, you act to create a new context or to change an existing

Figure 9.6   The alcoholic's paradox.

Adapted from "Between Text and Context: Toward a Rhetoric of Contextual Reconstruction" by Robert J. Branham and W. Barnett Pearce, in *Quarterly Journal of Speech* 71 (1985): 26. Reprinted by permission of the author and publisher.

one. Implicative force might come into play, for example, if your family did not value college and never encouraged its children to go on to school. You might take it upon yourself to change this situation, to create a new family definition, to make the family proud of one of its members for getting a degree. In this kind of situation, you would actually be trying to change the context of family expectations.

In modern society a person is part of many systems, each with its own set of meaning and action rules. The rules are learned through interaction in social groups. Over time, individuals internalize some of these rules and draw on them to guide their actions. The basic problem of communication is that when an individual enters an interaction, that person has no way of knowing precisely what rules the other participants will be using. The primary task in all communication, then, is to achieve and then sustain some form of coordination. *Coordination* involves meshing one's actions with those of another to the point of feeling that the sequence of actions is logical or appropriate. The communicators in an exchange need not interpret the events the same way, but each must feel, from within his or her own system of rules, that what is happening makes sense—that is the essence of coordination.

Figure 9.7 shows how coordination occurs.[33] Person A acts in a particular way in response to prior conditions or to achieve something. The act is taken as a message by person B, who uses meaning rules to interpret the message. Person A's act thus becomes an antecedent event to which person B responds, based on B's action rules. B's act is in turn interpreted by A as a message from the standpoint of A's meaning rules, and B's act becomes the consequent to A's initial move. If A and B are operating with substantially different rule structures, they will quickly discover that one person's behavior does not represent the consequent intended, and they will readjust their rules until some level of coordination is achieved.

Consider the simple example of a child trying to get back a ball after accidentally having thrown it

through a neighbor's window.[34] The adult begins with the following rule structure:

• *Constitutive rule:* If I say, "Is this ball yours?" in a stern fashion, this act will be taken as anger, a demand for a confession, and a threat.
• *Regulative rules:* My act, taken as anger, will elicit crying and apologies. I, in turn, will become less angry and will give back the ball.

The child, on the other hand, has a very different set of rules:

• *Constitutive rules:* When the neighbor says, "Is this your ball?" he is asking for information. My statement, "Give it back," will be taken as a request.
• *Regulative rules:* When the neighbor requests information, I will respond with a factual answer, "Yes, it is." I will say, "Give it back," and he will give it back.

Now observe the actual conversation:

NEIGHBOR: Is this your ball?
CHILD: Yes, it is. Give it back.

Obviously, the neighbor did not get the expected response and will interpret the child's remark as impudence rather than the simple request intended by the child. At this point the interaction is not coordinated. Now the neighbor must adjust the regulative rule by trying a different approach:

NEIGHBOR: Give it back? This ball went through my window. Do you know that?

If the child has a sufficiently complex rule structure to provide options, he may adjust so that a successful outcome can be achieved. If not, coordination may not be achieved. Consider:

Unsatisfactory outcome (no enmeshment):
CHILD: Give my ball back. I'll tell Daddy if you don't give it back.
NEIGHBOR: Get out of my yard, kid.

33. Pearce and Cronen, *Communication*, p. 174.

34. This example is adapted from Pearce and Cronen, *Communication*, pp. 162–164. Originally, the example was developed in K. T. Alvy, "The Development of Listener Adapted Communication in Grade-School Children from Different Social Class Backgrounds," *Genetic Psychology Monographs* 87 (1973): 33–104.

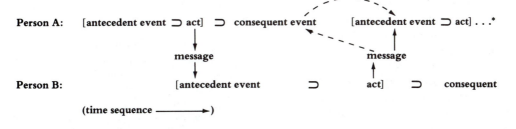

Figure 9.7   Enmeshment process.

*Solid arrows denote constitutive rules. Broken arrows denote the coorientational state of comparing the subsequent message to the anticipated consequent event in anticipation of the next act. From *Communication, Action, and Meaning* by W. Barnett Pearce and Vernon Cronen. Copyright © 1980 by Praeger Publishers. Reprinted by permission of the author.

Successful outcome (coordination achieved):

CHILD: I'm sorry. I didn't mean to do it, and I will be careful in the future.

NEIGHBOR: Okay. Here's your ball.

An important contribution of CMM is the idea that people can have perfectly satisfactory coordination without understanding one another. In other words, communicators can organize their actions in ways that seem logical to all parties, yet they understand what is going on in a variety of different ways. For example, a speaker and audience may mesh very well. The speaker is dynamic and effusive, and the audience responds enthusiastically. The speaker thinks she is educating and persuading the audience, but the audience is merely entertained and forgets the point of the message within hours. Here, both sides are satisfied, and each thinks what happened was appropriate; yet what the speaker thought was happening did not happen.

As an example of the latter, Uma Narula and Barnett Pearce studied the communication patterns of development in India.[35] Development is the process of improving economic conditions in a country, and the Indian government has had such a program for many years. The cornerstones of this program have been legislation, direct action, and "communication." The communication aspect of

the program was designed to make the people aware of the extent of their problems and to get them involved in local improvement projects. The result was that they became very aware of problems and the potential for improvement but they did not become involved in their own development. This is a case of coordination without understanding.

The rules used by the population to interpret and respond to the development campaigns were different from those of the government. The government intended to have the people become directly involved in development projects of their own. The people saw the direct action of the government as the answer and expected the government to do it all. This led to a pattern of "passive involvement," in which the population became increasingly critical of the government for not solving their problems for them. The government thought its communication program had been a failure, when in fact it had been very successful. The government did not realize that its own direct action was also taken by the population as a message, the message that problems could be solved by the government alone.

Language and Culture

In the final section of this chapter, we examine some prominent theories of culture and language. All theories presented in this chapter deal with this

---

35. Uma Narula and W. Barnett Pearce, *Development as Communication: A Perspective on India* (Carbondale: Southern Illinois University Press, 1986).

subject in a sense because they all show ways in which communication patterns create and reflect the reality of a social group, society, or culture. Generally speaking, the study of the relationship between language and culture is known as sociolinguistics. This material is somewhat related to theories of cultural interpretation presented in Chapter 10. Sociolinguistics is a very broad term covering any study of language that makes significant use of social data, or, conversely, any study of social life that makes use of linguistic data. Although this label would not be adopted by all students of language and culture, it is certainly the most commonly understood term for this kind of research and theory.

Sociolinguistics contrasts sharply with the structural approaches covered in Chapter 4, which view language as essentially independent from the ways in which it is used. Today, most students of language believe that language is affected by both intrinsic structural properties and sociocultural factors.[36]

We turn now to two important theoretical contributions to language and culture, both classic theories of this genre.

Linguistic Relativity

The *Sapir–Whorf hypothesis*, otherwise known as the theory of linguistic relativity, is based on the work of Edward Sapir and his protégé Benjamin Whorf.[37] Whorf is best known for his fieldwork in linguistics; his analysis of the Hopi is particularly well known. In his research Whorf discovered that fundamental syntactical differences are present among language groups. The Whorfian hypothesis of linguistic relativity simply states that the structure of a culture's language determines the behavior

and habits of thinking in that culture. In the words of Sapir,

> Human beings do not live in the objective world alone, nor alone in the world of social activity as ordinarily understood, but are very much at the mercy of the particular language which has become the medium of expression for their society. It is quite an illusion to imagine that one adjusts to reality essentially without the use of language and that language is merely an incidental means of solving specific problems of communication or reflection. The fact of the matter is that the "real world" is to a large extent unconsciously built up on the language habits of the group. . . . We see and hear and otherwise experience very largely as we do because the language habits of our community predispose certain choices of interpretation.[38]

This hypothesis suggests that our thought processes and the way we see the world are shaped by the grammatical structure of the language. As one reviewer reacted, "All one's life one has been tricked . . . by the structure of language into a certain way of perceiving reality."[39]

Whorf spent much of his life investigating the relationship of language and behavior. His work with the Hopi illustrates the relativity hypothesis. Like all cultural groups, the Hopi possess a reality, which represents their view of the world at large. One area of Whorf's extensive analysis of Hopi thought is the analysis of time. Whereas many cultures refer to points in time (e.g., seasons) as nouns, the Hopi conceive of time as a passage or process. Thus, the Hopi language never objectifies time. The Hopi would not refer to summer as "in the summer." Instead, the Hopi would refer to the passing or coming of a phase that is never here and now but always moving, accumulating. In our culture three tenses indicate locations or places in a spatial analogy: past, present, and future. Hopi verbs have no tense in the same sense. Instead, their verb forms relate to duration and order. In the Standard Average European (SAE) languages, including

36. Gillian Sankoff, *The Social Life of Language* (Philadelphia: University of Pennsylvania Press, 1980), p. xvii.

37. Edward Sapir, *Language: An Introduction to the Study of Speech* (New York: Harcourt, Brace & World, 1921); Benjamin L. Whorf, *Language, Thought, and Reality* (New York: Wiley, 1956). In the Whorf, the following articles are most helpful: John B. Carroll, "Introduction," pp. 1–34; "The Relation of Habitual Thought and Behavior in Language," pp. 134–159; "Language, Mind, and Reality," pp. 246–269.

38. Quoted in Whorf, *Language, Thought, and Reality*, p. 134.

39. Carroll (in Whorf's *Language, Thought, and Reality*), "Introduction," p. 27.

English, we visualize time as a line. The Hopi conception is more complex, as illustrated in the following example.[40]

Suppose that a speaker reports to a hearer that a third person is running: "He is running." The Hopi would use the word *wari*, which is a statement of running as a fact. The same word would be used for a report of past running: "He ran." For the Hopi, the statement of fact (validity) is what is important, not whether the event is presently occurring or happened in the past. If, however, the Hopi speaker wishes to report a past event of running from memory (the hearer did not actually see it), a different form would be used, *era wari*. The English sentence "He will run" would translate *warikni*, which communicates running as a statement of expectation. Again, it is not the location in past, present, or future that is important to the Hopi but the nature of validity (observed fact, recalled fact, or expectation). Another English form, "He runs [on the track team]," would translate *warikngwe*. This latter Hopi form again refers to running but in the sense of law or condition.

As a result of these linguistic differences, Hopi and SAE cultures will think about, perceive, and behave toward time differently. For example, the Hopi tend to engage in lengthy preparing activities. Experiences (getting prepared) tend to accumulate as time "gets later." The emphasis is on the accumulated experience during the course of time, not on time as a point or location. In SAE cultures, with their spatial treatment of time, experiences are not accumulated in the same sense. Elaborate and lengthy preparations are not often found. The custom in SAE cultures is to record events such that what happened in the past is objectified in space (recorded). Whorf summarizes this view: "Concepts of 'time' and 'matter' are not given in substantially the same form by experience to all men but depend upon the nature of the language or languages through the use of which they have been developed."[41]

Notice that the theory of linguistic relativity is different from the social constructionist theories discussed earlier in the chapter. In social constructionism people are believed to create their realities in the process of interaction, whereas Whorf and Sapir teach that reality is already embedded in the language and therefore comes preformed. Both theories deal with cultural reality, but they approach the topic differently.

Elaborated and Restricted Codes

One of the most important sociolinguistic theories is that of Basil Bernstein on elaborted and restricted codes.[42] This theory shows how the structure of the language employed in everyday talk reflects and shapes the assumptions of a social group. Bernstein is especially interested in and concerned about social class and the ways in which the class system creates different types of language and is maintained by language.

The basic assumption of this theory is that the forms of relationship established within a social group affect the type of speech used by the group. The structure of the language used by a group makes different things relevant or significant in communication. This condition results because different groups have different requirements of life and the language used emerges from what is required to maintain relationships within the group. In other words, people learn their place in the world by virtue of the language codes they employ.

For example, in one family where a strict authoritarian control system is used, children learn that they must respond to simple commands of the family authority, the mother perhaps. In this kind of family, persuasive appeals based on one's own desires would be not only irrelevant but counterproductive. This kind of talk is therefore not learned.

For Bernstein, role and language go hand-in-hand. The kinds of roles that children learn are

---

40. Adapted from Whorf, *Language, Thought, and Reality*, p. 213.

41. Ibid., p. 158.

42. Basil Bernstein, *Class, Codes, and Control: Theoretical Studies Toward a Sociology of Language* (London: Routledge & Kegan Paul, 1971).

reinforced by the kind of language employed in the agencies of socialization, including perhaps most importantly, the family. The term *code* refers to a set of organizing principles behind the language employed by members of a social group. Two children who both speak English might employ very different codes because the nature and organization of their talk is different.

Bernstein's theory centers on two codes—elaborated and restricted. *Elaborated codes* provide a wide range of syntactic or grammatical alternatives to the speaker. These allow speakers to make their ideas and intentions explicit. Because they are more complex, the use of elaborated codes requires more planning, explaining why people who employ these types of codes may pause more and appear to be thinking as they talk.

Restricted codes have a narrower range of options, and it is easier to predict what form will be chosen among speakers of restricted codes. These codes do not allow the speaker to expand on or elaborate their meanings and intentions.

Restricted codes are appropriate in groups in which there is a strongly shared set of assumptions about people and relationships. Because of the high coherence in the group's meanings, there is little need to elaborate on one's individual ideas. Elaborated codes are appropriate in groups in which perspectives are not shared, and this kind of language enables the members of the group to expand on what they as individuals mean. Restricted codes are oriented toward social categories, for which everybody has the same meaning, whereas elaborated codes are oriented to individualized categories that others might not share.

An example of a shared social category is gender. In some groups everybody knows the difference between masculine and feminine, and people are identified in terms of their sex. Everybody knows the place of a woman and a man, a girl and a boy. You can assume what people think and feel based on their gender identification. There is no need to explore individual ideas in this kind of system. In individualized systems, however, such social categories would not be as useful because there is not a common understanding of what masculine and feminine mean. Individuals' own perspectives must be shared, and the language must be elaborate enough to make this possible.

Thus, elaborated codes are used by speakers who value individuality above group identification. Because the intent of the speakers cannot be assumed by their role, they have to be able to express themselves individually in some detail. Bernstein offers the example of a couple that has just come out of a movie and goes to a friend's house. There, they discuss the film at some length. The other couple has not seen it but can understand their friends' ideas about the film anyway:

> An hour is spent in the complex, moral political, aesthetic subtleties of the film and its place in the contemporary scene. . . . The meanings now have to be made public to others who have not seen the film. The speech shows careful editing, at both the grammatical and lexical levels. It is no longer contextualized. The meanings are explicit, elaborated and individualized. . . . The experience of the listeners cannot be taken for granted. Thus each member of the group is on his own as he offers his interpretation.[43]

A primary difference between the types of groups that use these two codes is their degree of openness. A *closed-role system* is one that reduces the number of alternatives for the participants. Roles are set, and people are understood in terms of those roles. This understanding of who people are and how they should behave forms the basis of a common knowledge within the group. Because of this shared meaning in the group, an elaborated language is not necessary and therefore not cultured or learned.

An *open-role system* is one that expands the number of alternatives for individuals in the group. Roles are not categorical and simple; they are individualized and negotiated; they are fluid and change. Thus, there may be very little shared understanding of a person's identity within an open system, and an elaborated code is necessary for communication to take place in this system.

Two major factors contribute to the development of an elaborated or restricted code within a

43. Ibid., p. 177.

system. The first is the social structure of the major socializing agencies within the system, including the family, peer group, school, and work. Where the structure of these groups is well defined in terms of fixed roles, a restricted code is likely to develop. Where the structure of these groups is less well defined and has fluid roles, an elaborated code is more likely to be created. The second major factor is values. Pluralistic societies that value individuality promote elaborated codes, whereas monolithic societies promote restricted ones.

You can now see how codes are so strongly associated with social class. Bernstein says that members of the middle class use both types of systems. They may, for example, be exposed to rather open roles at home but somewhat closed roles in the workplace. Or peer groups may use closed roles, while the school employs open ones.

Members of the working class, however, are less likely to use elaborated codes. For working-class individuals, both the values and the role systems reinforce restricted codes. This leads Bernstein to write,

> Without a shadow of a doubt the most formative influence upon the procedures of socialization, from a sociological viewpoint, is social class. The class structure influences work and educational roles and brings families into a special relationship with each other and deeply penetrates the structure of life experiences within the family. . . . I shall go on to argue that the deep structure of communication itself is affected, but not in any final or irrevocable way.[44]

In a well-known study, Bernstein tape-recorded young men from the working class and the middle class in England, talking about capital punishment.[45] He analyzed samples of this speech and found interesting class differences. Even when the data were controlled for intelligence, the working-class speakers used longer phrases, shorter words, and less pausing than middle-class speakers. The interpretation is that with an elaborated code, the middle-class boys needed more planning time,

which explains their shorter phrases and longer pauses.

Many other differences found in this study illustrate elaborated and restricted codes. For example, middle-class speakers used "I think" significantly more than did working-class speakers. Working-class speakers made greater use of short phrases at the end of sentences to confirm the other person's common understanding, expressions like "isn't it?" "you know," and "wouldn't he?" Middle-class speakers had longer, more complex verb phrases, more passive verbs, more uncommon adverbs and adjectives. And middle-class speakers made more use of the personal pronoun *I*.

Elaborated codes are empowering because they enable universal appeals. They enable speakers to adapt to a wide range of audiences and appeal to widely different types of persons. On the other hand, elaborated codes can be alienating because, as Bernstein writes, they separate "feeling from thought, of self from other, of private belief from role obligation."[46]

Although he acknowledges the limitations of restricted talk, Bernstein does not devalue it: "Let it be said immediately that a restricted code gives access to a vast potential of meanings, of delicacy, subtlety and diversity of cultural forms, to a unqiue aesthetic the basis of which in condensed symbols may influence the form of the imagining."[47] However, Bernstein also notes that those in power in society often do devalue this type of speech, which further perpetuates the class system.

The family is especially important in the development of code. Two types of families correspond to the two types of codes. *Position families* have a clear and formally determined role structure. They tend to have a closed communication system and use restricted codes. Such families tend to have sharp boundaries in their use of space and in their conception of objects and persons. They define objects and people in terms of their position. *Person-centered families* determine roles on the basis of individuals' personal orientations rather than for-

44. Ibid., p. 175.
45. Ibid., pp. 76–117.

46. Ibid., p. 186.
47. Ibid., p. 186.

mally defined divisions. They tend to use open communication and elaborated codes. Roles and relations within these families tend to be unstable and constantly in negotiation. These families do not maintain sharp boundaries in their use of space or in their ideas about people and things.

Although a family may have a variety of means of exerting control and regulating behavior, there seems to be a predominant or preferred method employed, depending on the type of family. Some families prefer an *imperative mode* of regulation, which is based on command and authority. In this type of family, when Dad says, "Shut up," you do. This is preferred in hierarchical families in which certain members are defined as in control according to the role structure. This kind of control is delivered with a restricted code.

Other families prefer *positional appeals*, based on role-related norms. Here, control is exerted by relying on commonly understood norms associated with each role. Examples of this kind of appeal are "You are old enough to know better," or "Boys don't play with dolls." This kind of control can be expressed with restricted or elaborated codes, depending on the degree of differentiation in the system.

Finally, *personal appeals* are based on individualized characteristics and individualized rules, and these appeals often consist of giving reasons for why a person should or should not do something. Again, the code employed can be restricted or elaborated, depending on the degree of shared understanding in the family.

Commentary and Critique

For the most part, this chapter fills in the blanks left by symbolic interactionism in Chapter 8. We see here the many ways in which people construct reality through communication. The idea of social constructionism has won widespread favor because of its intuitive appeal. All theories in this chapter see a close relationship between language and reality. All show that the language used in a culture shapes the reality in which that culture lives.

We see from these theories that all aspects of reality are socially constructed, including, for example, the self and emotions. We have looked at the ways in which common forms of talk such as accounts contribute to the construction of reality within a social group or culture. Rules are an important part of a social reality, and they provide guidance for the communication that affects our sense of reality.

An important question deals with the role of interaction in this reality-constructing system. Symbolic interactionism assumes that language is an outcome of interaction and that interaction is therefore the basis of society. The social constructionists use this assumption as the basis for the idea that reality is constructed through communication. Some sociolinguists like Sapir and Whorf, on the other hand, assume that language precedes interaction and that our interaction patterns are a result, not a cause, of language structure. One can, of course, take a stand in the middle and suggest that both assertions are true. Interaction does shape language, but language itself in turn shapes interaction.[48] Most constructionists today would probably agree with this position.

Bernstein's work illustrates this idea very well. The type of interaction in the family and other socializing institutions determines the sort of language that is learned, but that language in turn reinforces the interaction patterns that led to it in the first place. We will return again to the issue of the primacy of language versus interaction in Chapter 10 in our examination of phenomenology and textual interpretation.

Although the social constructionist thesis is very popular, there is also a strong resistance to this idea from some quarters. Social constructionism remains controversial because it conflicts with the commonsense notion that reality is objective and independent, an idea deeply rooted in Western thought. Many social researchers and philosophers of science strongly believe that we use language to

---

48. This intermediate position is given weight by the influential theory of structuration, attributed most notably to Anthony Giddens. See, for example, *Profiles and Critiques in Social Theory* (Berkeley: University of California Press, 1982), chap. 1–3.

communicate about the objects in the world and that those objects exist prior to any communication about them.

Although it seems patently obvious to constructionists that human experience is formed largely in and through culture, many sociobehavioral scientists have not adopted this assumption at all. Much social science still rests on the assumption that the human experience is largely universal, owing to a common biological inheritance and common cognitive structures. Noam Chomsky (Chapter 4), for example, has taught that language structures are universal and that cultural differences in languages are merely superficial. Further, he believes that certain language universals are innate and that language is acquired by an interaction between experience and wired-in structures. Charles Osgood (Chapter 7) has come to the conclusion that the dimensions of meaning are universal, which is antithetical to social constructionism.

If these structuralists are right, then cultural relativists are barking up the wrong tree. We should not be looking for richly different language and meaning experiences; instead, we should discover the common universals that provide an explanatory basis for human behavior across the board. This is a debate that will not die, and we encounter it again at other points throughout this text.

Perhaps the most comprehensive critique of constructionism in recent communication literature is that of Richard Cherwitz and James Hikins.[49] These authors argue that although rhetoric is important in the communication and demonstration of truth, reality itself is independent from human subjectivity. Putting it bluntly, they remind us that nobody would test the social construction of reality by "venturing into the path of an oncoming locomotive on the assumption that the mind could alter the unpleasant consequences of the ensuing collision."[50] The locomotive, in other words, is not socially constructed!

Cherwitz and Hikins put forth five arguments

against the constructionist thesis. The first is the "naive" argument, which states simply that nobody really acts as though reality is socially constructed. We must assume in our daily actions that there is an independent reality. In other words, watch out for the train. Second is the evolutionary argument: If one believes that human experience is evolving from prehistoric times to the present, an objective sense of reality is required as a baseline with which to measure this evolution. Third, Cherwitz and Hikins argue from logical consistency, stating that without an outside reality, there is no way to test the validity or quality of socially constructed knowledge. Fourth, the anthropological argument claims that despite human variability there is in fact much commonality across cultures, to the point that "cross-cultural understanding can and does occur."[51] Finally, the argument from persuasive discourse advances the thesis that communication itself results in an undeniably objective world of discourse, speakers, audiences, and responses. In other words, the communication that supposedly "constructs" reality cannot be understood without reference to its own reality.

These authors do not deny the importance of communication and language to reality. In fact, they advance a theory of their own in which rhetoric takes a central role in the discovery, examination, and dissemination of truth. Truth claims describe reality, but these descriptions always occur through language. Communication is used to differentiate among things, to make inferences, to promote and preserve ideas, to evaluate claims, and to express perspectives on reality; but it does not construct the reality itself.

Social constructionists do not deny the facticity of objects in the world. The issue is not whether the locomotive exists apart from human construction but how it is seen, what it is, and how it relates to other objects in the person's experience. A locomotive is not in and of itself a locomotive but is created by human beings within a vast and rich context of social meanings, and the oncoming locomotive can never be viewed as meaningful apart from social interaction.

49. Richard A. Cherwitz and James W. Hikins, *Communication and Knowledge: An Investigation of Rhetorical Epistemology* (Columbia: University of South Carolina Press, 1986).

50. Ibid., p. 19.

51. Ibid., p. 121.

Rule theories further add to our understanding of social and cultural reality. The rule concept is appealing because it explains a mechanism by which people understand reality. As pointed out in Chapter 5, however, the rules concept is not particularly coherent because different theories use different definitions of rules. For example, Shimanoff is firm in stating that a rule must deal with overt behavior. She believes that the concept should not apply to interpretation, whereas Pearce and Cronen apply rules not only to overt behavior but also to internal meanings.

This lack of consistency in the use of rules has led to some confusion. For example, David Brenders in criticizing coordinated management of meaning relies on ideas from the rule-following tradition to show that Pearce and Cronen have blurred distinctions about meaning that Austin, Searle, and others (Chapter 5) thought important.[52] In their response, Cronen, Pearce, and Changsheng Xi argue that the ideas about meaning implied by this tradition are not appropriate for understanding communication as the process by which people shape their very experience.[53] If communication is used as a tool to relay meanings as Brenders suggests, the rules are followed to accomplish this task. If, on the other hand, communication is the process by which meaning itself is constructed as Pearce and Cronen assert, then rules themselves are part of the socially constructed reality, and rule-following approaches are not very useful.

Brenders's critique and the coordinated management of meaning response take us full circle back to the basic issue surrounding social constructionism: Is communication a tool for communicating accurately about the world, or is it the means by which the world itself is determined? I do not expect this controversy to be settled anytime soon.

52. David A. Brenders, "Fallacies in the Coordinated Management of Meaning: A Philosophy of Language Critique of the Hierarchical Organization of Coherent Conversation and Related Theory," *Quarterly Journal of Speech* 73 (1987): 329–348.

53. Vernon E. Cronen, W. Barnett Pearce, and Xi Changsheng, "The Meaning of 'Meaning' in the CMM Analysis of Communication: A Comparison of Two Traditions," *Research on Language and Social Interaction* 23 (1989–1990): 1–40.

Theories of Experience and Interpretation

The social sciences deal with human experience in its many forms. Communication studies are no exception. Indeed, we have previously learned that communication is one of the most central human experiences. The theories in this chapter are designed to tell us more about the nature of communication experience and how conscious experience can be understood.

The central assumptions of most theories discussed in this chapter are that people act in the world, that their actions are meaningful, and that interpretation is necessary to understand human experience. As opposed to many behavioral and cognitive theories, which deal with the "objects" of human social life, the theories we are about to discuss here relate to the "works" of human experience.

Interpretation, sometimes known by the German term *Verstehen* (understanding), attempts to explain this connection between action and meaning. Because an action may mean a number of things, meaning cannot be simply "discovered." Interpretation, by definition, is an active, disciplined process. It is a creative act of ascertaining the possible meanings of actions and messages.

This chapter deals with two converging lines of thought on interpretation—phenomenology and hermeneutics. Phenomenology is the study of the knowledge that arises in conscious experience. It is the study of the appearance of objects and events in everyday situations. Hermeneutics originally signified the interpretation of writings (texts) and in many circles still retains that designation; however, to many people, hermeneutics has come to designate any kind of interpretation. Today, phenomenology and hermeneutics are closely associated.

Phenomenology

Phenomenology is the study of the ways in which people experience the world. It looks at objects and events from the perspective of the perceiver, the individual who experiences those things. A *phenomenon* is the appearance of an object, event, or condition. Anything that is perceived and is known through perception is a phenomenon. Reality in phenomenology, then, is the way things appear in the conscious experience of the individual. This approach is a striking departure from objectivist methods that assume a reality apart from human consciousness or perception. Maurice Merleau-Ponty, a theorist of this tradition, expresses this point of view as follows:

> All my knowledge of the world, even my scientific knowledge, is gained from my own particular point of view, or from some experience of the world without which the symbols of science would be meaningless. . . . To return to things themselves is to return to that world which precedes knowledge, of which knowledge always speaks.[1]

In other words, phenomenology makes actual lived experience the basic data of knowledge. It avoids the application of arbitrary theoretical categories: "Phenomenology means letting things become manifest as what they are, without forcing our own categories on them."[2] A scientist hypothesizes a particular structure or relationship and then looks to see if it is there; a phenomenologist never posits but carefully examines actual lived experience to see what is there. If you want to know what love is, you would not ask the poets or psychologists; you would tap into your own consciousness of love in your life and in the lives of others.

Stanley Deetz summarizes three basic principles of phenomenology.[3] First, knowledge is conscious. Knowledge is not inferred from experience but is expressed in conscious experience itself. Second, meanings are assigned to things on the basis of the potential of those things for one's actions. How a person relates to an object determines its meaning. A set of keys, for example, becomes a paperweight when you consider its potential as a heavy object.

It becomes a weapon when you consider carrying keys between your fingers on the way to your car through a dark parking lot at night. Third, language is the vehicle through which meanings arise. We experience the world through the language used to define and express that world. We know keys because of the labels attached to the object: *lock, open, metal, weight, stab*, and so forth.

In this section we will look at three groups of phenomenological theories. The first, classical phenomenology, explores its roots in the work of Edmund Husserl. The second, social phenomenology, will examine the theories of Maurice Merleau-Ponty and Alfred Schutz, who have been particularly influential in the study of communication. The third, hermeneutic phenomenology, will include the theories of Martin Heidegger and Hans-Georg Gadamer, which address the way in which experience itself is an interpretive process. Gadamer's work is especially important because it has a foot in both phenomenology and hermeneutics and will make an excellent bridge to the second half of the chapter.

Classical Phenomenology

Edmund Husserl is usually considered the father of modern phenomenology.[4] Husserl, who wrote during the first half of the twentieth century, attempted to develop a method for ascertaining truth through focused human experience. For Husserl, no conceptual scheme outside of actual experience is adequate for uncovering truth; rather, the conscious experience of the individual must be the route for discovering the reality of things in the world. Only through conscious attention can truth be known. In other words, we can know the things of the world by carefully examining the way in which those things are presented to us in our consciousness. Phenomena present themselves to us,

1. Maurice Merleau-Ponty, *The Phenomenology of Perception*, trans. C. Smith (London: Routledge & Kegan Paul, 1974), pp. viii–ix. For an excellent general discussion of phenomenology, see also Michael J. Hyde, "Transcendental Philosophy and Human Communication," in *Interpersonal Communication*, ed. J. J. Pilotta (Washington, D.C.: Center for Advanced Research in Phenomenology, 1982), pp. 15–34.

2. Richard E. Palmer, *Hermeneutics: Interpretation Theory in Schleiermacher, Dilthey, Heidegger, and Gadamer* (Evanston, Ill.: Northwestern University Press, 1969), p. 128.

3. Stanley Deetz, "Words Without Things: Toward a Social Phenomenology of Language," *Quarterly Journal of Speech* 59 (1973): 40–51.

4. Edmund Husserl, *Ideas: General Introduction to Pure Phenomenology*, trans. W. R. B. Gibson (New York: Collier Books, 1962); *Phenomenology and the Crisis of Philosophy*, trans. Q. Lauer (New York: Harper & Row, 1965). For a brief summary of Husserl's ideas, see Zygmunt Bauman, *Hermeneutics and Social Science* (New York: Columbia University Press, 1978).

and we can know them by carefully analyzing our awareness of them.

Husserl believed that in everyday life (*Lebenswelt*) people experience things in a kind of *natural attitude*. This natural way of experiencing the world is affected by all kinds of beliefs and perceptions. There is nothing wrong with this kind of life, but to know the world requires a discipline that the natural attitude does not permit. To learn about an object phenomenologically then, the distractions of ordinary life must be bracketed out. The term *bracket* is especially useful because it suggests that we do not get rid of ordinary distractions of life but that we just put them off (in brackets) temporarily during a phenomenological investigation.

The term Husserl used to describe this process is *phenomenological reduction*, or *epoche*, which is the careful and systematic elimination of any subjective factors entering into one's pure experience of a thing. In reduction, one *brackets* subjective factors, including history, biases, and interests to eliminate these distorting elements of the natural attitude and concentrates on the object of interest.

When done effectively one's consciousness of the object reveals its true essence. Every phenomenon has a true essence that disciplined observers will agree is there if they carefully attend to their awareness of it.

Once an event is successfully reduced in this way, a second, *transcendental*, reduction can be made. This reduction brackets experience itself, leading to a true understanding of what Husserl called the *transcendental ego*, or pure state of consciousness. Social life, which leads to one's beliefs, attitudes, and values, can, like any other object or event, be bracketed and reduced. Doing so reveals the true essence of the human mind. Transcendental reduction is a psychological endeavor designed to uncover the nature of human being and thought. If I can attend to what I am doing when I am aware, then I gain insight into what it means to have consciousness.

Now let's look at an example of a phenomenological reduction. In this example a psychologist wanted to know more about the topic of learning. He interviewed a restaurant manager about an event in which the manager learned something. The psychologist then conducted a reduction of this interview to distill the essence of learning within the event. The following is the interview itself:

RESEARCHER: What did you find out?

MANAGER: I learned about these girls [waitresses]. Last night with the snow and all, the young crowd came here. This place was packed and business was great. Then I realized the girls were cheating. We must have cooked hundreds of hamburgers, but when I went over the slips only a few people had paid for hamburgers. The girls gave their friends all this food and only wrote them a slip for a coke or a cup of coffee. This has been going on for months. Last night I caught them. I really didn't know what to do. I felt like I wanted to hit them; then I felt like crying because of all my hard work trying to make a go of it here. I learned that after all these months these girls don't have any respect for me. . . . I also found out that they don't give a damn about their jobs. So I fire them, what do they care! All they are concerned about is getting a date for Friday night and giving away my food. . . .

RESEARCHER: How was it that you learned all this last night?

MANAGER: I don't know. I guess I was watching more than usual and I knew we had sold lots of hamburgers. I watched and listened to these kids. If I had stayed blind to this whole thing much longer, they would have walked off with the store. I was just too trusting and I wanted to be their friend. That doesn't work—you can't be the friend and the boss. You can't run a restaurant without respect. No sir, old Harry isn't going to be fooled any longer."[5]

This passage is presented within the natural attitude of the restaurant manager. His expression of anger and frustration about his employees is a natural *description*, the first step in a phenomenological analysis. In using a phenomenological method, the psychologist had to bracket everything in his own experience that could distract him from the essence of this event. The psychologist who ana-

5. Example taken from Amedeo Giorgi, "Phenomenology, Psychological Science and Common Sense," in *Everyday Understanding: Social and Scientific Implications*, eds. G. R. Semin and K. J. Gergen (London: Sage, 1990), p. 66.

lyzed the above passage describes how he applied phenomenology:

> Now, even though I am a psychologist, I am required by phenomenology to put out of play all my psychological "knowledge about" learning. Thus I do not think about reinforcement, learning curves, sign-Gestalt theory, or any other concept or specific study of which I am aware. I also acknowledge that I have performed many phenomenological psychological analyses of learning similar to this one before, but I also must not let those analyses influence this one. . . . The point for the issue at hand is that one must really get into the description or phenomenon under study in an experiential way.[6]

The psychologist also points out that he must bracket out all his personal experience with learning, restaurants, employees, or anything else that could bias his understanding of this subject's own conscious experience. The resulting reduction leads to the following description:

> Learning is awareness of the necessity to reorganize a personal project based upon the discrepancy between the implicit assumptions brought to a situation vital for the continuance of the project and the perception and understanding of the actions of others in terms of the project in the same situation. It is also manifested in S's [subject's] discovery of the fact that he is prereflexively and ambiguously living out two conflicting roles with respect to the others involved in the project and in the ability of S to circumvent the difficulty by imagining he can choose to live out the project in terms of the preferred role in an unambiguous way.[7]

This passage describes the phenomenological reduction. It is the essence of learning as embodied in the experience of the manager and as interpreted by the phenomenologist. We now see more clearly what a reduction is: It literally reduces the initial natural description of an experience to the essence of that experience.

Husserl believed that phenomena have true essences that are revealed in conscious experience. In other words, one can successfully understand the true nature of things by bracketing out their own

6. Ibid., p. 73.
7. Ibid., p. 67.

history and ideas. This is an idealistic notion, and it is controversial. Few phenomenologists today believe this, and many reject it completely. Because of the importance of language, communication, and social life to the conscious experience of people, many phenomenologists acknowledge our inability to divorce ourselves from these facts of life. We turn now to the work of two significant phenomenologists of the social tradition.

Social Phenomenology

Social phenomenology examines the experience of social relations, especially the use of language, in ordinary life. This school of thought acknowledges that our experience is inherently social and that consciousness cannot be divorced from language. Here, two significant social phenomenologists are discussed.

Maurice Merleau-Ponty was greatly influenced by Husserl, but he strongly rejected Husserl's idealism.[8] For Merleau-Ponty, the human being is an indivisible *"body-subject,"* a unified physical-mental being that creates meaning in the world. As a subject or knower, a person has a relationship to things in the world: Human life is both affected by the world and in turn defines and assigns meaning to the world. Merleau-Ponty is opposed to realism in that he does not believe that things exist in and of themselves. People give meaning to the things in the world, but there is no human experience outside the world. Thus, the human "body-subject" and the world of things and events exist in a give-and-take, or dialogic, relationship.

Communication is the vehicle by which people assign meaning to experience. Thought occurs in and through speech because meaning is created by speech. Thus, human experience is based in com-

8. Merleau-Ponty's most important work is *Phenomenology of Perception* (New York: Humanities Press, 1962); original published in 1945 in Paris. See also Richard L. Lanigan, *Phenomenology of Communication: Merleau-Ponty's Thematics in Communicology and Semiology* (Pittsburgh: Duquesne University Press, 1988); Remy C. Kwant, *The Phenomenological Philosophy of Merleau-Ponty* (Pittsburgh: Duquesne University Press, 1963); Samuel B. Mallin, *Merleau-Ponty's Philosophy* (New Haven, Conn.: Yale University Press, 1979); Wayne Froman, *Merleau-Ponty: Language and the Act of Speech* (Lewisburg, Pa.: Bucknell University Press, 1982). Many other secondary sources are available.

munication. Merleau-Ponty makes a distinction between the use of speech to create meaning, which he calls the *speaking word*, and speech used to convey meaning to others, which is the *spoken word*. This distinction captures the fact that persons both assign meaning and receive meaning. This distinction is similar to that of Saussure (Chapter 4) between *parole* (speech) and *langue* (language). When we communicate we may work out new ways of seeing the world through our interaction or the "speaking word." At the same time, we have available to us a whole range of understandings as part of the language or "spoken word" available to us in everyday life.

It should be clear, then, why Merleau-Ponty rejects Husserl's idea of essence. Things do not have essences that can become apparent to perception. Rather, the meanings of things are always created by the subject through speech. The language in force for a particular person at a particular time fixes a certain meaning to the object being studied, but that meaning is temporary and can change. For Merleau-Ponty, reduction to the essence is impossible.

How, then, does Merleau-Ponty conduct his phenomenology? He too calls for reduction of experience, but not to the true essence of a reality outside of the perceiver. Rather, we reduce experience to the meaning of the object as reflected in language. Bracketing must still be used. The researcher brackets any categories that could distract him or her from the task of concentrating on the meanings of the subject as expressed in the language of the subject.

In the case of the restaurant manager, for example, the reduction does not tell us about "learning" as an independent topic, but it tells us about the meaning of learning in the life of the manager based on the language used in its description. Remember, for Merleau-Ponty, you cannot separate the person from the world. Thus, the phenomenologist in this tradition concentrates on not only the thing itself but also the language used to describe the thing and the meanings reflected in this language.

This brand of phenomenology must assume that people who share a language also share meanings.

The analyst is therefore interested not in the subject's private meanings but in the public meanings available to everybody in the common language. Reduction, then, concentrates on the "spoken word," or *langue*, rather than the "speaking word," or *parole*.

To illustrate phenomenology in this tradition, Richard Lanigan has his students actually conduct this kind of research.[9] The students go through three exercises. In the first they explore their own experience by writing a description of an important event in their life that involves some kind of moral or social learning. In a phenomenological reduction, the students then look for particular words and phrases that reveal the meaning of the event. They then interpret this language and write a brief statement that captures the meaning of the event based on the language of the original description. In the second exercise, the students interview another person on the topic of body image and obesity. They go through the same process first by analyzing the audiotaped interviews and looking for important revealing words and phrases; second, by extracting the meaning from that language; and third, by writing a statement that distills the subject's meanings into a few words. In the third exercise, the students conduct another audiotaped interview in which they ask the subject a number of questions about this person's life. The same reductive procedure is then used to discover the meanings guiding the individual's life.

A contemporary of Merleau-Ponty was Alfred Schutz.[10] Schutz applies phenomenology to social life, investigating social events from the perspective of those actually participating in them. When individuals operate in everyday life, they make

9. Richard L. Lanigan, "Life History Interviews: A Teaching and Research Model for Semiotic Phenomenology," in *Phenomenology of Communication*, pp. 144–154.

10. Alfred Schutz, *The Phenomenology of the Social World*, trans. G. Walsh and F. Lehnert (Evanston, Ill.: Northwestern University Press, 1967); original published in 1932. For a clear summary of Schutz's ideas, see Robert A. Gorman, *The Dual Vision: Alfred Schutz and the Myth of Phenomenological Social Science* (London: Routledge & Kegan Paul, 1977). See also Richard Lanigan, "A Treasure House of Preconstituted Types: Alfred Schutz on Communicology," in *Phenomenology of Communication*, pp. 203–222.

three fundamental assumptions. First, they assume that the reality and structure of the world are constant—that the world will remain as it appears. Second, they assume that their own experience of the world is valid. Ultimately, individuals believe that their perception of events is accurate. Third, individuals see themselves as having the power to act and accomplish things, to affect the world.

The work of Schutz is important to communication theory because, like that of Merleau-Ponty, it makes communication central to the reality experienced by individuals. Our worlds depend on what we learn from others in our sociocultural communities. This knowledge is always part of an historical situation, and people in various times and places experience the world differently. Reality is socially constructed within the group, which is why no universal reality can be found. As one commentator puts it, "The world, when filtered through my biographical situation, becomes 'my' world."[11]

What is real for us depends on the categories employed within our culture. These categories are generalizations, which Schutz calls *typifications*. They are typical trees, typical children, typical love, typical greetings, ad infinitum; and trees, children, love, greetings, and everything else will vary from one social situation to another. Within a given social group then, people and things are understood and dealt with by being placed within a generalized category that "typifies" them.

Language and other signs consist of typifying categories. We use signs to communicate to other people. Signs are addressed to other people who we assume share our typifications. Communicators interpret signs on the basis of these shared categories, and communication can only be successful to the extent that individuals within the same community share meanings.

The problem is that if typifications and their associated meanings differ from group to group, from culture to culture, and from time to time, then how can we study social life at all? What can ever be known? This is the central problem of the social sciences, and Schutz's solution is to explore not

11. Gorman, *Vision*, p. 38.

universal categories of meaning but the socially approved typifications of particular cultures and social groups. General truths about human experience cannot be found, but specific truths of individual historical groups can be discovered. With this thesis Schutz brings us a long way from Husserl.

For Schutz, social knowledge consists of formulas or *social recipes*. These are typical, well-understood ways of doing things in particular situations. They enable people to classify things according to some kind of mutually understood logic, to solve problems, to take roles, to communicate, and to establish proper behavior in different situations. Conducting negotiations, getting married, worshiping, raising children, selling goods, and most other social activities proceed according to these recipes.

We can now see a rather clear progression of ideas among the chief phenomenologists. Husserl believed that you can understand events in and of themselves by reducing perception to its pure state. Merleau-Ponty rejected this idea by suggesting that all you can achieve is a sense of the meaning of events in the lives of subjects. Merleau-Ponty concentrated on public meaning, or that which is common to all subjects by virtue of their shared language. Schutz takes this thinking one step further by denying the importance of common knowledge. For him, meaning is particular and peculiar to individual social groups.

As social phenomenology Schutz's philosophy provides backing for the social constructionist movement discussed in Chapter 9. It is an important part of the philosophy of social relativism prevalent in much communication theory today and sensitizes us to the many ways in which human communities differ. Schutz's ideas also focus the observer on the individual meanings that different people bring to a communication encounter. These ideas have had particular impact on cultural interpretation, which will be discussed later in the chapter.

Hermeneutic Phenomenology

The ideas of classical phenomenology are understandably controversial. Their chief critic is the philosopher Martin Heidegger.[12] For Heidegger, phenomenology and hermeneutics become one in *hermeneutic phenomenology* or *philosophical hermeneutics*. Heidegger denies the ability to reach truth through any kind of reduction. Instead, what is most important in human life is the natural experience of merely being in the world. His philosophy has been called the "hermeneutic of *Dasein*," which means interpretation of being. In other words, Heidegger was interested in understanding as a mode of existence and as such was the originator of philosophical hermeneutics. For Heidegger, the reality of something is not known by careful analysis but by natural experience, and that natural experience emerges from communication or the use of language in everyday life. In sum, what is real is what is experienced through the natural use of language in context: "Words and language are not wrappings in which things are packed for the commerce of those who write and speak. It is in words and language that things first come into being and are."[13]

Hans-Georg Gadamer is today's leading proponent of philosophical hermeneutics.[14] A protégé of Heidegger, Gadamer is primarily interested in how understanding is possible in human experience. For Gadamer, individuals do not stand apart from texts in order to analyze and interpret them; rather, interpretation itself is part and parcel of being.

The central tenet of Gadamer's theory is that one always understands experience from the perspective of presuppositions. Our tradition gives us a way of understanding things, and we cannot divorce ourselves from that tradition. Observation, reason, and understanding are never objectively pure; they are colored by history and community. Further, history is not to be separated from the present. We are always simultaneously part of the past, in the present, and anticipating the future. In other words, the past operates on us now in the present and affects our conceptions of what is yet to come. At the same time, our present notions of reality affect how we view the past. We cannot exist outside an historical tradition.

That one is part of a tradition does not deny change. Indeed, over time one becomes distanced from events in the past. Our way of seeing things in the present creates a temporal distance from an object of the past such that artifacts have both a strangeness and a familiarity. We understand an artifact in terms of the categories provided by our tradition, but the unessential features of the artifact drop away, leaving a residue of highly relevant meaning. Interpretation of historical events and objects, like texts, is enhanced by historical distance. Thus, Gadamer would agree with Paul Ricoeur (discussed later) that understanding a text involves looking at the enduring meanings of that text within a tradition and apart from the original communicators' intentions. Texts therefore become contemporaneous and speak to us in our own time. The Gettysburg Address was originally a piece of spoken discourse designed to achieve a certain effect during the Civil War. Once spoken, however, the text lived on as an object of its own, rife with internal meaning. Unessential details—that it was written on the back of an envelope on the train by a tall, lanky president—drop away as the text itself reveals its meanings to us in our own time.

Hermeneutics is not only a dialogic process of questioning the text but also of allowing the text to question us. What questions does the text itself suggest, and when we ask those questions, what answers does the text offer? What questions does the text suggest for our own experience, and how do we respond to the questions of the text? This

---

12. Martin Heidegger, *Being and Time*, trans. J. Macquarrie and E. Robinson (New York: Harper & Row, 1962); *On the Way to Language*, trans. P. Hertz (New York: Harper & Row, 1971); *An Introduction to Metaphysics*, trans. R. Manheim (New Haven, Conn.: Yale University Press, 1959). For secondary treatments, see Bauman, *Hermeneutics*, pp. 148–171; Palmer, *Hermeneutics*, pp. 124–161; Deetz, "Words."

13. Heidegger, *Introduction*, p. 13.

14. Gadamer's major work is *Truth and Method* (New York: Seabury Press, 1975). An excellent secondary treatment can be found in Richard J. Bernstein, *Beyond Objectivism and Relativism: Science, Hermeneutics, and Praxis* (Philadelphia: University of Pennsylvania Press, 1983), pp. 107–169. See also Palmer, *Hermeneutics*, pp. 162–222; David Tracy, "Interpretation (Hermeneutics)," in *International Encyclopedia of Communications*, ed. E. Barnouw (New York: Oxford University Press, 1989), pp. 343–348.

interpretive process is paradoxical: We let the text speak to us, yet we cannot understand it apart from our own prejudices and presuppositions. Change results from the dialogue between the prejudices of the present and the meanings of the text. Thus, prejudice is a positive force, to be acknowledged and used productively in our lives. As one observer has noted, "The problem for the study of communication is not the existence of prejudices but the unawareness of their presence and subsequent inability to separate appropriate from inappropriate ones."[15]

Like Heidegger, Gadamer believes that experience is inherently linguistic. We cannot separate our experience from language. The perspectives of tradition, from which we always view the world, are embodied in words. Gadamer says,

> The linguistic word is not a "sign" which one lays hold of; it is also no existing thing that one shapes and endows with a meaning, making a sign to render some other thing visible. Both possibilities are wrong; rather, the ideality of the meaning lies in the word itself. Word is always already meaningful.[16]

Note how this conception differs from the structural view of language summarized in Chapter 4, in which language is seen as an arbitrary tool for expressing and referring to an objective reality. Gadamer's view is also different from the interactionist notion (even Schutz's), which suggests that language and meaning are created through social interaction. Gadamer's point is that language itself prefigures all experience. The world is presented to us through language. Thus, in communication, two people are not using language to interact with each other; rather, communication involves a triad of two individuals and a language.[17]

To get this idea across, Gadamer uses the analogy of the game. A game has its own nature and is independent from individual players. The game will exist and be the same whether it is being played or not and regardless of who is playing. Language and life are like games: We play them, just as we experience life, but they come to us preformed and remain intact after our particular playing is finished. One commentator explains it this way: "The world is already meaningful. That is, the world which comes to us in the only way that the human world can come to us, through language, is an already meaningful world.[18]

Gadamer brings phenomenology and hermeneutics together in one process. Phenomenology, or understanding through experience, and hermeneutics, or interpretation, are inseparable processes. Let us turn now in more detail to the field of hermeneutics.

Hermeneutics

Hermeneutics is the study of understanding, especially by interpreting action and text. There are several branches of hermeneutics, including interpretation of the Bible (exegesis), interpretation of literary texts (philology), and interpretation of human personal and social actions (social hermeneutics).[19]

Modern hermeneutics began in the early nineteenth century with Friedrich Schleiermacher.[20] Schleiermacher attempted to establish a system for discovering what authors meant in their writings, which involved reconstructing the mental lives of the authors. Schleiermacher had a scientific approach to text analysis, which he believed would be the key to authors' original meanings and feelings. Later in the century, Schleiermacher's biographer, Wilhelm Dilthey, was strongly influenced by these ideas.[21] For Dilthey, however, hermeneu-

15. Stanley Deetz, "Conceptualizing Human Understanding: Gadamer's Hermeneutics and American Communication Studies," *Communication Quarterly* 26 (1978): 14.

16. Gadamer, *Wahrheit und Methode* [*Truth and Method*] (Tuebingen, Ger.: Mohr, 1960), p. 394.

17. John Angus Campbell, "Hans-Georg Gadamer's Truth and Method," *Quarterly Journal of Speech* 64 (1978): 101–122.

18. Ibid., p. 107.

19. For an analysis of different approaches to hermeneutics, see Bauman, *Hermeneutics*. See also Tracy, "Interpretation."

20. Friedrich Schleiermacher, *Hermeneutik*, ed. H. Kimmerle (Heidelberg, Ger.: Carl Winter, Universitaetsverlag, 1959).

21. Wilhelm Dilthey, "The Rise of Hermeneutics," trans. F. Jameson, *New Literary History* 3 (1972): 229–244.

tics is the key to all humanities and social sciences; he believed that we come to understand human life and works in all areas, not by reductionistic methods as in natural science but through subjective interpretation. For Dilthey, the human world is social and historical and requires understanding in terms of the community in which human actors live and work. Humans are not fixed and cannot be known objectively. Dilthey therefore promoted a kind of historical relativism common in social sciences today.

Although classical hermeneutics, designed as a technical method for interpreting texts, is still very much in use in those disciplines concerned with understanding ancient scriptures and literature, the social sciences today treat hermeneutics more generally as the interpretation of social life and expressive forms. Just about any interpretive activity can be labeled hermeneutic: "Throughout, the goal of hermeneutic studies has been to develop understanding of human artifacts and actions by interpreting their nature and significance."[22] This may mean understanding another person's feelings and meanings, understanding the meaning of an episode or event, translating the actions of a group into terms understandable to outsiders, or uncovering the meaning of a written text. It also includes the general philosophical examination of understanding itself. One commentator put the matter succinctly: "The hermeneutical problem as a whole, I believe, is too important and too complex to become the property of a single school of thought."[23]

For our purposes, hermeneutic scholars fall into two general groups: (1) those who use hermeneutics to understand written texts and (2) those who use hermeneutics as a tool for interpreting actions. The first type is perhaps best described as *textual hermeneutics* and the second as *social or cultural hermeneutics*.[24] In this section we explore cultural her-

meneutics and textual hermeneutics in more detail. Generally speaking, *texts* are any artifacts that can be examined and interpreted.[25] Even some cultural interpreters refer to actions as texts, but more often, text hermeneutics deals with the interpretation of written documents and other records.[26]

Although little agreement exists on specific techniques of interpretation, almost all schools of thought rely on a common notion of its general process. This process is called the *hermeneutic circle*. One interprets something by going from general to specific and from specific to general. An interpreter looks at a specific text in terms of a general idea of what that text may mean, then modifies the general idea based on the examination of the specifics of the text. Interpretation is ongoing, as one goes back-and-forth between specific and general. One may look at the composite meaning of a text and then examine the specific linguistic structures of that text. Then the interpreter returns to the overall meaning, only to go back to the specifics again. This is nothing more than Gadamer's dialogue between the text and one's own tradition.

Further, within the circle, one always relates what is seen in the object to what is already known. The interpreter then alternates between a familiar set of concepts and the unfamiliar until the two merge in a tentative interpretation. In interpreting the actions of a foreign culture, for example, the anthropologist first tries to understand what is happening in terms of concepts that are familiar; later the anthropologist discovers how the natives understand what they do in their own concepts, and he or she can modify the beginning categories. This process continues back-and-forth until an adequate account is generated. So, too, with the interpretation of a written text: The interpreter begins by relating the text to what he or she already

22. John Stewart, "Philosophy of Qualitative Inquiry: Hermeneutic Phenomenology and Communication Research," *Quarterly Journal of Speech* 67 (1981): 110.

23. Palmer, *Hermeneutics*, p. 67.

24. For an analysis of the different approaches to hermeneutics, see Bauman, *Hermeneutics*.

25. For a good discussion of the various senses of the term *text*, see George Cheney and Phillip K. Tompkins, "On the Facts of the Text as the Basis of Human Communication Research," in *Communication Yearbook 11*, ed. J. A. Anderson (Newbury Park, Calif.: Sage, 1988), pp. 455–481, and attendant commentaries (pp. 482–501).

26. Actually, the concept of *text* is complex and should not be read simply as an object, action, or writing. For an excellent brief exposition of the concept, see Cheney and Tompkins, "Facts of the Text."

understands, looks for strange or unaccounted-for details in the text, modifies the original interpretation, reexamines the text, and so on.

Another point on which virtually all hermeneutic scholars agree is that interpretation is a process that can never be divorced from language. The very experience of understanding is linguistic, which means that one's linguistic categories become a crucial part of any understanding. Further, language comes to us with meaning and discloses meaning to us. It is not something we use only as a tool of expression but something that essentially forms reality for us. Here, we see one of the important links between hermeneutics and phenomenology.

Textual Interpretation

The interpretation of texts has long been the central problem of hermeneutics. Hermeneutics arose as a response to the problem of understanding ancient texts such as the Bible that can no longer be explained by an author. Today, virtually any text is open for interpretation, and whether the author is alive to explain what he or she meant is just not considered relevant. The text itself speaks to us; it has meanings of its own apart from what any author, speaker, or audience member might mean by it. The challenge of textual hermeneutics, then, is to ascertain the meanings of the text.

There are many prominent writers on text interpretation, but the most well known of these is Paul Ricoeur. Ricoeur is a current, major interpretive theorist who relies heavily on both the phenomenological and hermeneutic traditions.[27]

Although he recognizes the importance of dis-

27. Paul Ricoeur, *Interpretation Theory: Discourse and the Surplus of Meaning* (Fort Worth: Texas University Press, 1976); *Hermeneutics and the Human Sciences: Essays on Language, Action and Interpretation*, trans. and ed. J. B. Thompson (Cambridge, Eng.: Cambridge University Press, 1981); Don Ihde (ed.), *The Conflict of Interpretations: Essays in Hermeneutics* [by Paul Ricoeur] (Evanston, Ill.: Northwestern University Press, 1974).

course in actual speech events, most important for Ricoeur is text. Once speech is recorded, it becomes divorced from the actual speaker and situation in which it was produced. Texts cannot be interpreted in the same fashion as discourse because they have an enduring life of their own. Textual interpretation is especially important when speakers and authors are not available, as is the case with historical documents. However, it need not be limited to these situations. Indeed, the text itself always speaks to us, and the job of the interpreter is to figure out what it is saying.

The separation of text from situation is *distanciation*. The text has meaning irrespective of the author's original intention. In other words, you can read a message and get meaning from it despite the fact that you were not part of the original speech event. Thus, the author's intent does not prescribe what the text can subsequently be taken to mean, nor does any reader's peculiar understanding limit what the text itself says. Once written, the text can be consumed by anybody who can read, providing a multitude of meaning possibilities, and multiple readings (meanings) are definitely probable. The shared reality that made communication possible between the original author and the original audience may no longer exist. For these reasons the interpretation of textual material is more complex and more interesting than that of spoken discourse. For Ricoeur then, text interpretation is the central focus of hermeneutics.

This does not mean that hermeneutics should be limited to written material. In fact, any kind of action can be recorded. A text is essentially a recording, whether written, electronic, photographic, or preserved by some other means. The problem remains the same: How do we interpret a message that is no longer part of an actual event?

The problem is like interpreting a musical score. You may not know what mood and feeling Mozart had in composing and conducting the Jupiter Symphony, and you may be able to produce a number of interpretations of your own. But those interpretations are not unlimited; they are constrained by the musical notation itself. A conductor carefully studies the elements of the text to determine what meanings are embedded in it.[28]

The meaning of a text is always a pattern of the whole, never just a composite of individual elements. Ricoeur's version of the hermeneutic circle involves the fusion of explanation and understanding. *Explanation* is empirical and analytic: It accounts for events in terms of observed patterns among parts. In studying a book of the Bible, for example, you would carefully examine the individual linguistic elements of each verse and note the ways in which they form patterns of meaning. In the analysis of a text, an interpreter might look for recurring words and phrases, narrative themes, and theme variations. Ricoeur himself is interested in particular words that have metaphorical value, that point to meanings hidden below the surface of the writing. None of these structural elements is meaningful in and of itself but must be put together into a whole pattern in the understanding phase of interpretation.

Understanding is synthetic, accounting for events in terms of overall interpretation. So in continuing your study of the Bible, you would also look for a holistic, or general, meaning of the passage under consideration. In hermeneutics, one goes through both processes, breaking down a text into its parts and looking for patterns, then stepping back and judging subjectively the meaning of the whole. You move from understanding to explaining and back to understanding again in a continuing circle. Explanation and understanding, then, are not separate but are two poles in an interpretive process.

Interpretation is not merely a process of computing the meaning of the text in and of itself. Ricoeur agrees with Gadamer that an intimate interaction exists between text and interpreter. The text speaks to and changes the interpreter. Ricoeur refers to the act of being open to the meanings of a text as *appropriation*. If the interpreter is open to the message of a text, its meaning can be appropriated, or made personal. Interpretation begins in distanciation but ends in personalization. To interpret the sections of the Bible, you would remove your own interests from your study of the intrinsic meanings in the text, but then you would apply those meanings to your own situation.

An example of a Ricoeurian interpretation is Barbara Warnick's study of the Gettysburg Address.[29] In a careful examination of the text, Warnick isolates expressions of agent, place, and time. Agents include our forefathers, they who died here, we, and our progeny. Place references include our nation on the continent, the battlefield of this war, a small plot of ground, a nation on the earth. Time references include the far past ("four score and seven years"), the near past, a frozen present, and a possible future. The text can transcend the immediacy of the present situation by cycling back-and-forth from the present to other times, from immediate agents to other agents in past and future, and from this place to other places.

In so doing, the text tells a story of birth, adversity, recognition of values, rebirth, and perpetuation of the treasured values. In an appropriation move, Warnick notes that this story parallels that of the Christian narrative, which appeals to people so deeply in our society. The values of American culture are deeply embedded in the text. Warnick shows how the details of the text and the overall understanding of it as a projection of the American ideal go hand-in-hand. Warnick's overall understanding of the speech, then, is that it expresses values that are part of but transcend the immediate situation, and for this reason, the text speaks to generation after generation of Americans.

Cultural Interpretation

Cultural interpretation involves developing an understanding of the actions and meanings of a local group. Many cultural anthropologists are interpreters because they attempt to understand

---

28. The musical analogy of textual hermeneutics can be found in Ricoeur, *Interpretation Theory*, p. 75.

29. Barbara Warnick, "A Ricoeurian Approach to Rhetorical Criticism," *Western Journal of Speech Communication* 51 (1987): 227–244.

the practices of various cultural groups. Cultural interpretation involves a brand of hermeneutics or interpretation. The challenge is to observe and describe the actions of a local group, just as one might examine a written text, and to figure out what it means.[30] Another term for cultural interpretation is *ethnography*.

One of the leading cultural interpreters of our day is Clifford Geertz.[31] Geertz describes the process of *thick description*, in which the interpreter describes cultural practices "from the native's point of view." This level of interpretation is contrasted with *thin description*, in which one merely describes the behavioral pattern with very little sense of what it means to the actors involved.

Cultural interpretation involves the hermeneutic circle in what Geertz refers to as a movement from experience-near concepts to experience-distant ones. *Experience-near concepts* are those that have meaning to the members of the culture, and *experience-distant concepts* have meaning to outsiders. The cultural interpreter essentially translates between the two, so that observers outside can have an understanding of the insider's feelings and meanings in a situation. The interpretation process, then, is one of going back-and-forth in a circle between what appears to be happening from outside to what insiders define as happening. Slowly, a suitable experience-distant vocabulary can be developed to reflect the natives' point of view without forsaking their own experience-near concepts.

Ethnography, then, is a kind of cultural study in which an interpreter from outside the culture attempts to make sense of the actions of the group being studied. As such, it brings two worlds together so that one can be understood from the other. The ethnographer not only describes the actions of a group but also attempts to construct an interpretive model that enables one to understand those actions. The interpretive process is one of relating observed acts to larger patterns of acts in order to figure out the meanings of the part and the whole. The ethnographer's account would not be the same as the native's, but the native could certainly understand the ethnographer's view.

Ethnographic problems arise when an interpreter has a lack of adequate understanding. The researcher witnesses something that cannot be understood from his or her concepts and seeks to resolve the difficulty by creating an explanation that makes understanding possible. Ethnography attempts to achieve coherence by understanding practices that are otherwise foreign. How would you make sense of a cult's ceremony involving the fondling of rattlesnakes? Most of us have no frame for understanding such actions, but the ethnographer would—through careful examination, interviews, inference, and experience—create an explanation that would make such behavior understandable.

The ethnographic process is a gradual tacking back-and-forth between the concepts of the native, which are experience-near, and those of the observer, which are experience-distant. Eventually, a conceptualization is formed that enables the observer to make sense of the phenomena in a way that approximates the concepts of the participants themselves; yet the conceptualization of the ethnographer would be understandable to other outsiders.[32] Figure 10.1 illustrates the process. The figure shows how the observer goes through a series of schemas, or ways of understanding, which become increasingly refined and useful. One's first schema may not explain much, leading to a breakdown. After a series of breakdowns, a tentative resolution is achieved. The successful schema is then applied to other acts until further breakdowns occur, forcing the development of still further refined schemas.

The interpreter, of course, does not begin an ethnography empty-handed. Previous experience always provides some kind of schema for understanding an event, but ethnography is a process in

30. See Michael Agar, *Speaking of Ethnography* (Beverly Hills, Calif.: Sage, 1986).

31. See especially *The Interpretation of Cultures* (New York: Basic Books, 1973) and *Local Knowledge: Further Essays in Interpretive Anthropology* (New York: Basic Books, 1983).

32. Geertz, *Local Knowledge*, p. 57.

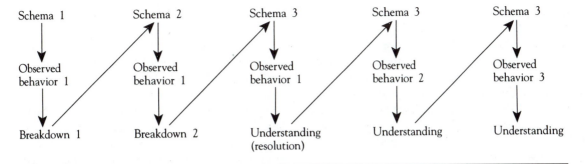

Figure 10.1 Ethnographic process of understanding.

Adapted from *Speaking of Ethnography* by Michael Agar. Copyright © 1986 by Sage Publications. Reprinted by permission of the publisher.

which one's understandings become increasingly more refined and accurate.

In this section we will look at three forms of cultural interpretation prominent in the communication field—the ethnography of communication, organizational culture, and media interpretation.

Ethnography of Communication

The ethnography of communication is simply the application of ethnographic methods to the communication patterns of a group. Here, the interpreter attempts to make sense of the forms of communication employed by the members of the group or culture. Gerry Philipsen isolates four assumptions of the ethnography of communication.[33] The first is that participants in a local cultural community create shared meaning. They use codes that have some degree of common understanding. Second, communicators in any cultural group must coordinate their actions. There must be some order or system to what is done in communication. Third, meanings and actions are particular to individual groups. In other words, they differ from culture to culture. Fourth, each cultural community has a set of distinct resources for understanding or assigning meaning to its actions. Not only are patterns of behavior and codes different

from group to group, but each group also has its own set of meanings with which to understand its own codes and actions.

The originator of this research tradition is anthropologist Dell Hymes.[34] Hymes suggests that formal linguistics is not sufficient by itself to uncover a complete understanding of language because it ignores the highly variable ways in which language is used in everyday communication. In Hymes's terms, "We deal here, in short, with the fact that the communicative event is the metaphor, or perspective, basic to rendering experience intelligible. . . . It is this fact that underlies the apparently central role of language in cultural life."[35] Communication, then, is the use of language in context, and culture constitutes a major part of any context.

What counts as a communicative event within a culture cannot be predetermined. Cultures use different practices for communication. Whatever the communication practice may be, however, it constitutes a message—which requires a shared code, communicators who know and use the code, a channel, a setting, a message form, a topic, and an event created by transmission of the message. An ethnographer's first schema for understanding com-

33. Gerry Philipsen, "An Ethnographic Approach to Communication Studies," in *Rethinking Communication: Paradigm Exemplars*, eds. B. Dervin et al. (Newbury Park, Calif.: Sage, 1989), pp. 258–269.

34. Dell Hymes, *Foundations in Sociolinguistics: An Ethnographic Approach* (Philadelphia: University of Pennsylvania Press, 1974).

35. Ibid., p. 16.

munication within a group might well begin with this model of the message. However, this model by itself is insufficient because it cannot tell you what specific practices meet these criteria. Anything may qualify as a message as long as it is construed as such by the natives. Is snake handling communication? Perhaps it is a shared code for expressing something among the members of the cult. We cannot know until further ethnographic study is undertaken.

Another communication ethnographer is Donal Carbaugh, who writes that communication ethnography addresses at least three types of problems.[36] The first is to discover the type of *shared identity* created by communication in the cultural community. This identity is a sense of who we are as a group. It is a common set of qualities with which all or most members of the community would identify, such as blacks, cheerleaders, Rotarians, Hispanics, or John's Autobody Bowlers. This identity consists not only of the identifying label but also a shared sense of what that label means in terms of qualities.

The second problem is to uncover the shared, public meanings that are used in the group. In other words, ethnography seeks to interpret the meanings that various performances have for members of the cultural community. What constitutes communication within the culture, and what meanings do the various displays evoke? What does playing the "dozens" mean in the black youth culture? What is communicated by cheerleaders at a high school basketball game? What meaning is assigned to the "fines" at a Rotary meeting?

The third is to explore the functions of communication in a *dialectical tension* of paradox in the community. Every culture has certain contradictions, or paradoxes. How are these handled through communication? How, for example, does the community handle the problem of giving its members a sense of individuality while providing a sense of community?

In attacking these ethnographic problems, three types of questions are pursued. *Questions of norms* look for the ways in which communication is used to establish a set of standards and the ways in which notions of right and wrong affect communication patterns. *Questions of forms* look at the types of communication used within the society. What behaviors count as communication, and how are they organized? *Questions of cultural codes* draw attention to the meanings of the symbols and behaviors used as communication in the cultural community.

An important extension of ethnography is comparative ethnography, which involves the creation of higher-level schema with which to understand and compare the practices of a variety of cultures. Hymes has been particularly emphatic about the need to establish comparative ethnography of communication: "What is needed, then, is a general theory and body of knowledge within which diversity of speech, repertoires, ways of speaking, and choosing among them find a natural place."[37] This statement calls for a movement between ethnographic description and generalized taxonomy. For Hymes, comparative ethnography is "a necessary part of the progress toward models . . . of sociolinguistic description, formulation of universal sets of features and relations, and explanatory theories."[38] Hymes suggests a set of nine "fundamental notions" that might be included in such a theory:[39]

1. *Ways of speaking*, or patterns of communication familiar to the members of the group

2. *Ideal of the fluent speaker*, or what constitutes an exemplary communicator

3. *Speech community*, or the group itself and its boundaries

4. *Speech situation*, or those times when communication is considered appropriate in the community

5. *Speech event*, or what episodes are considered to be communication for the members of the group

---

36. Donal Carbaugh (ed.), "Culture Talking About Itself," in *Cultural Communication and Intercultural Contact* (Hillsdale, N.J.: Erlbaum, 1990), pp. 1–9.

37. Hymes, *Foundations*, p. 32.

38. Ibid., p. 35.

39. Ibid., pp. 29–66.

6. *Speech act,* or specific set of behaviors taken as an instance of communication within a speech event

7. *Components of speech acts,* or what the group considers to be the elements of a communicative act

8. *The rules of speaking in the community,* or the guidelines or standards by which communicative behavior is judged

9. *The functions of speech in the community,* or what communication is believed to accomplish

This set of concepts is nothing more than a list of dimensions by which various cultures can be compared. Two cultures—the Apache and the Ilongot, for example—would have many different events that count as communication, varying behaviors that would be considered appropriate within those speaking events, and perhaps some distinct rules for how to communicate. On the other hand, they might have some similar types and functions of communication as well.

As an example of an ethnography of communication, consider the study of Tamar Katriel on Israeli "griping."[40] Based on her own experience as a "native griper" and about fifty interviews of middle-class Israelis, Katriel explains the common communication form *kiturim.* This form of communication takes place throughout adult Israeli society, but it is most often seen among the middle class and commonly takes place at Friday night social gatherings called *mesibot kiturim,* or griping parties.

This communication form is so common that it is widely recognized by Israelis as part of their national character. Griping does not deal with personal problems but national (and sometimes local) public ones. It seems to affirm the Israeli identity as having important common national concerns. These are concerns that society could do something about theoretically but that the individual has very little power to change. Thus, griping is a kind of shared venting of frustration. It is more

than this, however, as Katriel's informants told her that it provides a sense of solidarity and it is fun. In fact, griping and joke telling are often viewed together as the primary means of establishing cohesiveness in a social group.

Griping is ritualistic, and the content of the communication does not seem to be important. One must not mistake griping for serious problem solving on topics of concern. In fact, there is a strict prohibition against griping in the presence of non-Israelis like tourists. The reason for this rule is that outsiders do not understand the nature of griping and may take it literally, which would be embarrassing.

Griping follows a predictable pattern. It usually begins with an initial gripe, followed by an acknowledgement and a gripe by another person. The pattern of a griping session can go from general societal problems to local ones, or the other way around. Katriel found two interesting variants of the griping theme. *Meta-griping* is griping about the low morale of Israelis that makes them gripe too much. The other form is the *anti-gripe,* which takes the form: "Stop griping, and start doing something."

This study illustrates Hymes's categories of comparative ethnography very well. The griping session is a communication event, which consists of particular types of speech acts. It has rules and meets particular functions. The example also illustrates the ethnographic problems of identity, meaning, and tension. Griping reflects a certain national identity in Israel. It is understood among Israelis according to particular meanings, and griping is a mechanism for managing the tension between such opposites as serious concern and pleasant company.

Organizational Culture

Organizations can be viewed as cultures and as such present opportunities for cultural interpretation.[41] Organizations not only enable the achieve-

---

40. Tamar Katriel, "'Griping' as a Verbal Ritual in Some Israeli Discourse," in *Cultural Communication and Intercultural Contact,* ed. D. Carbaugh (Hillsdale, N.J.: Erlbaum, 1990), pp. 99–114.

41. For a brief description of this approach, see Michael Pacanowsky, "Creating and Narrating Organizational Realities," in *Rethinking Communication: Paradigm Exemplars,* eds. B. Dervin et al. (Newbury Park, Calif.: Sage, 1989), pp. 250–257.

ment of goals but are also a way of life for their members. In other words, an organization has a shared reality that distinguishes it from other cultures. Gareth Morgan explains:

> Shared meaning, shared understanding, and shared sense making are all different ways of describing culture. In talking about culture we are really talking about a process of reality construction that allows people to see and understand particular events, actions, objects, utterances, or situations in distinctive ways. These patterns of understanding also provide a basis for making one's own behavior sensible and meaningful.[42]

Organizational culture is produced by interactions of the members. Task-oriented actions not only achieve immediate objectives but also create or reinforce certain ways of understanding experience within the organization. But culture is created in other ways besides the "official" task behaviors of employees. Indeed, even the most mundane activities in the organization enter into the culture-producing process. Let us take a closer look at the ways in which communication practices in an organization establish and reflect its culture.

Michael Pacanowsky and Nick O'Donnell-Trujillo are leaders in the organizational culture movement. These theorists ask a set of questions about organizations designed to uncover cultural patterns in the organization. Pacanowsky and O'Donnell-Trujillo present a communication-centered theory of organizational culture, explaining the difference between their approach and traditional methods in these terms:

> We believe that an intriguing thing about communication is the way in which it creates and constitutes the taken-for-granted reality of the world. Social activity, as we see it, is primarily the communicative accomplishment of interrelated actions. So whereas the underlying motive of traditional research is coming to an understanding of how to make organizations work better, the underlying motive of the organizational culture approach is coming to understand how organizational life is accomplished communicatively.

To understand how organizational life is brought into being, we cannot let ourselves be limited to asking questions that require some implicit or explicit link to organizational productivity for their legitimacy.[43]

Because culture is sense making, the organizational culture approach must look for indicators of meaning in an organization. What do organizational members use to create and display their understanding of events within the organization? There are many indicators, including relevant constructs and related vocabulary, perceived facts, practices or activities, metaphors, stories, and rites and rituals. All these are "performances" in that they "display" the lived experience of the group. However, performances, like stage plays, are not only displays but also accomplishments; they bring something about—the reality of the culture: ". . . performance brings the significance or meaning of some structural form—be it symbol, story, metaphor, ideology, or saga—into being."[44] Following the lead of Victor Turner, these authors note that "performances are those very actions by which members constitute and reveal their culture to themselves and others."[45]

Pacanowsky and O'Donnell-Trujillo outline four characteristics of communication performances. First, they are interactional, more like dialogues than soliloquies. They are social actions, not solitary ones. Organizational performances are something people participate in together. Second, performances are contextual. They cannot be viewed as independent acts but are always embedded in a larger frame of activity. Context consists of the who, where, and when of the action. The performance both reflects and produces its context. Third, performances are episodes. They are events

---

42. Gareth Morgan, *Images of Organization* (Beverly Hills, Calif.: Sage, 1986), p. 128.

43. Michael E. Pacanowsky and Nick O'Donnell-Trujillo, "Communication and Organizational Cultures," *Western Journal of Speech Communication* 46 (1982): 121.

44. Michael E. Pacanowsky and Nick O'Donnell-Trujillo, "Organizational Communication as Cultural Performance," *Communication Monographs* 50 (1983): 129.

45. Pacanowsky and O'Donnell-Trujillo, "Organizational Communication," p. 131. See also Victor Turner, *Dramas, Fields, and Metaphors* (Ithaca, N.Y.: Cornell University Press, 1974).

with a beginning and an end, and the performers can identify the episode and distinguish it from other episodes. Finally, performances are improvised. There is flexibility in how a communication episode is played out, and although the same performances may be given again and again, they are never repeated exactly the same way.

From the many types of organizational communication performance, the authors present a suggestive list. The first is ritual. A *ritual* is a performance that is repeated regularly. It is an act that groups come to rely on as familiar and routine. Rituals are especially important because they constantly renew our understandings of our common experience, and they lend legitimacy to what we are thinking, feeling, and doing. Here is an example:

> Each and every day, Lou Polito, owner and general manager of Lou Polito Dodge, opens all the company mail. On those occasions when he is "free," he personally delivers this mail to the appropriate divisions in the company. This is just his way of letting his people know that he is keeping in touch with what they are doing.[46]

This is an example of a *personal ritual*. Another type is a *task ritual*, which is a repeated activity that helps members do their jobs:

> When a Valley View patrolman stops a driver for some traffic violation, he launches into a conversational routine that involves a question-answer sequence. "May I see your driver's license please?" "Is this your correct address?" "May I see your registration please?" "Do you know why I stopped you?" "Do you know what the speed limit is on this street?" "Do you know how fast you were going?" "Do you want to see the reading on the radar gun?" Although the officer has been taught this routine at the Police Academy as a way of being polite and professional, the Valley View police use it in order to see how the driver responds, to "size him up," and decide whether or not to give him any "breaks" in issuing a citation or warning.[47]

Social rituals are not task-related, yet they are important performances within organizations. The after-work drink is a good example: "Every Friday afternoon, the foremen from Steele Manufacturing go to the 'Pub,' one of the few places in their part of town that serves beer. The conversations are often filled with 'shop talk' but can range from sports . . . to politics . . . ."[48] Finally, *organizational rituals* are those in which an entire work group participates with some regularity: "Each year, the department of communication has its annual picnic, highlighted by the traditional softball game which pits the graduate students against the faculty. Competition is typically fierce; but alas for the graduate nine, they have had but one win in the last five years."[49]

The second category of performances is what the authors call *passion*. Here, workers put on performances that make otherwise dull and routine duties interesting or passionate. Perhaps the most common way in which this is done is by *story telling*. Almost everybody tells stories about their work, and the telling is often lively and dramatic. Further, these stories are told over and over, and people often enjoy telling one another the same stories again and again. We tell stories about ourselves (personal stories), about other people (collegial stories), or about the organization (corporate stories). Another way in which drama is created on the job is *passionate repartee*, which consists of dramatic interactions and the use of lively language: "The Valley View police, for example, do not deal with 'civilians,' but rather with 'assholes,' 'dirtbags,' 'creeps,' and 'maggots'—labels which serve as reminders that the 'negative element' is so much a part of the everyday experience of being a police officer."[50]

A third category of performances involves *sociality*. Such performances reinforce a common sense of propriety and make use of social rules within the organization. Courtesies and pleasantries are examples. Sociabilities are performances that create a group sense of identification and include things like joking, "bitching," and "talking shop." Finally,

---

46. Pacanowsky and O'Donnell-Trujillo, "Organizational Communication," p. 135.

47. Ibid.. p. 136.

48. Ibid., p. 137.

49. Ibid., p. 137.

50. Ibid., p. 139.

privacies are sociality performances that communicate sensitivity and privacy. They include such things as confessing, consoling, and criticizing.

A fourth category of performances involve *organizational politics*. These performances, which create and reinforce notions of power and influence, may include showing personal strength, cementing allies, and bargaining.

A fifth category is *enculturation*, or processes of "teaching" the culture to organizational members. We are always involved in enculturation throughout our careers in the organization, but certain performances are especially vital to this process. Orientation of newcomers is an example. On a less formal scale, "learning the ropes" consists of a series of performances in which individuals teach others how things are done. Although this can be accomplished by direct instruction ("That's how we do it here"), most often this kind of learning occurs when people talk about things that happened in a way that helps other individuals learn how to interpret events. After dealing with a rowdy drunk, an older officer (Davis) helps a rookie (Benson) interpret what happened: Benson says he heard that Davis almost got in a fight with the drunk, and Davis replies, "Not really. I didn't give the guy a chance to get mad at me."

> We take Davis' interaction with Benson as a unique enculturation performance, a metacommunicative commentary that instructs Benson in how he should interpret the prior performance. This metacommunication informs the rookie that the prior exchange was not an endorsement of fighting but was backstage "play." And, as the rookie observes more instances of this backstage "tough" talk, he comes to understand it as "not real," but serious nonetheless.[51]

This list of cultural performances shows us how organizations are indeed cultures and some of the ways in which individuals create and display them. Coming to understand the cultural meanings of an organization proceeds very much like any interpretive ethnography. The researcher first describes the actions of the organizational members and then constructs an interpretation of them in terms that

is not only faithful from the "native's point of view" but is also understandable by people outside the organization. This is in every way a hermeneutic process.

Interpretive Media Studies

Traditional media studies view media as channels for transmitting information to an audience (see Chapter 15). Another, increasingly popular way of approaching media is to think of the audience as numerous interpretive communities, each with its own meanings for what is read, viewed, and heard. Interpretive communities come into being around specific media and content. A community develops around a shared pattern of consumption: common understandings of the content of what is read, heard, or viewed, and shared outcomes. For example, a television audience consists of a number of "cultures," or communities of viewers, who use and perceive the medium, even individual programs, differently. Thus, if you want to discover how television affects the audience, you have to understand the cultures of these various communities.[52]

Because the outcomes of media assumption thus conceived depends on the cultural constructions of the community, this approach requires cultural interpretation.[53] One well-known researcher refers to this type of work as the "ethnography of mass communication."[54]

---

51. Ibid., p. 145.

52. The idea of an interpretive community was originally used by Stanley Fish, who applied the term to reading communities of written texts. See *Is There a Text in this Class?* (Cambridge, Mass.: Harvard University Press, 1980).

53. See, for example, Thomas R. Lindlof and Timothy P. Meyer, "Mediated Communication as Ways of Seeing, Acting, and Constructing Culture: The Tools and Foundations of Qualitative Research," in *Natural Audiences: Qualitative Research of Media Uses and Effects*, ed. T. R. Lindlof (Norwood, N.J.: Ablex, 1987), pp. 1–32; Thomas R. Lindlof, "Media Audiences as Interpretive Communities," in *Communication Yearbook 11*, ed. J. A. Anderson (Newbury Park, Calif.: Sage, 1988), pp. 81–107; Kevin M. Carragee, "Interpretive Media Study and Interpretive Social Science," *Critical Studies in Mass Communication* 7 (1990): 81–96; Klaus Bruhn Jensen, "When Is Meaning? Communication Theory, Pragmatism, and Mass Media Reception," in *Communication Yearbook 14*, ed. J. A. Anderson (Newbury Park, Calif.: Sage, 1991), pp. 3–32.

54. James Lull, "The Social Uses of Television," *Human Communication Research* 6 (1980): 197–209.

For example, a program like "Sesame Street" appeals to a variety of interpretive communities. One such community might be middle-class children whose parents encourage them to watch and who view the program and discuss it with their parents. Another community might be children who view the program on their own to kill time before dinner every evening. Another example of an interpretive community would be people who get their news by listening to National Public Radio's "All Things Considered" in the car on the way home from work. Still another might consist of people who watch a lot of weekend football for relaxation, entertainment, and social life.

Any person may be a member of a variety of interpretive communities, and particular social groups such as the family may be a crossing point for a number of such communities. For example, various members of a family may enjoy television news, top-40 radio programming, sitcoms, children's programs, and biographies.

Thomas Lindlof outlines three dimensions of an interpretive community.[55] Because interpretive communities define their own meanings for media, Lindlof refers to these elements as *genres*, or general types of media outcomes created by social interaction within the interpretive community. With this perspective then, the idea of the interpretive community is consistent with the social phenomenology of Schutz discussed earlier in this chapter and with social constructionism discussed in Chapter 9.

The first genre that characterizes an interpretive community is the genre of *content*. This consists of the types of programs and other media consumed by the community. One group shares an interest in televised football, another in mystery novels, and still another in music videos. It is not enough that a community share an interest in one type of medium content. It is a community because the members share some common meanings for that content. A mother who thinks "Sesame Street" is a cute and harmless pastime for her children, the children who become intimately involved with the characters day-after-day, the teenage son who thinks it is silly, and the grandfather who loves the

Muppets do not constitute an interpretive community because they see very different things in the content of that program.

Genres of *interpretation* capture this idea of meaning. Members of a community interpret the content of programs and other media in similar ways. They understand the content in similar ways, and the impact on their behavior, especially what they say about what they view and the language used to describe it, is similar. The phenomenon of the Tuesday morning quarterback is a good example. Members of the Monday night football club spend a good deal of time on Tuesday morning sharing their perceptions of the game.

Finally, genres of *social action* are shared sets of behaviors toward the media in the community. Genres of social action include not only how the media content is consumed (when and where it is viewed or read) but also the ways in which that content is included in the conduct of the members of the community. How are members' relationships among themselves affected by the media? Does a particular type of media content lubricate the relationship in some way? Do people talk to one another about what they have seen or heard? Do they use relationships viewed on television as models for their own relationships?

An example of a cultural analysis of media is Linda Steiner's investigation of the "No Comment" section of Ms. magazine.[56] For 10 years, between 1972 and 1982, Ms. magazine regularly published a page entitled "No Comment," featuring quotations and entries from other sources, sent in by readers, to illustrate the oppression of women in media. The title of the section implies that the negative quality of the quotation stands by itself without comment.

Items from other magazines—especially print ads—journals, newspapers, even textbooks and manuals found their way onto the "No Comment" page. All items were originally published with a particular meaning in mind, but the readers of Ms. read them differently. The fact that readers choose

55. Lindlof, "Media Audiences."

56. Linda Steiner, "Oppositional Decoding as an Act of Resistance," *Critical Studies in Mass Communication* 5 (1988): 1–15.

similar items again and again to make a point at odds with the original publisher's intent makes these readers an interpretive community. They are members of a community that share attitudes and perceptions and the desire to make their contrary reading of certain items public.

Steiner borrows Stuart Hall's (Chapter 11) concept of oppositional reading to characterize the binding element of this interpretive community.[57] An oppositional reading is deliberately assigning a meaning to a text that was not intended to contest the dominant ideology behind the original meaning. For example, an advertisement that is supposed to sell perfume by making a woman look glamorous might be taken by a feminist as showing the exploitation of women in advertising.

In her analysis Steiner isolates a number of alternative meanings for various items. For example, many depict women as the property of men. Some mock feminism as offensive. Others make use of women's bodies in ways that are exploitative. Still others promote sexual abuse and violence against women. In each case, the deliberate reading opposes that intended by the originator of the quoted item. Steiner shows how contributing to and reading the "No Comment" section solidifies a set of values and views shared by the interpretive community of *Ms.* readers.

All approaches discussed in this section—the ethnography of communication, organizational culture, and interpretive media studies—share cultural hermeneutics as a core element. In each, the meanings of various groups are studied and interpreted.

Commentary and Critique

The theories presented in this chapter are members of an extended family. Like any family, they have important differences but share a common relationship. These approaches privilege conscious human perception and experience in one form or another. In phenomenology the conscious experience of the individual provides an eye to truth. In hermeneutics the interpretation of a culture or text is a disciplined and conscious human task. We have seen several varieties of these two traditions, including essentialist, social, and hermeneutic phenomenology. We have also examined theories of cultural and textual hermeneutics.

Three serious debates surround phenomenology and interpretion. These approaches conflict first with traditional structural and cognitive perspectives summarized earlier in this book. They clash also with poststructuralism and critical theory (see Chapters 5 and 11). The third debate involves the tension between textual and cultural interpretation. Let us now consider each of these controversies in turn.

The structuralist critique is easily anticipated from ideas presented earlier in this book. We have encountered it before in the discussions of philosophical issues in communication theory and in the critiques of structuralism, cognitivism, and constructionism. The critique begins with the opposing assumption that structures are real apart from the human experience of them and that these realities impact human experience in ways neither anticipated nor understood by communicators themselves. For the structural or cognitive theorist, these powerful outside influences must be discovered by controlled observation, and hermeneutic interpretation is inadequate for this task.[58]

Traditional critics believe that interpretive approaches ignore important psychological and social structures that influence human behavior. By concentrating on conscious experience, they miss the ways in which outside factors affect human life. Interpretive media studies are an example. As Kevin Carragee points out,

> In their desire to examine audience interpretations and uses of media content, interpretive studies largely have ignored the organizational and economic factors

---

57. Stuart Hall, "Encoding/Decoding," in *Culture, Media, Language,* eds. S. Hall et al. (London: Hutchinson, 1980), pp. 128–138.

58. D. W. Hamlyn, "The Concept of Social Reality," in *Explaining Human Behavior: Consciousness, Human Action, and Social Structure,* ed. P. F. Secord (Beverly Hills, Calif.: Sage, 1982), p. 194.

that influence the media texts. . . . The interpretive project's failure to incorporate research examining encoding processes reduces media texts to autonomous signifying systems; they are cut off from their origin in organizational routines and procedures.[59]

According to the structural-cognitive critique, the structures that affect human life are largely unintentional and out of awareness. Cognition is a complex set of processes, many of which are hidden from the individual.[60] Although much of what we do is indeed conscious, many important structures governing social life are beyond awareness.[61]

Social structures, too, exist apart from any design or intention as people live their lives. Anthony Giddens calls these the "unintended consequences" of purposeful actions. As individuals go about their daily activities, certain outcomes that may not be intended nor even conscious come about, and these resultant structures have a serious impact on subsequent actions. Thus, structures are produced and reproduced in action. Interpretive approaches often ignore the unintended consequences of action. Giddens notes the importance of such structures:

> History is not an intentional project, and all intentional activity takes place in the context of institutions sedimented over long-term periods of time. The unintended consequences of action are of fundamental importance to social theory, especially insofar as they are systematically incorporated within the processes of the reproduction of institutions.[62]

This thesis flies in the face of phenomenology, which gives conscious experience great power to apprehend the structures of reality. Early phenomenologists like Husserl would probably agree that

the essence of reality is not normally within the awareness of the individual in the natural attitude, but they would suggest that what becomes conscious after distractions are bracketed is that which is essential and real about an experience. Later phenomenologists, especially of the social and hermeneutic traditions, would find the structuralist objection unacceptable in any version. For these theorists, reality is experience as lived.

Hermeneutics is a method that grants individuals the ability to interpret actions and texts. For theorists of this tradition, there is no structural reality outside of actions or texts, and ambiguity demands interpretation. Interpretation is a conscious human experience.

To the structuralist, on the other hand, people may not accurately understand, nor can they reliably report, their experience. If your intentions are elusive and important processes are hidden, then what is really going on in social life is not something a perceiver can tap into experientially. Instead, scientific methods of discovery are necessary. Research on attribution theory (Chapter 12) illustrates the difficulty of explaining one's own actions.[63]

Another objection of traditional social science is that interpretive methods tend to be case-oriented and do not lend themselves to generalization and theory building. In phenomenology each thing must be understood in and of itself by careful bracketing of experience. In hermeneutics one interprets a set of group actions or a text, but generalizations beyond the individual case are discouraged. Even comparative ethnography, though it may look for

59. Carragee, "Interpretive Media Study."

60. See, for example, Michael T. Motley, "Consciousness and Intentionality in Communication: A Preliminary Model and Methodological Approaches," *Western Journal of Speech Communication* 50 (1986): 3–23.

61. William Bailey, "Consciousness and Action/Motion Theories of Communication," *Western Journal of Speech Communication* 50 (1986): 74.

62. Anthony Giddens, "On the Relation of Sociology to Philosophy," in *Exploring Human Behavior: Consciousness, Human Action, and Social Structure*, ed. P. F. Secord (Beverly Hills, Calif.: Sage, 1982), p. 180.

63. R. E. Nisbett and T. D. Wilson, "Telling More Than We Can Know: Verbal Reports on Mental Processes," *Psychological Review* 84 (1977): 231–259. See also Pamela J. Benoit and William L. Benoit, "Consciousness: The Mindlessness/Mindfulness and Verbal Report of Controversies," *Western Journal of Speech Communication* 50 (1986): 41–63. Critics of attribution theory are quick to point out that the findings in this line of research do not accurately reflect the everyday experience of people acting in context. Indeed, this criticism has been leveled against all positivistic social science research. See, for example, John Shotter, *Social Accountability and Selfhood* (New York: Basil Blackwell, 1984), pp. 167–172; Kenneth Gergen, *Toward Transformation in Social Knowledge* (New York: Springer-Verlag, 1982), pp. 126–33.

commonalities, is equally interested in cultural difference. What, then, can be known from this method other than the facts of the case? For some, like Schutz, the facts of the case are good enough. These thinkers eschew theory as misleading because they espouse generalizations that are not there. For others, like Hymes, generalizations can be made after examination of several cases.

The culture approach to organizations illustrates the difficulty of generalization. If you assume that the social reality of an organization comes from the interactions among members of the organization and that organizational cultures thereby differ, you put yourself into the very difficult theoretical position of being unable to make generalizations or predictions about organizational life. Each organization must be studied independently, and generalizations become difficult.

An answer, of course, is that theories should not attempt to be predictive but should capture general categories of action, which we expect to be played out differently in various cultures. For example, although every organization is different, there are categories such as rituals and stories that all organizations can be expected to have. Such middle-range theories, like that of Pacanowsky and O'Donnell-Trujillo and of Hymes, enable us to observe cultures with a sensitivity to their rich individuality and their commonalities as well.

The structural-cognitive critique can be thought of as conservative because it argues from the tradition of Western thought and social science in the twentieth century. In a sense then, this first set of concerns is a critique from the right. The second debate relevant to the ideas in this chapter is a critique from the left. It comes from a movement that is by definition critical of traditional social science, a movement that aims to transform the work of social science. If the critique from the right accuses interpretive theories of ignoring, bending, or breaking traditional notions of reality and structure, the critique from the left accuses them of being overly conservative and insensitive to the need for change.

Poststructuralism was discussed briefly in Chapter 5 as a reaction against structuralism.[64] There, we saw that it denies the reality of universal structures of language and discourse. At the same time, poststructuralism also denies the existence of certain meaning in action or text. Poststructuralists see interpretive approaches as essentially foundationalist in that they seek some sort of essential meaning in practices and texts. Phenomenologists seek the essence of experience; poststructuralists deny essence. Hermeneutic scholars are devoted to finding the center or central meaning of texts; poststructuralists deny that there is any central meaning in text.

The version of poststructuralism most opposed to interpretation is *deconstructionism*, or the movement to obliterate the idea that texts mean anything.[65] Interpretation reconstructs meaning; deconstruction shows that whatever meaning is derived is wrong. Any meaning exists only by virtue of what it is not. A "house" can only be known because of what it is not, and every reference to "house" in a text implies that which it is not. Thus, an unending set of possible meanings exists in any text, which implies that there can be no central or true meaning at all.

As we will see in the following chapter, interpretive and critical approaches to communication theory have certain common principles. There is, however, a substantial difference between the two, which has become the source of a debate.[66] Critical theory is transformative: It not only presents a picture of society but also aims to change social structure by raising consciousness about power in society. Critical theory accuses interpretive approaches of being conservative and of failing to recognize their ideological character. In other words, understanding human action by itself does not go far

64. For an excellent summary of poststructuralism, see Art Berman, *From the New Criticism to Deconstruction* (Urbana, Ill.: University of Chicago Press, 1988).

65. The scholar most associated with deconstruction is Jacques Derrida. See *Of Grammatology*, trans. G. Spivak (Baltimore: Johns Hopkins University Press, 1974, 1976).

66. This debate is summarized in Brian Fay, *Social Theory and Political Practice* (London: George Allen & Unwin, 1975); and Ricoeur, *Hermeneutics*.

enough. Scholars must study the ways in which individuals are oppressed so that people can rise up and change the circumstances of their lives. The failure of interpretive scholarship to do so merely legitimizes repressive power structures and perpetuates oppression in society.

In fact, many critical scholars accuse interpretive theory of bolstering the dominant ideology. The cultural approach to organizational theory is an example. The downside to the organizational culture movement is that the empirically minded manager may come to think of culture as just another variable to be manipulated in the management of the organization. This idea can lead to the negative consequence of ideological control.

The above discussion implies that experiential and interpretive theories are a unified and cohesive block of ideas under attack from the outside. This is a misleading impression. In fact, substantial differences exist among the theories in this chapter. One of the most important is that between textual and cultural interpretation, which is a dispute about the locus of meaning.[67] For most cultural interpretivists, meaning is to be found in the practices of a culture. For most textual interpretivists, meaning is found in language and text. Indeed, Ricoeur's concept of distanciation is designed to capture the separation of text from cultural practice. The culture-interpretive view is that texts are a product of social interaction, whereas the text-interpretation view holds that texts prefigure culture in important ways.

Actually, cultural interpretation and social constructionism are closely related and could easily have been put in the same chapter of this book. Both are children of social phenomenology, and both see meaning as inherent in social practice. Thus, the tension between text and practice mirrors the debate between traditional text hermeneutics and social constructionism.

This controversy can be seen in debates on media. The idea of interpretive communities assigns great power to the practices of social groups in constructing the meaning of media and content in their own lives. Media text theorists, on the other hand, assign great power to the content of media in the creation of culture. Carragee continues his critique of interpetive studies in this way:

> Interpretive researchers need to devote far more attention to the properties and structures of media messages, to the symbolic power of texts. Characterizations of texts or indeed media as empty vessels deny the ways in which texts and media help to constitute meanings and realities for their audiences by highlighting certain meanings and values while excluding others.[68]

An important question at this juncture is whether the text–practice dispute is a true disjunction. Some important commentators believe it is not. It may be entirely possible—indeed desirable—to grant power both to text and cultural practice. Gadamer's work is especially important because he does precisely this. For Gadamer, readers cannot be separated from their interpretive communities in the way suggested by Ricoeur. This sort of distanciation is not possible. At the same time, the text itself does have inherent meaning, and readers must be open to a dialogue between the reader and the text. The text has rich meaning to convey, and the reader always approaches that text from within an interpretive tradition. The interpretive frame informs the reading of the text, whereas the text helps shape the interpretive frame itself.

In the following chapter, we continue the discussion of meaning and social power. The emphasis now switches from interpretation of text and action to their transformation.

---

67. This controversy is discussed by Berman, *From the New Criticism*, pp. 281–292.

68. Carragee, "Interpretive Media Study," p. 89.

CHAPTER **11**

Critical Theories

In general, criticism involves the application of values to make judgments for the purpose of accomplishing positive change. Criticism has been applied to a variety of communication phenomena. Rhetorical criticism, for example, carefully examines and judges the quality of discourse and other communication forms, and although an important topic, it is not the subject of this chapter.[1] Our subject here is with critical social science, which forms a critique of basic social structure.

Although there are several varieties of critical social science, all share three essential features.[2] First, critical social scientists believe it necessary to understand the lived experience of real people in context. As such, critical theories share the ideas and methodologies of some of the interpretive theories discussed in Chapter 10. What makes critical scholarship different from interpretive work is that it interprets the acts and symbols of society to understand the ways in which various social groups are oppressed.

Second, critical approaches examine social conditions in an attempt to bring often hidden structures to light. For this reason critical theories also borrow from structuralism (Chapter 4). Most critical theories teach that knowledge is power, for understanding the ways in which one is oppressed enables one to take action to change oppressive forces. Third, critical social science makes a conscious attempt to fuse theory and action. Such theories are clearly normative and act to accomplish change in the conditions that affect our lives.

Critical theories align themselves with the interests opposed to those of the dominant culture, and they often have partisan identification with particular groups whose interests are subverted by the interests of the dominant classes in society. Therefore, critical research asks questions about the ways in which competing interests clash and the manner in which conflicts are resolved in favor of particular groups. Such processes of domination are often hid-

1. See, for example, Sonja K. Foss, *Rhetorical Criticism: Exploration and Practice* (Prospect Heights, Ill.: Waveland Press, 1989.)

2. Brian Fay, *Social Theory and Political Practice* (London: George Allen & Unwin, 1975), p. 94.

den from view, and critical theory aims to uncover these processes.[3]

Critical social science is often economic and political in nature, but much of it concerns communication. Critical theorists are usually reluctant to separate communication and other elements from the overall system. Thus, a critical theory of communication (or economics, or politics) is necessarily part of a critique of society as a whole. Critical communication theory deals with a variety of relevant topics, including language, organizational structures, interpersonal relationships, and media. Here, we deal with two important genres of critical social science—feminist and Marxist.

Feminist Theory

Feminist theory is a generic label for a perspective or group of theories that explores the meaning of gender concepts.[4] Feminist theorists observe that many aspects of life are understood in terms of gender qualities, comprising not only biological sex but also virtually every facet of human life, including language, work, family roles, education, and socialization. The feminist critique aims to expose both the powers and limits of the genderized division of the world. Much feminist theory emphasizes the oppressive nature of gender relations under the domination of the patriarchy. As such it is in many ways a study of power distribution between the sexes.

Feminist theory begins with the assumption that gender is a pervasive category for understanding human experience. Gender is a social construction that, although useful, has been dominated by a male bias and is particularly oppressive to women. Feminist theory aims to challenge the prevailing gender assumptions of society and to achieve more liberating ways for women and men to exist in the world.

Feminist criticism has become increasingly popular in the study of communication.[5] Feminist communication scholars examine the ways in which the male language bias affects the relations between the sexes, the ways in which male domination has constrained communication for females, the ways in which women have both accommodated and resisted male patterns of speech and language, powers of women's communication forms, and other similar concerns.

For the feminist scholar, traditional methods of research and male-biased theories are not only misleading but also dangerous because they mute the experience of women and hide the values of women's experience. For this reason, feminist scholarship usually focuses on women's experience as central, legitimizing the value of women's experience itself. Women's experience includes a sense of interdependence and relationship, the legitimacy of emotionality, fusion of public and private realms of experience, egalitarian values, concern for process over product, and openness to multiple ways of seeing and doing.

Feminist theories acknowledge that the world can be understood in a variety of productive ways, and they resist the search for positive truth. They also see the feminine as a way of knowing that is distinct from the masculine, a view reflected, for example, in Carol Gilligan's well-known book *In a*

3. This characteristic of critical theory is discussed by Nancy Fraser, *Unruly Practices: Power, Discourse, and Gender in Contemporary Social Theory* (Minneapolis: University of Minnesota Press, 1989), p. 113.

4. Feminist theory is discussed in numerous sources. See, for example, Karen A. Foss and Sonja K. Foss, "Incorporating the Feminist Perspective in Communication Scholarship: A Research Commentary," in *Doing Research on Women's Communication: Alternative Perspectives in Theory and Method*, eds. C. Spitzack and K. Carter (Norwood, N.J: Ablex, 1989), pp. 65–94; Brenda Dervin, "The Potential Contribution of Feminist Scholarship to the Field of Communication," *Journal of Communication* 37 (1987): 107–120; Catharine A. MacKinnon, "Desire and Power: A Feminist Perspective," in *Marxism and the Interpretation of Culture*, eds. C. Nelson and L. Grossberg (Urbana: University of Illinois Press, 1988), pp. 105–122; Cheris Kramarae, "Feminist Theories of Communication," in *International Encyclopedia of Communications*, vol. 2, eds. E. Barnouw et al. (New York: Oxford University Press, 1989), pp. 157–160.

5. For a sampling of this work, see Fern L. Johnson, "Coming to Terms with Women's Language," *Quarterly Journal of Speech* 72 (1986): 318–352; Foss and Foss, "Incorporating."

Different Voice, in which she outlines the powers of the feminine values of intimacy, caring, and relationship.[6]

Feminism is not a single theory or even a single system of thought. It is a movement in which a variety of voices can be heard. Perhaps the most prevalent schools of feminist thought are liberal feminism and radical feminism. *Liberal feminism* was the foundation of the women's movement of the 1960s and 1970s. It is based in liberal democracy, or the idea that justice involves the assurance of equal rights for all individuals. Liberal feminists say that women have been oppressed as a group and that they have not had equal rights with men, as evidenced in such facts as the lower average income of women, the exclusion of women from centers of power and decision making, and the lack of opportunity for women to advance in careers of their choice. In short, liberal feminism deals primarily with the public image and rights of women.

Radical feminism is in some ways a reaction to liberal feminism. Proponents of this viewpoint believe that liberal democracy barely scratches the surface and that the oppression of women runs far deeper than public rights. For radical feminists, the problem is not just changing the law to give equal rights to women. The problem goes to the heart of our social structure, which is dominated by the patriarchy. The patriarchy perpetuates a set of gender-laden meanings that promote masculine interests and subordinate feminine ones. Women are oppressed because the very fabric of society is based on a constructed reality that devalues and marginalizes women's experience. If gender is a social construction, in our present order of things, it is a man-made construction. The term *radical* is appropriate for this movement because it goes to the "root" of social structure and demands "basic" redefinitions of all facets of society.

Whereas liberal feminists want women to be able to have what men already have, radical feminists do not see this as an answer. In fact, to emulate the status of men in society only perpetuates the patriarchal definition of the social order. So, for example, women not only must aspire to achieve the equal right to become a physician but society itself must also redefine the whole nature of medicine, especially in regard to how it treats the experience of women. Women not only should try to achieve equal representation among the ranks of business executives but also must strive to change the very definition of commerce and economy in society at large, so that it no longer damages the welfare of women and children.

Today, many radical feminists call for women to define their own reality and their own social order, to rely on their own instincts and experience as a guide to self-definition and interpersonal relationships. In other words, the answer can only be a complete restructuring of how our society defines human experience.

Feminism presents an increasingly popular challenge to mainstream communication scholarship. Sonja Foss, Karen Foss, and Robert Trapp discuss this challenge in terms roughly equivalent to the liberal and radical schools of feminism.[7] The first type of challenge, which these authors call the *inclusion stage*, is an attempt to get more public recognition for the contributions of women. It includes research on sexist language, including the ways in which language creates inequality between the sexes; sex differences in communication, including investigations into the real and imagined differences between the communication behavior of men and women; great women speakers, including research into the contributions of women to the history of public address; and women's culture, including writing about the differences between the ways in which men and women think and act and the legitimation of women's ways of knowing.

The *revisionist stage* is consistent with radical feminism in that it challenges the very definitions used to characterize communication in society. These writings aim to revise such definitions to include women's experience. Such issues as the definition of rhetoric, what constitutes effective speech, the eloquence of ordinary women's forms of

6. Carol Gilligan, *In a Different Voice* (Cambridge, Mass.: Harvard University Press, 1982).

7. Sonja K. Foss, Karen A. Foss, and Robert Trapp, *Contemporary Perspectives on Rhetoric* (Propsect Heights, Ill.: Waveland Press, 1991).

expression, the importance of communication in private settings, the nature of social movements, and the character of persuasion and influence are questioned and reformulated in this kind of work.

In this chapter we look at two prominent feminist theories of communication. The first is muted-group theory and the second is the theory of the patriarchal universe of discourse.

Muted-Group Theory

Anthropologists Edwin Ardener and Shirley Ardener originated muted-group theory.[8] Edwin Ardener observed that anthropologists tend to characterize a culture in terms of the masculine. In other words, ethnography seemed biased toward observation of males in a culture. On closer examination, however, it appeared to Ardener that the actual language of a culture had an inherent male bias, that men created the meanings for a group, and that the feminine voice was suppressed, or "muted." This silencing of women, in Ardener's observation, leads to women's inability to express themselves eloquently in the male parlance.

Shirley Ardener added to the theory by suggesting that the silence of women has several manifestations and is especially evident in public discourse. Women are less comfortable and less expressive in public situations than are men, and they are less comfortable in public situations than they are in private. Consequently, women monitor their own communications more intensely than do men. Women watch what they say and translate what they are feeling and thinking into male terms. When masculine and feminine meanings and expressions conflict, the masculine tends to win out because of the dominance of males in society, and the result is that women are muted.

Communication theorist Cheris Kramarae has expanded the muted-group theory by incorporating it with the results of research on women and communication.[9] She outlines the basic assumptions of muted group theory as follows:

1. Because men and women have different experiences based on the division of labor in society, they perceive the world differently.

2. Men are politically dominant in society, and their systems of perception are therefore dominant, which prevents women's perceptions from being publicly adopted.

3. Women must translate their own ways of understanding into the terms of the male worldview in order to participate in public life.

Kramarae suggests a number of hypotheses about women's communication based on research findings. First, women express themselves with more difficulty than do men. A common female experience is to lack a word for a feminine experience, apparently because men, who do not share that experience, have not developed a term for it. Women often report this experience. For example, a group of students when asked to create new words for aspects of their experience were able easily to do so. Some of the words they created as as follows:

> *soul rinse*—feeling after a big cry.
>
> *solo wholo*—used to describe a person not in a relationship with a significant other, not actively searching, yet not elminating the possibility, and perfectly satisfied with the way he or she is.
>
> *femipotent*—female virility.
>
> *silonuts*—no reaction from a male; domination by silence.[10]

Along the same line, linguist Suzette Elgin has created an entire language, Láadan, to reflect women's experience.[11]

---

8. Edwin Ardener, "Some Outstanding Problems in the Analysis of Events" (Paper presented at the Association of Social Anthropologists' Decennial Conference, 1973); "The 'Problem' Revisited," in *Perceiving Women*, ed. S. Ardener (London: Malaby Press, 1975); Shirley Ardener, *Defining Females: The Nature of Women in Society* (New York: Wiley, 1978). This theory is explored in some detail by Dale Spender, *Man Made Language* (London: Routledge & Kegan Paul, 1980), pp. 76–105.

9. Cheris Kramarae, *Women and Men Speaking: Frameworks for Analysis* (Rowley, Mass.: Newbury House, 1981), pp. 1–63.

10. Personal communication from Karen Foss, 1991.

11. Suzette Elgin, *A First Dictionary and Grammar of Láadan*, 2nd ed. (Madison, Wis.: Society for the Furtherance and Study of Fantasy and Science Fiction, 1988). See also Elgin's novel, *Native Tongue* (New York: Daw, 1984).

Kramarae's second hypothesis is that women understand men's meanings more easily than men understand women's. The evidence of this generalization has a number of corollaries:

1. Men may have distanced themselves from the expressions of women because they do not understand those expressions.

2. Women are subjected to language experiences that men have not had, such as lacking a word for something.

3. Men may suppress women and rationalize it on the grounds that women are not as rational or clear.

4. Women must learn the male system of communication, but men in return have isolated themselves from the female system.

The third hypothesis is that women have created their own means of expression outside the dominant male system. Letters, diaries, consciousness-raising groups, and alternative art forms are examples. Women rely more on nonverbal expression and use different nonverbal forms than do men because they are verbally muted. Some research has shown, for example, that facial expressions, vocal pauses, and bodily gestures are more important in women's discussions than they are in men's. Women also seem to display a wider variability of expression in their speech.

Fourth, women tend to express more dissatisfaction about communication than do men. Women may talk more about their problems in using language or their difficulty in using standard male tools of communication. Women poets often express these concerns, and writers and public speakers sometimes state their feelings of being constrained by the customary practices in those fields.

The fifth hypothesis follows from the fourth: Women often make efforts to change the dominant rules of communication in order to get around or resist conventional rules. Advocates for women's liberation, for example, have created new words such as *Ms.* and *herstory* and have developed different communication forms that incorporate women's experiences. Consciousness-raising groups are a good example of this.

Sixth, women are traditionally less likely to coin new words that become popular in society at large and feel excluded from contributing to language. Finally, women find different things humorous than do men. Because they have different methods of conceptualization and expression, relations that appear funny to men may not be humorous at all to women.

An example of research consistent with muted-group theory is the work of Foss and Foss on women's eloquence. Foss and Foss interviewed a number of women and examined their work. Their book *Women Speak: The Eloquence of Women's Lives* presents the work of these women in such a way as to challenge a number of assumptions about what constitutes eloquent communication.[12] The book shows that many of the forms of communication used by women are not viewed as significant in the masculine, public world but that these expressive forms have value in their own right. The book makes this kind of work more public in an attempt to give voice to women normally muted in society.

Two assumptions being challenged by the research of Foss and Foss are that significant communicators are men and that suitable frameworks for assessing communication are derived from male perspectives. The entire work is designed to refute these ideas. The book includes entirely the work of women, and this work reflects a variety of dimensions that come from the experience of women, not men.

Another assumption is that significant communication is produced by noteworthy individuals. Only two or three of the women included in the study come anywhere close to being famous. Many are ordinary acquaintances of the authors—a gardener, some mothers, an interior decorator, for instance. Another assumption is that significant communication is produced by historical individuals. Indeed, all women featured in this research are contemporary. The next assumption is that significant communication is produced by individuals, but the book includes groups such as a comedy

---

12. Karen A. Foss and Sonja K. Foss, *Women Speak: The Eloquence of Women's Lives* (Prospect Heights, Ill.: Waveland Press, 1991).

team, a family, two filmmakers who work together, two women who exchange letters, an artist who works with a whole team to complete a work, a newsletter-publishing group, and a reading group.

Yet another assumption is that significant communication occurs in the public realm. This work shows how women produce significant communication in private settings, and it honors and legitimizes this kind of eloquence, including, for example, family stories, journal writing, and mother–child interaction. Foss and Foss also challenge the assumption that speech making is the most significant form of communication: Only one speech is featured in their book. They also challenge the assumption that significant texts are finished products, which is refuted by the inclusion of such forms as journal writing, letter writing, and motherhood.

Muted-group theory is an excellent example of a critical communication theory. It focuses on the experience of particular groups in society, it exposes underlying structures causing oppression, and it suggests directions for positive change. Another consistent example of feminist communication theory is Julia Penelope's work on the oppressive nature of language.

The Patriarchal Universe of Discourse

One of the most highly recognized feminist communication theorists is Julia Penelope, who has developed a critical theory of the patriarchal universe of discourse.[13] For Penelope, who is a linguist, language is central to all human experience and society. The very way in which our experience is understood is prefigured by the elements of the language created by the culture. It comes as no surprise, then, that language is an instrument of oppression, and Penelope's theory deals with the ways in which language is patriarchal and oppressive to women. (She also acknowledges its oppression of many other groups.)

A *universe of discourse* is a set of language conventions that reflect a particular definition of reality. Those who accept the language essentially

13. Julia Penelope, *Speaking Freely: Unlearning the Lies of the Fathers' Tongues* (New York: Pergamon Press, 1990).

accept its categories of truth, and the vast majority of language users do so without question. Thus, a universe of discourse imposes certain meanings on members of a culture who employ it. For example, Penelope relates two incidents in which she was mistaken for a housewife, once when she was at home during the day and a salesman came to the door and once when she was called the "lady of the house" by a woman on the phone. Both of these people used common linguistic assumptions about what constitutes a household and a housewife: A household consists of a married man and woman, and any woman home during the day must therefore be a housewife. The conspicuous absence of the term *househusband* in common English reflects the same set of assumptions.

The definitions, meanings, and interpretations embedded in the patriarchal universe of discourse promote the interests of men and subordinate those of women. Most women do not question the categories of their language, so that they become co-opted into the male-dominant system. There is even a subcode used among many women in our society, the *cosmetic universe of discourse*, which signals recognition and approval of their own subordination. This female code includes such features as using the highest pitch range more often than men. It involves pausing more often than men and using a more questioning intonation than men. It includes a vocabulary of fashion, housework, and child rearing. Women also use more hedges like "well" or "sorta" than men typically use. They also tend to use more tag questions, which reflect uncertainty at the end of a statement, such as, "It's a nice day, isn't it?" Women also tend to use longer sentences than is customarily the case for men.

Penelope notes that language is a living, changing system. The problem is that most people fail to recognize that language is a human creation that is molded to meet human needs. The culprit in this misconception is *prescriptive grammar*, which is a codified set of rules written by men for the purpose of making a language seem pure and unchanging. The conventions of English—as with many other languages of the world—were established by aristocratic men in ways that promoted their own interests.

Penelope chronologically orders many standard rules of English to show how they were created, why they are arbitrary, and how they perpetuate the interests of white men over other groups. For example, one of the most important sets of conventions for the oppression of women is gender, which she calls "an essential element of the heterosexualization of grammar."[14] Although most people think that words really are masculine or feminine, gender is "among the most contorted constructions in which misogyny and prescriptivism cooperate to befuddle and mislead us."[15] According to Penelope the genderization of nouns goes back to ancient Greece, where Protagorus first classified nouns as masculine and feminine. Originally, *gender* referred to "race," "class," or "kind," but with the classification of words as masculine and feminine, this term became associated exclusively with biological sex. Penelope comments: "I do not know what motivated Protagorus to choose the adjectives *feminine* and *masculine* to describe noun classifications in Greek, and I haven't read a historian of grammars who has asked".[16]

For Penelope, classifying things into two categories based on biological sex is a distinctly male tendency. Even in English, where formal gender applies only to actual sexed animals and humans (e.g., bitch, husband, bull, daughter), the language implicitly defines particular attitudes, actions, and objects as feminine and others as masculine. This is a quality Penelope calls *sexual dimorphism*. Thus, for example, war, money, sex, cars, and sports are most often viewed as masculine, whereas babies, cosmetics, and recipes are feminine. Another example is the association of elements of nature with women because of the male tendency to use and manipulate objects in his environment, which Penelope believes comes from man's need to control.

Genderization is one of the most thoroughly and uncritically accepted features of language. What makes it especially insidious is that it is not just a bimodal classification system; it is a system in

which the masculine is considered the "normal" point of comparison, so the semantics of the language are divided into *male* and *nonmale* (female). Masculine is normal and healthy, whereas feminine is feminine. Even *androgyny*, the sought-after combination of both masculine and feminine traits, serves only to perpetuate the classification of concepts into these two categories.

To illustrate the point that masculine is normal, Penelope comments on the dictionary definitions of *manly, masculine, womanly,* and *feminine:*

> The qualities listed under *manly* and *masculine* are the "good" things an individual might wish to be: strong, brave, determined, honest, and dignified. Not a single one of the negative qualities commonly attributed to maleness are listed. . . . Look closely at the long list of characteristics in the definition for *manly* compared to the circularity of the pseudo-definition for *womanly*, "like or befitting woman." That's not a definition; it assumes that we already know the behaviors that "befit" a woman. The real definitions for *womanly* are implied as "oppositions" to "manly qualities". . . . Positive attributes commonly associated with females, nurturing, kind, and loving, have been omitted.[17]

You can see how the meanings of words have positive masculine or negative feminine connotations, but less obvious are the grammatical features of the patriarchal language. These are particularly oppressive because they enable people to use language subtly in a way that subverts the interests of women and other nondominant groups. False deixis is an example.

Deixis is the pointing feature of language, and deictic words point to specific objects. You might, for example, say, "Pass the salt," and everyone at the table knows exactly what you are referring to. A *false deictic* leads one to believe there is a specific object, but it fails to point it out precisely, resulting in confusion. It uses ambiguity to trick and manipulate. Penelope lists the following expressions as examples: "It's what's happening." (What is happening?) "You can't escape it." (What can't you escape?) "Don't throw it all away." (Don't throw

14. Ibid., p. 20.
15. Ibid., p. 20.
16. Ibid., p. 56.

17. Ibid., p. 53.

what away?) One of the most serious problems of false deixis is that it obfuscates and hides what we don't want to talk about. It is a way to avoid being honest and direct and to subvert the interests of important groups in society, such as women.

Another example of a grammatical feature of the patriarchal universe of discourse is the *missing agent*. This is the failure to identify the person or persons responsible for an action. It is especially common in the passive voice. For example, to say, "The woman was raped," avoids identifying the agent of the act. More direct would be, "The woman was raped by five men." These types of constructions enable speakers to victimize women and other groups because they focus on the object of an act without drawing attention to the perpetrator.

The solution to the patriarchal universe of discourse is, first, to reject the assumption that the categories of language are true and invariant; second, to become conscious of the ways in which language oppresses; and, third, to refuse to reinforce the categories of language or to resist the rules that oppress.

An example of research designed to accomplish these goals is *A Feminist Dictionary* by Cheris Kramarae and Paula Treichler.[18] This work attempts to capture the features of a feminist universe of discourse by including words with special meaning for women as well as definitions that are consistent, not with men's, but with women's experience. For example, *birth name* is "a term used by feminists as a more accurate label for the name received at birth than the older term *maiden name* which has sexual double standard implications."[19] *Birthing* is "another of the archetypal experiences exclusive to the female."[20] A *foremother* is "an ancestor."[21]

The *Feminist Dictionary* attempts to create a truly feminist universe of discourse, which is precisely what Penelope is calling for. Penelope capsulizes her project in these terms:

The purpose of my analysis is to show readers how to be self-conscious about their linguistic activities. . . . I want to provide information so that women can engage in communication more consciously. Whether we are speaking or listening, writing or reading, being conscious of the functions of linguistic structures when we try to communicate or interpret someone else's utterance enables us to identify immediately and in context uses of language that are dishonest, misleading, or manipulative. . . . If we are to protect ourselves against insidious uses of English, we have to be able to identify such uses and challenge them when someone tries to coerce us linguistically.[22]

Marxist Critique

One of the most important intellectual strands of the twentieth century is Marxist-based social theory. Originating with the ideas of Karl Marx and Friedrich Engels, this movement consists of a number of loosely related theories that challenge the dominant order of society. Virtually all branches of social science, including communication, have been influenced by this line of thought.[23]

Marx taught that the means of production in society determines the very nature of society.[24] This is the linear idea of the *base–superstructure* relationship: The economy is the base of all social structure, including institutions and ideas. In capitalistic systems, profit drives production and therefore dominates labor. Working-class groups are oppressed by the groups in power that benefit from profit. All institutions that perpetuate domination within a capitalistic society arise from this eco-

18. Cheris Kramarae and Paula A. Treichler, *A Feminist Dictionary* (Boston: Pandora Press, 1985).

19. Ibid., p. 72.

20. Ibid., p. 70.

21. Ibid., p. 166.

22. Penelope *Speaking*, p. xxxiii.

23. For a brief overview of the movement, see Tom Bottomore and Armand Mattelart, "Marxist Theories of Communication," in *International Encyclopedia of Communications*, vol. 2, eds. E. Barnouw et al. (New York: Oxford University Press, 1989), pp. 476–483. For coverage of a variety of Marxist-based ideas, see Cary Nelson and Lawrence Grossberg (eds.), *Marxism and the Interpretation of Culture* (Urbana: University of Illinois Press, 1988).

24. Karl Marx's most well-known works are *The Communist Manifesto* (London: Reeves, 1888) and *Capital* (Chicago: Kerr, 1909).

nomic system. Only when the working class rises up against dominant groups can the means of production be changed and the liberation of the worker be achieved. Such liberation furthers the natural progress of history in which forces in opposition clash in a dialectic that results in a higher social order. This classical theory is called the *critique of political economy*.

Today, Marxist-based critical theory is thriving, although it has become diffused and multitheoretical. Not all adherents to critical theory are strictly Marxist, but there is no question that Marx had an immense influence on this school of thought. Although few critical theorists today adopt Marx's ideas on political economy, the basic ideas of dialectical conflict, domination, and oppression remain important. In contrast with Marx's simple base–superstructure model, most contemporary critical theories view social processes as *overdetermined* or caused by multiple sources. They see social structure as a system in which numerous elements interact and affect one another (Chapter 3).

There are several different approaches to Marxist communication theory. These different theories deal with two major problem areas—the "politics of textuality" and the "problematic of cultural studies."[25] The politics of textuality has to do with the ways in which media producers encode messages, the ways in which audiences decode those messages, and the power domination apparent in these processes. The text scholar, for example, might study the ways in which certain kinds of media content, such as network news, are produced and how those depictions are understood by audiences so as to perpetuate or to oppose the power of certain dominant economic institutions such as government.

The problem of cultural studies examines more closely the relation among media, other institutions, and the ideology of culture. Cultural theorists are interested in how the dominant ideology of a culture subverts other ideologies through social institutions such as schools, churches, and the media. Both traditions are centrally concerned with the evils of class society and the struggles that occur among the different social forces. Both emphasize the ways in which social structures are produced and reproduced again and again in the actual daily activities of individuals, groups, and institutions.

Critical theorists view their task to be the uncovering of oppressive forces in society through dialectical analysis, which is designed to expose an underlying struggle between opposing forces.[26] The population generally perceives a kind of surface order to things, and the critical theorist's job is to point out the contradictions that exist. Only by becoming aware of the dialectic of opposing forces in a struggle for power can individuals be liberated and free to change the existing order. Otherwise, they will remain alienated from one another and from society as a whole.

Neo-Marxism places great emphasis on the means of communication in society. Communication practices are an outcome of the tension between individual creativity in framing messages and the social constraints on that creativity. Only when individuals are truly free to express themselves with clarity and reason will liberation occur, and that condition cannot come about in a class society. On the other hand, many critical theorists believe that contradiction, tension, and conflict are inevitable aspects of the social order and can never be eliminated. The ideal state is a social environment in which all voices can be heard so that no force dominates any other.

25. Lawrence Grossberg, "Strategies of Marxist Cultural Interpretation," *Critical Studies in Mass Communication* 1 (1984): 392–421.

26. See, for example, Robert Pryor, "On the Method of Critical Theory and Its Implications for a Critical Theory of Communication," in *Phenomenology in Rhetoric and Communication*, ed. S. Deetz (Washington, D.C.: Center for Advanced Research in Phenomenology/University Press of America, 1981), pp. 25–35; Jennifer Daryl Slack and Martin Allor, "The Political and Epistemological Constituents of Critical Communication Research," *Journal of Communication* 33 (1983): 128–218; Dallas W. Smythe and Tran Van Dinh, "On Critical and Administrative Research: A New Critical Analysis," *Journal of Communication* 33 (1983): 117–127; Everett M. Rogers, "The Empirical and the Critical Schools of Communication Research," in *Communication Yearbook 5*, ed. M. Burgoon (New Brunswick, N.J.: Transaction Books, 1982), pp. 125–144.

One of the chief constraints on individual expression is language itself. A class society is dominated by a language that makes it very difficult for working-class groups to understand their situation and to get out of it. It is a language that defines and perpetuates the domination of certain groups over others. It is the job of the critical theorist to create new forms of language that will enable the predominant ideology to be exposed and competing ideologies to be heard. This line of thought is obviously consistent with feminist views on language.

An *ideology* is a set of ideas that structure a group's notions of reality, a system of representations or a code of meanings governing how individuals and groups see the world.[27] In classical Marxism an ideology is a false set of ideas perpetuated by the dominant political force. For the classical Marxist, science must be used to discover truth and to overcome the *false consciousness* of ideology. Today, neo-Marxists tend to believe that there is no single dominant ideology but that the dominant classes in society are themselves constituted by a struggle among several. Many current thinkers reject the idea that an ideology is an isolated element in the social system; rather, it is deeply embedded in language and all other social and cultural processes.

Perhaps the most well-known ideology theorist is the French Marxist Louis Althusser.[28] For Althusser, ideology is present in the structure of society itself and arises from the actual practices undertaken by institutions within society. As such, ideology actually forms the individual's consciousness and creates the person's subjective understanding of experience. In this model the superstructure (social organization) creates ideology, which in turn affects individuals' notions of reality. This superstructure consists of *repressive state apparatuses* such as the police and the military and *ideological state apparatuses* such as education, religion, and mass media. The repressive mechanisms enforce an ideology when it is threatened by deviant action, and the ideological apparatuses reproduce it more subtly in everyday activities of communication by making an ideology seem normal.

We live within a real set of conditions, but we normally do not understand our relationship to actual conditions except through an ideology. The real conditions of existence can only be discovered through science, which Althusser poses in opposition to ideology. This idea has been highly controversial because it is based on a realist notion of truth, which much critical theory now opposes.

Most critical theories see society as the ground for a struggle among interests through the domination of one ideology over another. *Hegemony* is a process of domination, in which one set of ideas subverts or co-opts another. It is a process by which one group in society exerts leadership over all others. The concept was perhaps best elaborated by the Italian Marxist Antonio Gramsci.[29]

The process of hegemony can occur in many ways and in many settings. In essence, it happens when events or texts are interpreted in a way that promotes the interests of one group over those of another. This can be a subtle process of co-opting the interests of a subordinate group into supporting those of a dominant one. For example, advertisers often play into the "women's lib" theme, making it look as though the corporation supports women's rights. What is happening here is that women's interests are being reinterpreted to promote the interests of the capital economy. Ideology plays a central role in this process because it structures the way in which people understand their experience, and it is therefore powerful in shaping how they will interpret events.

27. For a brief discussion of theories of ideology, see Stuart Hall, "Ideology," in *International Encyclopedia of Communications*, vol. 2, eds. E. Barnouw et al. (New York: Oxford University Press, 1989), pp. 307–311.

28. Louis Althusser, *For Marx*, trans. B. Brewster (New York: Vintage Books, 1970); *Lenin and Philosophy*, trans. B. Brewster (New York: Monthly Review Press, 1971). Althusser's work is summarized by Stuart Hall, "Signification, Representation, Ideology: Althusser and the Post-Structuralist Debates," *Critical Studies in Mass Communication* 2 (1985): 91–114; Dennis K. Mumby, *Communication and Power in Organizations: Discourse, Ideology, and Domination* (Norwood, N.J.: Ablex, 1988), pp. 74–78.

29. Antonio Gramsci, *Selections from the Prison Notebooks*, trans. Q. Hoare and G. Nowell Smith (New York: International, 1971).

Dennis Mumby has presented a persuasive theory of hegemony within organizations that illustrates this process very well.[30] Mumby shows how organizations are sites in which hegemonic struggles occur. Power is established within an organization by the domination of one ideology over others. We saw in the previous chapter that communication in organizations functions in part to create an organizational culture. This occurs through rituals, stories, and the like, and Mumby shows how the culture of an organization is an inherently political process. Communication within the organization serves not only to establish meaning but also to create power and domination.

One way in which this happens is through story telling, or the use of narrative. Narratives are texts to be interpreted, and ideologies are created and perpetuated by particular interpretations of narrative texts. For example, Mumby discusses one story that was repeatedly retold among employees at IBM in which the chairman of the board was stopped by a 22-year-old female security guard because he did not have the appropriate badge to enter the area she was guarding. As the story goes, the chairman quietly secured the proper badge and got entry.[31] The story is remarkable only because of the power and status difference between these two individuals. The acceptance of the premises of the story lead to the uncritical acceptance of the power of management and owners to set rules that promote their own interests. The story also perpetuates status difference and gender-role expectations in the company. This process of domination is repeated again and again through communication in organizations and other settings in society.

The Frankfurt School and Universal Pragmatics

One of the longest and most well-known Marxist traditions is the Frankfurt School. The *Frankfurt School* is such an important tradition in critical

studies that it is often known simply as *Critical Theory*. These theorists originally based their ideas on Marxist thought, although it has gone far afield from that origin in the past 50 years, and communication takes a central place in this movement. Systems of mass communication have been an especially important focus in this work.

This brand of critical theory began with the work of Max Horkheimer, Theodor Adorno, Herbert Marcuse, and their colleagues at the Frankfurt Institute for Social Research in 1923.[32] The group was originally guided by Marxist principles, although they were never members of any political party, and their work was distinctly scholarly rather than activist. With the rise of National Socialism in Germany in the 1930s, the Frankfurt scholars immigrated to the United States and there became intensely interested in mass communication and the media as structures of oppression in capitalistic societies.

The early Frankfurt scholars reacted strongly to the classical ideals of Marxism and the success of the Russian revolution. They saw capitalism as an evolutary stage in the development, first, of socialism and then communism. Their ideas at that time formed a harsh critique of capitalism and liberal democracy. Since the early years of the Frankfurt School, however, there is no agreed-on unified theory that characterizes its members. The most well-known contemporary Frankfurt scholar is Jürgen Habermas, whose theory of universal pragmatics and the transformation of society has had considerable influence in Europe and an increasing influence in the United States. Habermas is clearly the most important spokesperson for the Frankfurt School today.[33] His theory draws from a wide range

30. Dennis K. Mumby, "The Political Function of Narrative in Organizations," *Communication Monographs* 54 (1987): 113–127; Mumby, *Communication and Power.*

31. Mumby, "Political Function," pp. 120–125; *Communication and Power*, pp. 115–124.

32. For a brief historical perspective, see Thomas B. Farrell and James A. Aune, "Critical Theory and Communication: A Selective Literature Review," *Quarterly Journal of Speech* 65 (1979): 93–120. See also Andrew Arato and Eike Gebhardt (eds.), *The Essential Frankfurt School Reader* (New York: Continuum, 1982).

33. The important works of Habermas include *Knowledge and Human Interests*, trans. J. J. Shapiro (Boston: Beacon Press, 1971); *Legitimation Crisis*, trans. T. McCarthy (Boston: Beacon Press, 1975); *The Theory of Communicative Action, Volume I: Reason and the Rationalization of Society*, trans. T. McCarthy

of thought and presents a coherent critical view of communication and society. We turn now to a closer look at the work of this man.

Habermas teaches that society must be understood as a mix of three major interests: work, interaction, and power. All three interests are necessary and inseparable from the human condition.

Work consists of the efforts to create necessary material resources. Because of its highly instrumental nature—achieving tangible tasks and accomplishing concrete objectives—this is basically a "technical interest." It involves an instrumental rationality and is represented by the empirical-analytical sciences. In other words, technology is used as an instrument to accomplish practical results and is informed by scientific research and development. It designs computers, builds bridges, puts satellites in orbit, administers organizations, and enables wonderous medical diagnoses.

The second major interest is *interaction*, or the use of language and other symbol systems for communication. Because social cooperation is necessary for survival, Habermas names this second item the "practical interest." It involves practical reasoning and is represented in historical scholarship and hermeneutics. The interaction interest can be seen in speeches, conferences, psychotherapy, family relations, and a host of other cooperative endeavors.

The third major interest is *power*. Social order naturally leads to power distribution; yet, a natural interest in being freed from the domination also comes from the application of power. Power leads to distorted communication, but by becoming aware of the ideologies that dominate in society, groups can themselves be empowered to transform society. Consequently, power is an "emancipatory

interest." The rationality of power is self-reflection, and the branch of scholarship that deals with it is critical theory. For Habermas, the kind of work done by the critical theorists discussed thus far in this chapter is emancipatory because it can empower otherwise powerless groups.

As an example of these interests at work, consider the study by Steven Ealy of a Georgia State job-classification survey in the 1970s.[34] At that time Georgia was strapped with the responsibility of reclassifying 45,000 state-job positions, a monumental task; according to Ealy, the result was a serious communication breakdown. The state employed a consulting firm to conduct the necessary survey, and a plan was drafted to collect information about each position, develop job specifications, classify the positions, and then assign compensation levels for the various positions.

A strong technical interest guided the reclassification study. There was a job to be done, and the consultants developed a method to achieve this goal. They proceeded as if the task could be solved by the use of "objective" or scientific procedures—gathering data, classifying jobs, and the like. The employees and the departments, however, did not think of the study in this way. They saw the study as a practical problem, one that affected their daily work and pay. For the departments, collecting data and implementing the results should have involved a good deal of interaction and consensus building. Immediately, then, there was a clash of interests.

Because they held the power, the organizational decision makers' technical interests prevailed, the consultants' methods were imposed, and all practical interests were eliminated. In other words, the employees were expected simply to comply with the survey without much discussion about their needs and the practical problems such as operational difficulties, management problems, and moral questions of reclassification might create. In short, the participants were unequal in power and knowledge, and the interests of workers were sub-

(Boston: Beacon Press, 1984). An excellent secondary summary can be found in Sonja K. Foss, Karen A. Foss, and Robert Trapp, *Contemporary Perspectives on Rhetoric* (Prospect Heights, Ill.: Waveland Press, 1991), pp. 241–272; see also Sue Curry Jansen, "Power and Knowledge: Toward a New Critical Synthesis," *Journal of Communcation* 33 (1983): 342–354; Mumby, *Communication and Power*, pp. 23–54; Richard L. Lanigan, *Phenomenology of Communication: Merleau-Ponty's Thematics in Communicology and Semiology* (Pittsburgh: Duquesne University Press, 1988), pp. 75–99.

34. Steven D. Ealy, *Communication, Speech, and Politics: Habermas and Political Analysis* (Washington, D.C.: University Press of America, 1981).

verted by those of management. The study lacked the kind of open communication that Habermas says is necessary in a free society. As a result the new classification system was not accepted by employees and was implemented only partially after many delays, new studies, lawsuits, and appeals.

As this case illustrates, human life cannot be properly conducted from the perspective of only one interest—work, interaction, or power. No single activity is entirely within any one of these but includes some combination of them. All three are necessary for a complete understanding of society. For example, the development of a new drug is a clear reflection of a technical interest, but it cannot be done without cooperation and communication, requiring an interaction interest as well. Within a market economy, the drug is developed by a corporation to gain a competitive advantage, which is clearly a power interest. If the Georgia merit-system managers had realized this, they could have prevented the reclassification fiasco.

The case also illustrates that no aspect of life is interest-free, even science. An emancipated society is free from unnecessary domination of any one interest, and everybody has equal opportunity to participate in decision making. Habermas believes that a strong public sphere, apart from private interests, is necessary to ensure this state of affairs.

Habermas is especially concerned with the technical interest's domination in contemporary capitalistic societies.[35] In such societies, the public and private are intertwined to the point that the public sector cannot guard against the oppression of private, technical interests, as the Georgia case illustrates. Ideally, the public and private should be balanced, and the public sector should be strong enough to provide a climate for free expression of ideas and debate. With the rise of private technocracy, however, that climate is stifled.

It is clear from the foregoing discussion that Habermas values communication as essential to emancipation. Language itself is central to human life, and language becomes the means by which the

emancipatory interest is fulfilled. Communicative competence is therefore necessary for effective participation in decision making. Competence involves knowing how to use speech appropriately to accomplish goals. This means communicating in such a way that your propositions are compelling to an audience and adapting your speech so that the listeners understand your intention.

Habermas's approach to communication is largely a reconstruction of speech act theory, which is summarized in Chapter 5. Habermas refers to his theory of speech acts as *universal pragmatics*, or the universal principles of the use of language. He outlines three types of speech acts. *Constatives*, or assertions, are designed to get across a proposition as true. For example, if you were involved in a labor–management dispute, you might accuse the union of engaging in unfair labor practices.

Regulatives are intended to affect one's relationship with another person or party through influence. Commands and promises are examples. In the labor–management example, your statement about unfair labor practices would be regulative if it were intended to bring the union to the bargaining table. Here, your purpose is to influence the other party in some way, to regulate their behavior, specifically, to initiate negotiations.

Finally, *avowals* are designed to express the speaker's internal condition, to affirm something about oneself. In labor–management negotiations, for example, participants often express anger over the other party's activities. Notice that any message you might present could embody any combination of these speech acts because you can achieve a number of intentions at once. So, for example, you might make an angry statement about unfair union practices. Your statement is an avowal because it expresses your internal condition (anger); it is a regulative because it is designed to get negotiations underway; and it is a constative because you are trying to prove the truth of your statement.

The nature of a speech act determines the kind of validity that one must meet in a statement. In a constative speech act, one must demonstrate the truth of the claim. In a regulative speech act, one must meet standards of appropriateness. And an

---

35. See especially, Habermas, *Legitimation Crisis*.

avowal must be sincere or truthful. Because a single speech act may fulfill any of the three types, various combinations of validity forms may also have to be met. For example, to meet all three validity requirements, your statement about union practices must be taken as true (that the union is indeed engaged in certain practices), as appropriate (that under the circumstances, bargaining is proper), and as sincere (that you are truly angry over the situation).

These validity claims are not always easy to secure. People do not always believe that one's statements are valid, and in the labor–management case, you might have some difficulty proving your case. We saw just this state of affairs in the Georgia reclassification case. Here, the management's validity claims about the new system were severely challenged in the form of objections, lawsuits, and individual appeals.

Habermas uses the term *discourse* to describe the special communicative action required when a speaker's statements are challenged. Unlike normal communication, discourse is systematic argumentation designed to bring special appeals to bear to demonstrate the validity of the statement. Truth claims are argued with *theoretic discourse*, which emphasizes evidence. For example, if the union denied your allegations of improper conduct, you would be pressed to make a case by using theoretic discourse. You would do this by expanding your argument to include evidence showing that the union did, indeed, participate in certain activities.

When appropriateness is being argued, *practical discourse*, which emphasizes norms, is used. If the union resisted your attempts to begin bargaining, you would have to create practical discourse to demonstrate the appropriateness of negotiations. Challenges to one's sincerity also require special action to demonstrate genuine concern, but this is usually direct action rather than discourse.

Of course, there is no guarantee that the union would agree with your evidence or the norms used to appeal for bargaining. Where communicators do not share the same standards or conceptual framework for evaluating the strength of an argument, they must move to a higher level of discourse,

which Habermas calls *metatheoretical discourse*. Here, communicators argue about what constitutes good evidence for a claim or what norms are indeed appropriate in the given situation.

There is even one higher level of discourse that is sometimes necessary—*metaethical discourse*. Here, the very nature of knowledge itself is under contention and must be argued. Such discourse is a philosophical argument about what constitutes proper knowledge. This is precisely what critical theory does, for it challenges the assumed procedures for generating knowledge in society.

Habermas believes that free speech is necessary for productive normal communication and higher levels of discourse to take place. Although impossible to achieve, Habermas describes the *ideal speech situation* on which society should be modeled. First, the ideal speech situation requires freedom of speech; there must be *no* constraints on what can be expressed. Second, all individuals must have equal access to speaking. In other words, all speakers are recognized as legitimate. Finally, the norms and obligations of society are not one-sided but distribute power equally to all strata in society. Only when these requirements are met can completely emancipatory communication take place.

Empancipatory communication in the form of higher levels of discourse is essential to transform society so that the needs of the individual can be met. Habermas believes that people normally live in an unquestioned *life-world*. The life-world is the ordinary, daily activities of people, and ordinary communication takes place within this realm. The life-world, however, is constrained by certain elements of the social system such as money, bureaucracy, and corporate power. We see here shades of Althusserian ideology in Habermas's theory—the idea that the superstructure creates an ideology that affects the ordinary understanding of citizens in their everyday lives. Habermas frames this problem as *colonization*, or the power of the system over individuals. When the life-world is colonized by the system, there is less opportunity to use language to achieve positive goals for individuals.

Here is where critical theory comes in. The primary function of critical theory is to raise questions and create problems about the life-world that make critical reflection and resolution necessary. Only when we are aware of the problems of our life-world and the ways in which the system influences our view of life can we become emancipated from the entanglements of the system. There is more opportunity to accomplish emancipation in modern society than in traditional society because of the relatively greater amount of conflict in modernity. In modernity we have the opportunity to hear a variety of viewpoints if the system will allow free expression. Modern capitalistic societies have not yet achieved emancipation, and critical theorists have a responsibility to work toward increasing freedom of higher levels of discourse to make this possible.

Cultural Studies

Another branch of Marxist theory is cultural studies, which involves the examination of the ways in which culture is produced through a struggle among ideologies. The most notable group of cultural scholars, British Cultural Studies, is associated with the Centre for Contemporary Cultural Studies at the University of Birmingham. The origins of this tradition are usually traced to the writings of Richard Hoggart and Raymond Williams in the 1950s, which examined the British working class after World War II.[36] Today, the leader of the movement is Stuart Hall.[37]

The cultural studies tradition is distinctly reformist in orientation. These scholars want to see

changes in Western society, and they view their scholarship as an instrument of socialist cultural struggle. They believe that such change will occur in two ways: (1) by identifying contradictions in society, the resolution of which will lead to change, and (2) by providing interpretations that will help people understand domination and the kinds of change that would be desirable. Samuel Becker describes this goal as follows: ". . . these communication scholars want to keep jarring both the audience and the workers in the media back from becoming too accepting of their illusions or existing practices so they will question them and their conditions."[38]

The study of mass communication is central to this work, for the media are perceived as powerful tools of the dominant ideology. In addition, they have the potential of raising the consciousness of the population about issues of class, power, and domination. We must be cautious in interpreting cultural studies in this light, however, because media in this tradition are part of a much larger set of institutional forces. Media are important, but they are not the sole concern of these scholars, which is why they refer to their field as "cultural studies" rather than "media studies."

What is meant by *culture* here? The answer to this question is in dispute, but essentially two meanings, which go back to Williams's writings, are implied. The first meaning of culture is the common ideas on which a society or group rest. It is collective ways in which the group understands its experience. The second meaning is the practices or the entire way of life of a group, what individuals do materially from day to day. These two senses of the word *culture* should not be separated. One contribution of the cultural studies program is to have us see how the ideology of a group is produced and reproduced in its practices. In fact, the general concern of cultural theorists is the link between the actions of societies' institutions such as the media and the culture. Indeed, texts as artifacts of a "culture" are not the culture itself, for practices and ideas must always be interpreted in light of the his-

36. Richard Hoggart, *Uses of Literacy* (London: Chatto & Windus, 1957); Raymond Williams, *The Long Revolution* (New York: Columbia University Press, 1961).

37. For a good survey of the work of Hall and others at the Centre, see Stuart Hall et al. (eds.), *Culture, Media, Language* (London: Hutchinson, 1981). See also, Stuart Hall, "Cultural Studies: Two Paradigms," in *Media, Culture and Society: A Critical Reader*, ed. R. Collins (London: Sage, 1986); and Hall, "Signification." Two secondary treatments were especially helpful: Samuel L. Becker, "Marxist Approaches to Media Studies: The British Experience," *Critical Studies in Mass Communication* 1 (1984): 66–80; Robert White, "Mass Communication and Culture: Transition to a New Paradigm," *Journal of Communication* 33 (1983): 279–301; and Ronald Lembo and Kenneth H. Tucker, "Culture, Television, and Opposition: Rethinking Cultural Studies," *Critical Studies in Mass Communication* 7 (1990): 97–116.

38. Becker, "Marxist," p. 67.

torical context in which they occur. For this reason, the cultural studies tradition is considered to be firmly materialist.

For example, one thing many people do everyday in society is watch television. The entire television industry is a cultural production because it is a means for creating, disputing, reproducing, and changing culture. The concrete or material practices involved in producing and consuming television is a crucial mechanism in the establishment of ideology.

Cultural theory posits that capitalistic societies are dominated by a particular ideology of the elite. For the workers of society, the dominant ideology is a false ideology because it does not reflect their interests. Instead, the dominant ideology is involved in a hegemony against that of powerless groups. Hegemony, however, is always a fluid process, what Hall calls a temporary state in a "theatre of struggle." We must therefore "think of societies as complex formations, necessarily contradictory, always historically specific."[39] In other words, the struggle between contradictory ideologies is constantly changing.

Social institutions like education, religion, and government are interlinked in ways that support the dominant ideology, making resistance difficult. Especially important is the link between infrastructure and superstructure. *Infrastructure* is sometimes referred to as the base, the basic economic resources and systems of a society, including buildings, monetary system, capital, machinery, and so on. The *superstructure* consists of societal institutions. The exact relationship between infrastructure and superstructure is in dispute. Early Marxist theory taught that the infrastructure (economic resource base) determined superstructure.[40] In cultural studies the relationship is believed to be more complex. The forces of society are considered to be overdetermined or caused by multiple sources.

Infrastructure and superstructure may therefore be mutually interdependent. Because of the complexity of causation in society, no one set of conditions is required for a particular outcome to occur.

The same is true of ideology. Multiple ideologies exist next to one another in dynamic tension. Hall puts the matter this way: "The important thing about systems of representation is that they are not singular . . . . As you enter an ideological field and pick out any one nodal representation or idea, you immediately trigger off a whole chain of connotative associations. Ideological representations connote—summon—one another."[41]

Communication, especially through the media, has a special role in affecting popular culture through the dissemination of information. The media are extremely important because they directly present a way of viewing reality. The media portray ideology explicitly and directly. This does not mean that opposing forces are silenced. Indeed, opposing voices will always be present as part of the dialectical struggle between groups in a society. But the media are dominated by the prevailing ideology, and they therefore treat opposing views from within the frame of the dominant ideology, which has the effect of discounting opposing groups as fringe elements. The irony of media, especially television, is that they present the illusion of diversity and objectivity, when in fact they are clear instruments of the dominant order.

Producers control the content of media by particular ways of encoding messages. As Becker describes the process,

> Events do not signify . . . to be intelligible events must be put into symbolic form . . . the communicator has a choice of codes or sets of symbols. The one chosen affects the meaning of the events for receivers. Since every language—every symbol—coincides with an ideology, the choice of a set of symbols is, whether conscious or not, the choice of an ideology.[42]

For example, advertisers carefully design television commercials to create a certain image and thereby sell the product. Other kinds of program-

---

39. Hall, "Cultural Studies," p. 36.

40. This problem and other issues facing the cultural studies program are discussed in Stuart Hall, "Cultural Studies and the Centre: Some Problematics and Problems," in *Culture, Media, Language*, eds. S. Hall et al. (London: Hutchinson, 1981), pp. 15–47.

41. Hall, "Signification," p. 104.

42. Becker, "Marxist," p. 72.

ming such as news and comedy may seem less ideological, but they are every bit as much so.

At the same time, however, audiences may use their own categories to decode the message, and they often reinterpret media messages in ways never intended by the source. As a result of alternative meanings, oppositional ideologies can and do arise in society. The intended meaning of a commercial may be completely lost on certain parts of the audience that interpret it in quite different ways. For example, an advertiser may use sex appeal for men, but feminist viewers may see the image as demeaning to women.

For Hall and his colleagues, the interpretation of media texts always occurs within a struggle for ideological control. Ronald Lembo and Kenneth Tucker describe the process as "a competitive arena where individuals or groups express opposing interests and battle for cultural power."[43] Rap music is a good example of this struggle. Does it reflect the genuine values and interests of the black youth culture, or is it a sign of the degeneration of society? The answer depends on which interpretive community is asked.

Hall is especially interested in the different situations in which decoding is consistent with and reproduces encoded ideology, decoding is inconsistent with the encoding and thereby resists ideology, and a negotiation between the decoding and encoding in which new meaning is created. The chief interest of cultural studies is to expose the ways in which the dominant class privileges certain interpretations of texts over others and the ways in which groups can resist these dominant interpretations. This kind of ideological resistance is encouraged by cultural studies because it empowers marginalized groups.

Usually in capitalistic societies, the ideology of dominate classes is perpetuated because of the infusion of the ideology in many realms of life. The audience is literally set up to read media texts in particular ways because of what they have learned in school, church, work, and throughout the cul-

ture. When the ideologies of powerful groups are accepted by members of the public as natural and true without question, those ideologies will prevail and the existing structure of power will remain in place. When oppositional meanings are given attention, new ideologies may arise, and a new, hopefully healthier distribution of power will result.

This process of domination by powerful groups may appear very much like a conspiracy, but Becker says that it is not:

> As far as I can see, no British scholar perceives the role of the media in the reproduction of the conditions of capitalistic production to be the result of a plot by capitalists or by the ruling classes. . . . They perceive, rather, that the medium's reflection of that ideology is a natural consequence of the system by which the medium operates and the larger system in which that operation takes place.[44]

The chief aim of cultural studies, then, is to expose the ways in which ideologies of powerful groups are perpetuated and the ways in which they can be resisted to disrupt the system of power that disfranchises certain groups.

Lawrence Grossberg's study of rock music is an especially interesting illustration of how cultural scholars work. In an his essay on the subject, he discusses a sweeping range of issues related to the meaning of rock and roll in contemporary culture, the role of punk, and the place of youth in society.[45] For Grossberg, rock and roll is an "apparatus" of culture, a disparate movement that is unified by the feeling it engenders among its fans. Like any cultural text, there is no privileged reading of it. Rock and roll of all types elicits a plethora of meanings in its various audiences and can be used for a variety of purposes. As such then, rock music has a strong potential for becoming oppositional. Grossberg points to the following evidence of rock and roll's oppositional nature:

> Rock and roll has, repeatedly and continuously, been attacked, banned, ridiculed and relegated to an

43. Lembo and Tucker, "Culture, Television, and Opposition," p. 100.

44. Becker, "Marxist," p. 71.

45. Lawrence Grossberg, "Is There Rock After Punk?" *Critical Studies in Mass Communication* 3 (1986): 50–73.

insignificant cultural status. The fact that so much effort has been brought to bear in the attempt to silence it, makes it reasonable to assume that some struggle is going on, some opposition is being voiced.[46]

Three characteristics demarcate rock and roll. First, it is associated with a particular group of fans, marking these individuals as somehow different from all others. Second, the music is involved in the everyday lives of its listeners and is part of the larger context of their lives. It is involved with numerous other social and cultural practices. Third, the entire rock apparatus provides intense pleasure to its fans, a pleasure of bodily sensation and emotional feeling. In short, it transforms the everyday lives of its fans: "The rock and roll apparatus is a kind of machine which, like a cookie cutter constantly changing its shape, produces or imprints a structure on the fans' desires and relations by organizing the material pieces of their lives."[47]

The primary way in which rock and roll is oppositional is that it gives character to the youth culture as being different from "straight" and "boring." If the predominant hegemonic ideology after World War II included a kind of serious depth, purpose, and order, rock music opposes this by concentrating on surface, style, and artifice: "The rock and roll apparatus not only energizes new possibilities within everyday life, it places that energy at the center of a life without meaning."[48] Grossberg identifies this primary oppositional character as the "attitude" of rock and roll.

Grossberg believes that the advent of punk had profound affect on the role of rock music as an oppositional force. Punk itself seems to say that anything goes and that nothing matters. It "deconstructed" all forms, including traditional rock and roll. As such punk itself became an oppositional force. Punk along with a host of other social and cultural factors have led to a deconstruction of the youth culture, which had been the the chief source of meaning for rock and roll among its fans: "Punk

attacked rock and roll for having grown old and fat, for having lost that which puts it in touch with its audience and outside of the hegemonic reality."[49] Grossberg is confident that youth is currently under reconstruction, but he is uncertain how.

Most of the work in critical studies has been applied to mass media of communication. The reason is clear: Media are powerful instruments of ideology in society. However, as the rock-and-roll case illustrates, the Marxist approach need not be limited to applications in media. Indeed, any aspect of social structure can be examined in this way.

Commentary and Critique

We have looked at two important areas of critical theory in this chapter—feminist and Marxist. Both explicitly display a set of values in the active attempt to raise consciousness and thereby empower people to resist dominant and oppressive ideological forces.

Feminist theory places the blame for the oppression of women on the patriarchy. Masculine values are believed to permeate society and govern all power centers, thus marginalizing the experience of women. This reasoning is not unlike that of the original Frankfurt School, which viewed capitalistic society as dominated by a singular hegemonic interest, the political economy. Although the reasoning used by the Frankfurt scholars and feminists is similar, their explanatory variables are different, and the Marxists would say that class, not gender, is the genesis of oppression.

The cultural studies tradition takes a more complex view. These scholars do not see any single set of ideas as perpetually dominant. Although various interests may dominate at any particular time and certain classes of people are almost always marginalized in this process, the field of ideological struggle is constantly in flux. This thesis is essentially a rejection of feminism's gender base. For the cultural

46. Ibid., p. 53.
47. Ibid., p. 55.
48. Ibid., p. 57.

49. Ibid., p. 62.

scholar, gender would be just one of many elements of society in dynamic tension with all others.

Feminist theory revolves around the conceptual division of masculine and feminine, but critics question the very utility of this dualism.[50] Although the masculine-feminine distinction has been useful, it may have oversimplified the situation and created a conceptualization that does not accurately reflect reality. Such labeling may, in fact, reify or reinforce distinctions that feminists themselves are trying to overcome. Linda Putnam states the point in these terms: "The problem of reification, the use of feminist labels has the double-edged effect of recognizing women while simultaneously isolating them."[51] And again, "Efforts to degenderize behaviors have the potential to liberate us from sex-role classifications that emanate from dualism."[52] The answer, according to Putnam, is not to abandon feminist theory or feminist ideals but to look at the process of communication differently. Instead of simply assuming that gender is the cause of other effects, we should also examine the ways in which communication patterns have led to gender distinctions themselves. If the cultural studies scholars are right, gender itself may be a construction of an ideology into which feminists themselves have been co-opted. This accusation is certainly relevant to liberal feminism, but less so to radical feminism.

Almost all versions of feminist and Marxist theory see the answer to domination and oppression as consciousness raising and empowerment. For the feminists, when women become conscious of their own oppression, they are empowered to create a reality of their own that gives voice to their interests. For contemporary Marxists, consciousness leads to the ability to create oppositional understandings that change the field of conflict in ways that promote a different, hopefully healthier, set of values in society. A common theme that seems to run through all critical theories, then, is giving voice to oppressed groups. The thesis of Habermas's work, for example, is precisely this: to create an ideal speech community in which all interests have an equal chance of being heard.

In Chapter 2 we discussed the value dimension of theory. The value issue can be stated in two ways, depending on whose perspective you take. From the perspective of traditional science, the issue is whether the theory contains value statements. From the perspective of critical theory, the issue is whether the theorist is conscious of inevitable values present in all theories.

The theories discussed in this chapter are unabashedly value-laden. Critical theorists would say that scholarship in other areas contain values as well but are dangerous because they do not recognize or acknowledge their interests. Critical studies therefore have a strange relationship with many of the other theories presented in this book. On the one hand, critical theories borrow liberally from relevant concepts of other theories, such as structuralism, interpretation, and social construction. On the other hand, they also constitute an oppositional critique of many of these other traditions. Critical theories represent a double critique, of society and of traditional social science. In a way, this is really the same critique because traditional social science is an institution within society that perpetuates its dominant interests.

Political scientist Paul Lazarsfeld was perhaps the first to label these two theoretical camps as administrative and critical.[53] *Administrative research* is designed to aid the administration of public and private programs, and *critical research* is designed to oppose and resist the administration of power in society. For critical theorists today, all research that is not critical is administrative because it automatically serves administrative interests.[54]

50. Linda L. Putnam, "In Search of Gender: A Critique of Communication and Sex-Roles Research," *Women's Studies in Communication* 5 (1982): 1–9.

51. Ibid., p. 4. See also, Julia T. Wood and W. Barnett Pearce, "Sexists, Racists, and Other Classes of Classifiers: Form and Function of 'ist' Accusations," *Quarterly Journal of Speech* 66 (1980): 239–250.

52. Putnam, "Search," p. 7.

53. Paul Lazarsfeld, "Remarks on Administrative and Critical Communications Research," *Studies in Philosophy and Social Science* 9 (1941): 2–16.

54. This division is amply discussed in the special edition of *Journal of Communication* entitled "Ferment in the Field," 33 (Summer 1983).

It is not surprising, then, to find a sharp line, even animosity, between theorists of traditional social science and those of the critical theory tradition. Critical theorists accuse traditionalists of conserving centers of power, of being naively oblivious to the ways in which their work perpetuates hegemonic interests, and of possessing a stubborn adherence to the belief in a realist epistemology.

Traditional social scientists are no less harsh in their criticisms of critical theories. They accuse their critical colleagues of rationalizing ideas without data, of pushing a narrow and ill-informed agenda, and of operating on the basis of a head-in-the-clouds utopianism. Television researcher James Lull comments: "Marxist and neo-Marxist criticism in particular now sound more like an echo in the hallway than a leading theoretical perspective."[55]

Jay Blumler summarizes the chief objections against critical theory.[56] First, even if media institutions should become more egalitarian, the critical approach does not provide sufficient guidance on how this is to be done: "But the critical paradigm, as so far enunciated, lacks a clarity of ethic and realism of political diagnosis that, when drawn on and applied, could help communication institutions to realize a vision of human beings as active, choosing, purposeful subjects."[57]

Second, the movement has a "self-defeating tendency to utopianism."[58] In other words, these theories downplay the realities of political life that require democracy, and they ignore the fact that media are required for democracy to work. Indeed, Marxist approaches are inherently antidemocratic: ". . . the critical perspective tends to slam shut, instead of prying open, doors of possible improvement in the contributions of journalism to democracy."[59]

Finally, administrative researchers deplore Marxist antipathy toward behavioral and social research. The Marxist claims are suspect because they are not supported by the kind of data traditional researchers find credible.

There are, of course, many differences among the various versions of feminist and Marxist theory. In a way this suits critical theory as a body of scholarship very well because of the common belief in the existence of contradiction. Society itself is filled with contradiction, so why should a body of theory be any different? In fact, one of the chief claims of critical theory is that we must be willing to acknowledge the presence of contradiction and learn to deal with it productively.

The problem for critical theory is determining where it stands in the absence of a unifying thesis. Feminism is an excellent case in point. On the one hand, feminists seem to be asking for equal rights for women, a public acknowledgment that women have the same qualities and powers as men and can perform as well in all walks of life. On the other hand, they also seem to be saying that women are different from men and that their powers and forms of expression should be valued in their own right. On one level of analysis, it may be that these are merely different brands of feminist theory. On another level these two theses, both of which seem to have validity, form a true paradox. For women to be valued and to have equal rights, the powers of the feminine must be acknowledged; but highlighting the powers of the feminine reinforces the patriarchal view that women have their place.

Similar contradictions can be found in Marxist thought as well. For example, even cultural studies scholars talk of domination and oppression, yet they see society as a constantly changing field of ideological struggle. At what point can you say that there is a dominant ideology, when no singular ideology can be found?

A contradiction common to almost all critical theories, certainly the ones in vogue today, is the one between their truth claims about the structure of society and their criticism of mainstream social science for making truth claims of their own. If social reality is indeed constructed, then is not the critical theorist simply constructing a useful reality

55. James Lull, "The Audience as Nuisance," *Critical Studies in Mass Communication* 5 (1988): 239.

56. Jay Blumler, "Communication and Democracy: The Crisis Beyond and the Ferment Within," *Journal of Communication* 33 (1983): 166–173. See also Michael Real, "The Debate on Critical Theory and the Study of Communications," *Journal of Communication* 34 (Autumn 1984): 72–80.

57. Blumer, "Communication," p. 168.

58. Ibid., p. 168.

59. Ibid., p. 169.

rather than making a valid truth claim? In other words, there seems to be some confusion in critical theory about whether theory is based on a structuralist or constructionist epistemology.

In the previous chapter, we noted the conflict between interpretive and critical theory on the issue of tradition. Critical theorists like Habermas accuse interpretive theorists such as Hans-Georg Gadamer of being too conservative. Indeed, the project of interpretation is to describe meaning structures, in texts and in social relations. Critical theory, on the other hand, is inherently radical. It aims to change the basis of society and is impatient with the conservative moves commonly found in phenomenology. This controversy raises the question of critical theory's relation to tradition.

Interpretivists like Gadamer revere tradition and accuse critical theory of trying to tear down the very history from which it can never escape. Interpretivists seek ways to uncover meanings and to overcome misunderstandings so that traditions can speak to us in positive ways, and they object to critical theorists' claims that such misunderstandings are systematic distortions by powerful groups. Finally, from their position of dialogue, interpretivists object to critical theorists' call for ideal communication designed to rescue society from its iniquities.[60] Instead, they believe, language and communication as naturally given in everyday life constitute a positive voice that should be heard. Gadamer says that you cannot remove yourself from tradition, that any intellectual project is always a part of a tradition that shapes its perspectives and values.

Two related issues are suggested by Gadamer's point. First, what is the cultural tradition from which critical theory arises, and how does this influence the truth claims being made by this movement? If critical theory is a soundly Eurocentric enterprise, how relevant is it to the dynamics of cultures other than Western societies? Second,

how do critical theorists get out of an ideology long enough to make judgments about ideology? Early Marxism had an easy answer; they deferred to science as nonideological.

Latter-day Marxists, however, are skeptical of this solution because they do not see science as interest free. Science itself promotes particular ideologies. The most promising resolution of this dilemma is that of Hall and his colleagues who claim that there will always be competing ideas and the aim of cultural studies is to expose the struggle, not to suggest a permanent solution. Cultural studies seem more interested in promoting oppositional readings of texts rather than pointing to any one ideology that should be overcome.

Paul Ricoeur crystallizes the perspectives of interpretive theory and critical theory in these terms:

> What is at stake can be expressed in terms of an alternative: either a hermeneutical consciousness or a critical consciousness. . . . In contrast to the positive assessment of hermeneutics, the theory of ideology adopts a suspicious approach, seeing tradition as merely the systematically distorted expression of communication under unacknowledged conditions of violence.[61]

Ricoeur himself argues for a "zone of intersection which . . . ought to become the point of departure for a new phase of hermeneutics."[62] Ricoeur believes that through distanciation (Chapter 10), one can understand texts in a way that reveals the limits of context. Once it is freed from situation and author, text provides insights into the problems of historical circumstances. In addition, when disembodied texts speak to us, they reveal our own limits and the limits of our own times. Such textual interpretation also opens up possibilities for new ways of being in the future. For Ricoeur then, interpretive theory and critical theory are not very far apart.

There is in cultural studies, as in all critical theory, confusion about the power of groups and indi-

60. The primary opponents in this debate have been Gadamer and Habermas. The debate is summarized by Paul Ricoeur, *Hermeneutics and the Human Sciences: Essays on Language, Action and Interpretation*, trans. and ed. J. B. Thompson (Cambridge, Eng.: Cambridge University Press, 1981), pp. 64–80.

61. Ibid., p. 64.
62. Ibid., p. 79.

viduals to accomplish opposition. At times cultural studies seems to view society as a complex machine in which ideologies are constantly in conflict. Other times they seem to want to give power to individuals to create oppositional readings to media texts, to take action to overcome hegemonic forces.

This is the old issue of the power of the subject. How much power do individuals have to use and assign meaning to messages? Are the minds of individuals shaped by social structure and language, or can individuals create their own structures and languages to meet their own ends? Feminist language theories such as that of Penelope waffle on this issue. If women are oppressed by patriarchal language, how can they find the power to overcome it?

In many ways the answers to these questions depend on the site of meaning. How is meaning established? If meaning comes prepackaged in language, as many feminists and Marxists suggest that it is, then the individual is left powerless to struggle against it. On the other hand, if meaning is constructed in social interaction, as other feminists and Marxists suggest that it is, then individuals do have some power to create new realities. This issue brings us full circle back to the question of a structural versus constructional epistemology. The interest of critical theory in creating social change requires a constructionist version of society, but the need for critical theory to prove conditions requiring change requires a structuralist one. This may be the ultimate contradiction of critical theory.

Contextual Themes

CHAPTER 12

Communication in Relationships

Communication always occurs in context. Four main contextual levels were described in Chapter 1: interpersonal communication, group communication, organizational communication, and mass communication. These contexts form a hierarchy in which each higher level includes the lower levels but adds something new of its own. For example, mass communication is a distinctive context, but it includes many of the features of interpersonal, group, and organizational communication.

In this part of the book, we explore a variety of themes related to these contexts. Each theme was chosen because of its centrality to one of the contexts and its importance in communication theory. Specifically, four themes are addressed—relationships, decision making, networks, and media. This chapter deals with communication in relationships, which has been a central concern in the study of interpersonal communication.[1] The chap-

ter is divided into three sections. The first deals with the theoretical foundations of relational communication, the second addresses relational dissolution, and the third applies relational themes to a variety of relational contexts.

Relational Communication

Relationships are based not only on the exchange of information but also on interpersonal perceptions. A relationship is defined not so much by what is said as by the partners' expectations for behavior. This idea lies at the heart of most relational communication theories, and we explore it in more detail here.

Relational Perception

Relationship is largely a matter of perception. The expectations that form a relationship are the

---

1. Interpersonal communication has been explored in some detail in the first three editions of this book, *Theories of Human Communication* (Columbus, Ohio: Merrill, 1978); (Belmont, Calif.: Wadsorth, 1983, 1989). See also, Sarah Trenholm and Arthur Jensen, *Interpersonal Communication* (Belmont, Calif.: Wadsworth, 1988), p. 29. Definitional issues of interpersonal communication are thoroughly explored by Joseph N. Cappella,

"Interpersonal Communication: Definitions and Fundamental Questions," in *Handbook of Communication Science*, eds. C. R. Berger and S. H. Chaffee (Newbury Park, Calif.: Sage, 1987), pp. 184–238.

product of our perceptions of other people's behavior and of their feelings. An important foundational theory in the relational communication tradition is that of psychiatrist R. D. Laing.[2] Laing's thesis is that a person's communicative behavior is largely shaped by his or her perception of the relationship with the other communicator.

Laing makes a distinction between experience and behavior. *Behavior,* which is the observable actions of another, is public; *experience* is private. Experience is the feeling that accompanies behavior or the perception of another's behavior. It consists of imagination, perception, and memory. We can imagine the future; we can perceive the present; we can recall the past. Such experiences are internal in the individual and not directly accessible to anyone else.

Although behavior can be observed, another person's experience cannot. Inferring experience from behavior is the heart of communication, but doing this is difficult, as Laing points out: "I see you, and you see me. I experience you, and you experience me. I see your behavior. You see my behavior. But I do not and never have and never will see your experience of me."[3] As implied in this quotation, experience is a personal matter, but experience is also affected by relations with others and how one perceives or experiences others. How we behave toward another person is a function of two related experiences, the experience of the other person and the experience of the relationship.

A person interacting with another has two levels of experience or perception, which Laing calls *perspectives.*[4] You can experience other persons in a *direct perspective* as you observe and interpret their behavior. You also experience the experience of other people when you assign meaning to what you imagine they are thinking and feeling. Laing calls this a *metaperspective,* and it involves imagining or inferring what the other person is feeling, perceiving, or thinking. Laing describes the process:

> I cannot avoid trying to understand your experience, because although I do not experience your experience, which is invisible to me (and nontastable, nontouchable, nonsmellable, and inaudible), yet I experience you as experiencing. I do not experience your experience. But I experience you experiencing. I experience myself as experienced by you. And I experience you as experiencing yourself as experienced by me. And so on.[5]

To use Laing's favorite characters, Jack perceives certain behaviors of Jill (direct perspective). He also infers or imagines Jill's perceptions (metaperspective). A relationship then is defined by the communicator's direct perspectives and metaperspectives. Theoretically, metaperception can proceed indefinitely through higher levels: Jack loves Jill; Jack thinks Jill loves him; Jack thinks that Jill thinks that he loves her; and so on. Further, because experience affects behavior, one often behaves in accordance with his or her metaperspectives. If Jack thinks Jill thinks he does not love her, he may try to change Jill's imagined perception. So metaperception is how communicators believe others see them.

Of course, metaperspectives may or may not be accurate, and the health of a relationship is greatly determined by perceptual accuracy. Three concepts are pertinent at this point. *Understanding* is the agreement or conjunction between Jack's metaperspective and Jill's direct perspective. If Jack correctly infers that Jill loves him, understanding results. *Being understood* is the inverse. It is the conjunction of Jack's meta-metaperspective and Jill's metaperspective. If Jack correctly infers that Jill believes Jack loves her, he is understood. But being understood is not the same as *feeling understood.* The latter is defined as the conjunction between Jack's direct perspective and his own metaperspective. If Jack infers that Jill believes he loves her, and he does, then he feels understood.

2. Laing's works most concerned with communication include *The Politics of Experience* (New York: Pantheon Books, 1967); *Self and Others* (London: Tavistock, 1969); and R. D. Laing, H. Phillipson, and A. R. Lee, *Interpersonal Perception* (New York: Springer, 1966).

3. Laing, *Politics,* p. 4.

4. Laing, Phillipson, and Lee, *Interpersonal.*

5. Laing, *Politics,* p. 5.

Because communicators attempt to behave in ways that they believe will affect others, *spirals* can develop wherein each person acts toward the other in such a way that particular metaperspectives such as mistrust become accentuated. The idea of spiral has been important for Laing as a psychiatrist because it explains various pathological relationships. For example, Jack, as a paranoid, mistrusts Jill. He does not believe she loves him. He then accuses her of having affairs with other men. Jill, in her metaperception of Jack's mistrust, attempts to prove her love. Jack sees this attempt as covering up her lack of love and accuses her of being a liar. The spiral will continue until the relationship is destroyed.

This is an example of a *unilateral spiral*, as Jack's mistrust of Jill becomes more and more accentuated. A *bilateral spiral* occurs when both parties move toward increasingly extreme metaperceptions. For example, Jack believes Jill wants too much from him and thinks she is greedy. At the same time Jill sees Jack as selfish. In other words, both feel the other is withholding what he or she needs. Because both parties feel misunderstood, they retaliate, causing their metaperceptions of greed and selfishness to increase. Such spirals need to be broken, or the relationship will be destroyed.

Laing's theory shows us the importance of perception in a relationship. We turn now to a theory that discusses the ways in which communication affects perception.

The Palo Alto Group

Most relationship theorists acknowledge the importance of the early work of Gregory Bateson, Paul Watzlawick, and their colleagues to our understanding of relationships. Bateson was briefly covered in Chapter 3, where we saw that his ideas about metacommunication have been highly formative in our field.

Bateson's early followers were known as the Palo Alto Group because they founded and worked at the Mental Research Institute based in Palo Alto, California. Their ideas are most clearly layed out in *Pragmatics of Human Communication*, now a clas-

sic.[6] In the book Paul Watzlawick, Janet Beavin, and Don Jackson present a well-known analysis of communication based on system principles. (A *system* is defined as a set of objects that interrelates with one another to form a unique whole.) Relationships are an important part of a system, and in defining interaction, the authors stress this idea: "Interactional systems then, shall be *two or more communicants in the process of, or at the level of, defining the nature of their relationship.*"[7]

Relationships result from interaction. People set up interaction rules, which govern their communicative behaviors. By obeying the rules, behaving appropriately, the participants sanction the defined relationship. In a marriage, for example, a dominance–submission relationship may emerge and be reinforced by implicit rules. The husband may send messages of command, which are followed by compliance by the wife, or vice versa. A status relationship in an organization may be observed in a subordinate's pausing at the supervisor's door to await an invitation to enter. Such implicit rules are numerous in any ongoing relationship, be it a friendship, business relationship, love affair, family, or any other type of relationship.

Watzlawick, Beavin, and Jackson present five basic axioms about communication. First, "one cannot not communicate."[8] This axiom has been quoted again and again in textbooks on communication. Its point is important, for the axiom emphasizes that the very attempt to avoid interaction is itself a kind of action. It also emphasizes that any perceivable behavior is potentially communicative.[9]

6. Paul Watzlawick, Janet Beavin, and Don Jackson, *Pragmatics of Human Communication: A Study of Interactional Patterns, Pathologies, and Paradoxes* (New York: Norton, 1967).

7. Ibid., pp. 120–121.

8. Ibid., p. 51.

9. This axiom has been challenged by Michael Motley, "On Whether One Can(not) Not Communicate: An Examination Via Traditional Communication Postulates," *Western Journal of Speech Communication* 54 (1990): 1–20. See also, "Forum: Can One Not Communicate?" *Western Journal of Speech Communication* 54 (1990): 593–623, which includes responses to the Motley article by Janet Beavin Bavelas and Wayne Beach and a rejoinder by Michael Motley. This exchange has important implications for the definition of communication.

Second, the authors postulate that "every communication has a content and a relationship aspect such that the latter classifies the former and is therefore metacommunication."[10] Here, we see the influence of Bateson's ideas about levels of communication. When communicating, we not only convey content but also signal perceptions of the relationship. When two people are talking, each is relating information to the other, and simultaneously each is also "commenting" on the information at a higher level. This simultaneous relationship talk, which often is nonverbal, is what is meant by *metacommunication*.

For example, on the content level, a teacher may tell you that a test will be given the next day. Many possible relationship messages may accompany this basic content message. The instructor may be making any of the following impressions: I am the authority in this classroom; I teach, you learn; What I have lectured about is important; I need feedback on your progress; I have a need to judge you; I want you to think I am fulfilling my role as professor; and so on. Of course, the students' responses also include a relationship dimension, which might express compliance, defiance, respect, fear, equality, or any of a number of other possible metamessages. In communicating about tests and all other topics, the teacher and student constantly define and redefine the nature of their relationship.

Note the connection between this axiom and Laing's ideas on perception. What a person says, the content of the message, can be directly observed, but more subtle aspects of the relationship arise from inferences that people make and expectations they communicate on the metaperceptual level.

Judee Burgoon and her colleagues have done research to discover the dimensions of this relational level of communication.[11] They conducted a

10. Watzlawick, Beavin, and Jackson, *Pragmatics*, p. 54.

11. Judee K. Burgoon and Jerold L. Hale, "The Fundamental Topoi of Relational Communication," *Communication Monographs* 51 (1984): 193–214; Judee K. Burgoon, David B. Buller, Jerold L. Hale, and Mark A. deTurck, "Relational Messages Associated with Nonverbal Behaviors," *Human Communication Research* 10 (1984): 351–378.

huge survey of the interpersonal communication literature to find possible elements of relational communication and isolated twelve common aspects of relationships that seem to be communicated. Relying on Aristotle's term for basic topics of communication, the theorists labeled these *fundamental topoi of relational communication*. They include varying levels dominance, intimacy, affection, involvement, inclusion, trust, superficiality, emotional arousal, composure, similarity, formality, and orientation toward task or social elements of the relationship. These topics were further narrowed into four basic, independent dimensions of relational communication:

1. Emotional arousal, composure, and formality
2. Intimacy and similarity
3. Immediacy (liking)
4. Dominance-submission

For example, in announcing an examination, the professor might communicate a sense prerogative with her formal role (dimension 1), distance from the student (dimension 2), neutrality toward individual students (dimension 3), and dominance (dimension 4). A student's questions about the exam could reflect anxiety (dimension 1), distance from the professor (dimension 2), dislike of the professor (dimension 3), and acceptance of her right to administer the exam (dimension 4). Another professor and student might have a very different relationship, which would be reflected in a very different set of messages on the same four dimensions.

Research shows that these four dimensions seem to characterize much relational communication. This important work tells us the kinds of perceptions that people get from the relationship messages of others. Burgoon and her associates further studied the question of how nonverbal behaviors specifically affect these perceptions, and some interesting results emerged. Four behaviors seem especially important in the relationship message. Proximity can be significant in communicating intimacy, attraction, trust, caring, dominance, persuasiveness, and aggressiveness. Smiling seems especially important in communicating emotional arousal, composure, and formality, as well as intimacy and liking. Touching, too, communicates intimacy. Eye contact is like an exclamation point in intensifying the effect of other nonverbal behaviors. It takes little imagination to see the nonverbal gestures used by the professor and student in the above example.

Watzlawick, Beavin, and Jackson's third axiom of communication deals with the *punctuation* of communication sequences. Interaction sequences, like sentences, cannot be understood as a string of isolated elements. To make sense they must be punctuated or grouped syntactically. In raw form an interaction consists of a move by one individual followed by moves from others. The objective observer would see a series of behaviors, or what Laing calls "direct perspective." Like the series of sounds in a sentence, however, these behaviors are not simply a chain. Certain behaviors are perceived to be a response to other behaviors. Behaviors are thus grouped or punctuated into larger units, which in the whole help define the meaning of the entire set of actions. This grouping is largely a matter of perception, or what Laing refers to as "experiencing" another's behavior.

Any given string of behaviors might be punctuated in various ways. One source of difficulty among communicators occurs when they punctuate differently. For example, consider a marriage involving nagging by the husband and withdrawing by the wife. This sequence can be punctuated in two ways. On the one hand, the wife's withdrawing may be a response to the husband's nagging: nag-withdraw, nag-withdraw. On the other hand, the opposite may be occurring: withdraw-nag, withdraw-nag. In the first case, the punctuation of nag-withdraw implies an attack–retreat relationship, but the husband's punctuation of withdraw-nag implies ignoring-imploring. It is all in the eye of the beholder.

The fourth axiom is that "human beings communicate both digitally and analogically," which implies two types of coding used in interpersonal communication.[12]

12. Watzlawick, Beavin, and Jackson, *Pragmatics*, p. 67. For a more detailed discussion of coding, see Chapter 4.

Digital coding is arbitrary. The sign and the referent, though associated, have no intrinsic relation to each other. The relationship between the sign and the referent is strictly imputed. The designation of a large black animal with claws wandering around the woods as a *bear* is entirely arbitrary. Second, the digital signs are discrete; they are "on" or "off," uttered or not uttered. You either say *bear*, or you do not; you can't say it partially. The most common digital code in human communication is language. Sounds, words, and phrases are digital signs that are arranged syntactically to communicate meanings. Certain nonverbal signs, especially discrete gestures like the victory sign or the "finger," are also digital.

The *analogic code* is different from the digital. First, an analogic sign is not arbitrary. Either it resembles the significate (as in the case of a photograph), or it is intrinsic to the thing being signified (as in the case of crying). Second, an analogue is often continuous rather than discrete; it has degrees of intensity or longevity. Most nonverbal signs are analogic. For example, a facial expression of surprise is not only a sign of a feeling or condition but is also actually part of the surprise itself. Its meaning is intrinsic, and the facial expression is not an either-or sign but is a continuous variable between no expression and extreme facial distortion.

Although the digital and analogic codes are different from each other, they are used together and cannot be separated in ongoing communication. For example, a digital word can be uttered in a variety of analogic ways (loud, soft; high, low; etc.). Similarly, a written message consisting of digital letters and words is presented on paper using various layouts, styles of handwriting or print, and other analogic codes.

Within the stream of behaviors in interaction, both digital and analogic coding blend. The theorists believe that they serve different functions. Digital signs, having relatively precise meanings, communicate the content dimension, whereas the analogic code—which is rich in feeling and connotation—is the vehicle for relationship messages. So while people are communicating content digitally, they are commenting about their relationship analogically. This idea is certainly consistent with Burgoon's research on the relational dimensions of nonverbal communication.

Suppose a father at a playground sees his daughter fall and scrape her knee. Immediately, he says, "Don't cry. Daddy is coming." The content meaning is clear. The child receives a message stating that her father is going to come to her. Imagine the large number of relationship messages that might be sent analogically with body and voice. The father might communicate his own fear, worry, anger, boredom, or dominance. At the same time, he might communicate a number of possible perceptions of his little girl, including "careless person," "attention getter," "injured child," "provoker," and so on. When it comes to relationships then, actions do speak louder than words.

The final axiom of communication deals with symmetrical and complementary interaction. When two communicators in a relationship behave similarly, the relationship is said to be *symmetrical;* differences are minimized. When communicator differences are maximized, however, a *complementary* relationship is said to exist.

In a marriage when two partners both vie for power, they are involved in a symmetrical relationship. Similarly, co-workers are communicating symmetrically when each wants the other one to tell him or her what to do. A complementary marital relationship would exist when the wife is domineering, and the husband responds submissively. In the work setting, a complementary relationship would exist when the boss gives orders, and the employee is happy to follow them.

The variable most often examined in regard to complementary and symmetrical relationships is *control.* To explore this idea, let us look at the work of Edna Rogers and Frank Millar. These investigators have been researching relational communication since the 1970s. Their work remains one of the most cogent and valuable statements about relational communication, and it provides a concrete extension of the work of the Palo Alto Group.[13] Although Millar and Rogers have discussed various dimensions of relationships, including trust and intimacy, most of their research has centered on control.

Control cannot be defined by examining a single message. Rather, one must look at the pattern of messages and responses over time. In other words, when one person makes a statement, another person's response defines a moment in the relationship. Consider the relationship between Bob and Mel. If Bob makes an assertive comment and Mel responds in a way that also asserts control, then Mel's response is said to be *one-up.* Making a one-up move is said to be *domineering.* On the other hand, if Mel responds in a way that accepts Bob's assertion of control, his message is *one-down.* If Mel's response neither asserts control nor relinquishes it, the message is *one-across.*

A complementary exchange occurs when one partner asserts a one-up message and the other responds one-down. When this kind of interaction predominates in a relationship, we can say that the relationship itself is complementary. The individual whose one-up message predominates at a given time is said to be *dominant.* Notice the difference here between dominance and domineeringness. A one-up move is domineering, but it is not dominant unless the other person accepts it. It is very possible for a person to be domineering without being dominant because the partner does not accept this control move.

A symmetrical exchange involves both partners presenting one-up or one-down messages, and a symmetrical relationship is marked by a preponderance of such exchanges. *Competitive symmetry* is the case of two people in a power struggle, each trying to assert control over the other. Here is a case of both partners being domineering and neither dominant. A third state, *transition,* exists when the partners' responses are different (e.g., one-up/one-

13. Although this work is explained in several sources, perhaps the most complete theoretical treatment is Frank E. Millar and L. Edna Rogers, "A Relational Approach to Interpersonal Communication," in *Explorations in Interpersonal Communication,* ed. G. R. Miller (Beverly Hills, Calif.: Sage, 1976), pp. 87–105. See also "Power Dynamics in Marital Relationships," in *Perspectives on Marital Interaction,* eds. P. Noller and M. Fitzpatrick (Clevedon, Eng.: Multilingual Matters, 1988), pp. 78–97; "Relational Dimensions of Interpersonal Dynamics," in *Interpersonal Processes: New Directions in Communication Research,* eds. M. E. Roloff and G. R. Miller (Newbury Park, Calif.: Sage, 1987), pp. 117–139.

across) but not opposite. Table 12.1 illustrates nine control states generated by combinations of these types of control messages.[14]

Control consists of two dimensions in a relationship. The first variable of control is the *rigid-flexible* dimension. The more flexible the relationship, the more control passes back-and-forth between the two parties. *Stability-instability* relates to the predictability of the control shifts. The more consis-

14. Millar and Rogers, "Relational Approach," p. 97.

tent the pattern of control over time, the more stable the control. One couple, for example, could have a very rigid relationship such that the husband is always dominant and the wife always submissive. Another couple might be quite flexible, so that the wife is sometimes dominant and the husband is sometimes so. Similarly, a stable relationship is one in which the husband is predictably dominant when it comes to the car, vacations, and the yard, and the wife is dominant when it comes to the house, family, and the social calendar. An

---

Table 12.1 Control Configurations

Control direction of speaker A's message	Control direction of speaker B's message		
	One-up (↑)	One-down (↓)	One-across (→)
One-up (↑)	1. (↑↑) Competitive symmetry	4. (↑↓) Complementarity	7. (↑→) Transition
One-down (↓)	2. (↓↑) Complementarity	5. (↓↓) Submissive symmetry	8. (↓→) Transition
One-across (→)	3. (→↑) Transition	6. (→↓) Transition	9. (→→) Neutralized symmetry

Control Pattern Examples

1. Competitive symmetry (one-up/one-up):
   A: You know I want you to keep the house picked up during the day.
   B: I want you to help sometimes.

2. Complementarity (one-down/one-up):
   A: Please help. I need you.
   B: Sure, I know how.

3. Transition (one-across/one-up):
   A: Let's compromise.
   B: No, my way is best.

4. Complementarity (one-up/one-down):
   A: Let's get out of town this weekend.
   B: Okay.

5. Submissive symmetry (one-down/one-down):
   A: I'm so tired. What should we do?
   B: I can't decide. You decide.

6. Transition (one-across/one-down):
   A: My Dad was pretty talkative tonight.
   B: You're right; he sure was.

7. Transition (one-up/one-across):
   A: I definitely think we should have more kids.
   B: Lots of people seem to be having kids these days.

8. Transition (one-down/one-across):
   A: Please help me. What can I do?
   B: I don't know.

9. Neutralized symmetry (one-across/one-across):
   A: The neighbor's house needs paint.
   B: The windows are dirty too.

unstable relationship is one in which you never know from day to day who will assert control on which issues.

Millar and Rogers believe that dominance and domineeringness are not very closely related. To find out whether this is true, they had forty-five married couples tape-record lengthy conversations on a variety of topics.[15] Using interaction analysis, they found little correlation between these two variables. It was clear from the study that, at least among these couples, a high level of domineeringness did not lead to a high level of dominance. In other words, one-up moves are not necessarily greeted by one-down moves. They also found that marital satisfaction was less in couples in which the wife was domineering and that satisfaction was higher in cases where the husband was dominant. This pattern may have something to do with the way in which one-up messages were delivered and the amount of support provided by the domineering partner.

The work of Rogers and Millar is consistent with system theory discussed in Chapter 3. Recall that an important systems tradition in the communication field involves the study of interaction, in which behaviors are analyzed only in relation to other behaviors. The interactional tradition includes research on small-group decision making, organizational networks, and even societal networks (see Chapter 3). The point is that the interaction–relationship tradition has been powerful not only in shaping thinking about the interpersonal context but also in all other contexts.

The Development of Relationships

Much has been written about relational development and dissolution, and it is clear that communication is a vital aspect in the initiation, growth, and decline of all kinds of relationships. In this section we discuss a number of communication theories related to these concerns.

Information and Uncertainty in Relationships

Information is a central part of all developing relationships. We seek information about other people, especially in the beginning of a relationship, and we give information about ourselves. An important aspect of relational communication therefore involves the exchange of personal information. An important theory on this subject is uncertainty reduction theory.

Uncertainty reduction theory is the brainchild of Charles Berger and his colleagues.[16] It deals primarily with the ways in which individuals come to know themselves and others in interaction.

The theory has two major concerns—self-awareness and knowledge of others. From research in social psychology, Berger observes that *self-awareness* varies from person to person and from situation to situation.[17] In *objective self-awareness*, the person centers on the self rather than other objects in the environment. *Subjective self-awareness*, on the other hand, puts the self in a peripheral position so that it blends into the momentary stream of experience. Research indicates that objective self-awareness is common because we are often required to concentrate on ourselves in various situations, but it tends to be an uncomfortable state. Although an individual's self-awareness will vary from

15. L. Edna Rogers-Millar and Frank E. Millar, "Domineeringness and Dominance: A Transactional View," *Human Communication Research* 5 (1979): 238–246.

16. The theory is clearly summarized in Charles R. Berger and James J. Bradac, *Language and Social Knowledge: Uncertainty in Interpersonal Relations* (London: Arnold, 1982). See also C. R. Berger and R. J. Calabrese, "Some Explorations in Initial Interaction and Beyond: Toward a Developmental Theory of Interpersonal Communication," *Human Communication Research* 1 (1975): 99–112; C. R. Berger, R. R. Gardner, M. R. Parks, L. Schulman, and G. R. Miller, "Interpersonal Epistemology and Interpersonal Communication," in *Explorations in Interpersonal Communication*, ed. G. R. Miller (Beverly Hills, Calif.: Sage, 1976), pp. 149–171; and Charles R. Berger and William Douglas, "Thought and Talk: 'Excuse Me, but Have I Been Talking to Myself?'" in *Human Communication Theory*, ed. F. E. X. Dance (New York: Harper & Row, 1982), pp. 42–60.

17. For more information on self-awareness, see, for example, S. Duval and R. A. Wicklund, *A Theory of Objective Self-Awareness* (New York: Academic Press, 1972).

moment to moment, each person has a relatively enduring norm of self-awareness. Some individuals are often or always self-aware, whereas others are rarely or never so.

The enduring trait of being objectively self-aware is *self-consciousness*, and this characteristic is dominated by a tendency to *self-monitor*, or "watch yourself." High self-monitors are guarded and careful about the impression they give to others. They are highly sensitive to the feedback of other people and try to adapt their behaviors to suit other people. Low self-monitors tend to be less sensitive to themselves or to others and are less concerned with making impressions. Whereas high self-monitors tend to be actors, low self-monitors tend to "tell it like it is."

When we encounter a stranger, we may have a strong desire to reduce uncertainty about that person by gaining information. Berger proposes that people have a difficult time with uncertainty, that they want to be able to predict behavior, and that they are therefore motivated to seek information about other people. Indeed, this kind of uncertainty reduction is one of the primary dimensions of a developing relationship.

Often, the normal behavior of the other person immediately reduces our uncertainty, greatly lessening the desire to get additional information. This is especially true when our involvement with the other person is limited to a particular situation and we have all the information we need to understand their behavior in this situation. For example, when you call a plumber, you probably feel you know all you need to know about him to discuss your plumbing problem.

However, under certain circumstances, the need to know more about a person is heightened. Such circumstances include abnormal behavior on the part of the other person, the expectation that we will be communicating with the other person in the future, or the prospect that the encounter will be especially rewarding or costly. Under these conditions, we will probably take action to get more information about the other person. For example, if a plumber noticed that you had a "Room for Rent" sign in your window and said she was interested in finding a new place to live, you would sud-denly have a great deal of interest in getting more information about her.

Berger believes that uncertainty is an extremely important variable in the development of relationships. So in initial interactions, people will talk a lot to get more information, and as uncertainty is eliminated, questioning and other information-seeking strategies will decline. This is not to say that people talk less after uncertainty is reduced, however, because the opposite is often the case. People may talk more after they get to know each other. Indeed, Berger believes that the level of intimacy definitely increases after uncertainty is reduced. This may be because liking is related to uncertainty: The less uncertain you are about someone, the more you tend to like him, other things being equal.

How, then, do you go about getting such information about others? Berger suggests a variety of strategies. *Passive strategies* are observational, whereas *active* ones require the observer to do something to get the information. A third class of strategies is *interactive* in that it relies directly on communication with the other person.

The first passive strategy is *reactivity search* in which the individual is observed actually doing something—reacting in some situation. For example, if you were interested in someone in a class, you would probably observe this person discreetly for a period of time. One of the most obvious things you would see would be the way in which he or she reacted to events in the class—questions from the instructor, class discussions, and so forth. Observers generally prefer to see how a person reacts when communicating with another person, so you would listen in on conversations this person was having with other people in class.

Disinhibition searching is another passive strategy in which people are observed in informal situations where they are less likely to be self-monitoring and are therefore behaving in a more natural way. You might therefore be especially interested in observing your classmate outside of class in settings such as the cafeteria or dormitory.

Active strategies of information involve asking others about the target person and manipulating the environment in ways that set up the target person for observation. You might, for example, maneuver to get assigned to a project group with the classmate you are interested in getting to know. *Interactive strategies* include interrogation and self-disclosure. Self-disclosure, which is discussed in more detail later, is a significant strategy for obtaining information because if you disclose something about yourself, the other person is likely to disclose in return. Once in the project group, you could actually talk to this other person, ask questions, and make disclosures about yourself.

To discover the ways in which strangers get information about one another, Charles Berger and Kathy Kellermann videotaped about fifty conversations in their laboratory.[18] The couples varied in terms of how much information they were told to get. Some participants were told privately to get as much information about the other person as possible, others were told to get as little as possible, and a third group was not given any instructions about how much information to get. Also, the dyads themselves were mixed, so that some consisted of couples in which both had been asked to get a great deal of information, some consisted of couples in which both had been asked to get little information, and some included one person from each category.

The videotaped conversations were coded by judges in a variety of ways. Chiefly, the researchers were interested in finding out what the communicators actually did to get or to resist getting information. Predictably, the most common strategy for getting information was to ask questions, but some other strategies were also used, such as putting the other person at ease so that they would feel comfortable talking and self-disclosure designed to elicit disclosure from the other person. Even the low-information seekers used questions, which shows how important questions are in structuring conversations, but their questions tended to be innocuous inquiries into the weather and other noninformative topics.

Individuals who were trying to get a great deal of

information asked significantly more questions than the low-information subjects. Those who were not given any instructions asked about the same number of questions as those who were told to get a great deal of information, which suggests that we normally tend to ask many questions when talking with strangers. This hypothesis is supported because the low-information seekers in this experiment had a harder time than did the high-information seekers and normal subjects. As expected, high-information seekers asked more open-ended questions and more questions that required an explanation than did low-information seekers.

William Gudykunst has done extensive research on the cross-cultural dimensions of uncertainty reduction, and he has found that whereas all cultures seek to reduce uncertainty in the initial stages of a relationship, they do so in different ways.[19] The key seems to be whether one is a member of a high-context culture or a low-context culture.[20] *High-context cultures* rely heavily on overall context to interpret events, whereas *low-context cultures* rely more on the explicit verbal content of messages to tell them what is going on. Members of high-context cultures are therefore more apt to rely on nonverbal cues and information about a person's background to reduce uncertainty, whereas members of low-context cultures are more apt to ask specific questions related to experience, attitudes, and beliefs.

The process of uncertainty reduction between people from different cultures is affected by additional variables. When you strongly identify with your own cultural group and you think the other person is typical of a different group, you will probably feel a certain amount of anxiety about interacting with him or her, and your uncertainty will be great. On the other hand, your confidence in

18. Charles R. Berger and Katherine Ann Kellermann, "To Ask or Not to Ask: Is That a Question?" in *Communication Yearbook 7*, ed. R. Bostrom (Beverly Hills, Calif.: Sage, 1983), pp. 342–368.

19. This work is summarized in William B. Gudykunst, "Uncertainty and Anxiety," in *Theories in Intercultural Communication*, ed. Y. Y. Kim and W. B. Gudykunst (Newbury Park, Calif.: Sage, 1988), pp. 123–156; and "Culture and the Development of Interpersonal Relationships," in *Communication Yearbook 12*, ed. J. A. Anderson (Newbury Park, Calif.: Sage, 1989), pp. 315–354.

20. This concept is developed by Edward T. Hall, *Beyond Culture* (New York: Doubleday, 1976).

getting to know the other person and your anxiety about doing so will be less if you expect the results to be positive. Experience and friendships with other people from different cultures may also increase your confidence when meeting a stranger from another group. Knowing the other person's language will also help, as will a certain amount of tolerance for ambiguity. When you are more confident and less anxious about meeting someone from a different group, you will probably do a better job of getting information and reducing uncertainty. Gudykunst continues to investigate a number of possible cultural variables in the uncertainty reduction process.

Berger's theory demonstates the importance of uncertainty and uncertainty reduction in relationships, especially in the initial stages of a relationship. Michael Sunnafrank suggests that the chief reason we seek information is not to reduce uncertainty per se but to assess the potential outcome of the communication. His *predicted-outcome value theory* suggests that people are motivated to reduce uncertainty because they want to know whether continued communication will be positive or negative.[21] So to return to our example of the plumber, the primary reason you would want to know more about this person is not just to reduce uncertainty but to know whether this person would be someone to whom you would want to rent your room. When you receive information that leads you to predict a rewarding outcome, you will probably be more attracted to the other person, and you will probably want to continue the association. On the other hand, if your initial information leads to a negative prediction, you will probably do all you can to decrease information and cut off the relationship.

Personal information exchange in a relationship is a two-sided coin. On the one side is information seeking, and the other is self-disclosure. We learned about the former from uncertainty reduction the-

ory, and we turn now to theories related to the latter.

Self-Disclosure

Disclosure and understanding were important themes in communication theory in the 1960s and early 1970s. Largely as a consequence of the humanistic school in psychology, an ideology of "honest communication" arose, and much of our thinking about what makes good interpersonal communication was affected by this movement. Spurred by the work of Carl Rogers, the so-called Third Force in psychology teaches that the goal of communication is accurate understanding of self and others and that understanding can only happen with genuine communication.[22]

According to humanistic psychology then, interpersonal understanding occurs through self-disclosure, feedback, and sensitivity to the disclosures of others. Misunderstanding and dissatisfaction in relationships are promoted by dishonesty, lack of congruence between one's actions and feelings, poor feedback, and inhibited self-disclosure.

Much self-disclosure research has emerged from this humanistic movement. One theorist who has investigated this process of self-disclosure is Sidney Jourard.[23] Jourard's prescription for the human being is openness or transparency.

Transparency is a two-sided coin. Being transparent means, on one side, allowing the world to disclose itself freely. The other side of the coin is the

21. Michael Sunnafrank, "Predicted Outcome Value During Initial Interactions," *Human Communication Research* 13 (1986): 3–33; "Predicted Outcome Value and Uncertainty Reduction Theories: A Test of Competing Perspectives," *Human Communication Research* 17 (1990): 76–103.

22. For a more complete summary of these theories, see the second edition of this book, *Theories of Human Communication* (Belmont, Calif.: Wadsworth, 1983), pp. 193–199. See also Carl Rogers, *Client-Centered Therapy* (Boston: Houghton Mifflin, 1951); "A Theory of Therapy, Personality, and Interpersonal Relationships, as Developed in the Client-Centered Framework," in *Psychology: A Study of Science*, vol. 3, ed. S. Koch (New York: McGraw-Hill, 1959), pp. 184–256; Abraham Maslow, *The Farther Reaches of Human Nature* (New York: Viking Press, 1971); Joseph R. Royce and Leendert P. Mos (eds.), *Humanistic Psychology: Concepts and Criticisms* (New York: Plenum, 1981); and Joseph Luft, *Of Human Interaction* (Palo Alto, Calif.: National Press Books, 1969).

23. Sidney Jourard, *Disclosing Man to Himself* (New York: Van Nostrand, 1968); *Self-Disclosure: An Experimental Analysis of the Transparent Self* (New York: Wiley, 1971); *The Transparent Self* (New York: Van Nostrand Reinhold, 1971).

person's willingness to disclose oneself to others. Thus, ideal interpersonal relationships require that people allow others to experience them fully and are open to experiencing others fully.

Jourard developed this idea after observing that his patients tended to be closed to the world. He found that they became healthy as a result of their willingness to disclose themselves to the therapist. Thus, Jourard equates sickness with closedness and health with transparency. Jourard sees growth, a person's moving toward new ways of behaving, as a direct result of openness to the world. The sick person is not willing to experience the world in various ways and is therefore fixed or stagnant. The growing person, being transparent, will come to new life positions. Such change is the essence of personal growth.

Personal growth is tied to interpersonal communication because the world is largely social. To accept one's own changes requires verification by being accepted by others. Growth is difficult if others around you are not open to your disclosures of change.

Since Jourard's ideas on self-disclosure were published, he and several others have conducted research that elaborates on the rudimentary notions.[24] Here are some of these research findings in general form:

1. Disclosure increases with increased relational intimacy.

2. Disclosure increases when rewarded.

3. Disclosure increases with the need to reduce uncertainty in a relationship.

4. Disclosure tends to be reciprocal (dyadic effect).

5. Women tend to be higher disclosers than are men.

6. Women disclose more with individuals they like, whereas men disclose more with people they trust.

7. Disclosure is regulated by norms of appropriateness.

8. Attraction is related to positive disclosure but not to negative ones.

9. Positive disclosure is more likely in nonintimate or moderately intimate relationships.

10. Negative disclosure occurs with greater frequency in highly intimate settings than in less intimate ones.

11. Satisfaction and disclosure have a curvilinear relationship; that is, relational satisfaction is greatest at moderate levels of disclosure.

The humanistic psychology movement presents a normative theory of communication. In other words, the theory tells us how we ought to communicate. Consequently, it embodies a very strong ideology of interpersonal relationships. As is always the case with normative theories, one may question the wisdom of the advice embedded in the values of the theory.[25]

The self-disclosure research, despite its ideological leanings, has been a significant and important line of inquiry in communication; but the research has not always supported the values of the original humanistic proponents like Jourard. Arthur Bochner recently reviewed the literature on self-disclosure and made the following qualified conclusions.[26]

First, people think it is appropriate to disclose to others they like; but, second, they overestimate the extent to which they in fact do so. Third, self-disclosure does not necessarily produce liking, and inappropriate disclosure can actually cause negative impressions. Fourth, liking may discourage self-disclosure because people do not want to risk

24. I have relied on the excellent analysis and summary of Shirley J. Gilbert, "Empirical and Theoretical Extensions of Self-Disclosure," in *Explorations in Interpersonal Communication,* ed. G. R. Miller (Beverly Hills, Calif.: Sage, 1976), pp. 197–216. See also P. W. Cozby, "Self-Disclosure: A Literature Review," *Psychological Bulletin* 79 (1973): 73–91.

25. A somewhat lengthy and penetrating critique of this ideology can be found in Malcom R. Parks, "Ideology in Interpersonal Communication: Off the Couch and Into the World," in *Communication Yearbook 5,* ed. M. Burgoon (New Brunswick, N.J.: Transaction Books, 1982), pp. 79–108. See also Daniel E. Berlyne, "Humanistic Psychology as a Protest Movement," in *Humanistic Psychology: Concepts and Criticism,* eds. J. Royce and L. P. Mos (New York: Plenum, 1981), p. 261.

26. Arthur P. Bochner, "The Functions of Human Communicating in Interpersonal Bonding," in *Handbook of Rhetorical and Communication Theory,* eds. C. C. Arnold and J. W. Bowers, (Boston: Allyn and Bacon, 1984), pp. 554–621.

damaging the relationship. The answer, in Bochner's reading, is not the lack of disclosure but thoughtful disclosure because discriminating disclosers seem more satisfied with their relationships than do undiscriminating ones. Bochner summarizes his overall impression from this literature:

> Thus self-disclosure appears to be a highly overrated activity. Perhaps the time has come to lift the fog of ideology surrounding the concept. The fact that there has been only mild, if any opposition to the thesis that openness leads to better and more satisfying relationships suggests that some investigators have been lulled into an uncritical acceptance of an untenable proposition. There is no firm empirical basis for endorsing unconditional openness. A critical evaluation of the evidence suggests at most a restrained attitude toward the efficacy of self-disclosure.[27]

Shirley Gilbert suggests three conditions necessary for Jourard's ideal of transparency to occur in a relationship: The participants must have healthy self-concepts; they must be willing to take relational risks; and they must be committed to unconditional positive regard in the relationship. Gilbert describes intimacy in these terms:

> There are interpersonal price tags attached to intimate relationships. Intimacy, as a dimension of affection, may not be a unidimensional construct. It seems to be comprised of not only feelings (satisfaction) but also commitment (willingness to risk). Intimacy refers not only to the depth of exchange, both verbally and nonverbally, but also to the depth of acceptance or confirmation which characterizes a relationship. Thus, "intimate disclosure" and "intimate relationships" need to be clearly conceptualized and differentiated in future disclosure studies. While disclosure has been established as an index of communicative depth in human relationships, it does not guarantee an intimate relationship.[28]

So far, all theories discussed in this chapter show how important information is in the establishment of a relationship. We constantly monitor information provided by other people and give out information about ourselves. Let us look more closely

now at the ways in which this process affects the development of relationships.

Social Penetration Theory

One of the most widely studied processes of relational development is social penetration. In a nutshell, this is the idea that relationships become more intimate over time when partners disclose more and more information about themselves. *Social penetration* is the process of increasing disclosure and intimacy in a relationship.

Gerald Miller and his colleagues literally define interpersonal communication in terms of penetration.[29] The more communicators know each other as persons, the more of an interpersonal character their communication takes on. The less they know each other as persons, the more impersonal that communication. Interpersonal communication is therefore the very process of social penetration:

> If the communicators continue their relationship—that is, if they are sufficiently motivated to exert the effort to continue it, and if their interpersonal skills are tuned finely enough to permit its growth—their relationship may undergo certain qualitative changes. When such changes accompany relational development, communicative transactions become increasingly interpersonal.[30]

Miller states that people have a natural tendency to predict the outcomes of their actions. In communication such predictions are largely based on the kinds of information they receive from and about other people. Three fundamental kinds of information are used. *Cultural information* is information about a person's most generally shared cultural attributes, including language, shared values, beliefs, and ideologies. If we know a person's culture, we have some information on which to predict how that person will respond in various situa-

---

27. Ibid., p. 608.

28. Gilbert, "Empirical," pp. 212–213.

29. G. R. Miller and M. Steinberg, *Between People: A New Analysis of Interpersonal Communication* (Chicago: Science Research Associates, 1975); G. R. Miller and M. J. Sunnafrank, "All Is for One but One Is Not for All: A Conceptual Perspective of Interpersonal Communication," in *Human Communication Theory: Comparative Essays*, ed. F. E. X. Dance (New York: Harper & Row, 1982), pp. 220–242.

30. Miller and Sunnafrank, "All Is for One," pp. 222–223.

tions like greetings and goodbyes; but cultural information by itself is shallow and impersonal. It assists communicators to perform acceptably in most general social situations but is not very helpful in relationships.

The second kind of information is *sociological.* Beyond cultural norms, sociological information tells us something about people's social groups and roles. You can be successful in communicating with your auto mechanic or dentist because you know something about that person's roles and affiliations, but you still know relatively little about the person as a person. Sociological information is more personal than cultural knowledge but is still abstract and general. Unless you know another person fairly well, however, you must rely heavily on sociological knowledge.

Psychological information is the most specific and intimate of the three. To know a person psychologically is to know individual traits, feelings, attitudes, and other important personal data. It is the most useful type of information in making predictions about how an individual will respond in communication. When one gears communication to psychological information, that communication is truly interpersonal.

Social penetration, in these terms, is the process of moving from cultural interaction to psychological interaction. You might, for example, go on a date with someone you barely know. With cultural information and perhaps a little sociological information, you may see some promise and agree to spend a little time with someone. The more you talk and the more often you see each other, the more sociological, and ultimately psychological, information you exchange with each other. If the relationship continues even for a short time, you will know each other personally.

The most well-known theory of the process of increasing intimacy is that of Irwin Altman and Dalmas Taylor, who coined the phrase "social penetration."[31] According to this theory, as relation-

ships develop, communication moves from relatively shallow, nonintimate levels to deeper, more personal ones. Communicators' personalities can be represented by a sphere with layers; it has both breadth and depth. Breadth is the array or variety of topics that have been incorporated into the individual's life. Depth is the amount of information available on each topic. On the outermost shell are highly visible levels of information, like dress and speech. Inside are increasingly private details about the individual's life, feelings, and thoughts. As the relationship develops, the partners share more aspects of the self, providing breadth as well as depth. Such communication involves exchanging information, exchanging feelings, and sharing activities.

Communication thus proceeds by levels. Once a certain level is reached, under the right conditions the partners share increasing breadth at that level. For example, after dating a few times a couple may begin discussing previous partners, and more and more information about previous partners will be revealed before moving to a still deeper level of disclosure such as sexual history.

Altman and Taylor's theory is based in large part on one of the most popular ideas in social science—social exchange. There are several theories of social exchange, but all are based in one way or another on the idea that relationships are sustained when they are relatively rewarding and discontinued with they are relatively costly.[32] According to Altman and Taylor, during relational development communicators not only assess the rewards and costs of the relationship at that moment but also use the information they have to predict the

31.   Irwin Altman and Dalmas Taylor, *Social Penetration: The Development of Interpersonal Relationships* (New York: Holt, Rinehart & Winston, 1973). For a recent update and summary, see Dalmas A. Taylor and Irwin Altman, "Communication in Interpersonal Relationships: Social Penetration Theory," in *Interpersonal Processes: New Directions in Communication Research*, eds. M. E. Roloff and G. R. Miller (Newbury Park, Calif.: Sage, 1987), pp. 257–277.

32.   An excellent summary of this entire line of work is Michael E. Roloff, *Interpersonal Communication: The Social Exchange Approach* (Beverly Hills, Calif.: Sage, 1981). The most well-known social exchange theory is that of John W. Thibaut and Harold H. Kelley, *The Social Psychology of Groups* (New York: Wiley, 1959); Harold H. Kelley and John, W. Thibaut, *Interpersonal Relations: A Theory of Interdependence* (New York: Wiley, 1978). For a brief summary of the theory, see the third edition of this book, *Theories of Human Communication.*

rewards and costs they think will occur later. If the partners judge that the rewards will be relatively greater than the costs, they will risk more disclosure, which has the potential of moving the participants to a deeper level of intimacy. Therefore, the greater the perceived rewards relative to cost, the more penetration will occur and the greater the rate of penetration. Altman and Taylor found that the most rapid penetration tends to occur in the early stages of development.

There are four stages of relational development. *Orientation* consists of impersonal communication, in which one discloses only very public information about oneself. Miller would call this a sociological stage. If this stage is rewarding to the participants, they will move to the next stage, the *exploratory affective exchange,* in which initial expansion of information and movement to a deeper level of disclosure takes place. The third stage, *affective exchange,* centers on more feelings at a deeper level. Such feelings may be evaluative and critical. The third stage will not be entered unless the partners have perceived substantial rewards relative to costs in earlier stages. Finally, *stable exchange* is highly intimate and allows the partners to predict each other's actions and responses very well. For Miller, this stage is clearly psychological and interpersonal.

Although social penetration is a process of progressing through these stages, it may not happen in a strictly linear fashion; instead, it may occur in a back-and-forth, cyclical fashion. A couple may go in and out of a stage as they test the rewards and costs, they may dwell at a stage for any length of time, or they may move on to the next one.

We saw that Gudykunst and his colleagues have been interested in uncertainty reduction across cultures, an interest that certainly extends to social penetration.[33] Gudykunst and his colleagues have found that, for the most part, these processes seem to be followed in other cultures and in relationships between cultures. There are differences, of course,

especially in the first stages of a relationship; but, in general, as people become friends, cultural differences seem to make less difference.

Where differences exist in social penetration between cultures, they seem to relate to a series of cultural dimensions.[34] Some cultures tend to avoid uncertainty more than others. Some are based more on individualism, whereas others are collectivist, or based on group identification. Some cultures are based on masculine norms and others more on feminine ones. Finally, some cultures make greater power distinctions than do others. You can see how these variables would affect social penetration within these respective culture types. For example, members of a collectivist culture would have more information about and develop relationships with other members of their in-group than with people who affiliate with other groups. That generalization might not hold for individualistic cultures where the qualities of the individual are considered more important than group affiliation.

Altman and Taylor show that relational development does not involve only increasing social penetration. All too often it also involves decreased intimacy, disengagement, and dissolution. Altman and Taylor suggest that as rewards are reduced and costs increased at the more intimate levels of communication, the social penetration process will be reversed. The process of relational dissolution is discussed next.

Relational Dissolution

Several theories of this reverse process have been advanced.[35] We discuss two of these here. The first, a dissolution "map," was developed by Steve Duck. It explains the process by which dissolution is accomplished. The second, based on the work of Leslie Baxter, discusses more directly the ways in which couples actually use communication to accomplish disengagement.

33. For a summary of this work, see Gudykunst, "Culture and Development."

34. G. Hofstede, *Cultures Consequences* (Beverly Hills, Calif.: Sage, 1980).

35. See Steve Duck (ed.), *Personal Relationships 4: Dissolving Personal Relationships* (London: Academic Press, 1982).

Mapping disengagement and dissolution. Steve Duck has proposed a general phase model of relational dissolution.[36] This model is predicated on the assumptions that dissolving a relationship involves complex decisions and that the relationship in the dyad, as well as the relationship with others outside, make such decision making difficult and nonlinear. In other words, the decision to break up occurs sporadically, inconsistently, and ambivalently over a period of time. There may be oscillation between attempts to reconcile and decisions to split. This rocky course is marked by certain thresholds or points of decision that define the boundaries of the stages.

In the *intrapsychic phase,* one focuses on his or her partner and assesses the dissatisfactions in the relationship. At this stage consideration of relationship problems remains pretty much on a private level with little intentional communication about the problems with the partner. In fact, there may actually be a decrease in communication in the relationship during this phase, while the partners seek comforting from others outside the relationship. The disillusioned partner spends time weighing costs and rewards and may decide to communicate explicitly about the relationship. The intrapsychic process involves perception, assessment, and decisionmaking. During this period, one or both partners are trying to figure out what is going on, evaluating the relationship, and making certain private decisions about how to deal with perceived problems.

In the second, *dyadic,* phase, the couple focuses on the relationship together. In this phase communication may be direct and confrontative while relational dynamics are discussed. One is forced to consider not only the partner's unsatisfying traits but also the partner's perspective and its implications for the relationship itself. There is much talk about how to solve the problems, whether to do so, or whether to separate. There may be considerable persuasion and argument during this period, as each partner tries to get the other to comply and change in desirable ways. The dyadic phase may end with a decision to repair the relationship, but if this does not work, the process will continue to the next stage, which is coping socially with the decision to break up.

The *social phase* requires a focus on the larger social group—family, friends, associates, and acquaintances. No relationship stands alone, and a couple do not just stop seeing each other without some impact on other people. At this stage then, the opinions and feelings of others are taken into consideration, and they may well affect what the couple decides to do. Major concerns during this period include what kind of relationship, if any, to continue and how to represent it to other people; to place blame, to save face, to create stories of what happened; and to seek the approval of significant others.

The final stage is called *grave dressing* because it occurs after the breakup has happened. Here, the partners each give their own accounts and in their own ways cope with and recover from the termination of the relationship.

Each phase involves certain communication challenges, which Duck calls "social management problems." In the intrapsychic phase, one must decide how to discuss the perceived problems with his or her partner. In the dyadic phase, the challenge is to negotiate the actual split. In the social phase, the problem involves how to discuss the situation with other people. In the grave-dressing stage, the couple must account for what happened and reach personal resolution.

36. Steve Duck (ed.), "A Topography of Relationship Disengagement and Dissolution," in *Personal Relationships 4: Dissolving Personal Relationships* (London: Academic Press, 1982), pp. 1–30; "How to Lose Friends Without Influencing People," in *Interpersonal Processes: New Directions in Communication Research,* eds. M. E. Roloff and G. R. Miller (Newbury Park, Calif.: Sage, 1987), pp. 278–298.

Strategies of relational disengagement. For several years, Leslie Baxter and her colleagues have conducted research on the disengagement process. These research results form the basis for a theory of the ways in which couples use communication to end relationships.[37] This program addresses three questions:

1. What communication strategies do couples use to break up a relationship?

2. Are the chosen strategies related to characteristics of the individual or the relationship?

3. What is the sequence of the disengagement process?

Baxter found that strategies of disengagement vary in *directness* and *concern* for the other person. Direct strategies involve the explicit statement of a desire to end the relationship, whereas indirect ones do not. Some people choose strategies that project concern for the other person, in an attempt to avoid hurt, whereas others choose strategies for their expediency. In addition, endings may be unilateral, in which only one member wishes to terminate the relationship, or bilateral, in which both parties feel that the relationship should end.

In *unilateral disengagement*, indirect strategies include withdrawal, pseudode-escalation, and cost escalation. *Withdrawal*, of course, is just avoiding the other person or reducing the amount of contact one has with a partner. Here is an example from one of Baxter's interviews: "I took a stand that related too much homework for an excuse to avoid her. She then initiated notes to me which contained certain things that both of us didn't like about the relationship. I never answered the notes."[38]

Pseudode-escalation is the lie that one just wishes to change the relationship to be a little less close. Here is an example: "I arranged to talk with her in a neutral location. . . . What I said basically was:

'Let's go back to being just friends' (knowing full well I meant I wanted to salvage my ego, and hers, by saying indirectly, the relationship was totally over)." *Cost escalation* is behaving in a way that makes it more difficult for the other person to continue the relationship. In other words, one deliberately makes the relationship more costly to the other person so that he or she will be able to tolerate, or even initiate, a separation: "I thought I would be an 'asshole' for a while to make her like me less."

In *bilateral disengagement, fading away* is common. Here, both parties acknowledge implicitly that the relationship is over: "My lover was a married man who was visiting overnight on his way through Portland. On the way to the airport the next day, we hardly spoke at all. When we did speak it wasn't concerning our relationship. We both knew that it was over." *Mutual pseudode-escalation* is also common in bilateral disengagement.

Two common forms of direct communication in *unilateral disengagement* are the *fait accompli*, or a simple direct statement that the relationship is over, and *state of the relationship talk*, which is an attempt to analyze the relationship. In bilateral disengagement, direct communication may take the form of attributional conflict or negotiated farewell.

Attributional conflict is basically a fight in which each party blames the other for the breakup. *Negotiated farewell* is a mutual parting of the ways without hostility. Among these strategies, cost escalation, fait accompli, withdrawal, and attributional conflict embody little or no concern for the other person. The other strategies include at least some attempt to smooth the waters and save face.

Baxter's second question is whether one's strategy choice is related to any personal or relational variables. She has done much research on this question, and her overall conclusion is that directness is most related to both individual and relational characteristics. This finding suggests that directness itself may be the primary issue in deciding how to end a relationship.

Some interesting findings related to strategies of disengagement are as follows. First, young children

37. The most comprehensive statement of this work is Leslie A. Baxter, "Accomplishing Relationship Disengagement," in *Understanding Personal Relationships: An Interdisciplinary Approach*, eds. S. Duck and D. Perlman (Beverly Hills, Calif.: Sage, 1985), pp. 243–266. See also William W. Wilmot, Donal A. Carbaugh, and Leslie A. Baxter, "Communicative Strategies Used to Terminate Romantic Relationships," *Western Journal of Speech Communication* 49 (1985): 204–216; Leslie A. Baxter, "Trajectories of Relationship Disengagement," *Journal of Social and Personal Relationships* 1 (1984): 29–48; Leslie A. Baxter, "Strategies for Ending Relationships: Two Studies," *Western Journal of Speech Communication* 46 (1982): 223–241.

38. All examples are from Baxter, "Accomplishing," p. 248.

have fewer strategies for disengagement than adolescents, and adults seem to have more strategies than adolescents. Preadolescents' strategies tend to be direct, whereas adolescents and adults choose more indirect strategies. At all ages, however, people seem to have a larger repertoire of communication strategies for beginning relationships than for ending them.

Baxter found no differences between men and women in her studies, but she did find that androgynous individuals, who have a balance of masculine and feminine traits, are more apt to use direct strategies than are either masculine or feminine sex-typed subjects. Baxter speculates that masculine and feminine individuals have different reasons for avoiding directness. Masculine individuals may have less concern for relationships generally, and feminine sex-typed persons may find direct strategies too assertive. Communication apprehension is also related to the manner in which an individual will terminate a relationship. Predictably, apprehensive individuals are less likely to use direct strategies than are nonapprehensive ones.

When one is involved in a close relationship, the tendency is to use direct strategies that also embody concern for the other person. Predictably, individuals in a particularly close relationship seem to want to reduce the potential pain involved in the breakup process. Along the same line, romantic partners tend to use direct strategies more than friends do.

The third question deals with the process of disengagement itself. Baxter found that disengagement is more complex than some other theorists believe. The dissolution of a relationship seems to be more than a mere backing out or reduction in the amount of intimacy of communication, as social penetration theory suggests. Disengagement often involves repeated attempts to reduce or end the relationship in a cyclical fashion, with the use of several different strategies at different points in the process. However, no one pattern fits all relationship endings.

Baxter refers to the course of a breakup as a *trajectory*, and she notes that the specific way in which partners accomplish it depends on a variety of sit-

uational conditions and personal decisions. The first is the nature of the precipitating events. Some relationships break up because of an incremental building of events, and others break up over a single critical incident. The second variable is whether the decision is one-sided or two-sided. Do both parties want to split, or is the breakup instigated by one? The third variable is how to discuss the problem with one's partner because essentially any strategy mentioned above might be used. Fourth, the way in which a partner reacts to mentioning the subject is also a concern. The fifth condition is whether either or both parties have ambivalence about breaking up and want to try to repair the relationship.

Depending on these conditions, a large number of possible trajectories or courses of action may result. To discover which trajectories are most common, Baxter asked about 100 volunteers who had experienced a breakup within the past year to provide information about what happened.[39] Each participant was given a stack of note cards and asked to write on separate cards each significant point in the dissolution process beginning with the problems that precipitated it. At the top of the card was to appear a single phrase that characterized the event and below was to appear a brief paragraph describing what happened at that point. Each deck of completed cards represented the story of an actual breakup. Baxter then analyzed the cards to discover what processes were employed in relational dissolution.

The most common pattern was unilateral, one person deciding he or she did not want to be in the relationship. In this pattern the initiating parties used indirect methods of communicating with their partners, and they had to try several times before getting through. Baxter calls this pattern *persevering indirectness*. About 30 percent of the participants experienced this trajectory.

Another trajectory type was *ambivalent indirectness*. It too was unilateral and indirect, but it did involve at least one attempt to repair the relationship before completely giving up. Eleven percent of

39. Baxter, "Trajectories."

the subjects experienced this kind of breakup. About the same number experienced *swift explicit mutuality*. Here, the termination was bilateral and direct. It did not take very long, and no attempt to repair the relationship was made.

Some people, about 9 percent of Baxter's subjects, experienced *mutual ambivalence,* in which they both initiated the split but were indirect about it, attempted several repairs, and took a long time getting around to the actual breakup. These were the most common types of trajectories, although she did find other ones as well.

We have looked at interpersonal perception and the communication of expectations in relationships, the role of information in relationship development, and relational dissolution. The theories discussed so far are rather general. In the following section, these ideas are applied specifically to particular contexts, including friendship, marriage, and conflict.

Relationships in Context

Communication in Friendships

One of the most recent theories of communication in relationships, William Rawlins's *dialectical theory of friendships,* is also one of the most intriguing and sophisticated.[40] Rawlins believes that friendship at any stage of life presents an interesting and often complex set of challenges. The challenges of friendship arise chiefly from the need to manage a variety of dialectical tensions.

A *dialectic* is a tension between two or more contradictory elements in a system that demands at least temporary resolution. Dialectical analysis looks at the factors in a situation in terms of their connections and reciprocal influences. It looks at the ways in which factors contradict one another and create conflicts. It looks at the ways in which

the system develops or changes, how it moves, in response to these tensions; and it looks at the strategic actions taken by a system to resolve dialectical tension.[41]

In a friendship, for example, you may experience a tension between being an individual and being a friend. Friends respect each other as individuals, but they are also loyal to each other and meet each other's needs. How can you accomplish both at the same time? This is an example of a dialectical tension that different friends handle in different ways.

Rawlins has done extensive research on friendships. He has surveyed the social science literature, examined reported case studies, read fictional accounts, conducted over 100 personal interviews, and conducted in-depth case studies of his own.[42] In his book he discusses the changing texture of friendships over the life span, including those in childhood, adolescence, young adulthood, middle adulthood, and old age. Although the demands on and challenges of friendship change over the life course, all people of all ages must manage dialectical tension in one way or another.

Rawlins suggests that two general classes of dialectics operate in friendships. The first, contextual dialectics, deals with the meaning of friendship within the broader culture. For example, what is the place of friendship in the American middle class? The second, interactional dialectics, deals with the ambiguities of everyday communication in any friendship.

Contextual dialectics relate to the question of the place of friendship in society at large. You cannot really characterize friendship in simple terms. Any definition must mediate two contradictions. The first contradiction is between the *public* and the *pri-*

40. William K. Rawlins, "A Dialectical Analysis of the Tensions, Functions and Strategic Challenges of Communication in Young Adult Friendships," in *Communication Yearbook 12,* ed. J. A. Anderson (Newbury Park, Calif.: Sage, 1989), pp. 157–189.

41. Another dialectical analysis of relationships has been developed by Leslie Baxter in "A Dialectical Perspective on Communication Strategies in Relationship Development," in *Handbook of Personal Relationships,* ed. S. Duck (New York: Wiley, 1988), pp. 257–273. Interestingly, Baxter's dialectics is similar to Rawlins's. Rawlins's theory deals with relationship changes across the life span, whereas Baxter's deals with the ways in which the tensions are actually worked out at different stages of a relationship.

42. William K. Rawlins, *Friendship Matters: Communication, Dialectics, and the Life Course* (Hawthorne, N.Y.: Aldine de Gruyter, in press).

vate. Friendship is inherently private. By definition it is something two people work out between themselves; and yet it is simultaneously governed by social and cultural expectations. The conflict here is between what society says a friendship should be (the public realm) and what the friends themselves have worked out between themselves (the private realm). This dialectic usually involves representing one's friendship to the world at large in a way that is socially acceptable.

An example of this tension occurs in cross-sex friendships. Because society more or less reserves such relationships for romance, love, and sex, a platonic relationship between a man and woman often has to be explained to others, and there may be a good deal of pressure by outsiders to move the relationship from a friendship to something more intimate.

The second contextual dialectic is that between the *ideal* and the *real.* Our culture gives us a set of ideals to achieve, and yet very few friendships meet this set of values. Friends must act in a way that accommodates this tension. For example, friends are supposed to be loyal and available to each other; yet, total loyalty may diminish one's own self-integrity, individuality, and freedom. How is this conflict managed? Again, different friends handle it in different ways.

You can see that the two contextual dialectics are related to each other because the public view of friendship is laden with ideals, whereas the private actuality is governed by real relations negotiated by the friends themselves.

The second set of tensions that affect friendships in middle-class American culture are *interactional dialectics.* These tensions involve the ambiguities and ambivalence that occur in communication within individual friendships. They include all conflicts that friends must endure and manage in order to sustain the friendship. Because these tensions govern communication in a friendship, Rawlins concentrates primarily on this area. He believes that four dialectical principles are used to manage the communication in friendships.

The first is to establish the *freedom to be independent* and the *freedom to be dependent.* People are supposed to let their friends lead their own lives, and

yet they are also supposed to be available to help, counsel, and guide one another. Every time you make a decision to back off or to engage a friend, you are dealing with this contradiction. There are various ways of achieving temporary resolution of the contradiction, one of the most common being to let the other person make his or her own choices, including the choice to ask for help.

One of Rawlins's cases is that of Lana and Darlene, 26-year-old women who had been friends since their freshman year in high school. Dependence and independence are important issues for Lana and Darlene. Over the years they have gone through several stages of both, and the friendship can accommodate both. At times either or both women desire independence, especially when their relationships with spouses and boyfriends were going well. At other times when one needs help and support, such as during Darlene's divorce, dependency is permitted.

The second principle is the dialectic of *affection* and *instrumentality.* Friendships often have a tension between valuing the friend as an end in itself versus using the friend as a means to some other end. This is a tension between affection and utility. Do you call a friend to help you move? You might think twice about it. Do you let a friend borrow your car? Probably so because that's what friends are for, or are they? How do people call on friends to help them do something without the risk of having the friend feel used? Again, people work this out in different ways. Often, for example, friends have developed particular ways of asking for help or have become particularly sensitive to the timing of such requests. Friends may work hard to ensure both genuine expressions of affection as well as the willingness to be of assistance.

Friendships during middle adulthood often arise from job contacts, especially for men. Here, friendships are clearly entangled with career advancement. Because the affection side of the tension is often unfulfilled in middle-aged men, they often feel that they have no best friend other than their wife. A male university professor, for example, said,

I have a lot of acquaintances, a lot of people I call friends that I only see once in a while.... Most of these are professional. Most of those are people I come in contact with through work and I consider friends that aren't really sharing kinds of friends. I have very, very few that I would consider true friends.[43]

Women during this period seem to balance the two sides of the dialectic more effectively and usually say they have a best friend other than their husband.

The third principle is the dialectic of *judgment* and *acceptance*. Friends are supposed to accept us as we are, but they are also called on to make judgments and give advice. Sometimes we criticize friends, and other times we try hard to refrain from doing so. When we criticize, we usually choose our words very carefully, and we often equivocate between expressing a judgment and accepting friends as they are. Again, each set of friends works out a pattern that manages this dialectic more or less effectively.

One of Rawlins's cases is that of Carol and Brent who in their early twenties had been close friends for 7 years. The tension between judgment and acceptance is a real issue in this friendship. In their interviews they both expressed how important acceptance has been in the friendship, and for this reason they have come to be very cautious about making judgments about each other. Carol, for example, most dislikes Brent when he comes off as a brother criticizing her boyfriends.

The fourth dialectic is that between *expressiveness* and *protectiveness*. To what extent can you express your feelings openly with a friend? Should you protect a friend from hurtful or difficult information? In many ways this is a tension between spontaneity and strategy. It is a tension between honesty and rhetorical adaptation. You want to feel that your friends are honest with you, but at the same time you do not want to hurt your friends. A frequent response to this dialectic is to try to accomplish both horns of the delimma at the same time, to be honest but to be careful in how that honesty is expressed. For most friends, this is a rhetorical feat.

Rawlins comments on the power of this dialectic in Darlene and Lana's friendship in these terms:

> Darlene and Lana recalled numerous instances when their desire to express misgivings or hurtful information was tempered by concern for the other's feelings, and when their voiced acceptance veiled deep-seated reservations and criticisms. They cautiously chose their moments for commenting and exercised great care in broaching subjects such as family members, relationships with men, husbands, details of their sex lives, and personal appearance.[44]

Friendships constitute a unique and interesting context in which relationships are developed. Another, very different context is marriage, to which we now turn.

Communication in Marriage

The foremost researcher on marriage in the communication field is Mary Anne Fitzpatrick, whose extensive research for the past decade has led to a widely recognized theory of marriage types.[45] Fitzpatrick's research employs a questionnaire, the Relational Dimensions Instrument, that asks individuals about various aspects of their marriages. It is based on the work of David Kantor and William Lehr, who argue that marriages can be characterized by how the partners use their space, time, and energy and the extent to which they express feelings, exert power, and share a common philosophy of marriage.[46] Fitzpatrick administered 187 questions on these topics to almost 1500 married persons. After the unreliable questions were eliminated, the questionnaire was narrowed down to 77 items. By a statistical procedure called factor analysis, Fitzpatrick discovered that these items measured three basic factors—ideology, interdependence, and conflict. *Ideology* is a variable between conventional and nonconventional notions of family. *Interdependence* is a variable reflecting the extent to which an individual is dependent on or

43. Ibid.

44. Ibid.

45. Mary Anne Fitzpatrick, *Between Husbands and Wives: Communication in Marriage* (Newbury Park, Calif.: Sage, 1988).

46. David Kantor and William Lehr, *Inside the Family* (New York: Harper & Row, 1975).

autonomous from his or her spouse. *Conflict* has to do with whether the couple engages each other in conflict or avoids disagreements. In additional research Fitzpatrick discovered that married couples tend to cluster into three distinct groups along these factors—the traditionals, the independents, and the separates.

The *traditionals*, the first group, tend to be conventional in their views of marriage and place more value on stability and certainty in role relations than on variety and spontaneity. They have strong interdependence and share much companionship. Although they are not assertive about disagreement, they do not avoid conflict.

A traditional wife, for example, would take her husband's name. Traditional couples would probably oppose infidelity, and they would share much time and space. They would try to work out a standard time schedule and spend as much time together as possible, and they probably would not have separate rooms for their own activities.

There is not too much conflict in a traditional marriage because power and decision making are distributed according to customary norms. Husbands, for example, may be in charge of certain kinds of decisions and wives in charge of others. Consequently, there is little need to negotiate and resolve conflict in these marriages. At the same time, there is little impetus for change and growth in the relationship. A traditional couple can be assertive with each other when necessary, but each person tends to support his or her requests with appeals to the relationship rather than by refuting each other's arguments.

Traditional couples are highly expressive and disclose both their joys and their frustrations. The communication in this kind of family seems to encourage expression of feelings, even from the men. They send many positive nonverbal cues and seem supportive of each other.

The second type of marriage is *independent*. These individuals tend to be nonconventional in their views of marriage, and they are not very interdependent. Although they may spend time together and share a great deal, they value their own autonomy very much and often have separate rooms in the house. They may also have separate interests and friends outside the family.

Because they do not rely on conventional roles, the relationship is constantly renegotiated. Because of their individuality, there is much conflict in a typical independent marriage. These individuals definitely do not avoid conflict and can be confrontative. They often vie for power, they use a variety of persuasive techniques, and they are not shy about refuting each other's arguments. Like the traditionals, the independents are also expressive. They respond to each other's nonverbal cues, and they usually understand each other very well.

The third type of marriage is the *separates*. These individuals seem to be ambivalent about their roles and relationship. They may have a fairly conventional view of marriage, but they are not very interdependent and do not share much. For this reason, Fitzpatrick refers to separates as emotionally divorced. They have their opinions and can be contentious, but conflicts never last very long because separates are quick to retreat from conflict. In this regard, they are definitely conflict avoiders. Actually, they do not seem able to coordinate their actions long enough to sustain a conflict. Their attempts to gain compliance rarely use relationship appeals and often mention the bad things that will happen if the spouse does not comply.

Separates have a watchful attitude. They ask many questions but offer little advice. Predictably, then, they are not very expressive, and they do not understand their partners' emotions very well.

About 60 percent of the couples Fitzpatrick has tested fall into one of these categories. In these cases the husband and wife agreed sufficiently in their answers to the questionnaires to classify them as purely traditional, independent, or separate. Obviously, spouses will not always agree, however, and a substantial number of Fitzpatrick's subjects did not. These couples are considered to be mixed and may be separate-traditional, traditional-independent, or independent-separate. The characterization of mixed types is naturally more complex.

We see from Fitzpatrick's work that the typology usefully classifies marriages into the pure and mixed types. We see also that couples in different types of marriages have different patterns of interacting and communicating. The natural question at this point is, What do these categories represent for the couples themselves? Fitzpatrick is now arguing that these categories are indeed psychologically real and that they truly reflect the way individuals in our culture think about marriage.[47] Thus, besides being marriage types, the categories of traditional, independent, and separate are cognitive schemas with which individuals understand marriage and all that it includes. When both partners have the same schema, they share a way of understanding, and they clearly fit one of the types. When the partners do not have the same schema, they are obviously mixed in type.

These schemas are used by individuals to understand their relationships with their spouses, and they are used to guide actions in relating and interacting with the spouse. You can see, for example, how the way in which conflict is handled in a marriage is very much a matter of the individual partner's cognitive categories for understanding what a marital relationship should involve and the manner in which spouses should communicate.

For example, independents, whose schema tells them that individuals count more than relationships, assert individual rights and negotiate solutions to problems. Such couples will find arguments and conflicts to be natural. Separates, on the other hand, who start with the premise that marriage partners should leave each other alone, will find conflict unnatural and uncomfortable.

Depending on your point of view, you may think that one of the marriage types is better than the others. Fitzpatrick takes a strong position against this view. In her research she has discovered that there are satisfied couples in every category and that one cannot judge a marriage on the basis of satisfaction alone. This means that there is no best form of marital communication. What is best depends on the needs of the couple.

The theory of marital types shows among other things that conflict is an important element of marriages. In the following section, we take a special look at this aspect of relationships.

Communication in Conflict

This section covers theories of relational conflict. Over the years many approaches to the study of conflict have emerged, and as in most theoretical areas, this work is not altogether consistent.[48] As a result defining conflict is difficult. Charles Watkins offers an analysis of the essential conditions of conflict, which form an operational definition.[49]

1. Conflict requires at least two parties capable of invoking sanctions on each other.

2. Conflicts arise due to the existence of a mutually desired but mutually unobtainable objective.

3. Each party in a conflict has four possible types of action alternatives:

   a. To obtain the mutually desired objective
   b. To end the conflict
   c. To invoke sanctions against the opponent
   d. To communicate something to the opponent

4. Parties in conflict may have different value or perceptual systems.

5. Each party has resources that may be increased or diminished by implementation of action alternatives.

6. Conflict terminates only when each party is satisfied that he or she has "won" or "lost" or believes that the probable costs of continuing the conflict outweigh the probable costs of ending the conflict.

47. This point is developed in Fitzpatrick, *Husbands and Wives*, pp. 255–256; and Nancy A. Burrell and Mary Anne Fitzpatrick, "The Psychological Reality of Marital Conflict," in *Intimates in Conflict: A Communication Perspective*, ed. D. D. Cahn (Hillsdale, N.J.: Erlbaum, 1990), pp. 167–186.

48. A number of reviews are available. See, for example, Dudley D. Cahn (ed.), *Intimates in Conflict: A Communication Perspective* (Hillsdale, N.J.: Erlbaum, 1990); Michael E. Roloff, "Communication and Conflict," in *Handbook of Communication Science*, eds. C. E. Berger and S. H. Chaffee (Newbury Park, Calif.: Sage, 1987), pp. 484–536; Alan Sillars and Judith Weisberg, "Conflict as a Social Skill," in *Interpersonal Processes: New Directions in Communication Research*, eds. M. E. Roloff and G. R. Miller (Newbury Park, Calif.: Sage, 1987), pp. 140–171; Joyce Frost and William Wilmot, *Interpersonal Conflict* (Dubuque, Iowa: Brown, 1978).

49. Charles Watkins, "An Analytic Model of Conflict," *Speech Monographs* 41 (1974): 1–5.

One advantage of Watkins's definition is that it includes the possibility for communication. Ironically, many theories of conflict have neglected the communication aspect, and there are frankly few communication-based theories of relational conflict. Two have been chosen for discussion here—game theory and attribution theory.

Game theory. Game theory was developed many years ago by John von Neumann and Oskar Morgenstern as a tool to study economic behavior and has since provided a base for popular research tools in a variety of disciplines.[50] For researchers studying the processes of decision making or choice making and goal competition or cooperation, game theory provides a possible approach. As a result it has been used extensively to study conflict.

Game theory itself is not a relational communication theory, although it has implications for relationships. Because game theoretic research involves the moves and countermoves of individuals, it is potentially useful in this area, as we will see.

Game theory includes several kinds of games. Two-person games, which are particularly useful in conflict research, consist of structured situations where two players take turns making choices that lead to payoffs. In all games the rational decision-making process is stressed. The question is how players behave in order to gain rewards or goals. Types of games vary in several ways, including the amount of information provided to players, the amount of communication permitted between them, and the extent of cooperation versus competition built into the payoff matrix. Thomas Steinfatt and Gerald Miller show how game theory is useful in studying conflicts:

> Game theory is concerned with how to win a game, with strategies of move sequences that maximize the player's chance to gain and minimize his chance for loss. Because a major ingredient in conflict situations

is the desire to gain something one does not possess and to hold onto that which one does possess, certain games are analogous to particular conflict situations and game theory serves as a model to predict the behavior of persons in such conflict situations attempting to gain those ends.[51]

Because game theory stresses rational decision making, it involves games of strategy. In such games a player makes moves (choices) that lead to rewards or punishments based on the moves of others. The object is to maximize gains and minimize losses.

For example, suppose that you and your spouse were having a disagreement about where to take your vacation; you would probably try to get your way. You might make a variety of moves, such as calling the travel agent, talking with friends, buying clothes, and discussing your preference with your partner. Each move is designed to win, to get the vacation you want. If you do, you have won, and your partner has lost.

One of the most commonly used games is the *prisoner's dilemma*.[52] This simple game is useful because it illustrates a number of salient features of games in general. Also, it is interesting as a *mixed-motive game* because players can choose between cooperating or competing, and genuine reasons are present for choosing either. Here is the situation: Two people are arrested for a crime. After being separated, each must choose whether to confess. If one confesses and the other does not, the confessor will be allowed to go free, and this person's testimony will send the other to prison for 20 years. If both confess, both will be sent to prison for 5 years. If neither confesses, both will go to prison for 1 year on a lesser charge. Figure 12.1 illustrates the choices. With no communication between players, they will not know the choice of the other. Each is in a dilemma on whether to trust the other prisoner and cooperate by remaining silent or to compete

50. John von Neumann and Oskar Morgenstern, *The Theory of Games and Economic Behavior* (Princeton, N.J.: Princeton University Press, 1944). Numerous secondary sources are also available. See, for example, Morton Davis, *Game Theory: A Non-technical Introduction* (New York: Basic Books, 1970).

51. Thomas Steinfatt and Gerald Miller, "Communication in Game Theoretic Models of Conflict," in *Perspectives on Communication in Conflict*, eds. G. R. Miller and H. Simons (Englewood Cliffs, N.J.: Prentice-Hall, 1974), pp. 14–75.

52. This game is explained in Davis, *Game Theory*, pp. 93–107. This book is an excellent source of real-world analogues for many types of games.

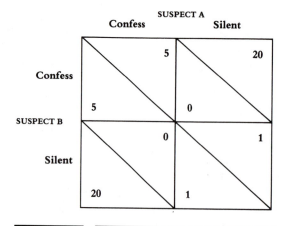

SUSPECT A

	Confess	Silent

Figure 12.1   Prisoner's dilemma.

with the other prisoner by confessing. If both are willing to cooperate by not confessing, the long-term payoff is maximized for both. But if one does not behave cooperatively, the other cannot cooperate. Over several trials, most players will move ultimately toward the noncooperative strategy.

Although our simple vacation example appears to be a win–win conflict, this kind of situation is usually not so simple; it is most often a mixed-motive conflict such as the prisoner's dilemma. You can either compete to get your way, or you can cooperate and come up with a vacation spot that suits both of you. If you compete and win, you will presumably enjoy your vacation more (although your partner will enjoy it less.) If you cooperate and compromise, you will still have a good time. Will you cooperate or compete? That is the question.

Steinfatt and Miller reviewed the literature in which games were used to investigate the process of communication in conflict. Using games as an analogue, Steinfatt and Miller list three ways in which parties in conflict come to assess each other's strategies. The first way is to observe the opponent's moves over several trials. In games such as the prisoner's dilemma, subjects play through a number of trials of the game. Typically, a player will observe the opponent's moves and decide what to do next. So, for example, if your partner goes out and buys beach clothes, you know that he is are serious about

going to the coast. So you go out and buy hiking boots to show that you are serious about going into the mountain wilderness.

The second way of assessing strategy is to observe the total conflict situation. In so doing a player makes inferences from the situation to the opponent's strategy. The player would study the game matrix and try to guess what the opponent's strategy is likely to be. Knowing your spouse as you do and having gone on many vacations together, you try to figure out what he likes and what he will do to get to go where he wants.

The third approach is direct communication. The authors point out,

> Ideally, communication makes it possible to conduct the entire conflict at the symbolic level, with each player stating how he would respond to the stated, rather than the actual, moves of the other. . . . Besides avoiding the hostility, disruption, and subsequent losses resulting from actual moves, negotiations allow the parties to move away from a winner-take-all position toward a solution that provides some rewards for everyone.[53]

If the players in the prisoner's dilemma game could communicate and agree to cooperate, both would receive lesser sentences. Similarly, if you just sat down and talked about your vacation, you would probably realize that there is a spot that both of you would like to visit.

It is interesting to speculate on how partners in different types of marriages would deal with their conflicts from a game theoretic point of view. Traditional husbands and wives would probably allow one or the other to decide based on their traditional power arrangement. Independents would probably talk about it and after much arguing agree to compromise. Separates would probably not talk about it and make inferences from each other's moves.

Steinfatt and Miller make three points about communication in conflict. The first point is that communication is symbolic and does not have the actual consequence of the real move. Thus, communication is a way to try out an idea rather than

53. Steinfatt and Miller, "Communication," pp. 32–33.

doing something that you may later regret. Second, communication changes the probability of moves and may reduce the amount of competitiveness on the part of the conflicting parties. So, for example, if your husband tells you why he wants to go to the beach, you may be more understanding and less inclined to block his decision. The third aspect of the model is that communication may result in changing the other person's orientations toward the problem. In other words, you may directly persuade him or her and change what he or she wants to do.

People in conflict are in a situation that has the potential of providing mutually exclusive payoffs, but by communicating the parties may reduce their own tendencies to behave chauvinistically. In fact, studies have shown that this is what tends to happen. Pregame discussions increase cooperation. The greatest effect occurs when communication exists from the beginning of the conflict. Studies also show that the fuller the communication, the more open the channels, and the greater the resultant cooperation.

Now that we have examined the basic game theoretic concepts of communication and conflict, we turn to a theory that attempts to explain the process of communication in real conflict situations.

An attribution theory of conflict.   Alan Sillars has developed a theory of conflict and conflict resolution based on attribution theory (see Chapter 7).[54] The premise of this approach is that when people are involved in conflicts, they develop their own "theories" to explain the conflict, and these theories are largely a product of their attributions. Further, the attributions have an important effect on how the partners will deal with the conflict.

Sillars maintains that three general strategies of conflict resolution are seen in interpersonal relationships. These include *passive* and *indirect methods*, which are primarily avoidance strategies; *distributive methods*, which aim to win favorable outcomes for oneself and losses for the other person; and *integrative strategies*, which aim to achieve mutual positive outcomes for both parties and perhaps for the relationship itself. Sillars has refined his scheme over the years and now refers to these categories simply as avoidance behaviors, cooperative behaviors, and competitive behaviors.

Avoidance behaviors employ no communication or, at best, indirect communication. *Competitive behaviors* involve negative messages, and *cooperative behaviors* entail more open and positive communication. Table 12.2 illustrates a variety of strategies found by Sillars in his research.[55]

As an example of how people use these different strategies in interpersonal conflicts, consider a study by Sillars and his colleagues on conflict communication in marriages.[56] In this study the researchers solicited the cooperation of forty married couples. Each couple was given a kit to take home to complete the study, consisting of a set of questionnaires for each spouse, a list of ten potential conflict areas, and an audiotape. Each couple was told to answer the questions separately and to seal them in an envelope before proceeding with the rest of the protocol. Then, the couple was to discuss each of the ten topics and to tape their discussions. The topics included such things as work pressures, lack of affection, how to spend leisure time, and child discipline.

Among the various questionnaires completed by the couples were a marital adjustment scale and Fitzpatrick's measure of marital types (discussed earlier). One objective of the study was to see how well-adjusted couples in each of Fitzpatrick's categories differed from less well-adjusted couples in

54. Alan L. Sillars et al., "Coding Verbal Conflict Tactics: Nonverbal and Perceptual Correlates of the 'Avoidance-Distributive-Integrative' Distinction," *Human Communication Research* 9 (1982): 83–95; Alan L. Sillars, "Attributions and Communication in Roommate Conflicts," *Communication Monographs* 47 (1980): 180–200; "The Sequential and Distributional Structure of Conflict Interaction as a Function of Attributions Concerning the Locus of Responsibility and Stability of Conflict," in *Communication Yearbook 4*, ed. D. Nimmo (New Brunswick, N.J.: Transaction Books, 1980), pp. 217–236.

55. Alan L. Sillars, *Manual for Coding Interpersonal Conflict* (Unpublished Manuscript, Department of Communication, University of Montana, 1986).

56. Alan L. Sillars et al., "Communication and Conflict in Marriage," in *Communication Yearbook 7*, ed. R. Bostrom (Beverly Hills, Calif.: Sage, 1983), pp. 414–429.

Table 12.2 Conflict Management Coding Scheme

Avoidance Behaviors

Denial and Equivocation

1. *Direct denial.* Person explicitly denies a conflict is present.
2. *Implicit denial.* Statements that imply denial by providing a rationale for a denial statement, although the denial is not explicit.
3. *Evasive remark.* Failure to acknowledge or deny the presence of a conflict following a statement or inquiry about the conflict by the partner.

Topic Management

4. *Topic shifts.* A break in the natural flow of discussion that directs the topic focus away from discussion of the issue as it applies to the immediate parties. Do not count topic shifts that occur after the discussion appears to have reached a natural culmination.
5. *Topic avoidance.* Statements that explicitly terminate the discussion of a conflict issue before it has been fully discussed.

Noncommittal Remarks

6. *Abstract remarks.* Abstract principles, generalizations, or hypothetical statements. Speaking about the issue on a high level of abstraction. No reference is made to the actual state of affairs between the immediate parties.
7. *Noncommittal statements.* Statements that neither affirm nor deny the presence of a conflict and that are not evasive replies or topic shifts.
8. *Noncommittal questions.* Unfocused questions or those that rephrase the questions given by the researcher.
9. *Procedural remarks.* Procedural statements that supplant discussion of the conflict.

Irreverent Remarks

10. *Joking.* Nonhostile joking that interrupts or supplements serious consideration of the issue.

Cooperative Behaviors

Analytic Remarks

1. *Description.* Nonevaluative, nonblaming, factual description of the nature and extent of the problem.
2. *Qualification.* Discussion explicitly limits the nature and extent of the problem by tying the issue to specific behavioral events.
3. *Disclosure.* Providing "nonobservable" information: i.e., information about thoughts, feelings, intentions, causes of behavior, or past experience relevant to the issue that the partner would not have the opportunity to observe.
4. *Soliciting disclosure.* Asking specifically for information concerning the other that the person himself or herself would not have the opportunity to observe (i.e., thoughts, feelings, intentions, causes of behavior, experiences).
5. *Soliciting criticism.* Nonhostile questions soliciting criticism of oneself.

Conciliatory Remarks

6. *Empathy or support.* Expressing understanding, support, or acceptance of the other person or commenting on the others' positive characteristics or shared interests, goals, and compatibilities.
7. *Concessions.* Statements that express a willingness to change, show flexibility, make concessions, or consider mutually acceptable solutions to conflict.
8. *Accepting responsibility.* Statements that attribute some causality for the problem to oneself.

Competitive Behaviors

Confrontative Remarks

1. *Personal criticism.* Stating or implying a negative evaluation of the partner.
2. *Rejection.* Rejecting the partner's opinions in a way that implies personal rejection as well as disagreement.
3. *Hostile imperatives.* Threats, demands, arguments, or other prescriptive statements that implicitly blame the partner and seek change in the partner's behavior.
4. *Hostile questioning.* Questions that fault or blame the other person.
5. *Hostile joking or sarcasm.* Joking or teasing that is used to fault the other person.
6. *Presumptive attribution.* Attributing thoughts, feelings, intentions, and causes to the partner that the partner does not acknowledge. This code is the opposite of "soliciting disclosure."
7. *Denial of responsibility.* Statements that deny or minimize personal responsibility for the conflict.

their conflict communication. The tape recordings were analyzed in terms of the amount of apparent conflict and the various types of strategies used by the couple in their discussion.

The investigators discovered that in all marriage types, more satisfied couples used a more positive tone of voice than less satisfied couples. Separates tended to be avoiders: They maintained a fairly neutral tone and kept their discussions of conflict areas to a minimum. The satisfied separates tended to be even more extreme in this regard. The independents, whether satisfied with their marriage or not, tended to express negative feelings. The more satisfied members of the independent category tended to use more description and self-disclosure than did the less satisfied members of this group. Finally, there was little difference between the satisfied and non-satisfied traditionals in the sample.

Perhaps Sillars's most important contribution is his use of attribution theory to explain conflict behavior. Recall from Chapter 7 that attributions are inferences made about the causes of behavior. One may make inferences about the causes of some effect, a disposition or trait of another person or oneself, or a predicted outcome of a situation. Whenever people try to explain an event by making inferences, attribution is involved.

Sillars believes that in at least three ways attributions are important determiners of the definition and outcome of conflicts. First, individuals' attributions in a conflict determine what sorts of strategies they will choose to deal with the conflict. This is true not only because one's reactions and feelings are colored by their attributions but also because future expectations are formed largely as a result of what has gone on in the past. If, for example, a partner in a relationship attributes cooperation to his or her partner, a cooperative strategy will probably be chosen, whereas attribution of competition may lead to a competitive approach. One's attribution of responsibility for the conflict is also important: Attributing blame to oneself may lead to the use of cooperative strategies; but when a person thinks the other communicator is responsible, a more competitive approach may be taken. Too, if one thinks his or her partner has certain per-

sonality traits that caused the conflict, he or she will be less likely to cooperate.

Second, biases in the attribution process discourage the use of integrative strategies. These include a tendency to see others as personally responsible for negative events and to see oneself as merely responding to circumstances. People believe that others cause conflict because of bad intentions, inconsideration, competitiveness, or inadequacy. Both partners in a conflict tend to believe that the other person caused it; people characterize their own behavior as merely responding to the provocations of others.

Third, the strategy chosen affects the outcome of the conflict. Cooperative strategies encourage integrative solutions and information exchange. Competitive strategies escalate the conflict and may lead to less satisfying solutions.

Commentary and Critique

In this chapter we have taken a brief look at some of the most significant theorizing in interpersonal communication. Many of the theories discussed here have been immensely popular and influential. Many of these theories de-emphasize individual traits and focus instead on the interactive and relational nature of interpersonal communication. This puts them in contrast with the more cognitive theories of message presentation and reception covered in Chapters 6 and 7.

Cognitive theories are psychological in orientation, explaining communication differences in terms of individual variables such as traits, behaviors, or cognitive structures. Relational theories are more interactional in looking at what goes on between communicators rather than within them.

Not all theories in this chapter are strictly relational in this sense, however. For example, uncertainty reduction theory and social penetration theory are based on psychological analysis because they concentrate on what individuals do, albeit in response to other individuals. Even Fitpatrick's theory of marriage types, although it appears to be relational on the surface, is based mostly on the individual perceptions of marriage partners. Baxter expresses the difficulty in these terms:

> [Psychological] theories share the assumption that relationship dynamics can be explained adequately by understanding the individuals who comprise the relationship. Theoretical frustration with this atomistic orientation is a frequently expressed complaint in the relationship communication literature; however, the relationships field still displays a paucity of genuine relationship-level theories.[57]

Nothing is inherently wrong with individualistic analysis, but it fails to capture important interactional dimensions of the relationship, such as conflict, control, power, mutual definition, and social meaning. For example, social exchange and social penetration theories put all their eggs in the cost–rewards basket and fail to deal with the relational processes by which rewards and costs are defined. Because they center on how persons weigh rewards against costs, these theories are ironically individualistic, despite their purported emphasis on the relationship.[58]

Social exchange theory and game theory are closely related: Both see relationships as a sequence of moves motivated by personal gain. Research in game theory and social exchange theory examines the choices people make in response to different reward and cost contingencies, using points or tokens as game outcomes; but we are not at all sure whether social rewards work in this way.[59] These theories assume that people behave rationally in making decisions and that they always want to maximize positive outcomes. However, in actual social life it is not a simple matter to establish exactly what outcomes people are seeking. How

people behave in real social conflict depends in part on their self-concept, motives, mental health, individual life goals, and an array of other complex factors. Steinfatt and Miller crystallize this objection: "In the daily political, economic, and social conflicts we all face, mutually advantageous solutions are seldom this sharply defined, and in seeking an acceptable solution, communication serves a myriad of cognitive and affective functions."[60]

The original work of the Palo Alto Group is an example of the relationship-level thinking that interaction theory strives to accomplish. The notion that communication patterns define relationships has been and remains its central idea. This idea is what makes the research of Millar and Rogers so interesting and important; it examines not individual messages but pairs of messages in response to each other. Relational dynamics are precisely what make Rawlins's work on friendship different from other kinds of research. Rawlins asks his subjects to report not just on what they personally feel but to reflect on the give and take between the partners in a friendship.

Of course, psychologically oriented theories do have an impact, and as this chapter and others in the book demonstrate, they can tell us a great deal about relationships. At the same time, although relationship-level theories have their own unique values, they are not without weaknesses. As a group relational theories display two limitations. First, they tend to suffer from conceptual confusion. Second, although as a group they paint a fairly complete picture, the individual theories can be myopic. Relational theories possess these faults in varying ways and to varying degrees, and the weaknesses of some of them are compensated by the strengths of others.

The first problem encountered in these theories

---

57. Baxter, "Dialectical Perspective," p. 258.

58. Teru L. Morton and Mary Ann Douglas, "Growth of Relationships," in *Personal Relationships 2: Developing Personal Relationships*, eds. S. Duck and R. Gilmour (London: Academic Press, 1981), pp. 3–26.

59. John L. LaGaipa, "Interpersonal Attraction and Social Exchange," in *Theory and Practice in Interpersonal Attraction*, ed. S. Duck (New York: Academic Press, 1971), pp. 129–164.

60. Steinfatt and Miller, "Communication," p. 70. For an excellent debate on the value of game theory in communication research, see Robert Bostrom, "Game Theory in Communication Research," *Journal of Communication* 18 (1968): 369–388; and Thomas Beisecker, "Game Theory in Communication Research: A Rejoinder and a Re-orientation," *Journal of Communication* 20 (1970): 107–120.

is conceptual confusion. The very term *communication* is fuzzy in much of the foundational work on relational communication. Watzlawick, Beavin, and Jackson's first axiom, that all behavior is communicative, places no limits on what communication is and essentially makes the concept meaningless.[61]

Another area of conceptual confusion is the distinction between the report and command functions, or metacommunication.[62] One critical treatment calls the concept "muddled and confusing." [63] The problem is that the Palo Alto Group, at different points in their writing, imply as many as three different meanings for metacommunication. (The use of other labels, such as command message and relational message, does not help in this regard.) At points metacommunication refers to a verbal or nonverbal classification of the content message, in which one's partner guides the coding of the content. At other times metacommunication refers to nonverbal statements about the relationship itself, such as control. Or, metacommunication sometimes refers to explicit discussion by individuals about the nature of their relationship. To make matters worse, metacommunication has been treated alternatively as strictly analogic, analogic and digital, nonverbal, and both verbal and nonverbal.

The second problem encountered in many of these theories is their limited focus. As a group the theories complete most of a rather intricate puzzle, but individually each leaves out important elements. Despite all their talk about how communication is used to define the nature of a relationship within a system, original relational theorists from the Palo Alto Group and disciples like Millar and

Rogers essentially ignore interpretation and cognition.[64] The research in this tradition deals with observable behavior, and the coding is done from the perspective of the outside observer, not from within the relationship. Although interaction analysis is powerful in detecting patterns of behavior, it tells us very little about what those patterns mean to the participants themselves. Here is where the later work by researchers like Fitzpatrick, Rawlins, Baxter, and Sillars fills in a gap.

An important contribution of some of the theories in this chapter is their process-oriented, developmental focus. Development is difficult to study, and it is tempting to oversimply the process of relational definition and development. Theories therefore often assume a single trajectory or a single set of processes without discriminating among types of relationships or variability among relationships. Social penetration theory, for example, assumes that all relationships develop along the same line, which is really too orderly.[65] Different relationships may have different processes operating, and we cannot assume that cost-reward operates in each phase of a relationship.[66] Social penetration theory teaches that dissolution is merely penetration in reverse; yet, relationships do not always follow this kind of simple backing-out, as Baxter's work illustrates. One of the advantages of Duck's model is that it recognizes the cyclical, back-and-forth nature of deteriorating relationships, and it does not try to predict the course of any one relationship. Duck's theory identifies certain threshold points, and he recognizes that within each stage there are several courses and outcomes. Baxter has done an excellent job of filling in the details in the complex picture of relational dissolution. The

61. See Motley, "On Whether."

62. This problem is discussed by William Wilmot, "Metacommunication: A Re-examination and Extension," in *Communication Yearbook 4*, ed. D. Nimmo (New Brunswick, N.J.: Transaction Books, 1980), pp. 61–69.

63. Arthur Bochner and Dorothy Krueger, "Interpersonal Communication Theory and Research: An Overview of Inscrutable Epistemologies and Muddled Concepts," in *Communication Yearbook 3*, ed. D. Nimmo (New Brunswick, N.J.: Transaction Books, 1979), p. 203.

64. Edna Rogers herself discusses this problem in "Analyzing Relational Communication: Implications of a Pragmatic Approach" (Paper presented to the Speech Communication Association, Washington, D.C., November 1983).

65. James L. Applegate and Gregory B. Leichty, "Managing Interpersonal Relationships: Social Cognitive and Strategic Determinants of Competence," in *Competence in Communication: A Multi-Disciplinary Approach*, ed. R. N. Bostrom (Beverly Hills, Calif.: Sage, 1984), p. 39.

66. Bochner, "Functions," p. 579.

major contribution of this theory is that it explic-itly identifies many of the communication behav-iors that other theories only indirectly and vaguely acknowledge.

Relational communication theory is an immensely interesting, important, and challenging field of study. We see in the theories established to date noble efforts to advance our understanding of one of the most difficult aspects of human life, and although any single theory leaves many questions unanswered, as a group they provide a great deal of insight.

CHAPTER 13

Communication in Group Decision Making

No contextual theme related to small-group communication has received as much attention as decision making. A number of contemporary source books on small groups reflects the breadth of work in this area.[1] In this chapter we look at some of the most interesting and insightful theories related to communication in small-group decision making.

What distinguishes the group? After summarizing several other definitions stressing different aspects of groups, Marvin Shaw provides his own interactional definition:

> A group is defined as two or more persons who are interacting with one another in such a manner that each person influences and is influenced by each other person. A small group is a group having twenty or fewer members, although in most instances we will be concerned with groups having five or fewer members.[2]

This definition is a good one for our purposes because it includes communication as the essential characteristic of the group. Shaw points out that the most interesting groups are those that endure for a relatively long period of time, have a goal or goals, and have an interactional structure.

1. See, for example, John F. Cragan and David W. Wright, "Small Group Communication Research of the 1980s: A Synthesis and Critique," *Communication Studies* 41 (1990): 212–236; Marshall Scott Poole, "Do We Have Any Theories of Group Communication?" *Communication Studies* 41 (1990): 237–247; Randy Y. Hirokawa and Marshall Scott Poole (eds.), *Communication and Group Decision-Making* (Beverly Hills, Calif.: Sage, 1986); Gerald M. Phillips and Julia T. Wood (eds.), *Emergent Issues in Human Decision Making* (Carbondale: Southern Illinois University Press, 1984); Dennis S. Gouran and B. Aubrey Fisher, "The Functions of Human Communication in the Formation, Maintenance, and Performance of Small Groups," in *Handbook of Rhetorical and Communication Theory*, eds. C. C. Arnold and J. W. Bowers (Boston: Allyn and Bacon,

1984), pp. 622–659; Marvin E. Shaw, *Group Dynamics: The Psychology of Small Group Behavior* (New York: McGraw-Hill, 1981).

2. Shaw, *Group Dynamics*, p. 10.

Foundations of Group Communication

The impetus for contemporary research and theory in group communication came from a variety of early twentieth-century sources. One such source was the work of Mary Parker Follett on integrative thinking.[3] Follett wrote in 1924 that group, organizational, and community problem solving is a creative threefold process of (1) gathering information from experts, (2) testing that information in everyday experience, and (3) developing integrative solutions that meet a variety of interests rather than competing among interests. Follett's notion reflects an idea that has gained much acceptance in twentieth-century American thought—dealing with problems and conflicts through discussion.

Another major influence on current theories was the group-discussion movement in the field of speech.[4] Here, students were taught how to speak productively with others in a small group, and such education is still a part of high school and college speech communication curricula. A third source of current group-communication theory was the tremendous body of group dynamics research in social psychology.[5]

For the most part, research on group dynamics follows an input–process–output model.[6] This

model segments the group experience into the factors that affect the group (input), the happenings within the group (process), and the results (output). For example, a study might examine the effects of heterogeneity of group members (input) on the amount of talking in a group (process) or the effect of interaction patterns (process) on member satisfaction (output).

Because of its impact on group-communication theory, the input–process–output model is discussed in some detail next.

The Input–Process–Output Model

This section is divided into three parts. First, we present a simple descriptive model of group action in the input–process–output tradition. Second, we look at theories of group effectiveness. Finally, we discuss two influential theories that focus on communication.

A General Organizing Model

Most of the work on group dynamics centers on task groups. Figure 13.1 is the model of Barry Collins and Harold Guetzkow.[7] This simple model captures the major themes of task–group research in general terms, and it illustrates the input–process–output approach very well.

Any task group is confronted with two types of problems: task obstacles and interpersonal obstacles. *Task obstacles* are the difficulties encountered by the group in tackling its stated assignment, such as planning an event or approving a policy. Group members deal directly with the problem—analyzing it, suggesting possible solutions, and weighing alternatives. Such efforts are task-related group behaviors, and they all in one way or another relate to decision making. Decision making in a group, however, is different because of interpersonal relations.

3. Mary Parker Follett, *Creative Experience* (New York: Longmans, Green, 1924).

4. For a brief summary of this work, see Dennis S. Gouran, "The Paradigm of Unfulfilled Promise: A Critical Examination of the History of Research on Small Groups in Speech Communication," in *Speech Communication in the 20th Century*, ed. T. W. Benson (Carbondale: Southern Illinois University Press, 1985), p. 90.

5. Shaw, *Group Dynamics*.

6. This model is discussed by Marshall Scott Poole, David R. Seibold, and Robert D. McPhee, "A Structurational Approach to Theory-Building in Group Decision-Making Research," in *Communication and Group Decision-Making*, eds. R. Y. Hirokawa and M. S. Poole (Beverly Hills, Calif.: Sage, 1986), pp. 238–240. See also Susan Jarboe, "A Comparison of Input-Output, Process-Output, and Input-Process-Output Models of Small Group Problem-Solving Effectiveness," *Communication Monographs* 55 (1988): 121–142.

7. Barry Collins and Harold Guetzkow, *A Social Psychology of Group Processes for Decision-Making* (New York: Wiley, 1964), p. 81.

SOURCE OF PROBLEM GROUP BEHAVIORS OUTPUTS REWARDS

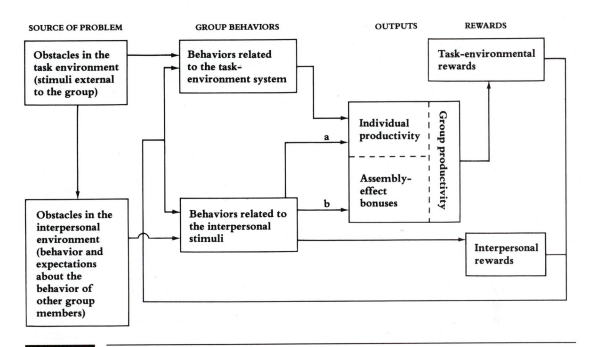

Figure 13.1 A simple working model of decision-making groups.

From *A Social Psychology of Group Processes for Decision-Making* by Barry Collins and Harold Guetzkow; John Wiley & Sons, publisher. Used by permission.

Whenever two or more people join together to handle a problem, *interpersonal obstacles* arise. Such obstacles include the need to make one's ideas clear to others, to deal with conflict among participants, to handle individual member differences, and so forth. Thus, in any group discussion, members will be dealing simultaneously with task and interpersonal obstacles.

The basic distinction between task work and interpersonal relations has been an overriding concern in the research and theory on small-group communication. Both types of behavior are important in accomplishing the task or in achieving group productivity. Any analysis of group problem solving must deal with both task and interpersonal demands. The outputs of a group are affected by members' task and interpersonal efforts.[8]

8. One proposed theory that explains leadership competence in terms of task and interpersonal variables is published in J. Kevin Barge and Randy Y. Hirokawa, "Toward a Communication Competency Model of Group Leadership," *Small Group Behavior* 20 (1989): 167–189.

Interpersonal and task factors interrelate, and group productivity results from both. Interpersonal relations can inhibit or enhance problem solving. The performance of a group depends primarily on its ability to integrate and organize the individual skills and resources of the members. When this integration is done effectively, an *assembly effect* occurs in which the group solution or product is superior to the individual work of even the best member. So, for example, if a club meets to plan a picnic and handles their interpersonal relations well, the event should turn out to be better than if it were planned by just one person.

Group rewards can be positive or negative. Successful goal achievement is usually positively rewarding to group members. In addition, the resolution of conflict and successful communication often reap interpersonal rewards. On the other hand, "rewards" can also be negative, something one would rather avoid. In any case outcomes are evaluated by group members as positive or negative, and these in turn affect future task and interpersonal efforts in the group, as indicated by the feedback arrows in Figure 13.1. A successful picnic, in other words, is a task reward, and the fun involved in planning it is an interpersonal reward. If the job is well done and enjoyed by the members, their future decision making will be affected in a positive way. If the task was not well done or the members did not handle their differences very well, negative feedback may make it more difficult next time.

Groups expend energy. Some of the effort goes to solve task obstacles, and some goes to deal with interpersonal ones. Because of interpersonal demands, energy must be expended to maintain relationships and overcome interpersonal barriers, which detracts from the amount of effort that can be put directly on the task. Raymond Cattell calls group effort *synergy*. The amount of energy devoted to interpersonal hassles is called *intrinsic synergy*. The resulting task effort is called *effective synergy*. If effective synergy is high, the task will be accomplished effectively. If not, it will be done poorly.[9]

The synergy of a group results from the attitudes of the members toward one another. To the extent that members have different attitudes toward the group and its operations, conflict will result, increasing the proportion of energy needed for group maintenance. Thus, the more that individuals possess similar attitudes, the less the need for an interpersonal investment, and the greater the effective synergy.

Let's use a simplified example to see how Cattell's theory explains real events. Suppose that in forming a study group, you discover that the members have varying attitudes toward the subject matter and differing manners of study. In your meetings you spend much time arguing about how to organize your efforts and learn the material. Much time and energy is spent working out these interpersonal problems. This is your intrinsic synergy. Now, after getting your test grade back, if you sense that the study group failed to achieve the goal of mutual

benefit, you will withdraw your energy and join another group or study alone. In this case the effective synergy of the group was so low that it did not accomplish more than you could have accomplished yourself.

But suppose that you join another group that agrees immediately on how to proceed and gets down to work. Because there are few interpersonal barriers to overcome, the group is cohesive. The effective synergy is high, and everyone does better on the examination than they would have done had they studied alone.

Janis's Groupthink Theory

The preceding ideas give us one answer to the question of the impact of interpersonal effects on group decision making. The *groupthink hypothesis* of Irving Janis constitutes a very different answer and a more complete view of synergy.[10] Janis examines in some detail the adequacy of decisions made by groups. He shows how certain conditions can lead to high group satisfaction but ineffective output.

Janis's theory is normative and applied. It is normative in that it provides a base for diagnosing problems and remediating weaknesses in group performance; it is applied to actual political groups. Janis has relied heavily on social-psychological research on group dynamics, integrating concepts such as cohesiveness in explaining actual observed group practices. Janis describes groupthink as a process in which poor decisions are reached because of the lack of critical thinking in the group:

> I use the term groupthink as a quick and easy way to refer to a mode of thinking that people engage in when they are deeply involved in a cohesive in-group, when members' strivings for unanimity override their motivation to realistically appraise alternative courses of action.... The invidiousness is intentional: Groupthink refers to a deterioration of mental efficiency, reality testing, and moral judgment that results from in-group pressures.[11]

9. Raymond Cattell, "Concepts and Methods in the Measurement of Group Syntality," *Psychological Review* 55 (1948): 48–63.

10. Irving Janis, *Victims of Groupthink: A Psychological Study of Foreign Decisions and Fiascos* (Boston: Houghton Mifflin, 1982).

11. Ibid., p. 9.

Groupthink is a direct result of *cohesiveness* in groups. There has been a great deal of research in group dynamics on cohesiveness. *Cohesiveness* was first discussed in some depth by Kurt Lewin in the 1930s and has come to be seen as a crucial variable in group effectiveness.[12] Cohesiveness is the degree of mutual interest among members. In a highly cohesive group, a strong mutual identification is found among members. This quality is what keeps a group together; without it the group will dissolve. Mutual identification is a function of the degree to which members are mutually attracted to certain goals or repulsed by certain negative forces. Cohesiveness is a result of the degree to which all members perceive that their goals can be met within the group. This does not require that the members have similar attitudes but that they are interdependent and rely on one another to achieve certain mutually desired goals. The more cohesive a group, the more force it exerts on its members, as participants are pressured by the group to conform to the group code.

Most small-group research and theory indicate that cohesiveness is a positive influence. In other words, effective synergy results from cohesiveness because cohesive groups need expend little intrinsic synergy. Although Janis does not deny the potential value of cohesiveness in decision-making groups, he also recognizes its dangers. He shows how highly cohesive groups may invest too much energy on maintaining goodwill in the group to the detriment of decision making.

The variable that can make cohesiveness negative is the person's need to maintain self-esteem. Such rewards as friendship, prestige, and mutually recognized competence are acquired in highly cohesive groups. With such rewards at stake, it is not surprising that group members invest intrinsic synergy to maintain solidarity. The doubts or uncertainties that arise may lead to an undermining of group confidence and hence of individual members' self-esteem.

Cohesiveness is a necessary but not sufficient condition for groupthink. Under conditions of low cohesiveness, factors may be present that prevent the illusion of unanimity. The natural conflict in noncohesive groups leads to much debate and consideration of all sides of an issue.

Janis's approach is intriguing. He uses historical data to support his theory by analyzing six national political decision-making episodes in which outcomes were either good or bad, depending on the extent of groupthink. The negative examples include the Bay of Pigs invasion, the Korean War, Pearl Harbor, and the escalation of the Vietnam War. Positive examples include the Cuban missile crisis and the Marshall Plan. These interesting historical examples once again illustrate how communication theory may be generated in a variety of arenas. One of the finest qualities of Janis's approach is that his theory involves small-group communication at the interface of psychology, political science, and history.[13]

Janis found in his historical research that groupthink can have six negative outcomes:

1. The group limits its discussion to only a few alternatives. It does not consider a full range of creative possibilities. The solution seems obvious and simple to the group, and there is little exploration of other ideas.

2. The position initially favored by most members is never restudied to seek out less obvious pitfalls. In other words, the group is not very critical in examining the ramifications of the preferred solution.

3. The group fails to reexamine those alternatives originally disfavored by the majority. Minority opinions are quickly dismissed and ignored, not only by the majority but also by those who originally may have favored them.

4. Expert opinion is not sought. The group is

---

12. Kurt Lewin, *Resolving Social Conflicts: Selected Papers on Group Dynamics* (New York: Harper & Row, 1948). For information on Lewin's theory of group dynamics, see the third edition of this book, *Theories of Human Communication* (Belmont, Calif.: Wadsworth, 1989), pp. 203–206.

13. For a laboratory test of the groupthink hypothesis, see John A. Courtright, "A Laboratory Investigation of Groupthink," *Communication Monographs* 45 (1978): 229–246.

satisfied with itself and may feel threatened by outsiders.

5. The group is highly selective in gathering and attending to available information. The members tend to concentrate only on the information that supports the favored plan.

6. The group is so confident in its chosen alternative that it does not consider contingency plans. It does not forsee the possibility of failure and does not plan for failure.

All these results are really a manifestation of a lack of critical thinking and overconfidence in the judgment of the group.

Janis maintains that groupthink is marked by a number of symptoms. The first symptom of groupthink is an *illusion of invulnerability*, which creates an undue air of optimism. There is a strong sense that, "We know what we are doing, so don't rock the boat." Second, the group creates collective efforts to *rationalize* the course of action decided on. It creates a story that makes its decision seem absolutely right. In other words, the group literally talks itself into thinking it did the right thing. Third, the group maintains an unquestioned belief in the its inherent *morality*, leading to a soft pedaling of ethical or moral consequences. It sees itself as being well motivated and working for the best outcome. Out-group leaders are *stereotyped* as evil, weak, or stupid. Not only is the group itself seen as right, but anybody who is outside and may oppose what the group is doing is seen as patently wrong. In addition, *direct pressure* is exerted on members not to express counteropinions. Dissent is quickly squelched, which leads to the sixth symptom, the *self-censorship* of disagreement. Individual members are reluctant to state opposing opinions and silently suppress their reservations. Thus, there is a shared *illusion of unanimity* within the group. In fact, the decision may not be unanimous, but the group rallies outwardly around a position of solidarity. Finally, groupthink involves the emergence of self-appointed *mindguards* to protect the group and its leader from adverse opinion and unwanted information. The mindguard typically suppresses negative information by counseling participants

not to make things difficult by stating their objections.

What is the answer to the problem of groupthink? Janis believes that decision-making groups need to recognize the dangers of groupthink and suggests steps to prevent it:

1. The leader of a policy-forming group should assign the role of critical evaluator to each member, encouraging the group to give high priority to airing objections and doubts.

2. The leaders in an organization's hierarchy, when assigning a policy-planning mission to a group, should be impartial instead of stating preferences and expectations at the outset.

3. The organization should routinely follow the administrative practice of setting up several independent policy-planning and evaluation groups to work on the same policy question, each carrying out its deliberations under a different leader.

4. Throughout the period when the feasibility and effectiveness of policy alternatives are being surveyed, the policy-making group should from time to time divide into two or more subgroups to meet separately, under different chairmen, and then come together to hammer out their differences.

5. Each member of the policy-making group should discuss periodically the group's deliberations with trusted associates in his own unit of the organization and report back their [sic] reactions.

6. One or more outside experts or qualified colleagues within the organization who are not core members of the policy-making group should be invited to each meeting on a staggered basis and should be encouraged to challenge the views of the core members.

7. At every meeting devoted to evaluating policy alternatives, at least one member should be assigned the role of devil's advocate.

8. Whenever the policy issue involves relations with a rival nation or organization, a sizable bloc [sic] of time (perhaps an entire session) should be spent surveying all warning signals from rivals and constructing alternative scenarios of the rivals' intentions.

9. After reaching a preliminary consensus about what seems to be the best policy alternative, the policy-making group should hold a "second-chance" meeting at which every member is expected to express as vividly as he can all his residual doubts and to rethink the entire issue before making a definitive choice.[14]

One of Janis's cases of successful decision making is the Kennedy administration's response to the Cuban missile crisis. In October 1962, Cuba was caught building offensive nuclear weapon stations and arming them with Soviet missiles. Kennedy had already suffered through one instance of groupthink in the Bay of Pigs invasion the year before, and he seemed to have learned what not to do in these kinds of international crises. He seemed intuitively to know how to avoid groupthink and invoked virtually all of what Janis would later prescribe. For example, he constantly encouraged his advisors to challenge and debate one another. He refrained from leading the group too early with his own opinion, and he set up subgroups to discuss the problem independently so as not to reinforce one another's opinions. Various members, including Kennedy, talked with outsiders and experts about the problem to make sure that fresh opinion was heard. In the end Kennedy successful invoked a military blockade and stopped the Cuban-Soviet development.

This groupthink theory involves in a practical setting some of the important concepts from other research and theory. It demonstrates the viability of group dynamics. In addition, it provides new understandings in its own right.

Group-Decision Quality

Janis emphasizes groupthink as one explanation for error in group decision making. This section examines a theory by Randy Hirokawa and his colleagues, which takes a more comprehensive look at a variety of error sources in group decision making with an eye toward identifying the kinds of things groups must address to become more effective.[15]

The theory begins with a general description of the process used by groups to make decisions.

Groups normally begin by *identifying and assessing a problem*. At this point the group deals with a variety of questions: What happened? Why? Who was involved? What harm resulted? Who was hurt? Next, the group *gathers and evaluates information* about the problem. As the group discusses possible solutions to the problem, information continues to be gathered.

Next, the group generates a variety of *alternative proposals* for handling the problem and discusses the *objectives* it wishes to accomplish in solving the problem. These objectives and alternative proposals are *evaluated*, with the ultimate goal of reaching consensus on a course of action. This general sequence of problem solving is depicted in Figure 13.2.[16]

This sequence of activity largely mirrors Thomas Dewey's problem-solving sequence, which since the publication of *How We Think* in 1910 has greatly influenced twentieth-century pragmatic thought.[17] Dewey's version of the problem-solving process has six steps: (1) expressing a difficulty, (2) defining the problem, (3) analyzing the problem, (4) suggesting solutions, (5) comparing alternatives and testing them against a set of objectives or criteria, and (6) implementing the best solution.

The factors contributing to faulty decisions are easily inferred from the decision-making process outlined in Hirokawa's theory. The first is *improper assessment* of the problem. This involves inadequate or inaccurate analysis of the problem or the situation in which the decision making occurs. The

14. Janis, *Victims*, pp. 262–271.

15. Randy Y. Hirokawa and Dirk R. Scheerhorn, "Communication in Faulty Group Decision-Making," in *Communication and Group Decision-Making*, eds. R. Y. Hirokawa and M. S. Poole (Beverly Hills, Calif.: Sage, 1986), pp. 63–80; Dennis S. Gouran and Randy Y. Hirokawa, "Counteractive Functions of Communication in Effective Group Decision-Making," in *Communica-*

tion and Group Decision-Making, eds. R. Y. Hirokawa and M. S. Poole (Beverly Hills, Calif.: Sage, 1986), pp. 81–92; Randy Y. Hirokawa, "Group Communication and Problem-Solving Effectiveness I: A Critical Review of Inconsistent Findings," *Communication Quarterly* 30 (1982): 134–141; Randy Y. Hirokawa, "Group Communication and Problem-Solving Effectiveness II," *Western Journal of Speech Communication* 47 (1983): 59–74; Randy Y. Hirokawa, "Group Communication and Problem-Solving Effectiveness: An Investigation of Group Phases," *Human Communication Research* 9 (1983): 291–305.

16. Hirokawa and Scheerhorn, "Faulty Group," p. 66.

17. John Dewey, *How We Think* (Boston: Heath, 1910).

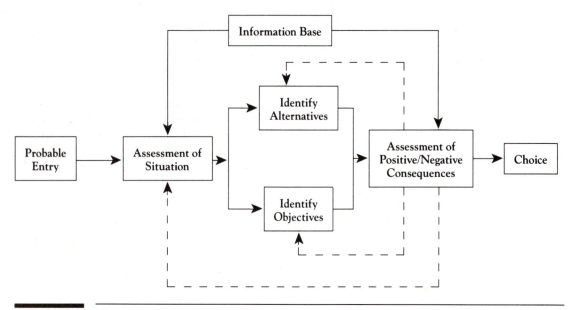

Figure 13.2 General model of the group decision-making process.

group may fail to see the problem, or it may not accurately identify the causes of the problem.

The second source of error in decision making is *inappropriate goals and objectives.* The group may neglect important objectives that ought to be achieved, or it may work toward unnecessary objectives. The third problem is *improper assessment of positive and negative qualities.* Here, the group cannot see the advantages and/or disadvantages of various proposals; or, conversely, the group may overestimate the positive or negative outcomes. Fourth, the group may develop an *inadequate information base.* This can happen in several ways. Valid information may be rejected, or invalid information may be accepted. Too little information may be collected, or too much information may cause overload and confusion. Finally, the group may be guilty of *faulty reasoning* from the information base.

Why do groups fall into these traps? These theorists believe that the errors most often arise from the communicative influences of group members. In other words, the group is swayed by certain members who unwittingly mislead the group in some way. Therefore, the solution to these problems must also be in the hands of individual mem-

bers. If someone can misguide the group, someone can also influence the group positively.

This is basically a functional theory of group decision making. In other words, for a group to make a successful decision, it must meet certain functions. To test this thesis, Hirokawa conducted a study of four potential functions of decision quality: appropriate understanding of the problem, appropriate understanding of the objective and standards of a good decision, appropriate assessment of the positive qualities of alternatives, and appropriate assessment of the negative qualities of alternatives.[18]

In his laboratory he formed about forty three-person groups and had them discuss what to do about a particular plagiarism case at the university. The discussions took from 17 to 47 minutes, and each was videotaped. Two professors with experience with student ethics cases judged the groups' decisions in terms of overall quality, and a panel of judges rated the extent to which each of the four

18. Randy Y. Hirokawa, "Group Communication and Decision Making Performance: A Continued Test of the Functional Perspective," *Human Communication Research* 14 (1988): 487–515.

critical functions was fulfilled. Statistical analysis showed that the quality of a group's decision is definitely related to the critical functions, and when the very best groups were compared to the very worst, there was a significant difference in the extent to which each function was fulfilled. Clearly, groups that were more effective in meeting the four functions made better decisions.

The Interactional Tradition

Group outcome depends greatly on the nature of interaction in the group. Theories of group interaction are especially important in this book because of their central concern for communication as the base of group productivity. We look at two theories of group interaction. The first, an old standard, is Robert Bales's interaction process analysis. The second modifies Bales's notion of interaction and takes interaction analysis in a different direction.

Interaction process analysis. One of the most prominent small-group theories is Robert Bales's *interaction process analysis.*[19] Bales's theory concentrates on interaction or communication per se. Using his many years of research as a foundation, Bales has created a unified and well-developed theory of small-group interaction. It is centered around the idea that people act and react in groups. As one person makes a comment, another person responds to the comment. Bales's aim, then, is to explain the pattern of responses in the small task group. He explains the value of his system:

> Interaction process analysis is built on a very simple common-sense base, and much that one intuitively believes about everyday conversation can be confirmed by it. The surprising thing, perhaps, is that it goes much further than one would suspect in revealing basic attitudes of people, their personalities, and their positions in a group.[20]

19. Robert F. Bales, *Interaction Process Analysis: A Method for the Study of Small Groups* (Reading, Mass.: Addison-Wesley, 1950); *Personality and Interpersonal Behavior* (New York: Holt, Rinehart & Winston, 1970); Robert F. Bales, Stephen P. Cohen, and Stephen A. Williamson, *SYMLOG: A System for the Multiple Level Observation of Groups* (London: Collier, 1979).

20. Bales, *Personality*, p. 95.

Figure 13.3 illustrates the categories of interactions.[21] Each category is a kind of comment that someone could make in a group. These twelve categories are grouped into four broader sets, as outlined at the left of the figure. In addition, the behavior types are paired, and each pair implies a particular problem area for groups, as labeled in Figure 13.3. For example, giving information is paired with asking for information, giving opinion is paired with asking for opinion, and giving a suggestion is paired with asking for a suggestion. These are all question–answer types. Agreement and disagreement, showing tension and dramatizing, seeming unfriendly and seeming friendly are positive, negative, and mixed emotional comments.

There are two general classes of group-communication behavior. The first is *socioemotional behavior,* represented by positive and negative actions like seeming friendly, showing tension, and dramatizing, and the second is *task behavior,* represented by suggestions, opinions, and information. (These are consistent with the same two categories found throughout the small-group literature and encountered earlier in this chapter.) In investigating leadership, Bales has found that typically the same group will have two different kinds of leaders. The *task leader,* who facilitates and coordinates the task-related comments, directs energy toward getting the job done. The emergence of the task leadership role is essential for the problem-solving activity in groups. Equally important is the emergence of a *socioemotional leader,* who works for improved relations in the group, concentrating on interactions in the positive and negative sectors. Usually the task and socioemotional leaders are different people.

The way a person behaves in a group depends on the role the individual takes and the person's personality. Role is situational and depends on the demands of the interpersonal dynamics of the group, including the expectations of others. The way a person behaves will lead to certain perceptions by the other group members.

Bales has shown how the perception of an individual's position in a group is a function of three

21. Adapted from Bales, *Personality*, p. 92.

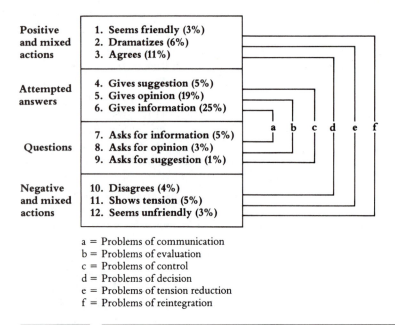

Positive
and mixed
actions

1. Seems friendly (3%)
2. Dramatizes (6%)
3. Agrees (11%)

Attempted
answers

4. Gives suggestion (5%)
5. Gives opinion (19%)
6. Gives information (25%)

Questions

7. Asks for information (5%)
8. Asks for opinion (3%)
9. Asks for suggestion (1%)

Negative
and mixed
actions

10. Disagrees (4%)
11. Shows tension (5%)
12. Seems unfriendly (3%)

a   b   c   d   e   f

a = Problems of communication
b = Problems of evaluation
c = Problems of control
d = Problems of decision
e = Problems of tension reduction
f = Problems of reintegration

Figure 13.3   Categories for interaction process analysis.

dimensions. These include (1) dominant versus submissive, (2) friendly versus unfriendy, and (3) instrumental versus emotional and expressive. These factors are visualized in a three-dimensional space, as shown in Figure 13.4. The axes of the space are labeled positive-negative, upward-downward, and forward-backward.

Within a particular group, any member's behavior can be placed in this three-dimensional space. An individual's position depends on the quadrant in which that individual appears (e.g., upward-positive-forward, or UPF); one's position within the quadrant is determined by the degree of each dimension represented. Thus, for example, a UPF could appear at various points in the space, depending on the degree of U, P, and F. Table 13.1 lists the behavior types and their value directions. When all group members' behavior types are plotted on the spatial graph, their relationships and networks can be seen. The larger the group, the greater the tendency for subgroups of coalitions to develop. These subgroups consist of individuals with similar value dimensions. Obviously, affinity exists among individuals who are close in value

dimension and direction, whereas distant individuals are not connected.

Not only can we predict the coalitions and networks of a group from a knowledge of the distribution of types, but Bales also has shown that behavior type is related to the nature of interaction in groups. The interaction that a person initiates and receives depends in part on his or her behavior type. Keep in mind at this point that one's behavior in a group is determined by both personality and role. Table 13.2 shows how interaction is related to value directions.[22]

One of Bales's most interesting categories is *dramatizing*. In Chapter 8 we looked at Ernest Bormann's development of this idea in symbolic convergence theory. Although convergence theory has been applied to a variety of contexts of communication, including public rhetorical communication, it has special application in small groups.[23]

22. Ibid., pp. 86–97.

23. Ernest Bormann, "Symbolic Convergence and Communication in Group Decision Making," in *Communication and Group Decision-Making*, eds. R. Y. Hirokawa and M. S. Poole (Beverly Hills, Calif.: Sage, 1986), pp. 219–236.

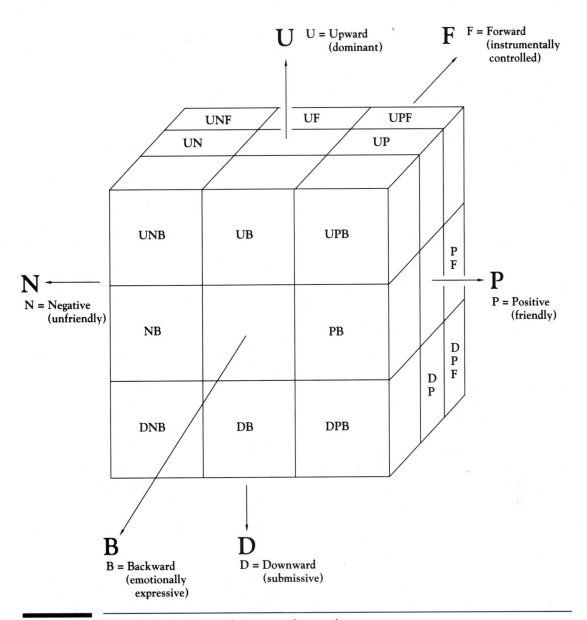

Figure 13.4   Three-dimensional space of interpersonal personality.

Adapted with permission of The Free Press, a Division of Macmillan, Inc. From *SYMLOG: A System for the Multiple Level Observation of Groups* by Robert F. Bales, Stephen P. Cohen and Stephen A. Williamson. Copyright © 1979 by The Free Press.

Bales found that one of the ways in which groups release tension is by telling stories or dramatizing. Bormann believes that this form of communication is very important not only in reducing tension but also in affecting the quality of group discussion in general. Stories are often told and retold within a group. They consist of *fantasy themes* or common elements of knowledge that build a common identity in the group. They constitute the mechanism by which cohesiveness is developed in a group, and we have already seen that cohesiveness can have both positive and negative effects on decision making.

Table 13.1   Types of Group Roles and Associated Characteristics

U:	Active, dominant, talks a lot
UP:	Extroverted, outgoing, positive
UPF:	A purposeful democratic task leader
UF:	An assertive businesslike manager
UNF:	Authoritarian, controlling, disapproving
UN:	Domineering, tough-minded, powerful
UNB:	Provocative, egocentric, shows off
UB:	Jokes around, expressive, dramatic
UPB:	Entertaining, sociable, smiling, warm
P:	Friendly, equalitarian
PF:	Works cooperatively with others
F:	Analytical, task-oriented, problem solving
NF:	Legalistic, has to be right
N:	Unfriendly, negativistic
NB:	Irritable, cynical, won't cooperate
B:	Shows feelings and emotions
PB:	Affectionate, likeable, fun to be with
DP:	Looks up to others, appreciative, trustful
DPF:	Gentle, willing to accept responsibility
DF:	Obedient, works submissively
DNF:	Self-punishing, works too hard
DN:	Depressed, sad, resentful
DNB:	Alienated, quits, withdraws
DB:	Afraid to try, doubts own ability
DPB:	Quietly happy just to be with others
D:	Passive, introverted, says little

Adapted with permission of The Free Press, a Division of Macmillan, Inc. From *SYMLOG: A System for the Multiple Level Observation of Groups* by Robert F. Bales, Stephen P. Cohen and Stephen A. Williamson. Copyright © 1979 by The Free Press.

Some fantasy themes relate to communication and problem solving itself. They express a group's feeling about its own communication and how decisions should be made. These visions shape the way in which the group actually does its work. Such fantasy themes can also affect the motivation of group members. For example, if fantasy themes relate to affiliation and enjoyment, the group may be motivated to meet for social purposes. On the other hand, if fantasy themes relate to task accomplishment and pride, a different set of motivations will operate. Bormann has also shown that a group's creativity can be affected by sharing fantasy themes. Dramatizing itself may provide space and time for group members to think up new ideas.

Fisher's interaction analysis. Aubrey Fisher and his associates have developed a theoretical perspective on group phases and decision emergence that stresses interaction and uses a system orientation. Because their theory is communication-oriented and incorporates much material of previous theories, we study it here in some detail. We look at the general orientation of the interact system model, Fisher's scheme for interaction analysis and the phases of decision emergence, and his ideas on decision making and decision modification.

Often the unit of analysis in group research is the individual's behavior. Aubrey Fisher and Leonard Hawes refer to this as the *human system model*.[24] Clearly Bales's method of analysis, though it is presented as "interaction" analysis, is really a human system approach because it focuses on individual behavior.

Fisher and Hawes believe that a more sensible approach for the study of group communication is the *interact system model*, in which the basic unit of analysis is not an individual act but an interact. An *interact* is the verbal or nonverbal act of one person followed by a reaction from another. Examples are question-answer, statement-statement, greeting-greeting. Here, the unit for analysis is not an individual behavior but a contiguous pair of acts. Fisher

24. B. Aubrey Fisher and Leonard Hawes, "An Interact System Model: Generating a Grounded Theory of Small Groups," *Quarterly Journal of Speech* 57 (1971): 444–453.

and Hawes observe that interacts seem to be organized over time in a hierarchical fashion. Three levels are defined.

The first level involves *interact categories*. These are the specific classes, or types, of interacts observed in groups. For example, an interpretation of a proposal might be followed by a comment seeking clarification of the proposal. A question asking for more information might be followed by someone offering that information. Over the entire discussion, the frequency of such interact categories would be studied to determine how they tend to cluster into interact phases, the second level of analysis.

A study of *interact phases* reveals the pattern of development in the group as it progresses toward task accomplishment. The discussion is not just a series of interacts, one after another. The task of making a decision consists of discernible phases, each characterized by the predominance of particular kinds of interacts. We will look at Fisher's ideas on phasing momentarily.

The third level of analysis is *cycles*. As the group proceeds through a number of tasks, the phases repeat themselves in cyclical fashion. This level of analysis is especially useful in an ongoing group like a club, a board of directors, a standing committee, or a family, where the group does not disappear after it makes a single decision. Fisher observes that such groups tend to work in cycles, repeating the same general trends over and over.

Now let's take a closer look at Fisher's method of interaction analysis. Interacts can be classified on two dimensions, the *content dimension* and the *relationship dimension*. Recall from Chapter 12 that communication messages have a content, or information, dimension and a relationship, or metacommunication, dimension. While a person is making a statement, the individual is also reflecting on the relationship with the other person in some way. For example, if someone were to ask you a question, you would probably answer it, but the manner in which you stated the answer might tip off the group that you thought it was a dumb question. Here, your answer is the content dimension, and your nonverbal comment on the question is the relationship dimension.

Despite the potential utility of analyzing the

Table 13.2 Relationship Between Interaction and Type

Category	Low initiation	High initiation	Low reception	High reception
Seems friendly	N	P	N	P
Dramatizes	DF	UB	NF	PB
Agrees	NB	PF	B	F
Gives suggestion	DB	UF	DN	UP
Gives opinion	B	F	NB	PF
Gives information	U	D	N	P
Asks for information	DN	UP	UF	DB
Asks for opinion	N	P	UP	DN
Asks for suggestion	UB	DF	B	F
Disagrees	P	N	DPB	UNF
Shows tension	UF	DB	DPF	UNB
Seems unfriendly	P	N	DPB	UNF

relational dimension in a group discussion, Fisher has concentrated on the content dimension. Because almost all comments in a task group are related in one way or another to a decision proposal, Fisher classifies statements in terms of how they respond to a decision proposal. The following outline is his classification scheme.[25]

- Interpretation
  - f   Favorable toward the decision proposal
  - u   Unfavorable toward the decision proposal
  - ab Ambiguous toward the decision proposal, containing a bivalued (both favorable and unfavorable) evaluation
  - an Ambiguous toward the decision proposal, containing a neutral evaluation
- Substantiation
  - f   Favorable toward the decision proposal
  - u   Unfavorable toward the decision proposal
  - ab Ambiguous toward the decision proposal, containing a bivalued (both favorable and unfavorable) evaluation
  - an Ambiguous toward the decision proposal, containing a neutral evaluation
- Clarification
- Modification
- Agreement
- Disagreement

Two essential differences exist between the theories of Bales and Fisher. First, Bales classifies a given act strictly in terms of its task or socioemotional function. Fisher assumes that any given act may fulfill either or both functions simultaneously. (Actually, Fisher finds it more appropriate to look at the content and relational dimensions of acts, although these divisions may in some ways be close to Bales's task and socioemotional categories.) Second, Bales classifies only single acts, whereas Fisher classifies interacts. In observing a group, Fisher will create a matrix with twelve rows and twelve col-

umns, corresponding to the twelve categories in his system. This matrix thus contains 144 cells, one for each potential type of interact. In other words, the observer will classify the first act and the second act, placing a mark in the appropriate cell between the two. In this way the researcher can actually see the character and frequency of act pairs in a group discussion. Fisher believes this kind of data is useful for understanding how groups function, how decisions are made, and how groups pass through phases as decisions emerge.

In his theory of decision emergence, Fisher outlines four phases through which task groups tend to proceed: orientation, conflict, emergence, and reinforcement.[26] In observing the distribution of interacts across these phases, Fisher notes the ways interaction changes as the group decision formulates and solidifies. The *orientation phase* involves getting acquainted, clarifying, and beginning to express points of view. A high level of agreement characterizes this stage, and comments are often designed to test the group. Thus, positions expressed are both qualified and tentative. In this phase people grope for direction and understanding.

The *conflict phase* includes a great deal of dissent. People in this second phase begin to solidify their attitudes, and much polarization results. The interacts in this phase tend to include more disagreement and unfavorable evaluation. Members argue and attempt to persuade at this point, and they may form coalitions. As people group together according to their common stands on the issues, polarization grows.

These coalitions tend to disappear in the third phase. In the *emergence phase*, the first inklings of cooperation begin to show. People are less tenacious in defending their viewpoints. As they soften their positions and undergo attitude change, their comments become ambiguous as they try to soften the attitude shifts through which they are going. The number of favorable comments increases until a group decision begins to emerge.

25. B. Aubrey Fisher, *Small Group Decision Making: Communication and the Group Process* (New York: McGraw-Hill, 1980), p. 117.

26. B. Aubrey Fisher, "Decision Emergence: Phases in Group Decision Making," *Speech Monographs* 37 (1970): 53–60; Fisher, *Decision Making*.

In the final phase, *reinforcement,* the group decision solidifies and receives reinforcement from group members. The group unifies, standing behind its solution. Comments are almost uniformly positive and favorable, and more interaction occurs on matters of interpretation. The ambiguity that marked the third phase tends to disappear.

To illustrate the phases of group development, Fisher presents an analysis of a mock jury deliberation in a lawsuit involving an automobile–pedestrian accident.[27] In the first phase, the jury explores its responsibility. What is it supposed to do, and how is it supposed to do it? What are the possible verdicts? Much uncertainty is expressed until clarification emerges. Considerable disagreement arises in the conflict phase as the jury argues over whether the defendant is negligent and the criteria by which they should decide. Here, the interaction tends to be somewhat emotional and heated at times.

In the emergence phase, the jury begins to agree that the defendant is not negligent and that the pedestrian could have avoided the accident. This agreement is somewhat tentative, and the jurors go back-and-forth on the issue, but the emotionality and debate definitely subsides during this period. In the final reinforcement phase, the jury is convinced and keeps saying so. Everybody affirms their agreement in this verdict.

The phases of group decision making characterize the interaction as it changes over time. An important related topic is that of *decision modification.*[28] Fisher finds that groups typically do not introduce only one idea at a time, nor do they introduce a single proposal and continue to modify it until consensus is reached. Rarely is parliamentary format the typical pattern in small-group discussion. Fisher theorizes on the basis of his group observations that decision modification is cyclical; several proposals are made, each discussed briefly, and certain of them reintroduced at a later time. Discussion of proposals seems therefore to proceed

27. Fisher, *Decision Making,* pp. 298–306.

28. Fisher, *Decision Making;* also B. Aubrey Fisher, "The Process of Decision Modification in Small Discussion Groups," *Journal of Communication* 20 (1970): 51–64.

in spurts of energy. Proposal A will be introduced and discussed. The group will suddenly drop this idea and move to proposal B. After discussion of this, the group may introduce and discuss other proposals. Then someone will revive proposal A, perhaps in modified form. The group finally will settle on a modified plan that was introduced earlier in the discussion in a different form.

Why does discussion usually proceed in such an erratic fashion? Probably because the interpersonal demands of discussion require "breaks" from task work. In effect, group attention span is short because of the intense nature of group work. Such an explanation suggests that "flight" behavior helps manage tension and conflict. The group's need to work on interpersonal dynamics is supported by other theories as well, including Collins and Guetzkow's ideas on interpersonal barriers and Bale's notion of socioemotional (versus task) interaction.

Fisher finds that in modifying proposals, groups tend to follow one of two patterns. If conflict is low, the group will reintroduce proposals in less abstract, more specific language. For example, in a discussion of a public health nursing conference, an original idea to begin "with a non-threatening something" was modified to "begin with a history of the contributions which public health has made to the field of nursing."[29] A group, as it successively returns to a proposal, seems to follow the pattern of stating the problem, discussing criteria for solution, introducing an abstract solution, and moving finally to a concrete solution. Keep in mind, however, that the group most likely will not move through these four steps with continuity. Rather, it will deal sporadically with these themes as members depart from and return to the proposal in a stop-and-start fashion.

The second typical pattern of modification occurs when conflict is higher. Here, the group does not attempt to make a proposal more specific. Because disagreement exists on the very nature of the proposal, the group introduces substitute proposals of the same level of abstraction as the origi-

29. Fisher, *Decision Making,* p. 155.

nal. In the first pattern, which involves making proposals more specific, the group task seems to be one of mutual discovery of the best specific implementation of a general idea.

Fisher's theory is an example of a phase model of group development. Phase models predict that groups go through a series of stages in dealing with a problem or set of tasks. Because there have been many such models in the history of small-group theory, the phase approach constitutes the dominant view of group development.[30] Recently, however, phase models have been criticized for being overly simple.[31] In the next section, we examine a theory that views group action and development in a more complex and potentially more useful way than have the preceding approaches.

The Structurationist Perspective

The input–process–output model has contributed much to our understanding of small-group decision making. However, it has emphasized only one aspect of the group process by taking a fundamentally deterministic approach. Largely ignored is the way in which individuals in groups act to create their realities. Recently, a group of communication researchers have recognized this problem and proposed a new perspective—the structurational approach.[32]

30. Some of the most prominent phase models are discussed in R. F. Bales and F. L. Strodbeck, "Phases in Group Problem-Solving," *Journal of Abnormal and Social Psychology* 46 (1951): 485–495; M. A. Bell, "Phases in Group Problem-Solving," *Small Group Behavior* 13 (1982): 475–495; W. G. Bennis and H. A. Shepard, "The Theory of Group Development," *Human Relations* 9 (1956): 415–437; R. Lacoursiere, *The Life Cycle of Groups* (New York: Human Sciences Press, 1980); Bruce Tuckman, "Developmental Sequence in Small Groups," *Psychological Bulletin* 63 (1965): 384–399.

31. These arguments are summarized in Marshall Scott Poole, "Decision Development in Small Groups, III: A Multiple Sequence Model of Group Decision Development," *Communication Monographs* 50 (1983): 321–342.

32. Marshall Scott Poole, David R. Seibold, and Robert D. McPhee, "Group Decision-Making as a Structurational Process," *Quarterly Journal of Speech* 71 (1985): 74; Poole, Seibold, and McPhee, "Structurational Approach."

Structuration Theory

Structuration theory is a general theory of social action. It is the brainchild of sociologist Anthony Giddens and his followers.[33] This theory says that human action is a process of producing and reproducing various social systems. Groups act according to rules to achieve their goals and in so doing create structures that in turn affect future actions. Structures like relational expectations, group roles and norms, communication networks, and societal institutions both affect and are affected by social action. These structures provide individuals with rules that guide their actions, but their actions in turn create new rules and reproduce old ones.

Giddens overcomes the debate between those who hold that human action is caused by outside forces and those who advocate the intentionality of human action; instead, Giddens claims that both sides in this dispute are right because social life is a two-sided coin. We do have intentions and act to accomplish these; at the same time, our actions have the unintended consequences of establishing or reinforcing structures that affect our future actions. Indeed, we do act to attain goals, and we monitor our actions and their outcomes; at the same time, however, we are unaware of many of the outcomes of action and their consequent structures.

Consider an example from group communication. A group member will talk to the group about certain concerns. In so doing, that individual is accomplishing specific objectives. At the same time, other group members come to see this person as one who has particular ideas and who can do special kinds of things. They will come to expect the person to behave in certain ways and to follow up on certain concerns. This is how the person's role is created. Over time the person's role, which was very much an unintended consequence of his or her action, will become a kind of structure that constrains that individual's future behavior in the

33. See, for example, Anthony Giddens, *New Rules of Sociological Method* (New York: Basic Books, 1976); *Studies in Social and Political Theory* (New York: Basic Books, 1977). For a brief summary of the theory, see *Profiles and Critiques in Social Theory* (Berkeley: University of California Press, 1982), pp. 8–11.

group. Giddens believes that this kind of "structuration" saturates all social life.

Giddens believes that structuration always involves three major modalities, or dimensions of structure, that affect and are affected by action. These are (1) interpreting or understanding, (2) a sense of morality or proper conduct, and (3) a sense of power in action. The rules we use to guide our actions, in other words, tell us how something should be understood (interpretation), what should be done (morality), and how to get things accomplished (power). In turn, our actions reinforce those very structures of interpretation, morality, and power.

In actual practice one's behavior is rarely affected by a single structure. Indeed, one's action of the moment is normally affected by and affects several different structural elements. Structures therefore relate to and affect one another. This can happen in two ways. The first is that one structure mediates another. In other words, the production of one structure is accomplished by producing another. For example, the group may produce a communication network, but it does so by establishing individual roles. Here, the role structure mediates the communication network.

The second way in which structures relate is through contradiction. Here, the production of a structure requires the establishment of another structure that undermines the first one. This is the stuff of classical paradox. Contradictions lead to conflict, and through a dialectic or tension between contradictory elements, system change results. The old problem of task and socioemotional work is a good example of contradictory structure. To accomplish a task, the group has to work on its interpersonal relationships, but working on relationships detracts from accomplishment of task. The consequences of this contradiction is already well explored by some of the theories presented earlier in the chapter.

Structuration and Decision Development

Relying on the ideas of Giddens and his followers, Scott Poole and his colleagues have been working on a structurational theory of group decision

making for several years.[34] This theory teaches that group decision making is a process in which group members attempt to achieve *convergence*, or agreement, on a final decision. Individuals express their opinions and preferences and thereby produce and reproduce certain rules by which convergence can be achieved or blocked.

In trying to achieve convergence, group members make use of Giddens's three elements of action—interpretation, morality, and power. Interpretation is made possible through language, morality is established through group norms, and power is achieved through the interpersonal power structures that have emerged in the group.

Suppose, for example, that a member of a group is interested in persuading other members to endorse a particular plan. He or she would express a shared understanding of the plan by using commonly understood language. The participant would behave in a way condoned by the group according to its norms. And the member would also attempt to persuade others and be effective in meeting the objective. To do this the speaker would make use of a variety of sources of power, like leadership ability or status. The speech delivered by this group member may or may not accomplish the objective, but it will certainly have the unintended consequence of helping reproduce the shared understandings and lingo, norms, and power structures of the group.

This theory of group decision making recognizes the importance of outside factors in influencing the group's actions; however, outside factors have meaning only insofar as they are understood and interpreted by the group, and these interpretations are negotiated through interaction within the group. One of the most important outside factors is task type, what the group has been given to do. The group's task makes certain rules appropriate and others inappropriate. For example, a study group

34. Poole, Seibold, and McPhee, "Group Decision-Making." For a recent overview of the entire project, see Marshall Scott Poole and Jonelle Roth, "Decision Development in Small Groups IV: A Typology of Group Decision Paths," *Human Communication Research* 15 (1989): 323–356; "Decision Development in Small Groups V: Test of a Contingency Model," *Human Communication Research* 15 (1989): 549–589.

will behave in one way when preparing for an upcoming exam and in an entirely different way when designing a group project for the class.

This theory also recognizes that the definition of persons in the group is always an outcome of structuration. We act toward others in ways that reflect our views of their place in the group, and in time a "group" definition of each person and the group as a whole emerges. This group definition subsequently affects the interaction among the members of the group and is thereby reproduced again and again. The key concept to understanding the definition of the person is role. The expected behavior pattern in a group is a structure that emerges from the actions of the group in its ongoing work. This role-establishing work is "microstructuration."

Poole and his associates believe that task groups are rife with contradiction. Consistent with Giddens, they see group structuration as deeply embedded in the process of producing and resolving these inherent tensions. For example, the group must meet certain time pressures, but they are also required to make good decisions, which may not be possible if done in a speedy fashion. They must attend to the requirements of the task, but in so doing they must also take care of their socioemotional needs, which by definition detract from task work. Members join the group to meet individual objectives, but they can only do so by attending to group objectives, which may undercut individual goals. Convergence can only come about through agreement, yet the group is told it must disagree in order to test ideas; by eliminating poor options, they can agree on the good options. In large measure, group structuration is a process of working through these contradictions.

One of the most interesting contributions of this theory is its version of the processes followed by groups as they make decisions. This theory contrasts with two other types of decision-development theories. *Unitary-phase models* such as that of Fisher suggest a singular set of stages through which all groups pass, and *nonphase models* characterize groups as erratic and unsystematic.

Poole and his colleagues have developed a *contingency theory* that takes an intermediate position on the issue of how organized groups are. It proposes that groups can follow a variety of paths in the development of a decision, depending on the contingencies with which they are faced. Groups sometimes follow a predictable procedure such as the one Hirokawa recommends, sometimes they are unsystematic, and sometimes they develop their own pathway in response to unique needs.

How a group operates depends on three sets of variables. The first is *objective task characteristics*, which are the standard attributes of the task regardless of the group or situation. These include the degree to which the problem comes with preestablished solutions, the clarity of the problem, the kind of expertise it requires, the extent of the impact of the problem, the number and nature of values implicit in the problem, and whether the solution is a one-shot action or will have broader policy implications.

For example, you might be involved in a club that has to decide whether and how to participate in a town festival. This may be a difficult decision because it involves many possible options, the potential number of values entering into the decision is fairly high, and what you decide to do this year may affect what you can do in subsequent years. This decision may take some time, and the decision path may be complex. On the other hand, if your group merely has to decide whether to have a taco booth, the decision is simple: The range of options is limited, the values involved in the decision are few, and the decision will have little impact outside the club. This decision will probably be made quickly and simply.

The second set of variables that affects the group's decision path is *group-task characteristics;* these are the characteristics of the task that will vary from group to group. They include the extent to which the group has previous experience with the problem, the extent to which an innovative solution is required as opposed to adoption of a standard course of action, and the urgency of the decision. In the case of deciding what to do in the town festival, your group may have previous experience (or not); it may choose a typical activity such as having a food booth (or create a new idea);

and it may or may not be urgent, depending on the deadline for applying to participate.

The third group of factors affecting the path of a group is *group structural characteristics*, including cohesiveness, power distribution, history of conflict, and group size. If your club has many members, gives the officers most of the power, and has a history of conflict, one kind of process will be used; but if it is small, cohesive, and has shared power, quite another would be predicted.

These three sets of factors will operate to influence the process adopted by the group, including whether it uses a standard or a unique path, the complexity of the decision path, the amount of organization or disorganization with which the task is handled, and the amount of time devoted to various activities. To continue our example, your club might use a standard method of solving problems, such as Hirokawa's pattern, or it might develop a different method. The club's procedure may turn out to be simple and brief, but it could become complex and contorted; similarly, it could turn out to be organized, even though complex, or it may be completely unsystematic.

To discover various decision paths adopted by different groups, Scott Poole and Jonelle Roth studied forty-seven decisions made by twenty-nine different groups.[35] The groups differed in their size, task complexity, urgency, cohesiveness, and conflict history. They included a medical school teaching team, an energy conservation–planning group, student term-project groups, a dormitory management committee, and a number of others. Each discussion was tape-recorded and analyzed. Each task statement in a discussion was classified by judges according to type, and these were combined into interacts similar to those of Fisher discussed earlier. Also, every 30-second segment was classified according to a set of relationship categories. With a sophisticated method of analysis, the researchers could see the various decision paths that emerged in these interactions on both the task and relationship tracks.

Three general types of paths were discovered. Some groups followed a standard *unitary sequence*, although not always exactly the same way. Several groups followed what Poole and Roth call a *complex cyclic sequence*. Most of these were problem–solution cycles, in which the group would go back-and-forth in concentrated work between defining the problem and generating solution ideas. The third type of sequence was *solution-oriented*, in which almost no problem analysis occurred.

The decision paths taken by a group consist of three interwoven activity tracks. The *activity tracks* are the courses along which the group develops or moves. A group may develop in different ways on each track, and the course of action taken on each track will be affected in part by the three contingency variables discussed above—objective task characteristics, group-task characteristics, and group structural characteristics.

There are probably many possible tracks, but three are elaborated in this theory—the task-process track, the relational track, and the topic-focus track. The *task-process track* consists of activities that directly deal with the problem or task, including, for example, problem analysis, designing solutions, evaluating solutions, and getting off on tangents. The *relational track* involves activities that affect interpersonal relationships in the group, such as disagreeing and making accommodations. These two correspond neatly with the task-maintenance duality encountered in several other theories presented in this chapter. The third track, the *topic-focus track*, is a series of issues, topics, or concerns of the group over time.

Figure 13.5 illustrates the activity tracks and how they work together.[36] The multiple-sequence model imagines that the group moves along the various tracks over time, as illustrated by the time scale at the bottom of the graph. At a given moment, the group may be at a particular "spot" in the development of each track. The figure shows the three tracks divided into various activity seg-

---

35. Poole and Roth, "Decision Development IV"; "Decision Development V."

36. Adapted from Poole, "Decision Development III," pp. 327, 329; Poole and Roth, "Decision Development IV," pp. 334–335.

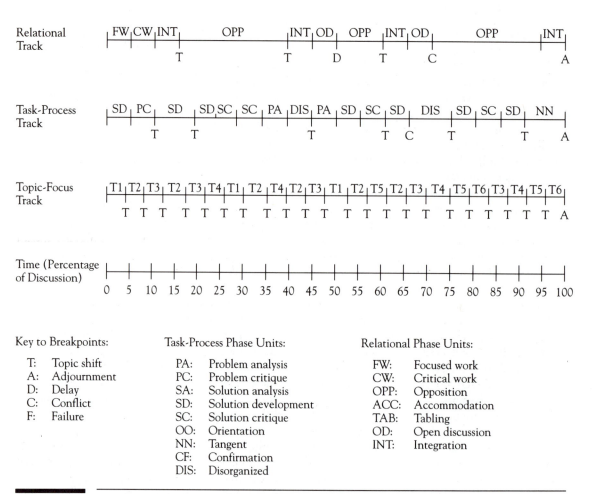

Figure 13.5   Sample discussion with activity tracks.

ments. The activity segments are identified by code letters above the line. (The letters below the line are breakpoints, which will be explained later.)

In the discussion depicted in Figure 13.5, the group begins with topic 1 (T1). In discussing this topic, the group is involved in focused work (FW) in the relational track and solution development (SD) in the task-process track. As they move to another topic, the group enters problem critique (PC) on the task-process track while they are engaged in critical work (CW) on the relational track. The discussion goes on for some time through a number of phases until the end, when they go off on a tangent (NN) on the task-process

track but accomplish integration (INT) on the relational track. Notice that the activity segments or phases on the different tracks in the discussion depicted in this graph do not necessarily correspond to one another, which adds to the complexity of the path.

During the discussion, breakpoints occur from time to time. A *breakpoint* is a point of transition in a track from one topic or emphasis to another. These are designated by a code letter below the lines in Figure 13.5. Sometimes a breakpoint will mark a change in a single track, but often it will mark changes in several tracks. Breakpoints are important because they signal important points in the development of the group's decision-making activity.

Three types of breakpoints are apparent. *Normal breakpoints* are the expected, natural points of termination or transition. They include such things as adjournment, caucusing, or topic shifts. *Delays* are unexpected problems that cause a pause in normal group functioning. Delays often consist of rediscussion of issues necessary for the group to resolve conflicts or establish understanding. Delays may be a sign of impending difficulty, or they may be a more positive sign of careful thought or creative activity. *Disruptions* are more serious. These consist of major disagreements and group failures. You can see in Figure 13.5 how the flow of activity in each track is interrupted by various types of breakpoints.

Although this is a somewhat complex and sophisticated theory, it expresses the structurational character of group decision making very well. It shows that groups do adopt particular courses of action to meet their needs but that in so doing they create structures that limit future action.

Commentary and Critique

Groups are important to individuals and society. As a person moves about in the world, cooperation becomes essential in achieving goals. People use communication to share resources in the solution of problems, and group communication thereby becomes not only an instrument for accomplishing tasks but also a means of group maintenance and cohesion.

Group communication can be viewed as a system of inputs, internal processes, and outputs. In decision making the inputs include information, group resources, and task characteristics. The process includes group interaction and decision development, and the outputs include completed tasks and solved problems.

Group communication is also a form of structuration. The practices of the group create structures that limit future practices. Input–process–output

models and structuration theories are not necessarily incompatible but provide two different ways of looking at group functioning. In many ways the theory of Poole and his associates is an input–process–output model because it posits a set of factors that affect processing, which in turn shapes outcomes. The difference is that this structurational model acknowledges the power of groups to shape the course of their own process to a certain extent.

Theories of small-group decision making form a distinct tradition. Their common threads and lines of influence are clear and provide a kind of coherence that binds this work. Certain basic ideas run through this history, as subsequent theories extend and develop earlier ideas. The division of group effort into task and socioemotional factors is a good example of this feature. It appears in almost all theories discussed in this chapter. Task energy is directed at problem solving, and socioemotional energy is directed at group maintenance and interpersonal relationships. Group effectiveness seems to depend on the balance between these two kinds of communication. Inadequate attention to these two factors can lead to dissatisfaction and poor decision making.

Perhaps the most influential theory to make the task–relationship distinction is Bales's foundational work. Bales's theory is an excellent beginning for understanding interaction in groups. His approach is highly parsimonious and internally consistent. It is built on a sensible and intuitively appealing conceptual base, from which a number of propositions about group interaction are derived.

Bales envisions the group as a body that swings between discussion of task matters and discussion of social matters, back-and-forth. Careful examination of groups in action, however, shows that task and socioemotional functions are thoroughly mixed. One can fulfill both task and social functions in a single statement, and in classifying group behavior, validly separating these functions is difficult. True, a given statement may be mostly task or mostly social but to separate them completely would be a mistake.

This theory is strictly act-oriented and fails to describe true interaction. It presumes that any statement will stand on its own apart from contiguous statements by other persons. Fisher, in contrast, shows how analyses that stop at the act level are not adequate. For Fisher, true interaction analysis must look at contiguous acts as the basic unit of analysis. Fisher's work, then, constitutes the second generation of interaction analysis. Although Fisher's theory admits to the existence of the relational dimension of interaction, it makes no attempt to correlate the content and relational aspects of group discussion.

In general, Bales's and Fisher's theories share a common strength and a common weakness. The strength is that interaction analysis, whether of the Bales or Fisher type, allows us to look carefully at the communication behavior of groups, correlating messages with other group factors. In other words, interaction analysis provides a way to analyze group communication. Thus, these theories are both appropriate and heuristic. These advantages, however, have been gained at the price of a trade-off, which leads to their common weakness. When individual acts (or interacts) are analyzed according to a classification scheme, rich idiosyncratic meanings are glossed over. The value of understanding general group trends is bought at the price of thorough understanding of particular events in groups.

The third generation of work on task and relationship communication is represented by the research of Poole and his colleagues. It is an advance on Fisher's theory because it accounts for both tracks at the same time. It also takes a step toward capturing the ideosyncratic nature of the group experience by showing how groups can create very different patterns of decision making.

A second theme of group decision making is group structure. Group structure occurs in a variety of ways. Individuals differ in the kinds of statements they make in a group. Bales's research in the early 1950s classifies statements according to various categories and relates individual actions to roles. He shows how the group interaction is shaped by the types of statements made and the roles assigned to individuals from their statements. He also shows how subgroups form according to the personalities of the individuals in the group.

Fisher uses somewhat different categories, and he is interested in how statements respond to one another in interacts. Even Poole's very sophisticated work begins with the classification of statements and interacts. Poole, however, goes far beyond any of his predecessors in showing how interacts combine into activity segments and how these segments combine into phases. Poole's notion of group structure is sophisticated and complex because he shows how several structures may be present in a group.

A third long-term theme in small-group research is decision development. Interaction differs from one time period within a discussion to another, and most theorists see this movement as a linear process of development. The precise nature of this development is still unclear and in dispute, but the theorists are still looking for it. Poole's theory has great potential for revealing the complexity and individuality of group-decision development.

The fourth trend in small-group theory is its interest in effectiveness. Janis's theory is appealing for this reason. It stems not only from laboratory research but also from field application and historical case study. It is a theory that demonstrates the utility of group-dynamics ideas in understanding actual groups at work. As we have seen repeatedly in this book, one of the failings of most communication theories is that they are based on limited perspectives or on limited types of research. Theories such as Janis's are like a breath of fresh air in this regard. In fact, if you look at the kind of data used throughout small-group research, you see a wide spectrum of variety and real-world application. Poole's use of real decision-making groups in the field is another example.

Janis's theory is different also because of its applied nature. It is a normative, or prescriptive, theory providing guidelines for improved group functioning. However, this aspect of the theory leads to one of its weaknesses, namely, that it does not take us very far in understanding or explaining how groups function. It suggests a way of guarding against one particular danger in groups, but it does not help us understand the nature of cohesiveness, conflict, roles, or communication. For this reason some scholars would be reluctant to call Janis's work a theory at all. Janis himself refers to this application merely as an hypothesis.

Hirokawa's theory is also highly normative. It is consistent with the everyday experience of groups in our society, and it seems to have practical potential in helping groups become more effective.

Hirokawa's theory also limits group functioning to a kind of rational task-only process. It fails to acknowledge the ways in which group successes and failures are a result of socioemotional or relational activity. In addition, the theory does not adequately integrate problems that are out of the control of the group, such as the vagaries of the situation or the pragmatic obstacles to information gathering.

Small-group theory is an interesting and important part of the overall study of communication, but it is not very popular now. This is puzzling because the work that has been done is important and sophisticated. In an article on small-group theory, Poole reflects on the status of the field.[37] He acknowledges that there have been substantial theoretical advances in small group–communication theory in the 1980s, but he feels that it lacks a spark. Specifically, Poole maintains that small-group theory lacks three critical qualities.

37. Poole, "Do We Have Any Theories?"

First, it lacks the kind of imagination that will attract attention and interest. It lacks a metaphor that could inspire creative involvement. Poole would like to see more use of such images as fantasy themes, which use a dramatistic metaphor. He suggests such metaphors as the group as clan or tribe, group communication as exchange, and group work as computer-like.

Second, the area has not persuasively framed its problems as intriguing puzzles. Group theorists need to show how their work has intellectual significance. The question of whether the group really matters in decision making is a good example of the kind of puzzle of which Poole is thinking. The issue of whether group work is primarily individual or social is another example. Here, the issue is where the locus of decision making really lies, in the group or in the individual.

Third, group-communication scholars need to show that their work has important real-world implications. Clearly, groups are important, but do the theories adequately capture this quality? Are the outcome measures realistic, and do the theories catch the essence of what real groups feel like?

Poole's concerns are thought-provoking and should challenge not only small-group theorists but also scholars in all areas of the field.

CHAPTER 14

Communication and Organizational Networks

According to sociologist Amatai Etzioni,

Our society is an organizational society. We are born in organizations, educated in organizations, and most of us spend much of our lives working for organizations. We spend much of our leisure time playing and praying in organizations. Most of us will die in an organization, and when the time comes for burial, the largest organization of all—state—must grant official permission.[1]

We know that a great deal of communication takes place in the context of the organization, and a large body of literature and theory has been written about human communication in organizations. In our search to understand the communication process, it is important for us to browse along the way in the area of organizational theory.

Organizations can be understood in a variety of ways. Gareth Morgan has written that the best approach to studying organizations is by using mul-

tiple perspectives because any one definition is too limiting.[2] Morgan outlines a number of metaphors that capture various aspects of organizations. One is the organization as *machine,* in which a product or service is produced by parts functioning together. Another is the organization as an *organism.* Like a plant or animal, the organization is born, grows, functions, and adapts to changes in the environment, and eventually it dies. Organizations are also like *brains:* They process information, they have intelligence, they conceptualize, and they make plans. Organizations are *cultures* because they create meaning, have values and norms, and are perpetuated by shared stories and rituals.

A complete explanation of an organization must also liken it to a *political system,* in which power is distributed, influence is exerted, and decisions are made. Morgan shows, too, that organizations are *psychic prisons* because in many ways they shape and

1. Amatai Etzioni, *Modern Organizations* (Englewood Cliffs, N.J.: Prentice-Hall, 1964), p. 1.

2. Gareth Morgan, *Images of Organization* (Beverly Hills, Calif.: Sage, 1986).

limit the lives of their members. He says that they are also *flux* and *transformation* because they adjust, change, and grow on the basis of information, feedback, and logical force. Finally, Morgan says that organizations are *instruments of domination:* They possess competing interests, some of which dominate others.

Organizational communication for many years has been an important part of the communication discipline. We have already encountered theories of organizational communication in earlier chapters on topics such as systems and interpretation. The theme chosen to organize a variety of theories of organizational communication in this chapter is the network. As a way of organizing or understanding, the network can be added to the list of metaphors on Morgan's list.

Networks are social structures created by communication among individuals and groups.[3] As people communicate with others, contacts and links are made, and these channels become instrumental in all forms of social functioning, in organizations and in society at large. Networks are a useful theme for organizing this material because they capture virtually all aspects of organizational communication in one way or another. They tell us about the structures and functions of an organization. They are the means by which social reality is constructed within the organization so that network communication is not only instrumental but also cultural. Networks are also the channels through which influence and power are exerted, not only by management in a formal way but also informally among organizational members.

Peter Monge and Eric Eisenberg see network theory as a way of integrating three traditions of organizational studies.[4] The first is the *positional tradition,* which has been concerned with formal structure and roles in organizations. The organization in this tradition is viewed as a set of positions, each with assigned functions. This tradition is an obviously structural approach that defines an organization as a stable set of formally defined relations.

Communication theories consistent with this tradition range from the old, still popular, and useful bureaucratic theory of Max Weber, to the often cited and controversial human relations theory of Rensis Likert, to the recently developed theory of George Cheney and Phillip Tompkins on organizational identification and control.

The second tradition related to networks is the *relational.* This tradition deals with the ways in which relationships naturally develop among participants in an organization and the manner in which networks emerge from these contacts. Here, the organization is seen as a living, changing system constantly shaped and given meaning by the interactions among members. Carl Weick's well-known theory of organizing is a good example of this tradition.

The third tradition is *cultural.* Here, symbols and meaning are central. The world of the organization is created by the members in stories, rituals, and task work. The real structure of the organization is not designed in a formal sense but emerges from the actions of the members informally in their daily work. Anthony Giddens's structuration theory, which we encountered in Chapter 13, shows how organizational structure is created in this way. Interpretive theories of organizations, which were encountered in Chapter 10, translate this structurational activity into cultural meanings.

In the following section, we look at an integrative network theory to discover the nature of networks, how they are formed, and what they do. Then, we look in turn at each of the traditions outlined by Monge and Eisenberg—the positional, the relational, and the cultural. According to Monge and Eisenberg, relational and cultural theories have much in common as each relates to emergent rather than formal networks. These theories are therefore treated in the same section in this chapter.

3. For a discussion of the network idea, see Peter R. Monge, "The Network Level of Analysis," in *Handbook of Communication Science,* eds. C. R. Berger and S. H. Chaffee (Newbury Park, Calif.: Sage, 1987), pp. 239–270.

4. Peter R. Monge and Eric M. Eisenberg, "Emergent Communication Networks," in *Handbook of Organizational Communication: An Interdisciplinary Perspective,* eds. F. M. Jablin et al. (Newbury Park, Calif.: Sage, 1987), pp. 304–342.

Networks: An Integrative View

The work of Peter Monge, Eric Eisenberg, Richard Farace, and several of their colleagues constitutes an excellent overview of network concepts.[5] Their writings integrate an eclectic set of ideas in an internally consistent fashion, providing a synthesis of the network view based on many of their own and others' research studies.

The authors define an organization as a system of at least two people (usually many more), with interdependence, input, throughput, and output. This group communicates and cooperates to produce some product by using energy, information, and materials from the environment. This definition follows the classic systems approach to organizations outlined in Chapter 3.

One of the most important resources in organizations is information. Using information theory (Chapter 3) as a base, these scholars define information in terms of the reduction of uncertainty. As a person becomes able to predict which patterns will occur in the organization, uncertainty is reduced, and information is gained. Communication requires the use of common symbolic forms that refer to mutually understood referents.

The authors delineate two types of communication, which correspond to two types of information. *Absolute information* consists of all pieces of knowledge present in the system. *Distributed information* is that which has been diffused through the organization. The fact that information exists in an organization therefore does not guarantee that it will be communicated adequately in the system. Questions of absolute information deal with what is known, whereas questions of distribution deal with who knows it. The practical implication of this theoretical distinction is that "failures in distribution policies are due to failures by managers to identify which groups of personnel need to know

certain things, or to establish where these groups are supposed to be able to obtain the information they need."[6]

These theorists use three analytic dimensions in their analysis. The first of these is the *level of analysis*—individual, dyadic, group, organizational, and interorganizational. The structure of the organization is built up as individuals communicate with others in dyads, as dyads cluster into groups, and as groups are linked into an overall network. Organizations themselves are interconnected with one another in the interorganizational network. Levels are addressed in more detail later.

The second dimension of analysis is the *function of communication*, including production, innovation, and maintenance. *Production communication* deals with the direction, coordination, and control of task activities, including what to, when to do it, and how to do it. *Innovation communication* generates change and new ideas in the system. It is the pathway through which suggestions and insights are communicated. *Maintenance communication* preserves individual values and interpersonal relations necessary to keep the system together. This type of communication includes workers' social and individual needs, the things that make working a pleasure in places where maintenance is well served. All these functions are accomplished by communicating in the dyad, in the group, and throughout the network.

The third dimension in the framework is *structure*. Whereas function deals with the content of messages, structure deals with the emergent patterns or regularities in the transmission of messages. Thus, for every level in the organization—individual, dyadic, group, and organizational—we can investigate the way that communication functions and how it is structured.

Let us turn our attention now to the levels of analysis, beginning with the individual. The key concept related to *individual communication* is load. Communication *load* is the rate and complexity of information. *Rate* is the quantity of inputs such as messages or requests, and *complexity* is the number

---

5. Monge and Eisenberg, "Emergent Communication"; Richard V. Farace, Peter R. Monge, and Hamish Russell, *Communicating and Organizing* (Reading, Mass.: Addison-Wesley, 1977).

6. Farace, Monge, and Russell, *Communicating*, p. 28.

of factors that must be dealt with in processing the information. In school, for example, you have times when you feel overloaded because of the amount of work you have to do. Your workload is a function of how many assignments you have been given (rate) and how difficult they are (complexity).

Two problem areas relate to load. *Underload* occurs when the flow of messages to a person falls below the person's ability to process them, and *overload* occurs when the load exceeds the person's capacity. For students, overload often occurs just before final examinations, and underload often happens at the end of vacation when boredom starts to set in. The concepts of load, underload, and overload can be applied to all levels of analysis, including dyadic, group, and organizational. Thus, for example, an entire organization might be underloaded or overloaded, as you have sometimes detected when an entire class complains that they can't get the work done.

The second level of analysis is the *dyad*. The key concept applicable to the dyad level of communication is rules. *Rules* or expectations about what people are supposed to do were discussed in some detail in Chapters 5 and 8. Organizations have explicit and implicit rules for communicating, which tell one how to communicate, when to communicate, with whom to communicate, and what to communicate about. Some common rule topics include the following: who initiates interactions; how delays are treated; what topics are discussed, and who selects them; how topic changes are handled; how outside interruptions are handled; how interactions are terminated; and how frequently communication occurs. Individual dyads are affected by these more general organizational rules, but they also develop idiosyncratic rules of their own.

The *links* between persons in a dyad are characterized by five properties. The first is *symmetry*, or the degree to which the members connected by a link interact on an equal basis. In a symmetrical relationship, the members give and take information relatively equally. An asymmetric link goes primarily one way, with a distinct information

sender and receiver, whereas a symmetric link flows both ways so that each participant is both sender and receiver. An army sergeant giving orders to a recruit is an example of an asymmetrical link, whereas two soldiers working side-by-side probably have a symmetrical link.

The second property of links is *strength*, which is a simple function of interaction frequency. Members who communicate more often have a stronger link, whereas those who communicate less often have a weaker one. Most professors probably have a pretty weak link to the dean, whereas two professors who do research together have a strong one.

Reciprocity, the third property of links, is the extent to which members agree about their links. If one person believes that he or she often communicates with another but the other denies it, the link is unreciprocated. The fourth property of links is the predominant *content* of the interaction— communication about work, social matters, or other topics. By probing the content of links in a network, we can discern the network's overall function. A *multiplex link* is one that has several types of content. The final property of links is *mode*. Here the question is, How is communication achieved? By what channel? Modes may be face-to-face conversations, group meetings, or communication via letter or telephone.

The third level of analysis is the *group*, or clique. Network researchers define a group by four criteria: (1) More than half of the members' communication is within the group; (2) each person must be linked with all others in the group; (3) the group will not break apart with the exit of one person or the destruction of one link; (4) the group must have at least three members. Through everyday contact among people in an organization, individuals in groups tend to work, interact, and communicate together. In fact, the structure of the overall organization depends on these groupings. Because people work together in different groups for different functions, different kinds of groups exist in an organization, and a given individual simultaneously may be a member of several groups. Carrying this analysis one step further, we must realize that the organization consists of multiple structures. For example, structures may be built on task relations, power relations, liking, and others. We will return to this idea of organizational structure in a moment. First, let's look at some characteristics of network groups.

To begin with, we note that groups themselves tend to have internal structures. Farace and colleagues outline three types of structure. The first, the communication pattern or *micronetwork*, is the lines of communication between the members of the group. The question here is, Who communicates with whom within the group? The second kind of structure involves *power*. Here the question is, Who has what kind of power over whom? The third type of structure stressed in this theory is *leadership*. Leadership structure deals with role distribution in the group, specifically the distribution of roles related to interpersonal influence of group members.

The fourth level of analysis is the organizational, or the *macronetwork*, a repetitive pattern of information transmission among the groups in an organization. It represents the organization's overall structure. An organization may consist of a number of networks, each providing a major function for the organization. Perhaps the most commonly understood network is the formal organizational chart, which is the prescribed task network. In addition, a number of informal networks may also exist. Any network consists of two fundamental parts: the members and their links. Clearly, any person may be a member of a number of groups within a number of networks, depending on his or her links with others in the organization.

As organizational members relate to one another, they take different network *roles*. Those who do not communicate with others in a network are *isolates*. *Bridges* are group members who are linked to a member of another group. *Liaisons* are not members of any group, yet they link two or more groups, as Figure 14.1 illustrates.[7] Some individuals are linked to a larger number of groups, and these people are called *stars*.

7. Ibid., p. 192.

Organizational networks can be characterized by a number of qualities. The first is *size*, or the sheer number of people in the network. The second characteristic, one of the most commonly studied, is *centrality*, or the degree to which individuals have access to one another. Centrality has a variety of manifestations. One is the number of contacts each person has with others in the organization. A person who has a number of contacts is considered to be central, and a network in which the average number of contacts is high has the characteristic of network centrality. Centrality may also involve "betweenness," or the opportunity to be a link between and among other people who are not directly connected. People who have this kind of liaison role are more central in the network than those who do not, and the network itself may possess centrality because of a number of people who take this kind of role. Finally, centrality can also be manifested in overall closeness or reachability. Some organizations are dispersed in such a fashion that it is difficult for any one person to make contact through the network with some other designated individual. Other organizations are tight in the sense that one could easily reach anyone else within just a few intermediaries.

The third network characteristic is *density*, sometimes called *connectedness*. This is the ratio of actual links to possible links. Very large organizations with a sparce network would be low in connectedness. A small organization with many links would be highly connected.

Another characteristic of networks is *multiplexity*, or network overlap. A multiplex is a network or part of a network that fulfills more than one function. A link between two people, for example, might be both task and social. Whenever a network or portion of a network contains more than one type of content, multiplexity exists.

We have now discussed the individual, dyad, group, and organization. The fifth level of analysis consists of *interorganizational* or *environmental* networks. The linkages between people from one organization to people in others comprise these networks. Through the links among their individual

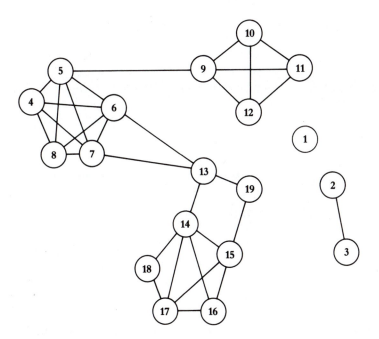

Groups:
Group 1—4, 5, 6, 7, 8
Group 2—9, 10, 11, 12
Group 3—14, 15, 16, 17, 18

Group Linkers:
Bridges—5, 9
Liaison—13
Other—19

Isolates:
True isolate—1
Isolated dyad—2, 3

Figure 14.1   Illustration of communication network roles.

From *Communicating and Organizing* by Richard V. Farace, Peter R. Monge, and Hamish Russell (Figure 8-5). Copyright © 1977 by Addison-Wesley. Reprinted by permission of Random House, Inc.

members, organizations can become tightly intertwined with one another. Employees, for example, may have contacts with suppliers, retailers, transporters, contractors, and many other types of organizations. Interorganizational networks demonstrate that an organization is never operating in isolation but that there is always an environment affecting its operation and culture.

There has been much research on almost all features of the networks described. We do not have sufficient space here to summarize the major findings, but they are readily available elsewhere.[8] To get an idea of how network analysis works, consider

8. See Monge and Eisenberg, "Emergent Communication."

the study of Karlene Roberts and Charles O'Reilly on the network of a large navy organization.[9] Each employee was asked three simple questions: (1) When you need technical advice in doing your job, who are the persons you are most likely to ask? (2) With which persons in this squadron are you most likely to have social conversations? (3) If you are upset about something related to the navy or to your job, to whom in the squadron are you most likely to express your dissatisfaction formally? The questionnaire was first administered when the

9. Karlene H. Roberts and Charles A. O'Reilly, "Organizations as Communication Structures: An Empirical Approach," *Human Communication Research* 4 (1978): 283–293.

organization was new and again 12 months later to see how the structure of the organization had changed. Almost 500 employees responsed to the first testing and 700 to the second, which constituted 80 percent of permanent personnel both times.

The data were analyzed by computer to determine every link mentioned by the respondents. The question about the technical advice was designed to discover an expertise network, the question about social conversations was designed to detect a social network, and the question about gripes was designed to find an authority network. About 80 percent of the employees were involved in the expertise and social networks, with about 20 percent isolates. The number of isolates increased substantially in the second testing for both networks. The number of isolates in the authority network was considerably greater at 57 percent, and that increased only slightly in the second testing.

The total number of links rose considerably from the first testing to the second, as people got to know one another better and as the kinds of problems with which they had to deal increased. There were about twenty-seven expertise groups, and that rose to forty-three in the second testing; there were sixteen social groups, which increased to thirty-eight; and the twelve authority groups rose to thirty during the 12-month period. The sizes of the groups remained about the same, about ten persons per group on the average in the expertise and social networks and about seven persons in the authority networks. The average group sizes, however, are deceiving because they ranged greatly from very small to very large groups.

Finally, the role properties of the networks were interesting. There were sixty-two liaisons and eighty-four bridges in the expertise network at the beginning, thirty-six liaisons and thirty-eight bridges in the social network, and only three liaisons and three bridges in the authority network. The number of individuals taking these roles increased drastically in every network in the year following the first testing. In fact, the number of liaisons in the authority network rose from three to eighty-seven, and the number of bridges in this network rose from three to ninety-seven during this period.

You can see from this study that the concepts of network theory are useful in providing a picture of the communication dynamics in an organization. These ideas provide a good beginning point for our exploration of organizational communication concepts.

The Positional Tradition and Formal Networks

The positional tradition consists of a number of theories of formal communication networks. These theories tend to take a managerial view and examine the ways in which management uses formal networks to achieve the stated objectives of the organization. A foundational theory of this genre is Max Weber's bureaucracy.

Classical Foundations: Weber

Certainly, Max Weber was one of the most prominent social theorists of all time. In his lifetime, from 1864 to 1930, he produced a great quantity of work on the nature of human institutions. One area for which he is best known is his theory of bureaucracy.[10] These ideas, developed at the beginning of the century, form an important part of the early classical theory of organizations.[11]

Weber defines an organization as follows: "An 'organization' is a system of continuous, purposive activity of a specified kind. A 'corporate organiza-

10. Max Weber, *The Theory of Social and Economic Organizations*, trans. A. M. Henderson and T. Parsons (New York: Oxford University Press, 1947). A lengthy interpretation and discussion of Weber's theory can be found in Parson's introduction to the above book. For a more complete bibliography of primary and secondary sources on Weber, see S. N. Eisenstadt, *Max Weber on Charisma and Institution Building* (Chicago; University of Chicago Press, 1968).

11. The most important classical theories are those of Henri Fayol and Frederick Taylor. See Henri Fayol, *General and Industrial Management* (New York: Pitman, 1949), originally published in 1925; and Frederick W. Taylor, *Principles of Scientific Management* (New York: Harper Brothers, 1947), originally published in 1912.

tion' is an associative social relationship characterized by an administrative staff devoted to such continuous purposive activity."[12] A central part of Weber's theory of bureaucracy is his concepts of power, authority, and legitimacy. For Weber, *power* is the ability of a person in any social relationship to influence others and to overcome resistance. Power in this sense is fundamental to most social relationships. When power is legitimate, or authorized formally by the organization, compliance is effective and complete. Whether communications will be accepted in an organization hinges on the degree to which the superior has *legitimate authority*.

The most common form of authority in bureaucracies is *bureaucratic*, or *rational-legal, authority*. The authorities in a bureaucracy derive their power from the bureaucracy's rules, which govern and are accepted by all organizational members. It is the kind of authority vested in supervisors and managers, for example.

Weber sees bureaucracy as the most efficient pattern for mass administration, and it is governed by a number of well-known principles. First, bureaucracy is based on rules. Such rules allow the solution of problems, standardization, and equality in the organization. Second, bureaucracies are based on the concept of sphere of competence. Thus, there is a systematic division of labor, each role having clearly defined rights and powers. Third, the essence of bureaucracy is hierarchy, which is seen in the formal organizational chart. Fourth, administrators are appointed on the basis of their knowledge and training. They are not generally elected, not do they inherit their positions, but gain them through training, experience, and selection. Fifth, the members of the bureaucracy must not share in the ownership of the organization. Sixth, bureaucrats must be free to allocate resources within their realms of influence without fear of outside infringement. Seventh, a bureaucracy requires carefully maintained records, a principle that has led to the very strong rule in most organizations to document all transactions.

Another feature of a bureaucracy is that it is usually headed by a nonbureaucrat. Nonbureaucratic heads are often elected or inherit their positions. They include presidents, cabinets, boards of trustees, and kings. Bureaucrats are dispensable; they may be replaced by similarly trained individuals, but the succession of the nonbureaucratic head may well be a crisis, precipitating innovation and change.

Weber's theory is included here primarily as a general background for the theories to come and to illustrate the positional tradition. In this regard it serves two functions. First, it provides a "classical," or standard, picture with which the other theories can be contrasted. Second, it presents the common traditional view of organizations, relating the essence of the classical notion of organizations. The theory has implicit ideas of what communication is like in organizations, but communication is not treated as an explanatory variable, nor is it seen as the essence of organizational life. As the upcoming sections indicate, this failure is significant.

Likert's Four Systems

Rensis Likert is a theorist in the human relations tradition. Human relations, in reaction to classical theories such as Weber's, focused on the workers, their feelings and needs. It was an especially popular movement from the 1940s through the 1960s. Human relations really has a foot in both the positional and relational traditions, but most of these theorists, Likert's included, looked at human relations from a production, management-oriented perspective. They taught that if you care for and nurture workers, the organization's operations will improve.[13]

Perhaps the most detailed theory of human relations, and surely the most explanatory, is that of Rensis Likert.[14] Likert outlines three broad groups of organizational variables. *Causal variables* are

12. Weber, *Social and Economic Organizations*, p. 151.

13. For a more detailed discussion and critique of the human relations movement, see Charles Perrow, *Complex Organizations: A Critical Essay* (Glenview, Ill.: Scott, Foresman, 1972).

14. Rensis Likert, *New Patterns of Management* (New York: McGraw-Hill, 1961); Rensis Likert, *The Human Organization* (New York: McGraw-Hill, 1967).

those that can be changed or altered. In this sense they may be considered as the independent variables in the model. *Intervening variables* are those that lead to the results of the causal manipulations. They reflect the general internal state and health of the organization. The *end-result variables*, the dependent variables or outputs, reflect organizational achievement.

An organization can function at any point along a continuum of four systems. System 1, at the extreme of the continuum, is the *exploitative-authoritative system*. Under this system the executive manages with an iron hand. Decisions are made by the executive, with no use of feedback. System 2, or *benevolent-authoritative leadership*, is similar to system 1, except that the manager is sensitive to the needs of the worker. Moving farther along the continuum, we come to system 3, which is *consultative* in nature. The authority figures still maintain control, but they seek consultation from below. At the other extreme of the spectrum, system 4 management, or *participative management*, allows the worker to participate fully in decision making. System 4 leads to high performance and an increased sense of responsibility and motivation. These relationships are illustrated in Figures 14.2 and 14.3.[15]

These figures illustrate that if management is authoritative, there is less group loyalty, more conflict, and consequently less mutual support. Workers have a lower attitude toward management and not much motivation to produce. The predictable result is lower sales, higher costs, and lower earnings. Consultative and participative management, on the other hand, leads to greater loyalty, higher performance goals, more mutual support, and more positive attitudes. The motivation to produce is higher, so that sales are greater, costs are less, and earnings are increased.

Likert treats communication as one variable among many. It is an intervening variable, related to the "interaction-influence system," which is a subpart of the "attitudinal, motivational, and perceptual variables." The relationship of communication variables to other variables is illustrated in Table 14.1.[16]

Here, we see that exploitative management does not think about communication very much except to express its desires clearly and forcefully to the workers. There is little upward communication, and what information that does go up the line tends to be distorted. Supervisors and subordinates are not very close to one another, and there is little accurate understanding between them. On the other hand, participative management includes strong upward and downward communication. This communication tends to be accurate and clear. Managers and workers tend to be close and understand one another well.

Although Likert's theory and the human relations movement have been criticized for being simplistic and ignoring important task variables, there does seem to be some truth to Likert's notion that exploitative systems have negative results, whereas participative ones have positive results, at least in some organizations. Virginia Richmond and James McCroskey conducted a study of employee satisfaction among 183 teachers in thirty-nine school districts.[17] The teachers were given a battery of tests related to, among other things, management style, manager's tolerance for disagreement, and satisfaction. Four styles were measured in the study, which are called "tells," "sells," "consults," and "joins." These are essentially identical to Likert's systems 1, 2, 3, and 4. The data showed a clear relationship between the perceived style of the manager and employee satisfaction. Employees who thought that their manager used a consulting or joining style were more satisfied than those who thought that a telling or selling style was used. The same relationship held for tolerance for disagreement. Employees who thought that their managers had less tolerance for disagreement were less satisfied

15. Likert, *Human Organization*, pp. 76–137.

16. Ibid., pp. 16–19.

17. Virginia P. Richmond and James C. McCroskey, "Management Communication Style, Tolerance for Disagreement, and Innovativeness as Predictors of Employee Satisfaction: A Comparison of Single-Factor, Two-Factor, and Multiple-Factor Approaches," in *Communication Yearbook 3*, ed. D. Nimmo (New Brunswick, N.J.: Transaction Books, 1979), pp. 359–373.

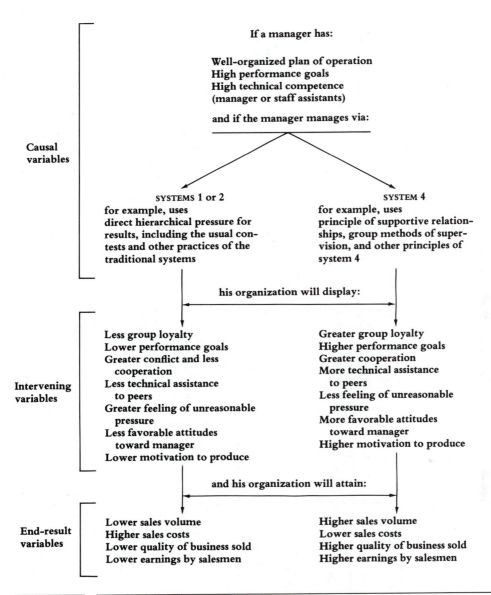

Figure 14.2 Sequence of developments in a well-organized enterprise, as affected by use of system 1 or 2 or system 4.

From "New Patterns in Sales Management," in *Changing Perspectives in Marketing Management*, ed. Martin Warshaw. Copyright © 1962 by The University of Michigan. Reprinted by permission of the publisher.

than those who thought their managers had a higher level of disagreement tolerance.

One function of formal communication in an organization is to elicit cooperation on the part of employees. Likert suggests that this can be done by participative management. The following theory

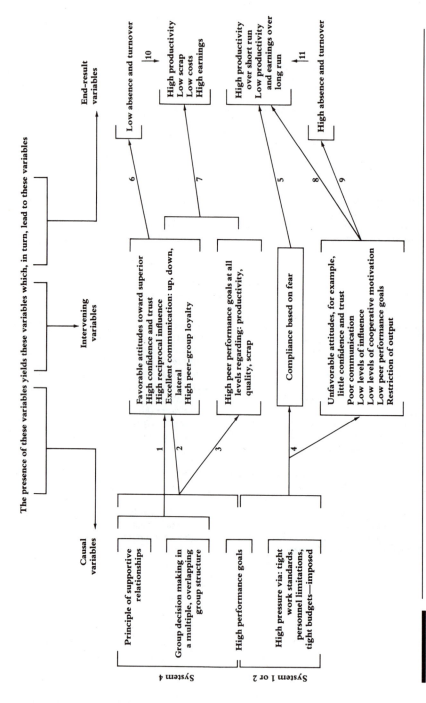

Figure 14.3 Simplified diagram of relationships among variables for system 1 or 2 and system 4 operations.
From *The Human Organization* by Rensis Likert. Copyright © 1967 by McGraw-Hill. Reprinted by permission of the publisher.

explores some of the less obvious ways in which control is exerted in organizations.

Unobtrusive Control and Identification

The theory of *organizational identification* is the product of Phillip Tompkins and George Cheney.[18] It integrates important existing theory into a fresh conceptualization of decision making in organizations.

According to the theory, control is exerted in organizations in a variety of ways. Tompkins and Cheney outline four processes by which control is accomplished.[19] The first is *simple control*, or use of direct, open power. This is very much like Likert's system 1 management in which management simply forces workers to comply. The second is *technical control*, or use of machinery. For example, if employees are given a computer and told to use it for their work, the computer itself limits what they can do and how they can do it.

The third form of control is *bureaucratic*, which involves the use of organizational procedures and formal rules. For example, employees may be given a manual that includes policies to be followed. Memos and reports are often used to communicate expectations to employees and to ensure compliance.

The fourth and most important for Cheney and Tompkins is *concertive control*, the use of interpersonal relationships and teamwork. This is the most subtle form of control because it relies on a shared reality and shared values. Concertive control is a central concept in this theory, as the authors explain:

> In the concertive organization, the explicitly written rules and regulations are largely replaced by the common understanding of values, objectives, and means of achievement, along with a deep appreciation for the organization's "mission." This we call—to modify a phrase in current use—the "soul of the new organization." [20]

With its emphasis on concertive control, this theory has a foot in both positional and relational traditions. Because the premises on which concertive control is based are managerial and because control is seen as communication at least in part through formal channels, it is included among the positional theories in this chapter.

Although the four types of control are normally found in various combinations within an organization, there is a trend away from simple, direct control toward the more subtle and complex form described as concertive. The theory of unobtrusive control deals primarily with the ways in which control is managed within the concertive system.

Following the classical work of Herbert Simon, Tompkins and Cheney show how control is accomplished by shaping the decisions made by organizational members.[21] Simon believes that organizational decision making follows a syllogistic pattern. In other words, decision makers reason deductively from general premises, and choices are based on those premises. Decisions are therefore shaped by organizational premises, and control is exerted by inducing workers to accept these general premises. The premises are accepted because of incentives like wages and the authority of people with legitimate power (see Weber).

This acceptance does not come automatically, however. Conflict often results from differences between employees' personal beliefs and the premises of the organization. Indeed, a substantial amount of industrial strife results from such differ-

18. George Cheney and Phillip K. Tompkins, "Coming to Terms with Organizational Identification and Commitment," *Central States Speech Journal* 38 (1987): 1–15; Phillip K. Tompkins and George Cheney, "Account Analysis of Organizations: Decision Making and Identification," in *Communication and Organizations: An Interpretive Approach*, eds. L. L. Putnam and M. E. Pacanowsky (Beverly Hills, Calif.: Sage, 1983), pp. 123–146; Phillip K. Tompkins and George Cheney, "Communication and Unobtrusive Control in Contemporary Organizations," in *Organizational Communication: Traditional Themes and New Directions*, eds. R. D. McPhee and P. K. Tompkins (Beverly Hills, Calif.: Sage, 1985), pp. 179–210.

19. Tompkins and Cheney base this conceptualization on the work of R. Edwards, "The Social Relations of Production at the Point of Production," in *Complex Organizations: Critical Perspectives*, eds. M. Zey-Ferrell and M. Aiken (Glenview, Ill.: Scott, Foresman, 1981).

20. Tompkins and Cheney, "Communication and Unobtrusive Control," p. 184.

21. Herbert Simon, *Administrative Behavior* (New York: Free Press, 1976). See also Perrow, *Complex Organizations*.

Table 14.1 Organizational and Performance Characteristics of Different Management Systems Based on a Comparative Analysis

Operating characteristics	System of organization			
	Authoritative		Participative	
	Exploitative-authoritative	Benevolent-authoritative	Consultative	Participative group
a. Amount of interaction and communication aimed at achieving organization's objectives	Very little	Little	Quite a bit	Much with both individuals and groups
b. Direction of information flow	Downward	Mostly downward	Down and up	Down, up, and with peers
c. Downward communication				
1. Where initiated	At top of organization or to implement top directive	Primarily at top or patterned on communication from top	Patterned on communication from top but with some initiative at lower levels	Initiated at all levels
2. Extent to which communications are accepted by subordinates	Viewed with great suspicion	May or may not be viewed with suspicion	Often accepted but at times viewed with suspicion. May or may not be openly questioned	Generally accepted, but if not, openly and candidly questioned
d. Upward communication				
1. Adequacy of upward communication via line organization	Very little	Limited	Some	A great deal
2. Subordinates' feeling of responsibility for initiating accurate upward communication	None at all	Relatively little, usually communicates "filtered" information but only when requested. May "yes" the boss	Some to moderate degree of responsibility to initiate accurate upward communication	Considerable responsibility felt and much initiative. Group communicates all relevant information.

3. Forces leading to accurate or distorted information	Powerful forces to distort information and deceive superiors	Occasionally forces to distort; also forces for honest communication	Some forces to distort along with many forces to communicate accurately	Virtually no forces to distort and powerful forces to communicate accurately
4. Accuracy of upward communication via line	Tends to be inaccurate	Information that boss wants to hear flows; other information is restricted and filtered	Information that boss wants to hear flows, other information may be limited or cautiously given	Accurate
5. Need for supplementary upward communication system	Need to supplement upward communication by spy system, suggestion system, or some similar devices	Upward communication often supplemented by suggestion system and similar devices	Slight need for supplementary system; suggestion system may be used	No need for any supplementary system
e. Sideward communication, its adequacy and accuracy	Usually poor because of competition between peers and corresponding hostility	Fairly poor because of competition between peers	Fair to good	Good to excellent
f. Psychological closeness of superiors to subordinates (that is, how well does superior know and understand problems faced by subordinates?)	Far apart	Can be moderately close if proper roles are kept	Fairly close	Usually very close
1. Accuracy of perceptions by superiors and subordinates	Often in error	Often in error on some points	Moderately accurate	Usually quite accurate

From *The Human Organization* by Rensis Likert. Copyright © by McGraw-Hill Book Company. Reprinted by permission of the publisher.

ences. How, then, do organizations achieve concertive control in the face of potential conflict? The answer lies in use of the organizational enthymeme.

Described by Aristotle over 2000 years ago, the *enthymeme* is a rhetorical device used to involve audiences actively in the advocate's reasoning process.[22] Aristotle wrote that the syllogism is a reasoning device for drawing conclusions but that the enthymeme is a "rhetorical syllogism" used for persuading audiences. In an enthymeme, one or more premises in a reasoning chain are left out, to be supplied by the audience. The audience is then expected to imagine particular conclusions based on these implicit premises. Sometimes the suppressed premises are widely accepted cultural values; other times they are inculcated by the advocate as part of the persuasion process.

For example, a speaker advocating the prohibition of offshore drilling might reason privately with this syllogism: (1) Offshore drilling will endanger the fragile coastal ecology; (2) coastal ecology is valuable and should be protected; (3) therefore, offshore drilling should be prohibited. In addressing a group of environmentalists, this speaker relies on the audience's acceptance of the second premise and works only to demonstrate the truth of the first. Once the environmentalists come to believe that drilling will hurt the environment, they will reason that it should be prohibited.

Enthymemes are used in all kinds of persuasion, but Tompkins and Cheney are especially interested in how they are used in organizations for unobtrusive control of decision making. These authors point out that when organizational members display loyalty and behave "organizationally," they are essentially accepting key organizational premises. Often organizations directly sell their premises to employees through house organs (company newsletters), training programs, and the like. Other times, organizations employ a variety of incentives

to induce employees to become loyal. In any case, once employees accept certain premises, their conclusions and decisions are controlled.

For example, one premise of many industrial firms is that obsolescence is positive because it maintains progress, sustains the market, and protects jobs. Once engineers buy this idea, they will opt for designs that include planned obsolescence. Engineering supervisors and executives do not have to order engineers to plan obsolescence into their designs; the engineers do so automatically because they accept the basic organizational premise. One could argue also that the scientists working on the Strategic Defense Initiative ("Star Wars") are able to proceed with the project because they have accepted the organizational premise that SDI will save the world from a nuclear holocaust.

The acceptance of organizational premises is part of a process of organizational identification.[23] Here, the theorists rely largely on the work of Kenneth Burke. (See the previous discussion of identification in Chapter 8.) *Identification* occurs when individuals become aware of their common ground. We identify with individuals with whom we share something in common; and the more two parties share, the more the potential identification between them. When employees identify with the organization, they are more likely to accept the organization's premises and make decisions that are consistent with organizational objectives. Tompkins and Cheney define organizational identification in terms of decision making: "A decision maker identifies with an organization when he or she desires to choose the alternative that best promotes the perceived interests of that organization."[24]

Identification is achieved through communication, and communicators often choose strategies that encourage identification. For example, Cheney examined samples of ten corporate house

22. Lane Cooper, *The Rhetoric of Aristotle* (New York: Meredith, 1932). See also Lloyd Bitzer, "Aristotle's Enthymeme Revisited," *Quarterly Journal of Speech* 45 (1959): 399–408; Jesse Delia, "The Logic Fallacy, Cognitive Theory, and the Enthymeme: A Search for the Foundations of Reasoned Discourse," *Quarterly Journal of Speech* 56 (1970): 140–148.

23. George Cheney, "The Rhetoric of Identification and the Study of Organizational Communication," *Quarterly Journal of Speech* 69 (1983): 143–158.

24. Tompkins and Cheney, "Communication and Unobtrusive Control," p. 194.

organs and discovered a variety of strategies aimed at increasing organizational identification, such as the common-ground technique.[25]

To explore organizational identification, Connie Bullis and Phillip Tompkins conducted a large study of the U.S. Forest Service.[26] These investigators interviewed 55 employees at national (Washington, D.C.) headquarters, three regional offices, two forest headquarters, and two ranger stations. In addition, they administered questionnaires to about 700 employees throughout the agency.

First, by comparing their findings with a study done 30 years before, they found that much more bureaucratic control is now being used and that concertive control is on the decline, as is organizational identification.[27] Still, some organizational identification obviously does exist, and employees vary substantially in their commitment to the ideals of the organization. Bullis and Tompkins found that employees who had the greatest identification with the organization subscribed much more readily to organizational premises such as the Forest Service goals, multiple-use management, and the public interest than do less committed employees. Those who do not identify that much with the organization are more concerned about such concerns as technical correctness or special interests.

The theory of organizational identification shows how control is exerted in organizations. It also illustrates some of the elements of relational and cultural networks. We move now to a more complete examination of these traditions.

The Relational and Cultural Traditions: Emergent Networks

Theories in the relational tradition are concerned with the ways in which organization is accomplished by interaction between individuals. These theories are less concerned with the lines of communication running through the organization and more concerned with the relationship among particular individuals and how they accomplish things together.

The cultural tradition in organizational studies emphasizes the ways in which persons enact an organizational reality. It is the study of an organization as a way of life, including meanings and values. It looks at the way in which individuals use stories, rituals, symbols, and other types of activity to produce and reproduce a set of understandings.[28]

These traditions see networks as emergent rather than prescribed. Such networks grow out of the natural interaction among the members of the organization. Here, we look first at the idea of organizational culture and then turn to some specific theories of the relational tradition.

The Idea of Organizational Culture

John Van Maanen and Stephen Barley outline four "domains" of organizational culture.[29] The first domain is *ecological context*. This is the physical world, including location, the time and history, and social context within which the organization operates. The second domain affecting the development of culture is *differential interaction*. Individuals interact with one another in certain patterns, and as we saw earlier in the chapter, networks emerge. Networks determine in large measure what kind of culture will result. The third domain is *collective understanding*, or common ways of interpreting events. This domain constitutes the "content" of the culture, its ideas, ideals, values, and practices. The fourth domain consists of *individuals* and their actions. It is through the practices of individuals that the culture is sustained and changed.

25. Cheney, "Rhetoric."

26. Connie A. Bullis and Phillip K. Tompkins, "The Forest Ranger Revisted: A Study of Control Practices and Identification," *Communication Monographs* 56 (1989): 287–306.

27. H. Kaufman, *The Forest Ranger: A Study in Administrative Behavior* (Baltimore: Johns Hopkins University Press, 1960).

28. See James A. Anderson (ed.), *Communication Yearbook 11* (Newbury Park, Calif.: Sage, 1988), pp. 310–405; Michael Pacanowsky, "Creating and Narrating Organizational Realities," in *Rethinking Communication: Paradigm Exemplars*, ed. B. Dervin et al. (Newbury Park, Calif.: Sage, 1989), pp. 250–257.

29. John Van Maanen and Stephen R. Barley, "Cultural Organization: Fragments of a Theory," in *Organizational Culture*, eds. P. J. Frost et al. (Beverly Hills, Calif.: Sage, 1985), pp. 31–54.

It is probably unrealistic to think of a large organization as a single culture. In most cases, subcultures will emerge. Subcultures identify themselves as distinct groups within the larger organization. You can imagine an organization as a set of Venn diagrams or overlapping cultural circles.

We encountered the cultural tradition in organizational studies earlier in Chapter 10, where we looked at Michael Pacanowsky and Nick O'Donnell-Trujillo's interpretive theory, which examines the ways in which the members of an organization create and perpetuate an understanding of their experience through stories, rituals, symbols, and other means.[30]

The Process of Organizing

One of the most influential theories of the relational genre is that of Carl Weick.[31] Weick's theory of organizing is significant in the communication field because it uses communication as a basis for human organizing and provides a rationale for understanding how people organize. Since its inception in 1969, it has received wide acclaim and some criticism as well.[32]

The feature that distinguishes this theory from those of the positional school is that Weick sees organizations not as structures based on positions or roles but as activities. It is more proper to speak of organizing than of organizations because organizations are something that people accomplish via a process that must be constantly reenacted. Thus, when people do what they do, their activities create organization.

The essence of any organization is that people are acting in such a way that their behaviors are interlocked: One person's behavior is contingent on another's. All organizing activities consist of behaviors that are interlocked through communication.

In this analysis, an *act* is a statement of communicative behavior of one individual, an *interact* involves an act followed by a response, and a *double interact* consists of an act followed by a response and then an adjustment or follow-up by the first person. This pattern is consistent with the focus of much of the relational tradition discussed in detail in Chapter 12. Weick believes that all organizing activities are double interacts. Consider an executive and a secretary as an example. The executive asks the secretary to undertake an activity (act); the secretary then asks for clarification (interact); and the executive explains (double interact). Or the executive asks the secretary a favor (act), and the secretary follows through (interact), after which the executive responds with a thank you (double interact). Simple? Yes, but these activities are exactly the kind of which Weick believes organizations are made.

Organizing activities fulfill the function of reducing the equivocality of information received from the environment. *Equivocality* is uncertainty and consists of complication, ambiguity, and lack of predictability. All information from the environment, according to Weick, is equivocal to some degree, and the organizing activities in the organization are designed to make the information unequivocal or to reduce its uncertainty.

Let's return to the example of the executive again. Suppose the executive receives a directive from the firm's president to solve a problem of plant safety. What is the nature of this problem, and how should the executive go about solving it? The answers to these questions are not clear, inasmuch as the problem can be defined and solved in a number of ways. In other words, the executive is faced with equivocal information.

Weick is saying that organizing activities, which consist of double interacts, interlocked behavior, or communication, are designed to make such situations clearer. Of course, the importance of information and the degree of equivocality in the information vary. The executive's asking the secretary a favor is an example of an insignificant piece of

30. Michael E. Pacanowsky and Nick O'Donnell-Trujillo, "Communication and Organizational Cultures," *Western Journal of Speech Communication* 46 (1982): 115–130. See also Michael E. Pacanowsky and Nick O'Donnell-Trujillo, "Organizational Communication as Cultural Performance," *Communication Monographs* 50 (1983): 126–147.

31. Carl Weick, *The Social Psychology of Organizing.* (Reading, Mass.: Addison-Wesley, 1969, 1979).

32. See for example the special section in *Communication Studies* 40 (Winter 1989): 231–265.

information, whose equivocality is low; but the example of solving safety problems illustrates a more significant problem that has a great deal of equivocality. This difference is not important to Weick. What is important is that organizing is accomplished through processes that are developed to deal with equivocal information. The exact nature of that information is irrelevant to the fact that organizational members engage in the processes to maintain organization. Interaction serves to achieve common meanings among group members, and the meanings that individuals together assign to information is the mechanism by which equivocality is reduced. In other words, as we interact we come to some amount of common understanding, which reduces uncertainty.

To test the relationship between equivocality and interaction, Gary Kreps studied the discussions of the Faculty Senate and the University of Southern California for a year.[33] He asked a sample of senate members to evaluate each of the twenty-four motions considered that year in terms of their equivocality. They filled out scales to test how complicated or uncomplicated, how predictable or unpredictable, and how ambiguous or unambiguous each motion was. Kreps then chose the five most equivocal and five least equivocal motions and counted the number of double interacts in the discussions of each of these. The difference is clear: Highly equivocal motions required much more discussion than did less equivocal ones. The average number of double interacts for less equivocal motions was seven, whereas that for highly equivocal ones was seventy-four.

We have discussed how individuals interact to deal with equivocal information from the environment. But what is the environment? Traditional theories of organization imply that the environment is a known entity outside the organization. This dualistic notion pits the organization against the environment as if each somehow preexists. Weick has a substantially different idea of environ-

ment. Organizers are always surrounded by a mix of stimuli to which they must respond, but the "environment" has no meaning apart from what the individual makes of it. In other words, the environment is a product of the person, not something outside the person. What makes the environment salient for the individual is the person's attention to particular aspects of the stimuli. People are selective in what they attend to in any situation and what is attended to at any moment is the environment.

Indeed, information from the environment is equivocal precisely because different individuals attend to different aspects of it. Interaction is the mechanism by which the individuals in the group reduce this equivocality. Hence, like every other aspect of the organizational reality, the environment is enacted by the people in the organization. People are continually reenacting their environments, depending on their attitudes, values, and experiences of the moment.

For example, the executive of our example is faced with a situation in which interpretation is necessary. Immediately, he or she will attend to certain aspects of the "safety problem." In enlisting the aid of others such as the secretary, the executive is beginning processes that will enable the group to treat the safety problem as its environment of the moment. To deal with this equivocal environment, group members make proposals (acts) to which others respond (interacts) so that the proposers can refine their initial proposals (double interacts). The executive may ask the secretary to check the files for accident records. This constitutes a proposal, an attempt to reduce the equivocality. The secretary may comply, pulling the appropriate file, so that the executive can be assured that the company knows the extent of the safety problem. Here, the sequence of the double interact would be as follows: request file (act), provide file (interact), take file and review it (double interact).

Weick views organizing as an evolutionary process that relies on a series of three major processes: enactment, selection, and retention. *Enactment* is the definition of the situation or registering equiv-

33. Gary L. Kreps, "A Field Experimental Test and Revaluation of Weick's Model of Organizing," in *Communication Yearbook 4*, ed. D. Nimmo (New Brunswick, N.J.: Transaction Books, 1980), pp. 389–398.

ocal information from outside. It is attention to stimuli and acknowledgment that equivocality exists. The mere acceptance of certain aspects of the environment removes some equivocality. Accepting the task of dealing with safety problems narrows the field for the executive, so that some uncertainty already is removed from the field of all possible problems that could be addressed.

The second process is *selection,* which enables the group to admit certain aspects of information and reject others. It narrows the field, eliminating alternatives with which the organization does not wish to deal. This process therefore removes even more equivocality from the initial information. For example, in dealing with the safety problem, the organization may decide to consider only the aspects of safety that management can control, eliminating all factors that relate to worker predispositions.

The third process of organizing is *retention.* Here, further equivocality is removed by deciding what aspects of the initial information will be saved for future use. Retained information is integrated into the existing body of information on which the organization operates. To continue our example, the safety group may decide to deal with safety problems that are caused strictly by machinery, rejecting all other kinds of problems. As you can see, the problem has become much less ambiguous; it has moved from equivocality toward clarity.

After retention occurs, organization members face a *choice point.* They must make two kinds of decisions. The first is whether to reenact the environment in some way. Here, they address the question, Should we (or I) attend to some aspect of the environment that was rejected before? The executive may decide, for example, to have the group review the rate of accidents that are not related to machinery. The second kind of choice is whether to modify one's behavior or actions. Here the question is, Should I take a different action than I did before? For example, the executive may decide that solutions for both machinery and nonmachinery accidents should be developed.

So far this summary may lead you to believe that organizations move from one process of organizing to another in lockstep fashion: enactment, selection, retention, choice. Such is *not* the case. Individual subgroups in the organization are continually working on activities in all these processes for different aspects of the environment. Although certain segments of the organization may specialize in one or more of the organizing processes, nearly everybody undertakes all of them in one form or another most of the time. Such is the essence of organizing.

Knowing the evolutionary stages of organizing helps us see how organizing occurs on a general scale, but this knowledge does not provide an explanation for how equivocality is removed from the information. To address this problem, Weick outlines two elements that occur within each of the three organizing processes. These are assembly rules and interlocked behavior cycles. *Assembly rules* guide the choice of routines that will be used to accomplish the process being conducted (enactment, selection, or retention). Rules are sets of criteria on which organizers decide what to do to reduce equivocality. The question answered by assembly rules is this: Out of all possible behavior cycles in this organization, which will we use now? For example, in the selection process the executive might invoke the assembly rule that "two heads are better than one" and on this basis call a meeting of plant engineers.

Behavior cycles are sets of interlocked behaviors that enable the group to come to an understanding about which meanings should be included and which rejected. Thus, the safety meeting called by the executive would enable interested individuals to discuss the safety problem and decide how to proceed in defining and solving it. Assembly rules and behavior cycles are a natural part of each of the three processes of organizing.

Now we have completed the basic elements of Weick's model. They are environment, equivocality, enactment, selection, retention, choices, assembly rules, behavior cycles, and equivocality removed. Weick envisions these elements working together in a system, each element related to the others. Weick's theory actually fits well with the idea of structuration, which is developed in more detail next.

Structuration in Organizations

In Chapter 13 we examined the theory of structuration and Scott Poole and his colleagues' application of this theory to group decision making. These researchers have also extended their application into the realm of organizational communication.[34]

Recall that the theory of structuration, attributable to sociologist Anthony Giddens, deals with the ways in which actions bring about unintended consequences, which in turn form social systems that affect future actions. The circle of actions and consequences is the mechanism by which sociocultural resources are produced and reproduced in all social systems.[35] Organizations, like any social structure, are produced through actions and interactions among individuals. As people rely on organizational resources such as roles, norms, and rules to guide their actions, they not only accomplish individual and organizational goals but also reproduce the organizational system itself. This process is what Weick calls enactment. Scott Poole and Robert McPhee have applied this idea to two aspects of organizational communication—structure and climate.

In an essay on the subject, McPhee recognizes the importance of organizational structure: "I would say that structure is a defining characteristic of an organization—it is what brings about or makes possible that quality of atmosphere, that sustained, routine purposiveness that distinguishes work in an organization from activities in a group, a mob, a society, and so forth."[36] As we saw earlier in the chapter, organizational structure provides the form necessary to accomplish a variety of functions. Structure is both a manifestation and product of communication in the organization. Consequently, McPhee refers to structure as "structure-communication."

The formal structure of an organization as announced in employee manuals, organizational charts, and policies and procedures is really two types of communication. First, it is an indirect way of telling employees about the organization—its values, procedures, and methods. Second, it is a form of metacommunication (Chapter 12) in which the organization addresses its own communication patterns directly.

Organizational structure is created when individuals communicate with others through certain channels. Such communication occurs in three metaphorical sites, or *centers of structuration*.[37] The first is the site of *conception*. This includes all those episodes of organizational life in which people make decisions and choices that limit what can happen within the organization. For example, when the curriculum committee of a university decides that a new college of creative arts will be established, the future lines of communication within the college will be "structured" by this decision.

The second site of organizational structuration is *implementation*, which is the formal codification and announcement of decisions and choices. Once the decision is made to establish the new college, the provost may send out a formal memorandum to the faculty and staff announcing the change. That

34. Marshall Scott Poole and Robert D. McPhee, "A Structurational Analysis of Organizational Climate," in *Communication and Organizations: An Interpretive Approach*, eds. L. L. Putnam and M. E. Pacanowsky (Beverly Hills, Calif.: Sage, 1983), pp. 195–220; Marshall Scott Poole, "Communication and Organizational Climates: Review, Critique, and a New Perspective," in *Organizational Communication: Traditional Themes and New Directions*, eds. R. D. McPhee and P. K. Tompkins (Beverly Hills, Calif.: Sage, 1985), pp. 79–108; Robert D. McPhee, "Formal Structure and Organizational Communication," in *Organizational Communication: Traditional Themes and New Directions*, eds. R. D. McPhee and P. K. Tompkins (Beverly Hills, Calif.: Sage, 1985), pp. 149–178.

35. Anthony Giddens, *Central Problems in Social Theory* (Berkeley: University of California Press, 1979); *Profiles and Critiques in Social Theory* (Berkeley: University of California Press, 1982).

36. McPhee, "Formal Structure," p. 150.

37. Robert D. McPhee, "Organizational Communication: A Structurational Exemplar," in *Rethinking Communication: Paradigm Exemplars*, eds. B. Dervin et al. (Beverly Hills, Calif.: Sage, 1989) pp. 199–212.

formal announcement itself will be instrumental in shaping the structure of the organization in the future.

Finally, structuration occurs in the site of *reception*, as organizational members act in accordance with the organizational decisions. Thus, after the decision is made to establish a new college, a dean will be recruited, certain department heads will meet with the new dean, and faculty lines of communication will change. In other words, the employees of the organization must live with the decision.

Although anyone in an organization may from time to time participate in communication at any or all three sites, structuration tends to be specialized. Top management usually is involved in conceptual communication, various staff personnel perform the job of implementation, and the general workforce itself participates in reception. Of course, the communication activities at these three sites are often difficult and conflict-laden. Indeed, rarely is a new college established at a university without considerable disagreement and resistance at all three stages, and this is the case with major changes in any kind of organization. The communication patterns at the three sites may be complex and time-consuming, and the outcome is very much affected by the skill of the people involved.

The second area in which Poole and McPhee have applied structurationist thinking is organizational climate.[38] Actually, climate has been a heavily researched topic in organizational communication.[39] Traditionally, climate has been viewed as one of the key variables affecting communication and the subsequent productivity and satisfaction of employees. For Poole and McPhee, climate is the general collective description of an organization or a part of the organization that shapes members' expectations and feelings and therefore the organization's performance. Climates are enacted by the members of the organization as they go through their daily activities, and any organization may

actually have a variety of climates for different groups of people.

Poole and McPhee define climate structurationally as "a collective attitude, continually produced and reproduced by members' interaction."[40] In other words, a climate is not an objective "variable" that affects the organization; nor is it an individual's perception of the organization. Rather, climate is an intersubjective phenomenon; it arises out of the interaction among those who affiliate with the organization. Climate is a product of structuration: It is both a medium and an outcome of interaction.[41]

Poole sees climate as a hierarchy of three strata. The first is a *concept pool*, or a set of basic terms that members use to define and describe the organization. The second is a *kernel climate*, or basic, highly abstract, shared conception of the atmosphere of the organization. Finally, the *particular climate* consists of groups' translations of the kernel climate into more concrete terms affecting their particular part of an organization. The kernel climate permeates the entire organization, but particular climates may vary from one segment of the organization to another.

The three layers in the hierarchy are linearly related. The concepts are the key to understanding what is going on in the organization. From these basic understandings, the kernel climate arises. Subgroups then translate these general principles into specific climate elements, which in turn affect the thinking, feeling, and behavior of the individuals.

An example of this process is found in a study of a consulting firm.[42] The firm consisted of two generations of employees—a group that had been with the firm a relatively long time and a group of more recent employees. The two groups seemed to expe-

---

38. Poole, "Communication and Organizational Climates"; Poole and McPhee, "Structurational Analysis."

39. This work is summarized in Poole, "Communication and Organizational Climates," pp. 79–97.

40. Poole and McPhee, "Structurational Analysis," p. 213.

41. For a contrast of the structurational approach to climate with traditional approaches, see Poole and McPhee, "Structurational Analysis."

42. This model of climate is based on a reinterpretation of a case study by H. Johnson. "A New Conceptualization of Source of Organizational Climate," *Administrative Science Quarterly* 3 (1976): 275–292.

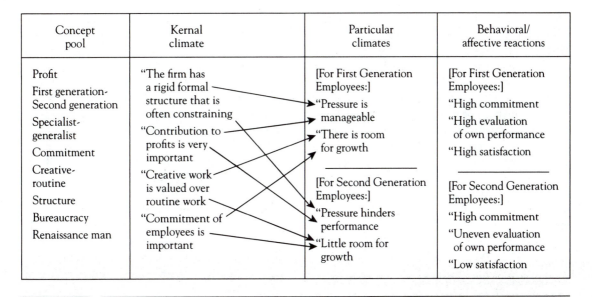

Concept pool	Kernal climate	Particular climates	Behavioral/affective reactions
Profit	"The firm has a rigid formal structure that is often constraining	[For First Generation Employees:] "Pressure is manageable "There is room for growth	[For First Generation Employees:] "High commitment "High evaluation of own performance "High satisfaction
First generation-Second generation			
Specialist-generalist	"Contribution to profits is very important		
Commitment			
Creative-routine	"Creative work is valued over routine work	[For Second Generation Employees:] "Pressure hinders performance "Little room for growth	[For Second Generation Employees:] "High commitment "Uneven evaluation of own performance "Low satisfaction
Structure			
Bureaucracy	"Commitment of employees is important		
Renaissance man			

Figure 14.4 Schematic of climate structure.

rience different climates. Both groups shared a common set of concepts.

From these core concepts, four key elements of a kernel climate emerged: (1) "The firm has a rigid formal structure that is often constraining." (2) "Contribution to profits is very important." (3) "Creative work is valued over routine work." (4) "Commitment of employees is important." These four elements of the kernel climate were translated differently into the particular climates of the two groups. The first-generation employees believed that "pressure is manageable, and that there is room for growth." The second-generation employees, however, believed that "pressure hinders performance and that there is little room for growth." [43] Figure 14.4 illustrates this example.

How do the elements of climate develop in an organization? We know already from a structurational perspective that the climate is produced by the practices of organizational members; and, in turn, climate affects and constrains those practices. Thus, climate is not static but constantly in the

43. Poole, "Communication and Organizational Climates," p. 98.

process of development. Three interacting factors enter into this developmental process.

The first is the *structure of the organization* itself. Because structure limits the kinds of interactions and practices that can be engaged in, it limits the kind of climate that can result from these interactions and practices. For example, if the organization is highly segmented with strong differentiation among employees and departments, individuals will have a limited pool of co-workers with whom they can communicate, which increases the chance of a "restrained" climate.

The second factor affecting climate is various *climate-producing apparatuses,* or mechanisms designed to affect employee perceptions and performance, such as newsletters, training programs, and the like. The third factor is *member characteristics,* their skills and knowledge. For example, if employees are sufficiently intelligent and reflective, they may challenge existing authority and "see through" apparatuses. Member characteristics also include the degree of agreement or coordination within work groups.

Both organizational climate and structure, then, are a manifestation of the structurational process.

This theory nicely extends Poole and McPhee's ideas about structuration in groups into the organizational climate. Like their group work, the theory shows much potential for providing a way of looking at group and organizational experience. Structuration is especially useful in the theory of organizations because it can integrate the otherwise disparate explanations of human action in organizations. On the one hand, ideas of structural causation show the ways in which the resources of the system constrain and affect the behavior of participants. On the other hand, ideas of practical action show how individuals act to accomplish goals in organizations. Both views are appropriate within a structurational frame.

Commentary and Critique

If we learn anything from the theories in this chapter, it is that organizations are created through communication as people interact to accomplish their individual and joint goals. The process of communication also results in a variety of structural outcomes such as authority relations, roles, communication networks, and climate. All these structural elements are results of the interaction between individuals and among groups within the organization, and all in turn affect future interactions within the organization.

The theme of networks was chosen to organize the material in this chapter because this term captures the interactive nature of organizational structure and function. Network theory is based on individual interactions among people, which build up into a macrostructure. The idea of multiple networks accommodates most of the ideas presented in this chapter, including bureaucracy, control, managerial style, culture, and structuration.

In this chapter we have looked at three traditions related to organizational networks—the positional, the relational, and the cultural. Strictly positional theories express a common structuralist mythology, but for the communication scholar, they omit a great deal. Classical theories such as

Weber's reflect and may have contributed to a powerful cultural norm about how organizing should occur. These theories, however, do not provide much of a sense of how the interaction among members results in any kind of meaningful outcome; one contribution of communication theory has been to provide additional insight into the interactive nature of organizations.

Likert's theory is somewhat better than earlier theories in showing the importance of communication, but even this theory fails to recognize the pervasiveness of communication as the very means by which organizing occurs. The theory is appealing because of its formalistic explanatory style. Communication is included in the matrix of variables used by Likert to explain organizational outcomes. This is a strictly linear theory, however, which leaves little to the imagination of individuals other than those who establish the managerial system of the company.

Likert's theory is part of the human relations movement. The movement helped practitioners and scholars understand that people have needs and values related to organizational functioning and that communication is an important aspect of organizational life. Likert's version, like several others, however, is simplistic in its linear, causal reasoning.

Human relations was criticized almost from its beginning.[44] Its problems are primarily attributable to its extreme position and simplistic view that high morale improves productivity. The correlations claimed to exist between human relations factors and organizational effectiveness have, for the most part, failed the test of empirical study. We reviewed one study in which a positive correlation was found between managerial style and satisfaction, but it does not say anything about productivity. In many cases the correlations have not been found in research, and where they do appear, serious methodological objections have been raised. In some ways what the human relations movement was trying to do has been more successfully accom-

---

44. For a comprehensive critique, see Perrow, *Complex Organizations*.

plished by the organizational culture movement, and this is to recognize and characterize the human needs within the organization.

Indeed, apart from achieving task-oriented goals, organizations are also human cultures, rich with tradition, shared meaning, and ritual. What people do in organizations creates and reflects the underlying culture of the organization.

The cultural approach to organizational theory is a major advance. It refocuses our attention on a set of processes that are not examined carefully in traditional management-oriented, variable-analytic studies. Traditionally, management is seen as a rational process of manipulating "things" for the benefit of the organization. The culture approach shows us that this is only partly true. In fact, a culture that is out of the conscious control of management is a major part of what characterizes an organization. The cultural approach refutes the idea that managers can somehow manipulate "objects" (like materials and machines) that are independent from the organization itself. The objects are only known through the meanings of the organizational culture, and those meanings will change from one organization, or even suborganization, to another. Organizations are not adapted to environments; rather, organizations in a very real way create their own environments based on shared conceptions and interpretations.

The downside to this observation is that the empirically minded manager may think of culture as just another variable to be manipulated and that the culture can be managed. This idea can lead to the negative consequence of attempted ideological control. Van Maanen and Barley's theory is an example of a cultural theory that could be used in this way. So is Cheney and Tompkins's theory of organizational identification. The answer to this criticism is that all forms of management exert some kind of ideological control. Let us therefore create the most humane and productive cultures possible.

Another disadvantage of the culture approach is one that is generally true of many interpretive theories of communication: If you assume that the social reality of an organization comes from inter-

actions among members of the organization and that organizational cultures thereby differ, you put yourself into the very difficult theoretical position of being unable to make generalizations or predictions about organizational life. Each organization must be studied independently, and generalizations become difficult. The answer, of course, is standard: Theories should not attempt to be predictive but should capture general categories of action, which we expect to be played out differently in various organizations. Such middle-range theories, like that of Pacanowsky and O'Donnell-Trujillo, enable us to observe organizations with a sensitivity to their rich individuality.

Organizational culture theories are not well suited to look at power and control in organizations. For organizational functions to be accomplished, coordination and control are necessary. Although control can be exerted in a variety of ways, communication is instrumental. As members accept the assumptions of the organization, they identify with the organization itself and work on its behalf.

Unobtrusive control theory on the other hand is fresh and valuable. Although it is well integrated with important standard theories of organizational decision making, it still advances those ideas. In addition, it brings insights from rhetoric into a field that badly needs outside perspectives. This advantage not only provides significant new perspectives for organizational theory but also helps to usefully combine divergent areas of the communication field. The theory is pragmatically helpful, while enabling interpreters and critics to uncover implicit organizational values and premises not normally available for inspection. It thereby paves the way for a necessary and significant critique of organizational communication. The theory seems to have much heuristic value and, in fact, has already generated much research.[45]

Both Weick's theory of organizing and McPhee and Poole's theory of structuration are middle-

---

45. Tompkins and Cheney summarize the research on the theory in "Communication and Unobtrusive Control," pp. 198–203. See also Bullis and Tompkins, "The Forest Ranger."

range theories of this type. They help us understand the process by which organizations are created without predicting specific outcomes.

The works of Weick and Giddens are consistent with each other in capturing the structurational character of interaction. In one way these theories bring us back full circle to networks as the essence of organizing. When people communicate they establish expectations that give shape to future interactions, and as we have seen repeatedly in this chapter, this structuration process is the heart of all organizing.

CHAPTER 15

Communication and Media

We are living in what Marshall McLuhan calls the "global village." Modern communication media make it possible for millions of people throughout the world to be in touch with nearly any spot on the globe. The omnipresent media present an important challenge to students in many disciplines.

George Gerbner points to the importance of the media in society:

> This broad "public-making" significance of mass media of communications—the ability to create publics, define issues, provide common terms of reference, and thus to allocate attention and power—has evoked a large number of theoretical contributions. Other theories of mass media have their origins in political thought, social-economic analysis, and historical-artistic-literary scholarship.[1]

Mass communication is the process whereby media organizations produce and transmit messages to large publics and the process by which those messages are sought, used, and consumed by audiences. Central to any study of mass communication are the media. Media are organizations that distribute cultural products or messages that affect and reflect the culture of society. Media provide information simultaneously to large heterogeneous audiences. Media systems are part of the larger societal context of political, economic, and other institutional forces.[2]

1. George Gerbner, "Mass Media and Human Communication Theory," in *Human Communication Theory*, ed. F. E. X. Dance (New York: Holt, Rinehart & Winston, 1967), p. 45. There are numerous surveys of mass-communication research and theory. See, for example, James A. Anderson, "Mass Communication Theory and Research: An Overview," in *Communication Yearbook 1*, ed. B. Ruben (New Brunswick, N.J.: Transaction Books, 1977), pp. 279–290; Joseph M. Foley, "Mass Communication Theory and Research: An Overview," in *Communication Yearbook 2*, ed. B. Ruben (New Brunswick, N.J.:

Transaction Books, 1978), pp. 209–214; Werner J. Severin and James W. Tankard, *Communication Theories: Origins, Methods, Uses* (New York: Hastings House, 1979); Charles R. Wright, "Mass Communication Rediscovered: Its Past and Future in American Sociology," in *Media, Audience, and Social Structure*, eds. S. J. Ball-Rokeach and M. G. Cantor (Beverly Hills, Calif.: Sage, 1986), pp. 22–33; Denis McQuail, *Mass Communication Theory: An Introduction* (London: Sage, 1984, 1987); Alexis S. Tan, *Mass Communication Theories and Research* (Columbus, Ohio: Grid, 1981); Robert White, "Mass Communication and Culture: Transaction to a New Paradigm," *Journal of Communication* 33 (1983): 279–301.

2. Definitions of mass communication are discussed in Sandra J. Ball-Rokeach and Muriel G. Cantor (eds.), *Media, Audience, and Social Structure* (Beverly Hills, Calif.: Sage, 1986), pp. 10–11; McQuail, *Mass Communication*, 1984, pp. 33–34, 1987, pp. 29–47.

Media, of course, imply *mediation*. Media go between the audience and something else. Denis McQuail suggests several views of mediation in mass communication: Media are *windows* that enable us to see beyond our immediate surroundings, *interpreters* that help us make sense of experience, *platforms* or *carriers* that convey information, *interactive communication* that includes audience feedback, *signposts* that provide us with instructions and directions, *filters* that screen out parts of experience and focus on others, *mirrors* that reflect ourselves back to us, and *barriers* that block the truth.[3]

An Organizing Model

Media scholars recognize two faces of mass communication. One face looks from the media to the larger society and its institutions. It reflects the link between the media and other institutions such as politics, economics, education, and religion. Theorists interested in the media–society link are concerned with the ways in which media are embedded in a society and the mutual influence between larger social structures and the media. This we could call the *macro* side of mass communication theory. The second face looks toward people, in groups and as individuals. This face reflects the link between the media and audiences. Theorists interested in the media–audience link focus on group and individual effects and outcomes of the media transaction. This is the *micro* side of mass-communication theory.[4]

Figure 15.1 illustrates mass communication and its two faces. The model may imply that the institutional link is distinct from the personal one, that the media's relationship to institutions is somehow different from the link to persons. Yet, this cannot be true because people, groups, and cultures com-

3. McQuail, *Mass Communication*, 1987, pp. 52–53.

4. This conceptualization is adapted from a discussion of mass-communication theory by McQuail, *Mass Communication*, 1984, pp. 53–57.

prise institutions. The relationship between media and institutions is possible only through the media's transaction with audiences; and the audience-media relationship is impossible to separate from the institutions of the society in which those audiences reside.

Thus, the model is not a map of the mass-communication process but is strictly intended to capture the different dimensions of media research and theory. This material defies tidy organization, and any ordering model would fail to characterize adequately the richness of the differences and similarities that abound in this field. The chapter is divided into five sections corresponding to the parts of the model: media content and structure, the media–institution link, the media–audience link, cultural outcomes, and individual outcomes.

Media Content and Structure

At the heart of mass communication are the media. Of course, media cannot be separated from the larger process of mass communication, nor can one examine media apart from their links with institutions and audiences as depicted in Figure 15.1. Yet certain theories have emphasized intrinsic structural properties of media over these other considerations. In this section we deal with two substantially different theories of media content and structure. Although these theories emphasize the makeup of media messages, they do not ignore media relationships. In fact, both theories show how media messages are understood by their relationship to other facets of society.

Innis and McLuhan

Marshall McLuhan is perhaps the best-known writer on mass communication among the general public. He has received attention primarily because of his interesting and bizarre style and his startling and thought-provoking ideas. At the same time, McLuhan has become one of the most controversial writers in the arena of popular culture.

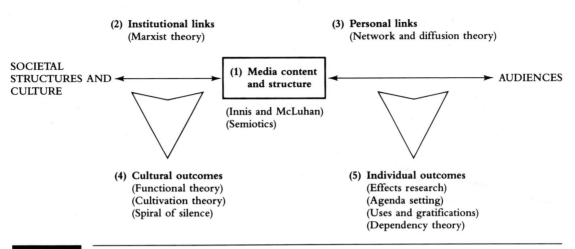

Figure 15.1 An organizing model.

Whether one agrees with him or not, his ideas have received too much publicity to be ignored.[5]

McLuhan's early ideas on the media of communication stem from his mentor Harold Adams Innis.[6] Both Innis and McLuhan treat communication media as the essence of civilization, and both see the course of history as a manifestation of the predominant media of the age.

Innis sees communication media as extensions of the human mind. He teaches that the primary interest of any historical period is a bias growing out of the predominant media in use. Heavy media such as parchment, clay, or stone are *time-binding*, providing a bias toward tradition. Time-binding

media facilitate communication from one generation to another. *Space-binding* media such as paper and papyrus, on the other hand, tend to foster empire building, large bureaucracy, and military interests. Space-binding media facilitate communication from one location to another. Speech as a medium encourages temporal thinking, which values knowledge and tradition and supports community involvement and interpersonal relationships.

Written media in opposition to oral produce different kinds of culture. The space-binding effect of writing produces interests in political authority and the growth of empires in a spatial sense. Innis teaches that the essence of Western culture has been shaped by a strong print or spatial bias. His own viewpoint is expressed as follows:

> Mechanization has emphasized complexity and confusion; it has been responsible for monopolies in the field of knowledge. . . . The conditions of freedom of thought are in danger of being destroyed by science, technology, and the mechanization of knowledge, and with them, Western civilization. My bias is with the oral tradition, particularly as reflected in Greek civilization, and with the necessity of recapturing something of its spirit.[7]

5. McLuhan's most well-known works are *The Gutenberg Galaxy: The Making of Typographic Man* (Toronto: University of Toronto Press, 1962); *The Mechanical Bride* (New York: Vanguard Press, 1951); *Understanding Media* (New York: McGraw-Hill, 1964); Marshall McLuhan and Quentin Fiori, *the Medium Is the Massage* (New York: Bantam Books, 1967). Other works by McLuhan are listed in the Bibliography. I have relied on the synthesis of Bruce Gronbeck, "McLuhan as Rhetorical Theorist," *Journal of Communication* 31 (1981): 117–128.

6. J. W. Carey, "Harold Adams Innis and Marshall McLuhan," *The Antioch Review* 27 (1967): 5–39. Innis's works include *The Bias of Communication* (Toronto: University of Toronto Press, 1951); *Empire and Communications* (Toronto: University of Toronto Press, 1950, 1972).

7. Innis, *Bias*, pp. 150–191.

One can easily see the connection between McLuhan's ideas and those of his predecessor, but McLuhan clearly has gone beyond the ideas of Innis in discussing the structure of media.[8]

McLuhan's most basic hypothesis is that people adapt to their environment through a certain balance or ratio of the senses, and the primary medium of the age brings out a particular sense ratio. McLuhan sees every medium as an extension of some human faculty, with the media of communication thus exaggerating this or that particular sense. In his words, "The wheel . . . is an extension of the foot. The book is an extension of the eye. . . . Clothing, an extension of the skin. . . . Electric circuitry, an extension of the central nervous system."[9] Whatever media predominate will influence human beings by affecting the way they perceive the world.

Before printing was invented, tribal people were primarily hearing-oriented communicators. They were emotionally and interpersonally close. For the tribal person, "hearing was believing." But the invention of the printing press changed this. The Gutenberg age brought a new sense ratio into being, in which sight predominated. McLuhan's basic premise about the development of Western culture is that the nature of print forced people into a linear, logical, and categorial kind of perception. For McLuhan, the use of the alphabet "fostered and encouraged the habit of perceiving all environment in visual and spatial terms—particularly in terms of a space and of a time that are uniform,

> c,o,n,t,i,n,o,u,s and
> c-o-n-n-e-c-t-e-d."[10]

We have entered a new age, though, according to McLuhan. Electronic technology has brought back an aural predominance. The Gutenberg technology created an explosion in society, separating and segmenting individual from individual; the electronic age has created an implosion, bringing the world back together in a "global village." As a result "it is forcing us to reconsider and reevaluate practically every thought, every action, and every institution formerly taken for granted."[11] McLuhan describes this impact:

> Electric circuitry profoundly involves men with one another. Information pours upon us, instantaneously and continuously. As soon as information is acquired, it is very rapidly replaced by still newer information. Our electrically configured world has forced us to move from the habit of data classification to the mode of pattern recognition. We can no longer build serially, block-by-block, step-by-step, because instant communication insures that all factors of the environment and of experience coexist in a state of active interplay.[12]

Thus, we come to the main thesis of McLuhan's work: "The medium is the message."[13] This catch phrase, at once curious and thought-provoking, refers to the general influence that a medium has apart from its context. Tom Wolfe puts it this way: "It doesn't matter if the networks show twenty hours a day of sadistic cowboys caving in people's teeth or twenty hours of Pablo Casals droning away on his cello in a pure-culture white Spanish drawing room. It doesn't matter about the content."[14] And here, of course, is where McLuhan parts company from most contemporary researchers in mass communication. What really makes a difference in people's lives is the predominant media, not content, of the period: "They are so pervasive in their personal, political, economic, aesthetic, psychological, moral, ethical, and social consequences that they leave no part of us untouched, unaffected, unaltered."[15]

McLuhan makes a distinction between the hot and the cool media of communication. These con-

---

8. Good brief summaries of McLuhan's theory can be found in the following: Kenneth Boulding, "The Medium is the Massage," in *McLuhan: Hot and Cool*, ed. G. E. Stearn (New York: Dial Press, 1967), pp. 56–64; Tom Wolfe, "The New Life Out There," in *McLuhan: Hot and Cool*, ed. G. E. Stearn (New York: Dial Press, 1967), pp. 34–56; Carey, "Innis and McLuhan."

9. McLuhan and Fiore, *Massage*.

10. Ibid.

11. Ibid.

12. Ibid.

13. McLuhan, *Understanding Media*, p. 7.

14. Wolfe, "New Life," p. 19.

15. McLuhan and Fiore, *Massage*.

cepts are the most confusing and probably the most controversial in his writing. McLuhan describes media in terms of the degree to which they involve people perceptually. *Hot media* are those that contain relatively complete sensory data, or high redundancy in the information-theory sense (Chapter 3). With hot media the perceiver has less need to become involved by filling in missing data. McLuhan refers to hot media as low in participation. Hot media, because they give us everything, create a dulling or somnambulism in the population.

Cool media, on the other hand, require the individual to participate perceptually by filling in missing data. This participation creates healthy involvement. It is important to realize that McLuhan's use of participation or involvement does not refer to the degree of interest or time spent attending to a particular medium of communication. Rather, he refers to the completeness (hot) or incompleteness (cool) of the stimulus itself.

Film, for example, is considered to be a hot medium because the image projected on the screen is complete in every detail. The viewer of a film is not required perceptually to fill in anything. In an information-theory sense (Chapter 3), we could say that the film has high redundancy, low information. Television, on the other hand, provides the viewer with only a sketch through the illumination of tiny dots. The viewer must perceptually fill in between these visual dots. In short, the viewer must become involved perceptually with the stimulus. This distinction is crucial, for McLuhan sees it as a fundamental point of impact on society. As he puts it, "So the hotting-up of one sense tends to effect hypnosis, and the cooling of all senses tends to result in hallucination."[16]

Given his definition of cool media, you can see why McLuhan believes that television is changing the fabric of society. But the advent of television brings its own problems. McLuhan makes clear that a shift from one kind of medium to another creates tremendous stresses in society. For example, if a hot medium such as radio is introduced into tribal or nonliterate cultures, which are accustomed to cool media, a violent reaction may occur. Similarly, the reorientation required for hot societies such as our own to adapt to the introduction of cool media such as television has been upsetting.

In the 1970s McLuhan's teachings changed substantially. In his earlier works, he strongly implies that the form of media in society affects or causes certain modes of perception on the part of society's members. In his later teaching, he seems much less certain of this causal link. Instead, McLuhan says that media resonate with or reflect the perceptual categories of individuals. Instead of envisioning a causal link between media and personal perception, he later saw a simultaneous outpouring of certain kinds of thought on the part of the media and the person. Media forms do not cause but bring out modes of thought that are already present in the individual. The lack of consonance between the individual's perceptual categories and the depictions of the media creates stress in society.

Semiotics

Semiotic theories of media are distinctly different in content and approach from those of Innis and McLuhan. Whereas McLuhan teaches that the media forms themselves constitute the primary message of mass communication, semiotics makes a sharp separation between a medium and its content. For the semiotician, content matters a great deal, and that content depends on the reading given to it by the audience member. Semiotics focuses on the ways in which producers create signs and the ways in which audiences understand those signs.

Semiotics was discussed in Chapter 4 as part of the general topic of language and coding. Recall that semiotics goes back to the work of Charles Peirce and has a long history of development in the twentieth century.[17] Chapter 4 discusses in some detail the contemporary theory of signs by Umberto Eco. Here we rely on the synthesis of

16. McLuhan, *Understanding Media*, p. 32.

17. Umberto Eco, *A Theory of Semiotics* (Bloomington: Indiana University Press, 1976); Arthur Asa Berger, *Signs in Contemporary Culture: An Introduction to Semiotics* (Salem, Wis.: Sheffield, 1989).

Donald Fry and Virginia Fry, who apply the ideas of Peirce and Eco to the study of media.[18]

Semiotics is the study of signification, or the ways in which signs are used in the interpretation of events. Semiotics looks at the way in which messages are structured, the kinds of signs used, and the meanings of signs intended and understood by producers and consumers. In short, semiotics is a tool for analyzing what the content of media messages mean.

Fry and Fry organize their discussion into three major postulates. The first is that media messages can elicit numerous meanings. In other words, the text is understood by audiences through interpretation, and there are several possible interpretations of any given message. Media producers do intend to convey particular meanings in their works, but audiences may or may not understand these messages in the ways intended. Consider music videos as an example:

> A music video is useful to illustrate that a particular expression can be correlated with a number of contents to produce different significations. For a teenager, video may be taken as a statement against the constraints that passing through adolescence seems to carry or as an image of the rebellious individual spurning social convention. A media researcher may study the video as a vehicle for the transmission of violent images to an audience. An executive of a record company may view the same video as an effective promotional device that is having a positive impact on sales of records. . . . In a cultural sense, the music video expression signifies different meanings for each because it is coded by each with different content planes.[19]

This discussion of individual interpretation does not mean that audience reaction is serendipitous. Indeed, producers go to some effort to predict the reactions of the audience and to use signs that will shape those reactions. Commercials are an excellent example. Although audience interpretations will vary, the advertiser certainly aims to elicit a predominant meaning and a particular response.

Denotation and connotation are central concepts in semiotics. *Denotation* refers to what a sign is believed to designate. Almost all literate consumers will get the denotation of a media message: You know a Preparation H commercial when you see one. If the actor says, "My mother-in-law is a doctor, and she likes Preparation H," you know what that means. What makes interpretations vary is not denotation but *connotation*, or the feelings, judgments, and assessments that you make about the message content ("Oh no, not another tacky hemorrhoid commercial"). Whereas denotations are stable, connotations vary because they are based on synthetic inferences or extensions from the denotation. Media producers try not only to present a denotation but also to affect the subsequent connotation.

An example of denotation and connotation can be seen in Farrel Corcoran's semiotic analysis of the news reporting of the crash of Korean Airlines flight 007 in 1983.[20] KAL 007, a commercial airliner that entered Soviet airspace, was shot down by a Soviet fighter, and all aboard were killed. Corcoran analyzed the reports of this event from the three major American newsmagazines, *Time, Newsweek*, and *US News and World Report*. Specifically, he was interested in the meanings attached to the event, the ways in which the event was used by these magazines as a symbol of something else. The author shows how these three magazines presented an amazingly similar interpretation of the disaster and how the overriding connotation was that the Soviet Union was an evil nation.

In the use of "perhaps the most vitriolic language in their history," these news magazines made a strong link between the airline incident and the entire Soviet system. This is an example of metonymy, or using a part of something to symbolize the whole. Russian stereotypes were used throughout the reporting to the effect that Russians are ignorant, drab, politically insensitive, tyrannical, and

18. Donald L. Fry and Virginia H. Fry, "A Semiotic Model for the Study of Mass Communication," in *Communication Yearbook* 9, ed. M. L. McLaughlin (Beverly Hills: Sage, 1986), pp. 443–462.

19. Ibid., p. 446.

20. Farrel Corcoran, "KAL 007 and the Evil Empire: Mediated Disaster and Forms of Rationalization," *Critical Studies in Mass Communication* 3 (1986): 297–316.

barbaric. In short, the incident was used as a "condensational symbol" for the polarization between the evil Soviet Union and the rest of the world.

The second of Fry and Fry's postulates is that media texts get their meaning through associations made by audience members. Here, the authors use Peirce's concept of interpretant, which is the meaning of a sign in the mind of the perceiver. Communication is made possible by a consensual meaning in society. This Peirce calls the "final interpretant"; but the final interpretant is still only one possible meaning for a sign. The audience member may have an *emotional interpretant* (a feeling associated with the content), an *energic interpretant* (an associated action such as compliance), and a *logical interpretant* (rationalization as to why a certain action is reasonable). For example, one of the most effective and interesting political spots in the 1984 presidential campaign was Ronald Reagan's "Morning in America" message. It was a series of beautiful photographic shots of morning in different places in the country. For many viewers, it left a feeling of warmth and contentment (emotional), it reinforced decisions to vote again for Reagan (energic), and it provided a cognitive rationalization that all is well in the country (logical).

Corcoran's study of the KAL 007 disaster shows how the final interpretant of this event in the United States was a generalized view of the Soviet Union as basically evil. The predominant emotional interpretant at that time was outrage. The energic interpretant was to speak out and act out against the Soviets for their deed. For example, *US News* showed liquor-store owners removing Russian vodka from their shelves. The logical interpretant is also shown to be operating here as the newsmagazines make overt statements about why their interpretation is reasonable and fail to consider any other possible interpretations.

Fry and Fry's third postulate is that the meanings of media texts are affected by events outside the texts themselves. The signs used in the text do play a role in shaping meaning, but numerous nontextual influences also bear upon the meaning that an individual will take from the text. The text will be influential to the extent that (1) the producer understands the kinds of content that will bring out certain meanings in the culture of the audience and (2) the actual structure of the text emphasizes specific meanings over others. For example, a producer of a sitcom may wish to elicit a feeling of warmth and amusement from the characters. Knowing the kinds of situations that appeal to the general American audience help writers develop situations that bring out those kinds of responses. Further, the writers and actors will concentrate on emphasizing a particular feeling for each character that will capture the attention of the audience.

The KAL 007 incident illustrates the way in which the media resonated with the feelings of the American public at that time. The media served as a virtual agent of the government in perpetuating an ideology of Good versus Evil in their reporting of the disaster. The newsmagazines ignored, downplayed, or dismissed alternative interpretations found commonly in the foreign press—the ideas that KAL 007 was on a reconnaissance mission, for example.

One objective of media is to get the attention of the audience. How is this done? Eco says that it occurs through a process of *semantic disclosure*. This is the use of signs to emphasize certain properties and to make other properties neutral. Out of everything that a person could "see" in a message, some are highlighted, and others are muted. Semantic disclosure in a sitcom might be accomplished by the character's costume, use of certain expressions in dialogue, and nonverbal demeanor. In fact, stereotyping is an important kind of semantic disclosure in media messages, as can be seen in the KAL 007 reporting.

Once again, however, the audience response is not totally predictable. Indeed, many extracodes, or outside factors, can influence meaning. *Overcoding* occurs when meanings normally attached to one kind of message or situation are used to interpret another. For example, at Christmas time Hallmark releases Christmas card commercials that just depict a beautiful scene without directly mentioning the product (cards). Viewers will still get that the company is trying to sell its product because of the standard interpretation given to all other commercials. *Ideological overcoding* is especially important. This occurs when the viewer's ideology affects the interpretation of a message, even when the ideological interpretation is not intended. For example, a feminist may consider certain commercials objectionable because they depict women in subordinate roles, a Marxist may view network television news as an instrument of oppression, or a union leader might read *The Wall Street Journal* as a house organ for industrial management.

Media as Social Institution

In communication studies, media are most often considered for their information-dissemination function, but we must remember that actual operating organizations within society comprise the media. In other words, they are an important social institution and are part of a complex matrix of societywide relations. McQuail discusses five major media links, which are depicted in Figure 15.2.[21] Here, the media themselves are shown in the center and include a management function, a professional set of personnel, and the technical element. Media are shown in this diagram to interact with various economic factors, social and political factors, events and happenings in society at large, and the audience.

Perhaps the most important line of theory to address media as institution includes various Marxist-based critical theories. Because we discussed critical theory in Chapter 11, we will not cover it in great detail here, but a general discussion is in order.[22]

Recall from Chapter 11 that Marxist-based theories are concerned with the distribution of power in society and the domination of certain interests over others. Clearly, the media are seen as a major

player in this ideological struggle. Dominant ideologies are perpetuated by the media, as we saw above in the case of the news reporting of the KAL 007 disaster. Most Marxist communication theories are concerned with mass media primarily because of their role in disseminating the dominant ideology and their potential for expression of alternative and oppositional ideas. For critical theorists, media are part of a culture industry that literally creates symbols and images that can oppress marginalized groups.

According to McQuail there are five major branches of Marxist media theory.[23] The first is *classical Marxism*. Here, the media are seen as instruments of the dominant class and as a means by which capitalists promote their profit-making interests. They disseminate the ideology of the ruling classes in society and thereby oppress other groups.

The second is *political-economic media theory*. It is close to classical Marxism in that it blames the structure of ownership in society for social ills. In this school of thought, media content is a commodity to be sold in the marketplace, and the information disseminated is controlled by what the market will bear. This system leads to a conservative, non-risk-taking operation, making certain kinds of programming and certain media outlets dominant and others marginalized.

The third line of theory is the *Frankfurt School*. This school of thought places more emphasis on ideas than on material goods. It sees the media as a means of constructing culture, which leads to the domination of the ideology of the elite. This outcome is accomplished by media manipulation of images and symbols to benefit the interests of the dominant class.

The fourth school is the *hegemonic theory*. *Hegemony* is the domination of a false ideology or way of thinking over other ways of understanding. Ideology is not caused by the economic system alone but is deeply embedded in all activities of society. Thus, ideology is not forced by one group on another but is pervasive and unconscious. The dominant ideology perpetuates the interests of cer-

21. McQuail, *Mass Communication*, 1987, p. 142.

22. See the Chapter 11 bibliography for readings in this area. McQuail's *Mass Communication* discusses Marxist theories of media in some detail. See also Lawrence Grossberg, "Strategies of Marxist Cultural Interpretation," *Critical Studies in Mass Communication* 1 (1984): 392–421.

23. McQuail, *Mass Communication*, 1987, pp. 63–68.

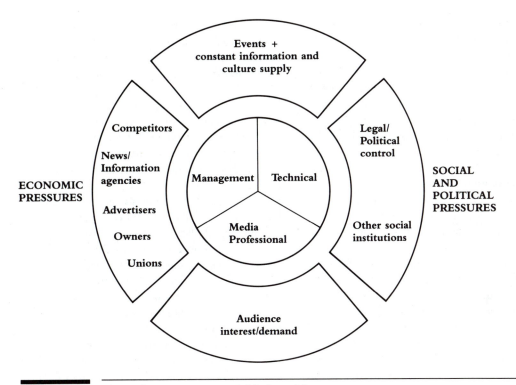

Figure 15.2   The media organization in a field of social force.

tain classes over others, and the media obviously take a major role in this process.

The final approach to Marxist media studies is the *sociocultural approach*. Relying in large measure on semiotics, this group of scholars is interested in the cultural meanings of media products. They look at the ways in which media content are interpreted, including both dominant and oppositional interpretations. Cultural studies sees society as a field of competing ideas in a struggle of meanings. The study by Corcoran of the news reporting of the KAL 007 disaster is very much in the cultural studies tradition.

Media and the Audience

The third part of the theory model outlined at the beginning of the chapter is the link between media and audience. Here, we are concerned with questions about the nature of the audience and how the media interact with them. No area in media theory has presented such theoretical quandaries and debates as studies of the audience. Media theorists are as far from consensus on how to conceptualize the audience as they are on how media influence audiences.

Disputes on the nature of the audience seem to involve two related dialectics. The first is a tension between the idea of audience as a mass versus the idea of audience as community. The second is a tension between the idea of audience as passive versus the the idea of audience as active. Let us consider each of these in turn.

Mass Society Versus Community

This controversy pits ideas about the audience as an undifferentiated mass against those of the audience as a highly differentiated set of small groups or communities. In the case of the former, audiences are viewed as a large population to be molded by the media. In the case of the latter, audiences are viewed as discriminating members of small groups who are influenced mostly by their peers.

The theory of mass society is a concept growing out of the large, complex, bureaucratic nature of the modern state.[24] The theory envisions a malleable mass of people in which small groupings, community life, and ethnic identity are replaced by societywide depersonalized relations. As William Kornhauser says, "All members of mass society are equally valued as voters, buyers, and spectators. Numerical superiority therefore tends to be the decisive criterion of success."[25] Greatness therefore comes to those who can effectively manipulate the mass.

This conception of society has led to widespread criticism of modern life. Critics of the mass society have suggested several propositions, summarized by Daniel Bell, as follows.[26] First, rapid developments in transportation and communication have increased human contact, and economic considerations have made people more and more interdependent. Thus, like a giant system, imbalance in one part affects everybody. The catch is that we are all more interdependent but have become increasingly estranged from one another. Community and family ties are broken, and old values are questioned. Second, because society is no longer believed to be led by the elites, morals, tastes, and values decline. Rapid changes in society hurl men and women into multiple-role situations, causing a loss of the sense of self. People become more anxious, and a charismatic leader ultimately may be required to lift society out of the abyss.

This dismal view has several implications for the mass media of communication. Critics of mass society fear that minds will be pounded and altered by propagandistic forces behind the media. Paul Lazarsfeld and Robert Merton express this fear: "There is the danger that these technically advanced instruments of mass communication constitute a major avenue for deterioration of aesthetic tastes and popular cultural standards."[27]

The theory of mass society is still prominent among the general population. There seems to be a popular belief that we are all "going to hell in a handbasket." Although this theory is not as prevalent among scholars today as it was a few decades ago, it still has an influence. McLuhan's theory is certainly a mass-society theory as are some of the Marxist theories. Certain "powerful-effects" theories (discussed later), including the well-known cultivation theory, are strongly influenced by mass-society thinking.

At the other end of the mass–community dispute is the idea that the audience cannot be characterized as an amorphous mass, that it consists of numerous highly differentiated communities, each with its own values, ideas, and interests. Media content is interpreted within the community according to meanings that are worked out socially within the group, and individuals are influenced more by their peers than by the media.[28] We explored the idea of media-interpretive communities in Chapter 10. There, we saw that the meanings of media messages are worked out interactively within groups of people who use a medium in a similar way.

The community view was given impetus by a now classic voting study in 1940 conducted by Lazarsfeld and his colleagues in Elmira, New York.[29]

24. The most prominent critics of mass society are José Ortega y Gasset, Karl Mannheim, Karl Jaspers, Paul Tillich, Gabriel Marcel, and Emil Lederer. Syntheses can be found in two critiques of the theory: Daniel Bell, "The Theory of Mass Society," *Commentary* (July 1956): 75–83; and R. A. Bauer and A. H. Bauer, "America, Mass Society and Mass Media," *Journal of Social Issues* 16 (1960): 3–66. See also Eliot Friedson, "Communications Research and the Concept of the Mass," in *The Process and Effects of Mass Communication,* eds. W. Schramm and D. Roberts (Urbana: University of Illinois Press, 1971), pp. 197–208; and William Kornhauser, "Mass Society," in *International Encyclopedia of the Social Sciences,* vol. 10 (New York: Macmillan, 1968), pp. 58–64.

25. Kornhauser, "Mass Society," p. 59.

26. Bell, "Theory of Mass Society."

27. Paul Lazarsfeld and Robert K. Merton, "Mass Communication, Popular Taste, and Organized Social Action," in *The Process and Effects of Mass Communication,* eds. W. Schramm and D. Roberts (Urbana: University of Illinois Press, 1971), p. 557.

28. For an excellent statement of this position, see Thomas R. Lindlof, "Media Audiences as Interpretive Communities," in *Communication Yearbook 11,* ed. J. A. Anderson (Newbury Park, Calif.: Sage, 1988), pp. 81–107.

29. Paul Lazarsfeld, Bernard Berelson, and H. Gaudet, *The People's Choice* (New York: Columbia University Press, 1948).

The researchers found an unexpected occurrence that implied a possible involvement of interpersonal communication in the total mass-communication process. This effect, which came to be known as the *two-step flow hypothesis*, was startling, and it had a major impact on our understanding of the role of mass media.

Since the original Elmira study, much additional data have come in, and the hypothesis has received substantial support.[30] Lazarsfeld hypothesized that information flows from the mass media to certain opinion leaders in the community, who facilitate communication through discussions with peers. For example, Lazarsfeld found that voters seem to be more influenced by their friends during a campaign than by the media.

The two-step flow theory is best summarized in Elihu Katz and Paul Lazarsfeld's classic work *Personal Influence*.[31] Central to the theory is the concept of *opinion leaders*—individuals in the community who receive information from the media and pass it to their peers. Opinion leaders are in all groups: occupational, social, community, and others. The opinion leader typically is difficult to distinguish from other group members because opinion leadership is not a trait. Instead, it is a role taken in interpersonal communication. Opinion leadership changes from time to time and from issue to issue. Katz and Lazarsfeld find that it differs in such areas as marketing, fashion, and public affairs. Interest in a particular issue is certainly an important determinant of opinion leadership, but leaders can be influential only when interest is shared by all members of the group.

Opinion leaders may be of two kinds: those influential on one topic, *monomorphism*, and those influential on a variety of topics, *polymorphism*. Monomorphism becomes more predominant as systems become more modern: "As the technological base of a system becomes more complex, a division of labor and specialization of roles result, which in turn lead to different sets of opinion leaders for different issues."[32] In this theory then, groups are the key to mass-communication influence, providing direction to individuals in terms of opinions, attitudes, values, and norms.

Research more recent than the Lazarsfeld study has shown that the dissemination of ideas is not a simple two-step process, and a *multiple-step model* of diffusion is now more universally accepted.[33] This model is similar to the two-step hypothesis but admits to more possibilities. Research has shown that the ultimate number of relays between the media and final receivers is variable. In the adoption of an innovation, for example, certain individuals will hear about it directly from media sources, whereas others will be many steps removed. This line of work is part of the interactional and network tradition discussed in some detail in Chapters 3 and 12–14. We saw in those chapters that interaction in networks plays an important role in relationships, small groups, and organizations. Here, we see that they play an important role in mass communication, too.

Active Audience Versus Passive Audience

Another controversy in the study of the audience deals with whether the audience is primarily passive and easily influenced in a direct way by the media or relatively active in structuring its own reality. This tension has to do with the extent to which audiences can be influenced by the media, and it is correlated with the mass–community tension. For the most part, mass theories tend to subscribe to a passive conception of audience, although not all passive-audience theories can legitimately be called mass-society theories. Similarly, most community theories subscribe to an active notion of audience, and although most active-audience theories would acknowledge the legitimacy of the community notion, they are not all directly based on it.

30. An excellent summary of this hypothesis is Elihu Katz, "The Two-Step Flow of Communication," *Public Opinion Quarterly* 21 (1957): 61–78.

31. Elihu Katz and Paul Lazarsfeld, *Personal Influence: The Part Played by People in the Flow of Mass Communications* (New York: Free Press, 1955).

32. Everett M. Rogers and F. Floyd Shoemaker, *Communication of Innovations, A Cross-Cultural Approach* (New York: Free Press, 1971), p. 224.

33. One of the best summaries of this extension can be found in Rogers and Shoemaker, *Innovations*, chap. 6.

These ideas about audiences are associated with various theories of media effects discussed later in the chapter. The "powerful-effects" theories tend to be based on the passive audience, whereas the "minimal-effects" theories are based more on an active one. The most well-known active-audience theory is uses and gratifications, which we will discuss in some detail later.

Frank Biocca discusses five characteristics of the active audience implied by the theories this genre.[34] The first is *selectivity*. Active audiences are considered to be selective in the media they choose to use. The second characteristic is *utilitarianism*. Active audiences are said to use media to meet particular needs and goals. The third characteristic is *intentionality*, which implies the purposeful use of media content. The fourth characteristic is *involvement*, or effort. Here, audiences are actively attending, thinking about, and using the media. Finally, active audiences are believed to be *impervious to influence*. In other words, they are not very easily persuaded by the media alone. These characteristics are antithetical to the passive notion of audience.

Many media scholars believe that the mass–community and active-passive dichotomies are too simple, that they do not capture the complexity of audiences. It may be that audiences have some elements of mass society and other elements of local communities. Audiences may be active in some ways and passive in others or active at some times and passive at other times. Rather than ask whether audiences are easily influenced by the media, it might be better to ask when and under what conditions they are influenced and when they are not.

Another way to view the tensions in the definition of audience is a natural contradiction of definition within society itself. In other words, sometimes society acts in ways that define the audience as a mass and sometimes as a community. Some-times society acts in ways that define an audience as active and at other times passive. This view changes the debate from one over what the audience really is to its meaning for people at different times and in different places.[35]

Theories of Cultural Outcomes

We turn now to a study of the outcomes of the media transaction. Of all areas of mass-communication research, outcome studies are the most prevalent, especially in the United States. A looming question throughout the history of media theory has been the effects of media on society and individuals.[36] The theories included here are divided into two sections, those focusing on general cultural outcomes and those focusing on individual effects. This section deals with the former, and the next section with the latter.

The Functions of Mass Communication

One of the earliest and best-known theorists of mass communication is Harold Lasswell. In his classic 1948 article, he presents the simple and often-quoted model of communication:[37]

> Who
> Says what
> In which channel
> To whom
> With what effect

35. This view is espoused by Martin Allor, "Relocating the Site of the Audience," *Critical Studies in Mass Communication* 5 (1988): 217–233.

36. For an exploration of media effects, see Jennings Bryant and Dolf Zillmann (eds.), *Perspectives on Media Effects* (Hillsdale, N.J.: Erlbaum, 1986).

37. Harold Lasswell, "The Structure and Function of Communication in Society," in *The Communication of Ideas*, ed. L. Bryson (New York: Institute for Religious and Social Studies, 1948), p. 37. For information regarding Lasswell's contribution to political science, see Arnold A. Rogow (ed.), *Politics, Personality, and Social Science in the Twentieth Century: Essays in Honor of Harold D. Lasswell* (Chicago: University of Chicago Press, 1969), especially the following articles: Heinz Eulau, "The Maddening Methods of Harold D. Lasswell: Some Philosophical Underpinnings," pp. 15–40; Bruce Smith, "The Mystifying Intellectual History of Harold Lasswell," pp. 41–105.

34. Frank A. Biocca, "Opposing Conceptions of the Audience: The Active and Passive Hemispheres of Mass Communication Theory," in *Communication Yearbook 11*, ed. J. A. Anderson (Newbury Park, Calif.: Sage, 1988), pp. 51–80. This article is an excellent discussion of the active-passive distinction and provides a review of the various theories on each side.

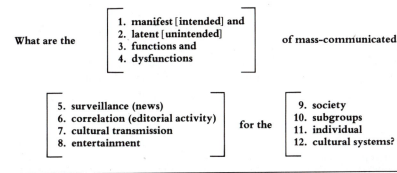

Figure 15.3 Wright's functional model.
From *Public Opinion Quarterly*, "Functional Analysis and Mass Communication," by Charles R. Wright. Copyright © 1960. Reprinted by permission of *The University of Chicago Press* and the author.

The model outlines the basic elements of communication that have received the most research attention. Indeed, the last element in the model directs us to the entire outcome research tradition.

Lasswell's work is paradoxical because it implies a linear process of mass communication, yet it also presents a set of functions fulfilled by mass communication, which are not easily classed as causal effects. Lasswell identifies three functions of the media of communication. These are *surveillance* (knowing what is going on), *correlation* (having options or solutions for dealing with societal problems), and *transmission* (socialization and education).[38]

Charles Wright has expanded on Lasswell's model. Starting with Lasswell's three basic functions, he developed a twelve-category model and a functional inventory for mass communication as shown in Figure 15.3 and Table 15.1.[39] The model is set up as a question, probing the various functions and dysfunctions of mass-communicated messages. Such functions are broken down according to social levels. The skeleton provided by the basic functional model is filled in, the questions answered, on the inventory. In Figure 15.3 we see a number of functions and dysfunctions of Lasswell's categories according to social level. Notice that

Wright added a fourth function, entertainment, to Lasswell's list.

The Diffusion of Innovations

We saw above that diffusion of information is one of the most significant outcomes of communication. One of the most fruitful theoretical areas contributing to our understanding of diffusion stems from the innovation research in rural agriculture, developing nations, and organizations. The diffusion of an innovation occurs when an idea spreads from a point of origin to surrounding geographical areas or from person to person within a single area.[40] Several prominent American and foreign researchers have been responsible for this line of research. The broadest and most communication-oriented theory is that of Everett Rogers and his colleagues.[41]

Rogers begins his theory by relating it to the process of social change in general. Social change consists of invention, diffusion (or communication),

38. Lasswell, "Structure and Function."

39. Charles R. Wright, "Functional Analysis and Mass Communication," *Public Opinion Quarterly* 24 (1960): 605–620.

40. For a general summary, see Torsten Hagerstrand, "Diffusion II: The Diffusion of Innovations," in *International Encyclopedia of the Social Sciences*, vol. 4, ed. D. Sills (New York: Macmillan, 1968).

41. Everett M. Rogers, *Diffusion of Innovations* (New York: Free Press, 1962); Rogers and Shoemaker, *Innovations*; Everett M. Rogers and Ronny Adhikarya, "Diffusion of Innovations: An Up-to-Date Review and Commentary," in *Communication Yearbook 3*, ed. D. Nimmo (New Brunswick, N.J.: Transaction Books, 1979), pp. 67–82; Everett M. Rogers and D. Lawrence Kincaid, *Communication Networks: Toward a New Paradigm For Research* (New York: Free Press, 1981).

and consequences. Such change can occur internally from within a group or externally through contact with outside change agents. In the latter case, contact may occur spontaneously or accidentally, or it may result from planning on the part of outside agencies.

Diffusion of innovations is a time-consuming process. Many years may be required for an idea to spread. Rogers states, in fact, that one purpose of diffusion research is to discover the means to shorten this lag. Once established, an innovation will have consequences, be they functional or dys-

---

Table 15-1   Partial Functional Inventory for Mass Communications.

	System under consideration			
	Society	Individual	Specific subgroup (e.g., political elite)	Culture
1. Mass Communicated Activity: Surveillance (News)				
Functions (manifest and latent)	Warning: Natural dangers Attack; war	Warning Instrumental	Instrumental: Information useful to power	Aids cultural contact Aids cultural growth
	Instrumental: News essential to the economy and other institutions	Adds prestige: Opinion leadership	Detects: Knowledge of subversive and deviant behavior	
	Ethicizing	Status conferral	Manages public opinion: Monitors Controls	
			Legitimizes power: Status conferral	
Dysfunctions (manifest and latent)	Threatens stability: News of "better" societies Fosters panic	Anxiety Privatization Apathy Narcotization	Threatens power: News of reality "Enemy" propaganda Exposés	Permits cultural invasion
2. Mass-Communicated Activity: Correlation (Editorial selection, Interpretation, and Prescription)				
Functions (manifest and latent)	Aids mobilization	Provides efficiency: Assimilating news	Helps preserve power	Impedes cultural invasion Maintains cultural consensus
	Impedes threats to social stability Impedes panic	Impedes: Overstimulation Anxiety Apathy Privatization		

functional, direct or indirect, manifest or latent. Change agents normally expect their impact to be functional, direct, and manifest, although this outcome does not always occur.

Although mass-communication channels may play significant roles in diffusion, interpersonal networks are most important. Networks are more than a simple information linkage between opinion leader and follower, which is implied in the flow models described earlier. How individuals understand ideas and the degree to which ideas are accepted and modified depend in large measure on

Table 15-1 Partial Functional Inventory for Mass Communications. (*Continued*)

	System under consideration			
	Society	Individual	Specific subgroup (e.g., political elite)	Culture
Dysfunctions (manifest and latent)	Increases social conformism: Impedes social change if social criticism is avoided	Weakens critical faculties Increases passivity	Increases responsibility	Impedes cultural growth

3. Mass-Communicated Activity: Cultural Transmission

	Society	Individual	Specific subgroup (e.g., political elite)	Culture
Functions (manifest and latent)	Increases social cohesion: Widens base of common norms, experiences, etc. Reduces anomie Continues socialization: Reaches adults even after they have left such institutions as school	Aids integration: Exposure to common norms Reduces idiosyncrasy Reduces anomie	Extends power: Another agency for socialization	Standardizes Maintains cultural consensus
Dysfunctions (manifest and latent)	Augments "mass" society	Depersonalizes acts of socialization		Reduces variety of subcultures

4. Mass-Communicated Activity: Entertainment

	Society	Individual	Specific subgroup (e.g., political elite)	Culture
Functions (manifest and latent)	Respite for masses	Respite	Extends power: Control over another area of life	
Dysfunctions (manifest and latent)	Diverts public: Avoids social action	Increases passivity Lowers "tastes" Permits escapism		Weakens aesthetics: "Popular culture"

the interaction along the links in the network. Interaction is important, for diffusion appears to be a product of give and take rather than the simple sending and receiving of information.

Communication in the process of diffusion is a convergence of meaning achieved by symbolic interaction.[42] The adoption, rejection, modification, or creation of an innovation is a product of this convergence process. Rogers obviously makes liberal use of symbolic interactionism, system theory, and network theory. (We looked at this aspect of the theory in Chapter 3.)

The diffusion of innovations is well illustrated by the family-planning program instituted in South Korea in 1968. This program involved the establishment of mothers' clubs in 48,000 villages throughout the nation for the purpose of disseminating information about family planning. Overall, the program was successful, and Korea saw a major decline in birth rate during this period. This program was built on the idea that interpersonal channels of communication would be crucial to adoption of birth control methods. Rogers and his colleagues studied the process in 1973.[43] They interviewed about 1000 women in twenty-four villages, seeking information about the networks the women used for information about family planning and other variables.

Initially the village leaders received their information about family planning from the mass media and family-planning worker visits, but interpersonal networks were crucial for ultimate dissemination and adoption of birth control methods. Two network variables were especially important. The first was the degree to which the mothers' club leader was connected in the network or the extent

of her relations with others in the village. The second was the amount of overlap between the family-planning network and the general village network. In other words, birth control adoption was greatest in the villages in which the leader talked to many people personally and the village women talked among themselves about it.

Public Opinion and the Spiral of Silence

As the research on family planning illustrates, communication has much to do with public opinion. One of the important outcomes of media communication, reinforced by interpersonal channels, is public opinion. The topic of public opinion has been of great concern in political science. The concept has come to represent opinions publicly expressed, opinions regarding public affairs, and opinions of the general public as a group rather than of smaller groups of individuals.

The previous section addressed the nature of the media–audience link. We saw there that individuals are not only exposed to media information but that they also talk among themselves, pass on information, and express opinions. Elisabeth Noelle-Neumann's theory of the "spiral of silence" continues this analysis by demonstrating how this interpersonal-media link operates in the development of public opinion.[44] As a political researcher in Germany, Noelle-Neumann observed that in elections certain views seem to get more play than others; her idea of the spiral of silence accounts for this.

The *spiral of silence* occurs when individuals who perceive that their opinion is popular express it, whereas those who do not think their opinion is popular remain quiet. This process occurs in a spiral, so that one side of an issue ends up with much publicity and the other side with little. In everyday life we express our opinions in a variety of ways: We talk about them, we wear buttons, and we put stick-

42. Lawrence Kincaid has been primarily responsible for the theory of convergence. See Rogers and Kincaid, *Communication Networks*, pp. 31–78; D. Lawrence Kincaid, "The Convergence Model of Communication," East-West Institute Paper No. 18 (Honolulu, 1979); D. Lawrence Kincaid, June Ock Yum, and Joseph Woelfel, "The Cultural Convergence of Korean Immigrants in Hawaii: An Empirical Test of a Mathematical Theory," *Quality and Quantity* 18 (1983): 59–78.

43. Rogers and Kincaid, *Communication Networks*. The Korean case is discussed throughout the book. See especially pp. 258–285.

44. Elisabeth Noelle-Neumann, *The Spiral of Silence: Public Opinion—Our Social Skin* (Chicago: University of Chicago Press, 1984). See also "The Theory of Public Opinion: The Concept of the Spiral of Silence," in *Communication Yearbook 14*, ed. J. A. Anderson (Newbury Park, Calif.: Sage, 1991), pp. 256–287.

ers on our car bumpers. According to this theory, people are more apt to do these kinds of things when they perceive that others share their opinion and less apt to do so when they do not.

This thesis rests on two assumptions. The first is that people know which opinions are prevalent and which are not. This is called the *quasi-statistical sense* because people have a sense of the percentages of the population for and against certain positions. People do not seem reluctant to make educated guesses about public opinion. The second assumption is that people adjust their expressions of opinion to these perceptions. Noelle-Neumann presents much research evidence to support these assumptions. In political elections, for example, people usually perceive quite accurately the prevailing opinion about the candidates and issues, and they are likely to express their preferences when these are shared by others.

An interesting test of the tendency to remain silent on unpopular positions is the "train test."[45] Here, respondents were asked whether they would be willing to discuss certain topics with someone with whom they shared a train compartment for 5 hours. Respondents were told that they were to imagine that the other person mentioned his or her opinion on the subject, which was either a popular or unpopular point of view. They were then asked, "Would you like to talk with this person so as to get to know their point of view better, or wouldn't you think that worth your while?" Topics ranged from whether it is acceptable to spank a child to one's approval of the performance of the very popular chancellor of Germany. Interviewers presented this problem to 3500 respondents, on numerous topics over several years. The overwhelming tendency was to freely discuss the topic when one agrees with the majority, but to let it slide when one does not. People simply did not want to make "waves" around strangers on the train.

Of course, other factors enter into the decision to express one's opinion. People and groups vary in their tendency to express ideas, regardless of the prevailing opinion. Young people are more expres-

sive than older people; educated individuals will speak up more than uneducated ones; men are generally more disclosive of their opinions than women. However, the spiral of silence is also a factor, and according to this research, a very powerful one.

The spiral of silence seems to be caused by the fear of isolation. As Noelle-Neumann puts it, "To run with the pack is a relatively happy state of affairs; but if you can't, because you won't share publicly in what seems to be a universally acclaimed conviction, you can at least remain silent, as a second choice, so that others can put up with you."[46] The spiral of silence is not just a matter of wanting to be on the winning side but is an attempt to avoid being isolated from one's social group. Threats of criticism from others were found to be powerful forces in silencing individuals. For example, smokers who are repeatedly criticized for advocating "smokers' rights" were found to remain silent rather than state their views on this subject in the presence of vocal nonsmokers.

In some cases the threat of expressing an opinion is extreme:

> Slashed tires, defaced or torn posters, help refused to a lost stranger—questions of this kind demonstrate that people can be on uncomfortable or even dangerous ground when the climate of opinion runs counter to their views. When people attempt to avoid isolation, they are not responding hypersensitively to trivialities; these are existential issues that can involve real hazards.[47]

One can easily see how the spiral of silence affects public opinion. Public opinion has been defined in numerous ways. For Noelle-Neumann, an operational definition is best: "Public opinions are attitudes or behaviors one must express in public if one is not to isolate oneself; in areas of controversy or change, public opinions are those attitudes one can express without running the danger of isolating oneself."[48] Stated differently, "public opin-

45. Noelle-Neumann, *Spiral*, pp. 16–22.

46. Ibid., p. 6.
47. Ibid., p. 56.
48. Ibid., p. 178.

ion is an understanding on the part of people in an ongoing community concerning some affect- or value-laden question which individuals as well as government have to respect at least by compromise in their overt behavior under the threat of being excluded or losing one's standing in society."[49]

There are, of course, exceptions to the spiral of silence. There are groups and individuals who do not fear isolation and who will express their opinions no matter what the consequences. This may be a characteristic of innovators, change agents, and the avant-garde.

The media are an important part of the spiral of silence. The media publicize which opinions are prevalent and which are not. When polled, individuals usually state that they feel powerless in the face of media. Two kinds of experience accentuate this feeling of helplessness. The first is the difficulty of getting publicity for a cause or point of view. The second is being scapegoated by the media in what Noelle-Neumann calls the *pillory function* of media. In each case the individual feels powerless in using or avoiding the media.

Although public opinion is formed by both personal observation and media, individuals mix the two and confuse what is learned through the media with what is learned through interpersonal channels. This tendency is especially true for television, with which so many people have a personal relationship. Noelle-Neumann addresses the complexity of media effects in the following excerpt:

> The longer one has studied the question, the clearer it becomes that fathoming the effects of the mass media is very hard. These effects do not come into being as a result of a single stimulus; they are as a rule cumulative, following the principle that "water dripping constantly wears away stone." Further discussions among people spread the media's messages further, and before long no difference can be perceived between the point of media reception and points far removed from it. The media's effects are predominantly unconscious; people cannot provide an account of what has happened. Rather, they mix their own direct perceptions and the perceptions filtered

through the eyes of the media into an indivisible whole that seems to derive from their own thoughts and experiences.[50]

It sometimes happens that journalists' opinions differ from that of the general public, and media depictions contradict the prevailing expressions of individuals. When this occurs, a dual climate of opinion results. Here, two versions of reality operate. Noelle-Neumann likens this event to an unusual weather situation—interesting and seemingly bizarre.

The spiral of silence, then, is a phenomenon involving personal and media channels of communication. The media publicize public opinion, making evident which opinions predominate. Individuals express their opinions or not, depending on the predominant points of view; and the media, in turn, attend to the expressed opinion, and the spiral continues.

Cultivation Analysis

Another theoretical program dealing with the sociocultural outcomes of mass communication is that of George Gerbner and his colleagues.[51] This theory deals with an important effect of television, which the theorists call cultivation. In a nutshell, television is believed to be a homogenizing agent in culture. Because television is the great common experience of almost everyone, it has the effect of providing a shared way of viewing the world:

> Television is a centralized system of storytelling. It is part and parcel of our daily lives. Its drama, commercials, news, and other programs bring a relatively coherent world of common images and messages into every home. Television cultivates from infancy the very predispositions and preferences that used to be acquired from other primary sources. Transcending

50. Ibid., p. 169.

51. George Gerbner, Larry Gross, Michael Morgan, and Nancy Signorielli, "Living with Television: The Dynamics of the Cultivation Process," in *Perspectives on Media Effects*, eds. J. Bryant and D. Zillmann (Hillsdale, N.J.: Erlbaum, 1986), pp. 17–40; Nancy Signorielli and Michael Morgan (eds.), *Cultivation Analysis: New Directions in Media Effects Research* (Newbury Park, Calif.: Sage, 1990).

49. Ibid., p. 179.

historic barriers of literacy and mobility, television has become the primary common source of socialization and everyday information (mostly in the form of entertainment) of an otherwise heterogeneous population. The repetitive pattern of television's mass-produced messages and images forms the mainstream of common symbolic environment.[52]

Cultivation analysis is concerned with the totality of the pattern communicated cumulatively by television over a long period of exposure rather than any particular content or specific effect. In other words, this is not a theory of media effects per se, but instead makes a statement about the culture as a whole. It is not concerned with what any particular strategy or campaign can do, but with the total impact of numerous strategies and campaigns over time. Total immersion in television, not selective viewing, is important in cultivation of ways of knowing and images of reality. Indeed, subcultures may retain their separate values, but general overriding images depicted on television will cut across individual social groups and subcultures, affecting them all. Too, television cultivation is not a linear effect of viewing per se but is a cumulative interactional outcome of the media–audience relationship. In other words, people respond to television, television responds to the world of the viewer, and over time a television "culture" results.

The theory predicts a difference in the social reality of heavy television viewers as opposed to light viewers. Heavy viewers will believe in a reality that is consistent with that shown on television, even though it does not necessarily reflect the actual world. Gerbner's research on prime-time television, for example, has shown that there are three men to every woman on television, there are few Hispanics and those shown are typically minor characters, there are almost entirely middle-class characters, and there are three times as many law enforcement officers as blue-collar workers.

One of the most interesting outcomes of television cultivation is the "mean-world syndrome." Although less than 1 percent of the population are

52. Gerbner et al., "Living," p. 18.

victims of violent crimes in any one-year period, "one lesson viewers derive from heavy exposure to the violence-saturated world of television is that in such a mean and dangerous world, most people 'cannot be trusted' and that most people are 'just looking out for themselves.'"[53]

Nancy Signorielli reports a massive study of the mean-world syndrome, in which violent acts in children's television programming were analyzed.[54] Over 2000 programs, including 6000 main characters, during prime time and weekends from 1967 to 1985 were analyzed with interesting results. About 71 percent of prime-time and 94 percent of weekend programs included acts of violence. Prime-time programs averaged almost five acts of violence each, and weekend programs averaged six. That amounts to over five acts per hour during prime time and about twenty per hour on weekends.

Next, people were surveyed on five occasions between 1980 and 1986 regarding their views of the state of the world. To measure feelings of alienation and gloom, they were asked whether they agreed with three statements: (1) Despite what some people say, the lot of the average man is getting worse, not better. (2) It's hardly fair to bring a child into the world with the way things look for the future. (3) Most public officials are not interested in the problems of the average man. In addition, they were asked three questions to measure feelings about a mean world: (1) Would you say that most of the time people try to be helpful, or are they mostly just looking out for themselves? (2) Do you think that most people would try to take avantage of you if they got a chance, or would they try to be fair? (3) Generally speaking, would you say that most people can be trusted, or you can't be too careful in dealing with people? The findings indicate that heavy viewers tend to see the world as gloomier and meaner than do light viewers, and

53. Ibid., p. 28.

54. Nancy Signorielli, "Television's Mean and Dangerous World: A Continuation of the Cultural Indicators Perspective," in *Cultivation Analysis: New Directions in Media Effects Research,* eds. N. Signorielli and M. Morgan (Newbury Park, Calif.: Sage, 1990), pp. 85–106.

heavy viewers tend to mistrust people more than light viewers do.

We see from this study that your viewing can correlate with your view of the world. Cultivation analysis has also found, however, that there is a general fallout effect from television to the entire culture. In this way culture is essentially homogenized and maintained by television. Television is not a force for change as much as it is a force for stability. Gerbner calls the homogenization effect of television *mainstreaming*: "Mainstreaming makes television the true 20th-century melting pot of the American people."[55] Mainstreaming can be seen in the mean-world data reviewed above. Even though heavy viewers scored higher on the mean-world index than did light viewers, a substantial number of light viewers also scored high. In fact, if you remove people with a college education from the sample, heavy and light viewers scored about the same.

Although cultivation is a general outcome of television viewing, it is not a universal phenomenon, despite the mainstreaming effect. In fact, different groups are affected differently by cultivation. Clearly, heavy viewers are more "cultivated" in this sense than are light viewers. The nature of one's personal interaction affects the tendency to accept the television reality. For example, adolescents who interact with their parents about television viewing are less likely to be affected by television images than are adolescents who do not talk with their parents about television. Interestingly, people who watch more cable television tend to manifest more mainstreaming than do people who watch less.

In short, Gerbner summarizes the cultivation theory in the following six propositions:

1. Television is a unique medium requiring a special approach to study.

2. Television messages form a coherent system, the mainstream of our culture.

3. Those message systems (content) provide clues to cultivation.

4. Cultivation analysis focuses on television's contributions over time to the thinking and actions of large and otherwise heterogeneous social aggregates.

5. New technologies [such as VCR] extend rather than deflect the reach of television's messages.

6. Cultivation analysis focuses on pervasive stabilizing and homogenizing consequences.[56]

The Agenda-Setting Function

Scholars have long known that media have the potential for structuring issues for the public. One of the first writers to formalize this idea was Walter Lippman, a foremost American journalist. Lippman is known for his journalistic writing, his speeches, and his social commentary.[57] Lippman took the view that the public responds not to actual events in the environment but to a *pseudoenvironment* or, as he described it, "the pictures in our heads."[58] Lippman's model interposes an image between the audience and the actual environment:

> For the real environment is altogether too big, too complex, and too fleeting for direct acquaintance. We are not equipped to deal with so much subtlety, so much variety, so many permutations and combinations. And altogether we have to act in that environment, we have to reconstruct it on a simpler model before we can manage with it.[59]

The agenda-setting function has been most described by Donald Shaw, Maxwell McCombs, and their colleagues.[60] In their major work on this

55. Gerbner et al., "Living," p. 31.

56. George Gerbner, "Advancing on the Path of Righteousness (Maybe)," in *Cultivation Analysis: New Directions in Media Effects Research*, eds. N. Signorielli and M. Morgan (Newbury Park, Calif.: Sage, 1990), p. 253.

57. See, for example, M. Childs and J. Reston (eds.), *Walter Lippmann and His Times* (New York: Harcourt Brace, 1959).

58. Walter Lippmann, *Public Opinion* (New York: Macmillan, 1921).

59. Ibid., p. 16.

60. Donald L. Shaw and Maxwell E. McCombs, *The Emergence of American Political Issues* (St. Paul: West, 1977). See also Everett M. Rogers and James W. Dearing, "Agenda-Setting Research: Where Has It Been, Where Is It Going?" in *Communication Yearbook 11*, ed. J. A. Anderson (Newbury Park, Calif.: Sage, 1988), pp. 555–593; Stephen D. Reese, "Setting the Media's Agenda: A Power Balance Perspective," in *Communication Yearbook 14*, ed. J. A. Anderson (Newbury Park, Calif.: Sage, 1991), pp. 309–340.

subject, Shaw and McCombs write about the agenda-setting function:

> Considerable evidence has accumulated that editors and broadcasters play an important part in shaping our social reality as they go about their day-to-day task of choosing and displaying news. . . . This impact of the mass media—the ability to effect cognitive change among individuals, to structure their thinking—has been labeled the agenda-setting function of mass communication. Here may lie the most important effect of mass communication, its ability to mentally order and organize our world for us. In short, the mass media may not be successful in telling us what to think, but they are stunningly successful in telling us what to think about.[61]

In other words, agenda setting establishes the salient issues or images in the minds of the public.

Agenda setting occurs because the press must be selective in reporting the news. The news outlets, as gatekeepers of information, make choices about what to report and how to report it. Therefore, what the public knows about the state of affairs at any given time is largely a product of media gatekeeping. Further, we know that how a person votes is determined mainly by what issues the individual believes to be important. For this reason some researchers have come to believe that the issues reported during a candidate's term in office may have more effect on the election than the campaign itself.

The agenda-setting function is a three-part linear process.[62] First, the *media agenda* itself must be set. This process raises the issue of how the media's agenda comes into being in the first place. Second, the media agenda in some way affects or interacts with the *public agenda,* or the public sense of issue importance. This process raises the question of how much power the media have in affecting the public agenda and how they do so. Finally, the public agenda affects or interacts in some way with the policy agenda. The *policy agenda* is what public and private policymakers think is important. In its sim-

plest and most direct version, the agenda-setting theory predicts that the media agenda affects the public agenda and the public agenda, in turn, affects the policy agenda.

Although a number of studies show that the media can be powerful in affecting the public agenda, it is still not clear whether the public agenda does not itself affect the media agenda. The relationship may be one of mutual causation rather than linear causation. Further, it appears that actual events have some impact on both the media agenda and the public agenda.

The prevailing opinion now among media researchers seems to be that the media can have a powerful effect on the public agenda, but not always. The power of media depends on such factors as media credibility on particular issues at particular times, the extent of conflicting evidence as perceived by individual members of the public, the extent to which individuals share media values at particular times, and the public's need for guidance. When media credibility is high, conflicting evidence is low, individuals share media values, and they have a high need for guidance, then the media are probably powerful in establishing the public agenda.

Karen Siune and Ole Borre studied some of the complexities of agenda setting in a Danish election.[63] In Denmark the election campaigns last only 3 weeks, and the number of political broadcasts are more limited than in the United States. This gave the researchers an excellent opportunity to study the agenda-setting process. Three kinds of political broadcasts on radio and television were aired in this election. These included programs made by the political parties, programs in which the candidates were asked questions by a panel of journalists and citizens, and debates. All these programs were recorded and content-analyzed by counting the number of statements made about each issue in the campaign. From these data the researchers could determine the media agendas of the politicians (from the debates and party pro-

61. Shaw and McCombs, *Emergence*, p. 5.
62. This idea is developed by Rogers and Dearing, "Agenda-Setting Research."
63. Karen Siune and Ole Borre, "Setting the Agenda for a Danish Election," *Journal of Communication* 25 (1975): 65–73.

grams), the press (from journalists' questions) and voters (from citizens' questions). This method shows that there is not just one media agenda but that there may be several.

In addition, about 1300 voters were interviewed at various points in the campaign to establish the public agenda. The authors add to agenda-setting theory by suggesting three kinds of agenda-setting effects. The first is *representation,* or the degree to which the media reflect the public agenda. In a representational agenda, the public influences the media. The second is *persistence,* or the maintenance of the same agenda by the public the entire time. In a persistent public agenda, the media may have little effect. The third is *persuasion,* or the media agenda influencing the public agenda. This kind of effect is exactly what classic agenda-setting theory predicts.

If you determine agendas at three points in a campaign—at the beginning (time 1), at the middle (time 2), and at the end (time 3), you can get a sense of these three effects. A correlation between the public agenda at time 1 and the media agenda at time 2 suggests representation, the media reflecting the public agenda. A correlation between the public agenda at time 1 and at time 3 suggests persistence, that the public agenda did not change despite whatever the media broadcast. Finally, a correlation between the media agenda at time 2 and the public agenda at time 3 suggests persuasion, the media influence the public agenda. It is possible for any combination of these three to occur at the same time.

In their Danish study, Suine and Borre found much persistence in the public agenda, but there was also some persuasion in the sense that the broadcasts seemed to affect the public agenda somewhat. The most persuasive effects seemed to come from those programs in which citizens set the media agenda. There was also a fair agenda-setting effect from the reporters and from the politicians themselves. The researchers did not find a representation effect in which the public affected the media.

A natural question is, Who affects the media agenda in the first place? This is a complex and difficult question. It appears that media agendas result from pressures both within media organizations and from outside sources.[64] In other words, the media agenda is established by some combination of internal programming, editorial, and managerial decisions and external influences from nonmedia sources such as social influentials, government officials, commercial sponsors, and the like.

The power of media in establishing a public agenda depends in part on their relations with these outside power centers. If the media have close relationships with the elite class in society, that class will probably affect the media agenda and the public agenda in turn. Many critical theorists believe that media can be an instrument of the dominant ideology in society, and when this happens, that dominant ideology will permeate the public agenda.

Four types of power relations between the media and outside sources can be imagined. The first is a high-power source and high-power media. In this kind of arrangement, if the two see eye-to-eye, the positive symbiotic relationship will exert great power over the public agenda. This would be the case, for example, with a powerful public official who has especially good relations with the press. On the other hand, if the powerful media and the powerful sources do not agree, a significant struggle may take place between them over the agenda.

The second kind of arrangement is a high-power source and low-power media. Here, the external source will probably co-opt the media and use them to accomplish its own ends. This is what happens, for example, when politicians buy airtime or when a popular president such as Reagan gives the press the "privilege" of interviewing him. In the third type of relation, a lower-power source and high-power media, the media organizations themselves will be largely responsible for their own agenda. This happens when the media marginalize certain news sources such as the student radicals in the 1960s. The fourth type of relation is where both media and external sources are low in power, and the public agenda will probably be established by the events themselves rather than the media.

---

64. Reese, "Setting the Media's Agenda."

Theories of Individual Outcomes

The theories summarized in the previous section emphasize societal and cultural outcomes of mass communication. Much research has also dealt with the individual effects of mass communication. In this section we discuss several of the theories that have come out of this tradition. Let us begin with a general discussion of effects research.

The Effects Tradition

The theory of mass-communication effects has undergone a curious evolution in this century. Early in the century, researchers believed in the "magic bullet" theory of communication effects. Individuals were believed to be directly and heavily influenced by media messages. In other words, media were considered to be extremely powerful in shaping public opinion.[65] Then, during the 1950s when the two-step flow hypothesis was popular, media effects were considered to be minimal. Later, in the 1960s, we discovered that the media have effects on audience members but that these effects are mediated by audience variables and are therefore only moderate in strength. Now, after research in the 1970s and the 1980s, scholars have returned to the powerful-effects model, in which the public is considered to be heavily influenced by media. This later research centers on television as the powerful medium.[66]

Limited or Powerful Effects?

Perhaps the most well-known early work on limited effects was the reinforcement approach most notably articulated by Joseph Klapper.[67] Klapper, in surveying the literature on mass-communication effects, developed the following propositions:

> **1.** Mass communication ordinarily does not serve as a necessary and sufficient cause of audience effects, but rather functions among and through a nexus of mediating factors and influences.
>
> **2.** These mediating factors are such that they typically render mass communication a contributory agent, but not the sole cause, in a process of reinforcing the existing conditions. . . .[68]

Raymond Bauer observes that the failure of many attempts at persuasion is due to the *obstinate audience*, an audience that is difficult to persuade.[69] He denies the idea that a direct hypodermic needle effect operates between communicator and audience. Instead, many variables involved in the audience interact to shape effects in various ways.[70] Two of the more important areas of audience mediation are group or interpersonal effects and selectivity. Studies have shown that audience members are selective in their exposure to information.[71] In its simplest form, the hypothesis of selective exposure predicts that people in most circumstances will select information consistent with their attitudes and other frames of reference.

The reinforcement approach was a definite step in the right direction at the time it was in vogue. Compared with the bullet theory, the reinforcement approach viewed mass communication as more complicated than had previously been imagined. It envisioned an audience and situation ripe with mediating variables that would inhibit media effects. The research in this tradition did identify some important mediating variables, completing a

65. For explorations of the history of the magic bullet or hypodermic needle theory, see J. Michael Sproule, "Progressive Propaganda Critics and the Magic Bullet Myth," *Critical Studies in Mass Communication* 6 (1989): 225–246; Jeffery L. Bineham, "A Historical Account of the Hypodermic Model in Mass Communication," *Communication Monographs* 55 (1988): 230–246.

66. This chronology is discussed by McQuail, *Mass Communication*, 1987, pp. 252–256.

67. Joseph T. Klapper, *The Effects of Mass Communication* (Glencoe, Ill.: Free Press, 1960).

68. Ibid., p. 8.

69. Raymond Bauer, "The Obstinate Audience: The Influence Process from the Point of View of Social Communication," *American Psychologist* 19 (1964): 319–328.

70. Raymond Bauer, "The Audience," in *Handbook of Communication*, eds. I. de sola Pool et al. (Chicago: Rand McNally, 1973), pp. 141–152.

71. Studies on selectivity are well summarized in David O. Sears and Jonathan I. Freedman, "Selective Exposure to Information: A Critical Review," in *The Process and Effects of Mass Communication*, eds. W. Schramm and D. F. Roberts (Urbana: University of Illinois Press, 1971), pp. 209–234.

more elaborate puzzle than had previously been constructed.

The problem of the limited-effects model is that it maintained a linear, cause-to-effect paradigm for research and theory.[72] It failed to take into account the social forces on the media or the ways that individuals might affect the process. The model remained one of active media and passive audience. In addition, the limited-effects model concentrated almost exclusively on attitude and opinion effects, ignoring other kinds of effects and functions. Finally, true to tradition, such research focused on short-term effects of mass communication without questioning whether repeated exposure or time latency might affect the audience.

The work of Klapper and others on limited effects resulted in two general types of response. The first was a rejection of limited effects in favor of powerful effects, and the second was an attempt to explain limited effects in terms of the powers of individual audience members, not of media.

Perhaps the most vocal contemporary spokesperson in favor of powerful effects is Noelle-Neumann.[73] She believes that limited-effects theory has "distorted the interpretation of research findings over the years," and "that the 'dogma of media powerlessness' is no longer tenable."[74] Noelle-Neumann claims that the pendulum, which began swinging in the other direction after Klapper's famous work, has now reached its full extension and that most researchers believe that the media indeed have powerful effects.

This critic thinks that the limited-effects model was an ideological response on the part of professional journalists, who did not want to see themselves as manipulative. Most limited-effects researchers were either academic journalists or people who held the media in a free society in high regard. These individuals were interested in painting a picture of the media as disseminators of information, but not of influence. If they were viewed as important, but not as controlling, the media would continue to have the freedom to investigate and report whatever they felt to be important at a particular time. This interest led to the tendency to "see" limited rather than powerful effects in media-research results. This Noelle-Neumann calls "the media's effect on media research."

There are still many who believe that this reaction to limited effects is extreme and oversimple. In the following sections, we review theories that take a more moderate stand than either the limited- or powerful-effects models.

Uses, Gratifications, and Dependency

One of the most popular theories of mass communication is the uses-and-gratifications approach. Until recently, uses and gratifications were considered to be a general approach to media with little theoretical coherence. In the 1980s, however, some important theoretical codification had taken place, making it a more acceptable theoretical area. We first examine the original idea of uses and gratifications and then look at some interesting extensions.

The original idea. The uses-and-gratifications approach focuses on the consumer, the audience member, rather than the message. This approach begins with the person as an active selector of media communications, a viewpoint different from the powerful-effects model.[75] The basic stance is summarized as follows:

> Compared with classical effects studies, the uses and gratifications approach takes the media consumer rather than the media message as its starting point, and explores his communication behavior in terms of

72. Criticism of the limited-effects approach can be found in Severin and Tankard, *Communication Theories*, p. 249.

73. Elisabeth Noelle-Neumann, "Return to the Concept of Powerful Mass Media," in *Studies of Broadcasting*, eds. H. Eguchi and K. Sata (Tokyo: Nippon Hoso Kyokii, 1973), pp. 67–112; "The Effect of Media on Media Effects Research," *Journal of Communication* 33 (1983): 157–165.

74. Noelle-Neumann, "Effect of Media," p. 157.

75. Elihu Katz, Jay Blumler, and Michael Gurevitch, "Uses of Mass Communication by the Individual," in *Mass Communication Research: Major Issues and Future Directions*, eds. W. P. Davidson and F. Yu (New York: Praeger, 1974), pp. 11–35. See also Jay Blumler and Elihu Katz (eds.), *The Uses of Mass Communication* (Beverly Hills, Calif.: Sage, 1974). See also the entire issue of *Communication Research* 6 (January 1979).

his direct experience with the media. It views the members of the audience as actively utilizing media contents, rather than being passively acted upon by the media. Thus, it does not assume a direct relationship between messages and effects, but postulates instead that members of the audience put messages to use, and that such usages act as intervening variables in the process of effect.[76]

The individuals most commonly associated with the uses-and-gratifications approach are Jay Blumler and Elihu Katz. These authors have outlined a number of basic theoretical and methodological assumptions. Three theoretical assumptions warrant discussion. The first is that the audience of mass communication is active and goal-directed. Unlike most effects theories, uses-and-gratifications theory assumes that audience members are not passive but take a proactive role in deciding how to use media in their lives. Second, the audience member is largely responsible for choosing media to meet needs. Audience members know their needs and seek out various ways to meet these needs. The third assumption, related to the other two, is that media compete with other sources of need gratification. In other words, out of the options that media present, the individual chooses ways to gratify needs.

Expectancy-value theory. Acknowledging the lack of theoretical coherence in early uses-and-gratifications work, Philip Palmgreen codified a theory of uses and gratifications based on his own work and that of several colleagues, including Karl Rosengren and others.[77] The theory is based on *expectancy-value theory*, which was discussed in Chapter 7. Perhaps the most well-known expectancy-value theorist is Martin Fishbein. According to this theory, people orient themselves to the world according to their expectancies (beliefs) and

evaluations. In Chapter 7 we noted that an attitude consists of a cluster of beliefs and evaluations. Viewing media gratifications as an application of the general expectancy-value phenomenon, Palmgreen and his colleagues have defined *gratifications sought* in terms of one's beliefs about what a medium can provide and one's evaluation of the medium's content. For example, if you believe that sitcoms provide entertainment and you evaluate entertainment as good, you will seek gratification of your entertainment needs by watching sitcoms. If, on the other hand, you believe that sitcoms provide an unrealistic view of life and evaluate such content as bad, you will avoid viewing sitcoms.

Rather than a single belief, an individual will have a number of beliefs about a program type, each associated with a particular evaluation. To determine the extent to which the person would seek gratification from that type of program, one would need to take the entire cluster of beliefs and evaluations into account. Palmgreen's formula for this, which mirrors the general expectancy-value formula discussed in Chapter 7, is as follows:

$$GS_i = \sum_1^n b_i e_i$$

where

$$GS = \text{gratification sought}$$
$$b_i = \text{belief}$$
$$e_i = \text{evaluation}$$

The extent to which one would seek gratifications in any segment of the media (a program, a program type, a particular kind of content, an entire medium, etc.) would be defined by the same formula. As one gains experience with this segment of the media, the perceived gratifications obtained will feed back to one's beliefs about that segment for future consideration, creating a cyclical process (Figure 15.4).[78]

You can easily see that a particular combination of beliefs and evaluations about a media segment could be either positive (in which case one will use that segment) or negative (in which case one will

76. Katz, Blumler, and Gurevitch, "Uses," p. 12.

77. Philip Palmgreen, "Uses and Gratifications: A Theoretical Perspective," in *Communication Yearbook* 8, ed. R. N. Bostrom (Beverly Hills, Calif.: Sage, 1984), pp. 20–55. See also K. Rosengren, L. Wenner, and P. Palmgreen (eds.), *Media Gratifications Research: Current Perspectives* (Beverly Hills, Calif.: Sage, 1985).

78. Palmgreen, "Uses and Gratifications," p. 36.

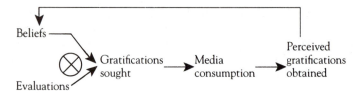

Figure 15.4   Expectancy-value model of gratifications sought and gratifications obtained.

avoid it). A person who relies on television sitcoms to meet a cluster of needs will have a positive orientation toward that program type, whereas an individual who avoids sitcoms because of an overall negative cluster of beliefs and evaluations will not rely on this type of program and will, in fact, avoid it.

To test the connection between expectancy values and media gratifications, David Swanson and Austin Babrow conducted a study of students' television news–viewing habits.[79] About 300 students at the University of Illinois were asked to fill out a questionnaire on their news viewing. To find out whether they watched the news and how they felt about it, the students were asked how many times a week they viewed network news and local news, how likely they were to view news in an average week, and whether other people thought they should watch the news. The questionnaire also tested the students' attitudes toward the news. To find out the extent to which the news gratified various media needs, the questionnaire asked whether each of a number of gratifications were met by watching the news. These included such items as keeping up on current events, getting entertained, and giving them things to talk about. In all, fourteen possible gratifications were included. The researchers found that the students' expectancy values (their attitudes) toward the news did relate to how much they used the news to gratify certain media needs.

Although the idea of expectancy and value is used as the basic explanatory mechanism for uses and gratifications, several other causal factors must be taken into account. Palmgreen has put togther a complex model to depict the process of media use that he sees reflected in the research literature. It is clear from the model in Figure 15.5 that uses and gratifications are not a simple linear process.[80] Rather, they involve a multiple causal chain.

One's beliefs about what certain media segments can provide are affected by (1) one's culture and social institutions, including the media themselves, (2) social circumstances such as the availability of media, and (3) certain psychological variables (e.g., introversion-extroversion or dogmatism). Values are affected by (1) cultural and social factors, (2) needs, and (3) psychological variables. Beliefs and values, as noted before, determine the gratifications sought, which in turn determine one's media-consumption behavior. Depending on what is consumed and what nonmedia alternatives are undertaken, certain media effects will be felt, and these in turn will feed back to one's beliefs about the media.

Dependency theory. The uses-and-gratifications approach is a limited-effects theory. In other words, it grants individuals much control over how they employ media in their lives. As we have seen, however, media scholars are divided about just how powerful the media are. Some have argued that the limited-effects and powerful-effects models are not necessarily incompatible, and dependency theory takes a step toward showing how both may explain media effects.

79. David L. Swanson and Austin S. Babrow, "Uses and Gratifications: The Influence of Gratification-Seeking and Expectancy-Value Judgments on the Viewing of Television News," in *Rethinking Communication: Paradigm Exemplars*, eds. B. Dervin et al. (Newbury Park, Calif.: Sage, 1989), pp. 361–375.

80. Palmgreen, "Uses and Gratifications," p. 47.

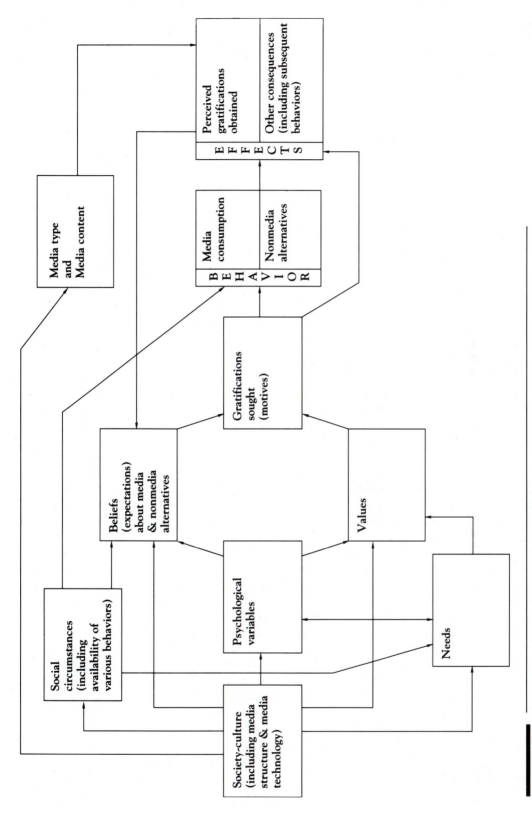

Figure 15.5 Integrative gratifications model of mass media consumption.

Dependency theory was originally proposed by Sandra Ball-Rokeach and Melvin DeFleur.[81] Like uses-and-gratifications theory, this approach also rejects the causal assumptions of the early reinforcement hypothesis. To overcome this weakness, these authors take a broad system approach. In their model they propose an integral relationship among audiences, media, and the larger social system: "It is through taking these sets of variables into account individually, interactively, and systematically that a more adequate understanding of mass communications effects can be gained."[82]

At the center of this theory is the notion that audiences depend on media information to meet needs and attain goals. This approach is consistent with the basic ideas of the uses model, but unlike the latter, the dependency model assumes a three-way interaction among media, audiences, and society. All three affect each of the others. The degree of audience dependency on media information varies, and the more dependent the audience becomes on a some aspect of the media, the more that will have an effect on them.

There are two sources of variation in the amount of dependency a person might experience. One is the *number and centrality of information functions* being served. We know that the media serve a gamut of functions such as monitoring government activities and providing entertainment. For any given group, some of these functions are more central or important than others. A group's dependence on information from a medium increases as that medium supplies information that is more central to the group.

The second source of dependency variation is *social stability*. When social change and conflict are high, established institutions, beliefs, and practices are challenged, forcing people to make reevaluations and choices. At such times reliance on the media for information increases.

81. Sandra J. Ball-Rokeach and Melvin L. DeFleur, "A Dependency Model of Mass-Media Effects," *Communication Research* 3 (1976): 3–21. See also Melvin L. DeFleur and Sandra J. Ball-Rokeach, *Theories of Mass Communication* (New York: Longman, 1982), pp. 240–251.

82. Ball-Rokeach and DeFleur, "Dependency," p. 5.

The dependency theory includes three types of effects: cognitive, affective, and behavioral. Mass-communication effects within these three areas are a function of the degree to which audiences are dependent on media information. Ball-Rokeach and DeFleur outline five types of *cognitive effects*. The first of these is *ambiguity resolution*. Events in the environment often create ambiguities, leading to a need for additional information. The media themselves often create ambiguity, and when it is present, dependence on media increases. At such times the power of mediated messages to structure understanding or to define situations may be great. At other times when the ambiguity is lessened, this effect may be much reduced.

The second cognitive effect is *attitude formation*. The selectivity and other mediational processes outlined by Klapper and the diffusion theorists probably come into play in this effect. Third, media communications create *agenda setting*, in which people use the media to decide what the important issues are, to decide what to be concerned about. Agenda setting is an interactional process. Topics are chosen by the media and disseminated through mass channels. From these topics people sort out information according to their individual interests and psychological and social characteristics.

The fourth cognitive effect is *expansion of the belief system*. Information may create a broadening of the number of beliefs within such categories as religion or politics, and it may also increase a person's number of categories or beliefs. The fifth cognitive effect, *value clarification*, may occur, for example, when the media precipitate value conflict in such areas as civil rights. Faced with conflicts, audience members are motivated to clarify their own values.

Affective effects relate to feelings and emotional responses. Such states as fear, anxiety, morale, or alienation may be affected by mediated information. Effects may also occur in the behavior realm. Activation, initiating new behavior, and deactivation, ceasing old behaviors, may occur as a result of information received from the media.

The important point from dependency theory is that mediated messages affect people only to the degree that persons depend on media information. In a nutshell, "when people do not have social realities that provide adequate frameworks for understanding, acting, and escaping, and when audiences are dependent in these ways on media information received, such messages may have a number of alteration effects."[83]

We have seen here that audiences can be affected by media to varying degrees, depending on their dependency on the media. Audiences do use media for their own ends but in the process may become dependent on them. Alan Rubin and Sven Windahl explain:

> Uses and gratifications, then, adds a voluntaristic element to dependency, just as dependency adds a more deterministic flavor to uses and gratifications. This makes a conceptualization of uses and gratifications more situational and context-bound . . . we propose that people's needs and motives vary as they evolve in interactions with societal and communication systems.[84]

Rubin and Windahl have created a model (Figure 15.6) to depict this process.[85]

This model shows that social institutions and media systems interact with audiences so as to create needs, interests, and motives in the individual. These in turn influence the individual to choose various media and nonmedia sources of gratification, which may subsequently lead to various dependencies. Consistent with dependency theory, individuals who grow dependent on a particular segment of the media will be affected cognitively, affectively, and behaviorally by that segment. Those dependencies, then, feed back to broader societal and media systems and institutions.

Dependency itself develops when certain kinds of media content are used to gratify specific needs or when certain media forms are consumed habitually as ritual, to fill time, or as an escape or distraction. People will fulfill their needs with media in different ways, and a single person may use media differently in different contexts. Further, one's "needs" are not always strictly personal but may be shaped by the culture or by various social conditions. In other words, individuals' needs, motives, and uses of media are contingent on outside societal and cultural factors that may be out of the individuals' control. These outside factors act as constraints on what and how media can be used and on the availability of other nonmedia alternatives.

For example, an elderly person who does not drive and has few friends nearby may come to depend on television in a way that other individuals, whose life situations are different, will not. A commuter may come to rely on radio for information and news. A teenager may become dependent on music videos because of certain norms in the social group. In general, "the more readily available, the greater the perceived instrumentality, and the more socially and culturally acceptable the use of a medium is, the more probable that media use will be regarded as the most appropriate functional alternative."[86] Furthermore, the more alternatives an individual has for gratifying needs, the less dependent he or she will become on any single medium. The number of functional alternatives, however, is not just a matter of individual choice or even of psychological traits but is limited also by sociocultural factors such as availability of certain media.

Commentary and Critique

Mass communication involves the dissemination of information and influence in society through media and interpersonal channels. It is an integral part of culture and is inseparable from other large-scale social institutions. Media forms like television, film, and print—as well as media content—affect our ways of thinking and seeing the world. Indeed, media participate in the very

83. Ibid., p. 19.

84. Alan M. Rubin and Sven Windahl, "The Uses and Dependency Model of Mass Communication," *Critical Studies in Mass Communication* 3 (1986): 186.

85. Ibid., p. 188.

86. Ibid., p. 193.

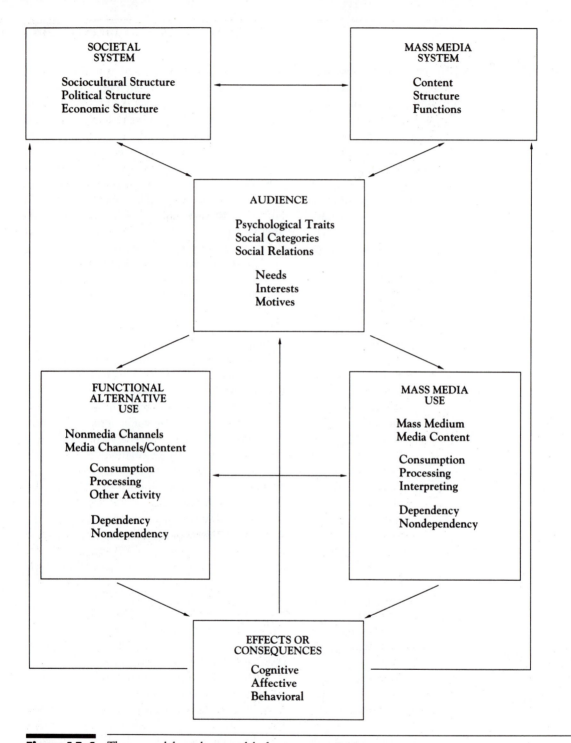

Figure 15.6 The uses and dependency model of mass communication.

From *Critical Studies in Mass Communication* by Alan M. Rubin and Sven Windahl. Copyright © 1986 by the Speech Communication Association. Reprinted by permission of the author and publisher.

creation of culture itself, and many believe that media are instrumental in the dissemination of power and domination in society and are thereby instruments of ideology and hegemony.

Mass communication fulfills a variety of functions in society. It provides information, entertainment, and interpretation of events, and it is certainly an instrument of public opinion. The media also appear to set the agenda of what is important in society. The extent and nature of media influence is a matter of dispute. Mass communication reinforces attitudes and opinions, and evidence suggests that media effects are often much more profound than is simple reinforcement. At the same time, however, people make active use of media to gratify their own needs. In fact, as people become dependent on certain types of media and content, the impact of those outlets may increase.

The outcome of the media-influence process is complex. In the final analysis, the outcome of mass communication may be a product of the interaction among various societal structures and individual needs, desires, and dependencies. The theories in this chapter emphasize different aspects of this complex relationship.

McLuhan's theory is not much in favor anymore, but few would deny that his basic idea—that media forms in and of themselves do have an impact on culture—has had a major effect on our thinking about media. Media scholars today are just less glib about what those specific effects are than was McLuhan.

McLuhan is in a world apart. His theory is not only unorthodox but also is rarely classified with other theories of a certain genre. However, to the extent that McLuhan conceives of media as affecting society in a general way without discriminating various kinds of effects among different groups, he must be considered among the critics of mass society. His ideas are almost impossible to criticize using standard categories of theory criticism. The reason for this difficulty is that his work is mostly an artistic-historical-literary treatment and does not constitute a theory in the standard sense. Yet, there has been no lack of criticism and commentary about the man.

McLuhan's ideas are useful for stimulating a fresh look at the subject matter, but they provide little guidance on how to understand the process of mass communication. They are valuable in that they point to the importance of media forms in society, but they do not give a realistic picture of the variables involved in the effects of media forms. In sum, Kenneth Boulding points out, "It is perhaps typical of very creative minds that they hit very large nails not quite on the head."[87]

More popular today is semiotics. This field has had a major impact throughout communication studies, and it has been especially popular in media scholarship. The reasons are clear. Semiotics provides a focus on what media messages mean and the ways in which they use a variety of symbols, verbal, auditory, and visual. Semiotics has also been useful to help explain why the media have differential effects. It is valuable, too, because it enables the observer to analyze the structure of media messages without ignoring the interpretive processes of the audience.

The primary objection to semiotics is that it grants too much power to the individual in determining the meaning of a message. Interactional theorists (Chapter 8) would say that semiotics downplays the ways in which meanings arise from social interaction. They would say that in media-interpretive communities, meaning results less from specific signs and more from how people interact in their daily lives around those signs. These critics would contend that meaning is not something that individuals confer upon texts but that meaning is a consensual product of communication in social groups. From this perspective then, our meanings for texts are worked out in interaction among people, not by peculiar and individualistic interpretation of signs.

This criticism reflects an abiding conflict in the study of mass communication. How powerful are media in the control of culture? Some, like McLuhan, argue that media are powerful forces in determining the character of culture and individual life. Other theories claim that individuals have much

87. Boulding, "The Medium," p. 68.

control over the outcomes of media transactions in their lives. Yet a third group believes that mass media are important, but that they are only part of a complex of factors involved in social domination and that individuals are influenced by the entire system of dominating forces.

One of the obvious issues in media studies is the role of groups and interpersonal communication in the mass-communication process. A whole line of research on diffusion of ideas and innovation supports the idea that interpersonal communication is a very powerful part of this process. Beginning with the work of Lazarsfeld, the research and theory of diffusion has been immensely successful. Dennis Davis and Stanley Baran remark of Lazarsfeld: "If one person deserves the title of founder of the field of mass communication research, that person is Paul Lazarsfeld. No one has done more to determine the way in which theory and research methods would be developed to aid our understanding of mass communication."[88]

The parsimony of diffusion theories has enabled observers to deal with a huge and complex phenomenon with relative ease. Additionally, these theories have been highly heuristic and have produced a large body of research. For many years the idea of the two-step flow (and later multiple-step flow) in the diffusion of information and innovation has been a mainstay of mass-communication theory.

Traditional diffusion theory uses a linear logic— messages flow from person to person along a network. Some contemporary diffusion theorists now believe that this logic does not explain enough. Research has not consistently supported this notion of how diffusion occurs. At times the media appear to inform the public directly, with little interpersonal involvement; at other times different forms of diffusion are revealed. Further, the strict dichotomy between opinion leaders and followers is overly simple. In the give and take of everyday conversation, people exchange information, question it, argue about it, and come to a shared understanding. Another problem with the linear model of diffusion is that it downplays context; the actual circumstances under which diffusion occurs may have a great deal to do with the pattern of dissemination used by individuals in sharing information and innovations. Dissemination is more a matter of convergence or the achievement of shared meaning than of strict linear influence.

One of the problems of diffusion theory is to explain why information sometimes does not flow in the network. An interesting explanation is the spiral of silence. The spiral of silence exemplifies careful theory development through research. Beginning with a mere hypothesis in the early 1970s, Noelle-Neumann undertook numerous studies designed to test the basic hypothesis, its assumptions, and ramifications.

At the same time, however, the theory does not seem to apply in all societies. Hernando González, for example, in a study of public opinion in the Philippine revolution, says that the Philippine experience is not consistent with the spiral of silence. Indeed, alternative media were heard, and no spiral of silence appeared to be in favor of a dominant opinion in this society.[89]

From another corner, cultural scholars and Marxists would point to this line of research as an example of the kind of work they most distrust. First, they believe that it is false to assume that one can find an underlying structure to public opinion through surveys. Social science methods cannot be trusted to reveal any kind of reality beyond the meanings assigned by observers. Second, the failure to acknowledge the ideological nature of the public opinion is a major oversight. Third, critical scholars would point out that the spiral of silence is one possible factor in a general hegemony, in which the interests of dominant groups in society are perpetuated. Fourth, these critics would object to the suggestion that the spiral of silence is a universal phenomenon. All social life must be viewed in the context of history; and the spiral of silence, like most traditional social science findings, abstracts

88. Dennis K. Davis and Stanley J. Baran, *Mass Communication and Everyday Life: A Perspective on Theory and Effects* (Belmont, Calif.: Wadsworth, 1981), p. 27.

89. Hernando González, "Mass Media and the Spiral of Silence: The Philippines from Marcos to Aquino," *Journal of Communication* 34 (1988): 33–48.

beyond the material world. Finally, this kind of research is truly "administrative" in the sense that it becomes a tool in which the dominant ideology can be managed or promulgated.

Another theory of cultural media outcomes is cultivation analysis. Cultivation analysis, which is bolstered by a decade of research on cultural indicators, calls our attention to the power of television; however, the cultivation hypothesis has not been without critique. In fact, television researcher Paul Hirsch has spoken out harshly against the cultivation effect. He reanalyzed Gerbner's data and failed to find evidence for cultivation. Hirsch concluded that "acceptance of the cultivation hypothesis as anything more than an interesting but unsupported speculation is premature and unwarranted at this time."[90] Gerbner and his colleagues have responded to this critique by reaffirming the validity of their findings and concluding that "Hirsch's analysis is flawed, incomplete, and tendentious."[91]

Another important cultural outcome of media communication is agenda setting. Agenda-setting theory is appealing for two reasons. First, it returns a degree of power to the media after an era in which media effects were thought to be minimal. Second, its focus on cognitive effects rather than attitude and opinion change adds a badly needed dimension to effects research. The idea of issue salience as a media effect is intriguing and important.

The basic problem with this line of work is that although the theory is clear in positing a causal link between media and issue salience, the research evidence on this point is not convincing.[92] Research has uncovered a strong correlation between audience and media views on the importance of issues,

but it does not always demonstrate that media choices cause audience salience. In fact, as we saw previously, some theorists argue that the emphasis given to issues in the media can be a reflection, not a cause, of audience agendas. This is a chicken–egg issue. Sometimes there may be an interaction between media and public in terms of the issue agenda, and situational factors probably always enter into how powerful the media are at any time in establishing the public agenda.

The uses-and-gratifications approach was like a breath of fresh air in media research. For the first time scholars in this tradition focused on receivers as active participants in the communication process, rather than the traditional viewpoint of the passive, unthinking audience. Indeed, this approach is certainly one of the most popular frameworks for the study of mass communication. However, a good deal of criticism has been leveled against it.[93]

The criticism of the uses and gratifications approach can be divided into three major strands.[94] The first set of objections deals with the lack of coherence and theory in the tradition. Although this objection had merit until recently, we have seen that more unified versions in the form of value-expectancy and -dependency theories are emerging.

The second line of criticism focuses on social and political objections, which come primarily from critical theory. The problem is that uses and gratifications is so functional in orientation that it ignores the dysfunctions of media in society and culture. It is conservative at heart and sees media primarily as positive ways in which individuals meet their needs, without any attention to the overall negative cultural effects of media in society.

90. Paul M. Hirsch, "The 'Scary World' of the Nonviewer and Other Anomalies: A Reanalysis of Gerbner et al.'s Findings on Cultivation Analysis," *Communication Research* 7 (1980): 404. See also, Paul M. Hirsch, "On Not Learning from One's Own Mistakes: A Reanalysis of Gerbner et. al.'s Findings on Cultivation Analysis, Part II," *Communication Research* 8 (1981): 3–38.

91. George Gerbner, Larry Gross, Michael Morgan, Nancy Signorielli, "A Curious Journal into the Scary World of Paul Hirsch," *Communication Research* 8 (1981): 39.

92. Criticism of this work can be found in Severin and Tankard, *Communication Theories*, pp. 253–254.

93. See especially Philip Elliott, "Uses and Gratifications Research: A Critique and Sociological Alternative," in *The Uses of Mass Communication*, eds. J. Blumler and E. Katz (Beverly Hills, Calif.: Sage, 1974), pp. 249–268; and David L. Swanson, "Political Communication Research and the Uses and Gratifications Model: A Critique," *Communication Research* 6 (1979): 36–53.

94. Denis McQuail, "With the Benefits of Hindsight: Reflections on Uses and Gratifications Research," *Critical Studies in Mass Communication* 1 (1984): 177–193.

Finally, some critics have objected to the instrumental philosophy of uses and gratifications. Uses and gratifications makes media consumption extremely rational, behavioristic, and individualistic. Individuals are believed to control their media-consuming behavior according to conscious goals. No attention is paid to the ways in which media may be consumed mindlessly or ritualistically. The theory does not study the ways in which media content form and reflect cultural values or patterns of action. In other words, much of our consumption of mass media may not be easily traced to individual needs, but rather to habits of the culture. Also, individuals may not be aware of many of the factors that enter into their consumption choices. Attribution theory, which was covered in greater detail in Chapter 7, suggests that people often misjudge the causes of their own behavior; some research indicates that this principle holds true for media consumption as well.[95]

McQuail, a noted researcher of uses-and-gratifications, takes this third point seriously and proposes that the traditional gratifications model is only part of what happens in media use.[96] He suggests that although individuals do use media for guidance, surveillance, and information, they also have a generalized arousal need that comes from and is informed by the culture. McQuail suggests that the uses-and-gratifications process is different between the, first, more cognitive process of media use and the, second, more cultural use. In the cultural model, individuals use media to achieve general arousal in the form of excitement, sadness, empathy, wonder, and so on.

Dependency theory makes an attempt to reconcile some of the problems of uses and gratifications with other more powerful-effects models. This theory accounts for both individual differences in responses to media and general media effects. As a systems theory, it shows the complexity of the interactions among the various aspects of the media transaction. The fusion of uses-and-gratifications and dependency theories provides an even more complete integration.

Like most of the theories in this chapter, however, both dependency theory and uses and dependency clash with the critical theory school. This clash points out a number of stasis points in media theory: Are media powerful in influencing culture, or are effects and cultural realities the accomplishments of individuals and interpretive communities? Do individuals make real choices, and how extensive are the cultural limits on individual media choice? To what extent should theory describe and explain, and to what extent should it reform? There will always be answers to these questions, but consensus will probably never be achieved.

95. See, for example, Dolf Zillmann, "Attribution and Misattribution of Excitatory Reactions," in *New Directions in Attribution Research,* vol. 2, eds. J. H. Harvey et al. (Hillsdale, N.J.: Erlbaum, 1978), pp. 335–368.

96. McQuail, "Hindsight."

PART IV

Capstone

CHAPTER **16**

Developing Core Communication Theory

Almost all communication and speech communication programs require one or more courses in communication theory. Why do so many professionals in our field consider this subject so important? Communication theory is the way in which those professionals express their understandings of the communication process.

We have come a long way from the days in which we thought we were developing theory to capture the truth about communication. Now, more realistically, the question is not what communication is but what we understand it to be. Consequently, communication theory may say more about us as a community of scholars than about communication as an object of study. Communication theory courses provide an exposure to these many understandings. Each theory has insights of its own, and each theory can help us see things in the communication process that might not otherwise be apparent. Communication theory, then, is like a kit of tools that can be used to take apart and put together a myriad of experiences encountered every day. Like a set of tools, different communication theories enable us to do different things. Some let us take a text apart, some let us

diagnose performance, some provide a lens for observing systemic relationships, and some uncover the meanings of groups and cultures. Although the items in the toolbox look very different from one another, each has its own function, and we can do a better job of understanding communication when all are available to us.

Over the years this book has been involved in the communication theory project of our field as a reporter and organizer. A quick review of the four editions of this book will reveal many changes in communication theory. Our toolbox is certainly growing. It used to consist of a few carpenter's tools, a couple plumbing devices, some electrical implements, not to mention a greasy wrench from the garage. Communication theory used to have little focus. Just about any theory dealing with psychological, social, or cultural matters was adopted. Now we have a much clearer sense of purpose. The focus of communication theory involves in one way or another the *message transaction, people generating and interpreting messages.*

The communication field probably always will have a diversity of voices, but they are finally shouting generally in the same direction. Communication theory as a field is maturing, and this sense of focus is just one sign. Another sign of this maturity is the development of several important theory programs by people trained in communication programs and working in communication departments throughout the world. Fewer and fewer theories are borrowed from other fields, and more and more are produced within our own. This is not mere playfulness in a field of ideas but the hard work of of tilling, planting, and harvesting those ideas. All of this reflects a genuine confidence and sense of integrity in our scholarship.

The Rise of Middle-Range Theory

Recall from Chapter 2 that theory is supposed to inform us about something bigger than an individual observation. If theories make statements about a general state of affairs, then they are predictive in some way, and they make statements on which we can rely. At the same time, we also know that people are purposeful and that they have intentions and goals. If this is so, how, then, can theory make general statements, and how can predictions be reliable? This is one of the most significant problems of communication theory—to predict and yet to allow for individual variation. If a theory is too general in its coverage and too specific in its predictions, then there is no room for individual choice and change. If, on the other hand, a theory is too specific, it does not really tell us anything we couldn't know from observing an individual case, and it certainly predicts nothing.

The answer to this dilemma lies in middle-range theory. Middle-range theories are based on the assumption of limited choice. That is, persons do make choices, and they do act to achieve goals; but they do not have free choice. Choices are restrained by all kinds of cognitive, social, cultural, and political conditions. Thus, we make choices within a range of alternatives. Middle-range theory specifies the range of choices available to people in different situations. As we have seen, there are numerous excellent theories of this type.

These theories specify the types of action possible in given situations with the knowledge that individuals may not always follow the expected course. Rules theory is an example because it tells us that people follow rules and it gives us some help in identifying what the rules are, but rules can be broken, sometimes intentionally.

These theories can also specify the general principles guiding or governing events without predicting how those principles will be played out or used by individuals at all times. Some cognitive theories are of this type. They tell us how the mind works, but they do not predict what the outcome of a particular operation will be.

This chapter addresses the aims of middle-range theories of communication. It looks at the elements of core communication theory, which are outlined in the following section.

Core Communication Theory

Theories are creations. They are made up of constructs that conceptualize various types of message transactions in a variety of situations and settings. Ernest Bormann divides communication theory into two types, special and general.[1] Special theories deal with specific types, settings, or situations: For example, theories of conflict, superior-subordinant communication, media effects, persuasion, and many more. These theories specialize in particular aspects of communication.

General theories deal with core processes common to all communication, such as meaning, coding and symbols, power, and a range of other elements and relations that work in any setting in which communication is involved.

General theories aim to define and explain basic processes essential to all communication. This is what I call *core communication theory*. The core concepts and process of communication could be outlined in a number of ways, and there would be sub-

---

1. Ernest Bormann, *Communication Theory* (New York: Holt, Rinehart, and Winston, 1980).

stantial disagreements about what these core processes are. This chapter suggests five elements that are strong candidates for the essential elements of all communication.

The first element is the *development of messages.* All communication consists of messages, and these have to be produced or generated in some way. Core communication theory attempts to explain the ways in which messages come into being. This core element consists of the cognitive, social, and cultural processes involved in creating messages in communication. It consists of notions of how messages are generated and constructed to accomplish various goals and intentions. Ideas about speaking and writing, thoughts about nonverbal coding and language, and hypotheses about the mental processes used to translate ideas into concrete form would all enter into the development of messages.

The second core element is *interpretation and generation of meaning.* Here we are looking at the cognitive, social, and cultural processes involved in understanding messages. This aspect of core theory addresses questions such as how people create meaning psychologically, socially, and culturally; how messages are understood mentally; how ambiguity arises and how it is resolved. Communication does not happen without meaning, and people create and use meaning in interpreting events.

The third element is *message structure.* This aspect of core theory looks at the ways in which texts are organized and how message organization itself may be an expression of meaning. Message structure involves the ways in which one message relates to another and the ways in which numerous messages may be organized into a coherent whole. What does a message look like, and how does its meaning depend on its organization? What makes a message or series of messages coherent? These are important considerations not only for communication face-to-face but also for communication across vast space and time. An interesting question is how the structure of a text that was produced long ago speaks to new readers in every generation.

The fourth element is *interactional dynamics.* This has to do with the relationships between and among people. It is involved with the ways in which individuals coordinate and mesh their behaviors, how they perceive one another and act on those perceptions. It deals with the organization and change of relational patterns over time—the development, maintenance, and even dissolution of relationships of all types.

The fifth element of core communication theory is *institutional dynamics.* This element deals with the political and societal forces of communication. It deals with the distribution of power and the ways in which power distribution affects all other aspects of communication on all levels—interpersonal, group, organizational, and mass communication. It also involves the ways in which communication itself is used to construct social and cultural institutions, including the power relations between classes, races, and sexes.

These five elements are not separate theories. Indeed, any core communication theory may treat any combination of them, although no one theory can probably touch on all. The five elements of core theory are not independent dimensions of communication but overlap subtantially with one another. So, for example, the development of messages is difficult to separate from meaning. Message structure and interactional patterns go hand-in-hand. People generate and interpret meanings in terms of the institutional dynamics that affect their lives.

These five elements, then, should be viewed more as dimensions or perspectives on the same process. Of course, we have no way to look at the process of communication other than from a particular angle, and each element outlined here is such an angle. These elements are like nonorthogonal or correlated factors of communication or like Burkeian ratios, where the meaning of each is enlightened by its relationship to all others.

The best research and theory programs in the field provide insight into the general communication process and thereby add to our body of core communication theory. In other words, theories should address one or more of the core elements and help us understand them in some productively new way. Some programs are designed directly to develop core theory in this way. Examples are semiotics; kinesics, proxemics, and other nonverbal communication studies; several cognitive theories like the action-assembly theory; symbolic interactionism and social constructionism; the coordinated management of meaning; and various feminist and critical theories.

Often, however, research addresses specific problems related to particular settings or types of communication. This work does not address core elements directly, but it may tell us a great deal about them indirectly. Just because a researcher is interested specifically in informal channels in organizations does not negate the value of this work in helping us understand communication in general. Indeed, it may say much about both institutional and interactional dynamics. Just because a theorist is interested specifically in marriage and family communication does not mean that the research will fail to address broader concerns. This type of research may indirectly address interactional dynamics and message organization in ways that can be generalized beyond the confines of the family. Just because a scholar is most interested in media effects does not negate the value of this work in telling us something about the ways in which power is distributed or messages are interpreted.

Most communication theories these days, whether general or special, have the potential to enlighten our understanding of core communication processes. For example, theories of interpersonal relationships tell us not only about relationships but also about such topics as the interpretation and generation of meaning and the structure of messages. Theories of group decision making tell us not only about group dynamics but also about institutions and interactions. Theories of organizational networks do not just address matters of concern to people working in business and other kinds of organizations. Indeed, communication scholars can learn about institutional dynamics, interactional dynamics, and message structure from these studies. Finally, theories of mass media may have a special focus, but they almost always say more about institutions, meaning, and messages than may be apparent on the surface.

These facts have special implication for how theory is produced and how it is read. Theory producers typically ask what their work says about the object of their study. They should ask a second question, too: What does their work say about communication in general? Those who read theory should read with two eyes: One looks at the substance of the theory, and the other looks at its broader implications for a fuller understanding of the communication process.

With these considerations in mind then, let us turn our attention to issues of core communication theory.

Issues in Core Communication Theory

Message Production

If communication involves message transactions, then the production of messages becomes an essential part of this process. Indeed, message production has captured a central place in communication theory. Some theories see message production primarily as an individual phenomenon, and others see it as institutional. Actually, both are probably correct. The real question is the extent to which the messages produced by individuals are influenced by larger system concerns.

With the exception of a few trait theorists, those who argue for individual message production usually take a cognitive perspective and explain the mental processes that govern message production. Action-assembly theory, for example, suggests that message production occurs by a hierarchical process of assembling information and action plans. Constructivism sees message production as a strategic endeavor in which perspectives are taken based on communicator's assessment of the situation and the needs of other people.

Rules theories add a social dimension to message production. Not only do individuals assess the situation, make plans, and follow strategies, but they also do so according to rules that are worked out interactionally. For most rules theorists then, message production is constrained by the social milieu.

Consideration of such social factors adds weight to the institutional side of the message-production controversy. If one's ability to produce messages is constrained by society, then institutions probably do have a much more powerful role in affecting the kinds of messages produced than psychologically oriented theorists would have us believe. This point of view would certainly be promoted by various organizational communication theories such as structuration and critical theories of all types.

The key consideration is not whether message production is cognitive or societal (it is obviously both), but which of these forces is most powerful in affecting messages. This is not a simple empirical question but goes to the very heart of how culture itself is defined. In the traditional liberal democractic perspective, the individual is given great power to make choices, but from a sociocultural perspective, the community is seen as the most important unit of analysis.

Although a variety of specific theoretical points can be debated in the attempt to explain message production, its essential character is a matter of dispute in the tension between individual and institutional forces.

Meaning

No discussion of communication is complete without consideration of meaning. Where is the site of meaning? How does meaning arise? What is the role of interpretation? These topics so permeate the theories discussed in this book that we cannot possibly summarize all positions here. At least three general approaches to these questions can be outlined at this point—the structuralist, the interactionist, and the cognitivist.

Structuralists see meaning in the arbitrary relationship between a sign and its referent. The hard version of this position says that meaning is an enduring relationship that is presented to people in messages. The meaning is in the sign; it is in the text. Classical semiotics takes this view, as do many hermeneutic scholars. Classical linguistics, too, has taken a firm structuralist approach.

The soft version of structuralism acknowledges

that signs come with alternative meanings, and individuals may choose from among these. Sometimes interpretation is a matter of conscious choice, as when an oppressed group chooses to assign meaning to messages that oppose dominant forces in society. Other times interpretation is colored by a host of cultural factors that are out of immediate awareness. Much semiotics show that meaning is determined in part by signs and in part by interpreters.

In opposition to the structuralist versions of meaning are the interactional-conventional ones. For theorists in the symbolic interactionist and social constructionist traditions, meaning is worked out interactionally within the social group. Whereas structuralists tend to take a universalist, synchronic view, interactionists take an historical, diachronic one. The interactional tradition is consistent with a variety of rules theories and certain discourse theories. Various ideas about cultural interpretation, including the ethnography of communication, organizational culture, and interpretive media studies also lie in this camp.

The third position on meaning is cognitive. Here meaning is seen as an active individual interpretive process. Meaning is a result of information processing; it is a product of mind. Some cognitivists like Charles Osgood and Noam Chomsky take a Kantian position by assuming certain universal categories of mind. Meaning is a result of applying these universal categories to information. Other theorists see meaning as a result of universal mental processes such as action assembly, attribution, and information integration. Here meaning is the result of certain kinds of mental work.

The tensions among the structuralists, the interactionists, and the cognitivists are true dialectics because, although their conceptual differences are clear, the tension can be only temporarily resolved by granting truth to one side or the other at given moments. Even the staunchest structuralists would admit that meanings receive local color by the way in which signs are used within the culture and that individuals do use some kind of cognitive process in dealing with messages. At the same time, the meanings of signs that arise from symbolic interaction within the social group come to have some structural force. They do endure, and they do affect future interactions, as Anthony Giddens so clearly points out. And, as the cognitivists constantly remind the interactionists, the participants in a social group do have separate brains.

This controversy of meaning deals with the power to define. Do people define their realities individually and culturally, or do people receive a set of realities predefined by language? Our answer to the meaning problem can only be that it is an outcome of the interplay between the structure of the message, the use of the message in actual situated interaction, and the mental process necessary to manage information and make interpretation.

Message Structure

Issues of message structure deal with the composition and organization of messages, individually and as a group. They deal with the structure of language, behavior, and other nondiscursive signs. In the parlance of linguistics, message structure is syntax.

Indeed, the traditional way of understanding message structure is linguistic. Here messages are seen as hierarchical structures built up from sounds to phrases, to sentences, to discourse. Even nonverbal behavior has been viewed this way, as in kinesics. The elements of a message are organized according to rules, and messages are meaningful because interpreters understand these rules.

Many of the issues of meaning discussed in the previous section also apply to the structure of messages. Are the rules of message structure given by language itself as assumed by structural linguistics, are they created through social interaction as assumed by symbolic interactionists, or are they a product of the individual mind, as assumed by generative grammarians? Here we see the inevitable theoretical link between message structure and meaning.

Theories of discourse are centrally concerned with message structure. What makes discourse coherent? How are individual messages patterned, and how are sequences of messages organized? When messages are exchanged in interaction, how do communicators mesh their messages with those of other communicators? Again, rules seem to be

the predominant explanatory mechanism at this level. Interpersonal message organization is necessary to achieve coherence or sensibility and to achieve coordination of actions.

The way in which messages and discourse are structured is not currently controversial. Although there are various versions of structure, they seem to deal with different aspects of the subject and do not clash with one another.

The consequences of message structure, however, are among the most hotly debated subjects in the field. For some, the linguists, theories of message structure merely explain how sounds are organized into coherent language structures. These scholars are message-centered, which explains why their work has been so influential in this aspect of communication theory. Their key question is how messages are intrinsically coherent.

For other researchers, message structure has implications for human relations. For these scholars, messages by themselves are not very important. Only when we see how language is used, how it is coordinated in ongoing interaction, do we get to the heart of the matter. The theory of the coordinated management of meaning is an example. Here the key question is how people coordinate their actions.

The third camp consists of the effectiveness researchers, who are concerned about the impact of message structure on individuals. How is information best organized to be understood? What kinds of structure bring about attitude and behavior change? Compliance-gaining research illustrates this group. Here the key question is how structure affects comprehension, attitudes, and behavior.

The fourth group consists of those who relate message structure to power. For them, the way in which a message is structured is not merely a curious intellectual puzzle. Particular message structures are powerful. They can promote interests and dominate entire classes of society. Much feminist and Marxist theory is of this type, as in the case of Julia Penelope's theory of the patriarchal universe of discourse.

Two tensions can be seen among these four groups. The first is the tension between description and prescription. On the one side are those who attempt merely to understand how various forms of discourse are organized. On the other side are those who are concerned with praxis, the pragmatic aspects of message design.

The second tension is between what has been called administrative scholarship and critical theory. Administrative approaches consist of two types of theories, those that attempt merely to describe and those that prescribe. Theorists of both approaches assume the basic correctness of their methods without questioning them, and their work can be used directly and indirectly to advance the institutional system of which they are a part. Critical theories on the other hand look at the ways in which message structures themselves communicate interests differentially in society. These theories question the values of the predominant system that supports administrative research.

Interactional Dynamics

The fourth element of core communication theory, interactional dynamics, has been addressed by a variety of theories. System theory gives impetus to this interest by stressing the ways in which elements of a system interact in dynamic tension. This idea has been picked up by scholars interested in interpersonal relationships, group and organizational development, and even the dissemination of ideas and innovations.

Symbolic interactionism, too, has been interested in the ways in which meaning arises out of interaction in small groups. Here is the site of self-presentation, fantasy themes, and narrative. It is the place where cultural values, norms, and rules are produced.

Interactional dynamics on the interpersonal level consist of social perception, self-disclosure, and uncertainty reduction. The establishment, development, and dissolution of relationships result from interactional dynamics of this sort. Group decision making is largely a product of the give and take between persons.

There can be no question that interpersonal relations are an important part of communication. Networks in organizations and in communities depend on the relationships established between individuals in small groups, and even the media

rely on these interpersonal processes to disseminate information and ideas.

The primary issue in this area of theory involves its relationship with institutional dynamics, as we see next.

Institutional Dynamics

Institutional dynamics relates to societywide processes and structures. How do the institutions of society affect communication and how are they affected by it? In what ways is power distributed in society, and how is this a function of communication? How is societal control exercised through communication?

There are three, not necessarily incompatible, approaches to these questions. The first is system theory, which sees society as a set of interrelated components that affect one another, adapt to the environment, and change as necessary. System theory has been applied to social groups such as the family, to organizations, and to the media.

The second approach is the conflict-of-interests view promulgated primarily by critical theorists. These scholars see societal dynamics as a series of conflicts among the interests of various groups in society, and they write that institutions such as education, religion, politics, and media are the vehicles by which these struggles are played out.

The third approach is the media-communication approach, which sees mass communication as the way in which society disseminates ideas and information and exerts control.

Unquestionably, communication consists of both interactional and institutional dynamics, but the relative positions of these two forces and their relationship to each other are in dispute. This dialectic between local community and societal institutions is the same tension we examined in regard to other areas of core theory.

From one perspective, institutional dynamics require interactional dynamics. In other words, institutions are merely higher-order products of interactions that occur within culturally situated social groups. This is a bubble-up theory. Carol Weick and Jay Blumer are two advocates of this perspective.

From another perspective, in a kind of trickle-down theory, interpersonal relations are shaped in large measure by the institutions of society. From this perspective, interpersonal relationships are either a tool for mass communication or they serve the hegemony of certain interests over others. Jürgen Habermas is a theorist in this group.

In many ways, the most important division among communication theories is not their substantive, conceptual differences but their positions on the bigger issues outlined in this chapter. A theory does tell us something about its appointed topic, but it does much more. It takes sides in a series of dialectical tensions related to message production, meaning, message structure, interactional dynamics, and institutional dynamics.

These debates will never be permanently resolved, for the philosophical divisions giving rise to them run too deep. At the same time, they can be temporarily resolved in the minds of communicators and scholars as we focus on particular moments and specific problems in communication. They are essential to "keep the conversation going."[2]

These debates should not be settled because to

do so would close off valuable ways of seeing, perspectives that are needed to produce alternative ways of viewing the process of communication.

In Closing

A legitimate question for students working their way through the communication curriculum is the difference between "communication theory" and "interpersonal communication" or "mass communication" or "organizational communication." The unique contribution of "communication theory" as a field of study is that it looks at the broader concerns addressed in this chapter. It should cast light on core communication processes and concepts.

After studying the various topics that arise in your classes, you certainly will know more about relationships, families, groups, organizations, media, and other topics. But you should also know more about communication itself, what is common to all forms of communication, what distinguishes communication from other human endeavors, and the big issues that separate different ways of thinking about communication. This is the goal of core communication theory.

---

2. Richard Rorty, *Philosophy and the Mirror of Nature* (Princeton, N.J.: Princeton University Press, 1979), p. 378.

Bibliography

Chapter One
Communication Theory and Scholarship

Barnlund, Dean C. *Interpersonal Communication: Survey and Studies*. New York: Houghton Mifflin, 1968.

Berger, Charles R., and Chaffee, Steven H., eds. "The Study of Communication as a Science." In *Handbook of Communication Science*. Newbury Park, Calif.: Sage, 1987, pp. 15–19.

Blalock, Hubert M. *Basic Dilemmas in the Social Sciences*. Beverly Hills, Calif.: Sage, 1984.

Bochner, Arthur P. "Perspectives on Inquiry: Representation, Conversation, and Reflection." In *Handbook of Interpersonal Communication*. Edited by Mark L. Knapp and Gerald R. Miller. Beverly Hills, Calif.: Sage, 1985, pp. 27–58.

Bormann, Ernest G. *Theory and Research in the Communicative Arts*. New York: Holt, Rinehart & Winston, 1965.

Bowers, John Waite, and Bradac, James J. "Issues in Communication Theory: A Metatheoretical Analysis." In *Communication Yearbook 5*. Edited by Michael Burgoon. New Brunswick, N.J.: Transaction Books, 1982, pp. 1–28.

Burrell, G. and Morgan, G. *Sociological Paradigms and Organizational Analysis*. London: Heinemann, 1979.

Cappella, Joseph N., ed. "Symposium on Mass and Interpersonal Communication." *Human Communication Research* 15 (1988): pp. 236–318.

Dallmayr, Fred R. *Language and Politics*. Notre Dame, Ind.: University of Notre Dame Press, 1984.

Dance, Frank E. X. "The 'Concept' of Communication." *Journal of Communication* 20 (1970): 201–210.

Dance, Frank E. X., and Larson, Carl E. *The Functions of Human Communication: A Theoretical Approach*. New York: Holt, Rinehart & Winston, 1976.

Delia, Jesse G. "Communication Research: A History." In *Handbook of Communication Science*. Edited by Charles R. Berger and Steven H. Chaffee. Newbury Park, Calif.: Sage, 1987, pp. 20–98.

de Saussure, Ferdinand. *Course in General Linguistics*. London: Peter Owen, 1960.

Diefenbeck, James A. *A Celebration of Subjective Thought*. Carbondale: Southern Illinois University Press, 1984.

Durkheim, Emile. *The Division of Labor in Society*. London: Collier-Macmillan, 1964.

Farrell, Thomas B. "Beyond Science: Humanities Contributions to Communication Theory." In *Handbook of Communication*

Science. Edited by Charles R. Berger and Steven H. Chaffee. Newbury Park, Calif.: Sage, 1987, pp. 123–139.

Farrell, Thomas B., and Aune, James A. "Critical Theory and Communication: A Selective Review." *Quarterly Journal of Speech* 65 (1979): 93–120.

Fay, Brian. *Social Theory and Political Practice*. London: George Allen & Unwin, 1975.

Fisk, Donald W., and Shweder, Richard A., eds. "Introduction: Uneasy Social Science." In *Metatheory in Social Science: Pluralisms and Subjectivities*. Chicago: University of Chicago Press, 1986, pp. 1–18.

Foss, Karen A., and Foss, Sonja K. "Incorporating the Feminist Perspective in Communication Scholarship: A Research Commentary." In *Doing Research on Women's Communication: Alternative Perspectives in Theory and Method*. Edited by Carole Spitzack and Kathryn Carter. Norwood, N.J.: Ablex, 1989, pp. 65–94.

Gergen, Kenneth J. *Toward Transformation in Social Knowledge*. New York: Springer-Verlag, 1982.

Giddens, Anthony. *Central Problems in Social Theory*. Berkeley: University of California Press, 1979.

———. *Profiles and Critiques in Social Theory*. Berkeley: University of California Press, 1983.

Glazer, Nathan. "The Social Sciences in Liberal Education." In *The Philosophy of the Curriculum*. Edited by Sidney Hook. Buffalo: Prometheus Books, 1975, pp. 145–158.

Greene, John O. "Evaluating Cognitive Explanations of Communicative Phenomena." *Quarterly Journal of Speech* 70 (1984): 241–254.

Grossberg, Lawrence. "Does Communication Theory Need Intersubjectivity? Toward An Immanent Philosophy of Interpersonal Relations." In *Communication Yearbook* 6. Edited by Michael Burgoon. Beverly Hills, Calif.: Sage, 1984, pp. 171–205.

Hanson, N. R. *Patterns of Discovery*. Cambridge, Eng.: Cambridge University Press, 1961.

Harper, Nancy. *Human Communication Theory: The History of a Paradigm*. Rochelle Park, N.J.: Hayden, 1979.

Hawkins, Robert P.; Wiemann, John M.; and Pingree, Suzanne; eds. *Advancing Communication Science*. Newbury Park, Calif.: Sage, 1988.

Hegel, G. W. F. *Phenomenology of Spirit*. Translated by A. V. Miller. Oxford, Eng.: Oxford University Press, 1977.

Holton, Gerald. "Science, Science Teaching, and Rationality." In *The Philosophy of the Curriculum*. Edited by Sidney Hook. Buffalo: Prometheus Books, 1975, pp. 101–108.

Jarett, James L. *The Humanities and Humanistic Education*. Reading, Mass.: Addison-Wesley, 1973.

Kincaid, D. Lawrence. *Communication Theory: Eastern and Western Perspectives*. San Diego: Academic Press, 1987.

Kuhn, Thomas S. *The Structure of Scientific Revolutions*. Chicago: University of Chicago Press, 1970.

Lakoff, George, and Johnson, Mark. *Metaphors We Live By*. Chicago: University of Chicago Press, 1980.

Littlejohn, Stephen W. "An Overview of the Contributions to Human Communication Theory from Other Disciplines." In *Human Communication Theory: Comparative Essays*. Edited by Frank E. X. Dance. New York: Harper & Row, 1982, pp. 243–285.

McKeon, Richard. "Gibson Winter's Elements for a Social Ethic: A Review." *Journal of Religion* 49 (1969): 77–84.

Meehl, Paul E. "What Social Scientists Don't Understand." In *Metatheory in Social Science: Pluralisms and Subjectivities*. Edited by Donald W. Fiske and Richard A. Shweder. Chicago: University of Chicago Press, 1986, pp. 317–319.

Miller, Gerald E., and Nicholson, Henry. *Communication Inquiry*. Reading, Mass.: Addison-Wesley, 1976.

Motley, Michael. "On Whether One Can(not) Not Communicate: An Examination Via Traditional Communication Postulates." *Western Journal of Speech Communication* 54 (1990): 1–20.

Pearce, W. Barnett. *Communication and the Human Condition*. Carbondale: Southern Illinois University Press, 1989.

———. "Scientific Research Methods in Communication Studies and Their Implications for Theory and Research." In *Speech Communication in the 20th Century*. Edited by Thomas W. Benson. Carbondale: Southern Illinois University Press, 1985, pp. 255–281.

Pearce, W. Barnett; Cronen, Vernon E.; and Harris, Linda M. "Methodological Considerations in Building Human Communication Theory." In *Human Communication Theory: Comparative Essays*. Edited by Frank E. X. Dance. New York: Harper & Row, 1982, pp. 1–41.

Pearce, W. Barnett, and Foss, Karen A. "The Historical Context of Communication as a Science." In *Human Communication: Theory and Research*. Edited by Gordon L. Dahnke and Glen W. Clatterbuck. Belmont, Calif.: Wadsworth, 1990. pp. 1–20.

Smith, Ted J., III. "Diversity and Order in Communication Theory: The Uses of Philosophical Analysis." *Communication Quarterly* 36 (1988): 28–40.

Snow, C. P. *The Two Cultures and a Second Look*. Cambridge, Eng.: Cambridge University Press, 1964.

Stewart, Jon. "Speech and Human Being." *Quarterly Journal of Speech* 72 (1986): 55–73.

Truzzi, M. *Verstehen: Subjective Understanding in the Social Sciences*. Reading, Mass: Addison-Wesley, 1974.

Winch, Peter. *The Idea of a Social Science and Its Relation to Philosophy*. London: Routledge & Kegan Paul, 1958.

Winter, Gibson. *Elements for a Social Ethic: Scientific and Ethical Perspectives on Social Process*. New York: Macmillan, 1966.

Chapter Two
Theory in the Process of Inquiry

Achinstein, P. *Laws and Explanation*. New York: Oxford University Press, 1971.

Andersen, Peter A. "The Trait Debate: A Critical Examination of the Individual Differences Paradigm in the Communication Sciences." In *Progress in Communication Sciences*. Edited by B. Dervin and M. J. Voight. Norwood, N.J.: Ablex, 1986.

Berger, Charles R. "The Covering Law Perspective as a Theoretical Basis for the Study of Human Communication." *Communication Quarterly* 25 (1977): 7–18.

Berger, Peter, and Luckmann, Thomas. *The Social Construction of Reality*. Garden City, N.Y.: Doubleday, 1966.

Black, Max. *Models and Metaphors*. Ithaca, N.Y.: Cornell University Press, 1962.

Bormann, Ernest G. *Communication Theory*. New York: Holt, Rinehart & Winston, 1980.

Bowers, John Waite, and Bradac, James J. "Issues in Communication Theory: A Metatheoretical Analysis." In *Communica-*

tion Yearbook 5. Edited by Michael Burgoon. New Brunswick, N.J.: Transaction Books, 1982, pp. 1–28.

Brinberg, David, and McGrath, Joseph E. *Validity and the Research Process.* Beverly Hills, Calif.: Sage, 1985.

Bross, Irwin B. J. *Design for Decision.* New York: Macmillan, 1952.

Brummett, Barry. "Some Implications of 'Process' or 'Intersubjectivity': Postmodern Rhetoric." *Philosophy and Rhetoric* 9 (1976): 21–51.

Chaffee, Steven H. and Berger, Charles R. "What Communication Scientists Do." In *Handbook of Communication Science.* Edited by Charles R. Berger and Steven H. Chaffee. Newbury Park, Calif.: Sage, 1987, pp. 91–122.

Coughlin, Ellen K. "Thomas Kuhn's Ideas About Science." *Chronicle of Higher Education* (September 22, 1982): 21–23.

Cushman, Donald P. "The Rules Perspective as a Theoretical Basis for the Study of Human Communication." *Communication Quarterly* 25 (1977): 30–45.

Cushman, Donald P., and Pearce, W. Barnett. "Generality and Necessity in Three Types of Theory about Human Communication, with Special Attention to Rules Theory." *Human Communication Research* 3 (1977): 344–353.

Dance, Frank E. X., and Larson, Carl E. *The Functions of Human Communication: A Theoretical Approach.* New York: Holt, Rinehart & Winston, 1976.

Dervin, Brenda; Grossberg, Lawrence; O'Keefe, Barbara; and Wartella, Ellen; eds. *Rethinking Communication: Paradigm Issues.* Newbury Park, Calif.: Sage, 1989.

Deutsch, Karl W. "On Communication Models in the Social Sciences." *Public Opinion Quarterly* 16 (1952): 356–380.

Fay, Brian. *Social Theory and Political Practice.* London: George Allen & Unwin, 1975.

Fisher, B. Aubrey. *Perspectives on Human Communication.* New York: Macmillan, 1978.

Fiske, Donald W., and Shweder, Richard A., eds. *Metatheory in Social Science: Pluralisms and Subjectivities.* Chicago: University of Chicago Press, 1986.

Gerbner, George, ed. *Ferment in the Field.* Special Issue of *Journal of Communication* 33 (Summer 1983).

Gergen, Kenneth J. "The Social Constructionist Movement in Modern Psychology." *American Psychologist* 40 (1985): 266–275.

———. *Toward Transformation in Social Knowledge.* New York: Springer-Verlag, 1982.

Gergen, Kenneth J., and Gergen, Mary M. "Explaining Human Conduct: Form and Function." In *Explaining Human Behavior: Consciousness, Human Action, and Social Structure.* Edited by Paul F. Secord. Beverly Hills, Calif.: Sage, 1982, pp. 127–154.

Habermas, Jürgen. *Knowledge and Human Interests.* Translated by Jeremy J. Shapiro. Boston: Beacon Press, 1971.

Hall, Calvin S., and Lindzey, Gardner. *Theories of Personality.* New York: Wiley, 1970.

Hamelink, Cees J. "Emancipation or Domestication: Toward a Utopian Science of Communication." *Journal of Communication* 33 (1983): 74–79.

Hanna, Joseph. "Two Ideals of Scientific Theorizing." In *Communication Yearbook 5.* Edited by Michael Burgoon. New Brunswick, N.J.: Transaction Books, 1982, pp. 29–48.

Hanson, N. R. *Patterns of Discovery.* Cambridge, Mass.: Cambridge University Press, 1961.

Harré, R., and Secord, P. F. *The Explanation of Social Behavior.* Totowa, N.J.: Littlefield, Adams, 1979.

Hawes, Leonard. *Pragmatics of Analoguing: Theory and Model Construction in Communication.* Reading, Mass.: Addison-Wesley, 1975.

Kaplan, Abraham. *The Conduct of Inquiry.* San Francisco: Chandler, 1964.

Kerlinger, Fred N. *Foundations of Behavioral Research.* New York: Holt, Rinehart & Winston, 1964.

Kibler, Robert J. "Basic Communication Research Considerations." In *Methods of Research in Communication.* Edited by Philip Emmert and William Brooks. Boston: Houghton Mifflin, 1970, pp. 9–50.

Kuhn, Thomas S. *The Structure of Scientific Revolutions.* Chicago: University of Chicago Press, 1970.

Littlejohn, Stephen W. "Epistemology and the Study of Human Communication." Paper delivered to the Speech Communication Association, New York, 1980.

———. "An Overview of Contributions to Human Communication Theory from Other Disciplines." In *Human Communication Theory: Comparative Essays.* Edited by Frank E. X. Dance. New York: Harper & Row, 1982, pp. 243–285.

Lustig, Myron W. "Theorizing About Human Communication." *Communication Quarterly* 34 (1986): 451–459.

MacIntyre, Alasdair. "Ontology." In *The Encyclopedia of Philosophy,* vol. 5. Edited by Paul Edwards. New York: Macmillan, 1967, pp. 542–543.

McNamee, Sheila. "Research as Social Intervention: A Research Methodology for the New Epistemology." Paper presented to the Fifth International Conference on Culture and Communication, Philadelphia, October 1988.

Miller, Gerald. "The Current Status of Theory and Research in Interpersonal Communication." *Human Communication Research* 4 (1978): 175.

Miller, Gerald E., and Nicholson, Henry. *Communication Inquiry.* Reading, Mass.: Addison-Wesley, 1976.

Monge, Peter R. "The Systems Perspective as a Theoretical Basis for the Study of Human Communication." *Communication Quarterly* 25 (1977): 19–29.

Pearce, W. Barnett. "Metatheoretical Concerns in Communication." *Communication Quarterly* 25 (1977): 3–6.

Pearce, W. Barnett; Cronen, Vernon E.; and Harris, Linda M. "Methodological Considerations in Building Human Communication Theory." In *Human Communication Theory: Comparative Essays.* Edited by Frank E. X. Dance. New York: Harper & Row, 1982, pp. 1–41.

Pepper, Stephen. *World Hypotheses.* Berkeley: University of California Press, 1942.

Polanyi, Michael. *Personal Knowledge.* London: Routledge & Kegan Paul, 1958.

Schutz, Alfred. *The Phenomenology of the Social World.* Translated by George Walsh and Frederick Lehnert. Evanston, Ill.: Northwestern University Press, 1967.

Secord, Paul F., ed. *Explaining Human Behavior: Consciousness, Human Action, and Social Structure.* Beverly Hills, Calif.: Sage, 1982.

Smith, Ted J., III. "Diversity and Order in Communication Theory: The Uses of Philosophical Analysis." *Communication Quarterly* 36 (1988): 28–40.

von Wright, Georg H. *Explanation and Understanding.* Ithaca, N.Y.: Cornell University Press, 1971.

Wallace, Walter L. *Sociological Theory: An Introduction*. Chicago: Aldine, 1969.

Williams, Kenneth R. "Reflections on a Human Science of Communication." *Journal of Communication* 23 (1973): 239–250.

Chapter Three
System Theory

Allport, Gordon W. "The Open System in Personality Theory." In *Modern Systems Research for the Behavioral Scientist*. Edited by Walter Buckley. Chicago: Aldine, 1968, pp. 343–350.

Ashby, W. Ross. "Principles of the Self-Organizing System." In *Principles of Self-Organization*. Edited by Heinz von Foerster and George Zopf. New York: Pergamon Press, 1962, pp. 255–278.

Asher, Herbert B. *Causal Modeling*. Beverly Hills, Calif.: Sage, 1976.

Bar-Hillel, Yehoshua. "Concluding Review." In *Information Theory in Psychology*. Edited by Henry Quastler. Glencoe, Ill.: Free Press, 1955, p. 3.

Bateson, Gregory. *Naven*. Stanford, Calif.: Stanford University Press, 1958.

Beach, Wayne. "Stocktaking Open-Systems Research and Theory: A Critique and Proposals for Action." Paper presented to the Western Speech Communication Association, Phoenix, November 1977.

Berger, Charles. "The Covering Law Perspective as a Theoretical Basis for the Study of Human Communication." *Communication Quarterly* 75 (1977): 7–18.

Bochner, Arthur P. "The Functions of Human Communication in Interpersonal Bonding." In *Handbook of Rhetorical and Communication Theory*. Edited by Carroll C. Arnold and John Waite Bowers. Boston: Allyn and Bacon, 1984, pp. 544–621.

Bochner, Arthur P., and Eisenberg, Eric M. "Family Process: System Perspectives." In *Handbook of Communication Science*. Edited by Charles R. Berger and Steven H. Chaffee. Newbury Park, Calif.: Sage, 1987, pp. 540–563.

Boulding, Kenneth. "General Systems Theory—The Skeleton of Science." In *Modern Systems Research for the Behavioral Scientist*. Edited by Walter Buckley. Chicago: Aldine, 1968, p. 4.

Broadhurst, Allan R., and Darnell, Donald K. "An Introduction to Cybernetics and Information Theory." *Quarterly Journal of Speech* 51 (1965): 442–453.

Buckley, Walter, ed. *Modern Systems Research for the Behavioral Scientist*. Chicago: Aldine, 1968.

———, ed. "Society as a Complex Adaptive System." In *Modern Systems Research for the Behavioral Scientist*. Chicago: Aldine, 1968, pp. 490–513.

———. *Sociology and Modern Systems Theory*. Englewood Cliffs, N.J.: Prentice-Hall, 1967.

Cherry, Colin. *On Human Communication*, 3rd ed. Cambridge: MIT Press, 1978.

Conant, Roger C. "A Vector Theory of Information." In *Communication Yearbook 3*. Edited by Dan Nimmo. New Brunswick, N.J.: Transaction Books, 1979, pp. 177–196.

Crowley, D. J. *Understanding Communication: The Signifying Web*. New York: Gordon and Breach, 1982.

Cushman, Donald. "The Rules Perspective as a Theoretical Basis for the Study of Human Communication." *Communication Quarterly* 25 (1977): 30–45.

Delia, Jesse. "Alternative Perspectives for the Study of Human Communication: Critique and Response." *Communication Quarterly* 25 (1977): 51–52.

Deutsch, Karl. "Toward a Cybernetic Model of Man and Society." In *Modern Systems Research for the Behavioral Scientist*. Edited by Walter Buckley. Chicago: Aldine, 1968, pp. 387–400.

Farace, Richard V.; Monge, Peter R.; and Hamish, Russell. *Communicating and Organizing*. Reading Mass.: Addison-Wesley, 1977.

Fisher, B. Aubrey. *Perspectives on Human Communication*. New York: Macmillan, 1978.

———. *Small Group Decision Making: Communication and the Group Process*. New York: McGraw-Hill, 1980.

Fisher, B. Aubrey, and Hawes, Leonard C. "An Interact System Model: Generating a Grounded Theory of Small Groups." *Quarterly Journal of Speech* 57 (1971): 444–453.

Garner, Wendell R. *Uncertainty and Structure as Psychological Concepts*. New York: Wiley, 1962.

General Systems: Yearbook of the Society for General Systems Research, 1956–present (annual).

Giddens, Anthony. *Profiles and Critiques in Social Theory*. Berkeley: University of California Press, 1982.

Grene, Marjorie. *The Knower and the Known*. Berkeley: University of California Press, 1974.

Guilbaud, G. T. *What Is Cybernetics?* New York: Grove Press, 1959.

Hall, A. D., and Fagen, R. E. "Definition of System." In *Modern Systems Research for the Behavioral Scientist*. Edited by Walter Buckley. Chicago: Aldine, 1968, pp. 81–92.

Handy, Rollo, and Kurtz, Paul. "A Current Appraisal of the Behavioral Sciences: Information Theory." *American Behavioral Scientist* 7, no. 6 (1964): 99–104.

Harris, Marvin. *The Rise of Anthropological Theory*. New York: Crowell, 1968.

Kaufmann, Walter, ed. *Hegel: Texts and Commentary*. Garden City, N.Y.: Anchor Books, 1966.

Kincaid, D. Lawrence, ed. "The Convergence Theory of Communication, Self-Organization, and Cultural Evolution." In *Communication Theory: Eastern and Western Perspectives*. San Diego: Academic Press, 1987, p. 15.

Kincaid, D. Lawrence; Yum, June Ock; and Woelfel, Joseph. "The Cultural Convergence of Korean Immigrants in Hawaii: An Empirical Test of a Mathematical Theory." *Quality and Quantity* 18 (1983): 59–78.

Koestler, Arthur. *The Ghost in the Machine*. New York: Macmillan, 1967.

Krippendorf, Klaus. "Information Theory." In *Communication and Behavior*. Edited by Gerhard Hanneman and William McEwen. Reading, Mass.: Addison-Wesley, 1975, pp. 351–389.

Littlejohn, Stephen W. *Theories of Human Communication*, 1st ed. Columbus, Ohio: Merrill, 1978.

"Ludwig von Bertalanffy." *General Systems* 17 (1972): 219–228.

Maruyama, Magoroh. "The Second Cybernetics: Deviation-Amplifying Mutual Causal Processes." *American Scientist* 51 (1963): 164–179 (Reprinted in *Modern Systems Research for the Behavioral Scientist*. Edited by Walter Buckley. Chicago: Aldine, 1968, pp. 304–316).

Millar, Frank E., and Rogers, L. Edna. "A Relational Approach to Interpersonal Communication." In *Explorations in Interper-*

sonal Communication. Edited by Gerald Miller. Beverly Hills, Calif.: Sage, 1976. pp. 87–203.

———. "Relational Dimensions of Interpersonal Dynamics." In Interpersonal Processes: New Directions in Communication Research. Edited by Michael Roloff and Gerald Miller. Newbury Park, Calif.: Sage, 1987.

Miller, Gerald R. "The Pervasiveness and Marvelous Complexity of Human Communication: A Note of Skepticism." Keynote address, Fourth Annual Conference in Communication, California State University, Fresno, May 1977.

Monge, Peter. "The Network Level of Analysis." In Handbook of Communication Science. Edited by Charles R. Berger and Steven H. Chaffee. Newbury Park, Calif.: Sage, 1987, pp. 239–270.

———. "The Systems Perspective as a Theoretical Basis for the Study of Human Communication." Communication Quarterly 25 (1977): 19–29.

Monge, Peter R., and Cappella, Joseph N. Multivariate Techniques in Human Communication Research. New York: Academic Press, 1980.

Monge, Peter R., and Eisenberg, E. M. "Emergent Networks." In Handbook of Organizational Communication. Edited by F. Jablin, L. Putnam, K. Roberts, and L. Porter. Newbury Park, Calif.: Sage, 1987.

Monge, Peter R. and Miller, Gerald R. "Communication Networks." In The Social Science Encyclopedia. Edited by A. Kuper and J. Kuper. London: Routledge & Kegan Paul, 1985.

Pask, Gordon. An Approach to Cybernetics. New York: Harper & Row, 1961.

Rapoport, Anatol. "Foreward." In Modern Systems Research for the Behavioral Scientist. Edited by Walter Buckley. Chicago: Aldine, 1968, pp. xiii–xxv.

———. "The Promises and Pitfalls of Information Theory." Behavioral Science 1 (1956): 303–309. (Reprinted in Modern Systems Research for the Behavioral Scientist. Edited by Walter Buckley. Chicago: Aldine, 1968, pp. 137–142.)

Rogers, Everett M. Diffusion of Innovations. New York: Free Press, 1962.

Rogers, Everett M., and Adhikarya, Ronny. "Diffusion of Innovations: An Up-to-Date Review and Commentary." In Communication Yearbook 3. Edited by Dan Nimmo. New Brunswick, N.J.: Transaction Books, 1979, pp. 67–82.

Rogers, Everett M., and Kincaid, D. Lawrence. Communication Networks: Toward a New Paradigm for Research. New York: Free Press, 1981.

Rogers, L. Edna. "Relational Communication Processes and Patterns." In Rethinking Communication: Paradigm Exemplars. Edited by Brenda Dervin, Lawrence Grossberg, Barbara O'Keefe, and Ellen Wartella. Newbury Park, Calif.: Sage, 1989, pp. 280–290.

Rosenbleuth, Arturo; Weiner, Norbert; and Bigelow, Julian. "Behavior, Purpose, and Teleology." Philosophy of Science 10 (1943): 18–24. (Reprinted in Modern Systems Research for the Behavioral Scientist. Edited by Walter Buckley. Chicago: Aldine, 1968, pp. 221–225.)

Ruben, Brent D., and Kim, John Y., eds. General Systems Theory and Human Communication. Rochelle Park, N.J.: Hayden, 1975.

Ruesch, Juergen, and Bateson, Gregory. Communication and the Social Matrix of Society. New York: Norton, 1951.

Shannon, Claude, and Weaver, Warren. The Mathematical The-ory of Communication. Urbana: University of Illinois Press, 1949.

Taschjan, Edgan. "The Entropy of Complex Dynamic Systems." Behavioral Science 19 (1975): 3.

Toda, Masanao, and Shuford, Emir H. "Logic of Systems: Introduction to a Formal Theory of Structure." General Systems 10 (1965): 3–27.

von Bertalanffy, Ludwig. "General Systems Theory: A Critical Review." General Systems 7 (1962): 1–20.

———. General Systems Theory: Foundations, Development, Applications. New York: Braziller, 1968.

Watzlawick, Paul; Beavin, Janet; and Jackson, Don. Pragmatics of Human Communication: A Study in Interactional Patterns, Pathologies, and Paradoxes. New York: Norton, 1967.

Weick, Carl. The Social Psychology of Organizing. Reading, Mass.: Addison-Wesley, 1969.

Wiener, Norbert. Cybernetics or Control and Communication in the Animal and the Machine. Cambridge, Mass.: MIT Press, 1961.

———. The Human Use of Human Beings: Cybernetics and Society. Boston: Houghton Mifflin, 1954.

Wilson, Donna. "Forms of Hierarchy: A Selected Bibliography." General Systems 14 (1969): 3–15.

Yum, June Ock. "Communication Diversity and Information Acquisition Among Korean Immigrants in Hawaii." Human Communication Research 8 (1982): 154–169.

———. "The Communication Network Paradigm and Intercultural Communication." In Rethinking Communication: Paradigm Exemplars. Edited by Brenda Dervin, Lawrence Grossberg, Barbara O'Keefe, and Ellen Wartella. Newbury Park, Calif.: Sage, 1989, pp. 486–496.

———. "Social Network Patterns of Five Ethnic Groups in Hawaii." In Communication Yearbook 7. Edited by Robert Bostrom. New Brunswick, N.J.: Transaction Books, 1983, pp. 574–591.

Chapter Four
Theories of Signs and Language

Berger, Arthur Asa. Signs in Contemporary Culture: An Introduction to Semiotics. Salem, Wis.: Sheffield, 1989.

Berman, Art. From the New Criticism to Deconstruction. Urbana: University of Illinois Press, 1988.

Birdwhistell, Ray. Introduction of Kinesics. Louisville: University of Louisville Press, 1952.

———. Kinesics and Context. Philadelphia: University of Pennsylvania Press, 1970.

Bloomfield, Leonard. Language. New York: Holt, Rinehart & Winston, 1933.

Burgoon, Judee K. "Nonverbal Communication Research in the 1970s: An Overview." In Communication Yearbook 4. Edited by Dan Nimmo. New Brunswick, N.J.: Transaction Books, 1980, p. 179.

———. "Nonverbal Signals." In Handbook of Interpersonal Communication. Edited by Mark L. Knapp and Gerald R. Miller. Beverly Hills, Calif.: Sage, 1985, pp 349–353.

Burgoon, Judee K.; Birk, Thomas; and Pfau, Michael. "Nonverbal Behaviors, Persuasion, and Credibility." Human Communication Research 17 (Fall 1990): 140–169.

Burgoon, Judee K., and Saine, Thomas. *The Unspoken Dialogue: An Introduction to Nonverbal Communication*. Boston: Houghton Mifflin, 1978.

Chomsky, Noam. *The Acquisition of Syntax in Children from 5 to 10*. Cambridge, Mass.: MIT Press, 1969.

———. Aspects of the Theory of Syntax. Cambridge, Mass.: MIT Press, 1965.

———. *Cartesian Linguistics: A Chapter in the History of Rationalist Thought*. New York: Harper & Row, 1966.

———. *Current Issues in Linguistic Theory*. The Hague: Mouton, 1970.

———. *Essays on Form and Interpretation*. New York: North Holland, 1977.

———. *Language and Mind*. New York: Harcourt Brace Jovanovich, 1972.

———. *The Logical Structure of Linguistic Theory*. New York: Plenum, 1975.

———. *Problems of Knowledge and Freedom*. New York: Pantheon, 1971.

———. *Reflections on Language*. New York: Pantheon, 1975.

———. *Rules and Representations*. New York: Columbia University Press, 1980.

———. *The Sound Pattern of English*. New York: Harper & Row, 1968.

———. *Studies on Semantics in Generative Grammar*. The Hague: Mouton, 1972.

———. *Syntactic Structures*. The Hague: Mouton, 1957.

———. "Three Models for the Description of Language." *Transactions on Information Theory* 1T-2 (1956): 113–124.

———. *Topics in the Theory of Generative Grammar*. The Hague: Mouton, 1966.

Dallmayr, Fred. *Language and Politics*. Notre Dame, Ind.: University of Notre Dame Press, 1984.

de Saussure, Ferdinand. *Course in General Linguistics*. London: Peter Owen, 1960.

Descartes, René. *Meditations on First Philosophy*. Translated by Lawrence J. LaFleur. Indianapolis: Bobbs-Merrill, 1960.

Eco, Umberto. *Semiotics and the Philosophy of Language*. Bloomington: Indiana University Press, 1984.

———. *A Theory of Semiotics*. Bloomington: Indiana University Press, 1976.

Ekman, Paul, and Friesen, Wallace. *Emotion in the Human Face: Guidelines for Research and an Integration of Findings*. New York: Pergamon Press, 1972.

———. "Hand Movements." *Journal of Communication* 22 (1972): 353–374.

———. "Nonverbal Behavior in Psychotherapy Research." In *Research in Psychotherapy*, vol. III. Edited by J. Shlien. Washington, D.C.: American Psychological Association, 1968, pp. 179–216.

———. "The Repertoire of Nonverbal Behavior: Categories, Origins, Usage, and Coding." *Semiotica* 1 (1969): 49–98.

———. *Unmasking the Face*. Englewood Cliffs, N.J.: Prentice-Hall, 1975.

Fisch, Max H. *Peirce, Semiotic, and Pragmatism*. Bloomington: Indiana University Press, 1986.

Fodor, J. A.; Bever, T. G.; and Garrett, M. F. *The Psychology of Language: An Introduction to Psycholinguistics and Generative Grammar*. New York: McGraw-Hill, 1974.

Fodor, Jerry; Jenkins, James; and Saporta, Sol. "Psycholinguistics and Communication Theory." In *Human Communication Theory*. Edited by Frank E. X. Dance. New York: Holt, Rinehart & Winston, 1967, pp. 160–201.

Fries, Charles. *The Structure of English*. New York: Harcourt, Brace & World, 1952.

Giddens, Anthony. *Central Problems in Social Theory: Action, Structure, and Contradiction in Social Analysis*. Berkeley: University of California Press, 1979.

Goudge, Thomas A. *The Thought of Peirce*. Toronto: University of Toronto Press, 1950.

Hall, Edward T. *The Hidden Dimension*. New York: Random House, 1966.

———. *The Silent Language*. Greenwich, Conn.: Fawcett Books, 1959.

———. "A System for the Notation of Proxemic Behavior." *American Anthropologist* 65 (1963): 1003–1026.

Harmon, Gilbert. *On Noam Chomsky: Critical Essays*. Garden City, N.Y.: Anchor Books, 1974.

Harper, Robert G.; Wiess, Arthur; and Motarozzo, Joseph. *Nonverbal Communication: The State of the Art*. New York: Wiley, 1978.

Harris, Zellig. *Structural Linguistics*. Chicago: University of Chicago Press, 1951.

Harrison, Randall. "Nonverbal Communication." In *Handbook of Communication*. Edited by Ithiel de sola Pool et al. Chicago: Rand McNally, 1973.

Hookway, Christopher. *Peirce*. London: Routledge & Kegan Paul, 1985.

Knapp, Mark. *Nonverbal Communication in Human Interaction*. New York: Holt, Rinehart & Winston, 1978.

Knapp, Mark; Wiemann, John; and Daly, John. "Nonverbal Communication: Issues and Appraisal." *Human Communication Research* 4 (1978): 271–280.

Langer, Susanne. *Mind: An Essay on Human Feeling*. 3 volumes. Baltimore: Johns Hopkins University Press, 1967, 1972, 1982.

———. *Philosophy in a New Key*. Cambridge, Mass.: Harvard University Press, 1942.

Lyne, John R. "Rhetoric and Semiotic in C. S. Peirce." *Quarterly Journal of Speech* 66 (1980): 155–168.

Martyna, Wendy. "What Does 'He' Mean?" *Journal of Communication* 28 (1978): 131–138.

Mead, George H. *Mind, Self, and Society*. Chicago: University of Chicago Press, 1934.

Morris, Charles. "Foundations in the Theory of Signs." In *International Encyclopedia of Unified Science*, vol. I, part 1. Chicago: University of Chicago Press, 1955, p. 84.

———. *Signification and Significance*. Cambridge, Mass.: MIT Press, 1964.

———. *Signs, Language, and Behavior*. New York: Braziller, 1946.

Ogden, C. K., and Richards, I. A. *The Meaning of Meaning*. London: Kegan, Paul, Trench, Trubner, 1923.

Peirce, Charles Saunders. *Charles S. Peirce: Selected Writings*. Edited by P. O. Wiener. New York: Dover, 1958.

Roskill, Mark. "'Public' and 'Private' Meanings: The Paintings of Van Gogh." *Journal of Communication* 29 (1979): 157–169.

Salus, Peter. *Linguistics*. Indianapolis: Bobbs-Merrill, 1969.

Silverman, Kaja. *The Subject of Semiotics*. New York: Oxford University Press, 1983.

Chapter Five
Theories of Discourse

Austin, J. L. *How to Do Things with Words*. Cambridge, Mass.: Harvard University Press, 1962.

———. *Philosophy of Language*. Englewood Cliffs, N.J.: Prentice-Hall, 1964.

Beach, Wayne. "Orienting to the Phenomenon." In *Communication Yearbook 13*. Edited by James A. Anderson. Newbury Park, Calif.: Sage, 1990, pp. 216–244.

Berger, Charles R. "The Covering Law Perspective as a Theoretical Basis for the Study of Human Communication." *Communication Quarterly* 25 (1977): 12.

Berman, Art. *From the New Criticism to Deconstruction: The Reception of Structuralism and Post-structuralism*. Urbana: University of Illinois Press, 1988.

Blair, Carole. "The Statement: Foundation of Foucault's Historical Criticism." *Western Journal of Speech Communication* 51 (1987): 364–383.

Buttney, Richard. "The Ascription of Meaning: A Wittgensteinian Perspective." *Quarterly Journal of Speech* 72 (1986): 261–273.

Campbell, Paul N. "A Rhetorical View of Locutionary, Illocutionary, and Perlocutionary Acts." *Quarterly Journal of Speech* 59 (1973): 284–296.

Cappella, Joseph N. "The Management of Conversations." In *Handbook of Interpersonal Communication*. Edited by Mark L. Knapp and Gerald R. Miller. Beverly Hills, Calif.: Sage, 1985, pp. 393–439.

Cooper, Martha. "Rhetorical Criticism and Foucault's Philosophy of Discursive Events." *Central States Speech Journal* 39 (1988): 1–17.

Craig, Robert T., and Tracy, Karen, eds. *Conversational Coherence: Form, Structure, and Strategy*. Beverly Hills, Calif.: Sage, 1983.

Cushman, Donald P. "The Rules Approach to Communication Theory: A Philosophical and Operational Perspective." In *Communication Theory: Eastern and Western Perspectives*. Edited by D. Lawrence Kincaid. San Diego: Academic Press, 1987, pp. 223–234.

———. "The Rules Perspective as a Theoretical Basis for the Study of Human Communication." *Communication Quarterly* 25 (1977): 30–45.

Delia, Jesse. "Alternative Perspectives for the Study of Human Communication: Critique and Response." *Communication Quarterly* 25 (1977): 54.

Derrida, Jacques. *Of Grammatology*. Translated by Gayatri Chakrovorty Spivak. Baltimore: Johns Hopkins University Press, 1974, 1976.

Ellis, Donald G., and Donohue, William A., eds. *Contemporary Issues in Language and Discourse Processes*. Hillsdale, N.J.: Erlbaum, 1986.

Foss, Sonja K.; Foss, Karen A.; and Trapp, Robert. *Contemporary Perspectives on Rhetoric*. Prospect Heights, Ill.: Waveland Press, 1991.

Foss, Sonja K., and Gill, Ann. "Michel Foucault's Theory of Rhetoric as Epistemic." *Western Journal of Speech Communication* 51 (1987): 384–402.

Foucault, Michel. *The Archaeology of Knowledge*. Translated by A. M. Sheridan Smith. New York: Pantheon, 1972.

———. *Discipline and Punish: The Birth of the Prison*. Translated by Alan Sheridan. New York: Vintage Books, 1979.

———. *The Order of Things: An Archaeology of the Human Sciences*. New York: Pantheon, 1970.

———. *Power/Knowledge: Selected Interviews and Other Writings 1927–1977*. Translated by Colin Gordon et al. Edited by Colin Gordon. New York: Pantheon, 1980.

Fraser, Nancy. *Unruly Pratices: Power, Discourse, and Gender in Contemporary Social Theory*. Minneapolis: University of Minnesota Press, 1989.

Gaines, Robert. "Doing by Saying: Toward a Theory of Perlocution." *Quarterly Journal of Speech* 65 (1979): 207–217.

Ganz, Joan. *Rules: A Systematic Study*. Paris: Mouton, 1971.

Garfinkel, Harold. *Studies in Ethnomethodology*. Englewood Cliffs, N.J.: Prentice-Hall, 1967.

Giddens, Anthony. *Central Problems in Social Theory: Action, Structure, and Contradiction in Social Analysis*. Berkeley: University of California Press, 1979.

Goodwin, Charles. "Turn Construction and Conversational Organization." In *Rethinking Communication: Paradigm Exemplars*, vol. 2. Edited by Brenda Dervin, Lawrence Grossberg, Barbara O'Keefe, and Ellen Wartella. Newbury Park, Calif.: Sage, 1989, pp. 88–102.

Grice, H. Paul. "Logic and Conversation." In *Syntax and Semantics*, vol. 3. Edited by P. Cole and J. Morgan. New York: Academic Press, 1975, pp. 41–58.

Hopper, Robert; Koch, Susan; and Mandelbaum, Jennifer. "Conversation Analysis Methods." In *Contemporary Issues in Language and Discourse Processes*. Edited by Donald G. Ellis and William A. Donohue. Hillsdale, N.J.: Erlbaum, 1986, pp. 169–186.

Jackson, Sally, and Jacobs, Scott. "Characterizing Ordinary Argument: Substantive and Methodological Issues." *Journal of the American Forensic Association* 22 (1986): 42–57.

———. "The Collaborative Production of Proposals in Conversational Argument and Persuasion: A Study of Disagreement Regulation." *Journal of the American Forensic Association* 18 (1981): 77–90.

———. "Conversational Relevance: Three Experiments on Pragmatic Connectedness in Conversation." In *Communication Yearbook 10*. Edited by Margaret L. McLaughlin. Newbury Park, Calif.: Sage, 1987, pp. 323–347.

———. "Structure of Conversational Argument: Pragmatic Bases for the Enthymeme." *Quarterly Journal of Speech* 66 (1980): 251–265.

Jacobs, Scott. "Language." In *Handbook of Interpersonal Communication*. Edited by Mark L. Knapp and Gerald R. Miller. Beverly Hills, Calif.: Sage, 1985, pp. 330–335.

———. "Recent Advances in Discourse Analysis." *Quarterly Journal of Speech* 66 (1980): 450–472.

Jacobs, Scott, and Jackson, Sally. "Argument as a Natural Category: The Routine Grounds for Arguing in Conversation." *Western Journal of Speech Communication* 45 (1981): 118–132.

———. "Building a Model of Conversational Argument." In *Rethinking Communication: Paradigm Exemplars*, vol 2. Edited by Brenda Dervin, Lawrence Grossberg, Barbara O'Keefe, and Ellen Wartella. Newbury Park, Calif.: Sage, 1989, pp. 153–171.

———. "Speech Act Structure in Conversation: Rational Aspects of Pragmatic Coherence." In *Conversational Coher-*

ence: Form, Structure, and Strategy. Edited by Robert T. Craig and Karen Tracy. Beverly Hills, Calif.: Sage, 1983, pp. 47–66.

———. "Strategy and Structure in Conversational Influence Attempts." *Communication Monographs* 50 (1983): 285–304.

Janik, Allan, and Toulmin, Stephen. *Wittgenstein's Vienna*. New York: Simon & Schuster, 1973.

Kellermann, Kathy, and Sleight, Carra. "Coherence: A Meaningful Adhesive for Discourse." In *Communication Yearbook 12*. Edited by James A. Anderson. Newbury Park, Calif.: Sage, 1989, pp. 95–129.

Lacan, Jacques. *The Four Fundamental Concepts of Psycho-Analysis*. Translated by Alan Sheridan. New York: Norton, 1981.

Littlejohn, Stephen W. *Theories of Human Communication*, 3rd ed. Belmont, Calif: Wadsworth, 1989.

Lyne, John. "Speech Acts in a Semiotic Frame." *Communication Quarterly* 29 (1981): 202–208.

Mandelbaum, Jenny. "Interpersonal Activities in Conversational Storytelling." *Western Journal of Speech Communication* 53 (1989): 114–126.

McLaughlin, Margaret L. *Conversation: How Talk Is Organized*. Beverly Hills, Calif.: Sage, 1984.

Mura, Susan Swan. "Licensing Violations: Legitimate Violations of Grice's Conversational Principle." In *Conversational Coherence: Form, Structure, and Strategy*. Edited by Robert T. Craig and Karen Tracy. Beverly Hills, Calif.: Sage, 1983, pp. 101–115.

Nofsinger, Robert. *Everyday Conversation*. Newbury Park, Calif.: Sage, 1991.

O'Keefe, Daniel J. "Two Concepts of Argument." *Journal of the American Forensic Association* 13 (1977): 121–128.

Pearce, W. Barnett. "Rules Theories of Communication: Varieties, Limitations, and Potentials." Paper presented at the meeting of the Speech Communication Association, New York, 1980.

Potter, Jonathan, and Wetherall, Margaret. *Discourse and Social Psychology: Beyond Attitudes and Behavior*. London: Sage, 1987.

Sacks, Harvey; Schegloff, Emanuel; and Jefferson, Gail. "A Simplest Systematics for the Organization of Turn Taking for Conversation." *Language* 50 (1974): 696–735.

Searle, John. "Human Communication Theory and the Philosophy of Language: Some Remarks." In *Human Communication Theory*. Edited by Frank E. X. Dance. New York: Holt, Rinehart & Winston, 1967, pp. 116–129.

———. *Speech Acts: An Essay in the Philosophy of Language*. Cambridge, Eng.: Cambridge University Press, 1969.

Shimanoff, Susan B. *Communication Rules: Theory and Research*. Beverly Hills, Calif.: Sage, 1980.

Sigman, Stuart J. "On Communication Rules from a Social Perspective." *Human Communication Research* 7 (1980): 37–51.

———. *A Perspective on Social Communication*. Lexington, Mass.: Lexington Books, 1987.

Silverman, David, and Torode, Brian. *The Material Word: Some Theories of Language and Its Limits*. London: Routledge & Kegan Paul, 1980.

Stewart, John. "Concepts of Language and Meaning: A Comparative Study." *Quarterly Journal of Speech* 58 (1972): 123–133.

Trapp, Robert. "The Role of Disagreement in Interactional Argument." *Journal of the American Forensic Association* 23 (1986): 23–41.

van Dijk, Teun A. *Macrostructures: An Interdisciplinary Study of Global Structures in Discourse, Interaction, and Cognition*. Hillsdale, N.J.: Erlbaum, 1980.

———. *News as Discourse*. Hillsdale, N.J.: Erlbaum, 1988.

———. *Studies in the Pragmatics of Discourse*. The Hague: Mouton, 1981.

Wittgenstein, Ludwig. *Philosophical Investigations*. Oxford, Eng.: Basil Blackwell, 1953.

———. *Tractus Logico-Philosophicus*. London: Routledge & Kegan Paul, 1922.

Young, Robert, ed. "Post-structuralism: An Introduction." In *Untying the Text: A Post-structuralist Reader*. Boston: Routledge & Kegan Paul, 1981, pp. 1–28.

Zimmerman, Don H. "On Conversation: The Conversation Analytic Perspective." In *Communication Yearbook 11*. Edited by James A. Anderson. Newbury Park, Calif.: Sage, 1988, pp. 406–432.

Chapter Six
Theories of Message Production

Andersen, Peter A. "The Trait Debate: A Critical Examination of the Individual Differences Paradigm in the Communication Sciences." In *Progress in Communication Sciences*. Edited by B. Dervin and M. J. Voigt. Norwood, N.J.: Ablex, 1986.

Applegate, James L. "The Impact of Construct System Development on Communication and Impression Formation in Persuasive Messages." *Communication Monographs* 49 (1982): 277–289.

Applegate, James L., and Sypher, Howard E. "A Constructivist Theory of Communication and Culture." In *Theories in Intercultural Communication*. Edited by Young Y. Kim and William B. Gudykunst. Newbury Park, Calif.: Sage, 1988, pp. 41–65.

Bellah, Robert N., et al. *Habits of the Heart*. Berkeley: University of California Press, 1985.

Burleson, Brant R. "The Constructivist Approach to Person-Centered Communication: Analysis of a Research Exemplar." In *Rethinking Communication: Paradigm Exemplars*. Edited by Brenda Dervin, Lawrence Grossberg, Barbara O'Keefe, and Ellen Wartella. Newbury Park, Calif.: Sage, 1989, pp. 29–46.

Cody, Michael J., and McLaughlin, Margaret L. "The Situation as a Construct in Interpersonal Communication Research." In *Handbook of Interpersonal Communication*. Edited by Mark L. Knapp and Gerald R. Miller. Beverly Hills, Calif.: Sage, 1985, pp. 263–312.

Cody, Michael J., et al. "Situation Perception and Message Strategy Selection." In *Communication Yearbook 9*. Edited by Margaret L. McLaughlin. Beverly Hills, Calif.: Sage, 1986, pp. 390–422.

Crockett, Walter H. "Cognitive Complexity and Impression Formation." In *Progress in Experimental Personality Research*, vol. 2. Edited by Brendon A. Maher. New York: Academic Press, 1965, vol. 2, pp. 47–90.

Darnell, Donald, and Brockriede, Wayne. *Persons Communicating*. Englewood Cliffs, N.J.: Prentice-Hall, 1976.

Delia, Jesse G. "Interpersonal Cognition, Message Goals, and Organization of Communication: Recent Constructivist Research." In *Communication Theory: Eastern and Western Perspectives*. Edited by D. Lawrence Kincaid. San Diego: Academic Press, 1987, pp. 255–274.

Delia, Jesse G.; Kline, Susan L; and Burleson, Brant R. "The Development of Persuasive Communication Strategies in Kindergarteners Through Twelfth-Graders." *Communication Monographs* 46 (1979): 241–256.

Delia, Jesse G.; O'Keefe, Barbara J.; and O'Keefe, Daniel J. "The Constructivist Approach to Communication." In *Human Communication Theory: Comparative Essays*. Edited by Frank E. X. Dance. New York: Harper & Row, 1982, pp. 147–191.

Friedrich, Gustav, and Goss, Blaine. "Systematic Desensitization." In *Avoiding Communication: Shyness, Reticence, and Communication Apprehension*. Edited by John A. Daly and James C. McCroskey. Beverly Hills, Calif.: Sage, 1984, pp. 173–188.

Garko, Michael G. "Perspectives on and Conceptualizations of Compliance and Compliance-Gaining." *Communication Quarterly* 38 (1990): 138–157.

Giles, Howard; Mulac, Anthony; Bradac, James J.; and Johnson, Patricia. "Speech Accommodation Theory: The First Decade and Beyond." In *Communication Yearbook 10*. Edited by Margaret L. McLaughlin. Newbury Park, Calif.: Sage, 1987, pp. 13–48.

Greene, John O. "Action-Assembly Theory: Metatheoretical Commitments, Theoretical Propositions, and Empirical Applications." In *Rethinking Communication: Paradigm Exemplars*. Edited by Brenda Dervin, Lawrence Grossberg, Barbara O'Keefe, and Ellen Wartella. Newbury Park, Calif.: Sage, 1989, pp. 117–128.

———. "A Cognitive Approach to Human Communication: An Action Assembly Theory." *Communication Monographs* 51 (1984): 289–306.

———. "Evaluating Cognitive Explanations of Communication Phenomena." *Quarterly Journal of Speech* 70 (1984): 241–254.

Greene, John O., and Sparks, Glenn G. "Explication and Test of a Cognitive Model of Communication Apprehension: A New Look at an Old Construct." *Human Communication Research* 9 (1983): 349–366.

Hale, Claudia. "Cognitive Complexity-Simplicity as a Determinant of Communication Effectiveness." *Communication Monographs* 47 (1980):304–311.

Harré, Rom. "Language Games and Texts of Identity." In *Texts of Identity*. Edited by John Shotter and Kenneth J. Gergen. London: Sage, 1989, pp. 20–35.

Hart, Roderick P. and Burks, Don M. "Rhetorical Sensitivity and Social Interaction." *Speech Monographs* 39 (1972): 75–91.

Hart, Roderick P.; Carlson, Robert E.; and Eadie, William F. "Attitudes Toward Communication and the Assessment of Rhetorical Sensitivity." *Communication Monographs* 47 (1980): 1–22.

Hewes, Dean E., and Planalp, Sally. "The Individual's Place in Communication Science." In *Handbook of Communication Science*. Edited by Charles R. Berger and Steven H. Chaffee. Newbury Park, Calif.: Sage, 1987, pp. 146–183.

Hull, C. L. *Principles of Behavior: An Introduction to Behavior Theory*. New York: Appleton, 1943.

Infante, Dominic A. "Aggressiveness." In *Personality and Interpersonal Communication*. Edited by James C. McCroskey and John A. Daly. Newbury Park, Calif.: Sage, 1987, pp. 305–316.

———. *Arguing Constructively*. Prospect Heights, Ill.: Waveland Press, 1988.

Infante, Dominic A.; Chandler, Teresa A.; and Rudd, Jill E. "Test of an Argumentative Skill Deficiency Model of Interspousal Violence." *Communication Monographs* 56 (1989): 163–177.

Infante, Dominic A., and Rancer, Andrew S. "A Conceptualization and Measure of Argumentativeness." *Journal of Personality Assessment* 46 (1982): 72–80.

Infante, Dominic A.; Rancer, Andrew S.; and Womack, Deanna F. *Building Communication Theory*. Prospect Heights, Ill.: Waveland Press, 1990.

Infante, Dominic A.; Trebing, J. David; Shepherd, Patricia E.; and Seeds, Dale E. "The Relationship of Argumentativeness to Verbal Aggression." *Southern Speech Communication Journal* 50 (1984): 67–77.

Infante, Dominic A., and Wigley, Charles J. "Verbal Aggressiveness: An Interpersonal Model and Measure." *Communication Monographs* 53 (1986): 61–69.

Kelly, George. *The Psychology of Personal Constructs*. New York: North, 1955.

Kline, Susan L., and Ceropski, Janet M. "Person-Centered Communication in Medical Practice." In *Emergent Issues in Human Decision Making*. Edited by Gerald M. Phillips and Julia T. Wood. Carbondale: Southern Illinois University Press, 1984, pp. 120–141.

Kling, J. W. "Learning: Introductory Survey." In *Woodward and Schlosberg's Experimental Psychology*. Edited by J. W. Kling and Lorrin Riggs. New York: Holt, Rinehart & Winston, 1971, pp. 551–613.

MacIntyre, Alistair. *After Virtue*. Notre Dame, Ind.: University of Notre Dame Press, 1984.

Marwell, Gerald, and Schmitt, David R. "Dimensions of Compliance-Gaining Strategies: A Dimensional Analysis." *Sociometry* 30 (1967): 350–364.

Matson, Floyd W. *The Idea of Man*. New York: Delacorte Press, 1976.

McCroskey, James C. "Classroom Consequences of Communication Apprehension." *Communication Education* 26 (1977): 27–33.

———. "The Communication Apprehension Perspective." In *Avoiding Communication: Shyness, Reticence, and Communication Apprehension*. Edited by John A. Daly and James C. McCroskey. Beverly Hills, Calif.: Sage, 1984, pp. 13–38.

———. "The Implementation of a Large-Scale Program of Systematic Desensitization for Communication Apprehension." *Speech Teacher* 21 (1971): 255–264.

McCroskey, James C.; Ralph, David C.; and Barrick, James E. "The Effect of Systematic Desensitization on Speech Anxiety." *Speech Teacher* 19 (1970): 32–36.

Miller, Gerald R. "Persuasion." In *Handbook of Communication Science*. Edited by Charles R. Berger and Steven H. Chaffee. Newbury Park, Calif.: Sage, 1987, pp. 446–483.

———. "Some (Moderately) Apprehensive Thoughts on Avoiding Communication." In *Avoiding Communication: Shyness, Reticence, and Communication Apprehension*. Edited by John A. Daly and James C. McCroskey. Beverly Hills, Calif.: Sage, 1984, pp. 237–246.

Norton, Robert. *Communicator Style: Theory, Applications, and Measures*. Beverly Hills, Calif., Sage, 1983.

O'Keefe, Barbara J. "The Logic of Message Design: Individual Differences in Reasoning About Communication." *Communication Monographs* 55 (1988): 80–103.

O'Keefe, Barbara J., and Shepherd, Gregory J. "The Pursuit of Multiple Objectives in Face-to-Face Persuasive Interactions: Effects of Construct Differentiation on Message Organization." *Communication Monographs* 54 (1987): 396–419.

O'Keefe, Daniel J. *Persuasion: Theory and Research.* Newbury Park, Calif.: Sage, 1990.

Planalp, Sally, and Hewes, Dean E. "A Cognitive Approach to Communication Theory: *Cogito Ergo Dico?*" In *Communication Yearbook 5.* Edited by Michael Burgoon. New Brunswick, N.J.: Transaction Books, 1982, pp. 49–78.

Schenck-Hamlin, William J.; Wiseman, Richard L.; and Georgacarakos, G. N. "A Model of Properties of Compliance-Gaining Strategies." *Communication Quarterly* 30 (1982): 92–100.

Schroder, Harold M.; Driver, Michael S.; and Streufert, Siegfreid. *Human Information Processing: Individuals and Groups Functioning in Complex Social Situations.* New York: Holt, Rinehart & Winston, 1967.

Siebold, David R.; Cantrill, James G.; and Meyers, Renee A. "Communication and Interpersonal Influence." In *Handbook of Interpersonal Communication.* Edited by Mark L. Knapp and Gerald R. Miller. Beverly Hills, Calif.: Sage, 1985, pp. 551–614.

Skinner, B. F. *Cumulative Record: A Selection of Papers,* 3rd ed. New York: Appleton-Century-Crofts, 1972.

———. *Verbal Behavior.* New York: Appleton-Century-Crofts, 1957.

Smith, Mary John. *Persuasion and Human Action.* Belmont, Calif.: Wadsworth, 1982.

Ward, Steven A.; Bluman, Dale L.; and Dauria, Arthur. "Rhetorical Sensitivity Recast: Theoretical Assumptions of an Informal Interpersonal Rhetoric." *Communication Quarterly* 30 (1982): 189–195.

Watson, J. B. *Psychology from the Standpoint of the Behaviorist.* Philadelphia: Lippincott, 1919.

Werner, H. "The Concept of Development from a Comparative and Organismic Point of View." In *The Concept of Development.* Edited by D. B. Harris. Minneapolis: University of Minnesota Press, 1957.

Wheeless, Lawrence R.; Barraclough, Robert; and Stewart, Robert. "Compliance-Gaining and Power in Persuasion." In *Communication Yearbook 7.* Edited by Robert N. Bostrom. Beverly Hills, Calif.: Sage, 1983, pp. 105–145.

Wiseman, Richard L., and Schenck-Hamlin, William. "A Multidimensional Scaling Validation of an Inductively-Derived Set of Compliance-Gaining Strategies." *Communication Monographs* 48 (1981): 251–270.

Chapter Seven
Theories of Message Reception and Processing

Ajzen, Icek, and Fishbein, Martin. *Understanding Attitudes and Predicting Social Behavior.* Englewood Cliffs, N.J.: Prentice-Hall, 1980.

Andersen, P. A. "Nonverbal Immediacy in Interpersonal Communication." In *Multichannel Integrations of Nonverbal Behavior.* Edited by A. W. Siegman and S. Feldstein. Hillsdale, N.J.: Erlbaum, 1985, pp. 1–36.

Anderson, Norman H. "Integration Theory and Attitude Change." *Psychological Review* 78 (1971): 171–206.

Aronson, Elliot. *The Social Animal.* New York: Viking Press, 1972.

Brehm, J. W., and Cohen, A. R. *Explorations in Cognitive Dissonance.* New York: Wiley, 1962.

Brown, Roger. *Social Psychology.* New York: Free Press, 1965.

Burgoon, Judee K. "Communication Effects of Gaze Behavior: A Test of Two Contrasting Explanations." *Human Communication Research* 12 (1986): 495–524.

Burgoon, Judee K., and Hale, Jerold L. "Nonverbal Expectancy Violations: Model Elaboration and Application." *Communication Monographs* 55 (1988): 58–79.

Burhans, David T. "The Attitude-Behavior Discrepancy Problem: Revisited." *Quarterly Journal of Speech* 57 (1971): 418–428.

Burleson, Brant R. "Attribution Schemes and Causal Inference in Natural Conversations." In *Contemporary Issues in Language and Discourse Processes.* Edited by Donald G. Ellis and William A. Donohue. Hillsdale, N.J.: Erlbaum, 1986, pp. 63–86.

Cappella, Joseph N., and Greene, John O. "A Discrepancy-Arousal Explanation of Mutual Influence in Expressive Behavior for Adult-Adult and Infant-Adult Interaction." *Communication Monographs* 49 (1982): 89–114.

Chapanis, Natalia P., and Chapanis, Alphonse. "Cognitive Dissonance: Five Years Later." *Psychological Bulletin* 61 (1964): 21.

Doelger, Joel A.; Hewes, Dean E.; and Graham, Maudie L. "Knowing When to 'Second Guess': The Mindful Analysis of Messages." *Human Communication Research* 12 (1986): 301–338.

Donnelly, J. H., and Ivancevich, J. M. "Post-purchase Reinforcement and Back-Out Behavior." *Journal of Marketing Research* 7 (1970): 399–400.

Festinger, Leon. *A Theory of Cognitive Dissonance.* Stanford, Calif.: Stanford University Press, 1957.

Festinger, Leon, and Carlsmith, James M. "Cognitive Consequences of Forced Compliance." *Journal of Abnormal and Social Psychology* 58 (1959): 203–210.

Fishbein, Martin, ed. "A Behavior Theory Approach to the Relations Between Beliefs About an Object and the Attitude Toward the Object." In *Readings in Attitude Theory and Measurement.* New York: Wiley, 1967, pp. 389–400.

———, ed. "A Consideration of Beliefs, and Their Role in Attitude Measurement." In *Readings in Attitude Theory and Measurement.* New York: Wiley, 1967, pp. 257–266.

———, ed. *Readings in Attitude Theory and Measurement.* New York: Wiley, 1967.

Fishbein, Martin, and Ajzen, Icek. *Belief, Attitude, Intention, and Behavior.* Reading, Mass.: Addison-Wesley, 1975.

Fishbein, Martin, and Raven, Bertram, H. "The AB Scales: An Operational Definition of Belief and Attitude." In *Readings in Attitude Theory and Measurement.* Edited by Martin Fishbein. New York: Wiley, 1967, pp. 183–189.

Hample, Dale. "Argument: Public, Private, Social, and Cognitive." *Argumentation and Advocacy* 25 (1988): 13–19.

———. "The Cognitive Context of Argument." *Western Journal of Speech Communication* 45 (1981): 148–158.

———. "A Cognitive View of Argument." *Journal of the American Forensic Association* 16 (1980): 151–158.

———. "A Third Perspective on Argument." *Philosophy and Rhetoric* 18 (1985): 1–22.

Heider, Fritz. *The Psychology of Interpersonal Relations.* New York: Wiley, 1958.

Hewes, Dean E., and Graham, Maudie L. "Second-Guessing Theory: Review and Extension." In *Communication Yearbook 12.* Edited by James A. Anderson. Newbury Park, Calif.: Sage, 1989, pp. 213–248.

Hewes, Dean E.; Graham, Maudie L.; Monsour, Michael; and Doelger, Joel A. "Cognition and Social Information-Gathering Strategies: Reinterpretation Assessment in Second-Guessing." *Human Communication Research* 16 (1989): 297–321.

Hewes, Dean E., and Planalp, Sally. "The Individual's Place in Communication Science." In *Handbook of Communication Science.* Edited by Charles R. Berger and Steven H. Chaffee. Newbury Park, Calif.: Sage, 1987, pp. 146–183.

Hovland, Carl I.; Harvey, O. J.; and Sherif, Muzafer. "Assimilation and Contrast Effects in Reactions to Communication and Attitude Change." *Journal of Abnormal and Social Psychology* 55 (1957): 244–252.

Jones, Edward E., et al., eds. *Attribution: Perceiving the Causes of Behavior.* Morristown, N.J.: General Learning Press, 1972.

Kelley, Harold H. *Attribution in Social Interaction.* Morristown, N.J.: General Learning Press, 1971.

———. "Attribution in Social Interaction." In *Attribution: Perceiving the Causes of Behavior.* Edited by Edward E. Jones et al. Morristown, N.J.: General Learning Press, 1972, pp. 1–26.

———. "Attribution Theory in Social Psychology." In *Nebraska Symposium on Motivation*, vol 15. Edited by David Levine. Lincoln: University of Nebraska Press, 1967, pp. 192–240.

———. *Causal Schemata and the Attribution Process.* Morristown, N.J.: General Learning Press, 1972.

———. "Causal Schemata and the Attribution Process." In *Attribution: Perceiving the Causes of Behavior.* Morristown, N.J.: General Learning Press, 1972, pp. 151–174.

———. "The Process of Causal Attribution." *American Psychologist* 28 (1973): 107–128.

Kiesler, Charles A.; Collins, Barry E.; and Miller, Norman. *Attitude Change: A Critical Analysis of Theoretical Approaches.* New York: Wiley, 1969.

McGuire, William J. "A Syllogistic Analysis of Cognitive Relationships." In *Attitude Organization and Change.* Edited by M. J. Rosenberg et al. New Haven, Conn.: Yale University Press, 1960, pp. 65–111.

O'Keefe, Daniel J. *Persuasion: Theory and Research.* Newbury Park, Calif.: Sage, 1990.

———. "Two Concepts of Argument." *Journal of the American Forensic Association* 13 (1977): 121–128.

Osgood, Charles. *Cross Cultural Universals of Affective Meaning.* Urbana: University of Illinois Press, 1975.

———. "The Nature and Measurement of Meaning." In *The Semantic Differential Technique.* Edited by James Snider and Charles Osgood. Chicago: Aldine, 1969, pp. 9–10.

———. "On Understanding and Creating Sentences." *American Psychologist* 18 (1963): 735–751.

———. "Semantic Differential Technique in the Comparative Study of Cultures." In *The Semantic Differential Technique.* Edited by James Snider and Charles Osgood. Chicago: Aldine, 1969, pp. 303–334.

Osgood, Charles, and Richards, Meredith. "From Yang and Yin to *and* or *but.*" *Language* 49 (1973): 380–412.

Patterson, M. L. *Nonverbal Behavior: A Functional Perspective.* New York: Springer-Verlag, 1983.

Petty, Richard E., and Cacioppo, John T. *Communication and Persuasion: Central and Peripheral Routes to Attitude Change.* New York: Springer-Verlag, 1986.

Petty, Richard E.; Cacioppo, John T.; and Goldman, R. "Personal Involvement as a Determinant of Argument-Based Persuasion." *Journal of Personality and Social Psychology* 41 (1981): 847–855.

Planalp, Sally, and Hewes, Dean E. "A Cognitive Approach to Communication Theory: *Cogito Ergo Dico?*" In *Communication Yearbook 5.* Edited by Michael Burgoon. New Brunswick, N.J.: Transaction Books, 1982, pp. 49–78.

Rokeach, Milton. *Beliefs, Attitudes, and Values: A Theory of Organization and Change.* San Francisco: Jossey-Bass, 1969.

———. *The Nature of Human Values.* New York: Free Press, 1973.

Seibold, David R., and Spitzberg, Brian H. "Attribution Theory and Research: Formalization, Review, and Implications for Communication." In *Progress in Communication Sciences*, vol. 3. Edited by B. Dervin and M. J. Voigt. Norwood, N.J.: Ablex, 1981, pp. 85–125.

Sherif, Muzafer. *Social Interaction—Process and Products.* Chicago: Aldine, 1967.

Sherif, Muzafer, and Hovland, Carl I. *Social Judgment.* New Haven, Conn.: Yale University Press, 1961.

Sherif, Muzafer; Sherif, Carolyn; and Nebergall, Roger. *Attitude and Attitude Change: The Social Judgment-Involvement Approach.* Philadelphia: Saunders, 1965.

Sillars, Alan L. "Attribution and Communication." In *Social Cognition and Communication.* Edited by Michael E. Roloff and Charles R. Berger. Beverly Hills, Calif.: Sage, 1982, pp. 73–106.

———. "Attributions and Communication in Roommate Conflicts." *Communication Monographs* 47 (1980): 180–200.

———. "The Sequential and Distributional Structure of Conflict Interaction as a Function of Attributions Concerning the Locus of Responsibility and Stability of Conflict." In *Communication Yearbook 4.* Edited by Dan Nimmo. New Brunswick, N.J.: Transaction Books, 1980, pp. 217–236.

Smith, Mary John. *Persuasion and Human Action: A Review and Critique of Social Influence Theories.* Belmont, Calif.: Wadsworth, 1982.

Snider, James, and Osgood, Charles, eds. *The Semantic Differential Technique.* Chicago: Aldine, 1969.

Sperber, Dan, and Wilson, Deirdre. *Relevance: Communication and Cognition.* Cambridge, Mass.: Harvard University Press, 1986.

Wyer, Robert S. *Cognitive Organization and Change.* Hillsdale, N.J.: Erlbaum, 1974.

Wyer, Robert S., and Goldberg, Lee. "A Probabilistic Analysis of the Relationship Between Beliefs and Attitudes." *Psychological Review* 77 (1970): 100–120.

Zajonc, Robert. "The Concepts of Balance, Congruity, and Dissonance." *Public Opinion Quarterly* 24 (1960): 280–296.

Chapter Eight
Theories of Symbolic Interaction, Dramatism, and Narrative

Bales, Robert F. *Personality and Interpersonal Behavior.* New York: Holt, Rinehart & Winston, 1970.

Becker, Howard. "Becoming A Marihuana User." *American Journal of Sociology* 59 (1953): 235–242.

Blumer, Herbert. *Symbolic Interactionism: Perspective and Method.* Englewood Cliffs, N.J.: Prentice-Hall, 1969.

Bormann, Ernest G. *Communication Theory.* New York: Holt, Rinehart & Winston, 1980.

———. "Fantasy and Rhetorical Vision: The Rhetorical Criticism of Social Reality." *Quarterly Journal of Speech* 58 (1972): 396–407.

———. "Fantasy and Rhetorical Vision: Ten Years Later." *Quarterly Journal of Speech* 68 (1982): 288–305.

———. *The Force of Fantasy: Restoring the American Dream.* Carbondale: Southern Illinois University Press, 1985.

Burke, Kenneth. *Attitudes Toward History.* New York: New Republic, 1937.

———. *Counter-Statement.* New York: Harcourt, Brace, 1931.

———. *A Grammar of Motives.* Englewood Cliffs, N.J.: Prentice-Hall, 1945.

———. *Language as Symbolic Action.* Berkeley and Los Angeles: University of California Press, 1966.

———. *Permanence and Change.* New York: New Republic, 1935.

———. *The Philosophy of Literary Form.* Baton Rouge: Louisiana State University Press, 1941.

———. *A Rhetoric of Motives.* Englewood Cliffs, N.J.: Prentice-Hall, 1950.

———. *A Rhetoric of Religion.* Boston: Beacon Press, 1961.

Collins, Randall. "Erving Goffman and the Development of Modern Social Theory." In *The View from Goffman.* Edited by Jason Ditton. New York: St. Martin's Press, 1980, pp. 170–209.

Coste, Didier. *Narrative as Communication.* Minneapolis: University of Minnesota Press, 1989.

Couch, Carl. "Studying Social Processes." Videotaped presentation, University of Iowa Media Center, Iowa City, 1984.

———. "Symbolic Interaction and Generic Sociological Principles." Paper presented at the Symposium on Symbolic Interaction, Boston, 1979.

Couch, Carl J., and Hintz, Robert, eds. *Constructing Social Life.* Champaign Ill.: Stipes, 1975.

Cragan, John F., and Shields, Donald C. *Applied Communication Research: A Dramatistic Approach.* Prospect Heights, Ill.: Waveland Press, 1981.

Delia, Jesse G. "Communication Research: A History." In *Handbook of Communication Science.* Edited by Charles R. Berger and Steven H. Chaffee. Newbury Park, Calif.: Sage, 1987, pp. 30–37.

Duncan, Hugh D. "Communication in Society." *Arts in Society* 3 (1964): 105.

Fisher, Walter R. "Clarifying the Narrative Paradigm." *Communication Monographs* 56 (1989): 55–58.

———. *Human Communication as Narration: Toward a Philosophy of Reason, Value, and Action.* Columbia: University of South Carolina Press, 1987.

Foss, Karen A., and Littlejohn, Stephen W. "*The Day After*: Rhetorical Vision in an Ironic Frame." *Critical Studies in Mass Communication* 3 (1986): 317–336.

Foss, Sonja K.; Foss, Karen A.; and Trapp, Robert. *Contemporary Perspectives on Rhetoric.* Prospect Heights, Ill.: Waveland Press, 1991.

Goffman, Erving. *Behavior in Public Places.* New York: Free Press, 1963.

———. *Encounters: Two Studies in the Sociology of Interaction.* Indianapolis: Bobbs-Merrill, 1961.

———. *Frame Analysis: An Essay on the Organization of Experience.* Cambridge, Mass.: Harvard University Press, 1974.

———. *Interaction Ritual: Essays on Face-to-Face Behavior.* Garden City, N.Y.: Doubleday, 1967.

———. *The Presentation of Self in Everyday Life.* Garden City, N.Y.: Doubleday, 1959.

———. *Relations in Public.* New York: Basic Books, 1971.

Gronbeck, Bruce E. "Dramaturgical Theory and Criticism: The State of the Art (or Science?)." *Western Journal of Speech Communication* 44 (1980): 315–330.

Hall, Peter M. "Structuring Symbolic Interaction: Communication and Power." In *Communication Yearbook 4.* Edited by Dan Nimmo. New Brunswick, N.J.: Transaction Books, 1980, pp. 49–60.

Hickman, C. A., and Kuhn, Manford. *Individuals, Groups, and Economic Behavior.* New York: Holt, Rinehart & Winston, 1956.

Johnson, C. David, and Picou, J. Stephen. "The Foundations of Symbolic Interactionism Reconsidered." In *Micro-Sociological Theory: Perspectives on Sociological Theory,* vol. 2. Edited by H. J. Helle and S. N. Eisenstadt. Beverly Hills, Calif.: Sage, 1985, pp. 54–70.

Kamler, Howard. *Communication: Sharing Our Stories of Experience.* Seattle: Psychological Press, 1983.

Kuhn, Manford H. "Major Trends in Symbolic Interaction Theory in the Past Twenty-Five Years." *Sociological Quarterly* 5 (1964): 61–84.

Kuhn, Manford H., and McPartland, Thomas S. "An Empirical Investigation of Self-Attitudes." *American Sociological Review* 19 (1954): 68–76.

Ling, David A. "A Pentadic Analysis of Senator Edward Kennedy's Address to the People of Massachusetts July 25, 1969." *Central States Speech Journal* 21 (1970): 81–86.

Littlejohn, Stephen W. *Theories of Human Communication,* 2nd ed. Belmont, Calif.: Wadsworth, 1983.

Lofland, John. "Interactionist Imagery and Analytic Interruptus." In *Human Nature and Collective Behavior.* Edited by Tamotsu Shibutani. Englewood Cliffs, N.J.: Prentice-Hall, 1970, p. 37.

Manis, Jerome G., and Meltzer, Bernard N., eds. "Appraisals of Symbolic Interactionism." In *Symbolic Interaction.* Boston: Allyn and Bacon, 1978, pp. 393–440.

———, eds. *Symbolic Interaction.* Boston: Allyn and Bacon, 1978.

McPhail, Clark. "Toward a Theory of Collective Behavior." Paper presented at the Symposium on Symbolic Interaction, Columbia, South Carolina, 1978.

Mead, George H. *Mind, Self, and Society.* Chicago: University of Chicago Press, 1934.

Meltzer, Bernard N. "Mead's Social Psychology." In *Symbolic*

Interaction. Edited by Jerome G. Manis and Bernard N. Meltzer. Boston: Allyn and Bacon, 1972, pp. 4–22.

Meltzer, Bernard N., and Petras, John W. "The Chicago and Iowa Schools of Symbolic Interactionism." In *Human Nature and Collective Behavior*. Edited by Tamotsu Shibutani. Englewood Cliffs, N.J.: Prentice-Hall, 1970.

Meltzer, Bernard N.; Petras, John; and Reynolds, Larry. *Symbolic Interactionism: Genesis, Varieties, and Criticism*. London: Routledge & Kegan Paul, 1975.

Mitchell, W. J. T., ed. *On Narrative*. Chicago: University of Chicago Press, 1980.

Mohrmann, G. P. "An Essay on Fantasy Theme Criticism." *Quarterly Journal of Speech* 68 (1982): 109–132.

Morris, Charles. "George H. Mead as Social Psychologist and Social Philosopher." In *Mind, Self, and Society* (Introduction). Chicago: University of Chicago Press, 1934, pp. ix–xxxv.

Rueckert, William, ed. *Critical Responses to Kenneth Burke*. Minneapolis: University of Minnesota Press, 1969.

Rowland, Robert C. "On Limiting the Narrative Paradigm: Three Case Studies." *Communication Monographs* 56 (1989): 39–54.

Sigman, Stuart J. *A Perspective on Social Communication*. Lexington, Mass.: Lexington Books, 1987.

Simons, Herbert W., and Melia, Trevor, eds. *The Legacy of Kenneth Burke*. Madison: University of Wisconsin Press, 1989.

Tedeschi, J. T., and Reiss, M. "Verbal Strategies in Impression Management." In *The Psychology of Ordinary Explanations of Social Behavior*. Edited by Charles Antaki. New York: Academic Press, 1981, pp. 271–309.

Tucker, Charles W. "Some Methodological Problems of Kuhn's Self-Theory." *Sociological Quarterly* 7 (1966): 345–358.

Verhoeven, Jef. "Goffman's Frame Analysis and Modern Micro-Sociological Paradigms." In *Micro-Sociological Theory: Perspectives on Sociological Theory*, vol. 2. Edited by H. J. Helle and S. N. Eisenstadt. Beverly Hills, Calif.: Sage, 1985, pp. 71–100.

Chapter Nine
Theories of Social and Cultural Reality

Alvy, K. T. "The Development of Listener Adapted Communication in Grade-School Children from Different Social Class Backgrounds." *Genetic Psychology Monographs* 87 (1973): 33–104.

Averill, James. "The Acquisition of Emotions During Adulthood." In *The Social Construction of Emotions*. Edited by Rom Harré. New York: Basil Blackwell, 1986, pp. 98–119.

———. *Anger and Aggression: An Essay on Emotion*. New York: Springer-Verlag, 1982.

———. "A Constructivist View of Emotion." In *Theories of Emotion*. Edited by K. Plutchik and H. Kellerman. New York: Academic Press, 1980, pp. 305–339.

———. "On the Paucity of Positive Emotions." In *Assessment and Modification of Emotional Behavior*. Edited by K. R. Blankstein, P. Pliner, and J. Polivy. New York: Plenum, 1980, pp. 7–45.

Berger, Peter L., and Luckmann, Thomas. *The Social Construction of Reality: A Treatise in the Sociology of Knowledge*. New York: Doubleday, 1966.

Bernstein, Basil. *Class, Codes, and Control: Theoretical Studies Toward a Sociology of Language*. London: Routledge & Kegan Paul, 1971.

Branham, Robert J., and Pearce, W. Barnett. "Between Text and Context: Toward a Rhetoric of Contextual Reconstruction." *Quarterly Journal of Speech* 71 (1985): 19–36.

Brenders, David A. "Fallacies in the Coordinated Management of Meaning: A Philosophy of Language Critique of the Hierarchical Organization of Coherent Conversation and Related Theory." *Quarterly Journal of Speech* 73 (1987): 329–348.

Buttney, Richard. "Accounts as a Reconstruction of an Event's Context." *Communication Monographs* 52 (1985): 57–77.

———. "Sequence and Structure in Accounts Episodes." *Communication Quarterly* 35 (1987): 67–83.

Carroll, John B. "Introduction." In *Language, Thought, and Reality*. Edited by Benjamin L. Whorf. New York: Wiley, 1956, pp. 1–34.

———. "Language, Mind, and Reality." In *Language, Thought, and Reality*. Edited by Benjamin L. Whorf. New York: Wiley, 1956, pp. 246–269.

———. "The Relation of Habitual Thought and Behavior in Language." In *Language, Thought, and Reality*. Edited by Benjamin L. Whorf. New York: Wiley, 1956, pp. 134–159.

Cherwitz, Richard A., and Hikins, James W. *Communication and Knowledge: An Investigation in Rhetorical Epistemology*. Columbia: University of South Carolina Press, 1986.

Cronen, Vernon E.; Chen, Victoria; Pearce, W. Barnett. "Coordinated Management of Meaning: A Critical Theory." In *Theories in Intercultural Communication*. Edited by Young Yun Kim and William B. Gudykunst. Newbury Park, Calif.: Sage, 1988, pp. 66–98.

Cronen, Vernon E.; Johnson, Kenneth M.; and Lannamann, John W. "Paradoxes, Double Binds, and Reflexive Loops: An Alternative Theoretical Perspective." *Family Process* 20 (1982): 91–112.

Cronen, Vernon E.; Pearce, W. Barnett; and Changsheng, Xi. "The Meaning of 'Meaning' in the CMM Analysis of Communication: A Comparison of Two Traditions." *Research on Language and Social Interaction* 23 (1989–1990): 1–40.

Cronen, Vernon; Pearce, W. Barnett; and Harris, Linda. "The Logic of the Coordinated Management of Meaning." *Communication Education* 28 (1979): 22–38.

———. "The Coordinated Management of Meaning." In *Comparative Human Communication Theory*. Edited by Frank E. X. Dance. New York: Harper & Row, 1982.

Geertz, Clifford. *Local Knowledge: Further Essays in Interpretive Anthropology*. New York: Basic Books, 1983.

Gergen, Kenneth J. "The Social Constructionist Movement in Modern Psychology." *American Psychologist* 40 (1985): 266–275.

———. *Toward Transformation in Social Knowledge*. New York: Springer-Verlag, 1982.

Giddens, Anthony. *Profiles and Critiques in Social Theory*. Berkeley: University of California Press, 1982.

Harré, Rom, ed. "An Outline of the Social Constructionist Viewpoint." In *The Social Construction of Emotions*. New York: Basil Blackwell, 1986, pp. 2–14.

———. *Personal Being: A Theory for Individual Psychology*. Cambridge, Mass.: Harvard University Press, 1984.

———. *Social Being: A Theory for Social Behavior*. Totowa, N.J.: Littlefield, Adams, 1979.

Harré, Rom, and Secord, Paul. *The Explanation of Social Behavior*. Totowa, N.J.: Littlefield, Adams, 1972.

McLaughlin, Margaret L.; Cody, Michael J.; and O'Hair, H. Dan. "The Management of Failure Events: Some Contextual Determinants of Accounting Behavior." *Human Communication Research* 9 (1983): 208–224.

McLaughlin, Margaret L.; Cody, Michael J.; and Rosenstein, Nancy E. "Account Sequences in Conversations Between Strangers." *Communication Monographs* 50 (1983): 102–125.

Narula, Uma, and Pearce, W. Barnett. *Development as Communication: A Perspective on India*. Carbondale: Southern Illinois University Press, 1986.

Pearce, W. Barnett. "The Coordinated Management of Meaning: A Rules Based Theory of Interpersonal Communication." In *Explorations in Interpersonal Communication*. Edited by Gerald R. Miller. Beverly Hills, Calif.: Sage, 1976, pp. 17–36.

Pearce, W. Barnett, and Cronen, Vernon. *Communication, Action, and Meaning*. New York: Praeger, 1980.

Sankoff, Gillian. *The Social Life of Language*. Philadelphia: University of Pennsylvania Press, 1980.

Sapir, Edward. *Language: An Introduction to the Study of Speech*. New York: Harcourt, Brace & World, 1921.

Schonbach, P. A. "A Category System for Account Phases." *European Journal of Social Psychology* 10 (1980): 195–200.

Schutz, Alfred. *On Phenomenology and Social Relations*. Chicago: University of Chicago Press, 1970.

Shimanoff, Susan B. *Communication Rules: Theory and Research*. Beverly Hills, Calif.: Sage, 1980.

———. "Rules Governing the Verbal Expression of Emotions Between Married Couples." *Western Journal of Speech Communication* 49 (1985): 147–165.

Shotter, John. *Social Accountability and Selfhood*. Oxford, Eng.: Basil Blackwell, 1984.

———. "Social Accountability and the Social Construction of 'You.'" In *Texts of Identity*. Edited by John Shotter and Kenneth J. Gergen. London: Sage, 1989, pp. 133–151.

Sigman, Stuart J. *A Perspective on Social Communication*. Lexington, Mass.: Lexington Books, 1987.

Smith, Mary John. "Cognitive Schemata and Persuasive Communication: Toward a Contingency Rules Theory." In *Communication Yearbook 6*. Edited by Michael Burgoon. Beverly Hills, Calif.: Sage, 1982, pp. 330–363.

———. "Contingency Rules Theory, Context, and Compliance-Behaviors." *Human Communication Research* 10 (1984): 489–512.

Whorf, Benjamin L. *Language, Thought, and Reality*. New York: Wiley, 1956.

Chapter Ten
Theories of Experience and Interpretation

Agar, Michael. *Speaking of Ethnography*. Beverly Hills, Calif.: Sage, 1986.

Bailey, William. "Consciousness and Action/Motion Theories of Communication." *Western Journal of Speech Communication* 50 (1986): 74.

Bauman, Zygmunt. *Hermeneutics and Social Science*. New York: Columbia University Press, 1978.

Benoit, Pamela J., and Benoit, William L. "Consciousness: The Mindlessness/Mindfulness and Verbal Report of Controversies." *Western Journal of Speech Communication* 50 (1986): 41–63.

Berman, Art. *From the New Criticism to Deconstruction*. Urbana, Ill.: University of Chicago Press, 1988.

Bernstein, Richard J. *Beyond Objectivism and Relativism: Science, Hermeneutics, and Praxis*. Philadelphia: University of Pennsylvania Press, 1983.

Campbell, John Angus. "Hans-Georg Gadamer's Truth and Method." *Quarterly Journal of Speech* 64 (1978): 101–122.

Carragee, Kevin M. "Interpretive Media Study and Interpretive Social Science." *Critical Studies in Mass Communication* 7 (1990): 81–96.

Carbaugh, Donal, ed. "Culture Talking About Itself." In *Cultural Communication and Intercultural Contact*. Hillsdale, N.J.: Erlbaum, 1990, pp. 1–9.

Cheney, George, and Tompkins, Phillip K. "On the Facts of the Text as the Basis of Human Communication Research." In *Communication Yearbook 11*. Edited by James A. Anderson. Newbury Park, Calif.: Sage, 1988, pp. 455–501.

Deetz, Stanley. "Conceptualizing Human Understanding: Gadamer's Hermeneutics and American Communication Studies." *Communication Quarterly* 26 (1978): 14.

———. "Words Without Things: Toward a Social Phenomenology of Language." *Quarterly Journal of Speech* 59 (1973): 40–51.

Derrida, Jacques. *Of Grammatology*. Translated by Gayatri Spivak. Baltimore: Johns Hopkins University Press, 1974, 1976.

Dilthey, Wilhelm. "The Rise of Hermeneutics." Translated by Fredric Jameson. *New Literary History* 3 (1972): 229–244.

Fay, Brian. *Social Theory and Political Practice*. London: George Allen & Unwin, 1975.

Fish, Stanley. *Is There a Text in This Class?* Cambridge, Mass.: Harvard University Press, 1980.

Froman, Wayne. *Merleau-Ponty: Language and the Act of Speech*. Lewisburg, Pa.: Bucknell University Press, 1982.

Gadamer, Hans-Georg. *Truth and Method*. New York: Seabury Press, 1975.

———. *Wahrheit und Methode* [*Truth and Method*]. Tuebingen, Ger.: Mohr, 1960, p. 394.

Geertz, Clifford. *The Interpretation of Cultures*. New York: Basic Books, 1973.

———. *Local Knowledge: Further Essays in Interpretive Anthropology*. New York: Basic Books, 1983.

Gergen, Kenneth. *Toward Transformation in Social Knowledge*. New York: Springer-Verlag, 1982, pp. 126–133.

Giddens, Anthony. "On the Relation of Sociology to Philosophy." In *Exploring Human Behavior: Consciousness, Human Action, and Social Structure*. Edited by Paul R. Secord. Beverly Hills, Calif.: Sage, 1982, p. 180.

Giorgi, Amedeo. "Phenomenology, Psychological Science and Common Sense." In *Everyday Understanding: Social and Scientific Implications*. Edited by Gun R. Semin and Kenneth J. Gergen. London: Sage, 1990, p. 66.

Gorman, Robert A. *The Dual Vision: Alfred Schutz and the Myth of Phenomenological Social Science*. London: Routledge & Kegan Paul, 1977.

Hall, Stuart. "Encoding/Decoding." In *Culture, Media, Language*. Edited by Stuart Hall et al. London: Hutchinson, 1980, pp. 128–138.

Hamlyn, D. W. "The Concept of Social Reality." In *Explaining Human Behavior: Consciousness, Human Action, and Social Structure*. Edited by Paul F. Secord. Beverly Hills, Calif.: Sage, 1982, p. 194.

Heidegger, Martin. *Being and Time*. Translated by John Macquarrie and Edward Robinson. New York: Harper & Row, 1962.

———. *An Introduction to Metaphysics*. Translated by Ralph Manheim. New Haven, Conn.: Yale University Press, 1959.

———. *On the Way to Language*. Translated by Peter Hertz. New York: Harper & Row, 1971.

Husserl, Edmund. *Ideas: General Introduction to Pure Phenomenology*. Translated by W. R. Boyce Gibson. New York: Collier Books, 1962.

———. *Phenomenology and the Crisis of Philosophy*. Translated by Quentin Lauer. New York: Harper & Row, 1965.

Hyde, Michael J. "Transcendental Philosophy and Human Communication." In *Interpersonal Communication*. Edited by Joseph J. Pilotta. Washington, D.C.: Center for Advanced Research in Phenomenology, 1982, pp. 15–34.

Hymes, Dell. *Foundations in Sociolinguistics: An Ethnographic Approach*. Philadelphia: University of Pennsylvania Press, 1974.

Ihde, Don, ed. *The Conflict of Interpretations: Essays on Hermeneutics* [by Paul Ricoeur]. Evanston, Ill.: Northwestern University Press, 1974.

Jensen, Klaus Bruhn. "When Is Meaning? Communication Theory, Pragmatism, and Mass Media Reception." In *Communication Yearbook 14*. Edited by James A. Anderson. Newbury Park, Calif.: Sage, 1991, pp. 3–32.

Katriel, Tamar. "'Griping' as a Verbal Ritual in Some Israeli Discourse." In *Cultural Communication and Intercultural Contact*. Edited by Donal Carbaugh. Hillsdale, N.J.: Erlbaum, 1990, pp. 99–114.

Kwant, Remy C. *The Phenomenological Philosophy of Merleau-Ponty*. Pittsburgh: Duquesne University Press, 1963.

Lanigan, Richard L. "Life History Interviews: A Teaching and Research Model for Semiotic Phenomenology." In *Phenomenology of Communication: Merleau-Ponty's Thematics in Communicology and Semiology*. Pittsburgh: Duquesne University Press, 1988, pp. 144–154.

———. *Phenomenology of Communication: Merleau-Ponty's Thematics in Communicology and Semiology*. Pittsburgh: Duquesne University Press, 1988.

———. "A Treasure House of Preconstituted Types: Alfred Schutz on Communicology." In *Phenomenology of Communication: Merleau-Ponty's Thematics in Communicology and Semiology*. Pittsburgh: Duquesne University Press, 1988, pp. 203–222.

Lindlof, Thomas R. "Media Audiences as Interpretive Communities." In *Communication Yearbook 11*. Edited by James A. Anderson. Newbury Park, Calif.: Sage, 1988, pp. 81–107.

Lindlof, Thomas R., and Meyer, Timothy P. "Mediated Communication as Ways of Seeing, Acting, and Constructing Culture: The Tools and Foundations of Qualitative Research." In *Natural Audiences: Qualitative Research of Media Uses and Effects*. Edited by Thomas R. Lindlof. Norwood, N.J.: Ablex, 1987, pp. 1–32.

Lull, James. "The Social Uses of Television." *Human Communication Research* 6 (1980): 197–209.

Mallin, Samuel B. *Merleau-Ponty's Philosophy*. New Haven, Conn.: Yale University Press, 1979.

Merleau-Ponty, Maurice. *Phenomenology of Perception*. New York: Humanities Press, 1962 (original published in Paris, 1945).

———. *The Phenomenology of Perception*. Translated by Colin Smith. London: Routledge & Kegan Paul, 1974.

Morgan, Gareth. *Images of Organization*. Beverly Hills, Calif.: Sage, 1986.

Motley, Michael T. "Consciousness and Intentionality in Communication: A Preliminary Model and Methodological Approaches." *Western Journal of Speech Communication* 50 (1986): 3–23.

Nisbett, R. E., and Wilson, T. D. "Telling More Than We Can Know: Verbal Reports on Mental Processes." *Psychological Review* 84 (1977): 231–259.

Pacanowsky, Michael. "Creating and Narrating Organizational Realities." In *Rethinking Communication: Paradigm Exemplars*. Edited by Brenda Dervin, Lawrence Grossberg, Barbara O'Keefe, and Ellen Wartella. Newbury Park, Calif.: Sage, 1989, pp. 250–257.

Pacanowsky, Michael, and O'Donnell-Trujillo, Nick. "Communication and Organizational Cultures." *Western Journal of Speech Communication* 46 (1982): 121.

———. "Organizational Communication as Cultural Performance." *Communication Monographs* 50 (1983): 129–145.

Palmer, Richard E. *Hermeneutics: Interpretation Theory in Schleiermacher, Dilthey, Heidegger, and Gadamer*. Evanston, Ill: Northwestern University Press, 1969, p. 128.

Philipsen, Gerry. "An Ethnographic Approach to Communication Studies." In *Rethinking Communication: Paradigm Exemplars*. Edited by Brenda Dervin, Lawrence Grossberg, Barbara O'Keefe, and Ellen Wartella. Newbury Park, Calif.: Sage, 1989, pp. 258–269.

Ricoeur, Paul. *Hermeneutics and the Human Sciences: Essays on Language, Action and Interpretation*. Translated and edited by John B. Thompson. Cambridge, Eng.: Cambridge University Press, 1981.

———. *Interpretation Theory: Discourse and the Surplus of Meaning*. Fort Worth: Texas University Press, 1976.

Schleiermacher, Friedrich. *Hermeneutik*. Edited by Heinz Kimmerle. Heidelberg, Ger.: Carl Winter, Universitaetsverlag, 1959.

Schutz, Alfred. *The Phenomenology of the Social World*. Translated by George Walsh and Frederick Lehnert. Evanston, Ill.: Northwestern University Press, 1967 (original published in 1932).

Shotter, John. *Social Accountability and Selfhood*. New York: Basil Blackwell, 1984, pp. 167–172.

Steiner, Linda. "Oppositional Decoding as an Act of Resistance." *Critical Studies in Mass Communication* 5 (1988): 1–15.

Stewart, John. "Philosophy of Qualitative Inquiry: Hermeneutic Phenomenology and Communication Research." *Quarterly Journal of Speech* 67 (1981): 110.

Tracy, David. "Interpretation (Hermeneutics)." In *International Encyclopedia of Communications*. Edited by Erik Barnouw. New York: Oxford University Press, 1989, pp. 343–348.

Turner, Victor. *Dramas, Fields, and Metaphors*. Ithaca, N.Y.: Cornell University Press, 1974.

Warnick, Barbara. "A Ricoeurian Approach to Rhetorical Criticism." *Western Journal of Speech Communication* 51 (1987): 227–244.

Chapter Eleven
Critical Theories

Althusser, Louis. *For Marx.* Translated by B. Brewster. New York: Vintage Books, 1970.

———. *Lenin and Philosophy.* Translated by B. Brewster. New York: Monthly Review Press, 1971.

Arato, Andrew, and Gebhardt, Eike, eds. *The Essential Frankfurt School Reader.* New York: Continuum, 1982.

Ardener, Edwin. The 'Problem' Revisited." In *Perceiving Women.* Edited by Shirley Ardener. London: Malaby Press, 1975.

———. "Some Outstanding Problems in the Analysis of Events." Paper presented at the Association of Social Anthropologists' Decennial Conference, 1973.

Ardener, Shirley. *Defining Females: The Nature of Women in Society.* New York: Wiley, 1978.

Becker, Samuel L. "Marxist Approaches to Media Studies: The British Experience." *Critical Studies in Mass Communication* 1 (1984): 66–80.

Blumler, Jay. "Communication and Democracy: The Crisis Beyond and the Ferment Within." *Journal of Communication* 33 (1983): 166–173.

Bottomore, Tom, and Mattelart, Armand. "Marxist Theories of Communication." In *International Encyclopedia of Communications,* vol. 2. Edited by Erik Barnouw et al. New York: Oxford University Press, 1989, pp. 476–483.

Dervin, Brenda. "The Potential Contribution of Feminist Scholarship to the Field of Communication." *Journal of Communication* 37 (1987): 107–120.

Ealy, Steven D. *Communication, Speech, and Politics: Habermas and Political Analysis.* Washington, D.C.: University Press of America, 1981.

Elgin, Suzette. *A First Dictionary and Grammar of Láadan,* 2nd ed. Madison, Wis.: Society for the Furtherance and Study of Fantasy and Science Fiction, 1988.

———. *Native Tongue.* New York: Daw, 1984.

Fay, Brian. *Social Theory and Political Practice.* London: George Allen & Unwin, 1975.

Farrell, Thomas B., and Aune, James A. "Critical Theory and Communication: A Selective Literature Review." *Quarterly Journal of Speech* 65 (1979): 93–120.

Foss, Karen A., and Foss, Sonja K. "Incorporating the Feminist Perspective in Communication Scholarship: A Research Commentary." In *Doing Research on Women's Communication: Alternative Perspectives in Theory and Method.* Edited by Carole Spitzack and Kathryn Carter. Norwood, N.J.: Ablex, 1989, pp. 65–94.

———. *Women Speak: The Eloquence of Women's Lives.* Prospect Heights, Ill.: Waveland Press, 1991.

Foss, Sonja K. *Rhetorical Criticism: Exploration and Practice.* Prospect Heights, Ill: Waveland Press, 1989.

Foss, Sonja K.; Foss, Karen A.; and Trapp, Robert. *Contemporary Perspectives on Rhetoric.* Prospect Heights, Ill.: Waveland Press, 1991.

Fraser, Nancy. *Unruly Practices: Power, Discourse, and Gender in Contemporary Social Theory.* Minneapolis: University of Minnesota Press, 1989.

Gerbner, George, ed. "Ferment in the Field," Special issue of *Journal of Communication* 33 (Summer 1983).

Gilligan, Carol. *In a Different Voice.* Cambridge, Mass.: Harvard University Press, 1982.

Gramsci, Antonio. *Selections from the Prison Notebooks.* Translated by Q. Hoare and G. Nowell Smith. New York: International, 1971.

Grossberg, Lawrence. "Is There Rock After Punk?" *Critical Studies in Mass Communication* 3 (1986): 50–73.

———. "Strategies of Marxist Cultural Interpretation." *Critical Studies in Mass Communication* 1 (1984): 392–421.

Habermas, Jürgen. *Knowledge and Human Interests.* Translated by Jeremy J. Shapiro. Boston: Beacon Press, 1971.

———. *Legitimation Crisis.* Translated by Thomas McCarthy. Boston: Beacon Press, 1975.

———. *The Theory of Communicative Action, Volume I: Reason and the Rationalization of Society.* Translated by Thomas McCarthy. Boston: Beacon Press, 1984.

Hall, Stuart. "Cultural Studies and the Centre: Some Problematics and Problems." In *Culture, Media, Language.* Edited by Stuart Hall, Dorothy Hobson, Andrew Lowe, and Paul Willis. London: Hutchinson, 1981, pp. 15–47.

———. "Cultural Studies: Two Paradigms." In *Media, Culture and Society: A Critical Reader.* Edited by R. Collins. London: Sage, 1986.

———. "Ideology." In *International Encyclopedia of Communications,* vol 2. Edited by Erik Barnouw et al. New York: Oxford University Press, 1989, pp. 307–311.

———. "Signification, Representation, Ideology: Althusser and the Post-Structuralist Debates." *Critical Studies in Mass Communication* 2 (1985): 91–114.

Hall, Stuart; Hobson, Dorothy; Lowe, Andrew; and Willis, Paul; eds. *Culture, Media, Language.* London: Hutchinson, 1981.

Hoggart, Richard. *Uses of Literacy.* London: Chatto & Windus, 1957.

Jansen, Sue Curry. "Power and Knowledge: Toward a New Critical Synthesis." *Journal of Communication* 33 (1983): 342–354.

Johnson, Fern L. "Coming to Terms with Women's Language." *Quarterly Journal of Speech* 72 (1986): 318–352.

Kramarae, Cheris. "Feminist Theories of Communication." In *International Encyclopedia of Communications,* vol 2. Edited by Erik Barnouw et al. New York: Oxford University Press, 1989, pp. 157–160.

———. *Women and Men Speaking: Frameworks for Analysis.* Rowley, Mass.: Newbury House, 1981.

Kramarae, Cheris, and Treichler, Paula A. *A Feminist Dictionary.* Boston: Pandora Press, 1985.

Lanigan, Richard L. *Phenomenology of Communication: Merleau-Ponty's Thematics in Communicology and Semiology.* Pittsburgh: Duquesne University Press, 1988.

Lazarsfeld, Paul. "Remarks on Administrative and Critical Communications Research." *Studies in Philosophy and Social Science* 9 (1941): 2–16.

Lembo, Ronald, and Tucker, Kenneth H. "Culture, Television, and Opposition: Rethinking Cultural Studies." *Critical Studies in Mass Communication* 7 (1990): 97–116.

Lull, James. "The Audience as Nuisance." *Critical Studies in Mass Communication* 5 (1988): 239.

MacKinnon, Catharine A. "Desire and Power: A Feminist Perspective." In *Marxism and the Interpretation of Culture*. Edited by Cary Nelson and Lawrence Grossberg. Urbana: University of Illinois Press, 1988, pp. 105–122.

Marx, Karl. *Capital*. Chicago: Kerr, 1909.

———. *The Communist Manifesto*. London: Reeves, 1888.

Mumby, Dennis K. *Communication and Power in Organizations: Discourse, Ideology, and Domination*. Norwood, N.J.: Ablex, 1988.

———. "The Political Function of Narrative in Organizations." *Communication Monographs* 54 (1987): 113–127.

Nelson, Cary, and Grossberg, Lawrence, eds. *Marxism and the Interpretation of Culture*. Urbana: University of Illinois Press, 1988.

Penelope, Julia. *Speaking Freely: Unlearning the Lies of the Fathers' Tongues*. New York: Pergamon Press, 1990.

Putnam, Linda L. "In Search of Gender: A Critique of Communication and Sex-Roles Research." *Women's Studies in Communication* 5 (1982): 1–9.

Pryor, Robert. "On the Method of Critical Theory and Its Implications for a Critical Theory of Communication." In *Phenomenology in Rhetoric and Communication*. Edited by Stanley Deetz. Washington, D.C.: Center for Advanced Research in Phenomenology/University Press of America, 1981, pp. 25–35.

Real, Michael. "The Debate on Critical Theory and the Study of Communications." *Journal of Communication* 34 (Autumn 1984): 72–80.

Ricoeur, Paul. *Hermeneutics and the Human Sciences: Essays on Language, Action and Interpretation*. Translated and edited by John B. Thompson. Cambridge, Eng.: Cambridge University Press, 1981.

Rogers, Everett M. "The Empirical and the Critical Schools of Communication Research." In *Communication Yearbook 5*. Edited by Michael Burgoon. New Brunswick, N.J.: Transaction Books, 1982, pp. 125–144.

Slack, Jennifer Daryl, and Allor, Martin. "The Political and Epistemological Constituents of Critical Communication Research." *Journal of Communication* 33 (1983): 128–218.

Smythe, Dallas W., and Dinh, Tran Van. "On Critical and Administrative Research: A New Critical Analysis." *Journal of Communication* 33 (1983): 117–127.

Spender, Dale. *Man Made Language*. London: Routledge & Kegan Paul, 1980, pp. 76–105.

White, Robert. "Mass Communication and Culture: Transition to a New Paradigm." *Journal of Communication* 33 (1983): 279–301.

Williams, Raymond. *The Long Revolution*. New York: Columbia University Press, 1961.

Wood, Julia T., and Pearce, W. Barnett. "Sexists, Racists, and Other Classes of Classifiers: Form and Function of 'ist' Accusations." *Quarterly Journal of Speech* 66 (1980): 239–250.

Chapter Twelve
Communication in Relationships

Altman, Irwin, and Taylor, Dalmas. *Social Penetration: The Development of Interpersonal Relationships*. New York: Holt, Rinehart & Winston, 1973.

Applegate, James L., and Leichty, Gregory B. "Managing Interpersonal Relationships: Social Cognitive and Strategic Determinants of Competence." In *Competence in Communication: A Multi-Disciplinary Approach*. Edited by Robert N. Bostrom. Beverly Hills, Calif.: Sage, 1984.

Baxter, Leslie A. "Accomplishing Relationship Disengagement." In *Understanding Personal Relationships: An Interdisciplinary Approach*. Edited by Steve Duck and Daniel Perlman. Beverly Hills, Calif.: Sage, 1985, pp. 243–266.

———. "A Dialectical Perspective on Communication Strategies in Relationship Development." In *Handbook of Personal Relationships*. Edited by Steve Duck. New York: Wiley, 1988, pp. 257–273.

———. "Strategies for Ending Relationships: Two Studies." *Western Journal of Speech Communication* 46 (1982): 223–241.

———. "Trajectories of Relationship Disengagement." *Journal of Social and Personal Relationships* 1 (1984): 29–48.

Beisecker, Thomas. "Game Theory in Communication Research: A Rejoinder and a Re-orientation." *Journal of Communication* 20 (1970): 107–120.

Berger, Charles R., and Bradac, James J. *Language and Social Knowledge: Uncertainty in Interpersonal Relations*. London: Arnold, 1982.

Berger, Charles R., and Calabrese, R. J. "Some Explorations in Initial Interaction and Beyond: Toward a Developmental Theory of Interpersonal Communication." *Human Communication Research* 1 (1975): 99–112.

Berger, Charles R., and Douglas, William. "Thought and Talk: 'Excuse Me, but Have I Been Talking to Myself?'" In *Human Communication Theory*. Edited by Frank E. X. Dance. New York: Harper & Row, 1982, pp. 42–60.

Berger, Charles R.; Gardner, R. R.; Parks, M. R.; Schulman, L.; and Miller, G. R. "Interpersonal Epistemology and Interpersonal Communication." In *Explorations in Interpersonal Communication*. Edited by Gerald R. Miller. Beverly Hills, Calif.: Sage, 1976, pp. 149–171.

Berger, Charles R., and Kellermann, Katherine Ann. "To Ask or Not to Ask: Is That a Question?" In *Communication Yearbook 7*. Edited by Robert Bostrom. Beverly Hills, Calif.: Sage, 1983, pp. 342–368.

Berlyne, Daniel E. "Humanistic Psychology as a Protest Movement." In *Humanistic Psychology: Concepts and Criticism*. Edited by Joseph Royce and Leendert P. Mos. New York: Plenum, 1981, p. 261.

Bochner, Arthur P. "The Functions of Human Communicating in Interpersonal Bonding." In *Handbook of Rhetorical and Communication Theory*. Edited by Carroll C. Arnold and John Waite Bowers. Boston: Allyn and Bacon, 1984, pp. 554–621.

Bochner, Arthur, and Krueger, Dorothy. "Interpersonal Communication Theory and Research: An Overview of Inscrutable Epistemologies and Muddled Concepts." In *Communication Yearbook 3*. Edited by Dan Nimmo. New Brunswick, N.J.: Transaction Books, 1979, p. 203.

Bostrom, Robert. "Game Theory in Communication Research." *Journal of Communication* 18 (1968): 369–388.

Burgoon, Judee K.; Buller, David B.; Hale, Jerold L.; and deTurck, Mark A. "Relational Messages Associated with Nonverbal Behaviors." *Human Communication Research* 10 (1984): 351–378.

Burgoon, Judee K., and Hale, Jerold L. "The Fundamental Topoi of Relational Communication." *Communication Monographs* 51 (1984): 193–214.

Burrell, Nancy A., and Fitzpatrick, Mary Anne. "The Psychological Reality of Marital Conflict." In *Intimates in Conflict: A Communication Perspective*. Edited by Dudley D. Cahn. Hillsdale, N.J.: Erlbaum, 1990, pp. 167–186.

Cahn, Dudley D., ed. *Intimates in Conflict: A Communication Perspective*. Hillsdale, N.J.: Erlbaum, 1990.

Cappella, Joseph N. "Interpersonal Communication: Definitions and Fundamental Questions." In *Handbook of Communication Science*. Edited by Charles R. Berger and Stephen H. Chaffee. Newbury Park, Calif.: Sage, 1987, pp. 184–238.

Cozby, P. W. "Self-Disclosure: A Literature Review." *Psychological Bulletin* 79 (1973): 73–91.

Davis, Morton. *Game Theory: A Non-technical Introduction*. New York: Basic Books, 1970.

Duck, Steve. "How to Lose Friends Without Influencing People." In *Interpersonal Processes: New Directions in Communication Research*. Edited by Michael E. Roloff and Gerald R. Miller. Newbury Park, Calif.: Sage, 1987, pp. 278–298.

———, ed. *Personal Relationships 4: Dissolving Personal Relationships*. London: Academic Press, 1982.

———. "A Topography of Relationship Disengagement and Dissolution." In *Personal Relationships 4: Dissolving Personal Relationships*. London: Academic Press, 1982, pp. 1–30.

Duval, S., and Wicklund, R. A. *A Theory of Objective Self-Awareness*. New York: Academic Press, 1972.

Fitzpatrick, Mary Anne. *Between Husbands and Wives: Communication in Marriage*. Newbury Park, Calif.: Sage, 1988.

"Forum: Can One Not Communicate?" *Western Journal of Speech Communication* 54 (1990): 593–623.

Frost, Joyce, and Wilmot, William. *Interpersonal Conflict*. Dubuque, Iowa: Brown, 1978.

Gilbert, Shirley J. "Empirical and Theoretical Extensions of Self-Disclosure." In *Explorations in Interpersonal Communication*. Edited by Gerald R. Miller. Beverly Hills, Calif.: Sage, 1976, pp. 197–216.

Gudykunst, William B. "Culture and the Development of Interpersonal Relationships." In *Communication Yearbook 12*. Edited by James A. Anderson. Newbury Park, Calif.: Sage, 1989, pp. 315–354.

———. "Uncertainty and Anxiety." In *Theories in Intercultural Communication*. Edited by Young Yun Kim and William B. Gudykunst. Newbury Park, Calif.: Sage, 1988, pp. 123–156.

Hall, Edward T. *Beyond Culture*. New York: Doubleday, 1976.

Hofstede, G. *Cultures Consequences*. Beverly Hills, Calif.: Sage, 1980.

Jourard, Sidney. *Disclosing Man to Himself*. New York: Van Nostrand, 1968.

———. *Self-Disclosure: An Experimental Analysis of the Transparent Self*. New York: Wiley, 1971.

———. *The Transparent Self*. New York: Van Nostrand Reinhold, 1971.

Kantor, David, and Lehr, William. *Inside the Family*. New York: Harper & Row, 1975.

Kelley, Harold H., and Thibaut, John W. *Interpersonal Relations: A Theory of Interdependence*. New York: Wiley, 1978.

LaGaipa, John L. "Interpersonal Attraction and Social Exchange." In *Theory and Practice in Interpersonal Attraction*. Edited by Steve Duck. New York: Academic Press, 1971, pp. 129–164.

Laing, R. D. *The Politics of Experience*. New York: Pantheon Books, 1967.

———. *Self and Others*. London: Tavistock, 1969.

Laing, R. D.; Phillipson, H.; and Lee, A. R. *Interpersonal Perception*. New York: Springer, 1966.

Littlejohn, Stephen W. *Theories in Human Communication*, 1st ed. Columbus, Ohio: Merrill, 1978.

———. *Theories in Human Communication*, 2nd and 3rd eds. Belmont, Calif.: Wadsworth, 1983, 1989.

Luft, Joseph. *Of Human Interaction*. Palo Alto, Calif.: National Press Books, 1969.

Maslow, Abraham. *The Farther Reaches of Human Nature*. New York: Viking Press, 1971.

Millar, Frank E., and Rogers, L. Edna. "Power Dynamics in Marital Relationships." In *Perspectives on Marital Interaction*. Edited by P. Noller and M. Fitzpatrick. Clevedon, Eng.: Multilingual Matters, 1988, pp. 78–97.

———. "A Relational Approach to Interpersonal Communication." In *Explorations in Interpersonal Communication*. Edited by Gerald R. Miller. Beverly Hills, Calif.: Sage, 1976, pp. 87–203.

———. "Relational Dimensions of Interpersonal Dynamics." In *Interpersonal Processes: New Directions in Communication Research*. Edited by Michael E. Roloff and Gerald R. Miller. Newbury Park, Calif.: Sage, 1987, pp. 117–139.

Miller, G. R., and Steinberg, M. *Between People: A New Analysis of Interpersonal Communication*. Chicago: Science Research Associates, 1975.

Miller, G. R., and Sunnafrank, M. J. "All Is for One but One Is Not for All: A Conceptual Perspective of Interpersonal Communication." In *Human Communication Theory: Comparative Essays*. Edited by Frank E. X. Dance. New York: Harper & Row, 1982, pp. 220–242.

Morton, Teru L., and Douglas, Mary Ann. "Growth of Relationships." In *Personal Relationships 2: Developing Personal Relationships*. Edited by Steve Duck and Robin Gilmour. London: Academic Press, 1981, pp. 3–26.

Motley, Michael. "On Whether One Can(not) Not Communicate: An Examination via Traditional Communication Postulates." *Western Journal of Speech Communication* 54 (1990): 1–20.

Parks, Malcolm R. "Ideology in Interpersonal Communication: Off the Couch and into the World." In *Communication Yearbook 5*. Edited by Michael Burgoon. New Brunswick, N.J.: Transaction Books, 1982, pp. 79–108.

Rawlins, William K. "A Dialectical Analysis of the Tensions, Functions and Strategic Challenges of Communication in Young Adult Friendships." In *Communication Yearbook 12*. Edited by James A. Anderson. Newbury Park, Calif.: Sage, 1989, pp. 157–189.

———. *Friendship Matters: Communication, Dialectics, and the Life Course*. Hawthorne, N.Y.: Aldine de Gruyter, in press.

Rogers, Carl. *Client-Centered Therapy*. Boston: Houghton Mifflin, 1951.

———. "A Theory of Therapy, Personality, and Interpersonal Relationships, as Developed in the Client-Centered Framework." In *Psychology: A Study of Science*, vol. 3. Edited by S. Koch. New York: McGraw-Hill, 1959, pp. 184–256.

Rogers, Edna. "Analyzing Relational Communication: Implications of a Pragmatic Approach." Paper presented to the Speech Communication Association, Washington, D.C., November 1983.

Rogers-Millar, L. Edna, and Millar, Frank E. "Domineeringness and Dominance: A Transactional View." *Human Communication Research* 5 (1979): 238–246.

Roloff, Michael E. "Communication and Conflict." In *Handbook of Communication Science*. Edited by Charles R. Berger and Steven H. Chaffee. Newbury Park, Calif.: Sage, 1987, pp. 484–536.

———. *Interpersonal Communication: The Social Exchange Approach*. Beverly Hills, Calif.: Sage, 1981.

Royce, Joseph R., and Mos, Leendert P., eds. *Humanistic Psychology: Concepts and Criticisms*. New York: Plenum, 1981.

Sillars, Alan L. "Attributions and Communication in Roommate Conflicts." *Communication Monographs* 47 (1980): 180–200.

———. *Manual for Coding Interpersonal Conflict*. Unpublished Manuscript. Department of Communication, University of Montana, 1986.

———. "The Sequential and Distributional Structure of Conflict Interaction as a Function of Attributions Concerning the Locus of Responsibility and Stability of Conflict." In *Communication Yearbook 4*. Edited by Dan Nimmo. New Brunswick, N.J.: Transaction Books, 1980, pp. 217–236.

Sillars, Alan, and Weisberg, Judith. "Conflict as a Social Skill." In *Interpersonal Processes: New Directions in Communication Research*. Edited by Michael E. Roloff and Gerald R. Miller. Newbury Park, Calif.: Sage, 1987, pp. 140–171.

Sillars, Alan L., et al. "Coding Verbal Conflict Tactics: Nonverbal and Perceptual Correlates of the 'Avoidance-Distributive-Integrative' Distinction." *Human Communication Research* 9 (1982): 83–95.

———. "Communication and Conflict in Marriage." In *Communication Yearbook 7*. Edited by Robert Bostrom. Beverly Hills, Calif.: Sage, 1983, pp. 414–429.

Steinfatt, Thomas, and Miller, Gerald. "Communication in Game Theoretic Models of Conflict." In *Perspectives on Communication in Conflict*. Edited by Gerald R. Miller and Herbert Simons. Englewood Cliffs, N.J.: Prentice-Hall, 1974, pp. 14–75.

Sunnafrank, Michael. "Predicted Outcome Value During Initial Interactions." *Human Communication Research* 13 (1986): 3–33.

"Predicted Outcome Value and Uncertainty Reduction Theories: A Test of Competing Perspectives." *Human Communication Research* 17 (1990): 76–103.

Taylor, Dalmas A., and Altman, Irwin. "Communication in Interpersonal Relationships: Social Penetration Theory." In *Interpersonal Processes: New Directions in Communication Research*. Edited by Michael E. Roloff and Gerald R. Miller. Newbury Park, Calif.: Sage, 1987, pp. 257–277.

Thibaut, John W., and Kelley, Harold H. *The Social Psychology of Groups*. New York: Wiley, 1959.

Trenholm, Sarah, and Jensen, Arthur. *Interpersonal Communication*. Belmont, Calif.: Wadsworth, 1988.

von Neumann, John, and Morgenstern, Oskar. *The Theory of Games and Economic Behavior*. Princeton, N.J.: Princeton University Press, 1944.

Watkins, Charles. "An Analytic Model of Conflict." *Speech Monographs* 41 (1974): 1–5.

Watzlawick, Paul; Beavin, Janet; and Jackson, Don. *Pragmatics of Human Communication: A Study of Interactional Patterns, Pathologies, and Paradoxes*. New York: Norton, 1967.

Wilmot, William. "Meta-communication: A Re-examination

and Extension." In *Communication Yearbook 4*. Edited by Dan Nimmo. New Brunswick, N.J.: Transaction Books, 1980, pp. 61–69.

Wilmot, William W.; Carbaugh, Donal A.; and Baxter, Leslie A. "Communicative Strategies Used to Terminate Romantic Relationships." *Western Journal of Speech Communication* 49 (1985): 204–216.

Chapter Thirteen
Communication in Group Decision Making

Bales, Robert F. *Interaction Process Analysis: A Method for the Study of Small Groups*. Reading, Mass.: Addison-Wesley, 1950.

———. *Personality and Interpersonal Behavior*. New York: Holt, Rinehart & Winston, 1970.

Bales, Robert F.; Cohen, Stephen P.; and Williamson, Stephen A. *SYMLOG: A System for the Multiple Level Observation of Groups*. London: Collier, 1979.

Bales, R. F., and Strodbeck, F. L. "Phases in Group Problem-Solving." *Journal of Abnormal and Social Psychology* 46 (1951): 485–495.

Barge, J. Kevin, and Hirokawa, Randy Y. "Toward a Communication Competency Model of Group Leadership." *Small Group Behavior* 20 (1989): 167–189.

Bell, M. A. "Phases in Group Problem-Solving." *Small Group Behavior* 13 (1982): 475–495.

Bennis, W. G., and Shepard, H. A. "The Theory of Group Development." *Human Relations* 9 (1956): 415–437.

Bormann, Ernest. "Symbolic Convergence and Communication in Group Decision Making." In *Communication and Group Decision-Making*. Edited by Randy Y. Hirokawa and Marshall Scott Poole. Beverly Hills, Calif.: Sage, 1986, pp. 219–236.

Cattell, Raymond. "Concepts and Methods in the Measurement of Group Syntality." *Psychological Review* 55 (1948): 48–63.

Collins, Barry, and Guetzkow, Harold. *A Social Psychology of Group Processes for Decision-Making*. New York: Wiley, 1964.

Courtright, John A. "A Laboratory Investigation of Groupthink." *Communication Monographs* 45 (1978): 229–246.

Cragan, John F., and Wright, David W. "Small Group Communication Research of the 1980s: A Synthesis and Critique." *Communication Studies* 41 (1990): 212–236.

Dewey, John. *How We Think*. Boston: Heath, 1910.

Fisher, B. Aubrey. "Decision Emergence: Phases in Group Decision Making." *Speech Monographs* 37 (1970): 53–60.

———. "The Process of Decision Modification in Small Discussion Groups." *Journal of Communication* 20 (1970): 51–64.

———. *Small Group Decision Making: Communication and the Group Process*. New York: McGraw-Hill, 1980.

Fisher, B. Aubrey, and Hawes, Leonard. "An Interact System Model: Generating a Grounded Theory of Small Groups." *Quarterly Journal of Speech* 57 (1971): 444–453.

Follett, Mary Parker. *Creative Experience*. New York: Longmans, Green, 1924.

Giddens, Anthony. *New Rules of Sociological Method*. New York: Basic Books, 1976.

———. *Profiles and Critiques in Social Theory*. Berkeley: University of California Press, 1982.

———. *Studies in Social and Political Theory*. New York: Basic Books, 1977.

Gouran, Dennis S. "The Paradigm of Unfulfilled Promise: A Critical Examination of the History of Research on Small Groups in Speech Communication." In *Speech Communication in the 20th Century*. Edited by Thomas W. Benson. Carbondale: Southern Illinois University Press, 1985, p. 90.

Gouran, Dennis S., and Fisher, B. Aubrey. "The Functions of Human Communication in the Formation, Maintenance, and Performance of Small Groups." In *Handbook of Rhetorical and Communication Theory*. Eidted by Carroll C. Arnold and John Waite Bowers. Boston: Allyn and Bacon, 1984, pp. 622–659.

Gouran, Dennis S., and Hirokawa, Randy Y. "Counteractive Functions of Communication in Effective Group Decision-Making." In *Communication and Group Decision-Making*. Edited by Randy Y. Hirokawa and Marshall Scott Poole. Beverly Hills, Calif.: Sage, 1986, pp. 81–92.

Hirokawa, Randy Y. "Group Communication and Decision Making Performance: A Continued Test of the Functional Perspective." *Human Communication Research* 14 (1988): 487–515.

———. "Group Communication and Problem-Solving Effectiveness I: A Critical Review of Inconsistent Findings." *Communication Quarterly* 30 (1982): 134–141.

———. "Group Communication and Problem-Solving Effectiveness: An Investigation of Group Phases." *Human Communication Research* 9 (1983): 291–305.

———. "Group Communication and Problem-solving Effectiveness II." *Western Journal of Speech Communication* 47 (1983): 59–74.

Hirokawa, Randy Y., and Poole, Marshall Scott, eds. *Communication and Group Decision-Making*. Beverly Hills, Calif.: Sage, 1986.

Hirokawa, Randy Y., and Scheerhorn, Dirk R. "Communication in Faulty Group Decision-Making." In *Communication and Group Decision-Making*. Edited by Randy Y. Hirokawa and Marshall Scott Poole. Beverly Hills, Calif.: Sage, 1986, pp. 63–80.

Janis, Irving. *Victims of Groupthink: A Psychological Study of Foreign Decisions and Fiascos*. Boston: Houghton Mifflin, 1982.

Jarboe, Susan. "A Comparison of Input-Output, Process-Output, and Input-Process-Output Models of Small Group Problem-Solving Effectiveness." *Communication Monographs* 55 (1988): 121–142.

Lacoursiere, R. *The Life Cycle of Groups*. New York: Human Sciences Press, 1980.

Lewin, Kurt. *Resolving Social Conflicts: Selected Papers on Group Dynamics*. New York: Harper & Row, 1948.

Littlejohn, Stephen W. *Theories in Human Communication*, 3rd ed. Belmont, Calif.: Wadsworth, 1989.

Phillips, Gerald M., and Wood, Julia T., eds. *Emergent Issues in Human Decision Making*. Carbondale: Southern Illinois University Press, 1984.

Poole, Marshall Scott. "Decision Development in Small Groups, III: A Multiple Sequence Model of Group Decision Development." *Communication Monographs* 50 (1983): 321–342.

———. "Do We Have Any Theories of Group Communication?" *Communication Studies* 41 (1990): 237–247.

Poole, Marshall Scott, and Roth, Jonelle. "Decision Development in Small Groups IV: A Typology of Group Decision Paths." *Human Communication Research* 15 (1989): 323–356.

———. "Decision Development in Small Groups V: Test of a Contingency Model." *Human Communication Research* 15 (1989): 549–589.

Poole, Marshall Scott; Seibold, David R.; and McPhee, Robert D. "Group Decision-Making as a Structurational Process." *Quarterly Journal of Speech* 71 (1985): 74.

———. "A Structurational Approach to Theory-Building in Group Decision-Making Research." In *Communication and Group Decision-Making*. Edited by Randy Y. Hirokawa and Marshall Scott Poole. Beverly Hills, Calif.: Sage, 1986, pp. 238–240.

Shaw, Marvin E. *Group Dynamics: The Psychology of Small Group Behavior*. New York: McGraw-Hill, 1981.

Tuckman, Bruce. "Developmental Sequence in Small Groups." *Psychological Bulletin* 63 (1965): 384–399.

Chapter Fourteen
Communication and Organizational Networks

Anderson, James A., ed. *Communication Yearbook 11*. Newbury Park, Calif.: Sage, 1988.

Bitzer, Lloyd. "Aristotle's Enthymeme Revisited." *Quarterly Journal of Speech* 45 (1959): 399–408.

Bullis, Connie A., and Tompkins, Phillip K. "The Forest Ranger Revisited: A Study of Control Practices and Identification." *Communication Monographs* 56 (1989): 287–306.

Cheney, George. "The Rhetoric of Identification and the Study of Organizational Communication." *Quarterly Journal of Speech* 69 (1983): 143–158.

Cheney, George, and Tompkins, Phillip K. "Coming to Terms with Organizational Identification and Commitment." *Central States Speech Journal* 38 (1987): 1–15.

Communication Studies 40 (Winter 1989): 231–265.

Cooper, Lane. *The Rhetoric of Aristotle*. New York: Meredith, 1932.

Delia, Jesse. "The Logic Fallacy, Cognitive Theory, and the Enthymeme: A Search for the Foundations of Reasoned Discourse." *Quarterly Journal of Speech* 56 (1970): 140–148.

Edwards, R. "The Social Relations of Production at the Point of Production." In *Complex Organizations: Critical Perspectives*. Edited by M. Zey-Ferrell and M. Aiken. Glenview, Ill.: Scott, Foresman, 1981.

Eisenstadt, S. N. *Max Weber on Charisma and Institution Building*. Chicago: University of Chicago Press, 1968.

Etzioni, Amatai. *Modern Organizations*. Englewood Cliffs, N.J.: Prentice-Hall, 1964.

Farace, Richard V.; Monge, Peter R.; and Russell, Hamish. *Communicating and Organizing*. Reading, Mass.: Addison-Wesley, 1977.

Fayol, Henri. *General and Industrial Management*. New York: Pitman, 1949.

Giddens, Anthony. *Central Problems in Social Theory*. Berkeley: University of California Press, 1979.

———. *Profiles and Critiques in Social Theory*. Berkeley: University of California Press, 1982.

Johnson, H. "A New Conceptualization of Source of Organizational Climate." *Administrative Science Quarterly* 3 (1976): 275–292.

Kaufman, H. *The Forest Ranger: A Study in Administrative Behavior.* Baltimore: Johns Hopkins University Press, 1960.

Kreps, Gary L. "A Field Experimental Test and Revaluation of Weick's Model of Organizing." In *Communication Yearbook 4.* Edited by Dan Nimmo. New Brunswick, N.J.: Transaction Books, 1980, pp. 389–398.

Likert, Rensis. *The Human Organization.* New York: McGraw-Hill, 1967.

————. *New Patterns of Management.* New York: McGraw-Hill, 1961.

McPhee, Robert D. "Formal Structure and Organizational Communication." In *Organizational Communication: Traditional Themes and New Directions.* Edited by Robert D. McPhee and Phillip K. Tompkins. Beverly Hills, Calif.: Sage, 1985, pp. 149–178.

————. "Organizational Communication: A Structurational Exemplar." In *Rethinking Communication: Paradigm Exemplars.* Edited by Brenda Dervin, Lawrence Grossberg, Barbara O'Keefe, and Ellen Wartella. Beverly Hills, Calif.: Sage, 1989, pp. 199–212.

Monge, Peter R. "The Network Level of Analysis." In *Handbook of Communication Science.* Edited by Charles R. Berger and Steven H. Chaffee. Newbury Park, Calif.: Sage, 1987, pp. 239–270.

Monge, Peter R., and Eisenberg, Eric M. "Emergent Communication Networks." In *Handbook of Organizational Communication: An Interdisciplinary Perspective.* Edited by Frederic M. Jablin, Linda L. Putnam, Karlene H. Roberts, and Lyman W. Porter. Newbury Park, Calif.: Sage, 1987, pp. 304–342.

Morgan, Gareth. *Images of Organization.* Beverly Hills, Calif.: Sage, 1986.

Pacanowsky, Michael. "Creating and Narrating Organizational Realities." In *Rethinking Communication: Paradigm Exemplars.* Edited by Brenda Dervin, Lawrence Grossberg, Barbara O'Keefe, and Ellen Wartella. Newbury Park, Calif.: Sage, 1989, pp. 250–257.

Pacanowsky, Michael E., and O'Donnell-Trujillo, Nick. "Communication and Organizational Cultures." *Western Journal of Speech Communication* 46 (1982): 115–130.

————. "Organizational Communication as Cultural Performance." *Communication Monographs* 50 (1983): 126–147.

Perrow, Charles. *Complex Organizations: A Critical Essay.* Glenview, Ill.: Scott, Foresman, 1972.

Poole, Marshall Scott. "Communication and Organizational Climates: Review, Critique, and a New Perspective." In *Organizational Communication: Traditional Themes and New Directions.* Edited by Robert D. McPhee and Phillip K. Tompkins. Beverly Hills, Calif.: Sage, 1985, pp. 79–108.

Poole, Marshall Scott, and McPhee, Robert D. "A Structurational Analysis of Organizational Climate." In *Communication and Organizations: An Interpretive Approach.* Edited by Linda L. Putnam and Michael E. Pacanowsky. Beverly Hills, Calif.: Sage, 1983, pp. 195–220.

Richmond, Virginia P., and McCroskey, James C. "Management Communication Style, Tolerance for Disagreement, and Innovativeness as Predictors of Employee Satisfaction: A Comparison of Single-Factor, Two-Factor, and Multiple-Factor Approaches." In *Communication Yearbook 3.* Edited by Dan Nimmo. New Brunswick, N.J.: Transaction Books, 1979, pp. 359–373.

Roberts, Karlene H., and O'Reilly, Charles A. "Organizations as Communication Structures: An Empirical Approach." *Human Communication Research* 4 (1978): 283–293.

Simon, Herbert. *Administrative Behavior.* New York: Free Press, 1976.

Taylor, Frederick W. *Principles of Scientific Management.* New York: Harper Brothers, 1947.

Tompkins, Phillip K., and Cheney, George. "Account Analysis of Organizations: Decision Making and Identification." In *Communication and Organizations: An Interpretive Approach.* Edited by Linda L. Putnam and Michael E. Pacanowsky. Beverly Hills, Calif.: Sage, 1983, pp. 123–146.

————. "Communication and Unobtrusive Control in Contemporary Organizations." In *Organizational Communication: Traditional Themes and New Directions.* Edited by Robert D. McPhee and Phillip K. Tompkins. Beverly Hills, Calif.: Sage, 1985, pp. 179–210.

Van Maanen, John, and Barley, Stephen R. "Cultural Organization: Fragments of a Theory." In *Organizational Culture.* Edited by Peter J. Frost et al. Beverly Hills, Calif.: Sage, 1985, pp. 31–54.

Weber, Max. *The Theory of Social and Economic Organizations.* Translated by A. M. Henderson and Talcott Parsons. New York: Oxford University Press, 1947.

Weick, Carl. *The Social Psychology of Organizing.* Reading, Mass.: Addison-Wesley, 1969, 1979.

Chapter Fifteen
Communication and Media

Allor, Martin. "Relocating the Site of the Audience." *Critical Studies in Mass Communication* 5 (1988): 217–233.

Anderson, James A. "Mass Communication Theory and Research: An Overview." In *Communication Yearbook 1.* Edited by Brent Ruben. New Brunswick, N.J.: Transaction Books, 1977, pp. 279–290.

Ball-Rokeach, Sandra J., and Cantor, Muriel G., eds. *Media, Audience, and Social Structure.* Beverly Hills, Calif.: Sage, 1986.

Ball-Rokeach, Sandra J., and DeFleur, Melvin L. "A Dependency Model of Mass-Media Effects." *Communication Research* 3 (1976): 3–21.

Bauer, Raymond. "The Audience." In *Handbook of Communication.* Edited by Ithiel de sola Pool et al. Chicago: Rand McNally, 1973, pp. 141–152.

————. "The Obstinate Audience: The Influence Process from the Point of View of Social Communication." *American Psychologist* 19 (1964): 319–328.

Bauer, R. A., and Bauer, A. H. "America, Mass Society and Mass Media." *Journal of Social Issues* 16 (1960): 3–66.

Bell, Daniel. "The Theory of Mass Society." *Commentary* (July 1956): 75–83.

Berger, Arthur Asa. *Signs in Contemporary Culture: An Introduction to Semiotics.* Salem, Wis.: Sheffield, 1989.

Bineham, Jeffery L. "A Historical Account of the Hypodermic Model in Mass Communication." *Communication Monographs* 55 (1988): 230–246.

Biocca, Frank A. "Opposing Conceptions of the Audience: The Active and Passive Hemispheres of Mass Communication Theory." In *Communication Yearbook 11.* Edited by James A. Anderson. Newbury Park, Calif.: Sage, 1988, pp. 51–80.

Blumler, Jay, and Katz, Elihu, eds. *The Uses of Mass Communication*. Beverly Hills, Calif.: Sage, 1974.

Boulding, Kenneth. "The Medium Is the Massage." In *McLuhan: Hot and Cool*. Edited by Gerald E. Stearn. New York: Dial Press, 1967, pp. 56–68.

Bryant, Jennings, and Zillmann, Dolf, eds. *Perspectives on Media Effects*. Hillsdale, N.J.: Erlbaum, 1986.

Carey, J. W. "Harold Adams Innis and Marshall McLuhan." *The Antioch Review* 27 (1967): 5–39.

Childs, M., and Reston, J., eds. *Walter Lippmann and His Times*. New York: Harcourt Brace, 1959.

Communication Research 6 (January 1979).

Corcoran, Farrel. "KAL 007 and the Evil Empire: Mediated Disaster and Forms of Rationalization." *Critical Studies in Mass Communication* 3 (1986): 297–316.

Davis, Dennis K., and Baran, Stanley J. *Mass Communication and Everyday Life: A Perspective on Theory and Effects*. Belmont, Calif.: Wadsworth, 1981.

DeFleur, Melvin L., and Ball-Rokeach, Sandra J. *Theories of Mass Communication*. New York: Longman, 1982.

Eco, Umberto. *A Theory of Semiotics*. Bloomington: Indiana University Press, 1976.

Elliott, Philip. "Uses and Gratifications Research: A Critique and Sociological Alternative." In *The Uses of Mass Communication*. Edited by Jay Blumler and Elihu Katz. Beverly Hills, Calif.: Sage, 1974, pp. 249–68.

Eulan, Heinz. "The Maddening Methods of Harold D. Lasswell: Some Philosophical Underpinnings." In *Politics, Personality, and Social Science in the Twentieth Century: Essays in Honor of Harold D. Lasswell*. Edited by Arnold A. Rogow. Chicago: University of Chicago Press, 1969, pp. 15–40.

Foley, Joseph M. "Mass Communication Theory and Research: An Overview." In *Communication Yearbook 2*. Edited by Brent Ruben. New Brunswick, N.J.: Transaction Books, 1978, pp. 209–214.

Friedson, Eliot. "Communications Research and the Concept of the Mass." In *The Process and Effects of Mass Communication*. Edited by Wilbur Schramm and Donald Roberts. Urbana: University of Illinois Press, 1971, pp. 197–208.

Fry, Donald L., and Fry, Virginia H. "A Semiotic Model for the Study of Mass Communication." In *Communication Yearbook 9*. Edited by Margaret L. McLaughlin. Beverly Hills, Calif.: Sage, 1986, pp. 443–462.

Gerbner, George. "Advancing on the Path of Righteousness (Maybe)." In *Cultivation Analysis: New Directions in Media Effects Research*. Edited by Nancy Signorielli and Michael Morgan. Newbury Park, Calif.: Sage, 1990, p. 253.

———. "Mass Media and Human Communication Theory." In *Human Communication Theory*. Edited by Frank E. X. Dance. New York: Holt, Rinehart & Winston, 1967, p. 45.

Gerbner, George; Gross, Larry; Morgan, Michael; and Signorielli, Nancy. "A Curious Journal into the Scary World of Paul Hirsch." *Communication Research* 8 (1981): 39.

———. "Living with Television: The Dynamics of the Cultivation Process." In *Perspectives on Media Effects*. Edited by Jennings Bryant and Dolf Zillmann. Hillsdale, N.J.: Erlbaum, 1986, pp. 17–40.

González, Hernando. "Mass Media and the Spiral of Silence: The Philippines from Marcos to Aquino." *Journal of Communication* 34 (1988): 33–48.

Gronbeck, Bruce. "McLuhan as Rhetorical Theorist." *Journal of Communication* 31 (1981): 117–128.

Grossberg, Lawrence. "Strategies of Marxist Cultural Interpretation." *Critical Studies in Mass Communication* 1 (1984): 392–421.

Hagerstrand, Torsten. "Diffusion II: The Diffusion of Innovations." In *International Encyclopedia of the Social Sciences*, vol. 4. Edited by David Sills. New York: Macmillan, 1968.

Hirsch, Paul M. "On Not Learning from One's Own Mistakes: A Reanalysis of Gerbner et al.'s Findings on Cultivation Analysis, Part II." *Communication Research* 8 (1981): 3–38.

———. "The 'Scary World' of the Nonviewer and Other Anomalies: A Reanalysis of Gerbner et al.'s Findings on Cultivation Analysis." *Communication Research* 7 (1980): 404.

Innis, Harold Adams. *The Bias of Communication*. Toronto: University of Toronto Press, 1951.

———. *Empire and Communications*. Toronto: University of Toronto Press, 1950, 1972.

Katz, Elihu. "The Two-Step Flow of Communication." *Public Opinion Quarterly* 21 (1957): 61–78.

Katz, Elihu; Blumler, Jay; and Gurevitch, Michael. "Uses of Mass Communication by the Individual." In *Mass Communication Research: Major Issues and Future Directions*. Edited by W. Phillips Davidson and Frederick Yu. New York: Praeger, 1974, pp. 11–35.

Katz, Elihu, and Lazarsfeld, Paul. *Personal Influence: The Part Played by People in the Flow of Mass Communications*. New York: Free Press, 1955.

Kincaid, D. Lawrence. "The Convergence Model of Communication." East-West Institute Paper No. 18, Honolulu, 1979.

Kincaid, D. Lawrence; Yum, June Ock; and Woelfel, Joseph. "The Cultural Convergence of Korean Immigrants in Hawaii: An Empirical Test of a Mathematical Theory." *Quality and Quantity* 18, (1983): 59–78.

Klapper, Joseph T. *The Effects of Mass Communication*. Glencoe, Ill.: Free Press, 1960.

Kornhauser, William. "Mass Society." In *International Encyclopedia of the Social Sciences*, vol. 10. New York: Macmillan, 1968, pp. 58–64.

Lasswell, Harold. "The Structure and Function of Communication in Society." In *The Communication of Ideas*. Edited by Lyman Bryson. New York: Institute for Religious and Social Studies, 1948, p. 3.

Lazarsfeld, Paul; Berelson, Bernard; and Gaudet, H. *The People's Choice*. New York: Columbia University Press, 1948.

Lazarsfeld, Paul, and Merton, Robert K. "Mass Communication, Popular Taste, and Organized Social Action." In *The Process and Effects of Mass Communication*. Edited by Wilbur Schramm and Donald Roberts. Urbana: University of Illinois Press, 1971, p. 557.

Lindlof, Thomas R. "Media Audiences as Interpretive Communities." In *Communication Yearbook 11*. Edited by James A. Anderson. Newbury Park, Calif.: Sage, 1988, pp. 81–107.

Lippmann, Walter. *Public Opinion*. New York: Macmillan, 1921.

McLuhan, Marshall. "At the Flip Point of Time—The Point of More Return?" *Journal of Communication* 25 (1975): 102–106.

———. "At the Moment of Sputnik the Planet Became a Global Theatre in Which There Are No Spectators but Only Actors." *Journal of Communication* 24 (1974): 48–58.

———. "The Brain and the Media: The 'Western' Hemisphere." *Journal of Communication* 28 (1978): 54–60.

———. "Communication: McLuhan's Laws of the Media." *Technology and Culture* 16 (1975): 74–78.

———. *The Gutenberg Galaxy: The Making of Typographic Man.* Toronto: University of Toronto Press, 1962.

———. "Implications of Cultural Uniformity." In *Superculture: American Popular Culture and Europe.* Edited by C. E. E. Bigsby. Bowling Green, Ohio: Bowling Green University Popular Press, 1975.

———. "Laws and the Media." *Et Cetera* 34 (1977): 173–179.

———. *The Mechanical Bride.* New York: Vanguard Press, 1951.

———. "Misunderstanding the Media's Laws." *Technology and Culture* 17 (1976): 263.

———. "The Rise and Fall of Nature." *Journal of Communication* 27 (1977): 80–81.

———. *Understanding Media.* New York: McGraw-Hill, 1964.

———. "The Violence of the Media." *The Canadian Forum* (September 1976): 9–12.

McLuhan, Marshall, and Fiori, Quentin. *The Medium Is the Massage.* New York: Bantam Books, 1967.

McQuail, Denis. *Mass Communication Theory: An Introduction.* London: Sage, 1984, 1987.

———. "With the Benefits of Hindsight: Reflections on Uses and Gratifications Research." *Critical Studies in Mass Communication* 1 (1984): 177–193.

Noelle-Neumann, Elisabeth. "The Effect of Media on Media Effects Research." *Journal of Communication* 33 (1983): 157–165.

———. "Return to the Concept of Powerful Mass Media." In *Studies of Broadcasting.* Edited by H. Eguchi and K. Sata. Tokyo: Nippon Hoso Kyokii, 1973, pp. 67–112.

———. *The Spiral of Silence: Public Opinion—Our Social Skin.* Chicago: University of Chicago Press, 1984.

———. "The Theory of Public Opinion: The Concept of the Spiral of Silence." In *Communication Yearbook 14.* Edited by James A. Anderson. Newbury Park, Calif.: Sage, 1991, pp. 256–287.

Palmgreen, Philip. "Uses and Gratifications: A Theoretical Perspective." In *Communication Yearbook 8.* Edited by Robert N. Bostrom. Beverly Hills, Calif.: Sage, 1984, pp. 20–55.

Reese, Stephen D. "Setting the Media's Agenda: A Power Balance Perspective." In *Communication Yearbook 14.* Edited by James A. Anderson. Newbury Park, Calif.: Sage, 1991, pp. 309–340.

Rogers, Everett M. *Diffusion of Innovations.* New York: Free Press, 1962.

Rogers, Everett M., and Adhikarya, Ronny. "Diffusion of Innovations: An Up-to-Date Review and Commentary." In *Communication Yearbook 3.* Edited by Dan Nimmo. New Brunswick, N.J.: Transaction Books, 1979, pp. 67–82.

Rogers, Everett M., and Dearing, James W. "Agenda-Setting Research: Where Has It Been, Where Is It Going?" In *Communication Yearbook 11.* Edited by James A. Anderson. Newbury Park, Calif.: Sage, 1988, pp. 555–593.

Rogers, Everett M., and Kincaid, D. Lawrence. *Communication Networks: Toward a new Paradigm for Research.* New York: Free Press, 1981.

Rogers, Everett M., and Shoemaker, F. Floyd. *Communication of Innovations, A Cross-Cultural Approach.* New York: Free Press, 1971.

Rogow, Arnold A., ed. *Politics, Personality, and Social Science in the Twentieth Century: Essays in Honor of Harold D. Lasswell.* Chicago: University of Chicago Press, 1969.

Rosengren, K.; Wenner, L.; and Palmgreen, P., eds. *Media Grat-ifications Research: Current Perspectives.* Beverly Hills, Calif.: Sage, 1985.

Rubin, Alan M., and Windahl, Sven. "The Uses and Dependency Model of Mass Communication." *Critical Studies in Mass Communication* 3 (1986): 186.

Sears, David O., and Freedman, Jonathan I. "Selective Exposure to Information: A Critical Review." In *The Process and Effects of Mass Communication.* Edited by Wilbur Schramm and Donald F. Roberts. Urbana: University of Illinois Press, 1971, pp. 209–234.

Severin, Werner J., and Tankard, James W. *Communication Theories: Origins, Methods, Uses.* New York: Hastings House, 1979.

Shaw, Donald L., and McCombs, Maxwell E. *The Emergence of American Political Issues.* St. Paul: West, 1977.

Signorielli, Nancy. "Television's Mean and Dangerous World: A Continuation of the Cultural Indicators Perspective." In *Cultivation Analysis: New Directions in Media Effects Research.* Edited by Nancy Signorielli and Michael Morgan. Newbury Park, Calif.: Sage, 1990, pp. 85–106.

Signorielli, Nancy, and Morgan, Michael, eds. *Cultivation Analysis: New Directions in Media Effects Research.* Newbury Park, Calif.: Sage, 1990.

Siune, Karen, and Borre Ole. "Setting the Agenda for a Danish Election." *Journal of Communication* 25 (1975): 65–73.

Smith, Bruce. "The Mystifying Intellectual History of Harold Lasswell." In *Politics, Personality, and Social Science in the Twentieth Century: Essays in Honor of Harold D. Lasswell.* Edited by Arnold A. Rogow. Chicago: University of Chicago Press, 1969, pp. 41–105.

Sproule, J. Michael. "Progressive Propoganda Critics and the Magic Bullet Myth." *Critical Studies in Mass Communication* 6 (1989): 225–246.

Swanson, David L. "Political Communication Research and the Uses and Gratifications Model: A Critique." *Communication Research* 6 (1979): 36–53.

Swanson, David L., and Babrow, Austin S. "Uses and Gratifications: The Influence of Gratification-Seeking and Expectancy-Value Judgments on the Viewing of Television News." In *Rethinking Communication: Paradigm Exemplars.* Edited by Brenda Dervin, Lawrence Grossberg, Barbara O'Keefe, and Ellen Wartella. Newbury Park, Calif.: Sage, 1989, pp. 361–375.

Tan, Alexis S. *Mass Communication Theories and Research.* Columbus, Ohio: Grid, 1981.

White, Robert. "Mass Communication and Culture: Transaction to a New Paradigm." *Journal of Communication* 33 (1983): 279–301.

Wolfe, Tom. "The New Life Out There." In *McLuhan: Hot and Cool.* Edited by Gerald E. Stearn. New York: Dial Press, 1967, pp. 34–56.

Wright, Charles R. "Functional Analysis and Mass Communication." *Public Opinion Quarterly* 24 (1960): 605–620.

———. "Mass Communication Rediscovered: Its Past and Future in American Sociology." In *Media, Audience, and Social Structure.* Edited by Sandra J. Ball-Rokeach and Muriel G. Cantor. Beverly Hills, Calif.: Sage, 1986, pp. 22–33.

Zillmann, Dolf. "Attribution and Misattribution of Excitatory Reactions." In *New Directions in Attribution Research*, vol. 2. Edited by J. H. Harvey, W. J. Ickes, and R. F. Kidd. Hillsdale, N.J.: Erlbaum, 1978, pp. 335–368.

Author Index

Subject Index